THE PRACTICE
OF MEDIATION

ASPEN COURSEBOOK SERIES

THE PRACTICE OF MEDIATION

A Video-Integrated Text

Second Edition

Douglas N. Frenkel
Morris Shuster Practice Professor of Law and Director of the Mediation Clinic
University of Pennsylvania Law School

James H. Stark
Professor of Law and Director of the Mediation Clinic
University of Connecticut

Wolters Kluwer
Law & Business

Printed in the United States of America.

3 4 5 6 7 8 9 0

ISBN 978-1-4548-0219-8

Library of Congress Cataloging-in-Publication Data

Frenkel, Douglas.
    The practice of mediation : a video-integrated text / Douglas N. Frenkel, James H. Stark. — 2nd ed.
        p. cm. — (Aspen coursebook series)
    Includes index.
    ISBN 978-1-4548-0219-8
    1. Mediation—United States. 2. Dispute resolution (Law)—United States. I. Stark, James H. II. Title.
        KF9084.F746 2012
        347.73'9—dc22

                                                                    2011053423

About Wolters Kluwer Law & Business

Wolters Kluwer Law & Business is a leading global provider of intelligent information and digital solutions for legal and business professionals in key specialty areas, and respected educational resources for professors and law students. Wolters Kluwer Law & Business connects legal and business professionals as well as those in the education market with timely, specialized authoritative content and information-enabled solutions to support success through productivity, accuracy and mobility.

Serving customers worldwide, Wolters Kluwer Law & Business products include those under the Aspen Publishers, CCH, Kluwer Law International, Loislaw, Best Case, ftwilliam.com and MediRegs family of products.

CCH products have been a trusted resource since 1913, and are highly regarded resources for legal, securities, antitrust and trade regulation, government contracting, banking, pension, payroll, employment and labor, and healthcare reimbursement and compliance professionals.

Aspen Publishers products provide essential information to attorneys, business professionals and law students. Written by preeminent authorities, the product line offers analytical and practical information in a range of specialty practice areas from securities law and intellectual property to mergers and acquisitions and pension/benefits. Aspen's trusted legal education resources provide professors and students with high-quality, up-to-date and effective resources for successful instruction and study in all areas of the law.

Kluwer Law International products provide the global business community with reliable international legal information in English. Legal practitioners, corporate counsel and business executives around the world rely on Kluwer Law journals, looseleafs, books, and electronic products for comprehensive information in many areas of international legal practice.

Loislaw is a comprehensive online legal research product providing legal content to law firm practitioners of various specializations. Loislaw provides attorneys with the ability to quickly and efficiently find the necessary legal information they need, when and where they need it, by facilitating access to primary law as well as state-specific law, records, forms and treatises.

Best Case Solutions is the leading bankruptcy software product to the bankruptcy industry. It provides software and workflow tools to flawlessly streamline petition preparation and the electronic filing process, while timely incorporating ever-changing court requirements.

ftwilliam.com offers employee benefits professionals the highest quality plan documents (retirement, welfare and non-qualified) and government forms (5500/PBGC, 1099 and IRS) software at highly competitive prices.

MediRegs products provide integrated health care compliance content and software solutions for professionals in healthcare, higher education and life sciences, including professionals in accounting, law and consulting.

Wolters Kluwer Law & Business, a division of Wolters Kluwer, is headquartered in New York. Wolters Kluwer is a market-leading global information services company focused on professionals.

To our awesome children. In a world so badly in need of constructive discourse and imaginative solutions, they give us reason to be hopeful.

SUMMARY OF CONTENTS

CONTENTS

CHAPTER 3
THE ROLE OF THE MEDIATOR

CHAPTER 4
PREPARING TO MEDIATE

CHAPTER 5

MEDIATION AS A STRUCTURED PROCESS   123

CHAPTER 6

OPENING THE PROCESS, DEVELOPING INFORMATION   133

CHAPTER 7

EXPANDING INFORMATION

CHAPTER **11**

CONCLUDING THE MEDIATION

CHAPTER **12**

THE ETHICS OF MEDIATING

CHAPTER 13

REPRESENTING CLIENTS IN MEDIATION

PREFACE TO THE FIRST EDITION

Eight years have elapsed since we first conceived the possibility of writing this book. Why did we undertake it? What were our goals?

First, candidly, we were frustrated. As longstanding teachers and practitioners of mediation, we had spent years looking for and trying to cobble together written materials that taught about the process and skills of mediation in effective, realistic ways. A good deal of the literature in the field seemed to us too simplistic; some seemed to hew to a single, monolithic view of the process and the "correct" role of the mediator.

We wanted to teach about mediation contextually, demonstrating—as our experience tells us—that the process cannot be reduced to a simple, "one-approach-fits-all" handbook, but rather looks quite different when applied in different conflict settings. At the same time, we appreciated that students needed a model to apply, and we set out to provide one. In doing so, we sought to equip them with the ability to assist in the whole spectrum of disputes—from tough, lawyered, zero-sum money problems to pure "relational" conflicts, and everything in between.

Second, as with other clinical fields that largely concern process, we believed that simply reading about mediation without seeing it in action was far from optimal. Perhaps because of teaching time limitations or the desire to portray mediation in ideal terms, many of the existing videos at the time were highly compressed and seemed to us rather unrealistic. Indeed, one could have concluded from some of this material that mediating was typically easy, even "magical" in its sudden, win-win endings.

We wanted to portray the process in all of its real-world richness complexity: its slowness; its "two-steps-forward, one-step-backwards" character; the arduous challenges mediators face when attempting to resolve deeply held or competitively bargained differences; the psychological, emotional, and strategic minefields that are often encountered in mediation; yes, the collaborative, reparative, and occasional transformative moments in mediation that can make the process so deeply rewarding.

Third, all teachers face the scarcity of classroom time and must deal with coverage concerns. Clinical teachers—preparing students to be able to perform as well as master theory—are especially pressed in this way and often must limit in-class use of video. We therefore decided to create and include in each copy of the text a DVD, depicting a wide variety of mediation problems, settings, and styles, that would enable students to view video extracts as part of their homework and help instructors save valuable class time.

Fourth, it seemed to us that much of the mediation literature was of two types: largely descriptive, anecdotal, and "how-to-do-it" writing about mediation by practitioners on the one hand, and deeply theoretical writing about disputing (sometimes not all that reflective of practice) on the other. We wanted to marry these two worlds if possible, grounding our text and videos in the most current research available from social science, communications, sales, and other disciplines, while at the same time exposing students to the insights and perspectives (even if untested) of experienced practitioners in the field.

Finally, we felt that a book written this way would help students perform generally in a stance that is pervasive in practice but largely ignored by contemporary legal education — that of the neutral. Whether they are counseling a client dispassionately, trying to break a negotiating logjam to solve a problem, adjusting differences between co-clients, chairing a potentially contentious departmental meeting or (as a few of our students will do early in their career) actually serving as a mediator — lawyers and other professionals must draw on mediative skills far more often than the partisan skills that are so prominently featured in law school classes and in popular culture. Thus the "voice" of this book, unlike most other books in the field, is decidedly that of the neutral.

This has been a long and happy partnership. One knows that a true collaboration has occurred when it is difficult to recall who wrote which paragraph, or came up with what phrase. We certainly did not anticipate when we started how much time it would take us to write the book, much less complete all the detail work involved in constructing, filming, and editing three mediation problems involving nine different neutrals, and deciding how to integrate these materials into the text. We have enjoyed (almost) every minute of it, cementing and deepening our friendship along the way.

We hope that you derive as much pleasure using these materials as we did preparing them. Please let us know what you think.

Doug Frenkel
Jim Stark
May 2008

The response to the first edition of this book — which married text and video while putting forth a contextually-driven model of mediation — exceeded our wildest expectations. Its widespread adoption by classroom teachers and professional mediation trainers here and abroad has validated our belief that effective acquisition of a new skill set requires both the ability to see differing professional models in action and the judgment to know how to adapt them to particular situations. New courses have sprung up, organized around the book's interactive pedagogy. But the most rewarding feedback of all has been the significantly accelerated and sophisticated mastery of both the theory and practice of mediation that our students have demonstrated in a semester's course.

This second edition builds on our efforts to harness new learning technologies and incorporate new mediation thinking into the refinement of our preferred model of practice. It represents our (and our publisher's) first foray into a SmartBook™ format that seamlessly links text and video. We have added new content in response to adopters' suggestions (e.g., co-mediation) and emerging trends in the field (e.g., increasing adoption of transformative mediation, mediating online). The "voice" of the text has been broadened so that, while the book remains fully at home in the law school classroom, it will be more readily accessible to students and professionals in other disciplines. We have expanded our discussion of effective mediator persuasion by incorporating what we think may be illuminating findings from social science research. And given the widespread application of mediation in the family context, we have expanded our video case study of a child custody dispute to include one full-length ("play all") treatment.

The growth of course offerings in mediation parallels its burgeoning use by individuals and institutions, and reflects the widespread recognition that the communications and problem-solving skills used by neutrals are among life's most important personal and professional competencies. It is our hope that this new edition will help fuel the development of a generation of skilled practitioners.

Doug Frenkel
Jim Stark
December 2011

ACKNOWLEDGMENTS

Many people have made this book possible and we are very grateful to all of them. We have been encouraged every step of the way by the editorial staff at Aspen, including especially Publisher Carol McGeehan, who believed in this project from its inception; Director of Sales Mike Gregory, who "took the leap" and supported us in our desire to integrate DVD material with the text; Eric Holt, our Development Editor, who nurtured the book with humor, flexibility and good judgment throughout its various stages of development; and Senior Editor Carmen Corral-Reid, who supervised the production of the first edition galleys through their final throes. For the second edition, we were ably assisted by Development Editor John Devins and by Gretchen Otto and her copyediting staff, who were patient with, and helped oversee, the many changes that we wanted to make in content and presentation. We thank also the anonymous faculty reviewers solicited by Aspen to read and comment on drafts of this book, and whose insights greatly improved it.

Of our colleagues in the world of mediation and dispute resolution, we especially wish to acknowledge the contributions of two individuals. Jon Hyman of Rutgers Law School worked closely with us for an extended period of time, developing ideas and providing insightful and very valuable comments for the book and the personal injury simulation, of which he is a coauthor. The time and effort he gave greatly exceeds the usual review and comment that one expects from professional colleagues. Carol Liebman of Columbia Law School, who has used this book in her mediation course, has our special thanks for her detailed suggestions on several chapters and for sharing her students' reactions to the manuscript. We also benefitted greatly from the feedback of mediation and clinical colleagues at the New York Clinical Theory Workshop and at presentations we made at the New England and Mid-Atlantic Regional Clinicians' meetings, the 11th Annual ABA Dispute Resolution Conference, and the AALS Annual Meeting.

We have also received a great deal of helpful feedback on a paper on social science findings pertaining to persuasion, portions of which we have incorporated into Chapter 9 of this second edition. We include in our thanks the participants at the 12th Annual ABA Dispute Resolution Conference, the Washington University School of Law ADR and Clinical Theory Workshop, the Quinnipiac-Yale Law School Dispute Resolution Workshop, the Mid-Atlantic Clinical Teachers' Workshop, the University of Connecticut Law School Faculty Workshop, the New York Law School Clinical Theory Workshop, and a Spring 2011 program hosted by the New York City office of JAMS. In addition, we want to express our thanks to Ian Ayres, Jon Bauer, Jennifer Brown, Peter Carnevale, Robert Condlin, Neil Feigenson, Rebecca Hollander-Blumoff, Jonathan Hyman, Daniel O'Keefe, Jennifer Robbennolt, Jon Romberg, and Karen Tokarz for their helpful insights and comments along the way.

We are enormously indebted to Pablo Colapinto, our creative, patient, hardworking videographer and the talented team he assembled. Without their help, the completion of the video portion of this project would not have been possible. Pablo filmed, edited, and authored the DVD selections, demonstrating the patience of Job as we tweaked and re-tweaked the material through its many stages of review. He combines artistry and attention to detail in just the right proportions.

We are very grateful to all the mediators and attorneys who "put themselves on the line" and agreed to participate in our filmed simulations: Cheryl Cutrona, Craig Lord, Judy Meyer, and Lee Rosengard in *Wilson v. DiLorenzo*; Mary Hanna, Sam Rossito, Jean Biesecker, and Don Weinstein in *Fitzgerald v. Fitzgerald*; and Harris Bock, Terry Lefco, Judy Greenwood, Chuck Forer, Lauren Levin Geary, and Dave Kwass in *Resnick v. Stevens Realty*. They have advanced our understanding of differing styles and approaches to mediating and to representing clients in mediation. Of course none of these professionals' efforts would have been as instructive had it not been for the work of the fabulous actors (Kimberly Fairbanks and Jerome Puma in *Wilson*, Suzanne Smart and Christopher Cline in *Fitzgerald*, Robert Toperzer and Bradley Wrenn in *Resnick*) who portrayed the disputants in these cases. It is a tribute to them that many of our students have had no idea that they are watching anything but real mediations as they read this text.

The video portion of this project was helped in large and small ways by many other people and we are indebted to all of them. Valerie Rose served as our "casting director," lining up our actors and keeping them happy. David Hofstein, Edward Polinsky, and Cynthia Arkin were instrumental in providing the office settings for these mediation filmings. Mark Pecci provided access to file documents in the matter on which the *Resnick* case was based. Ed Blumstein, Joni Berner, and Michael Becker, all first-rate neutrals, mediated a first take of the *Fitzgerald* case that fell victim to technical audio problems. The lessons of that ill-fated effort proved very helpful in completing the video portion of this project.

We have benefitted substantially from research support provided by our home institutions, and from the able student research assistance of Rachel Krinsky, Laura Johnson, Rebecca Mathis, Ndidi Moses, Justine Parker, Jaime Porter, Jon Sterling, Ami Tucci, and Matt Venhorst at Connecticut; Ben O'Glasser, Tom Devlin, Matt Funk, Emily Jane Schreiber, and David Merritt at Penn; and Eva Dowdell at Rutgers-Newark. At various stages of the project, Joan Wood, Judy Bigelow, Linda Kirk, Silvia Bloise, Yvette Scipio, Julie Green, Sean Goodbody, John Kuehne, and Leanne McCarron provided us with helpful assistance on manuscript and DVD transcript preparation. Our clinic students at Connecticut and Penn have given us feedback on the draft text, the problems, and the DVD extracts, and have asked great questions. We have incorporated a good many of their ideas and thank them for the improvements they have made to the finished product.

We thank the publishers who gave us permission to reprint excerpts of the following material:

Gary Bellow & Bea Moulton, The Lawyering Process: Materials for Clinical Instruction in Advocacy 458-462 (1978). Reprinted with the permission of Foundation Press.

Stephen Goldberg, Frank Sander, Nancy Rogers & Sarah Cole, Dispute Resolution: Negotiation, Mediation and Other Processes 4 (5th ed. 2007). Reprinted with the permission of Aspen Publishers.

Gary Goodpaster, A Guide to Negotiation and Mediation 95-96 (1997). Reprinted with the permission of Brill Publishers.

Leonard Riskin, Mediator Orientations, Strategies and Techniques, 12 *Alternatives to the High Cost of Litigation* 111-112 (1994). Reprinted with the permission of John Wiley & Sons, Inc.

Tolman Screening Model, reprinted (in modified form) with the permission of Professor Richard M. Tolman, University of Michigan School of Social Work.

Finally, we acknowledge the contributions of the hundreds of disputants, lawyers and student-mediators who have participated in mediations we have supervised as clinical teachers and conducted privately. They have provided us with a wealth of rich material and experience from which much of this book is drawn.

THE PRACTICE
OF MEDIATION

CHAPTER

1

"SO YOU WANT TO STUDY MEDIATION?"

An Introduction to the Processes of Mediation
and the Skills of Effective Mediators

■ §1.1 WHAT THIS BOOK IS ABOUT, AND A WORD ON ITS PERSPECTIVE

When you think about mediation, what images does it conjure up? A couple contemplating divorce? International diplomacy? The effort to avert a strike by public employees? Neighbors arguing about backyard noise?

Mediation is a growth industry. Once confined to specialized fields such as labor relations, today mediation is a process that cuts across almost every type of conflict or transaction that one might encounter in society — from small claims cases to multimillion dollar class actions; from family, community, minor criminal, education and workplace disputes to the most complex environmental, public policy and commercial matters. Mediation services are provided by a wide variety of private providers, with differing professional backgrounds and orientations, as well as by state and federal courts and administrative agencies, employers and community-based organizations. Participation in mediation is often voluntary, but in some instances may be mandatory. Above all, mediation is a flexible process — practiced in different ways depending on who the parties are, the nature of the dispute, the background and qualifications of the mediator and the culture of the particular setting in which mediation services are offered. As a result, people involved in conflict and those seeking to help them need to understand the many ways in which mediation is practiced and how mediation fits into the broader world of dispute resolution.

In the last two decades, American education has begun to treat dispute resolution as a discrete field of study. For example, most American law schools now offer courses that introduce students to negotiation, mediation and arbitration, as well as other subsidiary and hybrid processes offering alternatives to traditional litigation. Other graduate and undergraduate programs feature a wide array of conflict study courses. Many schools offer simulation courses in which students learn about these processes "from the inside out" rather than "from the outside in" — *by doing them*. And professional and undergraduate schools around the country now offer mediation practicums or clinics in which students are trained intensively to serve as neutrals in real disputes — in courts and administrative agencies, community mediation centers, on campuses and in other venues.

These developments are, in part, indicative of mediation's growth as a separate professional sphere in law and other professions. But mediation clinics and mediation simulation courses are also on the rise because they provide students with a sophisticated understanding of dispute resolution. Students in these courses and clinics build their arsenal of interpersonal and professional skills, confront the strategic and ethical demands of serving in a neutral capacity and become more sophisticated consumers of alternative dispute resolution (ADR) services. Much of the interest in studying mediation from the "inside" comes from analyzing in detail the communicative, strategic and ethical dimensions of specific interventions that mediators make — in the context of particular cases. And much of the interest in studying mediation from the perspective of the mediator comes from realizing just how challenging and rewarding the work is.

In this book, we place you primarily in the role of the mediator, recognizing that many of you will not in fact become professional mediators in your future careers. From time to time (in fact, starting in this chapter) we will vary the perspective of the book by asking you to consider mediation from the point of view of a disputant; or of an attorney or other advisor assisting a client at a mediation or counseling an individual or organizational client about dispute resolution options; or of a potential policy maker considering mediation from a legislative, judicial or regulatory perspective. But most of the time, we will study the psychology of conflict and the nature of conflict resolution processes from the distinctive perspective of the neutral.

Mediation is ubiquitous. Whether you are a student or team member seeking to cool down an argument between (or with) friends or colleagues; a CEO seeking to find common ground among warring departments; or the chairperson running a departmental or board meeting and having to organize an agenda, keep participants on task and search for consensus — you will find that you "mediate" often, at least in a broad sense of the term.

In other words, whether or not you want to become a "professional" mediator, this book will teach a great many transferable skills that will be valuable to you as lawyers or other helping professionals, managers or government officials. The skills taught in this book include effective interviewing and information development, agenda creation and control, persuasion and negotiation and — most important, we think — problem-solving. Good mediators must be able to understand conflict and work comfortably at the intersection of thought and feeling, helping people defuse tension and achieve solutions to difficult problems. These are not only important professional skills, they are fundamental life skills.

▪ §1.2 WHAT IS MEDIATION?

▪ **Assisted negotiation.** We begin with basic definitions. Mediation, broadly speaking, is a process of assisting the negotiations of others. A third party (usually someone with no involvement with the dispute or any of its participants) attempts to help the disputants discuss and try to resolve the problems they face. Mediation may be selected as a dispute resolution process because it has been difficult to get direct negotiations started or because negotiations between the parties have broken down. How mediation can improve on the negotiation process and help lawyers help their clients resolve their disputes are important subjects of this book.

■ **A consensual process.** Unlike a judge or arbitrator, a mediator has no power to issue a "ruling" or compel the parties to accept any particular resolution of their dispute. In certain court-connected settings or where a contract requires it, participation in mediation may be mandatory, but only in the sense that the parties are required to show up in the mediation room and give the process an initial try. Mediators may comment on the participants' settlement proposals or suggest ideas of their own for the parties to consider. But by definition, even if the parties enter into the process involuntarily, any decision to continue with mediation must be voluntary, and the only resolution that can be reached is one that is agreed to by the disputants themselves.

■ **An informal process.** A well-conducted mediation is a fair and structured procedure. But it is informal in the sense that participants are generally free to discuss anything that matters to them, unconstrained by rules of evidence, procedure or even substantive law. As one mediation scholar has written, "[i]n mediation . . . the ultimate authority resides with the disputants. The conflict is seen as unique and therefore less subject to solution by application of some general principle. The case is neither to be governed by a precedent nor to set one. Thus . . . whatever a party deems relevant is relevant."[1]

■ **Producing binding agreements.** Even though it is a consensual process, mediation can produce legally binding resolutions. Once an agreement is reached, it is often written up in the form of a contract and, in court-based matters, may be approved by a judge. Such agreements have the force of law: If any party breaches its terms, the contract may be enforced through court action.

■ **A private process.** Unlike public trials, mediations — even in well-publicized cases — almost always take place behind closed doors, generally with the expectation that party and mediator communications, and sometimes even the terms of substantive agreements reached, will be kept secret. Mediation confidentiality may be guaranteed by law or contractually agreed to by the parties. As we will see, the privacy of the mediation process is deemed by mediation proponents to be one of the core determinants of its success. To critics, however, it is a source of some concern.

In this book, we exclude from our main coverage substantial slices of the world of mediation. For example, we do not study in any detail the mediation

---

1. Leonard Riskin, *Mediation and Lawyers*, 43 Ohio St. L.J. 29, 34 (1982).

of everyday interpersonal conflicts. Nor do we focus on specialized applications of the process, such as mediation of public international disputes, the world of "managerial mediation"[2] in business organizations, "peer mediation" in elementary and secondary schools or mediation of urban planning and other public policy disputes.[3] We focus primarily on disputes, not deals and transactions. Having said this, the core of this text will generally be applicable to any setting in which mediation is practiced.

■ §1.3 WHERE DOES MEDIATION FIT IN THE RANGE OF DISPUTE RESOLUTION PROCESSES? WHAT ARE ITS DISTINCTIVE CHARACTERISTICS, ADVANTAGES AND DISADVANTAGES FOR POTENTIAL USERS?

We begin where the decision to mediate might be made — with two or more parties with a problem considering (perhaps with the aid of a lawyer or other advisor) possible ways to resolve it. For these individuals, a first question might be "What is the optimal process for this conflict from my vantage point?" Consider this situation:

▶ ▶ ▶ ▶   **Rosa Lopez and Texitron, Inc.**

Rosa Lopez is a fifty-one-year-old Mexican American woman who works for Texitron, a major U.S. producer of petroleum products and a Fortune 500 company. She has been employed at the company for almost twenty-five years, beginning as a shipping clerk, being retrained as a computer programmer and working her way up through the position of Senior Programmer to become an Assistant Director of Information Technology in one of the company's six divisions. Until recently, the company has treated her well, recognizing and rewarding her energy, inventiveness, teamwork and commitment to the company. She is well paid, especially considering that she started with only a community college degree. But three months ago, she was passed over for an IT director position for which she felt well qualified. A thirty-five-year-old male was hired for the position — someone from outside the company with good knowledge of information systems but no knowledge of the petroleum industry. And to her great frustration and anger, when she tried to get a better understanding of why she was passed over for the promotion, she was stonewalled by the manager who had made the decision.

How might Rosa Lopez handle this problem?

She could, of course, do *nothing*. The popular perception of America today is of a litigation-mad culture in which everyone sues everyone else at the drop of a hat. This perception — the belief that we are suffering a "litigation explosion" and

---

2. DEBORAH M. KOLB, *Labor Mediators, Managers and Ombudsmen: Roles Mediators Play in Different Contexts, in* Mediation Research 99 (Kenneth Kressel et al. eds., 1989).
3. *See* LAWRENCE SUSSKIND & JEFFREY CRUIKSHANK, Breaking the Impasse: Consensual Approaches to Solving Public Disputes (1987).

that courts cannot keep up with the increase of case filings — has had a good deal to do with the growth of alternative dispute resolution. But sociologist Marc Galanter has helped us understand that many experiences perceived as injurious are not necessarily perceived as potential *grievances* — experiences susceptible to a remedy.[4] Has Ms. Lopez been treated wrongfully in a legal sense? Has she been subjected to gender discrimination, age discrimination or discrimination based on her national origin? Is there some other basis in her contractual relationship with the company for a potential claim? She may not be able to tell without a lot more digging. She may not want to do that digging. And even if investigation reveals some possible claim against the company, Ms. Lopez might, like many potential claimants, decide to "lump it,"[5] perhaps because she is conflict averse or doesn't want to burn bridges or anticipates that other opportunities for advancement will eventually present themselves at the company. Or, she might prefer to put her energies into seeking a comparable position at a different company. *Avoidance* is a common and often appropriate conflict management strategy.[6]

But let us suppose that Ms. Lopez talks to other female managers and discovers some anecdotal evidence of a "glass ceiling" at the company for employees with her background and experience. Two senior female employees complain to Ms. Lopez that they also were passed over for promotions they expected, and younger men were hired instead. In addition, Ms. Lopez recently heard some newly hired managers exchanging ethnic jokes that made her uncomfortable. The more she thinks about her situation, the angrier she becomes. She resolves to speak with someone knowledgeable about dispute resolution processes. Assume that she consults you. How would you advise Ms. Lopez regarding the choices available to her?

The primary options available to Rosa Lopez are negotiation, mediation, arbitration and adjudication. The major characteristics of these processes, as they are classically defined, are summarized in the table on the following page. Note that only one of these processes (litigation) can be triggered unilaterally by Ms. Lopez, whereas the others (mediation, negotiation and arbitration) would generally — unless compelled by a court or by a preexisting employment contract — require the assent of both Ms. Lopez and her employer. Study the table carefully and consider: Assuming Ms. Lopez has a choice, what process or combination of processes would be most advantageous to her?

After examining the table, close the book and write down on a piece of paper: What are some of the most important *criteria* that might affect how someone in Ms. Lopez's situation might choose from among these options? If you were advising her, what considerations would you want to discuss with her?

---

4. MARC S. GALANTER, *Reading the Landscape of Disputes: What We Know and Don't Know (And Think We Know) About Our Allegedly Contentious and Litigious Society*, 31 UCLA L. REV. 4, 13 (1983). *See also* RICHARD E. MILLER & AUSTIN SARAT, *Grievances, Claims and Disputes: Assessing the Adversary Culture*, 15 LAW & SOC'Y REV. 525, 526-527 (1980-81).
5. GALANTER, *supra* note 4, at 14.
6. *Id.* at 14-15; R.H. KILMANN & K.W. THOMAS, *Developing a Forced-Choice Measure of Conflict-Handling Behavior: The Mode Instrument*, 37 ED. & PSYCH. MEASUREMENT 309 (1977).

"Primary" Dispute Resolution Processes[7]

Characteristics	Adjudication	Arbitration	Mediation	Negotiation
Basis of entry	Involuntary	Voluntary or compulsory	Voluntary or mandated	Voluntary
Effect of resolution	Binding; subject to appeal	Binding, subject to review on limited grounds	If agreement, enforceable as contract; sometimes agreement embodied in court decree	If agreement, enforceable as contract
Third party	Imposed, third-party, neutral decision maker, generally with no specialized expertise in dispute subject	Party-selected third-party decision maker, often with specialized subject expertise	Party-selected or appointed by a court, agency or outside provider, sometimes with specialized expertise	No third-party involved
Degree of formality	Formalized and highly structured by predetermined rules	Procedurally less formal; procedural rules and substantive law may be set by parties	Usually informal, no fixed rules	Usually informal, unstructured
Nature of proceeding	Opportunity to present proofs and arguments	Opportunity to present proofs and arguments	Unbounded discussion of evidence, arguments and interests	Unbounded discussion of evidence, arguments and interests
Outcome	Principled decision, supported by reasoned opinion	Sometimes principled decision, sometimes supported by reasoned opinion	Mutually acceptable agreement sought	Mutually acceptable agreement sought
Private/public	Public	Private, unless judicial review sought	Private	Private

---

7. This table is a slightly modified version of one that appears in GOLDBERG, SANDER, ROGERS & COLE, Dispute Resolution: Negotiation, Mediation and Other Processes 4 (5th ed. 2007). That text also identifies a number of "hybrid" dispute resolution mechanisms formed by combining elements of two or more of these "primary" processes.

What Does Ms. Lopez Want Exactly? How Much Does She Want It? Where Can She Get It? What Could Happen If She Tries?   In the fascinating, frustrating 1993 film, *The Story of Qiu Ju*, a peasant woman from rural mainland China tries to achieve justice for her husband after an altercation in which he is kicked in the groin by the village chief. Unable to resolve her problem informally, she begins a tortuous journey through various court processes newly established by the People's Republic of China. The court system fails her utterly, despite awarding her monetary damages, because it will not give her the only thing she ever really wanted as vindication for the humiliation her husband suffered — an apology. Moreover, her resort to the courts may actually have made things worse: As the film ends, she appears to be visibly pained on learning that her claim has resulted in the perpetrator's arrest — something she did not want or intend.

Our popular culture depicts dispute resolution almost exclusively in terms of the litigation process. So does the case method of instruction, used in the formative first year of every law school in America. Law schools teach students to fit facts into appropriate legal categories and to convert disputes into lawsuit-worthy claims. As a result, many lawyers and their clients are socialized early on to see litigation as the default "process of choice" for all potential legal problems. And if Ms. Lopez's primary objective is a job promotion and/or an award of damages, pursuing a civil rights lawsuit is an option she may want to (or have to) consider.

But maybe all she really wants, or what she mostly wants (because people rarely have just one motive for anything they do), is the dignity of a face-to-face meeting with the company manager who passed her over for a promotion. Or maybe she would like the opportunity to sit down with company officials and try to work out an entirely new relationship within the organization — something that a court could never compel. And could there be unintended consequences of suing? Might she be branded a troublemaker? Might her coworkers abandon her? These variables might influence her decision making.

The importance of the issues to Ms. Lopez — the *intensity* of her feelings about what has happened to her — will also be an important factor in any process choice she makes. For example, she may feel angry enough to want to try to negotiate some kind of informal resolution to her situation (either with or without representation) but not angry enough to "make a federal case out of it." Or, to the contrary, she may feel so furious that she will never agree voluntarily to sit down with "*that S.O.B.*" To make matters more complicated, her objectives and the intensity of her feelings about what has happened to her may shift as her dispute is processed. Which process is more likely to harden (or soften) her resolve to fight to the end? On what might this depend?

How Long Will This Take? How Much Will It Cost? How Involved Does Ms. Lopez Want to Be in the Resolution of Her Dispute?   Although for some disputants, delays are perceived as advantageous and cost is no object, most people are concerned about the efficiency — in both time and money — of the dispute resolution alternatives available to them.[8] Some processes tend to be more time-consuming and expensive than others.

---

8. Joseph B. Stulberg & Lela P. Love, Community Dispute Resolution and Training Manual 19 (Mich. Sup. Ct. 1991).

Litigation—at least if it reaches the formal court system that lawyers inhabit—is generally at the slow and costly end of the spectrum. But the fact that litigation may take a long time does not necessarily mean that it will take a lot of the litigant's time. A friend who is a very successful plaintiff's personal injury lawyer begins his relationship with new clients by telling them, "*If this case goes to trial, it will take [x] years to get there. I'll call you when I need you.*" For some clients, to have a possible trial—or even protracted discovery, settlement preparation and negotiation—hanging over them for years might be an excruciating experience. For others, so long as the principal burden is delegated to others (i.e., to their lawyer), that will be just fine.

One of the distinctive characteristics of mediation, compared to other processes, is that it tends to involve disputants directly in the resolution of their own conflicts. The growth of community mediation in the United States in the 1970s and 1980s reflected the ideal of democratizing justice and removing community problems from the exclusive control of courts, lawyers and other "experts."[9] In most forms of mediation, disputants sit at the negotiation table, with or without lawyers, and participate fully in crafting their own solutions to their own problems. For some people, this is one of mediation's most attractive features. For others, the prospect of facing an opponent at close range across the bargaining table is just too daunting; they prefer to have matters handled by a lawyer or other agent. Still others may prefer to cede control to a judge or arbitrator to decide their case, rather than having to engage in the hard work of trying to hash out a solution themselves or having to live with the tough compromises that "settling" may require.

How Strong Is Ms. Lopez's Case? Is There Enough Information to Predict The Outcome? How Risk Averse Is She?   Initiating litigation might make sense for Rosa Lopez if she has a strong legal claim, but might be too expensive and time-consuming judged against the potential payoff if she doesn't. Making an informed cost-benefit decision is often difficult when deciding whether to initiate court action, because important information about what has occurred may be lacking.

Note also that depending on the nature of their fee arrangement, lawyers and their prospective clients are likely to have different tolerances for risk when proceeding in the face of information gaps. An arrangement that makes the payment of fees and expenses contingent on a successful outcome will encourage more people to choose to litigate than one that requires an immediate and ongoing outlay of money. But the corollary is also true: Few lawyers will be willing to represent Ms. Lopez on a contingent fee basis unless her claim is deemed strong and her damages are substantial.

How Important Is Establishing a Precedent? How Does Ms. Lopez Feel About Publicity Versus Privacy? Formality Versus Informality?   If Rosa Lopez is concerned about publicly vindicating her position, or establishing a principle that will be applied to others, or combining forces with others who

---

9. SALLY MERRY & NEIL MILNER, The Possibility of Popular Justice: A Case Study of Community Mediation in the United States 10 (1993).

have experienced similar treatment, then she will most likely prefer litigation over other dispute resolution options. To the extent that she values the privacy of a mediation or arbitration setting and outcome or prefers the informality of mediation over the formality of a court or arbitration proceeding, those factors may loom large in her choice of process.

Will This Process Be Fair? Will Using It Lead To a Just and Durable Outcome?   This is the bottom line, of course. No one in Ms. Lopez's situation would deliberately choose a process that is unfair. Studies consistently demonstrate that mediation leads to high participant satisfaction and high rates of compliance with settlement terms.[10] But not all people have the verbal, intellectual and bargaining skills, or the ideal conflict management style, to use mediation effectively. Some individuals have overly accommodating bargaining styles that make it difficult for them to assert and protect themselves and who, even when they have lawyers present to protect them, may "give away the store." For such individuals, choosing mediation could be a risky option.

■ §1.4 VIEWS FROM THE "OUTSIDE": WHY ARE PEOPLE, COURTS AND OTHER INSTITUTIONS INCREASINGLY USING MEDIATION? WHAT CONCERNS MIGHT THIS RAISE?

The foregoing discussion should demonstrate that mediation is not a panacea for all individuals or all disputes; that there remains an important place for traditional adjudication in the resolution of disputes; and that selecting an appropriate dispute resolution process is a complex, sensitive and highly individualized task. There can be no doubt, however, that in the last twenty to thirty years, the use of mediation and other alternative forms of dispute resolution has risen substantially. (Some are fond of saying that these days the "A" in "ADR" stands for "appropriate," not "alternative," given the explosion in its use.[11]) With that rise in use, however, has come substantial criticism from scholars and practitioners.

Does Mediation Really Save Time and Money?   The perception that mediation is a faster, cheaper, more efficient process than litigation for resolving disputes is probably the most important reason for its explosive growth in legal matters. In his often-cited 1982 Report on the State of the Judiciary, U.S. Supreme Court Chief Justice Warren Burger attributed to Abraham Lincoln the following quotation: "Discourage litigation. Persuade your neighbors to compromise wherever they can. Point out to them how the nominal winner is often the real loser — in fees, expenses and waste of time."[12]

---

10. *See, e.g.*, ROSELLE L. WISSLER, *The Effectiveness of Court-Connected Dispute Resolution in Civil Cases*, 22 CONFLICT RES. Q. 55, 65-68 (2004) (review of empirical literature).
11. *See, e.g.*, CARRIE MENKEL-MEADOW, *Ethics in ADR: The Many "C's" of Professional Responsibility and Dispute Resolution*, 28 FORDHAM URB. L.J. 979 (2001).
12. WARREN BURGER, *Isn't There a Better Way?* 68 A.B.A. J. 274 (1982). Empirical research on court-based mediation programs is far from conclusive as to whether they are effective in cutting down on litigants' costs or litigation delays. *See, e.g.* JAMES S. KAKALIK et al., An Evaluation of Mediation and Early Neutral Evaluation Under the Civil Justice Reform Act (1996).

In reality, however, the most appropriate benchmark for evaluating the efficiency of mediation is not really adjudication; it is unassisted negotiation. Well over 90 percent of all cases filed in courts each year end before trial, sometimes by abandonment or court ruling on a dispositive motion, but most often by means of negotiation. Many thousands of additional disputes are settled each year by negotiation before they ever ripen into "cases." So the more relevant question is whether mediation is faster, cheaper and more efficient than direct negotiation between the parties. As it turns out, the empirical evidence on this question is inconclusive.

Does Mediation Produce Better Justice? Many mediation proponents believe that mediation produces outcomes that are substantively superior to those that courts—in their "limited remedial imagination"[13]—can dispense. Because mediation can explore the participants' real concerns and priorities, advocates argue, it stands a better chance of yielding satisfying solutions. By contrast, adjudication's exclusive focus on legal norms and legal rights tends to restrict most court judgments to binary, win-lose decisions based on a limited set of "legally relevant" claims and defenses.

Critics of mediation argue that it produces second-class justice.[14] Lacking the procedural and substantive protections afforded by adversary trials and meeting in secret behind closed doors, participants with less power — especially poor people, women and persons of color—are routinely disadvantaged by the mediation process, critics contend. They argue further that mediation cannot produce just outcomes if the parties lack equal bargaining power.

Is Mediation More Humane? Regardless of the outcome, advocates argue that mediation is a gentler, more humane process that reduces the emotional toll of protracted litigation and has the capacity to produce genuine catharsis. Empirical studies consistently demonstrate that participants in mediation are satisfied with the process when it is used appropriately and skillfully.[15]

Mediation critics worry that, as practiced in many settings, mediation can unduly dampen conflict, discourage participants from freely expressing their anger and deter them from vindicating important legal rights. Some critics believe that when disputants are urged to use mediation, they may be encouraged to sacrifice justice for peace. Anthropologist Laura Nader calls this "the ideology

---

13. CARRIE MENKEL-MEADOW, *Toward Another View of Legal Mediation: The Structure of Problem Solving*, 31 UCLA L. REV. 754, 791 (1984).
14. *See, e.g.*, RICHARD L. ABEL, *The Contradictions of Informal Justice, in* 1 The Politics of Informal Justice 270-295 (1982); RICHARD DELGADO, *ADR and the Dispossessed: Recent Books about the Deformalization Movement*, 13 LAW & SOC. INQUIRY 145 (1988); RICHARD DELGADO et al., *Fairness and Formality: Minimizing the Risk of Prejudice in Alternative Dispute Resolution*, 1985 WIS. L. REV. 1359, 1375-1378 (1985) (claiming that psychodynamic, social-psychological and economic factors contribute to prejudice in alternative dispute resolution); TRINA GRILLO, *The Mediation Alternative: Process Dangers for Women*, 100 YALE L.J. 1545, 1590 (1991) ("The very intimacy that renders mediation such a potentially constructive process may facilitate the mediator's projection of her own conflicts onto the parties, and the possibilities and dangers of transference and countertransference."); LAURA NADER, *Controlling Processes in the Practice of Law: Hierarchy and Pacification in the Movement to Re-Form Dispute Ideology*, 9 OHIO ST. J. ON DISP. RESOL. 1, 12 (1993) ("Mandatory mediation abridges American Freedom because it is often outside the law, eliminates choice of procedure, removes equal protection before an adversary law, and is generally hidden from view.").
15. *See* WISSLER, *supra* note 10, at 661, n.79 (summarizing studies).

of coercive harmony."[16] And recent studies are beginning to raise questions about how much people actually value "humane informality" in the resolution of their disputes.[17]

How Voluntary Is Mediation, Really?   Many of the claims made on behalf of mediation by its supporters — that it is more democratic, more creative, more humane — presuppose that individuals come to the mediation process voluntarily, that they choose it because it is "a better way." And there is no doubt that many people do freely choose mediation over other dispute resolution options available to them.

But increasingly, mediation and other forms of private dispute resolution are being forced upon disputants. For example, in Rosa Lopez's situation, she might have previously been required to sign, as a condition of employment, a pre-dispute mediation or arbitration clause that either waives her right to litigate claims against the company or conditions that right on first making a settlement effort. Such agreements have generally been upheld by the courts, but they have proved controversial.[18]

In a growing trend, courts, administrative agencies and other institutions with the power to resolve conflict have gotten on the mandatory ADR bandwagon by requiring that litigants attempt some form of alternative process before they are permitted to proceed to a hearing. Mediation advocates worry that, as mediation has been adopted in this way, it has been co-opted by these institutions and has become routinized and "lawyerized," more and more resembling the processes it was designed to replace.[19]

Is Private Justice Good for the Public?   Finally, there is the important question of whether the increasing privatization of justice is good social policy. Critics argue that private justice is antinormative: When disputants settle their claims privately, the public is deprived of the opportunity to learn about important social problems, and courts and other institutions are deprived of the opportunity to enunciate and enforce important public values.[20] Rosa Lopez's problem provides a case in point: If Ms. Lopez resolves her dispute informally, an opportunity may have been lost to expose and eradicate systemic discrimination at a large corporation. Mediation scholar Carrie Menkel-Meadow asks in response, "Whose dispute is it anyway?" and suggests that this debate pits those "who care more about the people actually engaged in disputes" against "those who care more about institutional and structural arrangements."[21]

---

16. NADER, *supra* note 14, at 7.
17. *See, e.g.,* DEBORAH HENSLER, *Suppose It's Not True: Challenging Mediation Ideology,* 2002 J. DISP. RESOL. 81 (2002) (arguing, based on twenty-five years of procedural justice studies, that many litigants prefer the formality of trials).
18. *Compare Gilmer v. Interstate/Johnson Lane Corp.,* 500 U.S. 20 (1991) and *Fisher v. G.E. Medical Systems,* 276 F. Supp. 2d 891 (M.D. Tenn. 2003), *with* KATHERINE STONE, *Mandatory Arbitration of Individual Employment Rights: The Yellow Dog Contract of the 1990s,* 73 DENV. U. L. REV. 1017 (1996).
19. NANCY WELSH, *Making Deals in Court-Connected Mediation: What's Justice Got to Do with It?* 79 WASH. U. L.Q. 787, 845 (2001).
20. OWEN FISS, *Against Settlement,* 93 YALE L.J. 1073 (1984). *See also* DAVID LUBAN, *Settlement and the Erosion of the Public Realm,* 83 GEO. L.J. 2619 (1995).
21. CARRIE MENKEL-MEADOW, *Whose Dispute Is It Anyway? A Philosophic and Democratic Defense of Settlement (In Some Cases),* 83 GEO. L.J. 2663, 2669 (1995).

▪ §1.5 THE MEDIATOR'S ROLE AND FUNCTION: AN INTRODUCTION

Assume that, after a period of unsuccessful negotiation but before any legal action is initiated, Rosa Lopez and Texitron both retain lawyers and agree to attempt mediation. Consider the following questions, all of which are debated in the mediation field and which this book will explore:

- **What qualifications and experience should their mediator possess?** Should the mediator be an attorney? A person with knowledge of potentially relevant civil rights laws? Someone with knowledge of information technology or the petroleum industry? How important is *substantive law* or *industry knowledge* compared to *process competence* as a mediator? What about using two co-mediators with differing expertise or (as this is a gender-discrimination case) genders?

- **What are the goals of the mediation?** Should the mediator's primary goal be to end this dispute on whatever terms the parties will accept? To improve communication and repair relationships? To help the parties make well-considered decisions for themselves, regardless of whether there is a settlement? How broadly or narrowly should the mediator define what can be discussed and resolved? Or is that a decision that the participants should make?

- **What are the roles of representatives in the mediation?** In community settings and some forms of legal mediation (in such areas as small claims and family disputes), parties commonly appear without attorneys. Here, Ms. Lopez and the company will each be represented by counsel. Should the mediator look primarily to the lawyers or to their clients when it comes time to speak? Who decides this? Should the mediator try to encourage the participants to talk directly to one another or primarily to her? In what ways might the presence of lawyers pose challenges for the mediator? Are there ways in which their presence might be an asset?

- **What is the place of feelings, as opposed to facts, in mediation?** How much anger and hurtful talk should the mediator permit during the course of the mediation? How might the expression of strong emotions help or hurt the process?

- **Is mediation about cooperative problem-solving or competitive bargaining?** If a resolution to the dispute is what the parties seek, is it the mediator's job to help the disputants bargain in a collaborative mode to reach a solution that can satisfy the needs of all? Or is it to help them engage (perhaps more effectively than they could do themselves) in competitive bargaining until a deal is struck? Is it important that mediators be good negotiators themselves?

- **Should the mediator hold joint or separate meetings?** Should mediation be conducted with everyone present at all times? Or should the mediator meet privately with the parties if that might make the task easier? When and why might separate meetings be useful or problematic?

■ **How directive or persuasive should the mediator be?** How much, if at all, should a mediator try to influence the shape and subject matter of the discussions? How active should he or she be in pointing out problems with each side's perspective or in urging disputants to change their stance? Should the mediator insist that all proposals for how to resolve the dispute come from the parties themselves, or should the mediator suggest possible ideas?

■ **Should the mediator provide legal or other evaluative feedback?** In a potential legal matter like the Rosa Lopez case, should a mediator express his or her views about the strengths and weaknesses of each side's position if this case were to go forward? Make a prediction about what might happen in an administrative hearing or trial? To what extent, if at all, should legal rules and legal norms guide the discussion?

■ **Is the mediator responsible for the fairness of the outcome?** What should a mediator do if the parties reach a solution that seems unjust or unwise?

The consistent and — for those seeking a simple model — frustrating answer to virtually all these questions is: *it depends*. At least that is our answer. It is not everyone's. There are some mediation theorists and practitioners who hew to a single vision of the way in which "good" mediation should be practiced.

But mediations today are conducted in so many different settings, in so many different kinds of disputes, with so many different kinds of participants, by so many different types of mediators, that it is difficult to make any universal statements about the way it is or should be practiced. For example, the mediation of a collective bargaining contract dispute by an experienced labor mediator might have little in common with a victim-juvenile offender conference conducted by a pair of volunteer community mediators. Or a court-ordered, single-session mediation of an automobile accident case involving experienced trial counsel and an insurance adjuster might not be best handled the same way as a private, multiple-session, parties-only divorce mediation that is conducted over a period of months.

The hallmark of mediation's power and potential lies in its flexibility — the fact that it can take different forms, depending on the needs and objectives of the parties, the mediator's background, the characteristics of the dispute and the setting in which the mediation is held. Many supporters of mediation celebrate the fact that it is eclectic. To critics, who see mediation as vague, amorphous and lacking standards, this flexibility is a source of concern. Commentators and performance evaluators sometimes disagree about the specific skills that constitute mediator competence.[22] Some even doubt that mediation can be reduced to a definable set of behaviors.[23] What implications does this have for you as you embark on the study of mediation?

---

22. *See* Society of Professionals in Dispute Resolution (SPIDR), *Ensuring Competence and Quality in Dispute Resolution Practice*, Report No. 2 of the SPIDR Commission on Qualifications (April 1995); ABA Section of Dispute Resolution Task Force on Improving Mediation Quality, Final Report (2008); STEPHEN B. GOLDBERG & MARGARET L. SHAW, *Further Investigation into the Secrets of Successful and Unsuccessful Mediators*, 26 ALT. HIGH COST LITIG. 149 (September 2008).

23. *See* SARA COBB & JANET RIFKIN, *Practice and Paradox: Deconstructing Neutrality in Mediation*, 16 LAW & SOC. INQUIRY 35 (1991).

■ §1.6 THE SKILLS OF EFFECTIVE MEDIATORS: AN INTRODUCTION

Based on our experience as teachers and trainers, we strongly believe that mediation skills can be taught and learned. We do have preferred approaches, which we will advance and explain. But there is no doubt that embracing the flexibility and variability of the mediation process complicates the task of skills training. Being a good mediator is not like preparing your favorite lasagna over and over again. There is no single recipe that you can follow in all cases. If you want to be an effective mediator, you will need to adapt your approach, if not your basic orientation and style, to the specific situation with which you are presented. In this book we will try to help you do that, by identifying the *factors* that may make one approach more appropriate to use than another in concrete settings and situations.

Nevertheless, we do believe that there are certain foundational skills that are at the core of all good mediation. Here are four of the most important skills themes we will explore in this book:

- ■ **Effective mediators possess good communication skills.** This includes the ability to listen, question, explain and facilitate the communication of others. It means being able to leave participants feeling "heard" and treated with dignity. No matter what the style of mediation or the setting in which the process is conducted, effective communication is the foundation of good practice.

- ■ **Effective mediators are skilled diagnosticians.** As information is presented, effective mediators are able to analyze the characteristics of the dispute and the disputants in order to determine whether mediation is an appropriate process for the case and what kind of mediation approach is needed. They are also adept at diagnosing the causes of the dispute and at perceiving or intuiting psychological and negotiating stumbling blocks that may impede its resolution.

- ■ **Effective mediators are able to establish a climate conducive to constructive negotiation.** This includes a number of skills: helping the parties determine their true interests and priorities; helping structure the participants' discussions; assisting the parties in developing creative, realistic resolution options; helping them assess these potential solutions; helping parties make and frame principled offers; managing reactions to offers in ways that enhance the chances of continued progress; and helping participants maintain a sense of optimism and cooperation in the face of potential impasse.

- ■ **Effective mediators are persuasive.** As we define this (somewhat controversial) term, it includes conditioning the parties to be open to changing their perspectives and to seeking a solution, encouraging them to question their stance and, when appropriate, providing feedback and evaluation in a way that can be received constructively.

■ §1.7 HOW THIS BOOK IS ORGANIZED

The remainder of this book is divided into three main sections. In Chapters 2 and 3, we consider the preconditions and foundations of the mediation process, starting with unaided negotiations and why they fail, followed by the major conceptual approaches or forms of mediation and, briefly, three fundamental ethical norms that guide all mediators, regardless of style. In Chapters 4 through 11, we explore in detail the stages of the mediation process and the skills of effective mediators. In Chapters 12 and 13, respectively, we provide a detailed analysis of the ethics of mediating and address the unique role and skills challenges for lawyers representing a client in mediation.[24]

Mediation is not a series of disembodied moves and techniques disconnected from particularized settings; as a result, it cannot fruitfully be studied in the abstract. The variability of the mediation process suggests that the subject can best be studied — perhaps can only be studied meaningfully — *in context.*

To accomplish this, in preparing this book we have created three mediation simulations, all based on actual cases, with varying subject matters and dispute characteristics. We asked nine experienced mediators, chosen for their differing styles, philosophies and backgrounds, to mediate one case each on videotape. The simulations were not scripted. The mediators were given only the kind of information that a mediator in the actual case would have seen prior to beginning the mediation. They were told to preside as they ordinarily would, making decisions as to how to conduct the process based on their usual style as well as their sense of the parties and the needs of the dispute. Disputants were also told to behave as they would in a real dispute by reacting to what happened in each session and to each mediator, and not according to a packaged "script."

We have organized substantial portions of the book around selected excerpts from these video case studies, which are briefly summarized below. They include essentially full-length ("Play All") examples, designed to give you a sense of one mediation from beginning to end, and shorter, "chapter-by-chapter" excerpts ("Video Clips"), depicting a particular stage in the mediation process or specific kinds of mediator interventions and challenges discussed in the text.

Our goal in integrating video and text is to help you analyze — in context and in action — the various stages of the mediation process, the different forms of mediation, the many constituent skills of effective mediators and the complex communicative, strategic and ethical choices (and mistakes) that experienced mediators make.

Video Case Summaries

Wilson v. DiLorenzo: **A Consumer Dispute.**   Homeowner Bernice Wilson sues contractor Frank DiLorenzo in small claims court in Hartford, Connecticut. She seeks to rescind the contract she entered into with him to renovate her kitchen and to recover actual and punitive damages. Her complaint alleges that she was promised that the work would be done in four weeks and that "more than three

---

24. While Chapter 13 focuses on attorney-representatives, its content may also provide guidance for non-lawyer representatives seeking to assist potential mediation participants.

months later, [it] is still not done. I am without a kitchen, and my house is a shambles. In addition, I have been defrauded by this contractor. He didn't tell me I needed new sheet rock on my walls. He used second-rate cabinet materials without telling me he was going to do so. The cabinets have not been hung properly, and the linoleum has an ugly seam. I seek return of my deposit, money necessary to hire a new contractor to complete the job properly, lost wages and punitive damages, in the amount of $14,927.50, plus the court filing fee."

The defendant's answer denies each of these claims and, as an affirmative counterclaim, alleges that the plaintiff "breached her contract with defendant by refusing to permit him entry into her house in order to complete the work contracted for." The defendant seeks $3,997.50 in damages for the unpaid balance owed under the contract.

As part of the court's Dispute Resolution Program, the parties were asked and have agreed to attempt mediation, using a mediator assigned to them. There is no cost for this service. If the case cannot be resolved after ninety minutes, it will be sent to court for an immediate trial. The defendant contractor is represented at the mediation by his attorney, "Barry Bowen."[25] The plaintiff homeowner appears *pro se* (without a lawyer).

The case was mediated three times by three different mediators.

G. Craig Lord
Mediator, Version 1
(Play All)

Cheryl Cutrona
Mediator, Version 2
(Play All)

Judith Meyer
Mediator, Version 3

Bernice Wilson
Plaintiff

Frank DiLorenzo
Defendant

Lee Rosengard
("Barry Bowen")
Attorney for Defendant

---

25. "Barry Bowen" is in fact Lee Rosengard, a Philadelphia lawyer and experienced mediation representative. In the other mediation involving lawyers (*see Resnick v. Stevens Realty*, which follows), we drop stage names.

***Fitzgerald v. Fitzgerald*: A Child Custody Dispute.**   Jane and Bob Fitzgerald are the parents of a four-and-a-half-year-old daughter and a three-year-old son. Each is seeking to become the children's primary custodian. The Fitzgeralds are currently living at separate addresses in Philadelphia, approximately eight miles apart, with Jane Fitzgerald living in the family house. Ms. Fitzgerald filed her petition for custody a couple of days after her husband's identical filing. At the time these petitions were filed (some five weeks ago), the children were listed as residing with their father. The court file also indicates that three-and-a-half months ago, Jane Fitzgerald sought and obtained a Philadelphia Family Court Protection from Abuse (PFA) Order, which ordered Bob out of the family home for sixty days, and that the order has now expired. The court file contains no indication that either party is represented by an attorney.

The judge to whom their case was assigned ordered the Fitzgeralds to try mediation under an experimental ADR program. The Fitzgeralds were given the choice of a free one-hour mediation session with a court staff mediator or up to three hours (two ninety-minute sessions) of private mediation for a fee of $300. They chose the latter option and were assigned a mediator from a panel of practitioners.

The case was mediated three times by four different mediators (two of whom worked as a lawyer-therapist co-mediation team). Only the initial ninety-minute sessions were filmed. They take place in the mediator's office.

***Resnick v. Stevens Realty, Inc.*: A Personal Injury Case.**   Plaintiff Josh Resnick, a former graduate student at Rutgers University, has sued Stevens Realty Inc., a New Jersey real estate company owned by Howard Stevens, for injuries suffered when he was bound, gagged, threatened and robbed at knifepoint by an

Samuel Rossito
Mediator Version 1

Jean Biesecker and
Don Weinstein
Mediator Version 2

Mary Hanna
Mediator Version 3
(Play All)

Bob Fitzgerald
Father

Jane Fitzgerald
Mother

unknown intruder in his apartment. The incident that is the subject of the lawsuit took place in Bloomfield, New Jersey, a middle-class suburb of Newark. Following the incident but before this court action was initiated, the plaintiff dropped out of his graduate program and moved back to Long Island to live with his parents.

The claim was filed in U.S. District Court for the District of New Jersey[26] alleging that the amount in controversy exceeds $75,000. Both parties are represented; defense counsel was retained by Stevens' liability insurer.

The plaintiff's complaint alleges that the defendant provided inadequate building security. Specifications of negligence include: failure to secure and lock all doors and windows to prevent unauthorized building access; failure to construct and maintain the fire escape so as to prevent unauthorized building access; negligent maintenance and/or construction of doors and windows; and failure to provide or maintain window gates on all fire escape windows.

The defendant's answer denies any negligence or any special knowledge of crime in the area and as an affirmative defense, alleges that the harm was caused by the plaintiff and his roommate, who left their apartment door unlocked. According to the defendant, the plaintiff's contributory negligence was greater than defendant's, if any, barring recovery under the applicable law.

The plaintiff alleges that he has suffered economic damages (loss of tuition) and other property loss (a new iPod and $300 in cash that were stolen by his assailant), as well as severe psychological injury (post-traumatic stress) as a result of this incident. Following the incident, he was in therapy with a psychiatrist for a period of five months.

The litigation has been pending for fifteen months. Both sides have conducted extensive discovery in the case and have decided to attempt mediation. Rather than accept a court-appointed mediator, the parties selected a private mediator, and the lawyers have each provided him a confidential memorandum describing their positions on the facts and law.

Two different mediators mediated the case, each for a period of about two hours. Different attorneys represented the parties in each version.

---

26. Federal jurisdiction is predicated on diversity of citizenship. New Jersey negligence law controls.

Version One

Harris Bock
Mediator
(Play All)

Arthur Lefco
Attorney for Defendant

Judy Greenwood
Attorney for Plaintiff

Howard Stevens
Defendant

Josh Resnick
Plaintiff

Version Two

Charles Forer
Mediator

Lauren Levin Geary
Attorney for Defendant

David Kwass
Attorney for Plaintiff

Howard Stevens
Defendant

Josh Resnick
Plaintiff

CHAPTER

2

NEGOTIATIONS, AND
WHY THEY FAIL

■ §2.1 WHAT DOES IT MEAN TO SAY THAT NEGOTIATIONS "FAIL"?

It may seem strange to talk about the "failure" of negotiations when so many commercial deals are completed by negotiation, so many international conflicts are resolved through diplomacy, so many disputes are resolved before they result in litigation and even where litigation has been initiated, the vast majority of lawsuits — well over 90 percent, according to most studies — are settled short of trial.[1] But negotiations fail every day, in ways and for reasons that are both obvious and subtle. Consider the following cases:

> • In September 2009, a local bar that caters to a primarily gay clientele and that has long provided support to persons with HIV and AIDS is raided without a warrant by the local police. Searches are conducted on patrons who are forced to the floor, an office door is kicked in and anti-gay slurs are uttered by police. Those few patrons who were arrested are acquitted or have their charges dismissed. The bar owner, its employees and a number of patrons, through their lawyer, offer to forego any claims they might have against the city if it apologizes. When the city refuses, a civil rights suit is instituted. After sixteen months of angry public wrangling that consumes the time of top city officials and galvanizes civic support for the bar, the already cash-strapped city agrees to pay over $1 million in damages and reform police practices — and it apologizes too.[2]

continues on next page >

---

1. *See generally* MARC GALANTER, The Vanishing Trial: An Examination of Trials and Related Matters in Federal and State Courts (2004).
2. *http://www.thegavoice.com/index.php/news/atlanta-news-menu/781-mayor-atlanta-eagle-attorney-share-testy-exchange-at-lgbt-town-hall-forum; http://www.thegavoice.com/index.php/news/atlanta-news-menu/1717-atlanta-eagle-co-owner-says-bar-is-not-1-million-richer-after-federal-lawsuit-settlement.*

21

- A Kentucky man is indicted on a charge of passing a forged check in the amount of $88.30. In plea negotiations, in the presence of the defendant's counsel, the prosecutor offers to recommend a sentence of five years in prison in exchange for the defendant's plea of guilty. The prosecutor expressly warns that if the defendant refuses the offer, he will seek an indictment under the Kentucky Habitual Criminal Act, under which the defendant, a twice-convicted felon, is subject to a mandatory sentence of life imprisonment. The defendant rejects the plea deal and, after re-indictment and a jury trial, is convicted and sentenced to life in prison. The United States Supreme Court upholds the conviction, noting that "the recidivist charge was fully supported by the evidence."[3]
- An agent for an aging rock star is negotiating with a noted concert promoter over payment for the rock star's appearance at a proposed summer concert at a large metropolitan arena. They finally reach an agreement on a compromise fee, but only after a bitter series of exchanges, and with the promoter paying more than he wants to and the rocker receiving less. Had they discussed the matter more openly, they would have discovered that they each had differing expectations regarding the probable size of the audience, and that both parties would have been happier with an arrangement in which the performer received a smaller fixed fee plus an agreed-upon percentage of the gate.[4]

When negotiation and mediation scholars talk about the failure of negotiations, they use the word "failure" in two different ways. Most obvious, of course, are the cases in which no agreement is reached — where individuals never talk at all or, having tried to talk, reach an impasse under circumstances where it would have been rational — at least in hindsight — to have resolved the dispute by negotiation. The first two cases would appear to fall into this category.

More subtle are cases where an agreement is reached, but only after the incurring of unnecessarily high costs or on terms that are less than optimal for the parties. Economists who study negotiation call such settlements "inefficient" because they involve excessive bargaining costs or fail to achieve all the gains that were jointly available to the parties.[5] The third case would appear to fall into this category.

"Rational" Negotiation Decisions.   It is important to emphasize that not every breakdown in negotiations represents a failure. Under some circumstances, it may be perfectly sensible for negotiators to walk away from a deal that is offered or to reject proposed settlement terms in a dispute and take their chances at a risky trial. Moreover, negotiating decisions cannot be evaluated by hindsight; sometimes vindicating an important principle is worth taking a big risk. (Viewed this way, the case of the Kentucky recidivist may look less like a negotiation failure.) "Rational" settlement decisions require that each negotiator carefully analyze the various alternatives to settlement, identify his or her best alternative

---

3. *Bordenkircher v. Hayes*, 434 U.S. 357, 359 (1978).
4. This is a slightly embellished version of a story told in David A. Lax & James K. Sebenius, The Manager as Negotiator 31-32 (1986).
5. Robert A. Baruch Bush, *What Do We Need a Mediator For?: Mediation's "Value Added" for Negotiators*, 12 Ohio St. J. on Disp. Resol. 1, 8 (1996).

to a negotiated agreement or "BATNA"[6] and reject any proposed settlement offer that is not as favorable as that alternative.

Key Concepts: Analyzing Alternatives in Transactions.   For example, in a transaction like that between our hypothetical concert promoter and the rock star, suppose that the rock star has set a minimum price of $80,000 for all appearances. He is concerned that if he lowers his minimum price, word will get out and this will impair his reputation and future value as a performer. He is also very rich and would rather vacation in the south of France than accept less than his minimum price. On the one hand, if the promoter knows that he can book another singer who will be as good a draw for $70,000, both negotiators will walk away from the deal, and it will be rational for each of them to do so: Each has an alternative that is better for him than the proposed transaction. Stated differently (and introducing some key negotiation concepts), there is no available *bargaining zone* in which the parties can negotiate, because there is no overlap between the respective *reservation prices, resistance points* or *bottom lines* of each negotiator. On the other hand, if the promoter were willing to pay up to $100,000 to sign the rock star, then he and the agent could negotiate within a bargaining zone of $80,000-$100,000. If, for some reason, their negotiations *still* broke down, that would represent a failure of bargaining.

Analyzing Alternatives in Legal Disputes.   When a lawsuit has been initiated (or threatened in a convincing way), the "alternative to a negotiated agreement" normally is litigation, and each side to the dispute must place an *expected value* on the case if it were to go to trial. Determining the expected value of the case helps each party make a rational decision whether to settle — and, in cases involving money, for what amount. As one commentator has written,

> [t]he basic theory of settlement has long been recognized. A rational party should settle only if it can obtain at least what it could achieve by proceeding to trial and verdict, taking into account all of the economic and non-economic costs of both settlement and trial. A plaintiff, for example, should never accept less in settlement than what it estimates it would receive in the way of a verdict at trial, discounting for the expected expenses of proceeding to trial and any other expected economic, social, psychological and legal costs. . . . The point where a party is indifferent to whether the case goes to trial or settles is the party's break-even point, or reservation price.[7]

The valuation process can be relatively simple or very complex, depending on the case. Consider a simple two-party bicycle accident case in which the defendant, an uninsured second-year MBA student, having had two beers at lunch forty-five minutes earlier, struck the pedestrian-plaintiff, knocking her down and breaking her leg as she was starting to cross the street at a crosswalk. The defendant claims he was not intoxicated and that the accident only occurred because, as he was slowing down to stop, he had to swerve hurriedly in order to avoid a stray dog that

---

6. Roger Fisher et al., Getting to Yes 100 (2d ed. 1991).
7. Peter Toll Hoffman, *Valuation of Cases for Settlement: Theory and Practice*, 1991 J. Disp. Resol. 1, 3-4 (1991). We have drawn on the analysis in this article in the discussion that follows.

darted in front of him. (Neither the plaintiff nor the one bystander who witnessed the accident saw a dog.)

Assume that there is no dispute that the plaintiff incurred $10,000 in out-of-pocket costs: $1,500 to replace a new laptop computer she dropped in the collision, $7,000 in unreimbursed medical expenses (she had no insurance) and missed work, resulting in lost income of $1,500. She also claims three months of pain resulting from her broken leg, although she concedes that this injury was not permanent. The defendant does not claim that the plaintiff contributed to her own injury. The matters in dispute are (a) whether the collision was caused by the defendant's negligence, or was instead an unavoidable accident; and (b) how to compensate the plaintiff for pain and suffering associated with her leg injury.

In a case like this, the rational plaintiff, considering a choice between settlement and trial, would take the following factors into consideration:[8]

- **What are the odds of establishing defendant's liability?** This requires a careful assessment of the available evidence regarding defendant's drinking, driving and control of the bike, and the claimed darting dog. Assume for purposes of discussion that plaintiff (or more likely her counsel) believes that there is a very good chance, say, roughly 80 percent, of establishing that defendant's negligence was the cause of the accident.

- **What is the most likely damages award?** We know that plaintiff has suffered $10,000 in out-of-pocket expenses. With the assistance of counsel, she must also evaluate the evidence regarding the seriousness of her leg injury, review reported jury verdicts and settlements in cases involving similar injuries and determine the most likely jury award, taking into account the unique facts of her case. Assume that after such research, plaintiff concludes that the most likely jury award for pain and suffering is $30,000, to be added to out-of-pocket costs of $10,000, for a total of $40,000. A preliminary "expected value" of the case can then be determined by multiplying the most likely total jury award ($40,000) by the chances of establishing liability (80%) to yield a gross settlement value of $32,000.[9]

- **What are the costs of trial versus settlement?** The plaintiff must then take into consideration the *comparative litigation costs* (attorneys' fees, filing and expert fees, etc.) of trial versus settlement. If the plaintiff will have to spend an additional $3,000 to prepare the case for trial rather than accept a

---

8. This is a classic claim in which monetary compensation would be the typical settlement outcome. The approach to decision making described in this section can also be applied to non-monetary claims, with values/preferences assigned to each item at risk.

9. In more complex cases, negotiators often use *decision-tree analysis*—a tool to evaluate closely the legal, factual and evidentiary strengths and weaknesses of the elements of each claim and affirmative defense. For some useful writings on decision-tree analysis, *see* MARJORIE CORMAN AARON & DAVID P. HOFFER, *Decision Analysis as a Method of Evaluating the Trial Alternative, in* Mediating Legal Disputes 312-317 (Dwight Golann ed., 1996) (showing that in decision-tree analysis, parties identify adjudicatory paths for resolution, estimate probability of success along each branch of the path and approximate the likely substantive outcome); JEFFREY M. SENGER, *Decision Analysis in Negotiation*, 87 MARQ. L. REV. 723 (examining how decision analysis can be used to assess the value of a case and help to determine the best strategy in a negotiation).

settlement now, then it would be rational for her to take $29,000, not $32,000, to settle the case.[10]

■ **How much interest could I earn on a settlement check received today?** The next consideration to take into account is the *time value of money*. Suppose that a trial of the case will not occur for two years. Money received today is worth more to the plaintiff than the same amount received in two years if it can be invested to earn interest or be used to pay bills that are now due. If the plaintiff were able to invest any money she received now at 6 percent, she would be better off accepting $26,000 to settle her case today than continuing the litigation.

■ **Accounting for psychological preferences and values.** The plaintiff may also wish to think about how comfortable she is with the risk of receiving nothing if she cannot establish the defendant's negligence.[11] Individuals have different levels of toleration of or aversion to risk, which often plays a critical role in their settlement decisions. In addition, individuals considering settlement versus trial are often strongly motivated by other psychological and social factors, such as the need for privacy or public vindication, the desire to create or avoid a precedent or the need for retaliation or closure. These preferences can be roughly quantified with the assistance of a skilled attorney to arrive at an actual "bottom line" for negotiating purposes. (*"OK; you've said that under no circumstances do you want to face the anxiety of a trial. How much less than $26,000 would you accept to avoid a trial?"*)

If both parties engage in this type of analysis, the negotiations should conclude "rationally," settling within the bargaining range created by each side's preference-adjusted "expected value," or breaking off if there is no bargaining range.

So Why Aren't Negotiators Rational?   To return to the three stories with which we began this chapter, all seem like negotiation failures, at least judged from the outside, on purely rational, cost-benefit terms. But we know that human beings (and organizations run and represented by them) do not necessarily act rationally when they negotiate. People are not "merely economic machines, motivated solely by reasons of profit and loss."[12] And while it may be difficult in any particular case to isolate the specific factors that cause a breakdown in negotiations, we know from a broad, interdisciplinary body of empirical and theoretical scholarship the kinds of barriers that, in general, make settlements difficult to achieve. These include:

■ *strategic* barriers caused by competitive bargaining tactics and the strategic withholding and manipulation of information during negotiation;

---

10. Such expenses are often referred to as "transaction" costs. Other kinds of "costs" could be factored into such an analysis as well: the value of foregone profits, leisure and other potential gains that could have been pursued but for a trial ("opportunity costs"); and the personal toll in stress and damaged relationships attributable to a trial ("human costs").
11. In situations (unlike this example) where the plaintiff might be assigned partial responsibility for the disputed incident, these risks would include receiving more than nothing but less than if she were fault-free.
12. HOFFMAN, *supra* note 7, at 33 (1991).

■ *psychological* barriers caused by the inherent emotionality of conflict;

■ *cognitive* barriers that cause predictable distortions in the way individuals pursue and process information, especially in the face of uncertainty;

■ *cultural* barriers posed by differences in negotiators' backgrounds that cause them to misinterpret each other's actions and motivations; and

■ *structural* barriers stemming from the composition or representation of a party that interfere with its ability to make good decisions.

In later sections of this chapter, we analyze these impediments to settlement, focusing primarily on strategic, psychological and cognitive problems. But to be able to assist the parties in overcoming these hurdles, mediators must first understand the wide variety of behaviors they are likely to encounter in negotiation and their possible causes. Accordingly, we first set out some basics of negotiation theory.

■ §2.2 INTRODUCTION TO NEGOTIATION THEORY: "COMPETITIVE" VERSUS "PROBLEM-SOLVING" NEGOTIATION

Take this situation:[13] You are a small-business owner who is very unhappy with the terms of your current four-year lease in a suburban shopping mall. With two years left to go on the lease, you would like to renegotiate its terms. The lease is a percentage clause lease, in which you pay a flat rental substantially below fair market value, plus 7.5 percent of your gross sales. The landlord, a close friend of your deceased father, originally suggested these terms as a personal favor, because you had little initial operating capital and your business concept was new and unproven. Now, two years later, the business has taken off, but the high percentage of sales you have been paying is strangling your profits and, in your view, unduly enriching the landlord. You want a fixed rental arrangement at fair market rates. And you need more space than your current 5,000 square feet.

You have recently been offered an attractive 9,000 square-foot space at a quite reasonable (fixed) rent in a large shopping mall across the street. In your last, angry conversation with the landlord, you threatened to move your business to the other mall, starting in a few months, if the lease is not renegotiated. In fact, the other mall space doesn't really meet your needs at all (it's too much space and rent), and you don't actually intend to move. What would really serve your interests is to figure out a way to expand your current space from 5,000 to 7,000 square feet. Your business projections suggest that, if you could do that, your profits would go up by 40-50 percent.

When you meet to negotiate with the landlord, will you disclose that you don't intend to move to the other mall but that you really need 2,000 extra square feet of space? Or will you use your threat to move as a bargaining chip to pressure the

---

13. Based on Joseph D. Harbaugh, *Whitmore & Rice, in* Lawyer Negotiation Training Materials (Practicing Law Institute, 1988).

landlord to renegotiate? If you disclose that your threat wasn't sincere, the landlord may well refuse to negotiate with you. (After all, there is a written contract and it's you who wants to breach it.) Alternatively, if he knows your threat to leave was a bluff, the landlord might be willing to renegotiate the lease but might hold out for a higher fixed rent than he otherwise would demand.

However, if you don't disclose your real desire to stay put but with additional space, there is little chance of learning whether your current space could be expanded in a way that serves that need, or to discern whether—and how strongly—the landlord wants to keep you as a tenant. This dilemma—between concealing information in order to avoid being exploited and sharing information to more fully meet your interests—is present in most negotiations. Where it is not resolved, some form of negotiation "failure" is likely.

The Tension Between Competing and Problem-Solving in Negotiation.

In order to perform effectively, mediators need to understand the strategic tension between *competing* (attempting to maximize one's own individual gain at the other's expense by getting the largest share of the limited "pie" to be divided) and *problem-solving* (attempting to identify and meet as many true needs of the participants as possible to create a larger pie to divide and give everyone a chance to get a larger slice). The essence of the tension is this: Despite the most careful preparation, negotiators usually lack critical information about each other's needs, interests, preferences and available alternatives to a negotiated settlement. Without freely sharing information, it is generally difficult to find trades that give each negotiator more of what he or she truly values, thereby expanding the amount of total satisfaction the parties can achieve. But if the negotiator openly discloses her preferences, she faces the risk of being exploited by a competitive opponent. She therefore has every rational incentive to hide or distort her preferences and to try to give the other negotiator a false sense of what she will settle for. If she does this, she may end up getting a larger share than might otherwise be available, but of a smaller pie than might have been created through more open information sharing. She also risks potential deadlock, especially if the other negotiator acts in a similar fashion.

This conflict has been called the tension between "creating value" and "claiming value."[14] And although many negotiators tend to view themselves as primarily competitive bargainers or primarily problem-solving bargainers, negotiation theorists have recently suggested that the tension is present—and must be managed—in most negotiations.[15]

To help negotiators manage this tension and negotiate more effectively, mediators need to understand something about the behaviors of competitive and

---

14. DAVID A. LAX & JAMES K. SEBENIUS, The Manager as Negotiator 30-35 (1986), ROBERT H. MNOOKIN, SCOTT R. PEPPET & ANDREW S. TULUMELLO, Beyond Winning 9, 11-43 (2000). The literature on competitive and problem-solving negotiation is vast. The sources we have relied on most heavily include DONALD G. GIFFORD, Legal Negotiation: Theory and Practice (2d ed. 2007); GARY GOODPASTER, A Guide to Negotiation and Mediation (1997); ROGER FISHER & WILLIAM L. URY, Getting to Yes (2d ed. 1991); MELISSA L. NELKIN, Negotiation: Theory and Practice (2d ed. 2007); HOWARD RAIFFA, The Art and Science of Negotiation (2005); and G. RICHARD SHELL, Bargaining for Advantage: Negotiation Strategies for Reasonable People (2d ed. 2006).

15. MNOOKIN, PEPPET & TULUMELLO, *supra* at 11-43.

problem-solving negotiators, who have differing goals with respect to the bargaining process. Because of their differing goals, they often use different strategies and tactics as well.

■ §2.3 BASICS OF COMPETITIVE (DISTRIBUTIVE) BARGAINING

The Goals of Competitive Bargainers.   Competitive bargainers (also known as *distributive* bargainers) generally see most matters as single-issue, zero-sum ("what I gain, you lose") problems and attempt to maximize their own individual gain. Their goal is to "claim value"—that is, to get the largest possible share of what is being bargained over or distributed. If a competitive negotiator bargains with a seller over the price of a used car or an existing business, every dollar more she is forced to pay the seller is a dollar less she can keep. In general, she wants more for herself if possible. Ours is a competitive culture, and distributive negotiation is what most Americans—not just lawyers—generally envision when they think about negotiation.[16]

Lawyers, especially those who primarily handle disputes, often make two additional assumptions that tend to make their negotiations distributive in character. The first is that the only available outcomes that the negotiators may consider are the kinds of limited remedies—in the vast majority of lawsuits, money—that a court can provide.[17] Legal dispute bargaining takes place in the "shadow" of the courts and the legal system.[18] Lawyers are taught from the first day of law school how to analyze claims and defenses and make predictions about what a court would do with a given state of facts.[19] This training causes lawyer-negotiators to tend to focus primarily on the *courtroom* merits of their cases—the legal rights and responsibilities of the parties—often to the exclusion of other potentially important (but legally irrelevant) values or concerns of their clients.

A second assumption affecting legal negotiations relates to the fundamental ethical obligation of lawyers to represent the interests of their clients "zealously."[20] Many lawyers negotiate in the belief that their job is to get a result as close to the other side's bottom line as possible, since to do anything less might constitute a dereliction of duty to their client. In their classic work, *The Lawyering Process*, Professors Gary Bellow and Bea Moulton set forth this traditional adversarial view—a view that, until quite recently, dominated the legal negotiation literature.

---

16. *Id.* at 18.
17. *See* Carrie Menkel-Meadow, *Toward Another View of Negotiation: The Structure of Problem-Solving*, 31 UCLA L. Rev. 754, 789 (1984).
18. *See* Robert H. Mnookin & Lewis Kornhauser, *Bargaining in the Shadow of Law: The Case of Divorce*, 88 Yale L.J. 950 (1979).
19. Leonard Riskin, *Mediation and Lawyers*, 43 Ohio St. L.J. 29, 43-48 (1982) (explaining how the "philosophical map," utilized by most legal practitioners and teachers and taught to law students, differs drastically from what a mediator may use). The "lawyer's standard philosophical map" is based on two assumptions—i.e., if one wins, the others must lose—and (2) that disputes are resolved through application, by a third party, of some general rule of law. *Id.* at 43-44. Conversely, underlying mediation are the assumptions: (1) that all parties can benefit through a creative solution to which each agrees; and (2) that the situation is unique and therefore not to be governed by any general principle except to the extent that the parties accept it. *Id.*
20. Model Rules of Prof'l Conduct R. 1.3 cmt. 1 (1983).

The Lawyering Process
Gary Bellow & Bea Moulton
458-462 (1978)

You will go into a negotiation with an idea of how much you are willing to pay, give up, or concede — but that is not all. You will also have an idea of the best deal you might be able to obtain, based on your assessment of your opponent's bottom line. What you predict will be your opponent's resistance point becomes your own target or goal. As a result, much of your effort in a particular negotiation will be directed toward trying to ascertain your opponent's resistance point while assiduously concealing your own. . . .

Suppose you represent a dog bite victim who is suing his next door neighbor for damages in a case where there is no question about liability. The two families have been friends and your client would not have brought the suit if he had not assumed the neighbor was insured. Nevertheless, relations between the families have become strained since the suit was filed and both parties are anxious to settle it. After a discussion with your client, you enter settlement discussions with the following goals:

- $2,000 in damages;

- $500 in costs and attorney's fees;

- An agreement to get rid of the dog or insure that this type of incident will not occur again.

This is the most you think you can possibly obtain. At bottom, your client is willing to settle for the agreement and $750, which would cover his actual expenses, court costs and attorney's fees. But he wants to obtain as much as possible. He also wishes to avoid the costs of failing to settle, which include not only monetary costs — such as higher court costs and attorney's fees, but also delay, a continuance of strained relations, and possible permanent damage to the friendship. . . .

In setting this goal of $2,500 you are, of course, making an estimate of your opponent's resistance point: it may be more than $2,500 and it may be less. . . . Thus you will also be trying to discover your opponent's actual limits — the most he or she is authorized to pay — and revising your goals accordingly. . . .

The problem, of course, is that in most negotiations in which lawyers engage information is imperfect, so that as an advocate you have no choice but to try to maximize your own client's satisfaction. For example, if the costs of deadlock are higher for your opponent than you realize (he or she may expect a jury verdict of at least $10,000 if the case should go to trial) your opponent might be satisfied with a settlement well above your original goal, and you would be doing your client a disservice if you did not try to find out about and press for that higher (and still mutually advantageous) figure. . . .

Assuming your original estimates are reasonably accurate, however, and a settlement acceptable to both parties can be reached anywhere between $750 and $2,500, how do you get your opponent to agree to a settlement on the high side of that range? Would you pay $2,500 if you believed your opponent would accept $1,000 or knew he or she would accept $750? This question answers itself, and it also illuminates the basic dynamic in this situation: since your opponent's goal is to pay the least you will accept, you must change his or her perception of your bottom line. You will obtain a settlement of upwards of $2,000 only if your opponent believes that a settlement below that figure is unacceptable. . . .

The Tactics of Distributive Bargainers: "Informational Bargaining."   As the above extract suggests, certain strategic behaviors are associated with competitive bargaining, and they generally follow predictable patterns. First, and before actual bargaining begins, effective competitive negotiators *bargain strategically* about, and for, *information*. As Melissa Nelkin has written of lawyers, "[i]n a distributive bargaining situation, where your goal is to maximize your client's gain, the single most useful information you could have about your opponent would be to know her walkaway point."[21] With this information in hand, a negotiator could simply offer that figure, not budge, and capture all the available (but concealed) surplus in the existing bargaining zone between her client's bottom line and that of the other side.

Of course, no effective negotiator readily discloses her bottom line, but good informational bargainers try to *discern* their opponent's resistance point and to hide their own by acquiring as much information as possible about their opponent's needs, alternatives and weaknesses, while at the same time attempting to avoid disclosing their own weaknesses. All of this leads to a highly strategic exchange of information, in which negotiators decide in advance:

- **Information to share.** What information they are willing to share freely with one another (because it strengthens their bargaining position);

- **Information to hide and tactics to hide it.** What information they wish to conceal from the other side and specific tactics to avoid answering questions in sensitive areas (ruling questions out of bounds, "over-answering" questions, answering unresponsively or partially, answering questions with questions, etc.);[22]

- **Information to "spin," and how to "spin" it.** How to package information in order to put a realistic but favorable gloss on bad facts or law;

- **Bluffing and other tactics to mislead.** When and how to mislead their opponents through such devices as bluffs, misstatements of intention, and false statements of value or worth;[23]

- **Information to seek from the other side.** What information they will try to learn about their opponent's non-settlement alternatives, priorities and weaknesses, and a detailed questioning strategy to obtain the maximum information possible.[24]

---

21. NELKIN, *supra* note 14, at 34.
22. HARBAUGH, *supra* note 13, at 82-86.
23. GOODPASTER, *supra* note 14, at 51-52 (1997). False statements as to material facts constitute unethical conduct if uttered by lawyers representing clients. *See* MODEL RULES OF PROF'L CONDUCT R. 4.1(a) (1983).
24. HARBAUGH, *supra* note 13, at 82-86.

Teddy Roosevelt's Photograph.   The importance of information bargaining is nicely illustrated by the following true story. In 1912, Theodore Roosevelt was campaigning for U.S. President. His staff had printed 3 million handbills containing the text of a campaign speech and a photograph of Roosevelt, for distribution on the campaign trail. Unfortunately, permission to reproduce the photograph had not been obtained in advance from the copyright holder, a Chicago photography studio. Roosevelt's campaign manager knew that he now had to negotiate to obtain copyright permission to use the photo, or else (a) reproduce 3 million new handbills without a photograph; (b) not use any handbills at all in campaigning or (c) go forward without permission and face the possibility of a copyright infringement lawsuit. None of these options was very attractive.

But the photography studio didn't know any of this, so Roosevelt's campaign manager sent a message to the studio stating that the campaign might be willing to use the photo, but only for a fee to be paid by the *studio. "This will be excellent publicity for you,"* he argued. The studio owner immediately agreed and eventually paid $250 to the campaign for the "privilege" of giving up his rights under copyright laws.[25] The moral for a distributive bargainer: If you don't ask questions that might reveal the other side's vulnerability, you are likely to end up paying for it.

Other Behaviors of Distributive Negotiators: Bargaining About Positions.
In addition to bargaining about information, distributive negotiators also bargain over positions—their stated stance regardless of what they actually need in a resolution. As Melissa Nelkin has written, the language of distributive negotiation is "self-centered": Competitive bargainers speak about what they *want*, they make *demands* of each other, and they threaten to *walk away* if their demands are not met.[26]

Effective distributive bargainers not only plan their walk-away point, but their *targets* as well. Targets are optimistic but realistic goals for the negotiation. Research suggests that negotiators who have high aspirations consistently do better in negotiation than those who do not.[27]

Making High Demands/Low Offers.   Psychological studies show that making high demands, low offers or otherwise taking aggressive positions often is effective in distributive negotiations, especially when the negotiator on the other side lacks information. This is because *anchors* strongly affect how we react to settlement offers when we are uncertain about the facts.[28]

Imagine that you are negotiating in a foreign bazaar for the purchase of a large Oriental rug. You have little idea of the rug's fair market value and no idea of the seller's actual cost. If the seller's first demand is $3,000 and you are able to able to whittle him down to $2,000, you may well feel good about the negotiated price and be happy to pay it. If, however, his first demand is $2,200 and you are "only" able to bargain him down to $2,000, you might feel less happy about the price and be more likely to turn down the deal, even though it is identical to the first.

---

25. Lawrence Bacow & Michael Wheeler, Environmental Dispute Resolution 73-74 (1984).
26. Nelkin, *supra* note 14, at 44.
27. *See* Russell Korobkin, *Aspirations and Settlement*, 88 Cornell L. Rev. 1, 23-25 (2003).
28. *See* Margaret A. Neale & Max H. Bazerman, Cognition and Rationality in Negotiation 48-50 (1991).

Bargaining with little information, you are only able to evaluate the negotiated outcome by reference to the seller's initial demand or "anchor." As this example demonstrates, making an initial, anchoring offer that is high (or low), but not so unreasonable as to risk impasse, is a rational and effective distributive negotiating strategy. Psychologically, the anchor pulls the bargaining toward the end of the bargaining range established by the negotiator who set it. It minimizes the risk of underestimating the other side's desire to settle. Equally important, it provides room for subsequent concessions—something the other side may expect and find satisfying.

Planning Offers and Concessions.   Having decided on their targets and walk-away points, effective distributive bargainers also plan in advance what *offers* and *concessions* they will make and how they will explain or justify those moves to their opponent. After making high but realistic opening demands, competitive negotiators attempt to communicate commitment to the positions they take by having well-articulated reasons for them and by appearing to be reluctant to make concessions. When a negotiation is conducted positionally, it often becomes a "stylized, linear ritual of struggle—planned concessions after high first offers, leading to a compromise point along a linear field of pre-established 'commitment and resistance' points."[29]

Distributive bargainers sometimes try to mislead their opponents regarding their own true goals and priorities by making false demands that they can "give up" in exchange for things they actually care about. A frequently cited (and controversial) example involves one parent (usually a father) bargaining hard for increased custodial time with the kids—an issue he doesn't really care about—in order to be able to trade apparent concessions on it for lower financial obligations, such as reduced alimony or child support.

Again, all such tactics are strategic: Since negotiators never know what the true bargaining range is in a negotiation, they can increase their negotiating leverage by manipulating their opponent's *perceptions* of the available bargaining zone.

In Professor Bellow and Moulton's dog bite case, how might such informational and positional strategies play out? It is easy to imagine a competitive negotiation in which one or both of the negotiators:

- Contend that their clients are not much concerned about improving strained neighbor-neighbor relations, even if they are in fact concerned, out of fear that such an admission might suggest that their clients would accept less (or pay more) to patch things up.

- Take exaggerated positions or make false demands on the question of what should be done with the dog ("*My client won't be satisfied unless your clients get rid of the damned dog.*" "*My clients have an absolute right to do what they want with their dog and won't be dictated to by your client.*") in order to trade apparent concessions on that issue for more (or less) money.

---

29. MENKEL-MEADOW, *supra* note 17, at 767.

■ Take extreme positions (compared to what they would actually settle for) on the money issues in the case. ("*My client won't accept a penny less than $10,000 to settle this case.*" "*My clients will pay $250 nuisance value to make this case go away, but only because they like your client.*") In legal dispute negotiations, denigrating the other side's legal position is often an associated tactic.

■ Make a "pre-condition" demand. ("*I won't even sit down with you to discuss a monetary settlement for my client's injury unless your clients first agree to install and pay for an electronic fence to keep the dog in.*") By establishing a pre-condition, a negotiator can sometimes gain a concession without giving up anything in return.

■ Make a "take it or leave it" offer. ("*I've researched all the dog bite cases in this jurisdiction and have determined that $4,000 is a fair sum to settle this case. My client has no interest in haggling. If you don't accept that figure, I am directed by him to proceed directly to trial.*") This form of threat — which can be genuine or a bluff — is also known as "Boulewarism," named after a General Electric vice president who frequently used it in collective bargaining negotiations. Note that this is an aggressive strategy that conveys the message, "*Since I've determined what a fair offer is, I'm not interested in your input.*" It can be effective against a weak opponent, but is likely to create anger and resistance as well.

■ Bluff, for as long a period as possible, about their clients' willingness to pursue the litigation process all the way to trial to create the perception of firm resolve. ("*The dog has to go, or we'll see you in court.*")

■ Make few concessions — slowly, reluctantly and in decreasing size — demanding reciprocal concessions each step of the way.

■ Make no further concessions once they have reached their *target* demand or offer.[30]

In a litigation context, such tactics are commonly played out — sometimes over a period of many months or years — until the negotiators come under the pressure of approaching trial deadlines. If competitive negotiations break down, it may be because the negotiators have been (too) successful in misleading each other about the existence of a bargaining range. If the bargaining does culminate in settlement, it may have been achieved at high cost in both money and strained relations. And, to the extent that information has been withheld or distorted, the resolution may be far from optimal in advancing the true interests of the parties.

Is Distributive Negotiation Necessarily a Bad Thing? What's Good About It? Despite these shortcomings, tough distributive negotiations offer several

---

30. This is just a small sample of competitive negotiation tactics. For a laundry list of additional, more hardball tactics, *see* GOODPASTER, *supra* note 14, at 33-50.

potential advantages over less adversarial forms of negotiation, at least in some circumstances:

■ **They can be relatively efficient.** Although competitive tactics can breed lengthy argument, begrudging movement and threats of stalemate, they may be less time-consuming than an approach that depends on obtaining interest-based information from reluctant, untrusting parties.

■ **They can be satisfying.** Despite the fact that a competitive fight can strain relationships and risk impasse, a hard-bargained distributive result can be emotionally rewarding for the participants. By virtue of having fought hard for each concession, each bargainer feels as if he or she has won things in the process, in that the other side was forced to make concessions it hated to make. This makes many bargainers feel good.

■ **They can avoid "negotiators' remorse."** What is the worst thing a car salesman can do to a prospective buyer? Accept his or her first purchase offer quickly, without haggling. Why? Most buyers will now feel that they paid too much, possibly to the point of wanting to renegotiate the sale price. Even where a deal has been concluded, such post-negotiation regret can threaten the stability of the resolution, manifesting itself in noncompliance with payment or other open obligations or the lodging of later complaints. Hard-fought negotiations avoid such consequences.

§2.4 BASICS OF PROBLEM-SOLVING (INTEGRATIVE) NEGOTIATION

The Goals of Problem-Solving Negotiators.   In contrast to the competitive negotiator, the problem-solver focuses on identifying his needs and interests and then negotiates in order to achieve a solution that satisfies them — even if means accommodating the interests of the other side and not maximizing his individual outcome. Problem-solving negotiations are generally less contentious than distributive negotiations, but they also require a greater degree of informational openness.

A number of years ago, a successful personal injury lawyer described one of his cases that illustrates something about the basics of problem-solving negotiation. The story is telling because negotiations in personal injury cases tend to be highly distributive in nature, and this one was not.

The case involved a single mother who had lost both of her teenage children when an allegedly defective product manufactured by the defendant failed. A typical distributive products liability negotiation would have pitted the lawyers against each other, arguing over issues pertaining to liability and trying to put a monetary value on the lives of the two deceased children. But the mother made it clear from the start that she would have nothing to do with a negotiation that treated her children like commodities with a disputed price tag. "*I cannot bear the thought of living a life without children,*" she told her attorney. "*What I really want is to be able to try to start over again — to adopt two children, to care for them without having to worry at all about how I am going to pay the bills, to give them the best possible opportunities for college—opportunities I never had myself.*"

Following her instructions, the woman's attorney was able to come up with a proposal to meet (i.e., integrate) both her short- and long-term interests and those of the defendant's insurer: The insurance company would pay a comparatively small sum to cover (in addition to her attorney's fees) the plaintiff's immediate adoption costs and projected annual child care expenses, and would invest money to ensure that when the children were of age, many years hence, a sufficient fund would exist to pay for two college educations. Because this proposal met the insurer's interests in limiting its total liability (including litigation costs), as well as closing the books on the case this fiscal year, it agreed to the settlement.

Problem-Solving Negotiation Is Based on Interests, Not Positions. Negotiators cannot engage in problem-solving negotiation unless they are able to look behind stated positions (both their own and those of the opposing party) and identify the true interests that underlie those demands. Interest analysis does not guarantee that problem-solving will occur in negotiation, but it is a necessary pre-condition for problem-solving.

What Are Positions? As noted earlier, positions are the concrete, tangible monetary and non-monetary demands and offers that bargainers make in negotiation: "*My client won't accept a penny less than $1 million to settle this medical malpractice claim*" or "*We cannot agree to this transaction unless your company can guarantee shipment of all 1,000 transformers by December 1*" or "*Mr. Jacobs will never agree to awarding physical custody of the children to Mrs. Jacobs unless a visitation schedule is put in place guaranteeing the boys will be with him at least two nights a week*" or "*We will not settle this case unless you get rid of that damned dog.*"

What Are Interests? Interests, Roger Fisher and William Ury tell us in their well-known book on problem-solving negotiation, *Getting to Yes*, are what cause people to take the positions they take. They are "the silent movers behind the hubbub of positions."[31] The most powerful interests are based on fundamental human needs, such as the need for physical safety, economic security, a sense of belonging, fair and respectful treatment and control over one's life.[32] And much of the potential power of interest-based bargaining lies in the fact that human beings are complex and make decisions for a wide variety of economic, social and psychological reasons.

The positions that negotiators state at the bargaining table are *always* proxies for their deeper-seated needs, fears and concerns. The seriously injured plaintiff wants monetary compensation, but why?: In order to pay for medical expenses and ease the way to a new life plan (and perhaps to punish the negligent driver a little for his carelessness). The plant manager opposes reinstating the worker he fired or paying her any lost wages (two positions) because he is worried about his perceived authority in the eyes of coworkers and his reputation at company headquarters

---

31. Fisher et al., *supra* note 6, at 41.
32. *Id.* at 48-49.

(two interests). The divorcing father demands visits with his sons *every* Sunday (a position) so that he can avoid further deterioration of his relationship with them and assure himself that the boys receive religious training (two interests). The angry eighty-year-old mother balks at moving to a nursing facility (a position) out of fear that she will never again be able to tend to her beloved roses (an interest).

Consider that in any bargaining process, the parties may be motivated by the following different interests, prioritized in many different ways:

- **Economic interests:** being well compensated, feeling financially secure; seeking a profit, reducing costs or developing new business opportunities;

- **Moral and psychological interests:** integrity, consistency, fairness, principled behavior, self-respect, excitement, freedom from anxiety and stress, retribution;

- **Ego or psychic interests:** personal satisfaction, accomplishment, autonomy, security and the respect of others;

- **Influence interests:** reputation, credibility, authority, status and good will;

- **Ideological interests:** religious, political or civic values and beliefs;

- **Social or relational interests:** maintaining and enhancing existing relationships, developing good future relationships, terminating detrimental relationships;

- **Freedom of action interests:** avoiding undesirable precedents and agreements that restrict future freedom of choice;

- **Efficiency interests:** resolving existing problems expeditiously, developing efficient and reliable procedures to resolve future problems.[33]

Many of these interests may be valued for *instrumental* reasons—because they favorably affect the negotiator's wealth, security or expected future dealings. But sometimes the most important interests are *intrinsically* valuable to negotiators, apart from their instrumental usefulness in the dispute or transaction.[34]

So, in Professor Bellow and Moulton's dog bite case, the injured plaintiff might simultaneously be concerned about securing her safety at all costs; recouping her medical expenses and legal fees; recovering something more for her pain and suffering; resolving the matter on the basis of governing legal norms if possible, so that she won't feel as if she has caved in; and patching things up with her neighbors so that she won't feel uncomfortable when she sees them on the street. The dog owners might be most concerned about keeping their dog to provide companionship for their children; providing fair but not exorbitant compensation to their neighbor for whose injury they feel responsible; patching up their relationship; and avoiding at all costs a trial judgment that, under local dog laws, would lead to their dog being destroyed if it ever bit another person.

---

33. This is a slightly modified version of a very helpful list of interests that appears in GOODPASTER, *supra* note 14, at 95-96.
34. DAVID LAX & JAMES SEBENIUS, *Interests: The Measure of Negotiation*, 2 NEGOTIATION J. 76, 78-80 (1986).

Mediators often can play a critical role in helping parties bring to the surface the differing needs and interests that may be motivating them — interests that they may be hiding for strategic reasons or that they may need help identifying because they operate at a subconscious level. Some needs and interests — for example, autonomy, financial security, personal accomplishment — can only be expressed in abstract, psychological terms that many disputants may be unaccustomed to using. (Can you see how talking with a party about "financial security" might have advantages over discussing "money" or "compensation"?) We explore how a mediator can probe for needs and interests in Chapter 7.

Comparing Shared and Differing Interests to Facilitate "Value-Creating" Trades. If the parties can identify and prioritize their own interests and then at the negotiation table are willing and able to explore each other's interests in an open way, they will often discover that some are *shared*, some are different but *complementary* and only some are *antagonistic*. The more interests that negotiators unearth and the more interests they are willing to lay on the table, the more likely they will be able to find trades that create value by giving everyone more of what they value most, making both sides better off or at least making one of the sides better off without hurting the other.

The discovery that bargainers have shared (or at least non-conflicting) interests is often what enables problem-solving negotiation to begin. For example, a reciprocal acknowledgment by both clients in the dog bite case that they share an interest in restoring their relationship and avoiding future dog bites might have a strong impact on the nature of their bargaining and put them psychologically on the "same side of the table." Discovering further that their interests with respect to the dog are different but not necessarily antagonistic (plaintiff wants security; defendants want companionship) might enable the negotiators to identify a variety of possible solutions short of getting rid of the dog (electronic fence, chain-link fence, dog run, etc.) that would accomplish both of their clients' objectives. Note that, in contrast to "take-it-or-leave-it" positions, a party's interests can almost always be met in multiple ways. Having a range of possible solutions greatly increases the chances that a mutually acceptable one can be found.

Trading on Differences. But it is the *differences* between the parties that are often most useful in facilitating integrative settlements. If the parties were identical in their resources, capabilities and preferences, they would have no way to benefit mutually by negotiation, and therefore would be relegated to negotiating in competitive (win-lose) fashion. Consider the following types of negotiation differences:[35]

> ■ **Different possessions, resources or capabilities.** These are fundamental to most business transactions. Acme Oil Company, best known as a producer and refiner, seeks to merge with BC Oil Company, whose strengths lie in oil trading, transportation and distribution. The merger will provide the newly formed company with market advantages that neither has by itself.

---

35. These differences have been adapted from David Lax & James Sebenius, The Manager as Negotiator 88-116 (1986) and Gerald Wetlaufer, *The Limits of Integrative Bargaining*, 85 Geo. L.J. 369 (1996).

■ **Different tastes, preferences and priorities.** The classic story tells of two sisters fighting over a single orange remaining in the refrigerator. The big sister could take the orange by force, but there might be negative consequences for her once mom and dad get home. Or the sisters could sulkily agree to split the orange in half or in some other proportion. In fact, one sister only wants the juice, the other the rind to bake a cake. If they are able to learn of each other's true preferences, they can both get more of what they want.

■ **Different predictions of future events.** We saw this earlier in the story of the rock star negotiating his fee. If the rocker and the concert promoter are willing to bet on their differing predictions over the likely size of the crowd, they can trade on those differences by negotiating a lower base appearance fee with a clause giving the rock star (who is more optimistic about drawing a large crowd) an agreed-on percentage of the gate.

■ **Different degrees of aversion to risk.** This is a special case of differently valued preferences. Suppose the defendants in the dog bite case are well off financially but want at all costs to avoid a trial because an adverse judgment exposes their dog to a future risk of being destroyed if it were aggressive again. Suppose that the plaintiff needs money now to pay for her expenses and is indifferent to the risks of a trial. The defendants might be willing to pay the plaintiff a monetary premium to obtain a quiet settlement with a confidentiality provision. If the parties are able to share their different priorities with respect to the risks of trial, they can both get more of what they want.

■ **Differences in time preferences regarding payment or performance.** This is another case of differently valued preferences. Go back to the product liability case involving the mother who lost both her children. Suppose that because she is not adept at managing money, the plaintiff prefers not to receive a lump sum payment, but rather a settlement under which she will receive a guaranteed annual income or annuity with a fixed, yearly inflation adjustment for the next thirty years. The defendant's insurance company is likely also to prefer such an arrangement, because it can now invest a smaller amount of money than it would otherwise have to pay to the plaintiff and let that money grow over time. (This is also an example of the parties' taking advantage of their differences in capabilities—in this instance, the insurer's superior expertise in money management.)[36]

Expanding *Issues* to Create Value and Ease the Negotiations.   Note an important corollary here: By focusing on the parties' actual concerns rather than the stances they take, negotiators often expand the number of negotiating *issues*—topics that can be discussed as part of a potential resolution. Adding issues to a negotiation is often what enables value-creating trades to be made. If negotiators have only one issue (a disputed amount of money allegedly owed in a

---

36. Such "structured settlements" are made even more attractive because both parties receive preferential tax treatment for the funds involved. *See* Internal Revenue Code, Sections 104(2)(2) and 130.

breach of contract case, the length of a twelve-year-old daughter's summer vacation with a non-custodial father in a child custody dispute, etc.) to talk about, their bargaining is likely to take on a zero-sum, tug-of-war character. But if negotiators are open with each other about their underlying interests, they will often find that there is more than one topic that can be addressed — each potentially with a variety of solutions.

For example, in the child custody scenario, if it is learned that the father cares about his daughter's learning Spanish (in addition to wanting to spend as long as possible with her) and the mother worries about her daughter's safety and well-being in traveling with a "risk-taking" father (in addition to wanting to limit the length of that vacation), a number of new options and trade possibilities arise (daughter attends language camp for a week of her time with him, mother gets advance notice of trip destinations so that she challenge them in court if she chooses) and each side may even get more of what it truly values.

■ §2.5 STRATEGIC BARRIERS TO SETTLEMENT AND THE MEDIATOR'S ROLE

So what are the main reasons that negotiations fail? The first has to do with the bargainers' competitive strategies. As we have seen, integrative bargaining maximizes the chances of securing satisfying, durable agreements. So why doesn't everyone aim to be a "problem-solver"?

To begin with, in the real world of dispute negotiation, problem-solving bargaining is hard to accomplish — even among those who negotiate frequently. An empirical study of New Jersey lawyers' settlement practices in non-matrimonial civil cases suggests that problem-solving negotiation is not nearly as common as positional bargaining, and even negotiators who would like to engage in problem-solving negotiation often find it difficult to do so.[37]

Certainly, the fear of exploitation is an important part of the reason why. As Robert Mnookin and his colleagues write, "Why don't negotiators just share all their information, search for value-creating trades, and both walk away happy? . . . A negotiator who freely discloses information about her interests and preferences may not be met with equal candor. . . . When disclosure is one-sided, the disclosing party risks being taken advantage of."[38] Moreover, the fear of exploitation may cause negotiators to choose a positional strategy in *anticipation* of the way they expect their opponent to behave, even if they would prefer to adopt a more problem-solving approach themselves.[39]

Other factors may also contribute to the prevalence of distributive bargaining. Despite the recent growth of "win-win" negotiation training, lawyers are still far less well versed in problem-solving techniques than they are in standard competitive modes of argument. In many legal quarters, problem-solving negotiation is perceived as weak. In large urban areas, lawyers are likely to negotiate against

---

37. *See* MILTON HEUMANN & JONATHAN M. HYMAN, *Negotiation Methods and Litigation Settlement in New Jersey: "You Can't Always Get What You Want,"* 12 OHIO ST. J. ON DISP. RESOL. 253, 255-256, 268, 284 (1997).
38. MNOOKIN, PEPPET & TULUMELLO, *supra* note 14, at 17.
39. HEUMANN & HYMAN, *supra* note 35, at 261.

lawyers who are strangers to them and who they therefore have no reason to trust. Traditional habits of legal negotiation, deeply rooted in lawyers' adversarial culture, die hard.[40]

Second, barriers are erected by the aggressive tactics that negotiators tend to employ, especially (although not exclusively) when pursuing a competitive strategy. Negotiators withhold and distort information in ways that make it hard to find a bargaining zone. They set extreme anchors and take positions that cannot be justified based on objective norms and standards. They make tiny concessions reluctantly, prompting tiny concessions in return, a pattern that can lead to deadlock. Such strategic aggressiveness sometimes turns personal, leading to a downward spiral of anger and mistrust that can itself produce an impasse.[41]

How can the presence of a mediator reduce the strategic tensions inherent in negotiation and help the parties avoid unnecessary impasses and reach more efficient, optimal agreements? By fostering effective problem-solving approaches where this is possible, and by helping the parties negotiate more effectively in a distributive mode where it is not. This will be a large part of our study of the skills of the effective mediator.

■ §2.6 PSYCHOLOGICAL BARRIERS TO SETTLEMENT

Several years ago, a student in a Negotiation course was assigned to negotiate a simulated personal injury case. His task was to represent a couple whose infant daughter had been burned in a hotel accident after she fell out of bed and hit her face against a hot radiator. It is a three-party negotiation:[42] The parents file a negligence lawsuit against both the hotel, which failed to provide a crib or insulate the radiators, and the airline, which selected the hotel and assigned the couple to it after their flight was canceled. There is no actual client in the role play; everything the students need to know is provided in a written profile. Students are assigned to negotiate with classmates as opposing counsel under conditions that make clear that: (a) the teacher will not observe the negotiation and (b) grades will not be affected by case outcomes or even demonstrated skill. The students are given ample bargaining authority to reach an agreement. Each year, most students reach agreement in the case, but occasionally some do not.

The student in this particular negotiation was older than most, having spent a number of years working in the construction business before entering law school. He was a gregarious and practical person, generally comfortable with conflict and

---

40. *Id.* at 307-309.

41. The dichotomy between distributive and problem-solving negotiation is a strategic one involving differing objectives, and should not be confused with the *style* of the individual negotiator. One can be a highly effective competitive bargainer, seeking to maximize individual gain, while at the same time speaking softly and treating the adversary with civility and good humor. Conversely, one can have a pugnacious personality and still pursue problem-solving, value-creating ends. In the hurly-burly of negotiation, it is often difficult—yet vitally important—for negotiators to discern whether the behaviors of their opponents are strategic or stylistic. In a 1991 study of civil settlements in Nebraska, Peter Toll Hoffman found that anger by litigants toward the opposing *lawyer* for their litigation and negotiation behaviors accounted for a substantial percentage of cases that did not settle. *See* HOFFMAN, *supra* note 7, at 36-37.

42. Based on JOSEPH D. HARBAUGH, *Milam v. Capri Hotel & Midwest Airlines, in* Lawyer Negotiation Training Materials (Practicing Law Institute, 1988).

with himself. During law school, he worked part time for a small law firm that did some plaintiff's personal injury work, so he approached this negotiation with some sophistication.

During the negotiation, the opposing "counsel" (a classmate with whom this student had no independent relationship) made a comment he felt to be disparaging of his "clients": a sarcastic remark to the effect that perhaps the couple (who the student had already said were financially strapped) ought to have sold one of their cars to pay for a psychiatric evaluation that might support their claim for pain and suffering damages. Furious, he clammed up for a significant period of time and eventually had to be coaxed back into the negotiations by another student.

What is interesting to us about this anecdote is not that a lawyer-to-be lost his temper in a negotiation or that the outcome was in jeopardy as a result. We all know of stories about lawyers who lose their cool in negotiations or whose own conduct or poor relationships with opposing counsel make resolving disputes harder, not easier. What is striking to us about this incident is that it occurred in the course of a *simulation*, in which there was no real client, in a situation with no real stakes at all.

What does this suggest for lawyers about the emotional content of *real* negotiations, with significant and lasting stakes? Even more important, what does this suggest about the emotional content of conflicts for those most directly affected by them — the *disputants themselves*?

The Emotionality of Conflict. Anyone who would serve as a mediator must understand a central truth about the negotiation process, and it is this: Strong emotions are not a side effect of conflict; they are often the central way in which disputants experience conflict.[43] When people have incompatible needs, positions, interests or goals, this often produces anger, fear, anxiety, guilt, shame and other strong feelings. Most disputes have both an objective and subjective element to those who are experiencing them. The subjective aspects of a dispute are frequently as — if not more — important to the disputants than the objective reality of the situation. Consider a real case example:

No White Pines, Please! A number of years ago, a mutual acquaintance of ours, who we will call Dan, bought a new condominium in an affluent community. The builders had developed a reputation among area homeowners for sometimes shoddy workmanship, price gouging and failure to remedy warranty problems on a timely basis. In addition, no one liked the project manager, a woman who could

---

43. *See* Tricia S. Jones & Andrea Bodtker, *Mediating with Heart in Mind: Addressing Emotion in Mediation Practice*, 17 Negotiation J. 217, 219 (2001) (arguing that emotion is the foundation of all conflict and emotion is central in all mediation contexts). Some other useful sources on the impact of mood and emotions on the disputing process include: Keith G. Allred, *Anger and Retaliation in Conflict: The Role of Attribution*, *in* The Handbook of Conflict Resolution (Morton Deutsch & Peter T. Coleman eds., 2000); Dwight & Helaine Golann, *Psychological Issues*, *in* Mediating Legal Disputes 187-216 (Dwight Golann ed., 1996); Nelkin, *supra* note 14, at 197-258; Douglas Stone, Bruce Patton & Sheila Heen, Difficult Conversations (1999); Robert Adler, Benson Rosen & Elliot Silverstein, *Emotions in Negotiation: How to Manage Fear and Anger*, 14 Negotiation J. 161 (1998); Clark Freshman, Adele Hayes & Greg Feldman, *The Lawyer as Mood Scientist: What We Know and Don't Know About How Mood Relates to Successful Negotiation*, 2002 J. Disp. Resol. 1 (2002); and Gerald Williams, *Negotiation as a Healing Process*, 1996 J. Disp. Resol. 1 (1996). *See also* Daniel Goleman, Emotional Intelligence (1995).

be rude and abrasive. Dan knew about these problems before deciding to buy but decided to proceed anyway because the house design and home site were beautiful. Despite some anxious moments, the construction process went pretty well; the few items on Dan's "punch list" at closing were remedied promptly.

About eight months after he moved in, the project manager contacted Dan and asked him if he would be willing to provide some kind of oral or written testimonial about recent improvements in warranty services. When Dan said he felt uncomfortable doing that, she invited him to lunch to share his experiences and views about the builders. "*I have found you to be a reasonable person,*" she said. "*We are interested in understanding what homeowners think about us, so that we can improve our service and our customer relationships in future phases of this development.*" A pleasant and candid discussion ensued in which Dan expressed the view that the developer created unnecessary ill will by taking a hard line on disputed small-cost items. Dan thought he had gotten his point across in a productive way and that the manager would take this to heart.

Two weeks later, the developers, without notice, planted three white pine trees in a common area about twenty feet from Dan's house and that of his neighbor. Dan had previous experience with white pines at his former home and knew them to grow exceptionally tall and wide with large root systems. Concerned that the pines might eventually dwarf his new home, he wrote a friendly e-mail to the project manager, asking that the trees be removed and offering to pay for replacement trees. The project manager e-mailed back, saying that "*Once they are in the ground, plantings are the responsibility of the homeowners' association, not the developers.*"

Upset, Dan sent a second, more sharply worded e-mail, this time directing the project manager's attention to a web site identifying white pines as the largest conifer in the Northeast and adding "*this is just the kind of issue that we talked about at lunch: small-cost matters that if not corrected, unnecessarily create bad feelings among homeowners.*" Dan's neighbor wrote a formal letter of complaint as well, pointing out how white pines planted just a few years earlier were already dwarfing several other homes in the community. Again, the project manager replied by e-mail stating, "*This is a matter of personal preference. You may pursue your request through the homeowners' association.*"

In the ensuing months the homeowners' association, using donated labor, replaced the offending white pines with shrubs bought by Dan and his neighbor. Many months after this incident, Dan told us, he was still filled with rage. "*It's not that we had to pay for replacement shrubs,*" he said. "*It did rankle me to have to fork over a dime to replace those completely inappropriate trees, of course. But I had already offered the project manager to pay for new plantings.*"

"*What is it, then, that still makes you so angry?*" we asked. "*First, it was the fact that the project manager never addressed the merits of our concerns. She never presented a different perspective—for instance, do these trees grow smaller when planted in groups?—but instead just kept spouting the 'company line.' It was just so disrespectful. Even more to the point, I now see that our lunch had been a complete charade. . . . I was used.*"

A few months later, Dan served as the chair of a homeowners' association committee responsible for selecting an attorney to represent the association in a lawsuit against the developer for a wide variety of construction defects, including those involving landscaping. Postscript: that lawsuit eventually resulted in a (mediated) settlement of almost $1 million.

The Roots of Anger.   What are the root causes of anger? Generally, social psychologists tell us, it is not the merits of the dispute—the "who's right and who's wrong" questions—on which disputants tend to focus. Conflicts become emotional when a person experiences:

- external threats to safety or self-identity, including the feeling of being attacked, misunderstood, snubbed or treated unfairly;

- perceived violations of rules or norms of honesty, trustworthiness and fair dealing;

- the perception of intentional wrongdoing; and

- abrasive, scornful or disrespectful treatment.[44]

Ask yourself: when someone tailgates you on the highway, how do you feel and why? What about when you're stuck in the express supermarket line behind a customer who has thirty, rather than the permitted ten items? Suppose that you ask what you think is a perfectly reasonable and relevant question in class and—in front of all your peers—your teacher seems to dismiss it as tangential? In each of these cases, the act itself may be less significant than the meaning we ascribe to it. The feeling of being threatened or disrespected is what gives such incidents the power to enrage.

In their book, *Difficult Conversations*, negotiation scholars Douglas Stone, Bruce Patton and Sheila Heen provide another useful way to understand these kinds of events. They argue that there is an underlying structure to every difficult interaction in life in which, at least internally, three separate conversations are going on at once. First, there is the "what happened" conversation, in which people argue about and struggle to determine who's right and who's wrong. Second, there is the "feelings" conversation, in which people identify their feelings and ask "are my feelings valid?" Third, there is the "identity" conversation, in which people try to determine what a conflict situation means to them in terms of their own sense of competence and self-worth.[45]

When we talked about these concepts with Dan, he could immediately relate to them. "*At one level, to be sure, this dispute was about the merits of white pines on the site where they were planted,*" he said. "*But the process of being jerked around was what really infuriated me.*"

"*I also consider myself a person who responds in a mature and balanced way to rational arguments,*" Dan continued. "*Here, I felt so powerless—just like I felt when I was eight years old and my parents said I had to do something because 'we say so.' I'm also angry at myself for being so gullible. I took it on faith that the project manager was really interested in my views and I gave a lot of time and thought to what I said. Afterwards I felt like a complete fool. These aren't feelings I can let go of easily.*"

The Moral of the Story.   For mediators, the moral of this story is that, to be effective, they must be attentive to the psychological aspects of the conflicts they enter. In addition to helping the parties analyze the merits of their claims, they need

---

44. *See, generally,* ADLER, ROSEN & SILVERSTEIN, *supra* note 43.
45. STONE, PATTON & HEEN, *supra* note 43, at 7-8.

to be able to "look under the hood" to discern the disputants' fundamental feelings about the dispute they are in and the meaning they ascribe to dispute-related events. As one article puts it, "[i]n many cases, the key to successful negotiation is not in the treatment of the technical details, but in the proper treatment of the emotions that drive the parties to settlement."[46] What specifically do we know about the effects of emotions on the negotiating process?

Ripeness: Emotions and the Parties' Willingness to Work Toward Resolution.   The first thing a mediator must consider is the impact of emotions on the parties' willingness even to try to resolve their dispute. The governing concept here is one of *ripeness*: There must be some minimal readiness on the part of the disputants to de-escalate their conflict; otherwise mediation probably will not work.[47]

The concept is familiar to most of us. How many times have you been involved in a serious argument with a friend, associate or family member? The other person gives signals of wanting to discuss the conflict with you. But you put it off because your feelings are still too raw, the prospect of dealing with the conflict is too frightening or you simply want to punish the other person for a little while longer.

Some scholars talk about *distortion, hostile attribution bias* and *rigid thinking* as common psychological responses to conflict.[48] When one perceives another person's behavior as threatening or demeaning, there is a tendency to assign entirely innocent motives to oneself and entirely hostile motives to the other person; and to try to root out of one's mind all inconsistent thoughts. In such a biased state of mind, all slights are perceived to be intentional. Hostility is triggered not only by actual external threats, but by "internal scripts" in which disputants rehearse their negative emotions over and over in their minds.[49]

Scholars who study intractable conflicts tell us that as the hostility and separation between contending parties increase, the disputants' self-identity comes to depend on defining oneself as the other's *enemy*.[50] The process of demonizing one's adversary makes violence and bloodshed more acceptable. Even with the aid of the most highly skilled interveners, such conflicts may be impervious to change.

Other negotiation scholars theorize that there is a cycle and a predictable series of stages that disputants must move through if they are going to be able to work toward resolution of their conflict.[51] Gerald Williams suggests that disputants often start off in a state of *denial*, characterized by "a tendency to see the other side as wholly at fault, and to see oneself as innocent and deserving of vindication."[52] Denial is an unconscious defense mechanism, a form of self-protection that enables people to allay their anxieties by disavowing feelings and ideas that

---

46. ADLER, ROSEN & SILVERSTEIN, *supra* note 43, at 162.
47. LOUIS KRIESBERG, *Timing and the Initiation of De-Escalation Moves, in* Negotiation Theory and Practice 223-224 (J. William Breslin & Jeffrey Z. Rubin eds., 1995).
48. LOUIS KRIESBERG, Social Conflicts 69-72 (1982).
49. JONES & BODTKER, *supra* note 43, at 230-231.
50. PETER COLEMAN, *Intractable Conflict, in* The Handbook of Conflict Resolution, *supra* note 43, at 428-435.
51. WILLIAMS, *supra* note 43, at 42-56. *See also* KRIESBERG, *supra* note 47, at 17-21.
52. WILLIAMS, *supra* note 43, at 43-44. (Source omitted.)

would be intolerable if made conscious.[53] Denial can take the extreme form of refusing even to acknowledge that a dispute is occurring. In divorce mediations it is not uncommon for one spouse to indicate a belief that *"this isn't really happening to me."* In such cases, one of the first tasks for the mediator is to help the spouse in question come to terms with the real possibility of divorce.

The conflict resolution process can only be successful, according to Professor Williams, if disputants are able to work past their denial, to accept the possibility that they themselves may be part of the problem, to admit that possibility to the other party and to make some sort of "sacrifice" in order to move the situation to resolution — in other words, to work through the conflict cycle from denial, polarization and blame to communication and a mutual search for resolution.[54]

The important practice point for beginning mediators is this: *You can only work with people at the stage of the conflict cycle they are in.* No matter how skilled you are as a mediator, you may not be able to convince parties to come to the bargaining table. Once they are there, you may not be able to help them resolve their dispute unless they are psychologically ready to do so. (Note also an important corollary point: To the extent this is true, you cannot judge your effectiveness as a mediator based on the number or percentage of cases that settle.)

Does this mean that the situation is hopeless any time a party, on considering mediation or at its start, says *"I'm not going to budge one inch. He was totally to blame"?* Of course not. Although disputants may psychologically arm themselves for negotiation like gladiators, their sense of rightness and their demonizing of the other side often dissipate in the face of rational discussion, upon confronting the legitimate perspectives of the other party. Beginning mediators are often amazed when disputes they thought could never be resolved do end up settling.

At the Table: Dealing with Anger, Fear and Other Psychological Variables. Preliminary research studies suggest that all kinds of positive and negative moods, even mild ones, can have a significant effect on the negotiation process.[55] Negotiators who are in good moods achieve larger joint gains than negotiators in neutral or negative moods. People in positive moods are more likely to honor their agreements than people in negative moods. The research suggests that mediators who can effectively manage the emotional climate in the negotiation room — maintaining hope, optimism and good humor, for example — are more likely to be successful than those who cannot. But of all the various emotions a mediator is likely to confront, anger and fear are the most critical, because they have the greatest potential to derail the negotiation process.[56]

"Emotional Flooding": The Effects of Anger and Fear on Our Ability to Think, Speak and Process Information. "Anger is short madness," the Latin poet Horace observed more than 2,000 years ago.[57] Put differently, social psychologists have found that "at high levels of emotional arousal, people can't think

---

53. *Id.* at 43, n.124.
54. *Id.* at 45-56.
55. The findings in this paragraph are reported in Freshman, Hayes & Feldman, *supra* note 43.
56. Adler, Rosen & Silverstein, *supra* note 43, at 163.
57. *Id.* at 168.

straight."[58] Neurological and psychological studies consistently demonstrate that when people are swamped by intense feelings of anger or fear — a state that some theorists call "emotional flooding"[59] — they are impaired in their ability:

- to think clearly and strategically, with complexity and nuance;

- to analyze problems objectively and dispassionately, taking into account not only their own views but the perspective of others;

- to decode accurately and without distortion other people's verbal and non-verbal behaviors;

- to express themselves dispassionately, without accusation, hostile attribution or threat;

- to engage in creative problem-solving; and

- to focus on their rational self-interest rather than on retribution and retaliation.[60]

Why do human beings become emotionally flooded when angry or afraid? As one article puts it, "evolutionary dynamics have developed our 'negative' emotions (e.g., fear and anger) to engage more quickly and with greater force than our positive emotions (e.g., joy and serenity) because the former carry greater survival potential."[61]

It is the familiar "fight or flight" phenomenon: When people become emotionally flooded, sometimes they will seek to escape from conflict and sometimes they will immediately engage it. But, in either case, intense levels of emotional arousal cause people to be unable to organize their thoughts, consider other people's perspectives, interpret others' conduct and communication accurately, process new information or make well-considered negotiation decisions. To be effective, a mediator must be able to recognize emotional flooding when it occurs and take steps to minimize its potentially harmful effects on the bargaining process.

"Emotional Contagion": The Impact of One Person's Moods and Emotions on Others.

Another potential psychological barrier to negotiation is "emotional contagion" — the tendency human beings have to "automatically synchronize facial expressions, vocalizations, postures and movements with those of another person and, consequently, to *converge* emotionally."[62] Do depressed and cynical people bring you down? Do your own feelings of hopefulness improve when you are around positive, upbeat friends? The idea behind emotional contagion is that human beings are natural mimics, and their emotional

---

58. Eileen Kennedy-Moore & Jeanne C. Watson, Expressing Emotion 220 (1999).
59. *Id. See also* Jones & Bodtker, *supra* note 43, at 228-232.
60. Kennedy-Moore & Watson, *supra* note 58, at 220.
61. The emotions of anger and fear are located in a portion of our mid-brain region (sometimes called the "lizard brain") called the amygdala. When human beings feel threatened, the amygdala responds instantaneously, before the cerebral cortex can assess a situation, sense subtleties and help us to respond rationally. Intense emotions prevent the brain from accessing information from the neocortex. The amygdala sacrifices accuracy for speed, because it is necessary for human survival. *See* Adler, Rosen & Silverstein, *supra* note 43, at 164-165.
62. Elaine Hatfield, John T. Cacioppo & Richard L. Rapson, Emotional Contagion 5 (1994).

states and expression are affected by the feedback of others' moods. Therefore people "tend to 'catch' each other's emotions"[63] — negative as well as positive.

Negotiation theorists have noted the tendency of destructive conflicts to perpetuate themselves through a process of escalating anger, mistrust and competition.[64] Mediation theorists argue that effective mediators can intervene to prevent destructive conflict resolution behaviors from occurring, model more productive and cooperative behaviors and positively affect the mood in the negotiation room. To the extent this is true, the presence and skilled intervention of a mediator may make the difference between a successfully resolved negotiation and one that, through its contagious effects, spirals out of control.[65]

Projection: Attributing Our Own Undesirable Traits to Others.

Do you know people who are super-competitive themselves but are always complaining about other people trying to take advantage of them? Or people who lie or cheat but see everyone else as dishonest? Such conduct is characteristic of the common psychological phenomenon of projection — perceiving others as having traits, impulses or desires that we possess but which are unacceptable to us and about which we are not conscious. We tend to see people as *we* are, not as *they* are.

In the context of dispute resolution, when a hostile negotiator unfairly accuses an opposing negotiator of being aggressive, this may be a projection of his or her own aggression onto the opponent. Such conduct often can begin a cycle of conflict. And because hostility, like other emotions, can be contagious, it may be reciprocated. Unless the mediator identifies this and intervenes to prevent it, such a dynamic easily can result in a downward spiral of mistrust and bad feeling.

Conflict Management Styles and Their Impact on Negotiations.

A final psychological variable that may create impediments to effective negotiation is the way individuals cope with conflict situations generally. In 1977, social psychologists K.W. Thomas and R.H. Kilmann hypothesized that individuals tend to be "competitors," "collaborators," "compromisers," "accommodators" or "avoiders" in their personal and professional conflicts.[66] The instrument they devised to test this defines these five modes of behavior as reflecting two fundamental personality traits — assertiveness and willingness to cooperate — in different combinations. Thomas and Kilmann contend that most individuals use all these strategies at one time or another, that all have value depending on the specific context, but that most people have a "default" style to which they will tend to revert in conflict situations.[67]

■ The *competing* personality is both highly assertive and uncooperative, a "me first," power-oriented response to conflict.

■ The *avoiding* mode of conflict is both unassertive and uncooperative. Conflict avoiders neither actively pursue their own interests nor the interests of others with whom they are in conflict.

---

63. *Id.* at 47.
64. *See generally* Morton Deutsch, The Resolution of Conflict: Constructive and Destructive Processes (1973).
65. *See generally*, Jones & Bodtker, *supra* note 43.
66. R.H. Kilmann & K.W. Thomas, *Developing a Forced-Choice Measure of Conflict-Handling Behavior: The Mode Instrument*, 37 Educ. & Psych. Measurement 309 (1977).
67. *Id.*

■ The *accommodating* personality is cooperative but unassertive, tending to neglect his or her own interests in deference to the interests of others.

■ Those who are *compromising* in their approach score in the middle range in both assertiveness and cooperation. Compromisers tend to want to "split the difference" as a way of finding a mutually satisfactory solution to a dispute.

■ The *collaborating* mode is simultaneously assertive and cooperative. Collaborators tend to want to work hard to find solutions that satisfy the interests of all disputants.[68]

Problems can arise when people with differing conflict management styles face each other in negotiation. A conflict avoider might choose to terminate a negotiation if it becomes too aggressively competitive. A competitive negotiator may overreach an accommodating negotiator and produce a one-sided agreement that feels like a big "win" but may have little durability. A skilled mediator may be able to recognize these dynamics as they are occurring and intervene appropriately. For example, she might coach the competitive negotiator on the potentially negative impact of aggressive tactics on the other side. Or she might speak to an accommodating negotiator in a private caucus to ensure that a proposed settlement agreement he is leaning toward accepting really meets his needs. In intervening in this way, a reflective mediator must also be aware of her *own* conflict management style and monitor her own behaviors to be sure that they serve the needs of the parties and not just her own preferred way of dealing with conflict situations.

Addressing Emotional Barriers: The Mediator's Role.   At this point, some of you may be saying to yourselves: "I am not trained in clinical psychology! Is all this stuff really necessary?"

In all honesty, we think it is. This does not mean you need a background in a mental health discipline to be effective as a mediator, as helpful as that training might be. What it does mean is that you need to be willing to address the psychological aspects of disputing, recognizing the critical (and in legal education, largely ignored) role that emotions can play in the conflict resolution process. As the negotiation scholar Melissa Nelkin has written about lawyers: "Client dissatisfaction with legal representation often results from the lawyer's inability to see the client's emotional self as anything but an impediment to the sensible, rational management of the legal problem the client brings. . . . Clients inevitably suffer when lawyers insist on divorcing the professional encounter from the emotional underpinnings of the dispute involved."[69] If a willingness to deal with emotional issues is important for lawyer-advocates, it is even more critical for mediators, whose central job it is to "enter" the parties' dispute[70] and to help guide it in more productive directions.

We will return to these subjects in more detail in Chapters 6, 7 and 9, when we analyze specific ways in which a mediator can lower tension, improve

---

68. *Id.*
69. NELKIN, *supra* note 14, at 235.
70. ROBERT A. BARUCH BUSH & JOSEPH P. FOLGER, The Promise of Mediation 70 (1994).

communication and ameliorate the harmful and distorting effects of strong emotions on the negotiation process.

■ §2.7 COGNITIVE BARRIERS TO SETTLEMENT

Most people like to think of themselves as rational people who make well-considered, logical decisions. But human beings are subject to pervasive judgmental biases that cause us to misinterpret and distort information and to depart from rationality in our decision making. These cognitive biases exist even under benign conditions, when we are not feeling angry or pressured. When combined with the kinds of strategic and emotional barriers we have just discussed, they make the pursuit of settlement a lot more challenging.[71]

Moreover, these judgmental biases are insidious, because they affect us even when we are unaware of them. If, as a potential future professional, you think that you will be immune to these biases and distortions, think again. Research consistently demonstrates that these cognitive biases affect laypersons and experts alike.

In this section, we present the cognitive and judgmental biases that are most likely to affect each stage of the negotiation process. First, we examine the cognitive distortions that may occur when a negotiator prepares and evaluates her own case for settlement purposes. Second, we consider the judgmental biases that can affect the negotiator's planning, including her prediction of what the other side will want and how he is likely to behave in the negotiation. Third, we examine the distortions that may affect how a negotiator reacts to an opponent's offers and concessions at the bargaining table.[72]

■ §2.7.1 DISTORTIONS IN DEVELOPING AND EVALUATING A CASE FOR SETTLEMENT

In legal matters, experienced lawyers generally have confidence in their ability to develop their cases thoroughly and assess them accurately for settlement purposes. But even the most capable lawyers are susceptible to biases that can distort their judgment in preparing a case and in assessing its chances of success. Why does this happen?

---

71. There is a substantial experimental literature on cognitive barriers to settlement. Helpful sources include KENNETH ARROW, DANIEL KAHNEMAN & AMOS TVERSKY, *Conflict Resolution: A Cognitive Perspective, in* Barriers to Conflict Resolution (Kenneth Arrow et al. eds., 1995); MAX H. BAZERMAN, Judgment in Managerial Decision Making (5th ed. 2001); MARGARET A. NEALE & MAX H. BAZERMAN, Cognition and Rationality in Negotiation (1991); LEIGH THOMPSON & JANICE NADLER, *Judgmental Biases in Conflict Resolution and How to Overcome Them, in* Handbook of Conflict Resolution (Morton Deutsch & Peter T. Coleman eds., 2000); LEIGH THOMPSON, The Mind and Heart of the Negotiator (2d ed. 2001); RICHARD BIRKE & CRAIG R. FOX, *Psychological Principles in Negotiating Civil Settlements*, 4 HARV. NEGOT. L. REV. 1 (1999); RUSSELL KOROBKIN & CHRIS GUTHRIE, *Psychological Barriers to Litigation Settlement: An Experimental Approach*, 93 MICH. L. REV. 107 (1994); and JANE GOODMAN-DELAHUNTY et al., *Insightful or Wishful? Lawyers' Ability to Predict Case Outcomes*, 16 PSYCHOL. PUB. POL'Y & L. 133 (2010).

72. This way of thinking about the effects of cognitive biases on negotiation and of organizing the discussion closely follows BIRKE & FOX, *supra* note 71.

Egocentric Biases and Negotiator Overconfidence.   The first problem is that human beings tend to pursue and interpret information in self-serving, biased ways. They are characteristically overconfident about their own abilities in relation to others and their own capacity to control outside forces. This causes them to be unrealistically optimistic in their predictions about future events, including both negotiation and litigation in which they are involved.

The problem of egocentric bias exists even when human beings are dealing with precisely the same information. For example, in one negotiation study eighty University of Texas undergraduates and eighty University of Texas law students were given identical transcript excerpts and documents from an actual motorcycle accident case in which the injured plaintiff had sought $100,000 in damages from the defendant driver. Assigned arbitrarily to one of two groups — one representing plaintiff, one representing defendant — the students were asked to predict whether the judge would rule for the plaintiff and, if so, for what amount. On average, students assigned to the role of plaintiff's lawyer predicted that the judge's award would be $14,527 higher than those assigned to the role of counsel for the defendant.[73] In other words, even when participants were *arbitrarily assigned* a role, and even when they were given precisely the *same information*, they interpreted that information in optimistic, self-serving ways consistent with their assigned positions.

However, in actual negotiations parties and their lawyers (if they are represented) usually do not have the same information. In general, both disputes and transactions are characterized by "information asymmetry": Each side knows more about its own positions and interests, and the facts supporting them, than it knows about the positions and interests of the other side. And a number of studies demonstrate that — *even when they know they are lacking important information* — disputants are unable to make proper allowances for that missing information when they evaluate their cases for settlement.

In one negotiation experiment, participants were divided into three subgroups. All subgroups were given the same background facts about several actual court cases. One subgroup was given only the plaintiffs' arguments construing the shared facts. Another subgroup was given only the defendants' arguments construing the background facts. (These arguments contained no new information; they were simply closing-argument-style characterizations of the facts from one partisan perspective or the other.) A third subgroup was given both defendants' and plaintiffs' arguments.

The three groups were then asked to predict how the juries decided these cases. Not surprisingly, the subgroup given both sides' arguments predicted the jury awards most accurately, and the two subgroups given one-sided information were less accurate in their predictions. But, even though they were aware that they were receiving one-sided information, these same two subgroups were generally more *confident* in those predictions than was the subgroup that received two-sided information![74]

---

73. George Loewenstein et al., *Self-Serving Assessments of Fairness and Pretrial Bargaining*, 22 J. Legal Stud. 135 (1993). Anecdotally, we have observed the same phenomenon in simulations conducted in our own negotiation courses.
74. Arrow, Kahneman & Tversky, *supra* note 71, at 46-50.

The overconfidence problem can be compounded by how we take in and seek out new information. In one interesting experiment, proponents and opponents of capital punishment were presented with two opposing studies, one supporting its effectiveness as a deterrent to crime, the other providing evidence showing no deterrent effect at all. After reading the two studies, each group thought that the study supporting their preexisting views was logically superior to the study opposing them. Not only that, but after reading *mixed* evidence from a combination of the two studies, each side felt more committed to its original position than before.[75]

Human beings also tend to *pursue* new information in biased, one-sided ways. Imagine that you have just come across a long magazine article lauding the many wonderful accomplishments of a well-known political, theatrical or sports figure. Are you more likely to take the time to read this article if you already greatly admire or if you intensely dislike this figure? Psychological studies suggest that people are generally more likely to pursue new information when it confirms, rather than contradicts, their preexisting views.[76]

The social science literature also suggests that negotiators may overestimate their own abilities, causing additional optimistic illusions about their cases. Negotiation scholars Richard Birke and Craig Fox write:

> . . . most people think they are more intelligent and fair-minded than average. Ninety-four percent of university professors believe that they do a better job than their colleagues. . . . [M]ost negotiators believe themselves to be more flexible, more purposeful, more fair, more competent, more honest, and more cooperative than their counterparts. . . . When lawyers try to anticipate the outcome of a trial or motion, there are many factors outside their control. . . . Nevertheless, the lawyers may overestimate their ability to control a trial's outcome, and in turn, overvalue the claim.[77]

When negotiators overestimate their chances of winning at trial or only listen with a partisan ear during the bargaining, their overall flexibility is likely to be limited, inhibiting settlement by reducing or eliminating the bargaining zone in which settlement can occur.[78]

The Jackpot Syndrome.   Negotiator overconfidence is also sometimes caused by the "jackpot" syndrome, caused by the fact that vivid, personal stories exert great, often undue influence on our decision making.[79]

---

75. CHARLES G. LORD, LEE ROSS & MARC R. LEPPER, *Biased Assimilation and Attitude Polarization: The Effect of Prior Theories on Subsequently Considered Evidence*, 37 J. PERSONALITY & SOC. PSYCHOL. 2098 (1979).

76. BIRKE & FOX, *supra* note 71, at 16.

77. *Id.* at 16-17 (citing studies). The predicted risks of negotiator overconfidence on the negotiation process are borne out by direct experimentation. A number of studies have been done of "final offer arbitration," a dispute resolution process (used in major league baseball salary disputes) in which an arbitrator, after conducting a hearing, may not freely make his or her own award, but must choose one of two final settlement offers submitted by the negotiators. In one study, in which there was on average only a 50 percent chance that any final offer would be accepted, participants on average estimated that there was a 68 percent chance of their offer being accepted. *See* BAZERMAN, *supra* note 65, at 140-141.

78. *Id.* at 141. Recall from §2.1 above that the first step in evaluating a case for settlement involves predicting the probable likelihood of a successful outcome.

79. NEALE & BAZERMAN, *supra* note 71, at 50-53.

Why is this so? When making decisions, human beings use a variety of mental shortcuts (*heuristics*). The shortcut we are talking about here is something psychologists call the "availability heuristic"—the tendency of decision makers to assess the frequency, likelihood and probable causes of events by the degree to which other similar events are readily available in their memories. Because vivid and recent stories are more easily recalled than bland and colorless statistics are, they often exert undue influence on our decisions.[80]

In the context of negotiation, this tendency can sometimes cause negotiators to exaggerate the value of their claims or the strength of their defense. Unusual legal events that have been prominently reported in the media—for example, the McDonald's coffee jury verdict, in which McDonald's was found liable for millions of dollars in damages[81] for overheating its coffee and failing to warn the plaintiff that her coffee was hot—can have a disproportionate effect on negotiators' case evaluations. The plaintiff's lawyer litigating his first medical malpractice case may know that a recent $12 million verdict against the local hospital was widely reported in the press only because the (extremely high) jury award was an aberration. Nevertheless, that award may unconsciously affect his and his client's negotiation expectations and demands. They hope to hit the jackpot too.[82]

The "Certainty" Effect.   Psychologists have demonstrated that people will pay an unwarranted, irrational premium to convert a strong probability into a certainty.[83] In the context of litigation, the certainty effect may cause lawyers to engage in over-investigation and over-discovery. They may spend more of their client's money than is warranted by the likely payoff to try to turn up that last bit of information—the "smoking gun"—that will turn an extremely strong case into a surefire winner or a slam-dunk loser into a case that could possibly be won.[84]

For a mediator trying to help parties resolve a lawsuit, this potentially presents two problems: The negotiators may be unrealistic about their cases, hoping against hope to find new and better information soon. Or, in more formal litigation, the negotiators may be unwilling to attempt settlement at all until discovery is completed.

Loss Aversion.   Psychologists have also shown that people are generally averse to suffering what they perceive to be losses and therefore often overcommit to a losing course of action. Take this example, suggested by negotiation scholar

---

80. *Id.* at 6-7, 15-16.

81. The initial jury award of $2.9 million was subsequently reduced to a total of $640,000. *www.nytimes.com/1994/10/ . . . /coffee-tea-or-ouch.html.*

82. BIRKE & FOX, *supra* note 71, at 5-11.

83. For example, in one study participants were shown a can of insecticide at a stated price. After reading warnings describing two different risks (inhalation and child poisoning), each with a .0015 probability, they were asked how much more they would be willing to pay for the insecticide if they could reduce these risks to (a) .0005 or (b) zero. On average, respondents were willing to pay $2.38 more to reduce the risks by .0010 to .0005 but were willing to pay an additional $5.71 to eliminate the last .0005 of risk to zero. In other words, they were willing to pay *more than twice as much to eliminate half of the risk to achieve a certain result. See* ARROW, KAHNEMAN & TVERSKY, *supra* note 71, at 52-53 (study citations omitted).

84. BIRKE & FOX, *supra* note 71, at 22.

Richard Shell: You have been standing in line for five minutes to go on a popular ride at an amusement park when a park employee announces that the total waiting time will be an hour and a half. Do you stick with it or choose another ride?

Now consider a second case, a variation on the first: You have been waiting in line for forty-five minutes when the employee announces that the total waiting time will be an hour and a half. Will you stick with it then? Here is what Shell says:

> Research on overcommitment suggests you are more likely to quit the line in case 1 than in case 2, even though the total waiting time is identical. Why? Because in case 2, you have invested a full forty-five minutes that you will "lose" by dropping out of line. In case 1, you "lose" only a few minutes. Once you have made an initial significant investment in waiting, you are inclined to invest more time to achieve a realizable goal.[85]

A similar distortion occurs when we incur *financial* costs that will be lost or "sunk" if we shift our course of action. Economists warn that we should not consider past or sunk costs in evaluating future courses of action, but instead should focus on the *prospective* costs and benefits of the decisions we make. But most human beings are unable to follow this advice, escalating their commitments in order to justify their past actions.[86]

Take this example, which happened to some married friends of ours. On a trip to Indonesia to visit their daughter several years ago, they stopped over in Bali, went shopping one day and saw an unusual teak bench that they loved. The cost was $220, plus another $130 to ship it to New Jersey. They made the purchase. Several months later, they discovered that the bench had been languishing in a New Jersey port for four weeks while they were still out of the country and had accrued $560 in storage fees. Not only that, but it would cost another $150 to ship it to their home, if they wanted to avoid additional storage fees of $20 per day until they could come pick it up themselves. At this point, they had a choice: either pay all the extra costs or let the bench be sold at auction without any further legal obligation to pay. Did they pay all the extra costs? Yes, they did, although the "$350" bench cost them more than $1,000 by the time they were done.

"*Would you have paid $1,000 for the bench if you had known from the start how much it would end up costing you?*" we asked them. "*Of course not, not even half that*" they laughingly replied. "*Well, why did you do it then?*" we asked. "*We had invested so much money in the damn thing that we just couldn't let it go,*" they replied.

In a lawsuit context, when clients and their attorneys invest a lot of time and money on a claim or defense that is not as strong as they initially believed, it is often difficult for them to admit to a losing course of action. They may choose to incur large additional costs in pursuing a long-shot victory rather than settling the litigation, even for a favorable amount, if it does not enable them fully to recoup their investment.

---

85. SHELL, *supra* note 14, at 182-183.
86. MAX BAZERMAN, *Negotiator Judgment: A Critical Look at the Rationality Assumption*, 27 AM. BEHAV. SCI. 211 (1983).

■ §2.7.2 DISTORTIONS IN PLANNING FOR NEGOTIATION: THE PROBLEM OF THE MYTHICAL FIXED PIE

Negotiation textbooks advise negotiators, when planning for a bargaining session, to think "outside the box," to put themselves in their negotiation counterpart's place and imagine what *they* want out of the negotiation. Only by doing this, negotiation planners are told, can they identify potential interests that are shared, interests that are different but compatible as well as interests that are truly conflicting. And it is only by doing this that many negotiations can be moved away from being a competitive struggle over dividing a "pie" that is fixed in size.

As we saw in §2.5, such planning is hard to carry out in actual negotiations. Problem-solving negotiation requires some openness about the parties' underlying interests; strategic concerns—specifically, the fear of being exploited—often make negotiators reluctant to freely share this information.

But the impediments to problem-solving negotiation are not only strategic; they are cognitive as well. Human beings are often unable even to *imagine* that they have interests that are not opposed to the interests of the other side. We tend to exaggerate the conflicts we have with others and often ignore signs from our counterparts that might suggest the existence of shared interests and concerns.

Theorists call this the "mythical fixed pie" or "exaggeration of conflict" bias.[87] Whatever it is called, it can lead to undue pessimism and closed-mindedness in negotiation planning, and to missed opportunities for non-zero sum and creative exchanges.

Consider a debate that was raging on college campuses and that divided many faculties in the 1980s and 1990s: Should universities continue to teach the traditional humanities "Western canon"? Or should they embrace multicultural studies by introducing students to a broader array of non-male, non-Western, non-Caucasian writers, artists and thinkers? In 1996, two researchers canvassed English professors throughout California who were thought to represent either traditionalist or revisionist perspectives on this issue. They asked the professors in each camp to list fifteen books they would assign freshmen in an introductory literature course, and then to list the fifteen books that they thought professors on the other side of the debate would assign. Each side had dramatically overestimated the extent of conflict. In fact, the two groups agreed on seven out of fifteen books.[88]

Exaggeration of conflict often leads negotiators to assume, mistakenly, that "if it's good for them, it must be bad for us." This is the essence of what negotiation scholars Max Bazerman and Margaret Neale call the "*mythical* fixed pie"—a pervasive assumption that the parties' interests are diametrically in conflict. Negotiators tend to assume that all negotiations are like carving up a fixed-size pie, with each trying to get the largest slice. This assumption often prevents negotiators from finding creative, mutually satisfying solutions to their problems.

---

87. *See* THOMPSON & NADLER, *supra* note 71, at 220 (exaggeration of conflict bias); BIRKE & FOX, *supra* note 72, at 30-31 (fixed-pie bias).
88. ROBINSON & KELTNER, *Much Ado About Nothing? Revisionists and Traditionalists Choose an Introductory English Syllabus*, 7 PSYCH. SCI. 18-24 (1996), described in THOMPSON, *supra* note 71, at 324-325.

Studies consistently show that negotiators find it difficult to identify potential interests in common with their adversaries. For example, one multi-issue negotiation experiment found that even where two parties' interests with respect to a particular issue were *identical* (they both wanted *exactly the same outcome on that issue*), in 39 percent of the pairings the negotiators settled for something different from that outcome. The negotiators assumed that their interests had to be in conflict with their opponent's interests, and that they therefore would have to give up some of what they really wanted on that issue in order to achieve an overall agreement.[89]

§2.7.3 DISTORTIONS AT THE TABLE: MISINTERPRETING AND MISEVALUATING SETTLEMENT OFFERS

Once negotiators arrive at the bargaining table, it is often difficult for them to interpret the actions of their negotiation counterparts and evaluate their settlement offers accurately. Of the various cognitive distortions that scholars have identified, four are especially critical: negotiators' biased perceptions of fairness; negotiators' hypersensitivity to perceived *un*fairness; the tendency of negotiators to "reactively devalue" any offers made by their negotiation counterparts and the aversion negotiators have to suffering what are perceived to be "losses" — often causing them to escalate their commitment to a losing course of action. We take each of these in turn.

"Do You Want More Than What's Fair?"   We have already seen how egocentric biases distort the way in which people in disputes pursue and evaluate information when preparing a case for litigation or settlement. These same biases can also affect how negotiators evaluate the fairness of their own settlement proposals and those of their adversaries. The point is well illustrated in a negotiation teaching tape, the "Hacker-Star Negotiation," produced a number of years ago by the Harvard Program on Negotiation.[90]

The Hacker-Star negotiation concerns a dispute between two business partners in a small start-up computer software firm. Hacker, the partner with software development expertise, has been trying to persuade Star, the partner with the capital, to support the development of a new software program (Power Star) as a company product. Star, who is conservative and risk averse, has repeatedly refused to support Hacker's proposal. Frustrated, Hacker finally goes off and develops the program on his own. He uses the company computer, working sometimes during office hours and often after hours to develop the new software. There is now a potential buyer for the new software program. Who owns the product, Hacker or the partnership? If the profits are going to be divided, what division is "fair"? Tensions over this issue, as well as others, threaten the continued existence of the partnership.

---

89. *Id.* at 20-21.
90. Videotape: Hacker-Star Negotiation (Harvard Program on Negotiation) (on file with the University of Connecticut School of Law Library).

Hacker believes that he owns the new product and that it is "immoral" and "unfair" for Star to ask to share in the profits from it. At most, he will offer Star 5 percent. After all, it was his idea, he did all the work, and Star repeatedly denigrated it, saying it wouldn't work. (Emotionally, this last point seems especially salient for Hacker.)

Hacker's lawyer insists that his client try to look at the issue from Star's point of view: Hacker diverted his time and attention away from company business to work on the product. He used company facilities to develop it. There is a clause in the partnership agreement that, while ambiguous, seems to suggest that any program developed by Hacker belongs to the partnership. Accepting only 5 percent of the profits would be felt by Star as "rewarding" Hacker for going behind Star's back. Finally, Hacker says, in exasperation, "*I don't want to recognize [his side of things] but if I put on my 'fair hat,' I know you're right.*" When his lawyer asks, "*do you want more than what's fair?*" Hacker sheepishly admits that he doesn't.

This short video segment illustrates several important points about fairness in negotiation. First, most people are concerned about fairness — being perceived as fair themselves as well as being treated fairly by others. Second, standards of fairness are inevitably subjective; reasonable people often disagree about what's fair depending on the norms that they choose to define "fairness." Third, because of egocentric biases and often without knowing it, people generally choose norms of fairness that favor their own positions.

So, in this example, Hacker did not think he wanted more than what's fair. But his ideas of fairness were biased by his own moral indignation — his sense that his ideas were disrespected and that it now would now be unfair for Star to share in any profit from them. It takes the skilled intervention of his lawyer to help him see that there are competing fairness norms he will need to consider if he wants to resolve the dispute with his business partner amicably.

Consider another example, a little closer to home. Suppose you are taking a negotiation seminar. Without explicitly weighting the various factors, the instructor indicates in her syllabus that final grades will be a function of (1) conscientious class participation; (2) demonstrated negotiation skill and favorable outcomes in simulated negotiations and (3) the quality of each student's pre-negotiation planning and post-negotiation reflection, as demonstrated in a written journal.

If you were an effective natural negotiator but not especially active in class and not much good at planning or reflection, you will probably think that negotiation skill should be the most important grading criterion. Conversely, if you were not an especially effective negotiator but prepared detailed plans and wrote deeply and self-critically about your negotiations, you will probably think that good planning and reflection should be the most important criteria. And if you didn't perform especially well in any of these dimensions, you will probably conclude that all grades should be roughly equal.

It's not that we human beings *want* to be unfair; it's that our sense of fairness is affected by our strong tendency to protect our own egos. And it often happens without our knowing it. As Leigh Thompson and Janine Nadler have observed, "our psychological immune system is so efficient that we do not even realize our judgments are tainted with self-interest."[91]

---

91. THOMPSON & NADLER, *supra* note 71, at 219 (collecting sources).

Hypersensitivity to Perceptions of Unfairness.   A closely related point is that most people are extremely sensitive to the feeling of having been treated unfairly. Suppose that a recent graduate, having done quite well in school, takes an entry-level position as an associate in a big-city financial services company or law firm. At the end of his first year, the managing partner calls him in and tells him that he has been awarded a $15,000 bonus in recognition of his good work. He is thrilled by his bonus because he was not expecting it and because he feels well rewarded. That night, he goes out and celebrates with a close friend over a bottle of good French wine.

The next day, he learns that of the other five newly hired employees, three were awarded bonuses of $20,000. He doesn't think their work was any better than his. To make matters worse, one of the coworkers who got a higher bonus than he did was extremely dependent on him during the year, constantly stopping by his desk to ask simple-minded questions. Now how does he feel? If he is like most people, the bonus he was thrilled about yesterday in *absolute* terms infuriates him today because he feels he has been judged unfavorably—and unfairly—in *relative* terms.

Psychological studies confirm that people are highly sensitive to issues of comparative fairness and that they tend to become distressed when they think they have been treated unfairly by or in relation to others. When this happens, social psychologists tell us, people generally seek to restore "equity" in their relationships. In an employment situation, this might take the form of asking for a raise, working less hard (so as to justify the smaller bonus), taking home office supplies or quitting.[92]

Equity-seeking behaviors affect negotiation as well, although the choices available to the negotiator to restore equity are more limited. If Jim believes that negotiator Jane has treated him poorly in the past or is demanding more in the bargaining process than she is entitled to or deserves in relation to Jim's own demands, Jim may well reject Jane's settlement offer even though it fully satisfies his underlying interests and is preferable to his non-settlement alternative. Negotiators often act against their rational self-interest—"cutting off their nose to spite their face"—when they think they have been treated unfairly by their negotiation counterpart.[93] And because their notions of fairness are likely to be affected by self-interest in the first place, this sensitivity is heightened and can easily produce an impasse.

"Reactive Devaluation" of Opponents' Offers.   A number of years ago, an African American woman was involved in a fair housing case against a large local realty company. She alleged that she had been told that a rental apartment she had recently applied for was "unavailable" and had been "steered" to another building owned by the company, with a higher percentage of minority tenants and in a less

---

92. *Id.*
93. *See* KOROBKIN & GUTHRIE, *supra* note 71, at 144-147 (simulated landlord-tenant dispute involving claim for rent abatement based on landlord's persistent failure to fix heater; landlord's offer to settle for $900 was far more likely to be accepted when landlord's failure to return calls was explained on basis of family emergency than when no explanation was provided. Simulation shows result occurred even when subjects were told that small claims court result would not be affected by landlord's excuse for failing to provide heat).

prosperous part of town. Suspicious and upset, she refused that apartment and retained a law school legal clinic to represent her. Subsequent fair housing testing by the clinic confirmed that the first apartment she had applied for had in fact been available at (and after) the time she had applied for it. She filed a complaint against the company with the state human rights commission seeking damages for her (considerable) humiliation and anger.

After a year or so of litigation, the students began to counsel her about her goals for settlement. Based on much research, they advised her that a figure of $15,000 would represent an excellent outcome, especially considering that she had suffered no out-of-pocket losses or other financial consequences. In discussions with student attorneys in the clinic, she said that if $15,000 were offered, she would settle her case for that amount. Yet when during settlement negotiations that amount of money was actually offered by the company's president, she told her attorneys to reject it and subsequently went to trial.

For experienced litigators, the story is common enough. Empirical studies confirm that the *source* or *authorship* of a proposal often determines its attractiveness. Offers and concessions in the bargaining process are often "reactively devalued" simply because they come from the other side.[94]

Why do we devalue the offers of our negotiation opponents? One explanation is grounded in the mythical fixed-pie bias ("if it's good for them, it must be bad for me") that we have already discussed.[95] A second explanation of reactive evaluation is captured by the saying, "the grass is always greener." The idea is that human beings who want something often desire it less when it actually becomes attainable to them. Put another way, once a proposal has actually been offered, it becomes less attractive than other possible proposals that are available hypothetically but have not been offered.[96]

A third explanation of reactive evaluation is based more simply on anger and spite. In a study of reactive devaluation in a simulated litigation context, law professors Russell Korobkin and Chris Guthrie found that the effects of reactive devaluation appear to be strongest when the side making the offer is viewed by the other side as a hostile adversary.[97] If this is true, then reactive devaluation is "a visceral reaction primarily motivated by dislike for the adversary and the desire to say 'no' whenever the adversary says 'yes.' "[98] Viewed from this perspective, given her strong feelings about having been discriminated against, the woman's decision to go to trial was understandable.

Whatever the psychological mechanisms underlying reactive devaluation, note its potential for producing a bargaining impasse. *Reciprocation* is a fundamental ingredient for any successful negotiation.[99] If one negotiator believes that she has made a reasonable offer or significant concession and that her

---

94. *See* Lee Ross, *Reactive Devaluation in Negotiation and Conflict Resolution, in* Barriers to Conflict Resolution 27-42 (Kenneth Arrow et al. eds., 1995); Korobkin & Guthrie, *supra* note 71, at 150-160.
95. Birke & Fox, *supra* note 71, at 48.
96. Ross, *supra* note 94, at 35.
97. Korobkin & Guthrie, *supra* note 71, at 157-159. Of course, depending on the circumstances, it may be rational for a negotiator to be suspicious of an opponent's offers if the relationship between the parties has been hostile or unpleasant.
98. *Id.*
99. Robert Cialdini, Influence: The Psychology of Persuasion 17-57 (1984); Shell, *supra* note 14, at 59-60. We further discuss reciprocity as a negotiation norm in Chapter 9.

proposal is summarily dismissed by the other side, this can often lead to recrimination, distrust and anger in return.

Loss Aversion Revisited.   We have already seen how loss aversion can cause negotiators to "throw good money after bad" when developing their cases for settlement. Loss aversion and a related cognitive bias (the *endowment effect*) can also affect negotiators at the bargaining table, leading them to turn down settlement offers when it would be economically rational to accept them.

Psychological studies demonstrate that people will take greater risks to avoid what they perceive to be losses than they will take risks to achieve equivalent gains.[100] Suppose that an anonymous benefactor calls you up out of the blue and offers you either $1,000 cash, payable tomorrow, or a lottery ticket, whose drawing is also tomorrow, with a 50 percent chance of winning $2,400. If you are like most people, you will probably take the $1,000 in cash, the sure thing, rather than taking a chance of receiving nothing. This is so even though the expected value of the lottery (a 50 percent chance of winning $2,400, or $1,200) is greater than $1,000.

Now suppose instead that you live in a dictatorship. A government bureaucrat comes to your house and tells you that you have the choice of paying the government $1,000 of your own money today or subjecting yourself to a 50 percent chance that the state will take $2,400 of your money tomorrow. Most people in this situation would choose the riskier option, the chance of losing more than twice as much money (but also of paying nothing), rather than suffering a sure loss. Again, the economically rational decision would be to pay the government $1,000, because the expected value of the lottery (a 50 percent chance of losing $2,400, or $1,200) is more costly. But most people are averse to suffering what they perceive to be losses and will take great (even irrational) risks to avoid them. A related bias often affects decision making at the same time: Once people *own* or are *endowed* with something, they value it more highly than a non-owner would and are therefore more reluctant to give it up. This is what cognitive psychologists call the *endowment effect.*[101]

Loss aversion and the endowment effect can have a powerful combined effect on negotiators and cause them to dig their heels in when they shouldn't. For example, in collective bargaining negotiations, if union representatives are asked to give up a hard-earned wage increase negotiated last year in order to avoid layoffs this year, they may have difficulty rationally calculating the costs and benefits of making this concession. And defendants in civil litigation matters are often resistant to accepting objectively reasonable settlement proposals when it means giving up money that they already possess. All of these forms of loss aversion, if unaddressed, can lead to impasse.

---

100. Arrow, Kahneman & Tversky, *supra* note 71, at 54-60.

101. In one series of studies of the endowment effect, researchers divided participants into several groups. One group (the "sellers") was given a coffee mug and told they owned it but could sell it for an agreed-upon price. Another group (the "buyers") were given money and told they could either keep the money or buy the mug. Each group was then asked to place a value on the mug. The sellers' median valuation of the mug was $7.12. The buyers' median valuation of the same mug was $2.88. *See* Max H. Bazerman & Margaret A. Neale, Negotiating Rationally 35-37 (1992).

▪ §2.8 CULTURAL AND STRUCTURAL BARRIERS TO SETTLEMENT

Before leaving the subject of barriers to settlement, we want to touch on two additional kinds of problems that, while less pervasive than the obstacles already discussed, can negatively impact the negotiation process, sometimes in less-than-obvious ways. These are *cultural* barriers and *structural* barriers to resolution.

Cultural Barriers. By *cultural* barriers, we mean the kinds of communication impediments and value differences that can threaten a negotiation solely by virtue of disputants' ethnic, racial, religious, gender and other identity differences. It is a truism that we live in an increasingly global and heterogeneous society. When people from different backgrounds interact in conflict situations or negotiate, this brings with it a number of heightened risks, including:

- misunderstandings due to basic language differences;

- discomfort at raising or discussing certain subjects, due to cultural norms;

- hostile or inaccurate attributions concerning a person's past conduct or intentions, due to identity-rooted sensitivity;

- culturally based disagreements about substantive rights, morality or fairness; and

- incompatible, culturally influenced orientations to conflict and negotiating.

As a result, intercultural understanding is an increasingly important skill for both practicing mediators and negotiators. In individual cases, mediators must find effective means of recognizing, diagnosing and then addressing such obstacles without making unwarranted assumptions about the impact of differences or acting on stereotyped notions about entire cultural groups. We return to these important skill themes in a number of later chapters.

Structural Barriers. By *structural* settlement impediments, we mean barriers that stem from the environment in which the mediation is taking place that limit negotiating options or from the way in which the parties are constituted.[102] Compared with the obstacles already discussed, some impediments in this category will be obvious. But even if they may be easy to identify, they may nonetheless be difficult to surmount.

Settlement-inhibiting factors present in the environment or setting include tangible and physical constraints — for example, limits on the number of participants allowed or on the time available to mediate, crucial participants barred from attending, or limits on the kinds of outcomes that are permissible or on the confidentiality that can be guaranteed.

Other structural problems can arise because of tensions among the party's negotiating representatives or between the official negotiators and their constituents, each of which can make the bargainers reluctant to commit to any settlement or to render any negotiated agreement "weak." An obvious example is the union

---

102. *See* BERNARD S. MAYER, The Dynamics of Conflict Resolution 305 (2000).

negotiator bargaining on behalf of absent rank and file who must ratify an unpopular agreement for it to take effect. A less obvious example is a husband negotiating on behalf of not only himself, but his absent wife, who may not be satisfied with (and could undermine) the deal he wants to make. Another example might be where two department chairmen are appearing for a corporation at a mediation involving a claimed breach of contract, and neither wants his department's budget to be charged any of the monies needed to settle the case. We discuss who should attend the mediation in Chapters 4 and 13 and the "missing constituent" problem in Chapter 7.

Another sort of structural problem arises when bargaining agents disagree with the principals they represent or disserve them in ways that potentially jeopardize a good negotiated resolution. A classic example is one in which a party wants to accept a settlement, but her overbearing lawyer is urging her not to. Or where a lawyer is giving his client very bad legal advice, and this is getting in the way of possible resolution. We consider the challenges for mediators who seek to uncover and overcome such impediments in Chapters 7 and 12.

The most important message of this chapter is that there are many reasons why unassisted negotiations break down, never get started or fall short of their potential, and good reason to believe that skillful mediators, by accurately diagnosing barriers to settlement, can help disputants better achieve their goals. But working effectively as a mediator also requires an understanding of the major forms or styles of mediation, how one's overall approach to conducting the process can affect both the chances of resolution and its quality and the variables that make adoption of one style over another appropriate for a particular case. We now turn to these topics.

CHAPTER 3

THE ROLE OF
THE MEDIATOR

Differing Approaches, Fundamental Norms

This chapter contains extended video extracts from two, almost full-length mediations, totaling approximately two hours and fifteen minutes.

■ §3.1 THE MANY FACES OF MEDIATION

You may have entered this course with a single, unitary image of the mediation process and the role that mediators play. If so, it isn't that simple. Unlike other professions, there is no one standard conception of the mediator's proper role.[1] Instead, we find philosophical and professional debate over competing models.

Consider the following (real) cases:

> • A breach of contract case brought by a fired sales representative against his former employer was referred to mediation by the trial judge. The plaintiff alleged $7 million in damages; the parties' prior settlement discussions had suggested that the plaintiff would accept $750,000, with the defendant offering $350,000. Before the mediation began, based on private phone sessions and study of documents provided by counsel for the parties, the mediator, an experienced lawyer, formed his own estimate of the settlement value of the matter as between $500,000 and $600,000. The mediator then convened the mediation and, through a series of private sessions with the parties, attempted to move them toward a settlement by predicting that evidence harmful to one side would be admitted into evidence, advising the plaintiff to drop a "messy" claim for infliction of emotional distress, exhibiting disbelief at the plaintiff's continuing to demand more

continues on next page >

---

1. *Compare* DAVID LUBAN, Lawyers and Justice: An Ethical Study (1988) (discussing the "standard conception" of the role of the lawyer in the adversary system).

than the mediator's projected outcome (*"how greedy can you get?"*) and showing anger when the defense refused a $550,000 offer of settlement. After thirteen hours of nonstop talks during which the parties were separated at one point for seven hours, having rebuffed (*"to keep the heat on"*) the plaintiff's 11 p.m. proposal to adjourn for the night and suggesting that the trial judge would react adversely to the company's failure to *"live up to its moral obligations"* to settle, the mediator drove home a $550,000 installment payment resolution at 1 a.m.[2]

- The U.S. Postal Service offers a voluntary mediation program for employees who have filed complaints of race, age, gender or other unlawful discrimination, usually against their workplace supervisor.[3] A recent case involved a claim of race discrimination based on a supervisor's failure to approve a subordinate's request to attend a training program that could have enabled the worker to develop skills needed for promotion. The unrepresented claimant charged that the supervisor showed favoritism to other workers, a feeling she claimed that others shared. At times, the claimant would run on emotionally for ten or fifteen minutes, often repeating herself. The claimant could not substantiate the alleged favoritism with examples or data. The supervisor explained in detail the process for selecting from among the many training program applicants and stated performance-based reasons for the claimant's non-selection. He also showed that the eligible pool for the program consisted overwhelmingly of persons of the claimant's race and that the worker selected for the training was a person of the claimant's own race. Pursuant to program policy, the lawyer-mediator made no effort to limit the claimant's emotional displays, expressed no views on the likely outcome of the matter (despite his clear belief that the claimant's case lacked legal merit) and proposed no solutions. The four-hour meeting ended with no resolution. Just before leaving the session, the worker thanked the mediator for his time, reiterated her intention to take her complaint to "the next step," and added, *"at least now the supervisor knows how I feel. And maybe now he'll stop making decisions without giving people reasons."*

- A college campus was rocked by the allegation that a junior-year male honor student sexually assaulted a female classmate in his room after a party at a fraternity house. Sit-ins by the campus women's group demanding his expulsion threatened to disrupt final exams. The accused student, who had been temporarily suspended, denied the charges, claiming that the sex was consensual. The alleged victim filed a campus disciplinary complaint and, at the urging of her boyfriend, contemplated seeking criminal charges as well. The male student threatened to sue the university if his progress toward graduation was impeded. At the suggestion of the university administration, both students agreed to try to resolve the matter through mediation. The mediation team, consisting of a male and female faculty member, convened marathon sessions that explored the incident, the background, the parties' reactions to the incident and its aftermath, their plans and needs. After forty-two hours of meetings over four days, a resolution acceptable to both was reached, including withdrawals of all complaints, provisions for preventing contact by the parties (including a semester's leave of absence for the alleged perpetrator),

2. Lavinia Hall, *Eric Green: Finding Alternatives to Litigation in Business Disputes, in* When Talk Works: Profiles of Mediators 279, 299-300 (Deborah Kolb ed., 1994).
3. The U.S. Postal Service REDRESS (Resolve Employment Disputes Reach Equitable Solutions Swiftly) program is described at http://about.usps.com/what-we-are-doing/redress/welcome.htm.

university-paid counseling for the alleged victim and mandatory "date rape" education for all of the university's sponsored fraternities and sororities. Because of fears expressed by the female student before the start of the process, at no time during those forty-two hours, including the signing of the agreement, did the two students sit in the same room together.

- At a Texas prison, a woman and the convicted death row inmate who brutally murdered her daughter engaged in a lengthy and highly emotional face-to-face confrontation two weeks before the inmate's execution. The meeting took place as part of a state-sponsored "victim-offender" program. The woman had sought the meeting for twelve years; the inmate had only recently agreed to participate. For months prior to the meeting, a psychologist-mediator worked separately with the participants in order to increase the likelihood that the meeting would be productive and would not re-victimize the mother. Among other interventions, he coached the inmate on how to offer an effective apology. (Referring to the murder as *a "mistake"* would not be well received, the mediator urged.) The meeting only took place once the mediator determined that the parties were "ready." At the meeting, hours went by as the mother's outpouring of rage and grief was followed by a tearful, non-defensive apology and acceptance of responsibility by the murderer. Eventually, the mother offered a form of personal forgiveness (*"I can forgive you, but not what you did"*), for which the inmate thanked her. The mediator said almost nothing the entire day.[4]

At the outset of this book, we defined mediation as assisted negotiation in which a neutral third party attempts to help disputants resolve a dispute, without compelling them to accept any particular resolution. Here is another definition, with a slightly different emphasis: "a consensual process that seeks self-determined resolutions."[5]

Were each of the third parties depicted above practicing "mediation" within these definitions? What factors might account for the differences in the way each conducted the process? Is there a way to assess which of these approaches is preferable? Were any of them *in*appropriate? From whose vantage point would we conclude this? Would a uniform approach have been effective across all of these situations? What does "effective" mean in each of these cases?

Role Definition as Mission Statement.   Understanding one's proper role in an undertaking and the goals one is trying to achieve are critical first steps in learning any new set of skills. Without a sense of one's goals and a conception of appropriate and inappropriate means of achieving them, skills become a set of disembodied techniques, and the new practitioner has little grounding to rely on when a situation presents a choice as to how to proceed.

A mediator's basic conception of her role—both her general *goals* and the *actions* she believes are appropriate to achieve them—will affect virtually

---

4. *48 Hours: My Daughter's Killer* (CBS television broadcast, Feb. 4, 1999).
5. Jay Folberg & Alison Taylor, Mediation: A Comprehensive Guide to Resolving Conflicts (1984).

everything she does as a mediator. Her role conception will help her determine an overall plan for each mediation and specific techniques, or tactics, to carry out that plan. That strategy and how it is executed, in turn, will often have considerable influence on the kind of outcomes produced. This can be depicted as follows:

Role Conception —> Plan —> Techniques and Tactics —> Outcomes[6]

This chapter focuses primarily on issues of role definition, postponing issues of planning, tactics and techniques to later chapters. We introduce you here to the differing ways in which mediators conceptualize their role, the differing forms of mediation that result, the current debate over these different mediation models and our own views on these contested issues. We also present three mediation norms about which even mediators with differing philosophies appear to agree, although, as we will see, these "universal" norms have different shades of meaning and different degrees of primacy for different mediators. We conclude by identifying the principal *contextual* variables and constraints that — however a mediator conceptualizes her role in general — might may affect how she plans for and conducts herself in a particular case.

▪ §3.2 DIFFERING CONCEPTIONS OF THE MEDIATOR'S ROLE: HISTORICAL ROOTS

To appreciate (and, we hope, to begin to locate yourself in) the "ideological contest"[7] over the proper goals and methods of mediation, it may be helpful to examine the historical forces behind the rise in interest in alternatives to litigation generally, and mediation in particular.

Mediation in America experienced its first widespread use in the "relational" areas of labor-management relations and domestic relations, in response to the social cost of labor strife and the dramatic rise of divorce in the mid-twentieth century. "Conciliation" was viewed as the foremost goal of mediation in those spheres.[8] The 1960s and early 1970s saw the advent of community-based conflict resolution, which involved the mediation of low-level neighbor-neighbor disputes and minor criminal matters. The "neighborhood justice" movement viewed mediation as a means of providing access to justice for those who would not otherwise afford it and of promoting community harmony. The proponents of the neighborhood justice movement urged the creation of processes that were informal, not controlled by outside legal professionals or specialists, that elevated personal (rather than legal) norms in decision making and stressed the empowerment that comes from maximizing the disputants' participation and personal control of their own

---

6. *See* CARRIE MENKEL-MEADOW, *Toward Another View of Legal Negotiation: The Structure of Problem Solving*, 31 UCLA L. REV. 754, 760, (1984) for a similar graphic portrayal of the relationship between orientation and results in the negotiating context.

7. *See* JOHN LANDE, *How Will Lawyering and Mediation Practices Transform Each Other?* 24 FLA. ST. U. L. REV. 839, 854 (1997).

8. *See, e.g.*, LEO KANOWITZ, Alternative Dispute Resolution: Cases and Materials 77, 77-78 (1985) (discussing differences between mediators and conciliators, and presenting the example of EEOC-mandated conciliation under title VII of the 1964 Civil Rights Act). *See also* LON L. FULLER, *Mediation — Its Forms and Functions*, 44 S. CAL. L. REV. 305 (1971).

fates.[9] This democratic movement was not without its detractors. Critics expressed concern that "informal justice" without protection of legal rights would harm the very disadvantaged citizens that such processes were intended to reach and would fail to consider the impact of decisions on those not present and participating.[10]

The 1970s and 1980s saw the dawn of what most scholars consider the modern "ADR movement."[11] In this period, ADR's most ardent advocates saw litigation alternatives, including mediation, as a solution to many of the perceived problems of the public court system. Officials managing congested dockets amidst the arguable "litigation explosion" that took place in the post-Vietnam era decried the cost and delay that characterized public justice and urged the creation of backlog-clearing alternatives. This *quantitative* rationale for alternative processes was perhaps best summed up in Chief Justice Burger's call for "mechanisms that can produce an acceptable result in the shortest possible time, with the least possible expense and with a minimum of stress on the participants." "That," he argued, "is what justice is all about."[12]

At the close of the twentieth century, corporate America joined the chorus of proponents of mediation and began to use it with increasing frequency. This trend can be traced to concerns about increasing financial costs, publicity risks and lost managerial time associated with traditional litigation. During this period, both trial and appellate courts also began to mandate mediation with increasing regularity. These proponents elevated a new set of priorities for the process: efficiency and high settlement rates. They also created a new emphasis on law in the mediation process, as much mediation activity was now hosted by courts in the "shadow"[13] of the courtroom or purchased by private users who valued legal expertise as a critical mediator qualification.

During this era, another school of ADR proponents entered the scene, with a different ideological perspective. Their quarrel was with limitations in the *quality* of justice (in terms of both process and outcomes) obtainable in the public courts. Some pointed to the courts' focus on rights-based, win-lose decision making, in which remedies were constrained by legal entitlements and important non-legal interests were viewed as irrelevant. They argued that alternative processes that could redefine disputes broadly so as to explore non-legal concerns could produce outcomes that were substantively superior (tailored to the parties' needs, built to last, etc.) to those obtained in adjudication or in the unprincipled distributive bargaining that characterized much dispute-based negotiation.[14] Others in this

---

9. *See* Raymond Shonholtz, *Community Mediation Centers: Renewing the Civic Mission for the Twenty-First Century*, 17 Mediation Q. 4 (2000).

10. On a macro level, critics expressed concern that the increased use of private, unreported alternatives would undermine law reform efforts aimed at helping the same segments of the population and would deprive the courts and society of needed bodies of case decisions. *See* Owen M. Fiss, *Against Settlement*, 93 Yale L.J. 1073 (1984).

11. A. Leo Levin & Russell R. Wheeler eds., The Pound Conference: Perspectives on Justice and the Future (1979).

12. Warren E. Burger, *Isn't There a Better Way?* 68 A.B.A. J. 274, 275 (1982).

13. *See* Robert H. Mnookin & Lewis Kornhauser, *Bargaining in the Shadow of the Law: The Case of Divorce*, 88 Yale L.J. 950, 952-956 (1979).

14. *See generally supra* §2.2. *See, e.g.*, Roger Fisher & William Ury, Getting to Yes: Negotiating Agreement Without Giving In 41 (1983) (negotiation can produce more settlements that maximize welfare by responding to complex interests rather than exclusively to legal "rights"); Menkel-Meadow, *supra* note 6 (suggesting that lawyers and other professionals often incorrectly think of negotiation as a zero-sum game).

school focused on the human costs and relationship-destroying hyper-adversariness of court litigation and the competitive bargaining that it spawned and pointed to the more humane process that could be obtained through alternatives like mediation. This was especially important for, but not limited to, matters involving continuing relationships.

These diverse, often conflicting values for both processes and outcomes—reconciliation, community building, empowerment, freedom from law, speed, efficiency, party participation, cost savings, creativity, informality, fairness, expertise, privacy, humanity—have today all made their way into the macro world of mediation, championed by differing consumer, provider and policy-making groups in varying degrees. On a micro level, for the individual mediator, the pulls of these competing values can easily converge in a single case or even a single moment in a case, when the neutral is confronted with a choice of several ways to proceed.

§3.3 THE MEDIATOR'S GOALS IN ACTION: A CASE OF A BROKEN CAR MIRROR

To introduce this role debate in action, imagine that you have been assigned to mediate the following dispute, a real case that recently took place in a major city in the Northeast:

> A lawsuit is brought in small claims court against the owner of a car wash stemming from alleged damage to a customer's Nissan Maxima. The car owner claims that four months ago the car wash machine ripped the electric mirror from his car's body and that it will cost $485 to install a new one. A written estimate from a local Nissan dealership for this amount is attached to his complaint. The parties agree to try to resolve the matter through mediation at the court's dispute resolution program one week before the date set for the trial. Neither party is represented by an attorney.
>
> In the first few minutes of the mediation you learn the following: The car owner and his spouse, both of whom are African American, live several blocks from the car wash and, for several years before the dispute, had been regular customers. The defendant, a recent immigrant from Southeast Asia whose English is poor, purchased the car wash about a year ago with his brother. The plaintiff's car is less than one year old. Its passenger-side mirror came loose from the car near the conclusion of the wash cycle. The customer immediately sought out the car wash operator to report the damage. After inspecting the dangling mirror and denying responsibility, the operator offered to have his brother (who he said was a mechanic) fix or replace the mirror. When this offer was refused, the operator threw up his hands and began to walk away. At this, the car owner began yelling angry insults, threatened a lawsuit and left. Since the incident occurred, both he and his spouse have been using another car wash.
>
> In the mediation, the car wash operator repeats his claim that he was not responsible, that there must have been something already loose or defective about the mirror, because this had never happened before and his business washes thousands of cars a year. He adds that he felt the amount the plaintiff was claiming was "not

reasonable" and that his brother could have fixed the problem for one-third of the amount claimed. He expresses bewilderment and anger that his immediate offer to fix the mirror was rejected and that he has been sued. In response to questioning, he states that his insurance has a deductible of $1,000.00.

You know from reading recent newspaper articles that the car wash is located in an area of the city that has been the site of considerable conflict between the communities from which these parties come. Among the factors cited for this tension is the trend of entrepreneurial Asian immigrants moving into the area, buying existing businesses (often from white or African American owners) and then hiring Asians to replace existing (mostly African American) employees.

Imagine yourself in the mediator's seat at this juncture. What kind of *outcome* comes to mind? A negotiated compromise involving payment of some amount by the car wash operator to the car owner? Some re-establishment of the parties' prior business relationship? Some greater understanding between the parties based on exploring the strong feelings that their conflict engendered? Some agreement that attempts to address wider intergroup concerns in the neighborhood? Which of these came to mind first? Do any of these possible solutions seem unrealistic? Do any make you uncomfortable? What is your reaction based on?

Next, how do you see yourself *acting* as a mediator in this matter? Would you have the parties talk face to face, or do you envision separate meetings with them? Will you focus on the strong feelings already identified? Or will you try to minimize or avoid them? Would you try to harness what you knew about neighborhood tensions? If so, how and to what end? If you developed a view of the likely court outcome and the risks/costs each side faced in going to court, would that become relevant? If you were to interject that assessment, how forcefully would you do so? What factors explain your answers to these questions?

The mediator's role conception will depend on his or her answer to two primary questions:

- What kind of outcome should this process produce?

- How much influence should I exert in the process?

In the pages that follow, we summarize the major perspectives in the debate over each of these questions.

§3.4   MEDIATION OUTCOMES: SHOULD "SOLVING THE PROBLEM" BE THE GOAL? IF SO, WHAT PROBLEM AND WHAT KIND OF SOLUTION?

To most mediation practitioners and theorists, it is almost a matter of definition: The principal goal of mediation is to "solve the problem"—resolve the dispute, conclude the transaction, settle the lawsuit or, at the very least, narrow the issues in controversy. If asked for justifications for this approach, problem-solving mediators would cite the expectations of the participants, program, agency or court, as well as the societal benefit from assisting the parties in averting continuing conflict, litigation, stalemate or even violence.

As to the means for achieving this goal, there is less consensus. In Chapter 2, we described how adversarial bargaining is still quite prevalent in all realms of dispute negotiation. Competitive negotiation is likewise common when parties enter mediation. If asked, many (perhaps most) mediators would agree that a broad, interest-based approach to mediation is desirable (in terms of "maximizing value"), and many mediators do attempt it. But the real world of mediating legal disputes is also heavily characterized (and perhaps even dominated) by rights-based approaches that seek efficient resolutions by making heavy use of legal rules and arguments that frame the problem narrowly.

Thus, within the world of problem-solving mediators:

Narrow "Settlers"   tend to define problems by seeing them as they are framed by the parties in their negotiating positions or pleadings. Because these are most often couched in positional, distributive terms ("*We demand $6 million in damages*"; "*I want my daughter every weekend*"; "*We seek a $2 an hour pay raise*"; "*We won't buy the company for more than $3.2 million*") the narrow problem-definer will generally seek a compromise between the parties' positions that will simply end the matter. If the dispute is a threatened or actual litigation, the primary focus may be on the past event that spawned the dispute, with the mediator often leading the process toward a discussion of likely court outcomes and using each party's litigation risks and costs as a primary settlement guide.

The narrowest mediators tend to be law-trained or non-lawyer practitioners who work in court settings. Some may acknowledge the potential benefits of broadening the way the problem is defined but view the process of learning information about concealed interests as too time-consuming or requiring skills they lack. Outcomes produced by narrow mediation tend to be reached through competitive bargaining and tend to be settlement solutions. In our car wash case, such a narrow approach would seek a payment amount, somewhere between $0 and $485, which the plaintiff would accept to end the lawsuit. As should be obvious, this conception of the mediator's role is closely related to the push for speedier, less costly alternatives to litigation that began to hold sway at the beginning of the 1970s and to the increasing adoption of mandatory mediation by courts.

Broad "Problem-Solvers"   are also motivated to resolve or end disputes but see their purpose as attempting to solve the problem at hand on the most optimal and satisfying terms possible. Tracing their roots to the qualitative push for alternatives to litigation, these neutrals attempt to go beneath the parties' stated positions to find agreements that meet the parties' real concerns. By focusing on the parties' legal and non-legal interests, broad problem-definers hope to find true and lasting *resolutions* to the underlying conflict, not mere compromise *settlements*. This problem approach goes beyond a desire to create satisfying results. By trying to get the parties to see the problem broadly in terms of their interests, the often contentious bargaining that tends to accompany narrow, zero-sum problem definitions may be reduced, the likelihood of resolution enhanced and the mediator's job of managing the process made easier.

In litigation matters, broad problem-solving mediators frequently try to get the parties to focus on what they need in the future rather than solely on what occurred in the past. (Our Chapter 2 products liability case, with its eventual focus on educating the adoptive children, is a good example of this.) "Relational solutions," which seek to build on actual or potential future dealings between the parties, hold particular promise for a forward-looking approach. Mediators committed to this vision and to seeing most parties' problems as existing in a wider context affecting the interests of others might seek to extend the breadth of the problem to be solved still further. In the university campus dispute over an individual incident of alleged sexual misconduct, the mediators did just that, by proposing and brokering an agreement for mandatory fraternity date rape education as part of the overall solution.

In our car wash case (instead of or in addition to a financial resolution of the $485 damage claim), a broad problem-solver might explore:

■ a resumption of the pre-existing business relationship between the parties (possibly also including the customer's spouse);

■ an agreement under which the car wash owner fixes the broken mirror and gives the customer free car washes for a specified period;

■ some more personal reconciliation or education of the parties. This might include attempting to foster better understanding of the parties' respective roles in causing the underlying dispute and some personal connection of the parties by working through its emotional and/or cultural components;[15]

■ some progress on easing the tensions in the neighborhood, possibly via a public demonstration of mutual support by the parties or an arrangement under which the parties work jointly to bring in African Americans as employees and customers.

■ §3.5 THE TRANSFORMATION OBJECTIVE: EMPHASIZING PERSONAL GROWTH AND IMPROVED COMMUNICATION

An important third model of mediation, called transformative mediation, has gained attention, support and increased adoption in recent years.[16] To its proponents, the principal focus of a mediator's efforts should not be to vindicate rights, satisfy interests or secure an agreement that resolves the matter. Instead, the main goal should be to try to "transform" the parties' conflict, by improving their conflict interactions.[17]

---

15. Some might view this as a transformative, not problem-solving, objective. *See* §3.5 below.
16. This school has emerged in the wake of the publication of ROBERT A. BARUCH BUSH & JOSEPH P. FOLGER, The Promise of Mediation: Responding to Conflict Through Empowerment and Recognition (1994) (Bush & Folger I). A substantially revised second edition of this book was published in 2005. *See* BUSH & FOLGER, The Promise of Mediation: The Transformative Approach to Conflict (2005) (Bush & Folger II). *See also* ROBERT BARUCH BUSH & JOSEPH FOLGER, *Transformative Mediation: Core Practices*, in Transformative Mediation: A Sourcebook 31 (ROBERT BARUCH BUSH, JOSEPH FOLGER & DOROTHY DELLA NOCE, eds., 2010). For an example of institutional adoption, see the U.S. Postal Service's REDRESS Program at note 3, *supra*.
17. ROBERT BARUCH BUSH & JOSEPH FOLGER, *Transformative Mediation: Theoretical Foundations*, in Transformative Mediation Sourcebook, *supra* note 16, at 24-25.

Transformative mediation rests on a fundamentally different view of conflict than problem-solving mediation. Under the problem-solving model, transformative theorists argue, conflicts are treated as problems in satisfying disputants' incompatible needs and interests, with the mediator's job to help the parties generate an agreement that solves tangible problems in fair and realistic terms. He or she does this by identifying concrete negotiation issues, generating options and using persuasion to try to bring the parties closer together and hopefully find a settlement.[18]

Transformative mediation, by contrast, views conflict primarily as a "crisis in human interaction" that makes disputants feel "more vulnerable and self-absorbed than before the conflict" and causes their interactions to degenerate and assume a "mutually destructive, alienating and dehumanizing character."[19] This negative cycle, involving feelings of disempowerment and disconnection, transformative theorists argue, is what people tend to dislike most about interpersonal conflicts.[20] As they see it, the most important job of the mediator is to help reverse this negative spiral if possible and "reestablish a constructive (or at least neutral) interaction."[21]

Transformative mediators seek to use the mediation process to bring about two major effects on the parties: *empowerment* and *recognition.* "Empowerment" is defined as "restoration to individuals of a sense of their own value and strength and their own capacity to handle life's problems,"[22] including the enhanced personal ability to work through and resolve a conflict. "Recognition" involves evoking in each participant "acknowledgment and empathy for the situation and problems of others,"[23] including, of course, the current "opponent." What counts in transformative mediation are shifts in the quality of the conflict interaction, by which the parties "reclaim *both* their sense of strength/competence/agency *and* their understanding/responsiveness/connection to each other."[24] Because mediation is seen as unique among dispute resolution processes in its potential to bring about such personal change and growth, this capacity (its promise) should be tapped if possible. Rather than being the main goal, settlement is seen as the likely *byproduct* of a successful transformative mediation.

In making the case for this different priority, the transformation school criticizes three of the major underpinnings of settlement-oriented mediation. First, they see the goal of efficiency, if measured by settlement rates and time/cost measures of success, as "creat[ing] perverse incentives: it opens the door to, and indeed encourages, manipulative and coercive mediator behavior."[25] Alternatively, to the extent that mediators attempt to protect the legal rights of participants by ensuring that agreements reached are substantively "fair," the mediator's impartial stance is impaired.[26] Finally, they argue that as a practical matter, it is impossible for mediators to take a "macrofocus, concentrating on the parties' *situation* in

---

18. Robert Baruch Bush, *Handling Workplace Conflict: Why Transformative Mediation?* 18 Hofstra Labor & Employment L.J. 367, 368-69 (2001).
19. *Id.* at 369.
20. Bush & Folger II, *supra* note 16, at 45-62.
21. *Id.* at 53.
22. Bush & Folger I, *supra* note 16, at 2.
23. *Id.*
24. Robert Baruch Bush, *Taking Self-Determination Seriously: The Centrality of Empowerment in Transformative Mediation, in* Transformative Mediation Sourcebook, *supra* note 16, at 67.
25. Robert A. Baruch Bush, *Efficiency and Protection, or Empowerment and Recognition?: The Mediator's Role and Ethical Standards in Mediation,* 41 Fla. L. Rev. 253, 264 (1989).
26. *Id.* at 261-262.

order to grasp the nature of the problem and possible solutions," while also taking a "microfocus and concentrating on the parties' *interaction* to spot opportunities for empowerment and recognition."[27] Any attempt to integrate concerns about both practical solutions and intangible relationships will likely fail, they argue, and one set of concerns will be sacrificed to the other.

Not surprisingly, the goal of transformation, at least as an end in itself, has its own critics and skeptics. Many broad problem-solving mediators see the transformative approach — helping people make their own decisions and better understand the perspectives of others — as an important part of what they already do. They reject as unsubstantiated the claim that it is impossible to focus both on concrete problem-solving and personal growth and reconciliation in mediation. Others acknowledge the possible transformative elements in many disputes but refuse to elevate this goal above settlement.

Other commentators are more hostile. They consider transformative mediation to be *anti*-empowering for participants who may enter mediation seeking practical solutions to their problem that may not be forthcoming.[28] Some claim that the goal may inappropriately seek to turn mediation, a conflict resolution process, into a quasi-therapeutic enterprise that imposes the mediator's own agenda on parties who may not wish to make the effort.[29]

Still others point to the limited applicability of this model. One of the premises of transformative mediation is that conflict is a "long-term affair" in which the intervenor is stepping into an interaction that "in most cases will continue in some form after the intervention is finished."[30] But many disputes submitted to mediation are between strangers, who had no relationship before their dispute arose and will have no further dealings in the future. Moreover, in disputes involving large organizations, even if there is an ongoing relationship between the parties, achieving transformational goals may be difficult if the individuals whose decisions or actions are complained of are not present at the table.[31]

Whatever one's views on these differing models, there is no question that the mediator's goals for the process will have a significant impact on how the process is conducted and on the outcomes that are achieved. In our car wash case, both transformative and broad problem-solving mediators might attempt to focus on an exploration of the emotional themes in the dispute, including the car wash owner's reactions and conduct on the day of the incident, his sense of outrage at being rebuffed after offering to fix the problem and to then being sued, as well as the car owner's reactions to the aborted discussions and other aspects of this conflict. Provided the parties raised or suggested them as important themes, transformative neutrals might follow the problem-solver's inclination to explore the impact of shifting neighborhood demographics and business climate on the

---

27. Bush & Folger I, *supra* note 16, at 109. *See also 15 Minutes: Interview with Aaron David Miller, President, Seeds of Peace*, Stanford Social Innovation Rev. (Spring 2005).

28. *See, e.g.*, Lisa Gaynier, *Transformative Mediation: In Search of a Theory of Practice*, 22 Conflict Resol. Q. 397, 401, 403 (2005) (expressing ethical concerns that in transformative mediation, the values of the mediator may trump the participants' own values and needs).

29. *See* Carrie Menkel-Meadow, *The Many Ways of Mediation: The Transformation of Traditions, Ideologies, Paradigms, and Practices*, 11 Negotiation J. 217 (1995).

30. Joseph Folger & Robert Baruch Bush, *Transformative Mediation and Third-Party Intervention: Ten Hallmarks of a Transformative Approach to Practice*, Mediation Q. 263, 274 (1996).

31. David Hoffman, *Confessions of a Problem-Solving Mediator*, 23 SPIDR News No. 3 (Summer 1999).

reactions of the parties at the time of the incident or to the events that followed. Expressions of feeling would be encouraged and explored, not managed or squelched. Transformative mediators, even more than problem-solving mediators, might seek to exploit the conflict for its learning potential—trying to help the parties grow in learning about themselves and their conduct as consumers, as business operators and as disputants.

But at some point in the mediation, the goals and actions of broad problem-solving mediators and transformative mediators would diverge. Problem-solving mediators would eventually work to identify concrete issues about which the parties could negotiate and then manage a bargaining process designed to help them achieve an interests-based resolution. Transformative mediators, by contrast, would continue to "follow" the parties, looking for opportunities for empowerment and mutual recognition, but allowing them to take their conversation wherever it might lead—in the direction of settlement or not.[32] Finally, whatever the similarities and differences between broad problem-solving and transformative approaches to the car wash matter, both would likely look very different from a narrow, settlement-oriented process focused on finding a monetary compromise to end the dispute.

■ §3.6 FROM GOALS TO ACTIONS: HOW MUCH INFLUENCE SHOULD THE MEDIATOR EXERT?

In addition to differing over the most important goals of the process, mediators are strongly divided regarding the related issue of what kind of actions are appropriate for a mediator to use to achieve her goals. In particular, how should a mediator use—or not use—her considerable power?

The central disagreement here is referred to as the *facilitative-evaluative* debate, terms we will define shortly. But it is really part of a broader controversy over how active the mediator should be in attempting to produce a resolution or influence its terms. Each camp—the traditional facilitative and the evaluative school—has roots that can again be traced to forces influential in the rise of the mediation movement. And, as we shall see, this debate is largely, although not completely, about the wide array of meanings attached to the principles of mediator impartiality, neutrality and party self-determination. Before we examine the debate, however, it is important that we identify three ways in which a mediator can exert influence on the parties and the process:

■ **Influence over the structure and ground rules of the mediation.** Here we refer to how much control the mediator exerts over how the mediation process will operate, especially in its early stages. Sometimes called the "meta-process" or "the process about the process,"[33] this might include decisions about who will participate, the number and identity of mediators,

---

32. ROBERT BARUCH BUSH & JOSEPH FOLGER, *Transformative Mediation: Core Practices*, *in* Transformative Mediation Sourcebook at 45.
33. *See* LEONARD L. RISKIN, *Who Decides What? Rethinking the Grid of Mediator Orientation*, 9 DISP. RESOL. MAG. 22, 24 (2003).

time limits, procedures for exchanging information, whether or not private sessions will be used and conditions for terminating the process.

- **Influence over the process in operation.** Here the focus is on the mediator's influence over the way in which the participants' ongoing communications are managed. This encompasses the many decisions that must be made in the midst of the process, ranging from the sequencing of speakers or choice and sequence of topics to be negotiated, whether and how to control emotional exchanges, whether and when to separate the parties, when to take breaks, how long a session will last and whether and when to declare an impasse.

- **Influence over the outcome.** Here the debate centers on how much influence — if any — the mediator should exert over whether an agreement is reached or the specific terms of a resolution. Suppose that one or both parties is being unreasonable? What if one lacks basic information about his rights? Suppose the parties lack the creativity to come up with effective solutions to their dispute? What if they want help in deciding whether to accept a settlement proposal? Suppose they are considering a resolution that seems unwise to the mediator? What is the proper allocation of control over the outcome between the parties and the neutral?

Separating Process from Outcome?   In the world of mediators, it is common to hear the expression "the mediator is in charge of the process; the parties control the outcome." This allocation of decision-making responsibility has considerable intuitive appeal, inasmuch as it corresponds to the respective expertise of mediators (over process issues) and the parties (over their own fate and what matters to them.)[34] But as in law, attempts to draw a bright line between "procedure" and "substance" raise as many questions as they answer. Why is this so?

First, mediation is, if nothing else, a dynamic and fluid process. To suggest that one of the participants — the mediator — unilaterally controls even the most clearly "procedural" aspects of the enterprise is to ignore the reality that parties and their lawyers can exert great influence over process decisions. For example, in our car wash case, who is really controlling the process if, in the face of mediator "direction" to the contrary, the customer refuses to participate unless his (non-party) spouse is permitted in the room? Or suppose that the mediator does not generally believe in separating disputants, but one party refuses to discuss an important topic in front of the other party?

Second, mediator and participant views about how to define the problem to be solved are not static. Attitudes can be changed by events, people and ideas. In our car wash case, a mediator who starts out predisposed to try to re-establish business dealings between the owner and the customer might well abandon this goal in the face of party resistance, time limitations or information pointing to the likelihood of future conflict if relations were restored.

Third, as suggested earlier, process decisions often have an enormous impact on outcomes. In our car wash case, for example, a mediator's decision to conduct

---

34. *Compare* MODEL RULES OF PROF'L CONDUCT R. 1.2, 1.4 and 2.1 (2006) Appendix E, *infra* (similar allocation of decision-making as between lawyer and client).

the mediation through heavy use of private meetings with each side — perhaps to avoid a potentially destructive recurrence of some earlier emotional outburst — might all but foreclose any opportunity for the participants to gain the kind of trust and understanding needed to attempt a possible restoration of their relationship or some other interests-based solution to their dispute.

Still, in the world of mediation, there is greater consensus about this question than the question of whether the neutral should influence substantive outcomes. On the latter topic, deep ideological differences have arisen between "facilitative" and "evaluative" theorists and practitioners.

What Is "Facilitative" Mediation?   In the classic facilitative model of mediation, the mediator moderates a structured process of communication aimed at generating a negotiated outcome of the parties' own creation. In this model, the mediator studiously avoids interjecting her own opinions or ideas for solutions. Instead, facilitative mediators assume that, because the parties know their situation better than anyone else, they can create better solutions themselves than an outsider can propose, or impose. (Historically, this model can be traced directly back to the community mediation movement with its ideals of citizen empowerment and "de-legalizing" disputing.)

The facilitative mediator focuses on the negotiating process itself, seeking to create optimal conditions for the parties to determine whether and how to resolve their problem. To this end, facilitative mediators generally prefer that the parties negotiate face-to-face as much as possible. Such neutrals may be directive about structure and process: asking questions, suggesting an agenda of topics to be negotiated and deciding the sequence of discussions and whether and when to meet privately with the parties. They work to keep discussions and behavior productive and may ask questions or challenge the parties to try to get them to assess the options realistically. But while facilitative mediators may assist in analyzing or even suggesting options, they refrain from recommending solutions, giving advice, offering opinions or making predictions about the court (or other) alternative to a mediated resolution. For the most part, they reject pressure of any kind as a method of achieving resolution.

What is "Evaluative" Mediation?   In evaluative mediation, by contrast, the mediator assumes (or determines) that the parties want her to assist in obtaining a settlement by providing feedback on their viewpoints and positions and/or offering help or direction as to possible agreement terms. This guidance may be based on the mediator's "industry knowledge" or experience with similar matters.

A mediator's evaluation may be based on law, other specialized knowledge or her personal reaction to the parties' perspectives on the dispute or their settlement proposals. When a mediator with a background in commercial construction advises the parties that the solution they are considering is not viable from an engineering standpoint, that is evaluative mediation. If a mediator with a degree in family counseling tells a divorcing couple that a proposed parenting arrangement may be psychologically harmful to the children, she is evaluating. And when any mediator offers his view of the strength of an argument or the fairness, practicality, durability or wisdom of a proposal, he is evaluating as well.

Our primary focus will be on *legal* evaluations, by mediators with legal knowledge. Such interventions may include pointing out weaknesses and strengths in a party's position; predicting the court outcome or other consequences of failing to reach agreement; or critiquing, suggesting and recommending specific solutions. As evaluations are often most effectively delivered in private, evaluative mediators tend to make greater use of "shuttle diplomacy" than do facilitators. In highly directive forms of evaluative mediation, the mediator may also exert considerable pressure on the parties to reach a resolution. Many proponents of evaluative mediation are those who entered the mediation field to serve in court-based or private commercial settings, in which efficiency is valued and most participants are sophisticated and/or represented by counsel.

Before we examine the debate about how the mediator *should* act, it may be helpful to examine the following excerpt from the leading attempt to categorize how mediators (in litigated disputes) *do* behave in each of these mediator role conceptions, formed by varying combinations of a broad or narrow approach to defining the problem and a facilitative or evaluative orientation:

Mediator Orientations, Strategies and Techniques
Leonard L. Riskin
12 Alternatives 111, 111-112 (1994)

Each of the two principal questions—does the mediator tend toward a narrow or broad focus? And does the mediator favor an evaluative or facilitative role?—yield responses that fall along a continuum. Thus, a mediator's orientation will be more or less broad and more or less evaluative. . . .

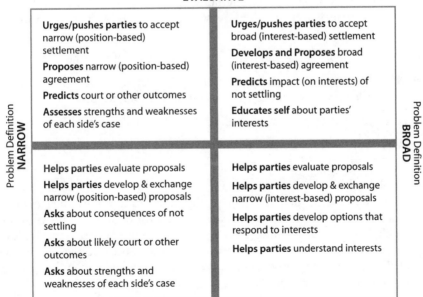

MEDIATOR TECHNIQUES
Role of Mediator

EVALUATIVE

Problem Definition NARROW	Problem Definition BROAD
Urges/pushes parties to accept narrow (position-based) settlement **Proposes** narrow (position-based) agreement **Predicts** court or other outcomes **Assesses** strengths and weaknesses of each side's case	**Urges/pushes parties** to accept broad (interest-based) settlement **Develops and Proposes** broad (interest-based) agreement **Predicts** impact (on interests) of not settling **Educates self** about parties' interests
Helps parties evaluate proposals **Helps parties** develop & exchange narrow (position-based) proposals **Asks** about consequences of not settling **Asks** about likely court or other outcomes **Asks** about strengths and weaknesses of each side's case	**Helps parties** evaluate proposals **Helps parties** develop & exchange narrow (interest-based) proposals **Helps parties** develop options that respond to interests **Helps parties** understand interests

FACILITATIVE

Evaluative-Narrow

The principal strategy of the evaluative-narrow mediator is to help the parties understand the strengths and weaknesses of their positions and the likely outcome at trial. To accomplish this, the evaluative-narrow mediator typically will first carefully study relevant documents, such as pleadings, depositions, reports and mediation briefs. Then, in the mediation, she employs evaluative techniques, such as the following, which are listed from most to least evaluative:

- Urge parties to settle or to accept a particular settlement proposal or range.

- Propose position-based compromise agreements.

- Predict court (or administrative agency) dispositions.

- Try to persuade parties to accept mediator's assessments.

- Directly assess the strengths and weaknesses of each side's case (usually in private caucuses).

Facilitative-Narrow

Like the evaluative-narrow, the facilitative-narrow mediator plans to help the participants become "realistic" about their litigation situations. But he employs different techniques. He does not use his own assessments, predictions or proposals. Nor does he apply pressure. Moreover, he probably will not request or study relevant documents, such as pleadings, depositions, reports or mediation briefs. Instead, because he believes that the burden of decision should rest with the parties, the facilitative-narrow mediator might ask questions — generally in private caucuses — to help the participants understand both sides' legal positions and the consequences of non-settlement. Also in private caucuses, he helps each side assess proposals in light of the alternatives.

Here are examples of the types of questions the facilitative-narrow mediator might ask:

- What are the strengths and weakness of your case? Of the other side's case?

- What are the best, worst, and most likely outcomes of litigation? How did you make these assessments? Have you thought about [other issues]?

- How long will it take to get to trial? How long will the trial last?

- What will be the associated costs — in money, emotions, or reputation?

Evaluative-Broad

The evaluative-broad mediator also helps the parties understand their circumstances and options. However, she has a different notion of what this requires. So she emphasizes the parties' interests over their positions and proposes solutions designed to accommodate these interests. In addition, because the evaluative-broad mediator constructs the agreement, she emphasizes her own understanding of the circumstances at least as much as the parties'.

Like the evaluative-narrow mediator, the evaluative-broad mediator is likely to request and study relevant documents, such as pleading, depositions, and mediation briefs. In addition, she tries to uncover the parties' underlying interests by such methods as:

- Explaining that the goal of mediation can include addressing underlying interests.

- Encouraging the real parties, or knowledgeable representatives (with settlement authority) of corporations or other organizations to attend and participate in the mediation. For instance, the mediator might invite such individuals to make remarks after the lawyers present their opening statements, and she might include them in most settlement discussions.

- Asking about the participants' situations, plans, needs and interests.

- Speculating about underlying interests and asking for confirmation.

Facilitative-Broad

The facilitative-broad mediator seeks to help the parties define, understand and resolve the problems they wish to address. She encourages them to consider underlying interests rather than positions and helps them generate and assess proposals designed to accommodate those interests. Specifically, she might:

- Encourage the parties to discuss underlying interests in joint sessions. To bring out such interests, she might use techniques such as those employed by the evaluative-broad mediator.

- Encourage and help the parties to develop their own proposals (jointly or alone) that would respond to underlying interests of both sides.

The facilitative-broad mediator does **not** provide assessments, predictions or proposals. However, to help the participants better understand their legal situations, she will likely allow the parties to present and discuss their legal arguments. In addition, she might ask questions such as those listed for the facilitative-narrow mediator and focus discussion on underlying interests.

In a broad mediation, however, legal argument generally occupies a lesser position than it does in a narrow one. And because he emphasizes the participants' role in defining the problems and in developing and evaluating proposals, the facilitative-broad mediator does not need to fully understand the legal posture of the case. Accordingly, he is less likely to request or study litigation documents, technical reports or mediation briefs.

However, the facilitative-broad mediator must be able to quickly grasp the legal and substantive issues and to respond to the dynamics of the situation. He needs to help the parties realistically evaluate proposals to determine whether they address the parties' underlying interests.

■ §3.7 THE FACILITATIVE-EVALUATIVE DEBATE: CASE EXAMPLES AND A HYPOTHETICAL DISCUSSION

Few mediation theorists or practitioners, we think, would quarrel with the propriety of a facilitative approach to mediation. Many would probably also agree that, in the abstract, a non-directive, non-evaluative stance is to be preferred. Yet in practice, for a variety of reasons, mediators often gravitate to a more directive or evaluative stance. Why is this so, and why is it controversial?[35] In order to explore some of the current controversies concerning facilitative and evaluative mediation, we present three actual cases, followed by an imaginary discussion.

Case One: An Incident of Vandalism

In Philadelphia, citizens can file private criminal complaints against those who have victimized them by conduct that, while technically "crimes," do not rise to a level at which the local prosecutor will generally file charges. Because of high volume and most judges' dislike of such "trivial" community matters, these cases are required to go through a mandatory mediation process before they can reach a judge for a trial.

A recent mediation was typical of those in the program: The complainant alleged threatening conduct and minor acts of vandalism (spray-painting a fence, dumping trash on the lawn) by his next-door neighbor and her teenage son. The volunteer mediator at the courthouse dispute resolution program spent the first hour of the two-hour session attempting to get the neighbors to talk with one another, examine the history of the problem and explore potential tension-avoiding solutions to their conflict. Throughout this period, the defendant, while not admitting guilt, appeared eager to work out "anything reasonable" for the future, including taking steps to control the son's hours outside. However, the complainant refused to discuss a resolution on these or any other terms, vowing to "see that justice is done" in court.

The mediator knows that no judge will listen to this case for more than a few minutes, that the almost certain resolution is a court-ordered "stay away" order (with no finding of guilt) and that another day in court will be costly for the disputants in terms of lost work time. She also has in mind specific ideas for an agreement that will meet the complainant's concerns for the future. What should she do?

Case Two: An Unsophisticated Husband

Husband and Wife recently separated and are locked in a bitter dispute over the custody of their five-year-old son. Wife has primary custody of the child by mutual agreement. At the start of this voluntary mediation, Husband seeks twice-weekly

---

35. For a summary of the controversy regarding evaluative mediation, *see* CHRIS GUTHRIE, *The Lawyer's Philosophical Map and the Disputant's Perceptual Map: Impediments to Facilitative Mediation and Lawyering*, 6 HARV. NEGOT. L. REV. 145, 146-154 (2001). *See also* LELA P. LOVE, *The Top Ten Reasons Why Mediators Should Not Evaluate*, 24 FLA. ST. U. L. REV. 937 (1997).

contact with the child, once on a week night, once on a weekend. Both Husband and Wife have bitter feelings about their separation and neither thinks that a reconciliation is feasible. Despite these feelings, neither has anything terrible to say about the other as a parent. After a considerable period of time attempting to resolve this through exploration of their schedules and relationships with the child, Wife (who has counsel present) proposes one afternoon visit every other weekend. The mediator knows the offer is way below what any court would award, but that the judge will also likely rubber-stamp any agreement reached in mediation and signed off on by a mediator. Husband, who has been quite passive throughout, is unrepresented (being unable to afford both counsel and his child support obligations) and is unaware of his rights. Bemoaning his circumstances but nevertheless seemingly poised to accept the offer, he twice asks the mediator his prediction of what would happen in court. What should the mediator do?

Case Three: A Serious Slip and Fall Accident

A personal injury suit was filed following an out-of-town tourist's slip on ice in front of a private home two winters ago. The plaintiff was quite seriously injured. After the start of discovery, the parties agreed to attempt to settle the claim through a half-day mediation effort. Both parties were represented by counsel and were present at the mediation, along with a representative of the defendant's insurance carrier. From their presentations and a summary of the proofs and experts they planned to produce at trial, it is clear to the privately retained mediator that there is considerable doubt about how a jury would decide as to both liability and damages and that each side would thus have significant risks if the case were tried. The parties, who have very different assessments of the likely trial outcome, are very far apart in their opening positions with respect to a dollar settlement. What should the mediator do?

What Should the Mediator Do in Each Case? An Imaginary Discussion Between Facilitative (F) and Evaluative (E) School Representatives

F: What is the one thing that is most unique about mediation, that most distinguishes it from other forms of dispute resolution? It is that the outcome is a self-determined, rather than an imposed decision. And true self-determination is premised on maximizing the participation of the parties, enabling them to choose the factors and norms on which they make decisions and encouraging them to create as many of the options for resolution as they can. This empowers people and makes them less dependent on law or lawyers in handling conflict. Injecting the law, legal predictions or the mediator's views, especially if no one asks for them, undermines this goal. Once an evaluation has been provided or a proposal recommended, the mediator becomes an authority figure, and the parties will see him or her as the repository of the solution. The mediator is simply steering the parties toward a resolution that he favors.

E: No one would quarrel with self-determination as a good thing. But so long as no one is being coerced in such a way as to override his or her free will, that principle is better honored by evaluative mediation. Your opposition to evaluation doesn't give disputants much credit. Why does their decisional autonomy suddenly disappear if the mediator floats an idea (perhaps one based on what the parties themselves have said)? Can't the participants hear a legal assessment without being overwhelmed? Indeed, telling the participants the mediator's assessment of the likely court outcome can actually *enhance* self-determination. It seems to me that a disputant can only exercise real self-determination if adequately informed of both his non-legal and legal alternatives to a mediated result. We are hardly empowering people if, as in the first two cases, we let them make important decisions when they are ignorant or mistaken about the law.[36]

Telling uninformed parties the law may further self-determination in another way. In my experience, most lay disputants are intensely interested in at least hearing a mediator's prediction of the court alternative and may be reluctant to make a decision without it. Providing legal information can actually *free* them from their curiosity about or overemphasis on the law as a decision factor or at least put it into some perspective as a guiding principle. To put it in process terms, one may have to evaluate *in order to* get to your beloved facilitative format. In the vandalism case, for instance, the complainant seemed to harbor a completely unrealistic hope of seeing his neighbor rot in jail. Only if he is disabused of that notion might he be open to talking with his neighbor and to engaging in finding practical alternative approaches to resolving the conflict.

To the extent that unrepresented parties are required by the court to take part in mediation prior to trial, it seems to me that the mediator has a special obligation to offer an evaluation. Parties forced into a process should not be allowed to reach final agreement without at least having some access to information about the court alternative[37] and fairness norms that are built into the law.[38] While it may be preferable to suggest that they get independent legal advice from their own lawyer,[39] that's simply not a realistic option for many unrepresented parties. Besides, if you're concerned about promoting mediation as an alternative to litigation, allowing unrepresented, uninformed litigants to make decisions that are unfair or out of line with likely court outcomes will come back to haunt all of us. How will Husband in the divorce case feel in a week or a month if

---

36. JAMES H. STARK, *The Ethics of Mediation Evaluation: Some Troublesome Questions and Tentative Proposals, from an Evaluative Lawyer Mediator*, 38 S. TEX. L. REV. 769, 776 (1997).

37. *See* JACQUELINE M. NOLAN-HALEY, *Court Mediation and the Search for Justice Through Law*, 74 WASH. U. L.Q. 47, 80 (1996); RUSSELL ENGLER, *And Justice for All — Including the Unrepresented Poor: Revisiting the Roles of Judges, Mediators and Clerks*, 67 FORDHAM L. REV. 1987 (1999).

38. JUDITH L. MAUTE, *Public Values and Private Justice: A Case for Mediator Accountability*, 4 GEO. J. LEGAL ETHICS 503 (1991).

39. *See* Model Standards of Conduct for Mediators §I(A)(2) (2005), Appendix B, *infra*.

he learns that he settled his case for far less than he would have gotten in court? Do you think he'll recommend mediation to his friends?

As for the slip and fall case, I see no problem with the mediator's evaluating. There is no danger of overreaching because the parties have lawyers to protect them and their self-determination. If they make a decision that they later regret, perhaps because of bad advice, this is still self-determined. The decision to hire the wrong lawyer or not to assert themselves with their lawyers, was theirs alone.

F: Are you done? (Pause) I have a problem with the premise of the whole evaluative school—that court outcomes can be predicted. Anyone who has seen courts in action knows that the predicted outcome of a trial-level proceeding is far from a scientific matter. The most an evaluator can do is provide an educated hunch about a range of likely outcomes, with a disclaimer. And, unlike an adjudicator, mediators who evaluate are doing so without the benefit of proofs, trial procedure, exclusion of improper evidence, etc.

E: Some information from a disinterested source—even if it's not perfect and which the parties are free to ignore or reject—is better than none at all, isn't it?

F: Providing legal information—whether in the form of a specific prediction about the outcome of a case or more generalized information (e.g., "*judges rarely jail people in these matters*" in the vandalism case)—is not likely to fall evenly on the parties. Someone—the defendant in Case One, Husband in Case Two—will be favored and the other person's position weakened. What about the promise (and the obligation) to be neutral and impartial?

Evaluating poses a serious risk to the parties' perception of the mediator's impartiality. Won't it seem that the mediator has either formed a preference for one side or isn't dealing evenhandedly with both? Even worse, won't the mediator *actually* be compromising that core principle by helping one side at the expense of the other? Rather than helping to resolve a matter, might that not actually harden the resolve of the party favored by the prediction? Might it not provoke anger, mistrust, the need to save face or even termination of the mediation by the disfavored party—especially if the evaluation contradicts that party's (or lawyer's) prior evaluation of the strength of his position?[40]

E: That's a possible risk, I agree. But the mediator's inaction can be just as problematic. Nothing could be *less* impartial than if, say in the divorce case, the mediator sits idly by while Wife and her lawyer take advantage of uninformed Husband. To do nothing would give the impression that Wife's proposed outcome would be perfectly acceptable to the court when that's not true. If he remains silent, the mediator is, in fact, favoring the wife. Evaluation is *needed* to remain impartial in fact.

---

40. Dwight Golann & Marjorie Corman Aaron, *Using Evaluations in Mediations*, 52 Disp. Resol. J. 26 (Spring 1997).

As to party perceptions, I think you underestimate the intelligence of most mediation participants. Most negotiators understand that an honest, objective evaluation does not mean that the mediator is biased.[41] Besides, since much evaluation is conducted in private session or caucus with each side, the other party need not even know what's being said.

F: Now we are getting to the heart of the problem — squandering and even perverting the real potential of the mediation process! The more that *private* evaluation creeps in, the further we get from the parties, as opposed to the mediator, being in control of what's being decided. Private sessions, while helpful for some purposes, ought not to become the place where most of the action takes place. By the end, the mediator may have orchestrated a deal, but the participants have not created it together in any meaningful sense and may largely be in the dark about what really took place. Any possibility for enhancing understanding or the ability to resolve future disputes by talking with each other have been undermined.

And another thing: Retreating to private meetings can easily lead to questionable mediator manipulation. We both know the kinds of things some mediators will do in order to broker a deal in a hard-fought case (like Case Three) in which no one can know for sure what the court outcome will be. To close the gap in positions, the mediator will use pressure or even slanted predictions focusing only on each side's weaknesses or risks.[42]

E: I'm not sure that is so troublesome, especially if it's done to neutralize the negotiators' overconfidence. But once we get away from the specific topic of offering legal predictions, I think our views are much closer than you realize. Almost all facilitators would agree that the mediator's role includes serving as an "agent of reality" by questioning a party's unrealistic or unwise expectations or demands. Facilitative types like you sometimes say that a good mediator asks questions rather than making statements.[43] But what's the difference between a facilitator's reality testing in the form of a skeptical or rhetorical question (To Husband in Case Two: "*How do you think you'll feel about this agreement in three months?*" To victim in Case One or Wife in Case Two: "*Do you think a court would think that a fair result?*") and a direct evaluation in the form of a stated prediction or opinion? It sounds to me as though you might want to examine your motives here. Is there some anti-law or anti-lawyer sentiment or turf issue operating here?[44]

F: I wouldn't say I'm hostile to law or lawyers in mediation. But the logical conclusion from *your* argument is that law training should be a

---

41. John Bickerman, *Evaluative Mediator Responds*, 14 Alt. High Cost Litig. 70 (1996).
42. Stark, *supra* note 36, at 774.
43. Lela Porter Love, *Mediation: The Romantic Days Continue*, 38 S. Tex. L. Rev. 735, 741 (1997) (encouraging mediators to focus on their roles as facilitators of communication between parties); John D. Feerick, *Toward Uniform Standards of Conduct for Mediators*, 38 S. Tex. L. Rev. 455, 472 (1997) (discussing the decision of the standards-drafting committee that "mediators should be effective facilitators and not necessarily evaluators").
44. *See* Ellen Waldman, *The Role of Legal Norms in Divorce Mediation: An Argument for Inclusion*, 1 Va. J. Soc. Pol'y & L. 87, 96-101 (1993) (reviewing and critiquing the anti-law bias sometimes found in the mediation literature).

requirement for mediating all law-related disputes. That would effectively bar many outstanding non-lawyers from mediating in areas in which skills other than legal analysis or argumentation should be most valued. Maybe we ought to not even call these two activities the same thing. Call one "mediation" and the other "neutral evaluation" and then at least the public will be able to make an informed choice[45] of the kind of neutral they want.

E: Now it sounds as if we've gotten down to a debate about labels or semantics. But even here we disagree. Many parties — in court and community mediations, for example — don't get to choose their mediator. More important, it's too late in the game to go back. All of the major forms of the process — from the narrowest of "settlement-oriented" to the most "therapeutic" — are widely understood to be "mediation." Usage determines meaning.[46] Moreover, except for the real purists out there, most mediators employ more than one style in the same case, depending on what's needed.

F: Would you at least agree that an evaluation shouldn't take place without the parties' consent?

E: Perhaps. . . .

■ §3.8   THREE FUNDAMENTAL NORMS: SELF-DETERMINATION, IMPARTIALITY AND NEUTRALITY[47]

The speakers in our hypothetical conversation make reference to three norms that are considered fundamental to the mediation movement: party self-determination, mediator impartiality and mediator neutrality. Each of these concepts is susceptible to different meanings and, in operation, is potentially in tension with the others. How do we define these terms? How might different shadings of meaning affect a mediator's philosophy and role conception?

■ **Party self-determination.** Most observers and the profession's ethical standards[48] proclaim this to be a foundational principle underlying mediation. Based on respect for individual autonomy, party self-determination is what differentiates mediation from all other processes in which a neutral third party intervenes in a conflict resolution capacity. It can be defined as the participants' right, once in mediation, to decide (a) whether to continue to participate and (b) on what terms, if any, to reach an agreement. We are talking about consensual decision making *in* mediation as opposed to

---

45. *See* Lela P. Love & John W. Cooley, *The Intersection of Evaluation by Mediators and Informed Consent: Warning the Unwary*, 21 Ohio St. J. on Disp. Resol. 45 (2005).

46. *See* Leonard L. Riskin, *Understanding Mediators' Orientations, Strategies, and Techniques: A Grid for the Perplexed*, 1 Harv. Negot. L. Rev. 7, 25 (1996).

47. A fourth — the principle of confidentiality — might also be considered a fundamental mediation norm. Because there is widespread general agreement as to its basic meaning and importance across all sectors of mediation practice, we discuss confidentiality in connection with our examination of mediator skills, starting in Chapter 6, and in our examination of mediator ethics in Chapter 12.

48. Model Standards of Conduct for Mediators §I (2005). *See* Appendix B, *infra*.

voluntariness about entering the process. Even those persons who are required to enter mediation have the right to discontinue negotiations or to refuse to reach resolution. At a minimum, self-determination means that participants have adequate capacity to make decisions and that their decisions are not the product of coercion. For some mediators, however, self-determination means more: the right to make decisions that are well considered and fully (or at least reasonably) informed.[49]

■ **Mediator impartiality.** "Impartiality," as we define the term,[50] means that the mediator does not favor — or appear to favor — any one party in a mediation over any other. Favoritism might be caused by a prior relationship or alliance with a mediation participant or by a personal bias — conscious or not — for or against a participant based on that person's identity, background, position, personality or behavior at the mediation. Impartiality thus means a freedom from bias regarding the mediation participants and, in action, treating them evenhandedly.

■ **Mediator neutrality.** Neutrality means that the mediator has no personal preference that the dispute be resolved in one way rather than another. The mediator is there to help the parties identify solutions that *they* find acceptable, not to direct or steer the parties toward results he favors.[51] Understood this way, neutrality means indifference regarding *outcomes*.

The ways in which neutrals define these norms and the relative values they assign to them may go a long way to determining the role orientation they adopt. Mediators who believe that party autonomy doesn't mean much if the parties lack basic information with which to exercise it are likely to adopt an evaluative orientation to their role. Mediators who have confidence in the parties' ability to make decisions and develop solutions based on their own values and interests and who worry about the potentially coercive effects of "expert" advice-giving are more likely to adopt a facilitative stance. Transformative mediators take the norm of non-directive party self-determination furthest, renouncing all efforts by the mediator to direct the flow of the disputants' conversation, including the topics they discuss, the perspectives they bring to their discussions and the choices they make. For a transformative mediator, assessments and evaluations are never appropriate because they involve mediator influence and are disempowering.[52]

Are "Impartiality" and "Neutrality" States of Mind? Or Are They Actions?   The answer is both, of course. As a state of mind, the mediation norms of impartiality and neutrality represent ideals. In many cases, it will be difficult for

---

49. ELLEN WALDMAN ed., Mediation Ethics 20-21 (2011).
50. In the literature, the terms "neutrality" and "impartiality" are sometimes used in different, even diametrically opposite, ways. *Compare* JOSEPH B. STULBERG, Taking Charge Managing Conflict 37 (1987) *with* CHRISTOPHER W. MOORE, The Mediation Process 53-55 (2003). *See also* EVAN M. ROCK, Note, *Mindfulness Mediation: The Cultivation of Awareness, Mediator Neutrality, and the Possibility of Justice*, 6 CARDOZO J. CONFLICT RESOL. 347, 354, n.27 (2005).
51. STULBERG, *supra* note 50, at 37. Neutrality is a fundamental norm, but it is not universally held. For example, in child custody mediation neutrality is not the governing norm, at least if the parties want to do something that is contrary to the best interests of the children.
52. WALDMAN, *supra* note 49, at 22-23. In Chapter 12, we examine the ethical dilemmas that can arise when these norms conflict.

the mediator to maintain a completely impartial and neutral state of mind. Mediators are human, after all, and we all have biases that affect how we react to different people (*"this person is obnoxious"*) or judge their ideas (*"that suggestion is really stupid"*). For example, returning to our case of the unsophisticated Husband, a mediator might simultaneously feel frustration and annoyance with Husband's passive, whiny bargaining style, while at the same time feeling antipathy for the solution that Wife proposes, because it is so one-sided.

The goal for the mediator is to be aware of her own biases, to monitor them during the mediation process and to try to demonstrate impartiality and neutrality at all times through her conduct. With regard to impartiality, this means treating the participants evenhandedly and in comparable ways during the mediation, so that neither party feels that the other has been favored. With regard to neutrality, this means making it clear that, even if the mediator makes suggestions or provides direction, the parties are entirely free to reject these suggestions and to reach their own decisions, based on their own interests, values and priorities. All of this is easier said than done, in part because it requires an awareness of how nonverbal cues can betray thoughts or feelings that one may be trying to keep under wraps.

■ §3.9 CONTEXTUALLY SENSITIVE MEDIATION: PLAYING THE RIGHT ROLE AT THE RIGHT TIME

Most mediators, we believe, have a preferred or "default" role orientation that — all things being equal — they bring to the mediation process. We do as well and it is set out in this book. Here is a summary:

We endorse a broad problem-solving approach wherever feasible. We believe that a broad approach to mediation — one that explores the parties' true interests, treats psychological issues as potentially important and seeks mutual perspective-taking and restoration of relationships — has the potential to produce better, more durable and more emotionally satisfying outcomes for participants — resolutions that "satisfy the heart."[53] Broad problem-solving can take much of the tension out of the process by reducing one of the major sources of hypercompetitive negotiation conduct — a fixed-pie or zero-sum view of the world. In addition, mediators sometimes talk about the "high" that comes from presiding over a process that does not just settle a case, but improves the climate of relationships and helps people see each other in new ways. We have experienced this feeling, and it is very gratifying.

Although we strongly believe that helping the parties learn to deal better with each other and with conflict are worthy goals in many mediation settings, and value making the most of possible educational "moments" in most mediations, this text neither emphasizes nor endorses the transformative model. First, as noted, we do not see an inherent tension between transformative and problem-solving objectives: Problem-solving processes can also develop mutual empathy and strengthen the conflict management capacities of their participants. Second, in our experience, most mediation participants enter mediation seeking practical

---

53. This is a Native American concept discussed in Jon Hyman & Lela Porter Love, *If Portia Were a Mediator*, 9 Clin. L. Rev. 157, 193 (2002).

solutions to real problems; we see the mediator's primary duty as attempting to serve the parties' own goals. Having said this, the model we will put forth does embrace several hallmark practices of transformative mediation. We will point these out as they arise in the text.

With regard to the facilitation-evaluation debate, we believe in acting in a facilitative mode and in avoiding legal evaluation unless and until it is needed in order to overcome barriers to resolution that are present in the dispute.[54] Helping parties make their own decisions without direction or advice best ensures "ownership" of those decisions. Moreover, some forms of evaluation are highly directive or even coercive: They seek to impose the mediator's preferred solution on the parties rather than simply providing information to parties to help them make better, more informed decisions. Under no circumstances do we endorse such practices.

But we also believe in the principle of informed decision making. Therefore, we do not reject the option of providing evaluations if they will assist the parties (especially those who are competitive bargainers) in accomplishing their goal of resolving their conflicts efficiently. In sum, we are comfortable with evaluation when appropriate and when properly executed. In Chapter 9, we analyze in detail the various ways this can be done.

As you start working as a mediator, you will begin to develop your own orientation toward the role. Your role conception will likely be affected by your own sense of the most important goals of mediation, your ideas about justice and fairness, your conflict management style and the degree of confidence you have in your overall judgment. Are you comfortable managing a process rife with emotion? Do you feel that you can make the "therapeutic" effort to encourage empathy or repair relationships? Do you feel that you have the legal or other relevant technical knowledge sufficient to support an evaluative orientation? Are you comfortable appearing authoritative?

The most effective mediators, we believe, are flexible — able to demonstrate behaviors associated with each of these different approaches depending on the context and circumstances of each dispute. Often they will use different approaches in the same case, depending on their reading of what is happening, then and there, in the room.[55] Of necessity, mediators make scores of choices during every mediation they conduct. The best mediators make their choices consciously and deliberately.

In short, we endorse a context-driven model in which the mediator begins with a preferred approach but also makes well-considered decisions about the problem to be addressed and the role to be played in response to specific variables present in each case. Some of these variables may affect the mediator's problem definition, some may affect the mediator's decisions regarding a facilitative or evaluative stance and some may affect the mediator in both dimensions. What are some of these variables?

---

54. MARJORIE C. AARON & DAVID P. HOFFER, *Decision Analysis as a Method of Evaluating the Trial Alternative, in* Mediating Legal Disputes 307-334 (Dwight Golann ed., 1996).
55. *See* DWIGHT GOLANN, *Variations in Style: How — and Why — Legal Mediators Change Style in the Course of a Case,* 2000 J. DISP. RESOL. 41, 42 (2000).

■ §3.10   VARIABLES IN DETERMINING THE RIGHT GOAL AND ROLE

The Parties.   The parties themselves often influence the process in crucial ways. Consider these variables:

■ **What are the parties' goals? How do they or their representatives want to define the problem?** In many cases, the disputants will be malleable and will take their cues about the goals of mediation from the mediator. But a more common scenario will be a highly interactive one, with the mediator and disputants jointly setting or negotiating goals for the process. As we have suggested, many participants will enter mediation with a narrow adversarial view of the problem and the kind of solution they think is possible or acceptable. They may wish a speedy end to the matter or be unwilling to share enough information to make a broad, interests-based approach feasible. A party uncomfortable with feelings may be unwilling to participate in any process that seems too "therapeutic." The mediator may or may not be able to transform such dynamics. But whatever happens, defining the problem is not just up to the mediator. Rather, it is likely to be a dynamic and interactive process, with the parties exerting great influence.

■ **Do the parties want a facilitative, evaluative or transformative mediator?** Have the parties chosen the mediator or was she appointed? Do they have an expectation as to how the mediator will carry out her role? Sometimes the parties or their representatives will want the mediator to play a purely facilitative role, sometimes they will seek evaluation, sometimes a transformative approach. (Often, they won't know or care.) Since much mediation is contractual, the mediator and the parties can often negotiate such questions in advance or change their preference during the process. Even where the mediator is appointed, role issues can be discussed and agreed to before or during the mediation process.

■ **Can each party negotiate effectively without the mediator's input?** Do the parties both have access to factual or legal information relevant to the dispute? Do they have comparable bargaining abilities? Is there a realistic opportunity for them to obtain independent advice before going to trial if the case does not settle? Will the parties be able to function adequately in court in the event of no resolution? These sorts of factors may have an effect on the perceived need for an evaluation.

■ **Are the parties sophisticated and/or represented by counsel?** This potentially cuts both ways. For some facilitative mediators, the fact that the parties are represented by counsel frees them from an arguable need to make evaluative statements about the law, the parties' risks or likely court outcomes. For other mediators, the fact that both parties are sophisticated about their rights and/or represented by counsel lessens the potential danger that they will be unduly influenced or coerced. In such cases, why not offer one's views? (Purely transformative practitioners would not provide an evaluation in any event.)

■ **How much hostility is there between the parties?** There is some empirical evidence that directive mediator approaches such as suggesting possible agreements are productive in producing settlements when hostility between the parties is low, but ineffective and even counterproductive when hostility between the parties is high.[56]

The Dispute.   The characteristics of the dispute itself may render it more or less suitable for one kind of approach or another. For example:

■ **Is this a single-issue or a divisible/multiple-issue problem?** Disputes defined in single-issue terms (*What price? How much in damages? What wage rate? Is the defendant guilty or not?*) tend to lend themselves to narrow problem definitions and to distributive bargaining. By contrast, potentially divisible issue or multi-issue problems (*"My price will be affected by your scheduling demands." "I want both weekend and weekday time with our son." "I'll take less in damages if you can pay me today in cash." "Can we trade a lower wage rate for better health benefits or improved safety?"*) are, by definition, more susceptible to interest-based trades.

■ **How predictable is the outcome in the court or other alternative?** Is the underlying legal dispute governed by well-established, "black-letter" principles? Are there clear industry or community standards to guide the transaction? The more settled the norms that relate to the dispute or transaction and the more clearly those "rules" apply to the facts of the case, the more likely that the participants will focus on their rights, and the law, in the mediation process. This often makes interest-based bargaining more difficult and may increase the mediator's temptation to provide a legal evaluation.

■ **Is this a "relational" dispute or one-time transaction?** Have any of the disputants had a past or ongoing relationship? Are those persons present at the mediation? Is there a possibility of future dealings? When the parties contemplate future interactions, they are more likely to be willing to explore each other's interests and be otherwise more open and cooperative — conditions conducive to the success of a facilitative approach. (Working on their ongoing relationship going forward might also argue for the transformative model.) When the parties are strangers and anticipate no future relationship, they are much more likely to take a narrow, settlement-oriented approach. Falling in the middle of the continuum are cases in which the parties in a dispute have had a past relationship but are ending it. While some disputants in this situation may be willing to explore their past relationship and try to clear the air, others may prefer to focus solely on getting the dispute settled as efficiently as possible.

■ **What are the main barriers to a negotiated resolution?** Recall the emotional, strategic and cognitive reasons why negotiations fail. The mediator's interventions may depend on her diagnosis of the barriers that may be preventing

---

56. Jean Marie Hiltrop, *Factors Associated with Successful Labor Mediation, in* Mediation Research 241, 254 (Kenneth Kressel et al. eds., 1989).

the parties from bargaining more productively. For example, a reflexively evaluative mediator who always tells the parties what he thinks about the settlement value of the case misses the boat entirely if the principal barrier to settlement is the parties' bad feelings about some angry words exchanged between them in their last meeting. (Note: Many of these dispute barriers could also be seen as part of the "parties" variable described above.)

External Factors. Finally, the setting in which the mediator works and other external factors can have a dramatic impact on the type of mediation practiced:

- **Are there significant time constraints?** Is there a time limit, an imminent related event (a trial, a strike) or similar constraint that places a premium on efficiency? If the mediation is conducted in a courthouse, is there a big caseload? Does the mediator or do any of the participants have to be someplace else soon? As negotiation scholars Douglas Stone, Bruce Patton and Sheila Heen have written, real conversations cannot be conducted "on the fly."[57] Because broad problem-solving, exploration of feelings and relationship-building or repair take time, mediations conducted under time pressure tend to be more narrow in their focus.

- **What is the mediation "culture?"** Does the host court, agency or institution have a clear agenda regarding the definition of a "successful" mediation? Does the mediator feel a sense of obligation to that agenda? Are there statutes, court rules or contractual provisions that require or prohibit the use of a particular role approach?

This listing is only suggestive of the complex currents and crosscurrents that will be unique in each case. As should be apparent from the list, some of these variables do not fall neatly on one side or another of the debate over what approach a mediator ought to adopt. Furthermore, the unique combination of party, dispute and external factor variables presented in any particular case may point the mediator in differing directions. To illustrate this, here are two different, essentially full-length mediations of the same consumer dispute (*Wilson v. DiLorenzo*). **Video Clips 3-A and 3-B.**

As you watch them, consider the following questions:

- How would you characterize the primary orientation of the male mediator? The female mediator? What were the most significant differences in their approaches? Be specific.

- What variables in this dispute made one or another mediator role preferable?

- How did their role conceptions affect their behaviors while conducting the mediation?

- Does each mediator adhere to his or her primary approach consistently throughout the mediation? If not, where did he or she deviate?

---

57. Douglas Stone, Bruce Patton & Sheila Heen, Difficult Conversations 140 (1999).

■ What did you like and not like about the way each mediator conducted the process? Be specific. Which mediator's approach did you prefer? Why? Would your views have similar or different if you had been one of the disputants?

■ Did their differing approaches affect the kind of outcomes produced? If so, how? Why?

These themes will come further alive as we begin to examine the mediation process in action. Chapters 4 through 11 of this book explore, in detail and in varied settings, the skills of effective mediators throughout the stages of the mediation process. We begin where all good professional practice should: with the subject of planning.

PREPARING TO MEDIATE

■ §4.1 INTRODUCTION: CAN MEDIATIONS BE PLANNED?

It may seem strange to think of mediations as events that can be planned for. Much of what takes place in negotiations (interpersonal reactions, emotional outbursts, distortions in decision making, etc.) cannot be known in advance by the participants, much less by a third person entering the situation for the first time. Given the nature of strategic behavior, much of what seems known in advance may be inaccurate. And the notion of having a plan may seem incompatible with the contextual flexibility that we have advocated as the hallmark of an effective neutral. Nonetheless, we think that the work of an effective mediator begins *before* meeting the participants to the dispute. An advertisement for a financial services company said about one's future, "You can't predict. You can prepare."[1] So it is with mediation.

In some settings (e.g., high-stakes commercial matters with privately selected mediators), the neutral will generally be provided with a great deal of information about the dispute in advance. In other contexts, such as small claims and community mediations, there may be little opportunity to learn about the matter before actually meeting the participants. In this chapter, we identify the main questions that a mediator should consider before meeting the parties and commencing the actual talks, regardless of how much he or she knows about the details of the dispute.

In almost all situations, pre-mediation plans will of necessity be tentative and subject to testing and revision as the case unfolds. Needless to say, planning adjustments must continue to be made throughout the entire mediation as the mediator responds to the unique dynamics of each dispute. But because the pre-mediation period can often be spent more deliberately than later phases and because early plans can serve as a guide to later inquiry and as insurance against oversights, we emphasize the importance of planning before sitting down with the parties. As with other skill-oriented chapters in this book, we will dissect this process in detail,

---

1. ®MassMutual Financial Group. *See http://www.my-life-insured.com/massmutual.php.*

knowing that, with experience, much of what you begin to do slowly and deliberately will end up becoming second nature.

■ §4.2 THE IMPORTANCE OF PLANNING: PROVIDING PROCEDURAL JUSTICE

Going through a deliberate planning effort may have a payoff beyond the natural desire to appear competent or feel less anxious on taking on a new professional task. Research is beginning to show that what many participants value in a dispute resolution process has at least as much to do with their sense of "procedural justice"—how fairly they feel the process was conducted—as with other measures of satisfaction, including the nature and size of the award or other outcome or the time or costs saved.[2] Disputants are especially concerned with whether they have had the opportunity for "voice": the chance to tell their story to a third party who listened and conducted a careful, unbiased and dignified proceeding. Studies also show that perceptions about process and outcome are interrelated: The better participants feel about the process, the better in general they will feel about the result.[3] The appearance—and reality—of a procedurally just process may be the most important attribute of the successful mediation. And good preparation can be crucial to delivering it.

■ §4.3 A KEY DETERMINANT OF THE EXTENT OF PLANNING: HOW THE CASE GOT TO MEDIATION

How much pre-mediation preparation is possible in a particular matter will often be determined by the manner in which a dispute found its way to a mediator in the first place. Here are the principal ways that mediators become involved in disputes:

■ **By party submission.** In this most voluntary of referrals, one or more of the parties seek to engage the services of a paid or volunteer mediator at a time when they are faced with an actual or threatened dispute. If fewer than all of the parties invite the mediator's entry, the proposed mediator must either bring the rest of the participants to the table or condition his service on the initiating party's arranging this. Mediations set up in this fashion can be tailored to the specific needs of the participants, although many consumers will agree to use the established procedures of the individual mediator or agency providing mediation services.

---

2. *See generally* E. ALLEN LIND & TOM R. TYLER, The Social Psychology of Procedural Justice (1988); NANCY WELSH, *Making Deals in Court-Connected Mediation: What's Justice Got to Do with It?* 79 WASH. U. L.Q. 787 (2001). *But see, e.g.,* YA-RU CHEN et al., *When Is It a "Pleasure to Do Business with You?" The Effects of Relative Status Outcome Favorability and Procedural Fairness*, 92 ORGANIZ. BEHAV. HUM. DEC. PROC. 1, 19-21 (2003) (study suggesting that in organizational hierarchies, "low status" employees care more about procedural fairness than "high status" employees, and calling for further research into the implications of this for procedural justice).
3. *See, e.g.,* KEES VAN DEN BOS et al., *How Do I Judge My Outcome When I Do Not Know the Outcome of Others? The Psychology of the Fair Process Effect*, 72 J. PERS. & SOC. PSYCHOL. 1034 (1997).

■ **By court or agency appointment.** In legal disputes, this is the most common method of submission of disputes to mediators. Courts and other forums responsible for resolving disputes seek to divert cases to mediation prior to (and, it is hoped, in lieu of) adjudicating them. Court referrals are used in settings that range from high-volume "people's courts" (e.g., small-claims courts and family courts in which many litigants are unrepresented by counsel), to major civil and appellate matters. Mediation is also employed by courts in minor criminal cases,[4] both before and after culpability has been established or acknowledged, and by government agencies charged with investigating and attempting to resolve conflicts prior to court intervention.[5] This kind of institutionalized mediation may be voluntary, mandated or something in between, as when an authoritative official like a judge "suggests" it.

Mediation in these programs is usually provided at no cost to the participants, with cases mediated by court staff or paid or unpaid outside neutrals selected with little or no say by the parties. These mediations are often time limited, due to resource limitations and the high volume of cases to be processed. Neutrals in such settings typically receive little pre-mediation information.

■ **On referral by other authorities.** Court officials are not the only persons outside of a dispute who may urge those in conflict to attempt mediation. It is not uncommon for organizational or workplace managers to refer staff or departmental conflicts to mediation. Police officers often suggest that neighborhood disputants seek the services of community-based mediaion providers. Although participation in such mediations is technically voluntary, the authority of the referral source enhances the likelihood that parties will agree to mediate.

■ **Pursuant to pre-dispute mediation clauses in contracts.** Parties in a contractual relationship are increasingly committing to mediating disputes that might arise in the future between them. Such mediation clauses usually preclude resorting to litigation until mediation has been attempted.[6] Contractual mediation clauses may name a specific mediator or agency in advance or specify a process of neutral selection in the event a dispute occurs.

■ **By requirement of law.** In a growing number of subject matter areas, federal, state or local laws mandate that disputes be mediated before resort can be had to any other dispute resolution mechanism. This can span subjects

---

4. In Philadelphia, for example, certain minor criminal matters emanating from the private complaints of the alleged victims are the subject of mandated pre-trial mediation. *See http://courts.phila.gov/ municipal/civil/* (last visited Sept. 19, 2007).

5. *See, e.g.,* Equal Employment Opportunity Commission, *http://www.eeoc.gov/eeoc/mediation/ index.cfm* (last visited Nov. 3, 2011).

6. Such clauses have generally been upheld by courts faced with challenges to their enforceability. *See, e.g., Fisher v. GE Medical Systems,* 276 F. Supp. 2d 891, 893 (M.D. Tenn. 2003).

ranging from family[7] and special education[8] cases to professional negligence[9] and labor[10] disputes. In such cases, neutrals are often appointed by the court or government agency ordering the mediation. In some settings, parties are permitted to select (and pay for) their own private mediators instead.

■ **By mediator initiation.** In certain disputes, a mediator or public conflict resolution entity will, uninvited, offer to assist the parties in efforts to end a conflict. This method of entry is most often used in community, family, institutional or international matters where the neutral third party perceives that he or she may have high credibility with the parties.[11]

In thinking about the materials in this chapter, it may be helpful to distinguish two related but conceptually distinct forms of planning: what we call *process planning* and *problem analysis*. Process planning involves thinking about possible ways of setting up the procedures and physical environment of a mediation for it to have the greatest chance of success. Problem analysis involves the mediator in examining what is known and forming tentative hypotheses about the participants and the conflict itself, with an eye toward possible ways to ease the negotiations and resolve the problem once the actual mediation begins. As you read the rest of this chapter, ask yourself how, if at all, the way the case got to mediation might affect these sorts of planning decisions.

■ §4.4 IS THIS CASE APPROPRIATE FOR MEDIATION?

Logically, this is the first question a mediator should ask because (a) a clearly negative answer stops the process in its tracks and (b) a possibly negative answer may lead to other important questions and planning steps. Consider this case:

> You have been selected to mediate a child custody dispute. The parties agreed three weeks ago to use the services of a private mediator after the judge to whom their case was assigned ordered them to try mediation. They both seek primary custody of their two children, ages three and four and a half. On reviewing the court's file, you notice that three months ago a Protection from Abuse order was issued by the court against the husband that immediately excluded him from the family home for

---

7. *See, e.g.,* Alaska Stat. §25.24.060; Cal. Fam. Code §3170; Iowa Code §598.41; Or. Rev. Stat. §107.755; Del. Fam. C. Rule 470 (authorizing local courts to mandate mediation). *But see Nelson v. Nelson,* 2004 WL 769450 (Neb. Ct. App. 2004) (ruling trial court exceeded its authority when it ordered parents to mediate future disputes).

8. *See, e.g.,* Minn. Stat. §125A.48. (In a special education case, if parent elects mediation, all other parties must participate.)

9. *See* Me. Rev. Stat. 24 §§2851-2859 (mandatory pre-litigation screening and mediation panels for claims of professional negligence); Wis. Stat. Ann. §655.43 (mandatory pre-litigation screening and mediation panels for claims of professional negligence).

10. Cal. Labor Code §1164; Montana Code §39-71-2408.

11. *See, e.g.,* RICHARD SONDOMIR, *Owners of Mets Finally Make a Deal,* N.Y. Times, Aug. 14, 2002, at A24.; Cease Fire-Chicago, an initiative of the Chicago Project for Violence Prevention, *http://www. nationalgangcenter.gov/SPT/Programs/139.*

a period of sixty days. That order has now expired. The file also reveals that the couple now lives at separate addresses in the city but that no divorce or child support proceedings have been initiated by either spouse.

Does this assignment raise concerns for you? Like some commentators,[12] you may believe that cases involving spousal abuse should not be mediated. You may be concerned, for example, that the wife may feel unsafe facing her husband in the private setting of a mediation; that fear of later reprisals could undermine her ability to negotiate effectively for herself; or that any agreement reached might be the product of an unbalanced, destructive power dynamic between the couple. If you feel this way, you may not trust your own ability to serve in an impartial and neutral fashion. You may believe that only courts should hear and decide such matters.

But what if the wife clearly expresses a desire to mediate and you believe that her choice is both voluntary and informed? Can you be sure how the psychological effects of any abuse will affect the negotiations? Does it matter whether the abuse was a single incident or is ongoing? Whether the allegation of abuse is disputed or not? How far should you go to protect potentially vulnerable parties from the consequences of their own decisions? If your overall reaction to these questions is "*I'm not sure I would mediate this case*," are you confident that the courts would do a better job of protecting the potentially weaker party?[13]

We are reluctant to adopt a categorical approach to the question of what kinds of cases should and should not be mediated, at least when the parties have expressed an initial willingness to proceed. Instead, we believe that mediators should consider several questions in deciding whether mediation is an appropriate process, both before the process begins and as it gets under way.[14] These include:

- Might the validity of any agreement reached be brought into question because a party appears unable to bargain adequately on his or her own behalf due to a mental impairment, cognitive deficit or fear of the other side?

- Does it appear that one of the parties seeks to use the mediation for purposes other than resolution, including delay, discovery or intimidation?

- Is there a serious question regarding the authority of the parties present to resolve the matter? Are all necessary parties present?

- Even if all parties have expressed a willingness to mediate, is this a case where one side is unable or unwilling to negotiate in good faith or compromise at all? For example, does one party cling to a position

---

12. *See, e.g.*, Penelope E. Bryan, *Killing Us Softly: Divorce Mediation and the Politics of Power*, 40 Buff. L. Rev. 441 (1992).

13. *See* U.S. Comm'n. on Civ. Rts., Under the Rule of Thumb: Battered Women and the Administration of Justice (1982); Adele Harrell and Barbara E. Smith, Effects of Restraining Orders on Domestic Violence Victims in Do Arrests and Restraining Orders Work? (Eve S. Buzawa & Carl G. Buzawa eds., 1996) (citing unavailability and weak enforcement of protective orders).

14. The parties in a potential domestic relations mediation are commonly asked a series of questions about their interpersonal history and negotiating comfort prior to the mediator's deciding whether to proceed. One formal screening device in the area of domestic violence is the Tolman Screening Model, set forth in Appendix F. For an example of domestic violence screening in action, see Video Clip 6-TM-5, Appendix A *infra*.

unacceptable to the other side out of genuinely held moral, religious or other personal convictions? Or is there someone at the table who, for political or other reasons, cannot accept responsibility for entering into a voluntary agreement but rather seeks the "cover" of an imposed result?

Some scholars have argued that there are other matters that should not be resolved by private agreement.[15] Examples might include issues of great public, moral or legal concern — for example, the legality of a state legislature's restrictive new abortion counseling regulations or a public university's plan to bolster its affirmative action hiring — issues that arguably cry out for a judicial ruling; or situations in which a private, confidential settlement seems inappropriate — for example, the terms of the cleanup of a hazardous waste site, in which the public-at-large has a substantial stake. Even "garden variety" cases can present similar concerns. For example, should a mediator in a small claims court consumer matter assist in settling the dispute privately if she learns that the merchant has been found to be a predator on elderly and unsuspecting consumers in poor neighborhoods?

Note that there will be many situations where one or both parties assert, prior to meeting, that the dispute ought not be mediated because *"it can't be settled"* or because (in mandatory mediation settings) they would prefer not even to try. Although mediation efforts may turn out to be futile, for now we simply remind you that such statements may be strategic in nature; the product of anger, fear or other psychological barriers; or simply a function of not knowing how mediation might be helpful even in a seemingly hopeless situation. Many such cases are in fact ideal candidates in which to proceed.

▪ §4.5 AM I THE RIGHT MEDIATOR?

Both new and experienced mediators often ask themselves — and should ask themselves — this question. They may be concerned about lacking experience as a mediator, lacking knowledge in the subject matter area in dispute or both. Occasionally the question is triggered by doubts about the wisdom of serving in the face of knowing a disputant or having some familiarity with, or preexisting viewpoint about, the specific conflict. In some situations, there is little or no choice as to who will be the mediator. But even in such settings, raising the question: "Am I the right mediator?" can be useful in planning.

Is Subject Matter Knowledge Important?

Imagine yourself assigned to mediate a dispute over a public school district's refusal to provide what the parents feel are appropriate special education services for their daughter. The seven-year-old child has been diagnosed with mild autism. Her parents, whose limited means have precluded hiring a lawyer, are concerned that she

---

15. *Compare* Owen J. Fiss, *Against Settlement*, 93 Yale L.J. 1073 (1984) *with* Carrie Menkel-Meadow, *Whose Dispute Is It Anyway? A Philosophical and Democratic Defense of Settlement (in Some Cases)*, 83 Geo. L.J. 2663 (1995).

> will not progress with the level of resources the school district is providing. The district has taken the position that the current placement is all that it is required to fund. The district will be represented at the mediation by the director of pupil services, who has a Ph.D. in Special Education. If the matter is not resolved there, an attorney will represent the district at the subsequent due process hearing.

This case may seem daunting to you. You may feel that you have enough to worry about at this stage just trying to master mediation process skills without concerning yourself with technical aspects of autism or special education law. Assuming you become skilled at the process we are about to study, however, will that be enough? How important is knowing about the subject matter of the dispute? This turns out to be a topic of considerable disagreement among theorists and practitioners.[16]

In the special education case, suppose the parents don't know what their rights are and that they ask you, as the mediator, what their child is entitled to. How will you respond if you don't know special education law? What if the school district appears to be trying to take advantage of the parents' ignorance — or yours? Can you assess whether the parents' demands regarding needed services are reasonable if you know nothing about the nature of autism? If lack of resources or of alternative placement options is claimed as a justification for the district's position, might not knowledge of how public schools work or what private school alternatives are available in the area be useful, especially if the parties become "stuck" and no one proposes new ideas?

Note that some of these questions seem to presume a rather directive mediator who sees her role as bringing the law to bear on the process by evaluating party positions, proposing solutions that the parties haven't raised or otherwise trading on her knowledge of the subject matter. Facilitative mediators might argue that using one's subject matter expertise in these ways is not what mediators should do anyway. They might add that the parties can be asked to play an educative function in familiarizing the neutral about new areas. Some might argue that being a non-expert may actually be an advantage in terms of being perceived as open-minded and able to add a new perspective unconstrained by things "as they are."

However, at least for certain kinds of disputes, mediator subject matter knowledge is seen as desirable, if not essential. For example, a 2001 study of construction industry disputants indicated that subject matter knowledge was the most important criterion by a considerable margin for selecting a mediator, even over other attributes such as mediation experience or legal expertise. Moreover, these consumers *wanted* to receive the mediator's evaluation of the merits of the dispute, in forceful terms if necessary.[17] As a practical matter, then, neutrals with no subject matter experience are unlikely to be selected in certain technical and specialized areas. In fact, some mediation consumers are intolerant of even the

---

16. It is important to note that in most settings and jurisdictions there are no minimum subject matter competency requirements to which a neutral can look for guidance on whether to serve as a mediator. *But see e.g.*, 34 C.F.R. §300.506(b)(3)(i) (2006) (requiring special education mediators to possess knowledge in "laws and regulations relating to the provision of special education and related services").
17. DEAN B. THOMSON, *A Disconnect of Supply and Demand: Survey of Forum Members' Mediation Preferences*, 21 CONSTRUCTION LAWYER 17 (2001).

slightest mediator learning curve. But does this necessarily mean that only a specialist can successfully mediate such matters? Might not an intelligent non-specialist learn enough, even in a technical area, by self-study or by reading pre-mediation submissions? And if parties seek a prediction of how a lay jury would see the merits of a case in litigation, who is better equipped to provide this — an expert or a non-expert?

For beginning mediators, the most important points are these: To the extent that you are called upon to mediate disputes about which you have limited subject matter knowledge, you may be more competent to handle them than you think. If you choose to do so, however, to the extent that some subject matter knowledge might serve as a plus for you and the parties, familiarizing yourself with that subject matter before the mediation begins would seem to be highly desirable.

Can I Appear to Be — and in Fact Be — Neutral?   Imagine that you have been asked to mediate the following conflict:

> In a suburban Pennsylvania hospital a dispute erupted between supervisors and the maternity staff over the supervisors' acceding to an expectant father's demands that no minority group member of the maternity staff be allowed to enter his partner's room or assist her in giving birth.[18] A suit was filed after three African American staff members were told that they would not be able to perform their customary duties in the delivery process.

What about this one?

> A large congregation in a major U.S. city recently fired its religious school director, despite the fact that he had been doing a good job, after it became known that he was gay. While the decision was officially based on assertions that homosexuality is antithetical to the faith's Biblical teachings, it was also viewed as reflecting the demands of powerful board members who feared that families would otherwise leave the church in droves. This action, not yet made public, has split the board and is likely to cause a rift in the membership. Although the fired employee has talked of possible legal action, religious organizations are exempt from the local laws pro-hibiting discrimination in employment.

These cases, both of which are actual disputes, may trigger strong feelings in many of you. If you feel predisposed toward one side and against the other, should this disqualify you from serving? How strong must your feelings be to warrant recusal? Do you think you could put these feelings aside sufficiently in order to act

---

18. OLIVER PRICHARD, *Three Workers Sue Hospital over Racist Incident*, Philadelphia Inquirer, Sept. 16, 2005, at B3.

impartially? What if your own group identity (race, sexual orientation or religious affiliation) were aligned with one side of the case?

Developing sympathy—or the opposite, antipathy—toward one or more participants or perspectives in a dispute is often unavoidable, sometimes before a mediator enters a mediation but, more commonly, once it is under way. Effective neutrals become skilled at keeping their reactions under sufficient control in order to honor the pledge of neutrality and impartiality and to maintain the parties' confidence.[19] But can we trust ourselves to remain neutral and act impartially in the face of strong feelings? And, more important, even if we think we can, can we *appear* neutral and impartial to the disputants both during and after the mediation—resolution or not?

What If I Have Had Past Dealings with a Party or Involvement in the Dispute? What about situations in which the proposed mediator has had dealings with a participant or the situation that is at the heart of the dispute? Can such a third party pass the test of impartiality and neutrality? Might familiarity with the specific parties and the dispute be a *benefit* in enabling the parties to talk more easily and openly with the neutral?

Being neutral and impartial plainly does not require being a stranger. In some cases, the fact that the mediator knows the parties is the reason why he or she is invited to serve in a neutral capacity. For example, trusted village elders and clergy have historically been chosen to mediate conflicts precisely because of their close ties to a community and its members.

Indeed, there are examples of mediators who not only have relationships with the parties, but also a stake in the outcome. For example, when the feuding co-owners of the New York Mets baseball club could not agree on a price at which one would buy out the other, their litigation threatened to air publicly certain dirty laundry that could have embarrassed Major League Baseball (MLB). This included allegations that MLB had supported efforts to force one of the partners to accept lower-than-market value for his share because a showing of depressed values was part of the sport's strategy to deal with a threatened players' strike. Who entered the fray to mediate and ultimately assisted in resolving the buyout dispute? None other than Commissioner Bud Selig, the chief executive of MLB![20]

The model of an authoritative mediator[21] with some interest in the outcome is not so unusual. Consider the common scenarios of a factory manager attempting to improve the working relationship between two antagonistic subordinates, an elementary school principal seeking to bring about a truce between two fighting students, or a U.S. President trying to broker a Middle East peace accord. Neutrality is thus neither a universal concept nor a pure one.[22]

---

19. To bolster awareness of and to reduce the impact of prejudices and automatic responses, and to awaken themselves to the importance of remaining open to all perspectives, some mediators make an effort to clear their minds through a form of meditation before embarking on the task. *See* LEONARD L. RISKIN, *The Contemplative Lawyer: On the Potential Contributions of Mindfulness Meditation to Law Students, Lawyers, and Their Clients*, 7 HARV. NEGOT. L. REV. 1 (2002). *See also* Video Clip 6-TM-1, Appendix A *infra*.

20. SONDOMIR, *supra* note 11.

21. CHRISTOPHER W. MOORE, The Mediation Process 44-45 (3d ed. 2003).

22. For further discussion of the norm of neutrality, *see* §12.3, *infra*.

Disclosure Issues.   In all of these situations, however, any prior dealings with the participants or loyalties and affiliations that might, if discovered later, appear to conflict with the neutral's duty of impartiality must be disclosed fully to the parties for their consideration and consent before proceeding.[23] But even if the parties consent, the potential mediator should still satisfy himself as to two questions: (a) Can I truly be impartial and (b) even if I can, could the appearance caused by my affiliation affect the proceedings, cause a party to seek to invalidate an agreement that is reached or negatively impact the public's perception of the profession? If the answer to question (b) is yes, wisdom may suggest declining to serve.

▪ §4.6 SHOULD I HAVE PRE-MEDIATION CONTACTS WITH THE PARTIES?

In many court and community-based mediations, the initial contact between the mediator and the disputants takes place at the first mediation session. In other settings, there may be telephone or other communication with the parties or their representatives prior to the start of face-to-face meetings. These discussions can help the neutral decide whether she is willing to mediate, determine whether her credentials and her proposed approach are acceptable to all parties or set the terms under which she will serve. In other situations, a mediator who has already been retained can use such contacts to identify subject matters that may be helpful to study in advance in view of the complexity of the dispute. Pre-mediation activities in such cases may also include:

- ▪ gathering initial data from the parties about the nature and history of the dispute,[24]

- ▪ obtaining shared or confidential submissions from the parties that summarize their perspectives, positions and interests,

- ▪ explaining the process and the mediator's role orientation and making arrangements about how the matter will proceed.

Pre-mediation discussions may also include questions about who will participate[25] as well as mediator coaching on how participants — especially those inexperienced in mediation — might conduct themselves most effectively at the table. For example, a lawyer inclined to "hardball" might benefit from well-explained[26] mediator advice about effective mediation representation, including moderating extreme and time-consuming positional demands, considering the potential

---

23. *See* Model Standards of Conduct for Mediators §III(C) (2005) ("A mediator shall disclose, as soon as practicable, all actual and potential conflicts of interest that are reasonably known to the mediator and could reasonably be seen as raising a question about the mediator's impartiality. After disclosure, if all parties agree, the mediator may proceed with the mediation."). *See infra* §12.2 for a further exploration of this issue. For an example of such a disclosure, see Video Clip 12-A.
24. In especially complex matters, this can involve a substantial amount of time and effort and may benefit from having a team of mediators engaged in getting this information. *See* Moore, *supra* note 21, at 122; Lee A. Rosengard, *Learning from Law Firms: Using Co-Mediation to Train New Mediators*, 59 Disp. Resol. J. 16, 19 (2004).
25. *See infra* §4.8.
26. Explaining the staged structure of the process and its rationale can assist in convincing a party or representative of the value of adopting a mediation-sensitive approach. *See* Chapter 5.

advantages and requirements of an effective apology[27] and accepting the (often foreign) notion of giving up some — or even considerable — control of the proceedings to the parties themselves.[28]

Such pre-mediation contacts, which can include private communications by each disputant with the neutral, mark the effective beginning of the process. In these discussions and submissions, parties often begin to try to persuade the neutral about the validity of their perspectives and positions. As a result, pre-mediation contacts can produce progress in defining the dispute and the challenges it will present. The mediator must, of course, make clear to the parties in advance which of these private communications, if any, will be regarded as confidential.

■ §4.7 SHOULD THERE BE A WRITTEN MEDIATION AGREEMENT?

In situations in which a mediator is privately retained, a contract for the mediator's services is often negotiated prior to commencing the process. Even if a mediator is serving in a setting in which the participants have had no say in selecting the neutral (and, in mandatory mediations, over whether to participate at all), the process to be followed must be agreed to. In court and community-based programs, the terms may be discussed at the initial meeting, with the disputants sometimes asked to indicate their agreement by signing a preprinted form. Mediations conducted under the auspices of an organizational provider of such services often incorporate the host agency's mediation rules.

Agreements to mediate typically cover:

- ■ a description of the process, its ground rules and the mediator's responsibilities, including, in some cases, the mediator's philosophy and how she will define her role;

- ■ any compensation the mediator will receive and the person(s) responsible for payment;

- ■ any conflicts of interest or other disclosures that the mediator has discussed with the parties; and

- ■ the scope of confidentiality promised by the mediator and the parties' agreement not to seek to compel her testimony in any later proceedings.[29]

- ■ In legal matters, the acknowledgment that a law-trained mediator is not serving as the lawyer for either party.

Where state or local law governs the mediator's ethical duties, the scope of confidentiality or other terms, mediation agreements often reflect these requirements. One area of controversy stands out in an otherwise straightforward area: Mediators occasionally try to obtain the parties' agreement not to hold them liable

---

27. *See* Chapter 9 for a discussion of the role of apology in mediation.
28. *See* Chapter 13 for an in-depth discussion of the role of party representatives in mediation.
29. Agreements in complex matters may be more comprehensive. For examples of such agreement forms, *see* DWIGHT GOLANN, Mediating Legal Disputes: Effective Strategies for Lawyers and Mediators §§4.3-4.6 (1996).

for any act or omission in connection with the mediation. What is your reaction to such clauses?

■ §4.8 WHO SHOULD (AND WHO SHOULD NOT) BE PRESENT AT THE MEDIATION?

In many cases, it is clear that participation by certain people is not only appropriate but indispensable to the proceedings. For example, in the mediation of a matter that is in litigation, the named parties have a right to be present. Moreover, if one or more of the parties (or at least someone authorized to act on their behalf) is absent, no meaningful mediation can take place. Similarly, where one of the participants does not speak the language being used in the process, a translator's participation will be essential.[30]

At the other end of the spectrum, there are situations in which the presence of certain individuals may be prohibited. For example, certain court programs limit participation to the named parties; witnesses, family members or other supporters are barred from the proceedings.[31] Some courts and agencies refuse to allow lawyers to appear with their clients or confine counsel to a nonspeaking role.[32]

Stakeholders and "Interested Others."   Between these clear cases lie many situations in which the mediator must exercise discretion in determining whether certain individuals should be permitted to attend or whether, conversely, someone not yet proposed should be added to the roster of participants. Consider the following real case examples and ask yourself: Who should attend the mediation?

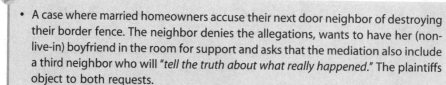

- A case where married homeowners accuse their next door neighbor of destroying their border fence. The neighbor denies the allegations, wants to have her (non-live-in) boyfriend in the room for support and asks that the mediation also include a third neighbor who will *"tell the truth about what really happened."* The plaintiffs object to both requests.
- A claim by an African American restaurateur that a white neighborhood association engaged in race discrimination by successfully opposing a zoning variance

---

30. Where a party has a disability (e.g. deafness) that might impair his or her ability to communicate in mediation or understand what is being said, the provision of a sign language interpreter may be legally required. *Cf. Settlement Agreement Between the United States of America and Gregg Tirone, Esq.*, Dept. of Justice Complaint 202-53-20 (2004) (available at *http://www.ada.gov/tirone.htm*) (private attorney obligated to provide such services for hearing disabled clients under the ADA).

31. *See, e..g.*, Washington Supreme Court Rules, §LSC 4 (a), *http://www.courts.wa.gov/court_rules/ ?fa = court_rules.rulesPDF&ruleId = districtdisclr44&pdf = 1* (prohibiting witnesses from attending mandatory small claims mediations).

32. *See* Cal. Fam. Code §3182, 4351.5(e); Kan. Stat. Ann. §23-603; Fla. R. Civ. P. 1.720(d). *See generally* CRAIG MCEWEN, NANCY ROGERS & RICHARD MAIMAN, *Bring in the Lawyers: Challenging the Dominant Approaches to Ensuring Fairness in Divorce Mediation*, 79 MINN. L. REV. 1317, 1362 n.261 (1995) (citing statistics showing that lawyers are allowed to participate actively in only a fraction of family court mediations). The special education mediation program in Pennsylvania does not permit parents to be represented by attorneys. *See http://odrpa.org/due-process/faqs/legal-representation/*.

that would have permitted him to open a sidewalk café in the area. The local NAACP chapter is not a party to the claim but supports it and wants to take part in the mediation.

In the case involving the fence dispute, including the boyfriend in the mediation might or might not benefit the process. On the one hand, his presence might comfort the defendant in not being outnumbered at the table. He might also be able to help his girlfriend think through her options clearly and make decisions without concern about his later disapproval. On the other hand, his presence might raise the emotional stakes and complicate the mediator's process management tasks. What would you think about conditioning the boyfriend's attendance on his agreeing not to speak when the plaintiffs are present but only to consult in private about possible resolutions?

While the proposed neighbor-witness may help the mediator understand what happened, is it the mediator's function to "get to the bottom of things?"[33] If the witness is heard, might this turn the mediation into a trial-type adversarial proceeding? If the witness is not heard, will this heighten the chances of the defendant's refusing to participate in a serious way and insisting on going to court?

What about the zoning dispute? What do you see as the pros and cons of allowing an NAACP representative to attend the mediation? On what factors would this depend?

Overall, we think it is useful to try to ascertain *why* a potential participant's presence is proposed or opposed by a party. Once these reasons and concerns are fleshed out, disagreements may soften or disappear, or conditions may be established that will address objections and clear the way for talks to begin.

In addition, we think that there is wisdom to the expression that it is easier to add than to take away. When in doubt, the safer course is to start with a small group and to add requested "others" as the need for their presence becomes apparent. This also avoids the awkwardness of seeking to remove someone who is already present and taking part in the discussions.[34]

What about an absent nonparty stakeholder—someone who is not present but is likely to be affected by the talks or who may have the ability to undermine the effectiveness of any resolution that is achieved? How, for example, would you proceed as the mediator in the following two (real) cases?

- A child custody case in which the parents of a thirteen-year old child—engaged in heated negotiations over where their son will spend weekend, summer and

continues on next page >

---

33. Although a full hearing of each side's perspective may serve important goals in a mediation, a trial-type determination of the facts in dispute may actually be problematic in terms of establishing a non-adversarial climate in the process, preserving the mediator's appearance of neutrality and achieving a resolution. *See* §7.5.8, *infra*, for a discussion of the benefits of factual uncertainty and doubt in promoting settlement.

34. This approach is also the more cautious one regarding any risks to confidentiality posed by the presence of non-parties.

> holiday time — describe the son as "sulking" in the wake of his parents' separa-
> tion. The father, while offering the mother some access to the child, says the son
> *"doesn't want to see his Mom"* and urges you to bring the boy in to solicit his views.
> * A dispute over the location of a proposed city recreation area in which an object-
> ing neighbor refuses to participate in a mediation aimed at arriving at an agreed
> siting of the facility and threatens to sue *"no matter what you all may agree."* In
> addition, certain homeowners who could be affected by changing traffic patterns
> do not even know about the talks.

In the child custody case, should a thirteen-year old be placed in the apparent position of choosing sides in a contested mediation between his parents?[35] Suppose he does attend and states a preference for spending more time with his mother. Might this help getting to an agreement? If no agreement is reached and his stated preferences are ignored by his disputing parents, might that worsen things at home? Alternatively, if failing to involve the child could lead to his later under-mining any agreement his parents reach, is that reason enough to include him?

In the recreation facility case, a failure to include any of the traffic-impacted homeowners could create a risk of their attacking a mediated agreement later on. This argues for inviting the neighbors to take part. And if some of these neighbors do attend, could there be a benefit (despite a lengthier process) in reaching at least some agreement that deals with traffic patterns that can then be "sold" to absent stakeholders or to a court that later hears objections?

In certain cases, mediators use the planning stage to try to ensure, apart from those who *must* be there, that key decision makers and the right party representatives attend. If a local corporation is being sued in a $50 million case, it is probably naive to think that a resolution can be reached without the participation of at least some representatives of the board of directors. An indecisive widower may be unlikely to conclude a matter affecting family finances if forced to attend the talks alone, without assistance by an accountant or financial advisor.

A mediator can also use the pre-mediation period to try to ensure that orga-nizational parties bring to the table individuals whose presence will enhance the odds of success or, at a minimum, not jeopardize them. For example, the perma-nently paralyzed victim of an allegedly defectively designed snowmobile might respond more favorably if the manufacturer were represented at mediation by its president rather than its risk manager. In such a case, the presence of the snowmobile designer might prove problematic if he were to come across as defensive about his design, no matter how much he might add to the company's factual presentation.

In trying to secure the presence of helpful participants, mediators often con-front the problem of attempts by busy persons either to delegate their involvement to subordinates or to attend via telephone or other more convenient means. Even if such persons are standing by, ready to be contacted by their representatives, such

---

35. This question has psychological implications that might well warrant the mediator's consulting an outside expert for advice. *See* Model Standards of Conduct for Mediators §IV(B) (2005) (providing that a mediator concluding that she does not have sufficient knowledge to effectively mediate a dispute may "request . . . appropriate assistance" to remedy the insufficiency). *See also supra* §4.5, Am I the Right Mediator?

"participation by proxy"[36] can seriously hinder the chances for success, in a number of ways:

- It can insult the opposing party by suggesting that the matter is not important enough to warrant high-level attention;

- It can deprive the absent decision maker of personal access to important information, including the genuineness and credibility of key figures on the opposing side;

- It can deprive the person who is present of direct access to the person who he or she may think is the most significant actor in the case and frustrate his or her desire to confront, persuade or simply be heard by that person;

- It can reduce the absent person's investment in the process and in making the hard decisions that may be required to achieve settlement.

Finally, in disputes involving many parties or large membership groups, mediators must take care to limit the roster of mediation participants in order to make the process manageable. For example, where a large tenants' association objects to an apartment building rent increase, the mediator might help the organization designate a smaller group of representatives to speak for the association as a whole.

■ §4.9 HOW SHOULD THE PHYSICAL SETTING BE ARRANGED TO ENHANCE THE LIKELIHOOD OF SUCCESS?

We are all familiar with the effects of physical space arrangements on human interactions. Parents typically sit at the head of the table. Those who are royal subjects are made to walk a long carpet leading to the raised platform holding the monarch's throne. (Ditto judges.) "Conversation pits" are often sunken and small in comparison to their surroundings. Indeed, such is the perceived importance and symbolism of physical arrangements that the negotiations to end the Vietnam War were stalled for a year over the shape of the bargaining table. (No one wanted the reduced status of having someone else at the head of the table.)[37]

Social science[38] has provided us with some helpful data about how spatial arrangements are related to behavior. In one well-known study, for example, researchers observed that when people sat at a rectangular cafeteria table, those sitting cater-cornered (i.e., at right angles diagonally across a corner) struck up twice as many conversations as those sitting side by side and six times as many conversations as those who sat across the thirty-six-inch-wide table.[39] In a similar study dealing with attitudes and seating orientation, subjects who sought to cooperate said they would sit side by side; those who came to compete would sit across

---

36. *See* GOLANN, *supra* note 29, at §5.1.3. New technologies may obviate these concerns to some extent. See the discussion of online options at §4.9, *infra.*
37. ANDREW D. SEIDEL, *The Use of the Physical Environment in Peace Negotiations*, 32 J. ARCHITECTURAL ED. 19, 19-23 (1978).
38. The study of spatial relationships and their effect on behavior is known as *proemics.*
39. EDWARD T. HALL, The Hidden Dimension 108-109 (1966).

the table from each other and those who sought to avoid interaction sat as far apart as possible.[40]

Intimacy and the desire to talk can be fostered by good eye contact. (So can honesty: It is harder to lie to someone who is looking you in the eye.) Thus, sitting opposite someone can actually *facilitate* communication,[41] provided it is at a comfortable distance. What distance is that? For North Americans, it is somewhere beyond "personal distance" (defined as between one and a half and four feet) but less than "public distance" (greater than twelve feet), probably around the near end of "social distance" (four to twelve feet), the range within which most "impersonal business" is transacted.[42] In other cultures, these measures of personal comfort or safety may be different. When trying to persuade or to foster agreement, nearer is generally better. Studies show that at close proximity, the incidence of nonverbal signs of agreement with a speaker's statements of opinion, measured by assenting head nods, increases dramatically.[43]

The "props" in any physical setting also convey symbolic meanings. Depending on their size and bulk, tables may signal business-like formality for some, create inhibiting barriers for others or provide comfort and protection to those who enter feeling vulnerable. Circular tables are nonhierarchical, while different seats at rectangular tables may confer differing status. Obviously the other trappings of any setting — the location, what people wear, the pleasantness or unpleasantness of the surroundings — can also affect attitudes and thus communications. In some cultures, food is seen as an important ingredient of serious cooperative work.[44] In lengthy negotiations, providing time for food breaks may be essential to prevent the participants' energy and morale from flagging.[45]

All of this probably confirms your own experiences and intuitions. But what does it tell us about planning the optimal physical environment for a mediation? Consider the following scenario:

> A water purification company sues an architect for $2.5 million, claiming architectural malpractice consisting of the allegedly defective design of the company's futuristic new corporate headquarters. A malfunctioning central fountain, roof

---

40. Robert Sommer, *Further Studies in Small Group Ecology*, 28 Sociometry 337, 344 (1965).
41. *Id.* at 340-341.
42. *Id. See also* Ivannia Jimenez Arias, *Proxemics in the ESL Classroom*, 34 English Teaching Forum 32 (1996), available at *http://www.au.af.mil/au/awc/awcgate/state/proxemics.htm.*
43. Robert Kleck, *Interaction Distance and Non-Verbal Agreeing Responses*, 9 Br. J. Soc. & Clin. Psychol. 180 (1970).
44. *See, e.g.,* Mary Weismantel, *Making Kin: Kinship Theory and Zumbagua Adoption*, 22 American Ethnologist 685 (1995) (describing the importance of food as a signaling mechanism in a South American context). *See also* Claudia Nolte-Schamm, *The African Traditional Ritual of Cleansing the Chest of Grudges as a Ritual of Reconciliation*, 13 Ritual & Theology 90, 103 (2006) ("People who do not trust one another and do not consider one another as belonging together, abstain from eating together.").
45. Carol B. Liebman, *Mediation as Parallel Seminars: Lessons from the Student Takeover of Columbia University's Hamilton Hall*, 16 Negotiation J. 157 (2000).

leaks and facade problems will require considerable repair and have precluded the company from moving in. In addition to disputing responsibility, the architect alleges that the company has wrongfully tarnished his reputation and counterclaims for $2 million for prospective loss-of-business damages.[46]

If you were asked to mediate this dispute, where would you hold the first meeting, and why? Your office? If there are lawyers, in one of the lawyers' offices? What would be the pros and cons of convening at the building site? Do you want a table? Why or why not? If so, what shape of table would be best? If each participant appeared with a lawyer, where would you want the various participants to sit? Where at the table will you be?[47] What might be the effect of your sitting closer to one party than to the other?[48]

Now consider the setting you would choose for the initial session in a child custody mediation involving two unrepresented spouses. How, if at all, does it differ from how you would set up the space in the architect malpractice case? Why? If on first greeting the parents you noticed that they were sitting far apart in the waiting area, would this influence your thinking about the desirable furniture or seating arrangements? If so, how? In each case, will you tell the participants where to sit or leave this to them? What are the pros and cons of each approach?

Examine the space-planning choices you made in each scenario. What do they say about your own objectives for this session and the tone you wish to set? In each case, what assumptions about the participants and their preferences, needs or concerns are reflected in the arrangements you would orchestrate? Does your view of your own role affect your choices? Is there a correlation between where you fall on the facilitative-evaluative continuum and your ideal seating plan? One related point: If a "shuttle diplomacy" model of private meetings is envisioned, good pre-mediation preparation would take into account the need for at least two (if not three) separate, sound-insulated spaces as well as facilities to help participants make productive use of "down" time.

Note that location and space arrangements (like other mediation plans) may be subject to modification over the course of the mediation. For example, the optimal setting for an opening session, in which often-tense parties first state their views about the conflict to the neutral and each other, might differ from the setting for the mediator's later efforts to gain agreement through persuasion, after having created a climate of cooperation. Indeed, deliberately moving people from familiar seats and thus disturbing their established territoriality (a classroom proxemics concept well known to students) can be effective in getting disputants "unstuck" from earlier positions and perspectives in a tough mediation.

Finally, many of these same considerations apply in court-based and community settings even though the location and room setup may be fixed, conditions may be less than ideal and the mediator may be meeting the parties for the first

---

46. *The Mediation Process: A Construction Case Study* (Videotape: Douglas N. Frenkel & American Arbitration Association, 1990).

47. Sitting nearest the door might have the effect of discouraging parties from walking out. *See* JOSEPH B. STULBERG, Taking Charge Managing Conflict 63 (1987). In some settings, it may allow mediators to leave the room quickly in case they feel their safety is at stake.

48. *Id.*

time at the mediation. Under these constraints there are still choices to be made: Where should the participants be placed (or should they seat themselves)? Will I augment the program's limited resources by providing paper and pencils for note taking? A laptop for agreement drafting? Drinking water or (as one of our European students was fond of doing) cookies, in order to create an atmosphere of warmth?

Mediating Online.   Up to now, we have concerned ourselves with preparing for proceedings in which all of the participants will be physically present at one location. But this traditional format may not work in many situations. In some cases, legal impediments prevent disputants (e.g., prisoners or those with visa restrictions) from traveling to a mediation site. In others, cost considerations or scheduling conflicts make in-person attendance impractical. In yet others, physical safety or other prudential concerns make face-to-face mediation problematic.

At the same time, technology-based modes of communication—from telephone (with and without video) to e-mail to Internet videoconferencing— have opened up viable alternatives for conducting mediations, at least for those with access to these mediums. Online dispute resolution (ODR) raises a number of unique pre-mediation considerations for the mediator. Consider the following scenario:

> You are a mediator for the local board of realtors assigned to mediate a dispute arising from the sale of a condominium in your Florida beachfront community. (The parties signed a form mandatory mediation clause as part of their agreement of sale.) The property was sold a month ago; one week after the sale was completed, the apartment was flooded from an undisclosed exterior leak that the buyer feels the seller should repair. The seller claims he had no knowledge of the leak and that the buyer's home inspector should have detected any potential problems. Estimates to do the work average $19,000. The buyer lives in Brazil but speaks good English; the seller is now visiting family in California. The parties met only once when the buyer toured the property for ten minutes. Both want to avoid traveling to Florida for the mediation.

If all options were available, which mode(s) of communication—text, voice or visual—would you want to use? Why? What are the pros and cons of each? Can this work at all? Might ODR work *better* than the traditional face-to-face format? Additional planning questions:

- Would the process be better conducted synchronously (with all taking part at the same time) or should an asynchronous model—taking turns, with breaks between contacts—be used?

- Will the choice of technology affect the mediator role orientation(s) that might be called for here?

- How can confidentiality—especially regarding disclosure of the discussions to undisclosed persons—be ensured?

To the extent you prefer one medium over others because of its ability to foster an advantageous connection between the parties, are you sure which it is?[49] Can a mediator satisfactorily develop trust and "read" the participants without a visual connection? Does a computer video image satisfactorily replicate the "psychological presence"[50] of in-person contact?

Depending on the intensity of the conflict and the nature of the parties, might an e-mail discussion have advantages in making people (perhaps with the mediator's help) more careful about the wording they choose and reducing the amount of extreme posturing or even lying that might occur in any bargaining that might take place?[51] But then, with only the written word to go on, might e-mailing lead to more untested assumptions and hostile attributions? Might the creation of a written "record" inhibit openness and spontaneity, notwithstanding the promise of confidentiality? If the problem is one that is likely to be negotiated in a competitive fashion, which medium(s) give the mediator the best chance of avoiding impasse? Which makes it hardest for parties to "walk away" from the process?

Given the newness of some of these options, there is little research-based guidance available. In many situations, lack of access to technology or the number of times zones to be traversed will dictate the format to be used. In the not-too-distant future, however, an appreciation for the comparative merits of new technologies will likely become an essential part of the planning process for many mediators.

■ §4.10   HOW FORMAL OR INFORMAL SHOULD I BE?

As you can see, several of the pre-mediation decisions confronting the mediator involve choices about how formal the process should be. Although mediation is often spoken of as "informal," that term is usually used to contrast it with the rule-bound, hyperformal traditions of the court system that many users of mediation seek to avoid. The label really provides little guidance for the mediator who is thinking about how to approach a specific dispute.

Assume you have been assigned to mediate a court-mandated child custody case at the local courthouse and will meet the parties there for the first time. How will you go about deciding whether to wear a suit or to dress in "business casual"?[52] Whether to use the room in the courthouse that has a conference table or the room with a sofa and chairs? Whether to announce a set of procedural ground rules or to invite the parties to assist in creating them?

---

49. *Compare* Michael W. Morris, Janice Nadler, Terri Kurtzberg & Leigh Thompson, *Schmooze or Lose: Social Friction and Lubrication in E-mail Negotiations*, 6 Group Dynamics 89 (2002) *with* Joseph B. Walther, Tracy Loh & Laura Granka, *Let Me Count the Ways: The Interchange of Verbal and Nonverbal Cues in Computer-Mediated and Face-to-Face Affinity*, 24 J. of Language and Social Psychology 36 (2005).

50. Robert M. Bastress & Joseph D. Harbaugh, *Taking the Lawyer's Craft into Virtual Space: Computer-Mediated Interviewing, Counseling and Negotiating*, 10 Clinical L. Rev. 115, 130 (2003).

51. *See* Jeffrey T. Hancock, Jennifer Thom-Santelli & Thompson Ritchie, *Deception and Design: The Impact of Communication Technology on Lying Behavior*, CHI Letters 6(1), 129.

52. Societal meanings attached to other appearance choices — for example, two days of beard stubble, nose rings, exposed tattoos, etc. — seem to be evolving. Do any of these seem inappropriate in a mediation setting? Does the kind of case matter?

Our answer is: *In general, and when in doubt, start formal.* Here are three reasons why:

First, it's the safer route. Have you ever been contacted by a cold-calling telemarketer who, in an effort to ingratiate himself, addresses you by your first name? ("*Hi, Marlene, this is John at CNS Cablevision.*") How do you react? If you are like many people, you may think it presumptuous for this stranger to take the liberty of familiarity. Have you ever shown up at an event only to be surprised that you were dressed much more casually than the other invited guests? Were you at all concerned that you might offend the host? Were you embarrassed that other guests might think you looked inappropriate?

Although some participants may warm to efforts to create a friendly environment and may prefer to avoid the trappings of traditional institutions and processes, others won't. Moreover, you cannot know this in advance. In mandated mediations, some participants might enter the room with concerns about being unprotected in the absence of a lawyer. Some might resent having been ordered to take part in an alternative to the formal court option. Still others might react negatively, at least initially, to a proceeding that looks very different from their image of court and may even equate informality with a lack of respect.

To reduce the risk of alienating any of the participants unnecessarily, the more cautious approach is to err on the side of formality. Later on, if parties signal receptivity, you can change to a more casual style. Note the strategic advantage of this approach: A move in the direction of informality can suggest that tensions are abating or progress is being made in the mediation, which itself can spur further momentum.

Second, at least in the early phases, a more formal approach underscores the serious expectations for the upcoming effort at resolution and can signal the difference between mediation and the failed negotiations that may have preceded it. This aspect of orchestrating a "settlement event"[53] can send an important message to disputants who may be participating reluctantly.

Third, formality is more likely to satisfy the participants' need for procedural justice. As discussed earlier, empirical research is beginning to tell us what litigants value in any dispute resolution process. Among the attributes most highly valued in measuring consumer satisfaction is a perception of procedural care,[54] defined as thoroughness and procedural regularity. The importance of procedural care may be connected to disputants' overarching need to feel that they are being heard and are being treated fairly. Erring on the side of more deliberate and formal procedures, especially at the start, may comfort the parties, help them invest in the process and increase the odds that they will come away from the mediation feeling that justice was done.

Are there any settings that would warrant departing from this approach? For example, suppose you were assigned to mediate (as part of a gang violence

---

53. *See* GOLANN, *supra*, note 29, at §2.1.1.
54. *See* DEAN J. PRUITT et al., *Long-Term Success in Mediation*, 17 LAW HUM. BEHAV. 313 (1993). *See also* JOHN T. CHANG et al., *Patients' Global Ratings of Their Health Care Are Not Associated with the Technical Quality of Their Care*, 144 ANN. INTERN. MED. 665 (2006) (reporting that procedural elements of patient care were more determinative of satisfaction than technical propriety of treatment approach).

prevention program) a dispute between two rival youth groups over their access to a local gym. How, if at all, would your approach to issues of formality change?

■ §4.11 WHEN SHOULD THE MEDIATION TAKE PLACE? HOW LONG WILL IT LAST?

Depending on the setting, pre-mediation planning may concern itself with two aspects of scheduling: (a) when in the life cycle of a dispute to begin the process and (b) the duration of the proceedings, or at least of the first meeting. Getting the timing right can greatly enhance the chances of achieving a resolution. Poor scheduling or allocating insufficient time are at the root of many mediation failures.

Timing of Entry.   As to when to attempt mediation, some situations will dictate the answer. For example, any effective mediator intervention into a conflict over how to treat a near-death hospital patient will have to be immediate.[55] By contrast, seeking to resolve a major commercial lawsuit before the defendant has seen the court papers is likely to be futile. In some settings, scheduling may be determined by administrative convenience regardless of whether it is optimal in a particular matter. This is true of many court-based programs, in which mediators have little or no say in scheduling decisions. Similarly, the length of time allotted for each session may be circumscribed by perceived limits on what can be asked of volunteer mediators, by work schedules or child care needs of the disputants and the like. But in many disputes, court-based or otherwise, there will be an element of control over the scheduling in which the mediator will have a say.

So what is the optimal time to enter a dispute as a mediator? A vineyard used to boast "we'll sell no wine before its time"[56] to suggest that there is a point of grape maturity before which wine should not be drunk. Given the significance of emotional "readiness" that we discussed in Chapter 2, one might think that the same reasoning applies to starting a mediation. But it isn't that simple. Consider the following dispute in which litigation has been threatened but not initiated:

> An employment discrimination case in which a just-fired female associate asserts that her law firm passed her over for partnership for reasons relating to gender and that the firm created a hostile environment for women through the behavior of some of its older male partners — ranging from offensive water-cooler humor to directing or condoning sexist remarks to the complainant and to women lawyers generally.

What might be the optimal timing for entry by the mediator? Early intervention, before the matter becomes public, might yield the best prospect for an

---

55. *See* CAROL B. LIEBMAN & NANCY N. DUBLER, Bioethics Mediation: A Guide to Shaping Shared Solutions 27 (2004).
56. *See* television advertisement for Paul Masson Wine, available at *http://www.youtube.com/watch?v=bpj0t2ozPWY*.

efficient resolution if both the employer and the employee seek to avoid publicity and the incurring of unnecessary expenses. Early mediation might also avoid hardening of positions and compounding of bad feelings that often accompany contentious and prolonged litigation. And if repair or restoration of the parties' relationship is feasible, its best chance may be prior to the initiation of formal legal action.[57]

But other factors may suggest that it is too soon to try mediation. In any complex case, provision needs to be made for all sides to feel they have accumulated enough information so that a decision to resolve the dispute is both informed and defensible to constituents. Some parties try to gain leverage and test the other side's will by demonstrating their staying power and ability to inflict punishment before they will enter serious negotiations. (Inflicting some harm, especially if seen as equalizing the pain already imposed by the other side, may satisfy a strong emotional need as well.) And as we have discussed, it may be fruitless to attempt to mediate a resolution before the parties are at a stage where they are emotionally "vented" — ready to let go of the conflict and work on a possible solution. In the case of the fired associate, this might include moving through the grief and the sense of loss of identity that often come from losing a job. Although a good mediator might be able to overcome some of these obstacles to early entry,[58] it could be an uphill battle.[59]

Duration of the Process and Length of Session(s).   If there is a choice, how much time should be allotted for the mediation? Should there be just one meeting or more than one? In the fired female associate case, how long would you estimate the process should take?

It is often difficult to predict in advance how long any particular mediation will last. You may be able to guess, based on the submissions you have received in advance and your sense of the number and complexity of the issues. Sometimes your predictions will be right. However, as often as not, the duration of the mediation will be dictated less by the complexity of the case than by the degree of cooperation between the parties, their emotional state and their respective bargaining styles.

It is easy to underestimate the amount of time that the process can consume, especially if there are strong feelings to work through at the outset. For each brief incident of emotional flooding, many minutes may be required to return to equilibrium. Thus, where there is a choice, many mediators try to allow a considerable period of time for the early phases of the process, asking the participants to keep

---

57. Dwight Golann, *Is Legal Mediation a Process of Repair-or Separation? An Empirical Study, and Its Implications*, 7 Harvard Negot. L. Rev. 301 (2002).
58. For example, if lack of adequate information is cited as the impediment, the mediator might arrange a schedule for exchange of needed data or interviews. If the emotions of one of the parties are too raw to be dealt with productively in mediation, the mediator might arrange for a postponement until that person can work through such issues with a therapist.
59. Some commentators suggest that even where a lawsuit has been filed, mediation should not be attempted until a true impasse has occurred. In this view, most lawsuits can be settled by the litigants without assistance; knowing that they will have access to a mediator will simply give the parties an excuse to put off any serious efforts to settle until the mediation. *See* F.A. Perez, *Evaluation of Mediation Techniques*, 10 Labor L.J. 116 (1959).

their schedules flexible the first day and to refrain from committing to a firm time limit for the overall effort.

Some mediators and agencies set aside (and bill for) a fixed amount of time — for example, a half day or full day — for their mediations, regardless of actual duration. Some commentators believe that creating specific time limits or deadlines are helpful in creating a sense of urgency,[60] especially for those parties who might be dragging their heels in negotiations. Such announced time limits and deadlines can present their own problems, however. How might a hardball negotiator seeking to maximize gain behave if a firm ending time has been announced in advance? What effect might there be if the mediator ends up relaxing that time limit?

In certain settings, such as court-based programs, there is often limited time allowed for each matter and the mediator has little if any control over scheduling. If a dispute optimally requires at least two hours to work through, what might be the consequences of having to try to resolve it in half that time or less?

There is probably a limit to how long a single session should last, given people's needs for food, movement, outside air and time to reflect. Indeed, it is for this very reason that some settlement-oriented mediators try to keep promising talks going beyond the comfort level of the participants. Although this can capture momentum toward resolution and underscore the importance of "keeping at it," is this ethical behavior? Recent empirical research suggests that human beings' capacity to make good decisions deteriorates as the day goes on, after strenuous physical or mental activity, and/or when blood glucose levels decline.[61] This can cause different effects: the loss of willpower, on the one hand; a preference for the status quo or reluctance to make difficult trade-offs on the other.[62] What duties, if any, might this suggest for the mediator? In general, what would you see as the optimal time of day to schedule a mediation, and the maximum amount of time that should be devoted to any single session?

■ §4.12 SUBSTANTIVE PREPARATIONS: ANTICIPATING AND ANALYZING THE PROBLEM

Once the procedural choices for conducting the mediation have been considered, the planning process turns to the problem itself. Here the mediator tries to form tentative hypotheses about the dispute: in a legal matter, this centers on its legal, factual, evidentiary and procedural dimensions; in all situations, it involves identifying possible barriers to resolution created by the disputants' attitudes about the conflict or each other or by their communication or bargaining styles. This advance analysis is aimed at having a leg up on fruitful areas of information to seek and possible ways of easing the negotiations or resolving the problem once the actual talks begin.

As we have said, this degree of preparation will not be possible in every case. Some mediation programs discourage or even preclude their mediators from learning in advance about the particulars of the matter to be mediated, on the theory

---

60. *See* GOLANN, *supra* note 29, at §6.1.
61. JOHN TIERNEY, *Do You Suffer From Decision Fatigue?* N.Y. Times Magazine (Aug. 17, 2011), *http://www.nytimes.com/2011/08/21/magazine/do-you-suffer-from-decision-fatigue.html?pagewanted = 1&sq = baumeister&st = cse&scp = 3.*
62. *Id.*

that reading pleadings or submissions beforehand may bias the neutral and make it difficult to listen to both parties with an open mind. This is not a silly idea. We all make judgments on the basis of limited information, and those judgments often turn out to be wrong.

However, programs of this kind are the exception rather than the rule. Most mediators are able to obtain at least some information about the dispute and the parties prior to meeting with them. Moreover, they find that this is useful and that the risks of forming biases or of diagnosing and even judging the problem prematurely, real as they may be, are outweighed by the advantages of pre-mediation problem analysis.

We believe that hypothesizing in advance about the problem and analyzing possible approaches to the mediation can be very useful, especially for beginning mediators. To see what we mean, assume you have been assigned to mediate the small claims case described in the following court complaint filed by a car buyer and the defendant car dealer's response (answer and counterclaim):[63]

▶ ▶ ▶ ▶

Complaint

Six months ago, I went to Ace Auto Sales after I see a newspaper ad for a Chevy pickup for $5,995 with low miles. When I get there and tell them that I need reliable transportation for my drive to and from work (seventy-six miles each way), this salesperson tells me that a different truck, a seven-year-old Dodge, would be better for my needs. I test-drive it, agree to buy it for $6,495 and pay $3,000 down. The rest I agree to pay on time for three years ("dealer financing").

The second day I had the car, the oil light comes on while I drive to work. I brought it to Ace (losing a half day of work), and they claim they fixed the problem.

They didn't fix the problem. Five weeks later, while driving to work, the oil light comes on again. On my way home from work two days later, the car starts smoking and flames start shooting up. I had to have the car towed to a local service station, which told me that the engine had burnt out from driving without enough oil. They offered to install a rebuilt engine and other needed repairs for $2,700 or buy the car from me for $500. What could I do? I sell it to them. I miss four more days of work because of this, and now I have no car.

Because of Ace's fraudulent and negligent conduct, I lost $2,500 on that car. I want my money back plus the return of my first two monthly payments ($234), four-and-a-half days of lost wages ($720), the towing fee of $50, plus punitive damages ($5,000) for a total of $8,504.00 plus court costs.

Answer

1. The money terms of purchase as recited in the Complaint are admitted.
2. The allegations of the Complaint are in all other respects denied, including:
   • that plaintiff stated any particular purpose in purchasing an automobile;

---

63. This is adapted from *Valley Marine Bank v. Terry James*, a hypothetical case developed by the Office of Program Support of the National Legal Services Corporation in 1975 to train staff attorneys in negotiation. *See* CARRIE MENKEL-MEADOW, *Toward Another View of Legal Negotiation: The Structure of Problem Solving*, 31 U.C.L.A. L. REV. 754, 772, n. 75 (1984).

- that any representation was made concerning the fitness of the Dodge pickup for any purpose;
- that there was a "problem" that needed repairing two days after plaintiff purchased the vehicle;
- that defendant warranted the vehicle at all beyond the thirty days stated in the contract of purchase; to the contrary, plaintiff specifically declined the option to purchase a longer warranty.

3. Defendant is without knowledge of the truth of any of the other allegations in the Complaint and thus denies them. Defendant further avers that any harm suffered by Plaintiff was solely the result of his own negligence.

4. Wherefore, defendant claims it is without any liability to Plaintiff.

Counterclaim

1. Plaintiff signed a Note in the total amount of $4,040 (including interest on the financed balance of $3,495).

2. Plaintiff has failed to make three months' payments despite demand for same. Moreover, Plaintiff's Complaint constitutes a repudiation and breach of his obligations under the Note, triggering its acceleration clause. Because of Plaintiff's subsequent actions, defendant is unable to repossess the vehicle or otherwise attempt to mitigate its damages.

3. Wherefore, defendant seeks a judgment against Plaintiff for the unpaid balance on the Note of $3,806 plus interest and attorney's fees.

What crossed your mind as you read these pleadings? For some of you, the answer may be simply that you digested the allegations, perhaps felt comfortable that the subject matter was not totally foreign to you, but that's it; you'll await the start of the mediation to think about the problem in any concerted way. But for most of you, reading the complaint probably caused your mind to race ahead. For example:

Did you form any impressions of the parties based on reading the pleadings? What impressions? Would you Google Ace Auto Sales? What if a search turned up many complaints against them? How might this affect your mediation planning?

Did you have any reactions in terms of responsibility or liability? Did you wonder if there was anything in the sales documents about the condition of the vehicle at sale or whether an extended warranty was provided? Or whether there are any writings that might document what the problem was on day two? Or what the customer did when the oil light appeared again a month later? Or whether he ever had the oil checked? Whether "steering" a customer away from an advertised "special" and toward a particular car for sale could be illegal dealer conduct? Whether the service station operator is available to provide helpful evidence and how the plaintiff can otherwise prove his claim?

What about whether the Note specified a right on the part of the defendant to recover its attorneys' fees? Or whether the law (or this small claims court) would permit an award of lost wages, punitive damages or attorneys' fees (even if provided for in a contract) to the victorious party?

Perhaps you began to anticipate how the disputants might view and feel about the conflict. Will the plaintiff see this as a matter of principle, wanting to vindicate himself and other potential victims of this car dealer? Will the car dealer be self-righteous? Defensive? Concerned about protecting its reputation in the area? How much anger is likely to be expressed in this dispute?

Maybe your mind moved to possible solutions to the problem. If you thought about money as a solution, maybe you wondered how the complainant came up with his damages calculation and if it is excessive. Or maybe you thought about non-monetary, even relational solutions, such as an agreement in which the dealer might provide the plaintiff with a substitute vehicle, perhaps with a warranty. Perhaps you imagined other solutions.

Having reviewed the court filings in a legal matter or learned the background descriptions of other kinds of disputes, it is almost impossible to approach mediating a case without formulating some questions and speculating about the problem. This inclination is more than idle curiosity; it is a useful form of conjecture geared toward maximizing one's effectiveness once the process begins. Especially when mediation time is limited, forming pre-mediation hypotheses can provide topical outlines for potentially fruitful information gathering and persuasion, a start on possible ideas for solutions to the problem and a basis for thinking about the mediation approach you may wish to adopt. Forming hypotheses about the dispute can also help in making ultimate decisions about space arrangements, who should participate, whether negotiation coaching is needed and other process considerations discussed earlier in this chapter.

The following questions may provide a helpful outline[64] for analyzing most disputes at this stage:

- What do I know about the participants themselves and their likely emotional state and bargaining approach?

- Are the parties likely to see matters of principle in this dispute? Can these be converted into concrete subjects that can be negotiated?

- What are the perceived stakes here? Can they be lowered or put into better perspective in the parties' minds?

- Can an apparent one-time transaction be converted to a situation in which future dealings are possible?

- Can the parties' conflicting positions or win-lose vision of the problem be converted into an approach that has integrative solution possibilities?

- What are the legal principles, industry standards or norms of fairness that might affect this dispute? Based on the possible legal and factual issues, are there areas of doubt that might be used as a basis for persuasion?

A few caveats need to be raised at this juncture: Like a good physician, the mediator must keep her pre-mediation diagnosis of the dispute in proper perspective. *Actually* analyzing the conflict, the parties' needs and perceptions and devising ways to meet or transform them can only take place once the

---

64. *See* LEONARD GREENHALGH, *SMR Forum: Managing Conflict*, SLOAN MANAGEMENT REV. 45 (Summer 1986) (outlining a conflict diagnostic model in the organizational context).

mediator has met with the parties and listened to them in person. Overreliance on tentative pre-mediation hypotheses about the problem or its roots can interfere with openness in listening. Failing to keep hypotheses about potential solutions in check can lead to over-directiveness and interfere with the goal of having the parties devise their own solutions to their problem.

On balance, however, we see this kind of pre-mediation thinking as very helpful. Indeed, rather than interfering with mediator listening, openness and flexibility, we find that anticipating the problem in this way can actually free the mediator to listen *more* deeply and attentively and to withhold ideas for solving the problem, secure in the notion that she has certain potential interventions already thought out if the need arises.

Anticipating Cultural Barriers.   Sometimes information will be available before the mediation begins suggesting the possible presence of cultural impediments to resolution. These can include obvious barriers, such as evident language difficulties or likely unfamiliarity with domestic legal norms, as well as problems that may or may not arise at the bargaining table (e.g., culturally-based and differing attitudes toward conflict, information openness, expressing or discussing emotions, or other differences in social norms.) Should a mediator devote pre-mediation effort to researching the cultures of the parties?[65] If so, what are the objectives of such research? Is it to learn about "typical" cultural tendencies or attitudes of groups or nationalities? How might this be helpful? Could it be problematic?

■ §4.13 A FINAL CONSIDERATION: SHOULD THIS CASE BE CO-MEDIATED?

As can be seen from this chapter, planning for mediation can involve many complex considerations. As future chapters will demonstrate, effectively conducting the mediation process requires utilizing a variety of different skills, often at the same time, requiring a kind of mental multi-tasking. Given the demands of the role, might there be advantages to having two people share it? Disadvantages? In what kinds of cases should co-mediation be considered?

Perhaps because of added scheduling complexities and presumed cost considerations, most mediations today are conducted by one neutral, working alone.[66] But there are certain kinds of cases and settings in which co-mediation is more commonly used. For example, possible concerns about a mediator's competence,

---

65. Some writers have suggested the importance of researching participants' cultural practices and the explanations for them (while being aware of one's own cultural lens), especially where the mediator's sense of fairness may conflict with a party's beliefs in an area concerning basic rights (e.g., the rights of women to own property). *See* Commentary of Harold Abramson *in* Ellen Waldman, Ed., Mediation Ethics: Cases and Commentary 327-335 (2011).

66. Are there potential efficiencies to be gained through co-mediation that can compensate for the extra costs of hiring a second neutral? Commentators disagree. *Compare* Joe Epstein & Susan Epstein, *Co-Mediation*, 35(6) Colorado Lawyer 21, 22 (2006) (co-mediation results in shorter, more efficient mediations) *with* Lela Love & Joseph Stulberg, *Practice Guidelines for Co-Mediation: Making Certain that "Two Heads Are Better Than One,"* 13 Mediation Q. 179, 180 (1996) (co-mediation can be more time-consuming than solo mediation, as co-mediators have to negotiate the tasks they will perform).

bias or group identity might be addressed by creating a team of mediators, balanced in composition.[67] Thus, it is not uncommon for family disputes to be mediated by male-female or lawyer-therapist teams,[68] for employment discrimination cases to be mediated by co-mediators of different (and, sometimes, party-matching) races, genders or ethnic backgrounds,[69] or, occasionally, for medical malpractice and other complex torts cases to be mediated by one mediator with a background doing plaintiffs' work and another who represents defendants. In cases involving specialized knowledge (such as our earlier special education example involving an autistic child), it may be possible to bring in a second neutral with greater substantive knowledge of the field, to supplement the non-specialist mediator. In cases where a mediator has had significant prior contacts with one of the disputants, it may be desirable to involve a second mediator who knows some of the other disputants, or is a stranger to all.

Co-mediation is commonly used in community and court-based mediation programs (as well as in school-based mediation programs and clinics) as a method of training new mediators, who work either under the auspices of a more seasoned supervisor-practitioner or on a peer-to-peer basis with another apprentice mediator. Co-mediation in this context offers the considerable benefit of being able to debrief the mediation experience with a partner and to give and receive constructive feedback while practicing new skills.[70]

Co-mediators can work together in a variety of ways, ranging from having one mediator closely observe the disputants and take detailed process notes, while the other neutral takes the lead in conducting the session, to full partnering on a more or less coequal basis. It has been noted that when mediators fully share the burden of being on the line, this can result in increased mediator patience and perseverance compared to working solo, given the considerable demands of the role.[71] Mediators who are working "in sync" can support each other at times when their partner is taking the more active role, engaging in deep observation of what is occurring in the room and coming to the rescue if he or she encounters difficulties.[72] Conversely, if partners find themselves disagreeing in the midst of a mediation about how to proceed, they can sometimes model constructive communication by discussing and resolving any differences transparently.[73]

Obviously, however, a dysfunctional co-mediation partnership serves no one's needs. Teaming can be challenging. At the very least, it requires having a partner with whom you feel you can work cooperatively and who shares your basic vision of the goals of the process.[74] But beyond that, it requires coordination regarding task allocation, as well as developing effective modes of communication for the many process decisions that must be made "on the fly."

---

67. Rosengard, *supra* note 24, at 18 (2004).
68. Forrest Mosten & Barbara Biggs, *The Role of the Therapist in the Co-Mediation of Divorce: An Exploration by a Lawyer-Mediator Team,* 9(2) J. Divorce 27 (1985).
69. Lorig Charkoudian & Ellen Kabcenell Wayne, *Does It Matter if My Mediator Looks Like Me? The Impact of Racially Matching Participants and Mediators,* Dispute Res. Mag. 22 (Spring 2009).
70. Paul Hutcheson & Palmerston North, *Co-Mediation: A Practical Guide,* New Zealand L.J. 251, 252 (July 2000).
71. Love & Stulberg, supra note 66, at 180.
72. *Id.*
73. *Id.*
74. *Id.* at 181.

For example, for what stages of the process and/or what types of mediator tasks and interventions will each co-mediator be primarily responsible? Why? With regard to communication, how will partners signal each other if they want to take a private "mediator's caucus" to strategize about what to do next? What if (as is often the case) there is no time for a caucus and decisions must be made spontaneously, in response to unexpected turns in the discussions? How will co-mediators handle such situations? How can co-mediators ensure that they will not undermine each other's authority or "step on each other's toes"? These kinds of challenges can generally be worked out, but they require mutual trust, and, as with other aspects of the process discussed in this chapter, benefit greatly from having spent adequate time preparing in advance.

CHAPTER
5

MEDIATION AS A
STRUCTURED PROCESS

▪ §5.1 INTRODUCTION

In the chapters that follow, we set out a model structure for conducting a mediation. Before we examine the structure stage by stage, this chapter provides an overview of the whole process. Like a good architectural plan, each stage of a mediation and its sequence in the overall structure is important to understand in functional terms — the goals the mediator seeks to accomplish during that stage, the skills called for to achieve them and how one stage relates to the next.

Why is structure important? A process that is well organized can provide comfort to participants and a sense of assurance that order will triumph over the drama of their dispute. Beyond this, a well-orchestrated, well-timed and well-structured process has important instrumental value in helping the parties achieve resolution.

Mediation is, above all else, a process of change. Albert Einstein once noted that "[t]he significant problems we face today cannot be solved with the same level of thinking we were at when we created them."[1] Success at resolving conflict through mediation necessarily requires shifts in how the participants think and feel about the dispute they are in, as well as the prospects of ending it. Even if the parties are ready to enter the process, movement from being in conflict to giving it up tends to be gradual and difficult, and calls for a methodical and progress-oriented[2] approach to challenging and potentially destructive

---

1. LYNN C. HOLADAY, *Stage Development Theory: A Natural Framework for Understanding the Mediation Process*, 18 NEGOTIATION J. 191, 205 (2002).
2. This emphasis assumes the goal of assisting the parties in achieving a resolution to the problem. Mediators whose objectives are less settlement-focused — for example, those with a transformative orientation — are likely to deemphasize structure in favor of following the parties' lead. *See generally* ROBERT A. BARUCH BUSH & JOSEPH P. FOLGER, The Promise of Mediation: Responding to Conflict Through Empowerment and Recognition (1994).

discussions. To appreciate these ideas, consider what happened in the following mediation:

A fifty-nine-year-old woman who had worked as a midlevel corporate manager for eleven years was denied a promotion for which she applied. The job went to a more recently hired male employee in his late thirties, on the ground that his "potential" was much greater. The woman felt that she had an excellent work record, and she was hurt and offended. Needing a job, however, she bit her tongue. But when soon thereafter her job was eliminated in an administrative reorganization, she consulted a lawyer and, with his assistance, filed a charge of age and gender discrimination with the U.S. Equal Employment Opportunity Commission (EEOC). The company responded to these allegations with a blanket denial of all charges, claiming that its decisions were lawful and justified by legitimate business considerations. When contacted by the EEOC several months later to see whether this matter might be mediated, both parties accepted the invitation.

The claimant was fearful of going to trial. She wanted and needed to work and was concerned about the possible harm to her prospects of finding a new position if viewed by others as litigious. At a pre-mediation conference, her lawyer, after briefly describing mediation, advised her that her case had possible legal weaknesses. On considering this, she informed him that, while she wanted the best deal he could get her, what she really wanted (assuming the company would not rehire her) was some fairly quick money. She was beginning to deplete her savings to pay for health insurance now that her month's severance pay and her unemployment benefits had run out. Most important, she wanted the case to end as soon as possible, because, despite entering therapy to deal with her problems, it was affecting her sleep, impeding her job search and hampering her personal life. Her bottom line: she would accept any offer that would net her $60,000 after deduction of her lawyer's one-third contingency fee if it would end things immediately.

The first session of the mediation was attended by the claimant, her lawyer, the company human resources director and its outside lawyer. It began with the mediator welcoming the parties to *"this effort aimed at reaching a settlement in this matter"* but dispensing with a lengthy description of the process *"since the lawyers have already done that."* On being invited to state her side of the case, the claimant's lawyer laid out a ten-minute summary of the facts and the law that supported her claim and damages, demanding *"$450,000 to resolve this."* Asked by the mediator if she had anything to add, the claimant began to provide an emotional account of her employment history, weeping openly while recounting the early days of the job and how gratifying it had been. At this point, the company's attorney apologetically interrupted her, telling the mediator that *"We, of course, could offer a different view of all of this. But perhaps we can make some progress if we try to deal with the money issues instead of rehashing contested allegations."* The mediator, acknowledging that *"these matters are tough,"* asked the claimant to *"try to put aside excessive emotion."* *"I think I'll let my lawyer do my talking from now on,"* she replied. After the company briefly repeated its denial of any unlawful conduct and summarized the justifications for its decisions, the mediator asked the claimant and her attorney to leave the room so that he could meet alone with the company's representatives. As the claimant rose from her chair, she was fuming.

The forty-minute session with the company representatives was marked by its defense of its actions and by the mediator's efforts to underscore the company's legal risks in face of the claimant's credibility and the sympathy she might evoke at trial. This produced a settlement offer of $35,000, an amount the company estimated as its legal costs to defend the case during the EEOC investigation and, if needed, to seek to have any court case dismissed. On next meeting privately with the claimant, the mediator's announcement of *"encouraging progress"* was met with a barrage of lawyerly argument reiterating the claimant's claims, as well as a lengthy, tearful outburst from the claimant about her work record, how poorly the company had treated her and how unemployment felt. The mediator raised questions about some of the potential weaknesses in her claim and pressed for an expression of flexibility. In response, claimant's counsel "reluctantly" lowered his demand to $320,000, citing his concession of a "25 percent risk" of not winning at trial.

Another one-hour private meeting with the company produced an increase in their offer to $100,000. When the mediator relayed this offer to the claimant, she immediately rejected it, calling it *"another insult from those bastards."* When pressed for a counteroffer, her lawyer, after thirty minutes of resisting, replied "$285,000."

The mediator then reconvened all of the participants and announced, *"We've been at it for nearly three hours and you're miles apart. Anyone got any ideas?"* Greeted with a lengthy silence, he terminated the mediation.

■ §5.2 THE NEED FOR STRUCTURE: LESSONS FROM A STORY

Recall that the claimant told her attorney before the mediation began that she would settle her case for $60,000 after payment of her attorney's fees. But when the company offered $100,000 — a figure that would net her $6,000 more than that, she turned it down instantly. Something happened here that turned a resolvable dispute into an apparent impasse. What lessons might we draw from this case?

Lesson One: Successful De-Escalation of Conflict Requires Time.   For conflict to ripen into a dispute can take considerable time. But *de-escalating* a conflict, especially after it has gotten to the point of threatened or actual coercion through litigation, is more complex and time-consuming than the buildup that led to it. Nikita Khrushchev, the Cold War Soviet leader, described this through the metaphor of two men tugging on a tangled rope, creating a knot. Untying the knot requires changing tactics completely and moving to a cooperative effort that is much more complicated than merely stopping pulling.[3] This notion has also been captured this way: One can do harm faster than good.[4]

This phenomenon is common in mediation. After a period of conflict escalation, the time it takes to produce a peace through talking tends to be substantial — for several reasons. First, the process is likely to start off on a note of mistrust and suspicion, given the buildup that produced the dispute. Even if the parties have

---

3. CHARLES F. HERMANN ed., International Crises: Insights From Behavioral Research 215 (1972).
4. *See* HO-WON JEONG ed., Conflict Resolution: Dynamics, Process and Structure 45 (1999).

agreed to a cease-fire and to attempt a resolution through mediation, this may be viewed more as a self-serving move to "stop the bleeding" than as an affirmative act of cooperation. (And where parties are *required* to mediate, there isn't even this level of pre-mediation agreement for a mediator to build on.) Once mediation talks begin, it may become clear that the words or actions that led to the conflict have inflicted deep wounds that may be very difficult to heal. Good mediation takes time. And the astute mediator structures the talks with this in mind.

The employment mediator in the case above, especially in the early stages, seemed to value efficiency over the importance of addressing the claimant's deeply hurt feelings. Sometimes the slow way is the fast way.[5]

Lesson Two: Participants Must Traverse Emotional and Behavioral Stages in Order to Reach Resolution.   As we noted in Chapter 2, research tells us that the process of resolving conflict requires most people to pass through discernible stages of emotion and that each such shift is important for them to experience. This has been described in several ways.[6]

Some writers focus on the evolving *feelings* that disputants — both those who feel wronged and those accused of wrongdoing — experience as a successful negotiation progresses. This involves moving from:

- angry denial and a sense of blamelessness; to

- acceptance of the conflict and some sense of shared responsibility; to

- the willingness to sacrifice to end the conflict.[7]

Others focus more on the negotiating *behaviors* associated with these feelings, which can progress from:

- seeking to punish and coerce others out of a sense of being wronged; to

- trying to win by seeking an authority's approval of the strength and rightness of one's position; to

- negotiating in ways that integrate the other person's needs, as well as one's own, into an workable resolution.[8]

While some mediations begin with one or more disputants at an advanced stage of emotional readiness to resolve the dispute, others involve participants who may need to move through the entire cycle of emotion and behavior before resolution is possible. In some situations, time constraints or a disputant's personal limitations may mean that the best that can be hoped for is to move a party up a single rung in the ladder. But the key point is that these stages are developmental: Most people must go through one stage before reaching the next. Related to this, many disputants will need an opportunity to give voice to their emotions — even at

---

5. See JEROME F. WEISS, *Slow Down, You Move Too Fast . . . A Helpful Mediation Hint* (2003) available at *http://www.mediate.com/mediationinc/docs/You%20Move%20Too%20Fast.pdf*. Cf. THOMAS JAMES, *The Hare and the Tortoise, in* Aesop's Fables 39, 40 (1848) ("Slow and steady wins the race.").
6. This way of looking at the steps in moving from conflict to resolution are examples of the larger school of stage development theory. For further discussion of stage development theory, see sources cited in HOLADAY, *supra* note 1, at 209, n.2 (2002).
7. *See, e.g.,* GERALD R. WILLIAMS, *Negotiation as a Healing Process*, 1996 J. DISP. RESOL. 1.
8. HOLADAY, *supra* note 1, at 203-204 (discussing the "integrative stage" of conflict resolution).

the risk of escalating the conflict—before being able to move forward.[9] As a consequence, attempts by the mediator to short-circuit the process are very likely to fail. The mediator must structure the talks—their duration and pace, the balance between uninterrupted expression and party interaction as well as between joint sessions and private meetings—to allow for these stages to be played out sequentially and constructively.

There is also an important *diagnostic* benefit to understanding the emotional and behavioral stages of conflict. Understanding how in general disputants' feelings about disputes tend to evolve over time can give the mediator a means of appraising realistically the progress (or lack of progress) of the discussions in a particular case. As a result, even in seemingly hopeless situations, the patient neutral can retain a sense of optimism from the ability to "trust the process," confident that, with enough time and the right conditions for receiving and processing information, even the most contentious disputants may well reach agreement in the end. If communicated to the parties, such optimism can itself be an ingredient in producing further progress.

Our employment mediator seemed oblivious to these emotional stages. He allowed virtually no time for the claimant to express her anger and hurt (loss of identity, grieving the loss of the job, etc.) or to direct it at the person she felt had wronged her. Had he done so, she might have been more open to understanding the employer's perspective and to negotiating toward resolution.

Lesson Three: Mediation Must Allow for the Strategic Stages of Competitive Negotiation.   A structured mediation process is often necessitated by a third factor: the strategic patterns of competitive negotiation and the barriers to resolution that can be presented by that bargaining approach. Many if not most mediation participants start negotiations in an adversarial fashion—they seek to maximize gain or, at a minimum, to protect themselves from being exploited by an untrustworthy opponent. As a result, certain tactics—for example, extreme positioning or argumentation, guardedness or caginess about information—are to be expected, especially in the early stages.[10] When parties emphatically commit to positions, movement off these positions is generally slow, because an element of face-saving is required. If a positional approach to the bargaining persists, it is often manifested by threats, bluffs and increasingly begrudging concessions as part of a ritualized, competitive "dance" that, if concluded at all, converges somewhere in the middle of the established bargaining zone.

To complicate matters, as noted in Chapter 2, a tough distributive bargaining approach is often exacerbated by cognitive distortions such as loss aversion, reactive devaluation, partisan norms of fairness and overconfidence bias, which may create additional barriers to resolution. While effective mediators can lower these barriers, it is clear that a mediation in which the participants are bargaining competitively must provide a structure that includes adequate time and appropriate

---

9. Bernard Mayer, Beyond Neutrality: Confronting the Crisis in Conflict Resolution 181-214 (2004).
10. *See, e.g.*, Christopher W. Moore, The Mediation Process 166-2007 (2003) (discussing the prevalence of emotions and extreme positioning in early-stage negotiations and suggesting tactics for overcoming such factors).

settings (including private consultation periods) to allow these stages to run their course.

Although one cannot know this with certainty, the mediator in the employment case may have lost a potential resolution by failing to appreciate the progress of concessions that had begun, by underestimating (or being insufficiently patient about) the time that each side might need to move toward convergence or by assuming that the requisite movement could be accomplished in a single mediation session. The mediator may have read too much into the fact that no one was willing to "blink" during the final joint session, or may have erred in thinking that, at that stage in the process, a joint session format would yield further gap-narrowing proposals.

Lesson Four: A Structured Approach Can Enhance the Perception of Procedural Justice and Mediator Impartiality.   As we have already noted, the kind of process a mediator orchestrates is an important part of the product she delivers. This is not simply a matter of appearing organized or knowledgeable about how to mediate, important as these things are. For mediation consumers to feel that procedural justice has been done, they must feel that they have been treated fairly and their voices truly heard. This underscores the importance of time, focus and attention to participants' needs that only a systematic approach can ensure.

Having an organized structure also enhances the odds of the mediator's acting, and being seen as acting, impartially — an important component of consumer satisfaction. Conducting the talks in stages, with an awareness of the purpose of each step, can heighten the mediator's understanding of the state of each party's emotions and bargaining strategy in that stage, and allow her to put them in proper perspective. This can protect the mediator from feeling overwhelmed when the parties exhibit strong emotions or from forming biases when they engage in aggressive, adversarial conduct. And this, in turn, can lead to levelheaded strategies for dealing with problem behavior while maintaining an impartial stance.

Lesson Five: Structure Is Crucial to Widening and Deepening the Information Flow.   *The* major factor in producing change through mediation is improving upon the prior flow of information — reducing communication distortions, uncovering undisclosed interests, expanding upon what has been said previously, adding new perspectives on that information and helping the participants take in such information in a way that will help them shift their perceptions of the situation and of the other side. (This is also important in trying to obtain resolutions that will last. When settlement agreements are violated or ignored, it is often because of insufficient information gathering — the mediation failed to uncover or address an important need of a party or missed an important issue.)

Resolution-enhancing information comes from both the words that are spoken and impressions that those words create. It can come from what the parties say to the mediator and what she says to them. Examples of potentially useful information flowing *from* the parties include

■ the parties' complete account of the problem and its history;

■ their views on possible solutions — both optimal and acceptable;

- how a party really feels about the dispute and his or her role in creating it;

- the parties' real willingness to compromise from stated positions;

- the parties' true (and perhaps undisclosed) interests and private settlement facts, such as their financial situations, attitudes about risk and alternatives to a negotiated settlement;

- whether they will appear sympathetic and believable as possible future witnesses;

- whether a party will follow through on commitments made or can be trusted in a future relationship.

The mediator adds to the communication flow as well. Examples of potentially useful information the mediator provides *to* the parties include

- feedback on how a party's negotiating stance or conduct is affecting the talks;

- statements of optimism about progress made, agreements reached and signals about possible areas of future agreement;

- a detached view on how a party's perspective or position might be viewed by others;

- basic legal information about, or the mediator's evaluation of, the dispute;

- new ideas for resolving the problem.

Not all of this information will come out quickly or be heard easily. Some information — for example, the history of the dispute and the feelings it has generated — may emerge spontaneously but may also trigger emotions that require time-consuming management. Some information will generally be withheld in the early stages for strategic reasons, or until trust in the other side has been established. Some information (e.g., admissions of weakness and interests risky to disclose) may only be provided in private. Some information, such as ideas for resolution, may only be possible once previously withheld information has been revealed. Finally, some information provided by the mediator, such as disinterested feedback or evaluation, will only be accepted by the parties after the mediator has earned their confidence, a process that almost always takes time.

Optimizing the output and impact of information is not a matter of chance. Success depends on creating conditions that are conducive to openness and receptivity — the comfort of the parties, the right balance of plenary and private discussions, the expectations created by the mediator's questioning and the trust in the process that has been built. Establishing such conditions requires a deliberately structured process.

In the employment mediation, limiting the parties' face-to-face contact may have prevented the employer from hearing important information from the claimant that might have induced a change in the company's view of her and her claim. The mediator's immediate focus on persuasion and settlement rather than information expansion may have come at the expense of learning critical information about feelings, motivations and interests.

Lesson Six: The Trappings of Ceremony Can Aid the Settlement Effort. In mediation, as in other areas of life, ceremonies often underscore the importance of events. Beginning a mediation in a fairly formal, ceremonial fashion can cement the parties' investment in the effort about to begin, thus differentiating it from the failed negotiations that may have preceded it.[11] Moving from opening formality to increasing informality as tensions ease and trust develops can graphically signify the progress that has been made. And a final closing stage may benefit from a return to formality that conveys the significance of the agreement reached or of the failure to conclude one.

A closing ceremony that results in settlement may take the form of celebration, especially if the conflict has been protracted and settlement has been hard to achieve. But even failed mediations need not be somber occasions: They can be used to put tense parties at ease or set a constructive tone. For example, the mediator can point to differences that have been aired, partial agreements that have been reached and beneficial learning that has taken place. If conducted in a positive and optimistic manner, closing ceremonies can enhance the possibility of future cooperation.

The mediator in the employment dispute conducted a very stunted opening session by dispensing with any real introduction or description of the process that would follow and depriving the parties of much opportunity to express themselves or to interact. In the final session, he ended the effort without even acknowledging the positive: that in less than three hours, the gap between the parties had narrowed by nearly 60 percent—from $450,000 to less than $200,000. Different approaches at these two junctures in the process might have yielded different attitudes and feelings, if not results.

Lesson Seven: The Structure Itself Can Be a Catalyst Toward Progress. Mediations that end in agreement often have clear turning points. Indeed, deliberate transitions from one stage to the next (e.g., from gathering data to listing topics for negotiation) can themselves signal and encourage a sense of forward momentum. Similarly, changing the setting—such as by moving from joint sessions to private caucuses—can demonstrate the need for greater openness in information or greater flexibility in bargaining.

■ §5.3 THE PROGRESSIVE STRUCTURE OF A MODEL MEDIATION

Like most good stories, a well-organized mediation moves logically from beginning to middle to ending stages. And like many stories, its emphasis moves from the past (the events that produced the conflict) to the present (organizing the things that need to be discussed) to the future (whether and how the conflict will

---

11. *See* DWIGHT GOLANN, Mediating Legal Disputes §§2.1.1 and 6.1 (1996) (discussing the need for the creation of "settlement events").

be resolved). Once the parties are seated at the table,[12] effective mediations have four stages:

- **Stage One: Opening the Process, Developing Information.** With all participants present, the mediation begins somewhat ceremoniously. It establishes the mediator's role, the agreed procedure to be followed and, one hopes, universal commitment to the settlement effort. Each party provides an uninterrupted account of the conflict from his or her perspective, after which the participants respond to each other, and the mediator clarifies and summarizes but provides minimum direction.

- **Stage Two: Expanding the Information Base, Identifying Issues, Organizing an Agenda.** The mediator then moves to a more active stance by probing to obtain deeper and more detailed information about the background and context of the dispute and possible barriers to resolution. The mediator probes in both joint and private sessions, to find additional potential subjects for negotiation, uncover the parties' true interests and flesh out details that may assist in any evaluation or persuasion that may be required in later stages. Based on the information developed, the mediator identifies the negotiable issues and, with the parties, organizes them into a comprehensive agenda to be discussed. No attempt is made at this stage to solve the problem.

- **Stage Three: Problem-Solving and Persuasion.** The mediator then attempts to act as the orchestrator of party negotiations and, if necessary, inventor of potential options. This stage is often conducted in both joint sessions and caucus; "shuttle diplomacy" may be used to coach the parties about their negotiating conduct, obtain or transmit offers and encourage open responses. In this stage, mediators engage in problem-solving, persuasion and/or evaluation to try to increase the parties' flexibility and encourage movement.

- **Stage Four: Dealing with Impasse, Closing.** When the psychological timing is right (or the scarcity of time demands it), the mediator attempts to bring closure to the negotiations by helping the parties choose from among the options being considered. If an apparent impasse has been reached, the mediator attempts to diagnose the remaining barriers to settlement and intervenes strategically to deal with them. While joint sessions are preferred if closure can be obtained by face-to-face final bargaining, private sessions are often used in competitive bargaining situations. The mediation concludes with a ceremony in which the agreement (or lack of one) is confirmed. If there is an agreement, it is memorialized, with the mediator attempting to ensure that all important contingencies have been considered. If there is no final agreement, the mediator may confirm or suggest alternative processes for resolving disputed issues that remain.

---

12. The process of preparing for the mediation, covered in Chapter 4, could be considered the first stage in the overall effort. *See, e.g.*, MOORE, *supra* note 10, at 68-69, Fig. 2.3 (illustrating a twelve-stage process in which the first five stages precede the mediator's meeting with the parties).

Our recommended structure aims to create the conditions — safe face-to-face contact; comfort, sufficient time and, if needed, privacy for good communication and information flow; organized discussions, opportunities and incentives for inventing and evaluating options; and a sense of urgency appropriate to the problem — that are most conducive to participants' voluntarily reappraising their views of the dispute and their role in it. In our model, the mediator becomes progressively more active over time — moving from communication facilitator to developer of information to organizer and moderator of the negotiations, and finally to an advocate for resolution.[13]

█ §5.4 THE LIMITS OF A MODEL STRUCTURE

Mediations are obviously not as neat as the words on a printed page. Many disputes will not permit an orderly, logical progression from one stage to the next. Emotions may run so high or strategic maneuvering may be so pronounced as to challenge even the best attempts to impose structure on the process. Stages can repeat themselves or require revisiting, such as when previously withheld information surfaces at a later stage of a mediation, requiring additions or changes to the negotiating agenda. One stage may not be finished in the mediator's mind when another is begun by the participants, thus requiring the mediator to multi-task and think about the functions of more than one phase at a time. In short, the mediator must react while she orchestrates, and both lead and follow at the same time.

While some mediations are multisession events, taking place over months or years, others must be concluded, if they are going to be concluded, in a matter of hours or even minutes, especially if the duration is constrained by the external demands of courts, participant time limitations and the like. In some settings, certain stages of the mediation must therefore be compressed or skipped over entirely, potentially impeding the development of rapport and the uncovering of important information. In others, participants enter the process closer to resolution than our model suggests, enabling the mediator safely to shorten or even dispense with certain stages of the process.

In short, there are limits to any model, and the effective mediator needs to develop the ability to adapt quickly to the situation in which he or she is working. However, recognizing these realities does not in any way diminish the value of a model and the value of working through as many of its stages, in their optimal duration and sequence, as is possible under the circumstances.

The next six chapters will analyze this staged model in detail.

---

13. The model of mediation we have set forth reflects our preferred approach to the process, summarized in Chapter 3. The structure of any mediation is likely to be determined in large part by the orientation of its mediator. For example, the time and emphasis devoted to information expansion or the balance of public versus private discussions might vary considerably depending on whether the neutral were a facilitator or an evaluator.

CHAPTER 6

OPENING THE PROCESS, DEVELOPING INFORMATION

This chapter contains fourteen video clips, totaling approximately fifty-five minutes.

■ §6.1 THE MEDIATION BEGINS

The participants are seated and the mediation is about to begin. As the mediator, how should you conduct yourself? What should you say and do? This chapter analyzes the opening stage of mediation, in which the mediator introduces herself, explains the mediation process, provides the parties with an opportunity to make opening statements and then begins to manage a process of exchanging and developing information. In this chapter, we also introduce skills that are stressed in the opening stage but that continue to be important throughout the process: effective questioning, listening and note-taking and managing the expression of strong feelings.[1]

Making good choices about one's conduct as a mediator requires having well-developed objectives for each stage of the process. Here, we think, are three key goals for the beginning of the mediation:

"Safety First." You will want to make the participants feel as safe and as comfortable as possible. They may know little (or even be misinformed) about the mediation process and how it will work. They may feel defensive or frightened to be confronting their opponents and need assurance that the proceedings will be orderly and safe. They need to be provided with an overview of the process, and your role and their roles within it. Think of yourself as an attentive host at a dinner party and act accordingly. The mediation is not about you; it's about the participants.

---

1. In order to isolate the central themes in carrying out the mediation role, we use a two-party dispute as our primary paradigm. Some mediated disputes, of course, involve three or more parties, creating additional process management demands for the neutral.

Develop Empathy and Trust: The Importance of Tone.   Whatever you say at the beginning of the process, *how* you say it is also very important. Good mediators, we believe, are able to convey a tone of respect, self-confidence, patience, attentiveness, seriousness and simplicity.[2] As we will see, developing empathy, authoritativeness and trust at the start of the process helps establish a foundation for later efforts to aid the actual negotiations.

Develop Empathy and Trust: The Importance of Good Listening.   Since mediation is first and foremost a helping process, the participants must trust you and feel that you have their best interests in mind. Good mediators convey a sincere desire to understand all participants' perspectives and concerns. The effective mediator treats "everyone as a person, not a case."[3] Giving each participant an opportunity to speak fully, without interruption, is crucial, as is attentive and respectful listening.

■ §6.2 THE MEDIATOR'S OPENING STATEMENT

All mediators begin the process with some kind of mediator's introduction or opening statement. The length of this opening statement will vary depending on the nature of the case and the parties' familiarity with the process. In court-connected mediations in which there is a premium on efficiency or with highly experienced "repeat players," the mediator's opening remarks might be relatively brief. In complex, multi-session matters, the introduction might be longer and quite detailed, tailored to the nature of the dispute. In a private divorce mediation, for example, the mediator would likely discuss a host of topics, such as the role that attorneys will play in the process; the potential need for family or child counseling; the need for complete financial disclosures and an explanation of the documents that will have to be exchanged or that the mediator will use, as well as fee arrangements.

Whatever the length and content of the introduction, we recommend an inter-active, conversational style. The participants may be nervous at the very outset. They may be rehearsing to themselves what they will say when their turn comes to speak. Although the mediator's opening may provide them with time to acclimate themselves and get comfortable, they will probably not be able to digest a long, boring speech.

Interaction during the mediator's opening can be initiated by the mediator or by the parties themselves. The neutral can engage the parties in conversation by asking questions (*"Have you ever participated in mediation before? Tell me about that experience. . . . " "Did you know that this process is confidential?"*) or otherwise trying to draw the parties out, or the mediator can invite the participants to ask questions in order to clarify points in his opening statement or raise concerns about any other matters. In cases of mandatory mediation, it is not uncommon for parties to interrupt the mediator's opening by expressing resistance to participating. Newer mediators are often put off by such interruptions, deferring responses

---

2. Jennifer E. Beer & Eileen Stief, The Mediator's Handbook 70 (3d ed. 1997).
3. *Id.* at 71.

so that they can finish their prepared remarks first. Why might it be desirable to address such interjections when they arise?

The Mediator's Opening

What are some key components and objectives of a mediator's opening statement?

- **Introductions.** If the mediator has not already done so, she will want to introduce herself to the participants and have them introduce themselves to each other and to her. The mediator should not assume that everyone knows one another; there may be attorneys or others at the table who have not previously met.
- **Key Elements of the Process.** The mediator will want to describe the key elements of the process, explaining the reasons why things will be done, in understandable terms. This allows the participants, if they have not already done so, to make an informed decision whether (and how) to participate. It sometimes includes "ground rules" that all agree will govern the mediation. These can provide the participants with a sense of security and direction as the process moves forward.
- **The Mediator's Function.** Most mediators say something about their part in the mediation — what they will (and will not) do.
- **Touting the Benefits of Mediation.** Many mediators try to explain the potential advantages of the process, especially for first-time users and parties who have been mandated by the courts to participate. This is designed to instill optimism and increase their "buy-in" to the process.
- **Confirm the Presence and Bargaining Authority of Necessary Parties.** In appropriate cases, the mediator may want to confirm that all persons whose presence is necessary to settle the case are on hand and that they have authority to negotiate and resolve the matter.
- **Establishing a Positive Tone.** As an overarching goal, the mediator works to establish a positive tone for the discussions that will follow.

Video Illustrations

Here are excerpts of some mediator opening statements from our three video case studies. To remind you, one case involved a couple with a dispute about the custody of their children. Another involved a dispute between a contractor and a homeowner over a kitchen renovation. The third case was a premises liability case in which a tenant, claiming inadequate security, sued his former landlord for injuries suffered when he was accosted in his apartment by an intruder.

Watch first as one of our child custody mediators introduces the mediation process to Bob and Jane Fitzgerald. What do you like about this (fairly complete) opening? Is there some aspect you don't like? What, if anything, would you have said or done differently? To what extent has the mediator accomplished the objectives listed above? Would his approach have been appropriate in a different kind of case — for example, a commercial dispute between hardheaded businessmen, with lawyers on both sides? If not, what might be changed to accommodate that setting? **Video Clip 6-A.**

Next we will focus more closely on some of the specific components of our mediators' openings, across different types of cases. As you watch these extracts, closely analyze the mediators' language and consider the following questions:

Introductions and Ice-breaking.   It is not uncommon for mediators to introduce themselves by their first names and to seek permission to call the parties by theirs.[4] By doing so, they signal to participants that the mediation process is a less formal process than litigation. What are the case, party and mediator variables that make the use of first names appropriate or not? What kind of small talk, if any, is appropriate at the beginning of the process? **Video Clip 6-B (1–2).**

Describing and Touting the Process, Gaining Commitment.   With a limited time to speak before the participants may start to get restless, mediators must decide how much they want to say about the mediation process. What features of the process do these particular mediators emphasize? What additional points should they have made? The line between describing the mediation process and "selling" it is a fine one. Is it appropriate for a mediator to tout the benefits of mediation in order to try to *convince* reluctant disputants to participate? If it is proper, what are the most effective mediation selling points in court-based cases? **Video Clips 6-C (1–2) and 6-D (1–3).**

Some mediators also try during their openings to obtain a verbal commitment from the parties to make a serious effort to seek a solution. What might be gained by doing this?

Role Definitions.   In Chapter 3, we discussed different conceptions of the mediator's role. Because of mediation's variability, many mediators believe that it is important to tell the participants at the outset about their philosophy of mediation and how they will define and carry out their role. In the extracts that follow, what are the commonalities and differences between these mediators' conceptions of their roles? Can you tell the preferred role orientation of each? **Video Clip 6-E (1–4).**

Ground Rules.   As noted in Chapter 2, effective mediators must be adept at managing conversations in which strong feelings abound and angry words are exchanged. Some mediators seek to establish ground rules as a way to try to avoid talk that is too hostile, chaotic or potentially demeaning to the other side. ("*No personal attacks,*" "*no foul language*" or "*we ask that everyone treat each other with respect*" are some typical formulations.) What are the pros and cons of ground rules? Is it better to try to preempt interruptions, rude conduct and expressions of hostility before they occur or to assume that such conduct will not occur and deal with it only if it does? Is it better to set the rules yourself or involve the parties in devising them? If you were a participant, how would you react to these two mediators' approaches to setting ground rules in the following video excerpts?

---

4. When a mediator has had past dealings with or other connections to the parties or their lawyers, some kind of conflict of interest disclosure is generally required, as Video Clip 12-A illustrates. The beginning of the mediation is the time for such disclosures to be made. We discuss this in greater length in Chapter 12.

Which approach is more likely to promote respect for the process? If the parties have questionable communication skills or a history of stormy relations, is ceding authority to them over how communications will be structured in the mediation a wise idea? **Video Clip 6-F (1–2).**

Explaining the Confidentiality of the Process. An operating principle to which all mediators subscribe is that *confidentiality of the process* is an essential protection that enables mediation to work effectively. It is widely believed that parties to legal disputes will be less willing to discuss their interests candidly, acknowledge responsibility for their acts or take the risk of proposing difficult compromises if they believe that their statements can be used against them if their case does not settle and goes to trial.[5]

By "confidentiality of the process," we mean that statements made during mediations — by the parties and by the mediator — should have some expectation of privacy and protection against being disclosed to the outside world. In legal disputes, this means that neither the mediator nor the parties may testify at a later hearing about what was said in the mediation in an attempt to reach settlement.

This is to be distinguished from *confidentiality within the process*, which applies to information revealed during caucuses (i.e., private sessions between the mediator and each party). The added protection for caucus discussions enables the mediator to speak confidentially with each of the disputants and obtain information from them that they might not be willing to discuss in front of their opponent.[6] The typical mediator's opening statement mentions both kinds of confidentiality.

In the extracts that follow, we have two examples of mediator statements regarding confidentiality. The scope of protection to be given to private mediation information is the subject of considerable debate — and great variation — around the country.[7] If a state's mediation law contains exceptions to confidentiality, should the mediator warn the parties about these limits? If so, how, specifically? **Video Clip 6-G (1–2).**

The Order of Topics. Note finally that psychological studies demonstrate that, other things being equal, people tend to remember the first and last statements in any list of ideas better than items placed in the middle. (Psychologists call this the law of "primacy" and "recency.")[8] So, in addition to considering what topics she wishes to emphasize in her opening, the mediator needs to consider the order in which to discuss them. In general, what themes would you think it desirable to start and end with in the mediator's introduction? Why?

---

5. *See* L. Freedman & M. Prigoff, *Confidentiality in Mediation: The Need for Protection*, 2 Ohio St. J. on Disp. Resol. 37, 39 (1986).
6. We will return in detail to the subject of caucusing in Chapters 7 and 9.
7. *See infra* §12.4 for an extended discussion of this topic.
8. *See, e.g.,* Psychology and Law: An Empirical Perspective 301 (Neil Brewer & K.D. Williams eds., 2007).

§6.3 DEVELOPING INFORMATION: MEDIATION AS AN INTERVIEW

Having introduced the process, the mediator now shifts his focus to the parties: For the process to succeed, they will need to provide information to the neutral and to each other that might bring about changes in thought and feeling as well as the seeds of potential solutions needed to resolve the conflict. How is this accomplished?

It may be useful to think of mediation as a kind of three-way, goal-oriented "interview." This interview ideally begins open-endedly, in what could be called a "helping" mode, in which the parties are assisted in describing the problem as they see it. It then moves to more probing interventions, in order to uncover new (and sometimes sensitive) information. Eventually, it involves persuasive efforts, using both the information gathered from the participants and some that the mediator may provide, to help the parties see the conflict differently and achieve movement from earlier stances.

Three Types of Interviews.   To help understand these ideas, consider that, broadly speaking, there are three major kinds of interviews:

- The *problem-solving* or *helping* interview, in which professional counselors or advisors or lay persons help clients, friends, associates or family members confront personal, business or financial problems, develop greater insight about those problems and take productive action.

- The *probing* interview, commonly associated with journalists, survey takers, police officers, physicians, insurance adjustors and the like. The central purpose of the probing or investigative interview is to obtain relevant information accurately and completely.

- The *persuasive* interview, commonly used by sales, recruiting, fund-raising and political campaign interviewers. In persuasive interviews, the interviewer wants to influence how the interviewee thinks and feels to persuade him or her to take action.[9]

For neutrals of most role orientations, mediation involves aspects of helping, probing and persuasion. To be effective, they must therefore master skills and techniques useful in all three types of interviews.

Mediation as a Problem-Solving or Helping Interview.   All neutrals and disputants would agree that mediators seek to "help" in some fashion; most judge the effectiveness of a mediation by whether and how the problem that the parties face is resolved. Depending on their style and the nature of a particular conflict, mediators help disputants:

- communicate and hear each other's perspectives — both the facts of the dispute and the feelings associated with it;

---

9. *See* CHARLES J. STEWART & WILLIAM B. CASH, Interviewing: Principles and Practices 301-344 (10th ed. 2003).

■ understand their own interests, values and priorities and those of the other party;

■ negotiate effectively and make good decisions about continuing versus resolving the conflict;

■ learn through this experience how to deal more effectively with conflict situations

Like other helpers, mediators help people confront difficult issues, develop insight and decide what action, if any, they want to take. And like other helpers, they accomplish this largely by establishing an empathic collaboration with the disputants so that they feel listened to, heard and respected.[10]

Mediation as a Probing Interview. But mediators also must be effective investigators: They must probe for salient details and explore potentially sensitive matters that the parties may not have broached themselves, may be reluctant to discuss openly for strategic reasons or may even be unaware of at a conscious level. This includes:

■ **Probing the History of the Dispute, Including Legally Relevant Facts and Evidence.** By asking probing questions, the mediator helps each party unpack and elaborate his or her "story" and hear how it stands up against competing versions. In legal dispute mediations, the parties often expect that the facts — including harmful ones — will be carefully developed and that applicable legal principles will be considered.[11]

■ **Probing for Interests, Priorities and Constraints.** A mediator cannot help the parties problem-solve effectively unless she learns what they really need, why they care about it and what their constraints and alternatives to a negotiated settlement are.

■ **Probing About Options and Terms for a Settlement "Deal."** Like a business lawyer's or sports agent's interview of a client concerning a proposed contract with a third party,[12] mediators probe for information to help the parties create possible terms for resolving the dispute, asking them questions regarding what future arrangements are acceptable, workable, indispensable or "deal-breakers."

■ **Probing for Weak Points.** Effective mediators often must ask direct yet tactful questions designed to expose weak points, discrepancies and significant omissions in each party's position that might explain their false bravado,[13] plant the seeds of doubt or otherwise set the stage for bargaining flexibility. How is this accident victim going to prove this difficult element of his claim? How does that accused offender reconcile her two seemingly inconsistent statements?

---

10. CLARA E. HILL, Helping Skills: Facilitating Exploration, Insight and Action 25 (1999).
11. *See supra* §4.2.
12. *See* D. BINDER, P. BERGMAN, S. PRICE & P. TREMBLAY, Lawyers as Counselors: A Client-Centered Approach 208-233 (2d ed. 2004).
13. On the poses and masks people wear to conceal what they truly feel, *see* KENNETH CLOKE, Mediating Dangerously 32-36 (2001).

Mediation as a Persuasive Interview.   Finally, consistent with the norms of self-determined party decision making and mediator neutrality, most mediations include significant elements of persuasion, and appropriately so. These can include:

- attempting to convince resistant mediation participants to give mediation a good faith try;

- trying to assist the parties to empathize with the "opponent" or to see the dispute the way a third party might;

- trying to convince mediation participants to put aside irrational ideas and objectively weigh the risks and benefits of different solutions;

- trying to persuade parties not to give up in the face of apparent impasse; and

- helping the participants to recognize the benefits of settlement and the risks and costs of continuing the conflict.[14]

§6.4 A PROGRESSIVE MODEL OF INFORMATION GATHERING IN MEDIATION: MOVING FROM NON-DIRECTIVE AND PARTY-CENTERED TO MORE DIRECTIVE AND MEDIATOR-GENERATED QUESTIONING

As the mediation process unfolds, shifting from helping to probing to a more persuasive mode, this generally means progressing from *a non-directive, party-centered* focus to a more *directive, mediator-driven* one.

Non-Directive Interviewing.   In a non-directive interview, the interviewer cedes control to the interviewee to select the topics that he or she wishes to talk about; to decide whether, when and how particular issues are discussed; and to control the structure and pace of the interview. The interviewer does not impose his ideas on the interviewee; he assumes that the interviewee knows best what information is most important and how it should be discussed.[15] Non-directive interviewers start by asking *open-ended* questions (*"Tell us about the situation that brings us here"*), and their follow-up questions tend to be *party-centered*, in that they arise directly from the topics that the *interviewee* has initiated. (*"You briefly mentioned that you had words with the landlord when you vacated the apartment. Can you tell us more about that?"*) Even when helping others to make decisions, non-directive interviewers tend to ask questions, rather than making statements. (*"The tenant has proposed that you and he split the difference on your claim for two months' unpaid rent. What are your thoughts about that proposal?"*)

---

14. While there is little doubt as to the prevalence of this part of what mediators do, there is disagreement about the proper bounds of mediator persuasion. We will return to this subject in Chapters 9, 10 and 12.
15. STEWART & CASH, *supra* note 9, at 348-349.

Directive Interviewing. In more directive forms of interviewing, the *interviewer* controls the structure, form, pace and length of the interview. A central premise of the directive interview is that the interviewer is an expert who best knows the relevant subjects of inquiry and who, by controlling the questioning, can best develop the necessary information to guide the discussions and efficiently resolve the dispute.[16] Directive interviewers tend to ask more *closed* questions, about *interviewer-selected* subjects they deem important to the case. (*"Did you provide the landlord your forwarding address? Was it orally or in writing? It is important that I know about that."*) When moving the process toward decision making, they tend to make more directive statements, guiding interviewees toward action. (*"The tenant has offered to pay you one month's rent in order to avoid going to court. It's your decision, of course, but that doesn't seem like a bad offer in light of your admitted litigation risks, does it?"*)

Because different kinds of inquiry tend to elicit different kinds of information, all mediators find it necessary to employ a combination of non-directive and directive and party-centered and mediator-driven approaches. How these will be combined in a particular mediation will depend on the mediator's role orientation, the nature of the dispute, the disputants' communication styles and the context of the mediation.[17] For example, because non-directive questioning can be time-consuming, external factors such as significant time constraints tend to lead to more directive mediator behaviors.[18] In disputes that are chaotic or very complex or where a participant has difficulty presenting basic information coherently, more structuring by the mediator may be required. That said, in this text we will put forward a model of information gathering in which the mediator moves very gradually from non-directive, party-centered questions and statements to more directive, mediator-generated ones.

■ §6.5 INVITING AND ASSISTING THE PARTICIPANTS' OPENING STATEMENTS

After the mediator introduces and opens the proceedings, it is time to give the participants their first opportunity to describe the problems that have brought them to mediation. Consistent with our model, how should the mediator approach the beginning of the information gathering process?

■ §6.5.1 IN GENERAL, BEGIN WITH VERY OPEN QUESTIONS

In problem-solving and helping interviews, most texts strongly recommend that the interviewer start the process non-directively.[19] In the great majority of cases, we believe that the mediator should likewise ask the most open-ended questions possible and allow the participants uninterrupted time to share their perspectives and concerns. During this stage, the neutral should listen closely, demonstrating

---

16. *Id.*
17. Readers may wish to review §3.9 at this point.
18. *See generally* NANCY WELSH, *The Thinning Vision of Self-Determination in Court-Annexed Mediation: The Inevitable Price of Institutionalization?* 6 HARV. NEGOT. L. REV. 1 (2001).
19. *See, e.g.,* BINDER, BERGMAN, PRICE & TREMBLAY, *supra* note 12, at 64-77.

this through good eye contact, attentive posture and the like; take minimal notes; and encourage further disclosures by means of unobtrusive verbal and non-verbal prompts such as head nodding, "uh-huh," "take your time" and "go on." As the objective at this stage is to encourage as much disclosure as possible, the parties' opening statements should be elicited with as little direction from, or intervention by, the mediator as possible. Why?

■ **Open Questions Demonstrate Respect.** First, open-ended, non-directive questioning demonstrates that the mediator trusts that each party knows what is most important and has the ability to communicate his or her concerns effectively. Eventually the mediator may need to probe for sensitive information or engage in various persuasive or even confrontational tactics. Allowing the parties to describe the problem in their own time and their own way, is an important and respectful first step in establishing a trusting relationship that will make these later interventions easier to accomplish.

■ **Open Questions Give the Parties "Voice."** Second, open-ended, non-directive questioning promotes what procedural justice studies tell us many people in disputes prize most: the opportunity to be given "voice." Regardless of whether people settle their disputes and regardless of the terms on which they settle them, disputants *independently* value the opportunity to tell their stories to persons who are really listening, in a non-judgmental way.

■ **Open Questions Are Efficient.** Third, open-ended, non-directive questioning is efficient. Although responses to such questions may be lengthy, they tend to provide a great deal of information to the mediator and the other side—including essential information about what is most important to the speaker.[20] Well-formulated broad questions tend to produce information not only about the history of the dispute, but also important data about feelings, motivations and interests. Such responses help the mediator gauge the emotional content of the dispute, assess how the parties think and express themselves, and may provide a start on identifying mediable issues and diagnosing the dispute resolution barriers that exist.[21]

■ **Open Questions Model Good Communication.** Fourth, by asking open-ended questions and listening attentively, mediators demonstrate to the participants communication techniques that are useful for effective problem-solving: respect, patience, the willingness to listen without

---

20. *See* GAY GELLHORN, *Law and Language: An Empirically-Based Model for the Opening Moments of Client Interviews*, 4 CLINICAL L. REV. 321 (1998) (empirical study demonstrating that clients reveal crucial self-information in the opening moments of lawyer-client interviews as soon as they are given the opportunity to do so and that attentiveness, non-interruption and encouragement of complete responses by the interviewer produces better information and, in turn, more comprehensive and accurate advice).
21. Beginning mediators sometimes express the view that open-ended questions are inefficient, because they can produce long-winded and repetitious responses. Certainly some people ramble when given the opportunity and this be trying for mediators who are in a hurry or focused solely on the facts. But the speaker's response, even (or, perhaps, especially) if rambling and repetitive, often provides important diagnostic clues about how—and how effectively—the speaker thinks and communicates and what he or she feels is important. The mediator needs this information to diagnose the dispute accurately and intervene appropriately.

interruption and, importantly, interest in the other person's perspective. If the mediator behaves in these ways, chances are better that the parties will too.

■ **Open Questions Encourage Party Participation and Control.** Finally, as we stated in Chapter 1, one of the hallmarks of mediation is that it seeks to involve those most affected directly in the resolution of their own disputes. Open questions put to the parties encourage their broad participation and control, allowing them to feel early on that it is *their* process, rather than *yours*.

Formulating Initial Open-Ended Questions: How Open Is Open?   The openness of a question is a function of how much freedom the question gives the respondent to answer. Questions are almost infinitely variable in their degree of openness. Suppose that Sonia is interviewing for her first job after college. Compare these alternative opening questions by the interviewer:

"Very nice to meet you, Sonia. Why don't you tell me about yourself?" or

"Very nice to meet you, Sonia. Why don't you tell me about your educational background?" or

"Very nice to meet you, Sonia. Why don't you tell me how you've liked college?"

These are all open-ended questions, but they are obviously not equally open-ended. The first question invites Sonia to disclose anything she may feel comfortable disclosing. To this question, she might plausibly respond, *"I like classical jazz, bird watching and sports cars."*

The second question invites Sonia to talk generally about her educational background — which might mean her elementary school, high school, or college background — at her discretion. (*"Well, I was raised right here in Birmingham and went to the local public schools. Then I decided to go north for college and attended Boston University. . . . "*)

The third question still gives Sonia somewhat wide berth but limits her answer to what she's liked about college. (*"Well, I really liked the summer internship I got, and my conflict studies course. And I know it's dorky, but I really liked astronomy club too. . . . "*) How questions are formulated matters, because people — especially those seeking professional help — look for and take direction from their questioners, often quite literally.

In the mediation context, how neutrals invite parties to describe their conflict at the beginning of the process can significantly affect the nature and breadth of the information the parties share. Consider the following alternatives in a small claims court dispute between two former friends (Angelo and Hector) concerning Hector's allegation that Angelo failed to repay a $250 personal loan:

"Hector, let's begin with you. From your perspective, what's the situation that brings us here today?"

"Hector, we have studied the complaint in this matter and we know that you are claiming that that you and Angelo were friends, that Anglo has refused to repay a debt and that Angelo denies it. Can you tell us more about the situation as you see it?"

"Hector, we know you have a claim against Angelo. Talk about when things began to go wrong between the two of you."

What are the pros and cons of each approach?

Video Examples.   Now watch three extracts, in which two mediators in our consumer case and one of our child custody mediators, having completed their own openings, invite the parties to talk about the dispute that brought them to mediation. What forms of questions do they ask? Is there a connection between their invitations to speak and the responses they receive? Are the question forms effective, given each context? **Video Clip 6-H (1–3).**

When Should a Mediator Depart from Asking Open Questions at the Beginning of the Process?   Note that the child custody mediator got very short answers to his initial questions. Why? Was his approach to initial questioning justified?

In *When Talk Works,* a collection of ethnographic essays analyzing the work of practicing mediators from widely different areas of practice, social psychologist Kenneth Kressel closely analyzed a child custody mediation conducted by Frances Butler, a highly successful family mediator. He noted with interest when Butler departed from the "received (mediation) canon" by not allowing each parent to provide his or her perspective in narrative fashion. Instead she asked the parents a series of focused questions on specific topics grounded in the legal realities of divorce law. Why did she do this, Professor Kressel wanted to know. "I think that most people in parenting conflict are totally incapable of explaining their situation in a rational way—together in the same room, on a first meeting," "Her solution . . . ? Structure and control."[22]

Perhaps it makes sense to pose narrow initial questions in cases that are very complex or extremely emotionally charged. This may be the case especially when the parties demonstrate an inability to sit quietly during long narratives by the other side, constantly interrupt each other or otherwise act in an unruly fashion. In addition, because responses to open-ended questions tend to take time, somewhat more directive questioning is prevalent in many court-annexed settings, where a premium is placed on mediating lots of cases quickly. More directive forms of questions also tend to be used by "narrow-evaluative" mediators, who focus exclusively on the facts, law and positions of the parties. The narrowest and most directive form of question is the leading question—one that suggests the answer (*"So you've brought this claim to get your job back, right?"*). Given the goals of the opening stage of mediation, such questions would almost never seem advisable at the beginning of the process.

In our experience, many newer and law-trained mediators tend to exercise too much control in their information gathering and revert to closed questions much too early, regardless of the circumstances. (Do any of the mediators you have seen on video thus far come to mind?) Our advice is: resist the tendency to do so. By questioning directively, you are saying to the parties, "*I know the important topics here and I will ask you about them.*" You may be right about what would be

---

22. Kenneth Kressel, *Frances Butler: Questions That Lead to Answers in Child Custody Mediation, in* Deborah Kolb, When Talk Works: Profiles of Mediators 25-26 (1994).

important to a court (or perhaps to you if you were in the parties' shoes), but at the outset of the mediation you will generally have little idea about what is really driving the dispute from the parties' perspective. In general, trust the participants to tell you what's most important to them, by asking the broadest questions possible.

■ §6.5.2 WHO GETS TO SPEAK FIRST?

The mediator's management of the process usually involves deciding who speaks first. This can be important to disputants, because it's hard to listen to a lengthy statement by the other side before getting a chance to speak for the first time oneself. In addition, there is some evidence that going first creates a rhetorical advantage: The first speaker gets to decide the topics of discussion, with the second speaker feeling as if she must respond to the first speaker's frame of reference.[23] But someone has to go first. Who?

Where Litigation Has Been Initiated or Threatened. In legal matters, where litigation has already been started or threatened, the decision is usually an easy one: It is customary and logical to begin with the party who initiated the claim. Most sophisticated litigants know this, but many disputants may not. As the mediator, you can ease any potential feelings of unfairness (*"Hey! Why does* <u>she</u> *get to go first?"*) by simply explaining this custom: *"It's typical in these cases for the person who brings the lawsuit, the plaintiff, to speak first. Mrs. Ramirez, I understand that you're the person who is bringing this claim. Please take your time and tell us, from your perspective, why we are here."* This sequence can also be explained based on enhancing the mediator's comprehension: *"I will probably be better able to understand both of you if I learn first what the grievance is that led to this lawsuit."*

Where One Side Seeks to Change the Status Quo. In some situations, it is more logical to begin with the person whose desire to change a longstanding situation is at the heart of the conflict — regardless of who initiated the claim or the mediation.

For example, where a father has threatened to take legal action to stop his wife from carrying out her sudden plan to remove their four-year-old son from their home in Miami to her parents' home in Central America, the mediator's need to understand the situation may suggest that the wife be invited to speak first — even if it was her husband who had requested the mediation or would be the plaintiff in any litigation: *"Ms. Pena, your husband claims you have plans to leave next month and to take Alejandro with you to live in El Salvador. Your husband was concerned about this and arranged for our mediation center to set up this chance to talk before any court case is filed. It probably makes sense for all of us to hear from you first. Can you tell us about the situation, as you see it?"*

---

23. *See* Sara Cobb & Janet Rifkin, *Practice & Paradox: Deconstructing Neutrality in Mediation*, 16 Law & Soc. Inquiry 35, 56–59 (1991).

Where Both Sides Jointly Seek Mediation.   What about cases in which there is no litigation on the horizon and both parties have jointly initiated mediation? For example, suppose that two brothers who are partners in a troubled printing ink company jointly seek to mediate their business problems in order to avoid resorting to the courts. In such cases, the mediator has two choices: arbitrarily pick someone to go first or let the parties decide themselves. Which shall the mediator choose?

In cases where the dispute dynamics seem "cool" — where, judging from their demeanor, both parties seem reasonably calm — it may be advantageous to let the parties decide themselves: "*Charlie and Frank, you've jointly decided to try to resolve your business problems through mediation, and I commend you for that. Both of you will have uninterrupted time to get out the concerns that brought you here. Who would like to go first?*" If the parties can agree on this procedural issue, it may also establish a positive momentum for the substantive discussions to follow.

But if either party seems tense or angry, it is probably best for the mediator to make a command decision herself, avoiding an unnecessary argument over procedure: "*Charlie and Frank, you've jointly decided to try to resolve your business problems though mediation, and I commend you for that. Both of you will have uninterrupted time to get out the concerns that brought you here. Charlie, why don't you go first? Frank, I've provided you with a notepad so that, while Charlie is speaking, you can jot down any thoughts that occur to you.*"

If a Party Is Represented by Counsel, Who Speaks on Behalf of That Party?   In many forms of mediation — even including some legal matters — disputants routinely participate on their own, without anyone present to represent or assist them. In other kinds of cases, it is common for one or both parties to be represented by an attorney or lay advocate. To whom should the mediator look when it comes time to ask a represented party to make an opening statement?

Some mediators and theorists seek to minimize the role of lawyers in mediation. They view lawyers as impediments to the process and state a preference that they take a back seat to their client. Mediators with such a view might ask each party to provide his or her own opening statement and instruct the attorneys that "*this process is about the parties,*" and that their role is to sit to the side and provide backup support.

Do you think this approach is realistic? Does your answer depend on the kind of dispute? If you were retained by a client to represent her in mediation and the mediator instructed you that you could only talk within limited constraints, how would you feel? How might your client? If you are like many lawyers, you might fight back. As attorney Brendan Sullivan famously declared in the Iran-Contra hearings when instructed by a United States Senator that his client, Oliver North, would have to object to senators' questions himself: "*Sir, I am not a potted plant. I am here as a lawyer!*"

The best advice we can give you when inviting a represented party's opening statement is to look generally in the direction of lawyer and client, say something like "*Mrs. Peterson, you initiated this mediation and it probably makes sense for you to begin. I would be glad to hear from either you or your attorney.*" In many cases, the lawyer will proceed to give the opening statement. (Even highly sophisticated and articulate clients probably want and expect it, and some lawyers want to be perceived by the client as earning their fee.) As the mediation unfolds, the mediator will ordinarily be able to find opportunities to involve the disputants more directly.[24]

In the extract that follows, watch how one of the mediators in our premises liability case (he is mostly off-camera) invites the plaintiff to participate in setting out his view of things and how his lawyer reacts to this suggestion. Did the mediator respond appropriately to the lawyer's stated concerns? Would you have handled this situation any differently? **Video Clip 6-I.**

§6.5.3 RESPONDING TO INITIAL PARTY NARRATIVES

If the first disputant provides a detailed narrative or impassioned, partisan response to your opening question, what should you do next? Tempting though it may be, asking follow-up questions is risky at this early stage. Remember that there are two (or more) disputants in this "interview," not just one. The other side may be anxiously waiting for his turn and hypersensitive to any hint of favoritism. Time spent asking follow-up questions (especially detailed follow-up questions) of the first speaker may seem unfair to the other party.

What If Your Open Questions Produce a Limited Response?   Sometimes disputants or their attorneys provide very limited opening statements in response to even the most open-ended invitations. There can be a variety of reasons for this. Some disputants may be distrustful of the mediation process or fearful of or reluctant to upset the other side. Some may be discomfited by the openness of a question or unsure about the boundaries of a proper or relevant response. Some people, for personal or cultural reasons, are uncomfortable being in the conversational limelight. Some attorneys, seeking to avoid predictable arguments or eager to start negotiating, prefer to shortcut this part of the process and to proceed to private caucuses as soon as possible; as a result, they provide cursory answers to even the most open-ended questions.

So what can you do if, having asked one side a question such as "*Tell us from your perspective why we're here,*" the respondent says something like "*Well, you've read the complaint, haven't you? It's all there. We're suing for $75,000 in damages, plus our attorney's fees. What do you want to know?*"

The one thing we think you should *not* do if this happens is to revert immediately to closed questions. There are a number of less directive options. You can:

■ Ignore the attempt to provide a limited response and persist tactfully in seeking a more narrative one, emphasizing your *own* need for information. ("*Of course I've carefully read your complaint and have a general sense of*

---

24. Our recommended approach here is a pragmatic one. As a philosophical matter, we believe that encouraging the participants to take an active role in mediation increases the chances of achieving quality resolutions. *See* Harold I. Abramson, Mediation Representation: Advocating as a Problem-Solver in Any Country or Culture 242 (2010). We return to the role of lawyers in mediation in Chapter 13.

the legal claims at issue. But for me to be helpful here, I need to know more about how each of you here sees what happened, and what's most important to you. So it would be very helpful if you could tell me in detail about the situation that brings us here, in your own words.")

- Emphasize *each party's* need to learn more about the other side's perspective. (*"Mediation participants often think that you know what the other side is going to say before they even say it. But I have found that people in disputes often have misunderstandings about each other's past conduct and intentions. It's important for this process that each of you gets the opportunity to hear how the other side views the situation, above and beyond any technical legal claims you may have.")*

- Use the information you have to ask focused but relatively open-ended questions. (*"I have carefully read your complaint and see that you have claimed wrongful termination and are requesting lost wages, emotional distress damages and attorney's fees. Perhaps we could start with your talking about your job history and the circumstances of your termination?"*)

- Use minimal prompts, followed by silence. *"Tell us more about your claims"* might work. In other situations, so might *"uh-huh"* or *"go on."* By using silence, coupled with continued eye contact and attentive posture, you convey the message that you eagerly await (and expect) the speaker's statements once she has gathered her thoughts. Most people are uncomfortable with silence and will fill in the "dead air."

Usually one or another of these approaches will cause people to speak more openly. If not, there may be some real impediment to their participation that needs to be explored before proceeding further.

Summarizing.   However the parties' opening presentations emerge, their conclusion presents an initial opportunity for the mediator to demonstrate understanding and develop rapport by synthesizing what has been said. For example: *"So, Mr. Muhammed, to summarize, you were hired as an account associate three years ago. You believe that you did everything that was asked of you and that your previous supervisor's evaluations were quite positive. As you see it, things turned bad when Ms. Collins, the new supervisor, took over a year and a half ago. You feel that her evaluations were unfair from the beginning and did not reflect the quality of the work you did. You believe that your ethnicity was the reason for your termination. Since your termination, you have not found another job and you have not been sleeping well. You are suing for lost wages and emotional distress damages. Does that capture the basic situation as you see it?"*

This task presents the neutral with a choice: summarize each party's opening immediately at its conclusion or wait until both sides have spoken to present two summaries back to back. What factors might argue for one approach versus the other? It also poses a decision as the content of a summary: What are the pros and cons of presenting a detailed as opposed to a more general recap? However this is accomplished, impartiality requires that if one side's opening is summarized, the other party receive a summary that is comparable.

■ §6.6 THROUGHOUT THE PROCESS: THE CRITICAL IMPORTANCE OF GOOD LISTENING

On the cable television program, "Inside the Actor's Studio," host James Lipton often asks his guests the following question: *"When working with other actors, how important is good listening?"* His guests, from Kevin Kline to Meryl Streep to Matthew Broderick, invariably give a version of the following answer: *"It's the most important thing. It's everything!"*

Ask mediators the same question, and you will likely get the same answer.

Good listening sounds easy, but it isn't. Listening effectively means listening and observing with a "quiet mind"[25] — with minimal distraction caused by your own reactions or concerns. (*"There were too many 'ums' and 'ahs' in my last question." "I don't believe that answer." "What should I ask next?" "Is that his real hair color?"*)

Listening well means paying careful attention; maintaining good eye contact, an open and attentive posture and an attitude of focus; and having patience without (at least for now) judging. It means being "in the moment,"[26] working hard to understand the situation as the speaker sees it. Perhaps because they are so very busy and tend to value talking more than listening, Americans in general are not good listeners.[27] (If you want to test yourself in response to this criticism, you might try keeping a running count of how many times your mind wanders during your next class or phone call with a friend!)

Kinds of Listening in Mediation. Good listening in mediation is all the more challenging because, as the process unfolds, effective mediators must listen and gather information for many different purposes. Because we will discuss this subject in greater detail in Chapter 7, here we emphasize six particularly critical kinds of listening in mediation:

- ■ **For Content.** Like all interviewers, mediators must attend carefully to the factual content of the parties' narratives. (*"When did your neighbor put up the fence?" "How many cabinets have been delivered and installed?" "What was the last offer the defendant made?"*)

- ■ **For Empathy.** Effective mediators must also listen in a way that demonstrates empathy — a nonjudgmental understanding of each party's view of things.[28] This requires that the mediator put herself in a "believing" mode[29]

---

25. Beer & Stief, *supra* note 2, at 68-69.
26. *Id.* at 68. *See also* Leonard L. Riskin, *The Contemplative Lawyer: On the Potential Contributions of Mindfulness Meditation to Law Students, Lawyers, and Their Clients,* 7 Harv. Negot. L. Rev. 1, 49-53 (2002). In seeking to enhance the likelihood that they and the parties will be open to hearing all perspectives and to otherwise being fully "present," some mediators begin the process with a meditative period of silence. For an example of such an opening, see Video Clip 6-TM-1.
27. *See, e.g.,* Stewart & Cash, *supra* note 9, at 38 (citing surveys of hundreds of U.S. corporations indicating that poor listening skills create a major barrier in nearly all positions from entry level jobs to CEOs).
28. *See, e.g.,* Robert H. Mnookin, Scott Peppet & Andrew S. Tulumello, Beyond Winning 47 (2000). (Pointing out that empathy is not the same thing as sympathy, which has to do with feeling "for" a person. Rather, empathy is a "value-neutral mode of observation" in which the listener tries to understand how the speaker sees the world, regardless of whether he agrees with it.)
29. Mark Weisberg & Jean Koh Peters, *Experiments in Listening,* 57 J. Legal Educ. 432-434 (2007).

in which she tries to put all skepticism out of her mind in order to under-stand and accept each person's perspectives. To the extent that those per-spectives include strong emotions, listening for empathy requires paying close attention to those feelings, both those that are expressed verbally and those that are revealed nonverbally.

■ **For Needs, Interests, Goals and Priorities.** Mediators must listen carefully to try to identify the parties' underlying interests, to get at the needs that explain why disputants are saying what they are saying or taking the posi-tions they are taking. (*"She says she won't agree to let the kids visit dad during the week. Hmmm . . . I wonder if that's because she's concerned that they won't keep up with their homework . . . "*)

■ **For Ultimate Negotiation Issues.** Mediators must listen carefully in order to identify the subjects to be negotiated if the matter is to be resolved, even-tually to be able to help the parties create a workable agenda for the bar-gaining/problem-solving phase of the process. (*"So it seems that one topic is what kind of time-sharing plan will work for both of you. Might another be how you help the kids make transitions from one household to the other?"*)

■ **For Evaluation.** Listening for evaluation means listening skeptically and doubtfully, with an eye to the possibility of providing helpful feedback later in the process.[30] It is the opposite of nonjudgmental, empathic listen-ing. In legal cases, it can involve considering how each side's factual account and the admissible evidence line up against governing legal or other appli-cable norms in order to assess the parties' competing claims. It also means actively indulging one's doubts about how the parties' ideas and proposed solutions stack up against external realities (*"I understand why you're mak-ing that offer, but can you borrow enough to make it work?"*) Listening for evaluation comes naturally to most lawyer-mediators and can pay off in the later stages of mediation. But because it can interfere with other kinds of attention, it must be kept within proper boundaries in the early going.

■ **For Diagnosis.** Finally, as Chapter 2 suggests, mediators listen for the purpose of discerning obstacles to settlement. Is a key barrier to negotiated resolution a lack of information on the part of one or more parties? Widely differing and overconfident assessments about the likely trial outcome? A counterproductive negotiating style? A misperception that the parties' interests are diametrically opposed? Listening for diagnosis helps the medi-ator determine what questions to ask and what statements to make throughout the mediation process and can sometimes produce surprising breakthroughs in the parties' conflict.

As an example of attempting to listen for diagnosis, watch the following extract from our child custody case, *Fitzgerald v. Fitzgerald*. (It may be helpful to review the summary of this case at the end of Chapter 1.) Based on this brief exchange, what are possible barriers to resolution in this dispute? **Video Clip 6-J.**

---

30. *Id.*

As you can see, mediators are concerned about information that goes well beyond the facts and evidence that support the parties' contentions. (Indeed, the deepest listening is often about what is *not* said.) Not all mediators listen on all these levels; the extent to which they do will depend on how they define their role, the nature of the dispute and the setting in which the mediation is occurring.

These multiple modes of listening will continue well beyond the early stages of the mediation we are discussing here. They will bear keeping in mind as we chronologically dissect the mediation process.

■ §6.7 A BRIEF NOTE ON NOTE-TAKING

While we are on the topic of listening, it makes sense to talk about note-taking as well, because the two subjects go hand in hand.

Note-taking in mediation, as in other professional interviewing, is a necessary evil, with pros and cons that will be obvious to you. As in a lecture course, good note-taking in mediation can improve your attention in important ways and make it more likely that you will process and later recall important information. In mediation, it can also be a sign to the participants that you are considering their competing presentations with "procedural care."

But a mediation is not a lecture course. It is a setting in which you are also trying to establish a positive connection with the parties, who may be under stress. Note-taking interferes with eye contact and rapport-building. It may prevent you from attending to important nonverbal cues. It can also bias the presentation of information: Taking a lot of notes can be inherently reinforcing to the speaker or conversely may distract the speaker from her "flow" because of anxiety about all that information you are scribbling down.

So how does a mediator maximize the advantages of note-taking while minimizing its disadvantages? While note-taking is a highly individual practice, here are a few suggestions:

> ### Suggestions for Note-Taking
>
> - **Ask permission and tell the parties what you are going to do with your notes when you are done.** *"Is it okay if I take notes? This will help me do a better job by helping me remember the key issues." "At the end of this mediation, I will destroy my notes, so you can be sure that this is a confidential process."*
> - **Take the fewest notes possible.** Early on, write down only the essential information in the case: for example, the parties' names, a chronology of key dates, essential facts and potential negotiating issues. Write down key words, noting topics that you want to come back to later. (Later on in the process, record specific offers, counteroffers that are mentioned and possible options for settlement that occur to you.) Use any form of shorthand or abbreviation that works for you. Less is more; your memory for the main points is probably better than you think. And you can always ask a participant to repeat or clarify details your notes leave out.
> - **Experiment with preselected categories of information about which you will keep notes.** If your note-taking is limited to just the *facts*, you are probably
>
> *continues on next page >*

missing the boat. As the parties speak, try to take deliberate note of their possible underlying *feelings* and *interests*; any dubious aspects of their presentations; the actual and potential negotiating topics they raise; and any *barriers to resolution* you can (at least tentatively) diagnose. Experiment with different ways of recording this information that work for you.

- **Try to maintain eye contact during your note-taking.** This is self-explanatory but not so easy to do. You don't want to have your head buried in a notepad rather than being attentive to the people in the room.
- **Take notes evenhandedly during each party's presentations.** Balance is necessary in order to be perceived as impartial.

In Chapter 4, we discussed co-mediation as an alternative to working alone. Might having a partner help alleviate some of the challenges of deep listening and note-taking? If so, how?

■ §6.8 ENCOURAGING AN UNSTRUCTURED CONVERSATION: THE PROCESS OF "EXCHANGE"

The last part of the opening stage of the mediation, utilized by mediators who seek to encourage open communication between the parties, is a process of "exchange," in which the mediator gives the parties an opportunity, for at least a few minutes, to respond to each other's initial presentations and arguments in an *unstructured* way, without imposing any kind of topical agenda on them.[31]

At first blush, this seems as simple as pie. When both parties have completed their opening statements, the mediator can turn to the first speaker and say something like, "*OK, Mr. Smith, both you and Ms. Jones have had an opportunity to set out your perspectives. Would you like to respond now to what Ms. Jones has just said?*" When Mr. Smith is done, the mediator can turn to Ms. Jones and say, "*Ms. Jones, would you care to respond to that?*" This kind of back and forth can go on, without interrupting or questioning, for as long as the mediator thinks it is productive.

 Watch how one of our mediators utilizes the exchange process in *Wilson v. DiLorenzo*. What do you think of this approach? **Video Clip 6-K.**

The Benefits from an Exchange.   Not all mediators utilize an exchange process. However, if handled well, it can serve a number of useful purposes:

■ First, open exchange continues the process of non-directive information gathering, signaling to the parties, "*this is your dispute, and you are encouraged to talk about whatever is important to you.*"

■ Second, whereas the parties' opening statements are likely to be rehearsed or even scripted, their subsequent exchanges will generally be spontaneous and often raw and impassioned. As a result, the mediator can learn more

---

31. *See* BEER & STEIF, *supra* note 2, at 37-41.

about the parties' real interests and needs — what is really important to them and is driving their stance. This can be critical in diagnosing barriers to settlement and in later coming up with ideas for resolution.

- Third, during such an exchange, additional negotiation issues often surface, going beyond the topics the parties identified in their (often canned) opening statements.

- Fourth, if managed well, exchange can be educational — a chance for the participants to communicate more effectively than in the past and to begin to understand each other's perspectives. But to accomplish this, the mediator must often play the role of conversation "traffic cop," intervening to correct distortions and setting and enforcing ground rules to ensure that expressions of strong feeling are stated productively, and that each side listens to the other even if the emotional temperature in the room is rising.

The Risks of an Exchange.   Because it is unstructured, it is during this stage of the process that disputants are most likely to express strong feelings of resentment, mistrust and anger. If a mediator does not exercise strong management skills, an unstructured exchange process can sometimes spiral out of control, leading to angry, chaotic discussions and even the threat of one side walking out. Therefore, if the disputants have exhibited great hostility during their opening statements, speaking over each other or otherwise acting rudely, it may be preferable to skip this stage and to proceed directly to a more structured effort at expanding information, in which the mediator plays a more active role. (We discuss this in detail in Chapter 7.)

Asking About Desired Outcomes?   At some point in the opening phase of the process, the mediator and the participants may begin to wonder what kind of resolution each party envisions. Assuming that neither side has offered this information, what do you see as the pros and cons of asking for it at this early stage? On what might your answer depend?

§6.9 KEY COMMUNICATION ENHANCING INTERVENTIONS

In this section, we explore techniques that are useful in encouraging constructive communication during the initial stages of the process and throughout the entire mediation:

- Active Listening
- Pointing Out Agreements
- Productive Reframing
- Clarifying Meaning
- Coaching People to Express Their Anger Productively
- Stating and Enforcing Ground Rules

■ §6.9.1 ESTABLISH EMPATHY AND ENCOURAGE COMMUNICATION THROUGH ACTIVE LISTENING

For those in the helping professions, the skill of active (also known as empathic or reflective) listening — paraphrasing back to the speaker the essential content, feelings or interests expressed in the speaker's statement — is an essential one to master.[32] Mediation is no exception. When a mediator is able to distill and reflect — without parroting — the key elements of a party's statement back to that speaker, at least five important objectives are achieved:

- ■ The speaker knows that what he said has registered and has been understood. The feeling that "*I am really being listened to*" is intrinsically rewarding for all human beings. When a person feels listened to, he is more likely to trust a person in a helping role and to accept his or her guidance.

- ■ The speaker knows that his ideas and feelings are acceptable and that he is not being judged. Effective active listening conveys the message that "*I understand what you are saying and feeling. It is your frame of reference that matters, not mine.*"

- ■ The speaker hears the essence of what the mediator thinks he has said and can verify or correct that understanding. This feedback process often encourages further elaboration and helps the speaker better understand his *own* feelings and motivations.

- ■ In the context of mediation, active listening can enable *the other party* to better hear (and perhaps empathize with) the speaker's message. Hearing an accepting message stated by a disinterested neutral can lend legitimacy to an opponent's previously discredited position or feelings.

- ■ By identifying the core interests and feelings embodied in participants' statements, the *mediator* is helped to understand the less tangible and often unspoken aspects of a dispute that may hold the key to identifying and improving on potential solutions later on.

Active listening statements in mediation are just that — statements embodying what the *speaker* — not the mediator — thinks and feels about the situation, with which the mediator is expressing empathy, not sympathy or agreement. (The latter could jeopardize the parties' perception of the mediator's impartiality.) Starting the statement with "*You*" can help ensure this; useful stems include "*It sounds as if you . . .* " or "*So you're saying that . . .* " or "*You're angry about . . .* " or "*What's important to you is that. . . .* " (It is generally better to avoid using the same formulations over and over.) If the mediator is not certain whether her statement has captured the speaker's meaning correctly or completely, she can add a verifying question such as "*Is that right?*" or "*Am I understanding you correctly?*"[33]

---

32. *See* ALFRED BENJAMIN, The Helping Interview 46-47 (2d ed. 1974); STEWART & CASH, *supra* note 9, at 39.
33. This technique of confirming the mediator's understanding has also been called completing an "empathy loop." *See* MNOOKIN, PEPPET & TULUMELLO, *supra* note 28, at 63-66 (2000). *See also* SHERRY CORMIER & BILL CORMIER, Interviewing Strategies for Helpers 107-108 (1998).

In addition to gaining clarity, such verifying questions show respect for a speaker by demonstrating a desire to get her meaning right. Finally, because active listening is aimed (in part) at conveying empathy, the mediator should endeavor to employ this tool evenhandedly with both parties.

Three Types of Active Listening.   As we have said, active listening responses can reflect back the *content, feelings* or *interests* underlying the speaker's statement. Suppose that the husband participating in a difficult divorce mediation says, with feeling: *"Ever since our separation, I've been completely unable to concentrate at my job. It's been going on now for over six months now. He hasn't said anything yet, but I can tell me boss is starting to lose patience with me!"* A mediator wanting to reflect the content of the husband's statement might say, *"So your separation has been seriously affecting your performance at work."* A mediator trying to reflect the feelings underlying the statement might say something like *"So is sounds like this whole thing, the separation and all, has been really quite stressful for you."* And a mediator wanting to reflect (and test out for diagnostic purposes) the interests underlying the statement might say *"So would I be correct in assuming that you're worried about job security and being the kind of family provider you want to be going forward?"*

Challenges in Active Listening.   Beginning mediators (and some experienced ones) often have difficulty learning to use and master active listening. Some neutrals are not wholly comfortable when dealing with strong emotions. Can a mediator to whom "feelings talk" does not come naturally overcome these inhibitions? If you are such a person, how might you do so?

Others learning the skill of active listening sometimes ask, "How frequently should one use this intervention before it begins to seem forced and loses its effectiveness?" In our experience, a little carefully chosen active listening generally goes a long way in mediation, especially when focused on unpacking psychological aspects of the conflict that seem most salient or highly charged to the disputants. If selectively and artfully done, it is a powerful communications tool. If overdone, it can appear manipulative and false.

Sometimes, challenges in the use of active listening are presented by the parties themselves. For example, while most participants convey at least a few perceptions or feelings with which one can empathize, in rare situations a party may come across as so unrealistic or unreasonable that it may feel false to appear to validate or accept (even momentarily) their perspective. What should a mediator who feels that way do? In other situations, use of this communications tool is challenging because feelings talk is resisted by one or more of the participants. (This may be a product of an individual's family or cultural background.) Should the neutral steer clear of feelings in such situations? If not, can such inhibitions be addressed and overcome? How?

Active Listening Examples.   Here are two examples of active listening in action. The first involves one of our child custody mediators working with Jane Fitzgerald, the mother. The second involves one of our consumer mediators working with Bernice Wilson, the homeowner. Do you think these examples are effective? If so, what makes them so? If not, why? **Video Clip 6-L (1–2).**

▪ §6.9.2 DECREASE PERCEPTUAL BARRIERS BY POINTING OUT AGREEMENTS AND COMMONALITIES

Recall from our discussion in Chapter 2 how people in conflict tend to exaggerate their differences, denying their own contributions to a dispute, seeing the other side wholly at fault and assuming that their interests are diametrically opposed. These perceptions are likely to be most pronounced in the beginning stages of the mediation, because the parties have been mentally rehearsing their arguments and gearing up for a fight. A mediator can moderate this dynamic and improve the climate for eventual negotiations by pointing out agreements and commonalities that come to light during the opening stage.

Pointing Out Common Goals and Interests.   As we discussed in Chapter 2, even people locked in bitter conflict often have shared, or at least compatible, interests. The mediator can periodically remind the disputants of these shared interests. In our child custody mediation, one of the mediators made statements like, "*You're both concerned about having a relationship with the children*" and "*You're both interested in developing a plan for an ongoing relationship with the children that does not depend on somebody else imposing a decision.*" In a similar vein, one asked Bob and Jane if either had brought photographs of the kids to the mediation. (They hadn't.) The basic message imparted was "*Keep all that you share in mind as you think about this current disagreement.*"

Pointing Out Positive Attributes and Relationships.   In cases where the parties have had a relationship, it is sometimes useful to ask them to acknowledge positive aspects of that relationship or of the other person. For example, if a landlord accuses a long-term tenant of scratching the living room floor as the reason for refusing to return a security deposit (an assertion the tenant vigorously disputes), the mediator can ask the landlord whether the tenant moved out when she said she would, whether all of her rental payments were made on time and whether the rest of the apartment was in good condition. Statements like "*It sounds as if you had a long history of working together*" or "*while you dispute some of her fees here, you do view her as an honest and competent accountant*" can sometimes help people stop from demonizing each other and reduce the tension of a difficult conflict.

Pointing Out Agreements as They Occur.   If the parties can reach agreement on even a small disputed matter, the mediator can reinforce it to create a sense of accomplishment. "*Great!*" the mediator can say. "*You've agreed to get a speech pathologist's opinion about Megan's language delays. You should feel good about that. Let's go on and discuss these two other issues.*" Or when weak claims or defenses in the pleadings are abandoned by one party or conceded by the other at an early stage of the mediation of a lawsuit, neutrals often commend this progress.

Pointing Out Common Predicaments.   In a pinch, where the participants seem to agree on nothing at all, the mediator can point out their common predicament. Statements like, "*Boy, this is a difficult situation for both of you*" can create a sense of a shared problem needing resolution. Indeed, it is the shared uncertainty about how a court might resolve contested claims that motivates many legal dispute settlements. We revisit this topic in later chapters.

■ §6.9.3 REDUCE PERCEPTUAL DISTORTIONS BY CLARIFYING MEANING

We saw in Chapter 2 that when people are in conflict and their strong emotions are engaged, they often are unable to listen to their counterparts without distortion. Consumed with their own thoughts and feelings, they mishear what the other person says, attribute hostile motives to their counterparts and misconstrue their conduct and intentions. When this occurs, effective mediators intervene promptly to reduce distortions and clarify meaning.

Clarifying the Other Side's Statements.   In one of our child custody mediations, Bob said, "*In terms of discipline, when I described to you the situation when I came home and found everything in chaos, that's very typical. You know, what she calls 'relaxed,' I call 'lax.' I mean you can take that too far. Relaxed is great, but lax is irresponsible when you are raising two small children. I think that Megan would be much more prepared to go to school and start succeeding in school right away had she had the cooperation in both parents in working on her verbal skills and encouraging her to read out loud more and to speak more and articulate things.*"

Suppose, in response to this, Jane had blurted out, "*You see? He thinks that Megan's speech delays are all my fault!*" After such an exchange, the mediator might inject, "*Is that what you are saying, Bob? Are you saying that Jane is solely to blame for Megan's speech delays?*" to which Bob might answer, "*Of course not. What I mean is that we both need to cooperate in treating this as a serious matter and get her the professional attention she needs.*" If the mediator thinks that Jane still doesn't "get" it, he can ask her for her understanding of Bob's message: "*OK, Jane; what is Bob saying?*"

Clarifying the Other Side's Intentions.   In our consumer mediation, Bernice Wilson was furious that none of her calls about construction delays to Frank DiLorenzo, the contractor, were ever returned. She felt totally disrespected. She said, "*I went through making fifty million phone calls because, see, the thing that really kills me is that had my check bounced, had the money not been there, you better believe I would have received a phone call. Had my answering machine not worked and the check bounced, they would have been sending me a letter in the mail. It would have been a certified letter in the mail. It could have been a sheriff at my door, could have been anything. . . . I am just still so upset.*"

A mediator who understood the feelings behind Bernice's statement might say: "*So it sounds as if you felt like Frank just blew you off.*" If Bernice responded "*Yes!*" the mediator could turn to Frank and ask, "*Was that your intention, Frank?*" (to which Frank might answer, for example, that he was stressed with too many jobs, that he didn't mean any disrespect and that he's sorry Bernice's job got lost in the shuffle). Intervening promptly to disentangle the *impact* of an actor's conduct from his or her *intent* can greatly improve the mediation climate.[34]

---

34. *See* Douglas Stone, Bruce Patton & Sheila Heen, Difficult Conversations 44-57 (1999).

▪ §6.9.4 REDUCE THE STING OF ANGRY, NEGATIVE STATEMENTS BY "PRODUCTIVE REFRAMING"

Reframing is an established counseling technique therapists use to help their patients see themselves in new, more constructive ways. A patient who thinks of himself as "stubborn" is encouraged to view himself as "valuing autonomy." A patient who sees herself as "perpetually lazy" is helped to see that if she is lazy at all, it is only in specific settings, not most of the time. The purpose of reframing is to reduce patients' negative generalizations about themselves and to redirect their focus to more positive aspects.[35]

In mediation, reframing is an important tool used to reduce the sting of disputants' hostile or otherwise unproductive statements about each other or the situation and to redirect how they see things. Mediators cannot prevent persons in the heat of conflict from making such statements, but they can try to minimize the destructive aspects of such statements while preserving their positive aspects. How?[36]

Reframing a Positional Statement as an Interest-Based Statement.   Suppose in our earlier dog bite case, the plaintiff said, "*My son already got bitten by their dog once and was seriously injured. We won't be satisfied unless they get rid of the mangy beast.*" The mediator could reframe this by saying, "*So your primary concern here is to ensure your son's and your family's physical safety?*" This reframing removes both the possibly extreme demand ("*get rid of*") and the negative characterization of the dog ("*a mangy beast*"), and focuses instead on the speaker's underlying interest in security.

Reframing a Judgment Statement as a Problem Statement.   Suppose a disputant says, "*Why should I trust her to pay me anything? She already stiffed me once. I wouldn't believe anything this woman tells me!*" The mediator could reframe this by saying, "*So from your perspective any acceptable resolution would have to contain a way of protecting you in the event of nonpayment?*" This removes the blame ("*she stiffed me!*") and judgments about trust and believability from the speaker's statement and focuses instead on the problem to be solved—the speaker's need to be reassured that any settlement he agrees to has "teeth."

Reframing a Statement About the Past as a Shared Problem About the Future.   Suppose that in our child custody dispute Jane said, "*I can't believe what Bob said about me in front of the kids when he brought them over last week. He said that he hoped at least that I had cleaned up the kitchen this month so that the kids wouldn't have to eat like pigs. Can you believe that?*" to which Bob responded, "*That's nothing compared to her telling them I'm a wife-beater.*" The mediator could reframe this by saying, "*So one of the issues we have to discuss is how you'll talk about each other in the presence of your children.*" This reframing shifts the focus from the past to the future and recasts each side's accusation as a mutual problem to be jointly solved.

---

35. Cormier & Cormier, *supra* note 33, at 395-399.
36. This discussion is adapted from an excellent treatment of the subject in Mark D. Bennett & Scott Hughes, The Art of Mediation 101-104 (2d ed. 2005).

Reframing an Individual Problem as a Shared Problem.   Suppose in our child custody case Bob said, "*I insist that the kids live with me and my parents. They can visit Jane on weekends.*" Jane says, "*I'm Megan and Ryan's mother! The kids should be with me. They can visit Bob on weekends.*" The mediator could reframe this exchange by saying, "*Both of you are very concerned about maintaining a strong relationship with your children and having quality time with them. I cannot say that about all the couples I meet.*" This reframing converts individual positions into statements of a shared problem and focuses on the positive aspects of the exchange.

Potential Risks in Reframing.   Like active listening, productive reframing, to be effective, must reflect some key element of the speaker's statement. But reframing is different from active listening in that the responder deliberately tweaks or "massages" the original message to make it more positive-sounding. By finding something productive in even the most negative of statements, the mediator tries to lower the emotional temperature in the room.

But note the risks in doing this: If the mediator appears to be a Pollyanna about conflict or overly manipulative, sweeping strong disagreements under the rug and pretending they don't exist, this can be upsetting and seem disrespectful to angry disputants. If in the process of reframing a message, the mediator *distorts* it, this can infuriate the speaker. Reframing is thus a technique that requires a good deal of practice to ensure that it retains the essence of the speaker's message, while also reducing its potential sting. Keeping this in mind, do any of the above examples seem disingenuous to you? Would you have confidence that all of them would be effective? And technique aside, might the goal of calming down a heated conflict be problematic in any way? How?[37]

■ **§6.9.5   REDUCE TENSION BY COACHING PEOPLE TO EXPRESS THEIR ANGER PRODUCTIVELY**

Effective mediators also assist mediation participants in expressing their feelings constructively, not destructively. As the mediation scholar Keith Allred has written,

> It has become popular, even in works that receive considerable attention in scholarly circles, to advise people to "vent" their anger. This advice draws on a metaphor that compares anger to a gas whose pressure in a sealed vessel is building and can only be released by releasing it. . . . [But] venting is . . . an exercise in rehearsing the very attributions that arouse anger in the first place. As a consequence, rather than giving psychological relief from anger, research indicates that venting actually makes the individuals even angrier.[38]

---

37. Some mediators—especially those with a transformative orientation—oppose softening or diluting conflict in this way. According to this view, intervening to defuse emotional exchanges is inconsistent with the disputants' choices regarding how they wish to talk about their conflict—matters that should be left within the control of the parties. *See, e.g.,* ROBERT A. BARUCH BUSH & JOSEPH P. FOLGER, The Promise of Mediation: A Transformative Approach to Conflict 153-154 (2d ed. 2005).

38. KEITH G. ALLRED, *Anger and Retaliation in Conflict: The Role of Attribution, in* The Handbook of Conflict Resolution 249-250 (MORTON DEUTSCH & PETER T. COLEMAN eds., 2000). The idea that expressing negative emotion is cathartic and that it reduces violence has a long and distinguished intellectual history, dating back to Aristotle, Sigmund Freud and Konrad Lorenz. But empirical research has consistently demonstrated that it is not true. *See, e.g.,* SUZANNE K. STEINMETZ, Violence in the Family 7, 14-16, 305-306 (1971); LEONARD BERKOWITZ, *Stimulus/Response: The Case for Bottling Up Rage,* 7 PSYCHOLOGY TODAY 24-31 (July 1973) (summarizing research).

It can be tempting to allow extended displays of strong emotion early in the process — in part because the parties seem to need to get things off their chests and because in their unrehearsed spontaneity they may reveal a great deal about their true concerns. But some expressions of feeling are more *de*structive than *constructive*. How can the mediator encourage emotional expressions while curbing their potentially negative impact?

Empirical studies suggest that mediators are most effective in resolving disputes when they neither squelch the expression of strong feelings nor let the expression of strong feelings get out of hand.[39] They allow disputants to talk to each other long and freely enough to permit them to express their feelings fully but do not let exchanges continue when the discussions begin to get hostile and polarized.[40] They are able to discriminate between constructive and destructive communication patterns and, during periods of increased conflict intensity, intervene more frequently in order to moderate the exchange.[41]

Encourage "I" Statements.   One way to help mediation participants express their anger productively is by helping them turn angry *"you"* statements into more productive *"I"* statements. A psychologist of aggression explains it this way:

> [There is] an important distinction between verbal aggression and talking about one's feelings. When a person attacks someone verbally (for example, when he curses *"you bitch,"* or screams *"I'll kill you"* . . .) he provides aggressive stimuli to himself and his listeners [that] can evoke further aggressive reactions. However, if he merely describes his own emotion (saying, for example, *"I'm boiling mad"*) . . . can be informative and even beneficial. You let the other person know how he has affected you, and this might cause him to make amends or change his behavior. You give him *cognitive* feedback so that he is less likely to hurt you inadvertently again.[42]

A powerful illustration of an "I statement" intervention occurred in one of our child custody mediations. By asking Jane to speak in "I" rather than "you" statements, the mediator helped move the conversation from one of recrimination and blame to one in which she was able to communicate her deepest needs to Bob. **Video Clip 6-M.**

▪ §6.9.6 ENSURE BALANCE BY STATING AND ENFORCING GROUND RULES

The mediator must exert control over the process so that it does not get out of hand, with one side dominating the discussion or intimidating the other, or with both sides engaging in downward, escalating expressions of hostility. One way to do this is to ensure balance by stating (or restating) — and enforcing — ground rules.

---

39. WILLIAM A. DONAHUE, *Communicative Competence in Mediators, in* Mediation Research 322, 327-331 (KENNETH KRESSEL et al. eds., 1989). *See also* J.Z. RUBIN, Dynamics of Third Party Intervention: Kissinger in the Mideast (1981).
40. DONAHUE, *supra* note 39, at 329.
41. *Id.* at 331.
42. BERKOWITZ, *supra* note 38, at 30.

As we discussed in §6.2, mediators often ask the parties to agree at the outset to abide by rules such as not interrupting each other, calling each other names or engaging in personal attacks. But even if ground rules are stated and agreed to at the beginning of the process, the parties may need frequent reminders. Being reminded of their earlier agreements is usually helpful in gaining compliance from parties who have strayed from their earlier commitments.

Review Problem: Dealing with Strong Feelings. Now watch and critique four different mediators' attempts to deal with Bob and Jane Fitzgerald's expressions of strong hurt and anger in their child custody mediation. As you observe these extracts, consider: Did these mediators exert enough control over the parties' expression of feelings? Too much control? How would you characterize their different approaches to displays of strong emotion? Which of the mediator's approaches do you think was most effective? Least effective? Why? **Video Clip 6-N (1–3).**

■ §6.10 THE CHALLENGES OF MULTI-TASKING IN THE OPENING STAGE OF MEDIATION

We have covered only the first stage of the mediation, in which the mediator opens the proceedings and then moderates a process in which the parties present their initial perspectives. It all may seem pretty straightforward.

But nothing could be further from the truth. Especially when they first begin mediating, mediators generally find this opening stage very complex and challenging, because there are so many mental tasks to juggle both while introducing the process themselves and then when the parties are talking. This form of multi-tasking has the neutral:

- developing trust and rapport

- obtaining participant "buy-in"

- listening for facts, feelings, interests and possible barriers to settlement

- looking for opportunities to listen actively

- answering participants' questions

- assessing the appropriateness of the case for mediation and the readiness of the parties to mediate

- deciding what notes to take

- thinking about what to ask next

- planning to summarize as appropriate

- reframing where appropriate

- deciding how much venting to allow and intervening to manage destructive modes of communication

- looking for weaknesses or flaws in the parties' perspectives or legal positions

- being aware of his or her own biases and keeping them in check

Observing this stage from the outside, it may seem as if mediators are not doing much. But from the *inside*, things feel very different.

In our experience, the challenges posed by this multi-tasking, especially in heated disputes, contribute to two common and problematic temptations—to caucus prematurely and to begin negotiations too soon. Both are worth mentioning briefly before we move on.

Premature Caucusing.   First, beginning (and some efficiency-driven) mediators often feel an urge to separate the parties too soon. Some cannot wait to adjourn to private sessions in order to seek information that is not being revealed by the parties. Others want to separate the parties at the slightest expression of anger, concerned that they will not be able to manage greater displays of emotion if they occur. (Lawyers who want to avoid "wasting time" often push mediators in this direction as well.) But remember: It is often the exchange of strong views and feelings that makes negotiation possible by allowing participants to let go of feelings they have been storing up for a long time.

The model of mediation that we will put forward begins with the participants face-to-face and continues with the mediator keeping them together for as long as possible. The full potential of mediation—in which the parties talk to each other, express their feelings, compare their different takes on the facts, become more "human" and trustworthy, and work jointly to resolve the problem—cannot be achieved if they are separated too soon. Private caucusing can be a very valuable tool. But if utilized too early in the process, it can interfere with some of the highest goals of mediation. So our advice is: Except in rare circumstances where the temperature is rising and you cannot get control of the room, keep the parties together until your (or their) efforts to learn useful information have been exhausted.[43]

▶ ▶ ▶ ▶   **Special Situations: Separating the Parties at the Outset**

In some models of mediation, or in special situations that arise at the table, the parties will be separated from the very beginning of the process or almost immediately thereafter. For example, in victim-offender mediation, where the mediator's goal is to prepare the way for acceptance of criminal responsibility and the offering and acceptance of apologies or other amends, a mediator might work separately with an offender and the victim for a considerable period of time before bringing the parties together.

In cases where the parties are mandated by a court or agency to participate in mediation, participants commonly indicate at the very outset a reluctance to say anything, much less work on the problem. When this happens, it can be helpful to meet with the recalcitrant party privately to explore the resistance further to see if concerns about the process can be identified and addressed.

And in domestic relations cases, a commonly used method of screening for mediation appropriateness has the mediators meeting privately with the parties

---

43. For a full discussion of the purposes and methods of informational caucusing, *see infra* §7.8.

before a substantive joint takes place. The purpose of such separate sessions is to explore in depth whether mediation poses a potential danger to any participant and whether the family dynamics (including any possible history of violence) make true negotiation possible.[44]

Can you think of other circumstances in which you would think it desirable to separate the participants at the start of a mediation or soon thereafter?

Premature Problem-Solving and Negotiation. A related tendency of beginning mediators is to assume mistakenly that their initial open-ended questions and the unstructured exchange that follows have uncovered most, if not all, of the information needed to resolve the dispute. Newer mediators, as well as those overly focused on efficiency, often want to move directly from the opening stage to try to solve the problems that brought the participants into mediation. (This again is a step often urged by parties or lawyers who have a narrow view of the problem and/or a competitive bargaining orientation.) But developing information takes a lot more time and a lot more effort than most beginning mediators imagine or than impatient neutrals can tolerate. It's like peeling an onion: For each layer you peel off, there are usually at least several more layers underneath. In general, until the mediator understands in greater detail not only the background of the conflict, but also how the parties feel about it and what they truly need, she cannot productively orchestrate a process of problem-solving and negotiation—at least not one that will leave the parties satisfied.

So that is the subject of our next chapter: How the mediator takes the (usually limited) data received in the opening stage of the mediation and then, in a systematic way, works to expand on it.

---

44. For an example of such a screening process in the *Fitzgerald* case, *see* Video Clip 6-TM-5. For an example of the kinds of questions often asked in such a screening, *see* Appendix F. Starting in caucus for this purpose can present its own challenges. For example, if confronted with seemingly hostile mother and father in a child custody mediation, how would you explain the reason for holding such private sessions before proceeding further?

CHAPTER 7

EXPANDING INFORMATION

This chapter contains ten video clips, totaling approximately twenty-seven minutes.

■ §7.1 INTRODUCTION

The opening stage of the mediation is over. The parties have made their initial statements and perhaps traded viewpoints back and forth about the dispute. Maybe some (or more than some) angry words have been exchanged. You have summarized the parties' positions, demonstrating that you have heard what everyone has had to say.

Now what?

As we have noted, if you are like many beginning mediators (and some less-than-patient seasoned ones), you may be tempted to begin working to resolve the dispute. And in some disputes, after relatively brief opening exchanges, the parties will be ready to do so. But these situations are rare. In general, premature attempts to solve the problem can lead to serious difficulties. Consider the following recent case:

> In the mediation of an alleged assault by one woman on her across-the-street neighbor, the staff mediator, feeling rushed to try to dispose of several cases in one morning, quickly grew tired of listening to a heated disagreement over who threw the first punch and whether the alleged victim had actually been hurt at all. Cutting off discussion after ten minutes and announcing that *"this case should be settled,"* the mediator proposed, and the women reluctantly agreed, that they would stay away from each other and that the defendant would reimburse the alleged victim's minor emergency room costs.
>
> Within three weeks, the neighbors were back in court, this time facing criminal charges. One of the women had smashed the other's car windshield. In retaliation, the car owner had set fire to the other woman's garage. An investigation by the local prosecutor revealed that the women had each been carrying on a love affair with the same man for more than a year and that one of them was now pregnant. The mediator who had "settled" their first dispute learned none of this.

Beware Premature Efforts at Settlement.   At the end of the opening phase of the mediation process, disputes are often in a state *least* conducive to a negotiated resolution. Here are some reasons why:

- **The parties have defined the dispute in the hardest-to-resolve way.** Where court is the alternative, parties in mediation are likely to see the problem and possible negotiation outcomes through the narrow lens of the law's definitions of what is relevant and the limited types of outcomes that characterize most court decisions over legal rights.[1] This may be because of the influence of lawyers,[2] of popular culture or because they simply don't know any other way of thinking about a legal problem.

  Problems defined in this way yield zero-sum negotiations: Anything one person gains produces a corresponding loss by the other. Most people do not like to make concessions in such a climate, especially when they feel that they are, even mostly, in the right.

  To make matters worse, disputes framed in this narrow way tend to be negotiated by positional bargaining tactics. At the beginning of the process, this commonly takes the form of overstatements about the rightness of each party's position and the weakness of the other side's. Such competitive tactics create further barriers to resolution, triggering feelings of anger that make negotiations more difficult.

  Following opening statements, then, the disputants are unlikely to feel, much less acknowledge, sympathy or empathy for each other. Their belief in their case is unlikely to have been shaken by the opponent's openings, much of which they may have heard before the mediation. For reasons outlined in Chapter 5, they are unlikely to be ready to let go of the conflict. Therefore, any effort by the mediator to bring about a change in feelings or perception at this juncture will likely be met with resistance.

- **Much of the most important information is likely not being disclosed.** As noted in Chapter 2, narrowly defined problems and competitive strategies severely limit what the parties will reveal. The parties' opening statements tend to be confined to only those facts and arguments that support the positions they espouse. Fearing potential exploitation by the "opponent," negotiators are reluctant early on to reveal information that may divulge their true needs, case weaknesses or other clues as to possible bargaining flexibility.[3] In other situations, nondisclosure may stem from *under*stated

---

1. Most court cases require judges or juries to make binary, win-lose decisions (guilty or not, liable or not), even in matters featuring closely conflicting evidence. Where formal pleadings are required, the filings in such cases are thus likely to consist of one-sided recitations stating, in minimally revealing terms, how each party is entitled to a favorable result under the law. MICHAEL MOFFITT, *Pleadings in the Age of Settlement*, 80 IND. L.J. 727, 738-739 (2005).

2. According to Carrie Menkel-Meadow, lawyers transform their clients' actual disputes to fit them into established legal categories and language. This may cause underlying issues to remain unexplored and unresolved. MENKEL-MEADOW, *The Transformation of Disputes by Lawyers: What the Dispute Paradigm Does and Does Not Tell Us*, 1985 MO. J. DISP. RESOL. 25.

3. Other cognitive and psychological factors further constrain information disclosure. Psychological research shows that disputants tend to recall past events consistent with their objectives or interests. As a result, ambiguities or potentially harmful information may actually be beyond their retrieval ability. DAVID A. BINDER, PAUL BERGMAN, SUSAN C. PRICE & PAUL R. TREMBLAY, Lawyers as

openings, with the parties fearful of expressing, or choosing to suppress, potentially important information that is at the core of their position but which might provoke, offend or humiliate the other side. These difficulties in obtaining complete and honest disclosures are compounded by the fact that the mediator hasn't done much yet to earn the parties' trust.

For these reasons, the early stages of mediation often reveal only the tip of the information iceberg — and *maybe even the wrong iceberg!*[4] As the story of the neighbor-neighbor dispute demonstrates, the problems that the parties identify at the beginning of the mediation process may not even be the real problems that have caused their conflict.

The Key to Overcoming These Obstacles: Expand the Information.   To narrow differences and achieve resolutions, something must change. That something is information. People involved in difficult disputes often suffer communication breakdowns. The initiation of litigation makes candid communication even harder. Most people entering mediation need to take in and assess new information before they will be comfortable revealing their own information or making concessions.[5] After all, if the parties do not learn something that adds to or challenges what they already know, why would they change how they feel about or perceive the conflict? Why would they modify their positions?

What This Chapter Covers.   In this chapter, we explore how a mediator works to expand and deepen the information base of a dispute beyond what the parties have initially revealed. We begin by discussing the goals of the mediator in information expansion — goals that are different in important respects from that of other professionals who conduct probing interviews. We then present a model of information expansion that can be used in the mediation process, including useful forms of questions, productive categories of information to explore and a recommended progression for inquiring about them. Our model is premised in part on the belief that it is desirable to develop the information base of the dispute as much as possible in joint session, rather than privately. But in some mediations, it is necessary to use caucuses to accomplish meaningful information expansion. We therefore conclude the chapter by analyzing some of the goals and mechanics of information caucusing.

Counselors: A Client-Centered Approach 351-352 (2d ed. 2004). It is therefore not surprising that the initial phase of mediation often features polarized, overly simplified and even distorted versions of the events that led to the dispute.

4. This metaphor was used to describe the similar and common problem of premature diagnosis of client problems by lawyers who fail to conduct thorough initial interviews. *See* David A. Binder & Susan C. Price, Legal Interviewing and Counseling: A Client-Centered Approach 55 (1977).

5. From the negotiators' perspective, this has been termed the "assessment" stage, in which information is sought about the other side, its needs and the strength of its case in order to test out the "confident expectations" or educated guesses with which they entered the bargaining. Robert M. Bastress & Joseph D. Harbaugh, Interviewing, Counseling, and Negotiating: Skills for Effective Representation 406 (1990).

■ §7.2 THE MEDIATOR'S GOALS IN INFORMATION EXPANSION

The mediator's goals in information gathering are both narrow and broad. What exactly is he or she looking for when seeking new information?

Probing for Facts.   Many law-trained mediators have a ready answer to this question: The mediator is looking for "the facts": What happened? Who did what? When? With what effects? Can each side's assertions be established? And these questions are all valid, at least as a starting point. When court is the alternative, most negotiators expect that the relevant, provable facts of the case, and how they may affect the parties' legal rights and responsibilities, will be considered. Even in non-legal disputes, mediation participants welcome the neutral's exploring the underlying events with care.

But mediations are not trials. If the participants want (or if the mediator thinks they need) an exhaustive exchange of evidence aimed at getting to the bottom of things, a trial-type proceeding may be more appropriate for them. On a practical level, most mediations cannot accommodate an exhaustive fact-finding effort while also allowing sufficient time for all of the other stages of the process to play out.[6]

More important, the mediator's objectives regarding legally relevant facts are different, and considerably narrower, than a court's. Since a voluntary resolution, not an imposed adjudication, of the dispute is the only achievable outcome, the mediator's objective is not to determine the truth of what happened; rather, it is to encourage movement away from early bargaining stances. One way of doing this is to sow doubt about the likely outcome in the mind of one or both parties, which may require digging for some greater level of factual and evidentiary detail than the parties have themselves offered. But how deeply? In what areas? And by what means?

Good investigative journalists look exhaustively under every rock to get the true story. Litigators press their clients for accuracy and detail on all potential claims and defenses in litigation, with an eye toward gathering sufficient evidence to win any trial that might ensue. How does the mediator's probing for details about the history of a dispute compare?

To us, the mediator's goals are to obtain enough detail to be able to point out honestly to each party other ways in which the situation could be viewed and the risks they might encounter in trying to persuade a third-party decision maker of their perspective. Doing this calls for far less detail than an advocate would need to prove or refute the case, or a judge would need to decide it. In operational terms, probing for legally relevant facts means:

- ■ determining what disputed factual areas are likely to be salient in a potential trial of the matter;

---

6. The mini-trial, a "hybrid" process, has been devised to combine aspects of trial presentation with a settlement effort, in recognition of the fact that some litigants may need aspects of both processes before they can resolve a matter. *See, e.g.,* RONALD OLSON, *An Alternative for Large Case Dispute Resolution,* 6 LITIGATION 22 (Winter 1980).

■ obtaining greater detail in areas that have been left to the realm of assertions, generalizations and conclusions;

■ probing how such key areas might be proven if a trial becomes necessary, including such factors as the availability of evidence and the credibility of potential witnesses.

Note that devoting even this much attention to facts, evidence and modes of proof may tend to polarize the discussions and limit the potential solutions that the parties will consider later. Depending on the parties' values, focusing on legally relevant evidence may be less important to them than exploring other factors, such as the reasonableness, moral justification or sympathy of a party's explanation of what happened. (The same might be true of some juries and, in reality, some judges as well.)

Probing for *Information*, Not Just *Facts*.   For most mediators, however, engaging in fact gathering about the legally relevant past is only a small part of the task. If a resolution is to be achieved in mediation, both the parties and the mediator need far more and different information than a judge would need to decide a case. What kinds of information?[7]

If he wants to help the parties resolve their conflict voluntarily, all kinds of information about the parties' feelings, motivations, relationships, values, standards and priorities — topics generally *irrelevant* to a judge or arbitrator — are important data for the mediator. For their part, the disputants may need information about the other side's perspectives, needs, constraints, trustworthiness and resolve before they will move off their positions. They may also need to understand or reconsider information about themselves: Did I overreact? What is really motivating me? What do I need in order to be satisfied?

■ §7.3   A MODEL OF INFORMATION EXPANSION IN MEDIATION

Is there a way to think systematically about what information to seek in mediation? Are there generally applicable categories or areas of helpful information and a logical order in which to pursue them? We believe so and in this section set out a recommended model of information expansion in the mediation context.

Our model is based on certain premises about what good mediation is and what the primary goals of the process should be. These include: (1) our preference, where possible, for a broad problem definition and interest-based bargaining as a means of producing better negotiation outcomes; (2) our belief that mediation is generally more successful, and more satisfying to disputants, when they persuade themselves that movement is desirable, rather than having the mediator try to convince them through more directive or heavy-handed tactics and (3) our view that mediation's capacity to restore relationships, as well as to settle controversies,

---

7. In §6.6, *supra*, we listed six kinds of listening in mediation. It may be helpful to review that section now.

is one of its distinct advantages over other forms of dispute resolution. Here is an outline of the model, followed by a detailed explanation:

> ### A Model of Information Expansion in Mediation
>
> **Organization:**
>
> - Focus on both the past and the future.
> - In general, question topically, not chronologically.
>
> **Progression:**
>
> - Begin by fleshing out the parties' own statements, ideas and feelings.
>
> **Then Probe for:**
>
> - Empathy and mutual understanding;
> - More issues, more people and resources;
> - Future dealings and interdependencies;
> - Readiness to mediate;
> - Previous discussions of the dispute and past negotiations;
> - Other persons who may be affected by a proposed resolution;
> - Needs, interests and priorities;
> - Uncertainty and doubt;
> - Negotiation norms, standards and past practices;
> - Alternatives to a negotiated settlement and the impact of non-resolution
>
> **Format:**
>
> - To the maximum extent possible, develop information with all parties present, not in caucus.

As this model suggests, we believe that in most cases there is a certain logical progression[8] in the way an effective mediator works to widen and deepen the information base of a dispute. Under our model, the mediator starts by delving into topics that the parties have been comfortable enough to share themselves. She then branches out to explore categories of information that offer the prospect of improving interparty understanding, easing the eventual negotiations and optimizing and strengthening potential outcomes in the case. By organizing her pursuit in this way, the mediator enhances her rapport with the parties and builds trust. As a result, later in the process she may be in a better position to use more confrontational information probes — such as probing for doubt — if she needs and chooses to do so.

In general, the information elicited in the earlier probing categories can more readily be discussed in joint session than some of the later ones, such as the parties' alternatives to a negotiated settlement. This progression thus enhances

---

8. "Sequence" would be too strong a word for this recommended progression. Every mediation is different, and the topics chosen to inquire about and their order will vary from case to case.

the prospect that the parties will be able to work together longer and to learn more from each other's perspectives.

Our model of information gathering will be helpful in a great many situations — even in cases in which, at first glance, it appears inapplicable. But like any model, it is not universal. First, not all mediators subscribe to the assumptions on which it is based.[9] Second, even if they do, the model is subject to significant real-world constraints, including time pressures, participant goals and expectations that may differ from the mediator's, and the fact that some problems are non-relational, zero-sum disputes no matter how the mediator tries to frame them. These constraints, and others, may require changing the order of topics probed or abandoning entire categories of potentially fruitful inquiry. Even with modifications, however, our overall approach to information gathering aims to maximize the quality of outcomes by increasing mutual understanding and by exposing as many needs as can be satisfied by a possible agreement. And so we recommend it to you.

■ §7.4 ORGANIZING THE INQUIRY

We begin with some general guidance. In seeking to expand on information that the parties present in the opening stage of the mediation, there are many possible ways to organize the inquiry. What should be the guiding focus of the mediator's questioning? What forms of questions are most useful for expanding information?

■ §7.4.1 FOCUS ON BOTH THE PAST AND THE FUTURE

Some mediators take the view that mediation is "about the future, not the past," and attempt to lead the participants as much (and as soon) as possible toward discussing forward-looking solutions rather than rehashing old events. Others tend to gravitate to the past, trying to get as complete a history as they can. (Mediators are often egged on in this effort by angry disputants wanting to rehash in detail the events that spawned the conflict.) How much time and effort should a mediator spend on the past? How much on the future? Striking an appropriate balance between past and future-oriented questioning is often key to successful information expansion.

Occasionally in negotiation, the past is irrelevant. If two strangers are bargaining over the sale of a house and the only issues are what furniture or appliances will be included with the home as part of the sale and for what price, the parties' sole focus will be on the future: Will the seller part with the corner curio cabinet and his favorite crystal chandelier? Will the buyer pay the seller's $1,500 asking price?

Other kinds of disputes, at least at first blush, seem exclusively about the past. Take a commercial dispute over a roof (now repaired) that began to leak only eight

---

9. Because transformative mediators reject the goal of "solving the problem," they also would reject many if not all of the mediator-driven informational topics recommended in this chapter. *See, e.g.,* Robert Baruch Bush & Joseph Folger, *Transformative Mediation: Core Practices, in* Transformative Mediation: A Sourcebook 31 (Robert Baruch Bush, Joseph Folger & Dorothy Della Noce, eds., 2010).

months after construction was completed. Can the fault be attributed to the roofing subcontractor, alleged to have used improper flashing? To some defect in the roofing materials, the responsibility of the manufacturer? Could the problem have been prevented by the general contractor had he overseen the project more diligently? In such cases, the mediator must work carefully with the parties to reconstruct past events.

In fact, information gathering in mediation is challenging because it usually requires a dual focus on the past and the future. Like a lawyer representing a client in a dispute, the mediator must probe for historical facts important to the parties' claims and defenses. But mediations are also transactional in the sense that any settlement agreement reached is a contract governing the future. Thus, like an agent representing a client in a possible "deal," the mediator must ask the parties probing questions about their present situation, needs, abilities and priorities to help them decide what future arrangements are acceptable.

Variables Affecting the Balance Between Past and Future Questioning.

In any particular matter, what variables affect the appropriate balance between past and future questioning?

- **The nature of the dispute.** The nature of the dispute itself will of course be a key factor. In some cases, the history of the problem will be brief and uncontested and will require little exploration; in others, the history of the conflict will be extensive and may require considerable probing.

- **The setting of the mediation.** The context of the mediation, and the time allotted to it, may strongly affect the balance between past and future questioning. In many court-based settings, only an hour or two (or even less) can be devoted to any one mediation. In such situations, detailed exploration of the past might have to yield — sooner than might otherwise be optimal — to an effort to find a solution.

- **When the parties are rights-conscious or want an evaluation from the mediator.** In some cases, especially when lawyers are present, little progress can be made unless the mediator engages in extensive questioning about past events with a view toward helping the parties evaluate their respective claims and defenses. Eventually, the mediator may be able to broaden the parties' focus, but until that happens, he has little choice but to explore the past history of the dispute in some detail.

- **Where looking back may be thawing or educational.** Many mediated disputes involve people (spouses, neighbors, business owners and their customers) who had a friendly or at least cooperative relationship before their conflict arose. Encouraging discussion of such earlier times can help put the current problem in perspective and remind the parties of the qualities they once saw in the other person.[10] If the parties' relationship was poor from the start, taking them back in time can help them appreciate the futility of

---

10. For this reason, marriage counselors and divorce mediators frequently start working with couples in this way. *See* DONALD T. SAPOSNEK, *Clarifying Perspectives on Mandatory Mediation*, 30 FAM. CT. REV. 490, 490-506 (1992).

attempting to repair the relationship, see the potential gain in putting further destructive dealings behind them, and, if they chose the relationship, appreciate their ability to learn from having made some bad choices.

■ **Where catharsis is important.** When a disputant feels seriously wronged, recounting what has happened in the past is almost always crucial to moving beyond it. As has been illustrated in efforts at achieving reconciliation after public atrocities, those who feel victimized may only engage in future-oriented efforts after a full airing of historical wrongs.[11] People involved in everyday disputes often feel seriously wronged as well. As we discussed in Chapter 5, providing the parties a chance fully to air their differing versions of past events and their impact may provide the emotional shift needed to "move on."

 Watch how one of our *Fitzgerald* child custody mediators, in response to a very angry exchange between the parents, rules "detailed arguments about the past" out of bounds. What are the potential consequences of doing this for the parties and the process? **Video Clip 7-A.**

■ §7.4.2 IN GENERAL, QUESTION TOPICALLY, NOT CHRONOLOGICALLY

The "story" of any dispute can be inquired about in two different ways: by questioning about the sequence or chronology of events ("*What was the first thing that happened when you boarded the Titanic?*" "*What happened next?*") and by questioning about various subject areas or topics,[12] including events, people, places, relationships, ideas and feelings. ("*Can you describe the iceberg?*" "*And what do you remember thinking and feeling as the ship went down?*") When gathering information about the background of a dispute, the mediator must make choices throughout the process about which approach — chronological or topical — to emphasize. Before we examine these choices, it may be helpful to look at the characteristics and advantages of each approach. Both chronological and topical questions can vary in their breadth, from very open-ended to very closed-ended. Mediators, like interviewers in general, must be adept at asking both kinds of questions.

Chronological Questions.   Open-ended chronological questions seek to elicit a sequential summary of the whole dispute: "*Please give us an overview of the situation that brings you here, Mr. Chen, starting at the beginning.*" "*How did this dispute between you and Ms. Hoyle come to pass?*" "*Take your time and bring us up to date about the problems that bring you here*" are examples of questions asking for a broad chronological outline of the problem.

More narrow chronological questions ask for a more detailed time line of specific events affecting the dispute. To obtain such a detailed chronology, a mediator might say: "*OK. I got that. Did anything significant happen between your*

---

11. Carrie J. Menkel-Meadow, *Remembrance of Things Past? The Relationship of Past to Future in Pursuing Justice in Mediation*, 5 Cardozo J. Conflict Resol. 97 (2004).
12. For some, the phrase "subject area" may have a broader connotation than the word "topic." In this chapter, we use the terms interchangeably.

June 14th conversation with Ms. Hoyle and the July 1st board meeting? . . . Okay. And what happened next?" Detailed chronological questions help piece together a time line — either of the entire dispute or of a particularly important time period — in a sequential order.

Topical Questions.   Open-ended topical questions focus generally on a particular subject area that has been mentioned or suggested by a party's own narrative or that the mediator is interested in exploring. For example: *"One of the items you said you are suing for, Mr. Gomez, is the damaged stove. Could you tell us more about that?"* Or: *"I know that you haven't talked about this, Mr. Gomez, but is there anything else other than the damage to the apartment that is causing you to want to evict Mrs. Thomas?"* Or: *"What for you are the pros and cons of settling this matter?"*

     Broad topical questions can then be followed by more closed or narrow topical questions seeking specific details that seem important, such as *"What did the stove cost?" "How old was it?"* Or: *"You say that Mrs. Thomas gave loud parties in her apartment. How often did she do that? What time did they end?"* Or: *"How much would you save in attorney's fees if this case were resolved today?"*

     Is there an optimal balance in mediation between chronological and topical questioning? Is it possible to identify the variables that might affect that balance?

     In our view, a general chronological overview of the whole dispute is almost always helpful, and a detailed chronology of portions of the dispute is often necessary. But a detailed chronology of the entire dispute is seldom necessary and is often impractical time-wise. We also think that, given the nature of the mediator's role, a topical approach to questioning has many advantages over a chronological one. Let us say more about these ideas.

Definitions.   First, what do we mean by a "general chronological overview" and how do we distinguish it from a "detailed chronology"? The difference is one of degree, best illustrated by an example. Suppose that you are mediating a special education dispute involving appropriate educational programming for the coming school year for a fourteen-year-old child with severe attention deficit disorder. The legal issue in the case is whether the specific program and services being offered to the child constitute a "free and appropriate education" for him, given his unique psychological and learning disabilities — an issue that depends in part on how he has responded to previous years' programs and services and how the programs and services now being offered compare.

     To obtain a "general chronological overview" of the case, a mediator might want to question the parties briefly about how long the child had been in the school system, what kind of programming he had received in the past, the overall trend in his progress and whether there had been a history of disputes between these parents and the school. Obtaining a "detailed chronology" would require far more: a specific review of each year's educational programming, what educational progress the child made each year, what problems were encountered, the content of discussions that preceded this year's dispute and so forth.

A General Chronological Overview Is Always Helpful.   Obtaining a general chronological overview of the dispute at the outset is always helpful because it helps the mediator understand, and sometimes diagnose, the presenting problem. In cases centering on past events, the parties' opening statements often describe the situation that led to the mediation in incomplete and confusing ways. For example, some disputants dispense with any discussion of past events and focus only on the remedy they seek. ("*We are next door neighbors, and his loud parties are intolerable and have to stop.*") Others skip backward and forward in time — starting in the middle of the history, skipping to the end and the relief they seek, then going back to the beginning. Do you find movies with a lot of flashbacks confusing? For most people, it is easiest to understand stories when they are told in chronological sequence.

A chronological overview also reduces the danger of prematurely misdiagnosing the problem and attaching significance to what later turn out to be unimportant events and topics. Like a good map, a chronological overview of the problem provides the mediator with the "big picture" of the route from start to finish and helps him decide which destinations to stop and explore and which to drive past.

Asking the parties to provide a chronological overview of the problem can sometimes yield crucial information about what lies beneath the surface of a dispute. In their opening statements, disputants will often stress the immediate events that precipitated the current conflict: the $26 worth of spoiled meat sold by the grocer, the child's being returned "dirty" the last time the father had a weekend visitation. Significant as these facts may be, they do not necessarily explain why the aggrieved person chose to initiate the dispute or why it has gotten to the point where a mediator's help is needed. In reality, it is often other factors (the grocer's hostile attitude toward minority customers, the father's recent remarriage to a longtime family friend) that are the root cause of the problem and help explain its intensity. These are more likely to emerge if parties are invited to talk about the problem from "the beginning."

A Detailed Chronology of Portions of the Dispute Is Often Necessary.
There are, however, times when a general chronological overview of the problem is insufficient, and precise chronological detail, at least regarding specific aspects of a dispute, is important to elicit. These include situations in which:

- **The parties' narratives are disjointed and hard to follow.** Disputants sometimes have difficulty relating their conflict in a logical, sequential way. Where the parties have weak communication skills or are "all over the place," the mediator may have to slow the process down and ask for a more detailed time line about particularly confusing portions of the narrative.

- **The parties forget important facts.** Occasionally, the parties have difficulty relating all the facts in a narrative because they have forgotten important details. Asking people to relate events from beginning to end can stimulate accurate recall.[13]

- **The parties' general chronological account seems to be missing something.** Sometimes an initial overview will leave a mediator sensing a gap or something illogical in the sequence of events as portrayed or in a party's

---

13. Research shows that the ability to recall and recount past events is enhanced by thinking about them in chronological fashion; both accuracy and retrieval of detail are increased by reliving the connection between sequential events. *See* BINDER, BERGMAN, PRICE & TREMBLAY, *supra* note 3, at 117.

described behavior. In such cases, obtaining a more detailed chronology may yield important diagnostic clues. For example, in a recent case in which a dentist's drill had nicked a patient's lip, the patient's anger and decision to pursue a large claim for pain and suffering seemed puzzling to the mediator, given the patient's full recovery without residual injury. Only after obtaining a more detailed chronological account (including events occurring before and after the legally relevant transaction) did the explanation become apparent: The dentist, with whom the patient had had a long relationship, never indicated any concern about the patient's condition or her recovery. When the underlying cause of a dispute from one party's perspective is surfaced, it will often come as news to the other side. This, in turn, can trigger a new level of understanding and promote resolution.

■ **The precise sequence of events affects the parties' rights and responsibilities.** In some cases, the precise sequence of certain events will be critical in proving — or at least suggesting inferences about — a key disputed factual proposition if the case goes to trial: In a housing discrimination case, was the rental apartment still available at 3:35 p.m. on May 12, when the African American couple applied for it and was rejected by the landlord? Or had the unit already been rented by a different rental agent to a Caucasian couple that morning? When a unit is rented, how quickly is the "available" listing generally removed from the Internet? In cases like these, a mediator may need to focus closely on the precise sequence of events to help the parties evaluate how their narratives hold up (or don't) and to help them appraise their risks of proceeding to trial.

A Detailed Chronology of the Entire Dispute Is Seldom Necessary, Generally Impractical and Often Counterproductive.

In our experience, law-trained mediators tend to want to probe the past in great chronological detail. Chronological questions come naturally to these mediators, because this is the way stories are elicited in trial-type settings, and many of them are also (or have been) trial lawyers or judges. Many of these mediators adopt an evaluative approach, using the process to predict (and if possible to get to) the "right" outcome, as measured by the likely court resolution of contested past facts.

In our view, seeking a detailed chronology of the entire dispute is usually misguided, for at least five reasons:

■ **It often isn't necessary.** While mediations often involve conflicting versions of past events, in many cases there will be no particular dispute about the *sequence* of those events. Suppose the central questions are: Did the residential tenant damage the bathroom tile or not, and what was the extent of the damage? In such a case, even a mediator with a highly evaluative orientation can assess and sow doubt about the dispute's potential legal outcome by probing *topically* rather than chronologically, such as, for example: *"How old was the tile?" "What kind of condition was it in at the beginning of this tenant's rental?" "What photographic evidence do you have, Mr. Landlord, of the broken tile?"*

■ **There isn't sufficient time.** In many mediated disputes, the history of the dispute is protracted and complex. Sometimes there are a great many documents reflecting that history, which may or may not have been exchanged before the mediation began. Imagine that you are conducting a one-day EEOC mediation in an age discrimination case involving a manager terminated after ten years of employment. As a practical matter, could you feasibly develop a complete chronological history of the plaintiff's employment? Review all his performance evaluations over the past ten years and compare them to other similarly situated employees who were not fired? As we have said, a mediation is not a trial; even if you wanted to learn as much as possible about the history of the dispute, there are far too many other tasks to attend to.

■ **It may create bad feelings.** Probing the history of a dispute in great chronological detail can rekindle angry feelings and stiffen commitments, jeopardizing the negotiations that will follow. It can make the mediation seem more like a trial (with the mediator playing inquisitor), in the process dampening candid and productive communication between the parties.

■ **It makes it hard to take turns.** Information gathering in mediation is challenging because there are two (or more) parties, each anxious to be heard. Spending too much time developing the historical details of one side's narrative creates the risk that the other party — left to "cool his heels" — will begin to feel aggrieved.[14] To maintain the appearance of evenhandedness, the mediator must find effective ways for the parties to take turns speaking. A detailed chronological approach to information gathering — especially where the history of the dispute is complex — makes it hard to do this.

■ **The parties may not want or value it.** In many situations in which disputes are voluntarily submitted to mediation instead of to arbitration or a full-blown trial, the parties are, in effect, saying that they place a higher value on other features of the mediation process and what it can achieve.

Take a look at our kitchen contract mediation, *Wilson v. DiLorenzo*. The history of this dispute is probably of about average complexity. This mediator, a former judge, tries to impose a strict chronological structure on the information-gathering process. As you watch this excerpt, ask yourself: Was learning the history in this level of chronological detail necessary in this dispute? If not, how else might the mediator's questions have been organized? **Video Clip 7-B.**

If you have already seen this version of *Wilson* in its entirety, did this approach to information gathering impact the process? The outcome? If so, how?

Now watch how two other mediators used topical questions to develop the information base of the disputes they were mediating. In the first extract, a mediator in the *Resnick* personal injury case used broad topics — liability and damages — to help organize the parties' initial presentations and facilitate taking turns. (By limiting the plaintiff's initial presentation to the topic of "liability facts," he permitted the defendant to be heard on those issues at an earlier stage, before tackling the issue of damages.)

---

14. *See* JAMES H. STARK, *Preliminary Reflections on the Establishment of a Mediation Clinic*, 2 CLINICAL L. REV. 457, 477-478 (1996).

In the second extract, a mediator in the *Fitzgerald* custody matter uses more narrow topical questioning to explore the topic of "structure" and the perceived impact to Bob and Jane of different custody arrangements on their kids' development. How do you assess her effort? **Video Clip 7-C (1–2).**

Topical Questions Have Many Advantages over Chronological Questions.
As noted, we generally favor a topical approach to information gathering in mediation over a detailed chronological approach. This preference arises not only from the practical difficulties of conducting detailed chronological questioning but also from the distinct nature of the mediator's role. As we have said, a mediator is not an advocate who must explore every nook and cranny of a client's case to investigate all possible claims and defenses. Nor is she a judge or arbitrator who must piece together the entire history of the dispute to decide what happened or who's right. Her primary purpose is very different: to unearth and develop information that will help the disputants achieve a resolution. This is best achieved by probing into certain categories of information that are present in most disputes and that have the potential of leading the parties to see the dispute differently or to find the seeds of possible solutions.

■ §7.4.3 BEGIN BY FLESHING OUT THE PARTIES' OWN STATEMENTS, IDEAS AND FEELINGS

However, before moving in directions that she selects, the astute mediator seeks clarification and expansion of the parties' *own* statements, for several reasons. First, when people first describe events, ideas and feelings to others, they often use unclear terms (*"He hurt me bad." "Her husband is strange."*) They combine several thoughts, conditions or events into one.[15] (*"My neighbor constantly has loud parties." "Our damages total $21,000."*) They speak in detail-omitting generalizations and conclusions. (*"He drove recklessly."*) If the participants (or the mediator) are from different backgrounds, their statements may be subject to cultural misunderstandings. Even when the parties appear to have explained themselves clearly, additional facts and feelings often lurk underneath apparently complete statements. Helping the parties to flesh out their perspectives is a way to avoid proceeding down wrong avenues, based on erroneous assumptions about what the parties mean.

This approach — beginning with non-directive, *party-centered* questions before moving to more directive, mediator-driven ones — has another advantage: By working with the parties to help them expand on their own expressed statements and feelings, the mediator signals that *"I am interested in learning more about what you have already chosen to tell me."* This helps build rapport and trust and establishes a foundation for more mediator-centered interventions later on.

"Could You Say More About That?"   One especially useful device to flesh out incomplete party statements and help people relate their own perspectives more fully is the simple but powerful "Tell me more about that" request or any

---

15. *See* BINDER, BERGMAN, PRICE & TREMBLAY, *supra* note 3, at 114-116 (discussing problem of "clumped" events in client interviewing).

of its variations. For example: "*You mentioned loud parties, Mrs. Jones. Why don't you expand on that?*" Or "*You say that your damages total $21,000, Mrs. Smith? Could you break that down for us?*" One reason why this question form is so useful is that it can be employed for any kind of subject, from legally relevant facts and evidence ("*Mr. Gomez, could you say more about the proof you have supporting your claim for damage to the linoleum?*") to inchoate feelings and emotions ("*Mr. Brown, you said earlier that 'his actions hurt you bad.' What did you mean by that?*")[16]

But the real power of the "could you say more about that?" question is that it helps the mediator emphasize topics that might improve the parties' understanding of each other[17] and increase their satisfaction with the process. The mediator who is listening carefully and who has some intuition about what is really motivating a party can try to flesh out that topic and, in doing so, increase that person's feeling of being heard. In addition, the mediator who senses that there are potentially persuasive details lurking behind overly generalized statements can use this question form to help parties elaborate their assertions more completely and, in the process, begin to plant the seeds of doubt, change and movement.

"T-Funneling."   When fleshing out details about a specific topic is important, the technique known as "T-Funneling," can be a very useful tool.[18] A T-Funneling probe is designed to explore a single topic thoroughly and systematically, starting with (multiple, if fruitful) open-ended questions (which tend to produce spontaneous but incomplete recall) and then proceeding to "drill down" by asking closed, mediator-generated questions (which can stimulate more specific memory) on selected and potentially important details suggested by the responses to open-ended questions before starting a new "T" on the next topic. It's called "T-Funneling" because it resembles a T and, like a funnel, starts broadly and ends narrowly:

Open Question ⟼ Open Question ⟼ Open Question ⟼ Open Question

Closed Question

Closed Question

Closed Question

Closed Question

To illustrate: Suppose that you are mediating a landlord-tenant dispute in which the landlord has sued the tenant for three-months' unpaid rent. In his

---

16. Naturally, the mediator needs to be tactful in choosing topics to pursue in this fashion in joint session, and should usually avoid or postpone potentially inflammatory subjects. For example, if one party says early in the mediation, "*Her husband is strange,*" the mediator probably does not want to ask the follow-up question, "*Could you say more about how you find him strange?*" in joint session.
17. Asking party-centered questions like "*say more about [X]*" can also be seen as a hallmark practice of transformative mediators, in that they involve the mediator's following the direction set by the parties rather than leading them. *See* Bush & Folger, *supra* note 9.
18. *See* Binder, Bergman, Price & Tremblay, *supra* note 3, at 167-180 (discussing the use of this tool in client representation).

introductory statement, the tenant alleges that the apartment was a "wreck" with all sorts of problems, including limited heat, and that he should not be required to pay any rent for this period. Under the governing law, substandard apartment conditions may reduce the tenant's duty to pay rent, but even deteriorated housing has some rental value, for which the tenant will still be responsible. The parties' dispute (which tracks the governing legal standard) is whether the landlord's rent claim should be adjusted downward because apartment conditions materially endangered the health or safety of its occupants.

Using a T-Funnel to help the tenant flesh out his position, the mediator might proceed as follows:

M: "Could you say more about the problems you experienced in the apartment?" (*Open question.*)

T: "Well, as I say, there was limited heat, and it was cold. After all, we're talking about November, December and January!"

M: "Any other problems?" (*Open question.*)

T: "Absolutely. There was a broken smoke detector in the kitchen that I complained to the landlord about and he refused to fix, and there was a bee problem. My daughter got stung twice before the problem got fixed."

M: "So there was a heat issue, a smoke detector issue and a bee issue. Anything else?" (*Summarizing and open question.*)

T: "Yeah. The landlord promised me a clean apartment when I moved in, but it was really dirty. The rug in the living room was disgusting."

M: "Anything else?" (*Open question.*)

T: "That's about all. Isn't that enough?"

M: "We'll talk about these problems one by one, OK? Let's start with the heat. Could you say more about that?" (*Choosing a specific and likely important topic and continuing with open questions.*)

T: "Well, I have no control over the heat; it's centrally controlled by the landlord. That's the first problem. This guy has a reputation among the tenants for turning off the heat entirely at night just to save a few bucks. It was barely tolerable most of November, because it was fairly warm that month. But it was really cold in December and January, and there were two weeks in January where the heat seemed to be entirely on the fritz."

M: "Putting aside the period in January for a minute, how cold would you say it was in the apartment at night during November and December?" (*Closed question.*)

. . . .

M: "And when exactly — at what time — would the heat come back on during this period?" (*Closed question.*)

. . . .

M: "And what would the temperature go up to during the day?" (*Closed question.*)

. . . .

M: "What time did you and your daughter generally leave the house on week-days?" (*Closed question.*)

. . . .

M: "During this period, before the period in January when the heat seemed 'completely on the fritz,' did you complain to the landlord about the heat?" (*Closed question.*)

T: "Well no; but other tenants did, I'm pretty sure."

M: "Can you name any who did?" (*Closed question.*)

. . . .

M: "OK; now let's talk about the heat in January. Tell me more about that, would you?" (*Open question, starting T-Funnel over again.*)

. . . .

M: "Before we go on to the next topic, why don't we give the landlord an opportunity to share his perspectives on these heating issues. Mr. Land-lord?" (*Open question to the landlord, starting the T-funneling process again with him.*)

As you can see from this example, one advantage of using a T-Funnel in mediation is that it helps in organizing the discussions by topic and taking turns with the parties, giving them each an opportunity to speak about specific dispute topics one at a time.

But using this tool, like deciding how deeply to investigate generally, poses diagnostic and strategic challenges for the mediator: Which topics are likely to be most salient? How deeply to probe on each? To get to the "bottom"? Just far enough to suggest uncertainty for one or both sides? Is exposing greater factual detail (or gaps) likely to overcome barriers to settlement here? Or would limited time perhaps be better spent in other ways?

▶ ▶ ▶ ▶   **Clarifying Cultural Meanings**

Information expansion can raise special challenges in mediations involving cultural differences. In some situations, statements or events can mean vastly different things to different participants by virtue of who they are, unless someone — usually the mediator — realizes this is happening and intervenes. Consider this recent example:

A small claims court mediation involved the customer of a local corner grocery store who had returned some allegedly "bad" milk he had purchased. Skeptical about the customer's claim, the grocer reluctantly agreed to the $2.85 refund. When the shopkeeper placed the money on the counter, an argument and then

continues on next page >

a shouting match erupted in two (non-English) languages, culminating in the customer's throwing the change at the grocer. The grocer later sued the customer, claiming he had incurred $365 in medical expenses to close a gash above his eye caused by one of the coins.

After the grocer finished his opening statement, the defendant angrily offered to pay $100, stating that he doubted the total being claimed, had not intended to injure the grocer and resented how he had been treated in the store. Sensing that the difference in nationalities might somehow have contributed to the incident, the mediator invited the customer to *"Say more about what happened that day to make you feel angry."* It was then that the defendant described how, in his country, it is a sign of disrespect not to place change directly in a customer's hand. On hearing this, the grocer expressed surprise and then apologized, explaining that in his country of origin, such touching, even in transferring money, is a source of discomfort. The dispute resolved quickly.

Sometimes cultural differences can lie at the heart of a dispute yet somehow remain hidden from the parties. How does a mediator (who cannot possess universal cultural literacy) "know" when there may be something cultural at work? Sensitivity to the possibility that the same conduct or event can appear different to people simply by virtue of their background or identity is, of course, crucial. So, too, is understanding the wide range of cultures that potentially can affect the dynamics of a dispute. Not all are as obvious as our consumer example. Differences in gender, race, age, heritage, geography, class, faith and even vocation or industry can all impact how events, gestures and words are perceived. Finally, the mediator must be attentive to potential — and often subtle — clues: Is there a puzzling aspect to the parties' disagreement? Does the level of upset seem disproportionate to the events? Do the parties seem unwilling or afraid to engage each other?

Obviously, awareness of the possible impact of culture is not a license to make unwarranted or stereotyped assumptions. Hypotheses in this realm must be tested very tactfully, such as, for example: *"I wonder: When he remained seated instead of getting up, did that have any particular meaning for you?"* Taking the plunge to ask such questions can feel intrusive. But the potential cost of *not* asking them can be very great.

◼ §7.5 GOAL-DRIVEN INFORMATION CATEGORIES AND A LOGICAL PROGRESSION FOR ASKING ABOUT THEM

Once a mediator has helped the participants expand on their own statements, the parties will commonly offer little else that is not repetitive, at least in joint session. This may be because of strategic reasons or because they do not know what else might be relevant or helpful. But if the objective is to bring about change in the parties' feelings and perceptions about the conflict, new information must be surfaced. This can be difficult for newer mediators, who often can feel stumped in terms of what to ask or feel inhibited from probing further with everyone present.

Is there a way around this stop sign? In this section, we present broad categories of information that have the potential to help the mediator diagnose, and the parties to resolve, a wide variety of disputes and what we think is a logical sequence in which to pursue them.

■ §7.5.1 PROBE FOR EMPATHY AND MUTUAL UNDERSTANDING

From the beginning of the information-gathering process, effective mediators look for early opportunities to make each party's past conduct, statements, goals, constraints and intentions "more intelligible" to the other.[19] This means probing to help parties more fully articulate their feelings and motivations toward each other and helping them to see each other in a fuller (and perhaps more favorable) light.

In seeking to promote greater openness and connectedness, it is helpful to choose topics introduced in the opening stage for which a more detailed description or explanation is likely to have the greatest impact, regardless of the topics' legal relevance. This includes the effects of the dispute on each disputant and the feelings caused by the other person's conduct. The goal here is for each party to develop empathy for the other side: to begin to see the situation as the other person has experienced it, regardless of whether they agree. Such thawing can occur only if the participants are encouraged to talk about their experiences in a deeper way than is typical in the opening phase and, of course, listen to each other when they do so.

Watch this probing (using a "tell me more about that" type of question) by one of the mediators in *Wilson v. DiLorenzo*. How would you characterize the topic on which she focuses? What is she trying to accomplish with her question? Is her choice of topic helpful? Why or why not? **Video Clip 7-D.**

Effective mediators also help parties explain the reasoning or motivations behind their conduct, using "why" questions, such as *"Why is it that Ms. Wilson's kitchen renovation took so long to complete?"* Where appropriate, this inquiry can be completed by disentangling the negative *impact* of the parties' acts from their *intentions*, as in *"So, in making Ms. Wilson wait so long for her kitchen renovation, was it your intent to convey disrespect to her?"* Such questions are the foundations for later persuasion, in that they can diminish hostile attributions, improve damaged relationships and make resolution more likely.

Note that the mediator in our *Wilson* video excerpt (Clip 7-D) probed a topic that the plaintiff had already raised herself. Sometimes the mediator may wish to probe for empathy in areas not mentioned in the parties' own opening presentations, including subjects the parties have deemed irrelevant or have chosen to avoid. For example, the mediator may have some sense that something one party did deeply upset the other, even if that party has said nothing explicit about it in her opening. Questions such as "Ms. Defendant, you haven't said anything about how (this event) (the dispute) (the plaintiff's conduct) has affected you or made you feel. Would you like to?" give the parties permission to broach these difficult topics.

---

19. This is also a major thrust of the transformative approach. Robert A. Baruch Bush & Joseph P. Folger, The Promise of Mediation: Responding to Conflict Through Empowerment and Recognition 101, 160 (1994).

Seeking to expand the flow of information in this way may strike you as a risky invitation to increased mutual hostility, especially because this form of probing must take place in joint session to be effective. At a minimum, it demands strong process management skills on the mediator's part. She may need to control inter-ruptions and ensure that the speaker is listened to. She may need to exhort the listener to put aside disagreements to try to understand the speaker's perspective. For parties who have a difficult time appreciating the opponent's perspective after listening, she may need to translate or reframe what has been said, usually in caucus, in order to open that party to hearing it more empathically. Despite these challenges, we think that these sorts of exchanges can be among the most powerful moments in mediation, especially if the participants are talking face-to-face for the first time about their problem.

■ §7.5.2 PROBE FOR MORE ISSUES, MORE PEOPLE AND MORE RESOURCES

As noted earlier, disputes perceived or defined as zero-sum problems can be the hardest to negotiate: There is only one fixed negotiating issue that everyone values equally, and everyone wants the most they can get of it. Since any increase in one side's share must correspondingly diminish the other's, an inherently competitive tension — with accompanying tactics — is triggered.

How can such a tug-of-war be eased? By increasing the number of topics that are up for grabs or adding more resources available to solve the problem, thereby increasing the size of the "pie" to be divided up (and thus the size of each potential "slice"). These possibilities often arise only as a result of the mediator's questioning.

More Issues.   Why expand the number of issues that might be negotiated? On the simplest level, going from one to two or more immediately opens up the pos-sibility of trading one for another ("Although we both want all of *A*, I'll give you some of *A* if you give me some of *B*"), potentially creating a climate of coop-eration and mutually beneficial exchange. If the parties should value those issues differently — with one preferring *A* and the other *B* — their amount of combined satisfaction can be increased because everyone can get something they value that does not come at the other's identical expense. Note an important paradox here: The negotiation can be made easier by making it more complex.

One way of increasing the number of things that might be negotiated is to ask the parties directly: "*Is there anything else — even if it's not relevant or part of this dispute — that you want to resolve or discuss with Jim?*" At other times, the medi-ator may be able to identify potential additional topics based on hints or overt statements by the parties, or his own intuitions. In a wrongful termination of employment case, would the parties be open to discussing a helpful job reference (almost costless to the employer but potentially very valuable to the worker), in addition to the already-demanded monetary settlement? In a dispute over unpaid rent, would the landlord be open to reducing the length of the existing lease (the tenant who is graduating from college in May having hinted that he might welcome this) in addition to negotiating the amount of money he will be paid?

Another approach is to break a single issue into possible sub-issues. What seem like simple, single-issue money claims almost always contain potential subcompo-nents. The mediator can ask questions such as: "*Let's take the money you are owed. Let's look at its possible components: When will it be paid? How much in total? In what form (cash, personal check, cashier's check, etc.)?"* To a cash-strapped creditor: *"Would you consider some discount if they could pay that amount in a lump sum in cash by next week?"* Conversely, to a debtor temporarily short on funds, *"Might you be willing to agree to pay a slightly larger total in exchange for their being willing to accept payments spread out over time?"*

More People and Other Resources. Creative mediators also try to bring new people or resources to the table to help to meet the needs of the claiming party. Obvious examples include adding insurers or additional defendants who, because of contractual or other potential legal responsibility, might shoulder or share the cost of resolving the claim — the second tenant on the lease who has not been sued for the rent arrears because he could not readily be located, for example.

Sometimes it is even possible to bring in other people or outside sources who, while not legally responsible, might be persuaded to help bridge a settlement impasse. Maybe a grandmother would be willing to help out on a regular basis with her grandson's transportation needs in order to help resolve her daughter's visitation dispute with the child's father. Maybe there is a social service agency that will provide short-term financial assistance to an out-of-work homeowner to help him pay his three-month mortgage arrearage and avoid foreclosure. Perhaps there is a person who does not have legal responsibility for a claim but feels some sense of moral responsibility for it — for example, the passenger who begged for a ride to the mall in a friend's uninsured car that then dented another car's fender in the parking lot.

Again, the way to find out about such potential resources is to ask directly about them: *"Can you submit this to your insurer?"* *"Would your frat brothers — even those who claim to have been asleep when the house party got out of hand — be willing to take part in fulfilling the 500 hours of public service work the injured students are asking for in exchange for dropping their claims?"* *"Is there anyone who could help you out with the payments (or services required) here or sign the agreement as guarantor?"* Parties are often unaware of the possibility of bringing additional resources to bear on a problem and sometimes are reluctant to do so even when the possibility is pointed out to them. Mediator probing is often needed both to raise the option and explore any resistance.[20]

■ §7.5.3 PROBE FOR FUTURE DEALINGS AND INTERDEPENDENCIES

Common sense tells us, and research confirms, that people who can foresee themselves interacting with each other in the future — and who therefore may be in a position to help or harm each other in the future — are more likely to be accommodating today than those who will never again deal with one another.[21] Mediators who are able to help the parties appreciate the possibility of future

---

20. As discussed in Chapter 4, sometimes this can be planned for before the mediation begins. At other times, the possibility of additional resources emerges only after the mediation has gotten under way.
21. Robert Axelrod, The Evolution of Cooperation 19-21 (1985).

relationships and interdependencies are often able to create a more productive negotiation climate.

Continuing Relationships.   In disputes involving squabbling neighbors or the divorcing parents of young children or union representatives and management under a long-term contract, it will be obvious that the parties will have to interact with each other going forward. In others, the possibility of such future dealings will be less obvious, even to the parties, but might come to light through probing. For example:

> In a recent mediation over the alleged fraudulent failure to disclose material defects in the sale of a house, the seller and the buyer were at an impasse. The buyer claimed that, within a month of moving in, he had discovered that the home was in much worse shape than had been evident on inspection or was represented in the disclosure document signed by the seller. The seller claimed that the problems complained of were neither known to him before moving out nor as serious as claimed, that the home and the neighborhood were "gems" and that the price paid reflected the need for some repairs.
>
> Looking for ways to break the logjam, the mediator asked the seller whether he maintained any ties to his old community. When the seller revealed that he planned to continue to attend his old church, the buyer remarked that he had just joined the same congregation. From that point on, the talks took on a somewhat more cordial atmosphere and a joint effort that eventually produced a resolution.

Restoring Past Relationships.   In many disputes — between businesses and their customers, for example — a prior relationship has soured. Nevertheless, the existence of a past relationship often makes it possible to consider renewed future dealings. For example, a catering establishment may be unwilling to refund the angry customer the entire $5,000 he is asking for the return of the deposit on his canceled wedding. But would the caterer be willing to provide a discount on a future event if the customer will renew his patronage? The only way to explore such possibilities is to ask about them: "*Is there any basis on which you would consider continuing to use their services?*" "*Are free future services or discounts on future work ideas that you would be willing to consider?*"

The *Wilson* "unfinished kitchen" case provides an interesting example of this kind of probing. Watch how one of our mediators explored with the plaintiff homeowner whether she might be willing to allow the defendant contractor to complete the job he started. Did she press this question too hard? If you had been the mediator, would you have accepted the homeowner's initial "no" answer? **Video Clip 7-E.**

Other Interdependencies.   Careful probing by the mediator can sometimes reveal other situations in which the parties are mutually dependent on each other, to the point of having an interest in the other party feeling satisfied with the negotiated outcome. For example, creditors seeking to collect money from debtors often moderate their demands for full and immediate payment if they learn (often through mediator questioning) that the debtor's likelihood of complying with any agreement they make would be enhanced by more lenient payment terms than they are currently offering. They do so after realizing that their interests and the debtor's are interdependent.

Or consider this more subtle example:

In a recent mediation, the plaintiff had suffered a serious fire in her home. With the proceeds from her insurance policy, she hired a company to move all her furniture out and to clean and restore any of it that could be salvaged. She later brought suit against the company, claiming that they had done a poor cleaning job and had damaged some of the furniture in transit. In the mediation, the company representative took a hard line, saying that it had done a fine job.

"How did you find this moving and cleaning company in the first place?" the mediator asked the plaintiff. When she revealed that her insurance company had recommended it, and (in questioning the defendant) that this insurance company's referrals were the moving company's largest source of business, the case quickly settled. It didn't take much coaxing for the mediator to convince the company representative that it was in its interest to be more generous in the negotiations in order to avert a possible complaint by the plaintiff to the insurer.

How do mediators uncover such relationships and interdependencies? By thinking and being curious about the parties' possible connections before and after the mediation and being cognizant that people often populate intersecting communities. And by asking questions such as *"How did you come to deal with each other in the first place?"* or *"Do you imagine there is any way in which you might come into contact with them again?"* or *"Are there ways in which they could help (hurt) you in the future?"* or *"Can you see any way in which you would be worse (better) off if they were worse (better) off in the future?"*

■ §7.5.4 PROBE FOR READINESS: ENSURING THAT THE MATTER IS RIPE FOR MEDIATION

We wrote in Chapter 2 about the stages of conflict resolution and the fact that sometimes disputants are not psychologically "ready" to work to end their dispute. In some situations, the mediator can discern that readiness is a potential problem by careful pre-mediation screening.[22]

But in other cases — especially where participation in mediation has been mandated by a court or where there has been no opportunity for the mediator to talk with the parties in a advance — the mediator may not discover a readiness problem until after the mediation begins, or indeed until late in the process, when the talk turns to actually ending the controversy. The problem can take one of two different

---

22. In commercial litigation, readiness problems often take the form of discovery processes that are incomplete. For example, in a case like *Resnick*, has the expert completed and made available his report on the permanency of plaintiff's post-traumatic stress injury? Problems of this nature (often due to denial that the marriage is in trouble) are so common in divorce mediation that some mediators routinely schedule pre-mediation conferences to assess the parties' readiness to proceed.

forms: Either one or more of the parties is not emotionally prepared to work toward resolving the dispute; or additional information (e.g., a psychologist's assessment where a child's developmental needs are in dispute, an accountant's review of the books in a contentious sale of a family business) is needed to achieve a resolution that one or both parties won't later regret. This impediment obviously does not arise in every case and not every expression of ambivalence is a true indication that a party is not ready to resolve things. But where the problem does suggest itself, the mediator must probe to ensure that the matter is truly ripe for mediation.

In *Fitzgerald*, the child custody mediation, the mediators faced a difficult problem: Bob and Jane Fitzgerald had a physical altercation resulting in a court-imposed order temporarily removing Bob from the marital home. After the order expired, Bob snatched the kids and took them to live with him at his parents' house. In the mediation, Bob and Jane acted out their extreme anger with each other in a variety of ways, but at the same time gave the mediators hints that they might still be open to reconciling. At the same time, both children may be experiencing developmental delays: Megan, age five, has some speech delays and Ryan, age three, still isn't fully toilet trained. In the mediation, Bob and Jane disagree about the extent of these problems and base their arguments about desirable custody arrangements on these concerns, so further expertise is needed. But school is starting in only six weeks, and Bob and Jane need to decide where Megan will go to school and where the kids will reside.

As you watch the following video extract, ask yourself: What exactly is the readiness problem (or problems) here, if any? Did the mediators deal adequately with readiness as an issue? If not, what might they have done differently? If there was a tension between a lack of readiness for mediation and a need for prompt decisions regarding the children, how might the mediators have helped Bob and Jane resolve this tension? **Video Clip 7-F.**

■ §7.5.5 INQUIRE ABOUT PREVIOUS DISCUSSIONS OF THE DISPUTE AND PAST NEGOTIATIONS

It is almost always helpful to ask the parties whether they have had any prior discussions about the dispute and to inquire about any previous efforts to resolve it. These kinds of questions serve important diagnostic purposes, by allowing the mediator to learn what is really motivating the disputants and what impediments to settlement may exist.

If the parties have not spoken at all about their dispute, the mediator can ask why. If they have engaged in previous negotiations that broke down, the mediator can probe each party's perspectives about the reasons for this. At the very least, the mediator will learn what offers (if any) were on the table prior to the mediation, and how well or badly those offers addressed the parties' interests. Especially where things have been adversarial, this information can be critical in understanding the negotiation "dance" that will likely follow. In most situations, the parties' responses to these questions will also yield valuable clues about psychological, strategic and other barriers to settlement that may be present.

If the climate of the prior discussions seems to have been friendly and candid, such questions can fruitfully be asked in joint session. More commonly, if the mediator wants to get unguarded information from the participants about potential barriers to settlement, she will pursue this topic in caucus.

A possible culmination of such probing might be to inquire about the parties' current stance: What are they demanding or offering today? What outcomes do they seek? What specific suggestions for resolution or offers might they be willing to put on the table from this point on? Some mediators ask such questions earlier, at the end of the parties' opening statements. What do you see as the pros and cons of asking for such information at that point in joint session as opposed to at a later stage of information development, typically in caucus?

§7.5.6 INQUIRE ABOUT OTHER PERSONS WHO MUST BE SATISFIED WITH A PROPOSED RESOLUTION

Mediations are private proceedings, generally closed to the outside world. But they rarely take place in a vacuum. Mediation outcomes are often of considerable interest to persons not present at the bargaining table. These missing persons or stakeholders can have a profound impact on the acceptability of proposed resolutions.

In some situations, these outside audiences or constituencies will be obvious to all of the mediation participants: the rank-and-file union members who, as a formal matter, must ratify any new contract negotiated by the union's elected representatives; the teenage child who can easily sabotage a custody and visitation plan devised without her input; the claims adjuster in the personal injury case who must approve any proposed payment to be made on behalf of the insured defendant.

In other cases, it may not be apparent that there are outsiders who must be satisfied with a proposed settlement. When a mediator fails to discover that there are persons not at the table who may care deeply about and could influence the negotiated outcome, this can pose a serious impediment to settlement.

A recent small claims mediation provides an example:

> A florist sued the father of a bride for breach of contract when he refused to pay the $7,000 balance of the $13,000 floral bill for his daughter's wedding. The mediation lasted more than three hours. At various points throughout the session, the father focused on the fact that, contrary to the terms of their contract, the roses were not all red (something that was very important to the bride and her mother) and that some had wilted before the party's end.
>
> The mediator grew quite frustrated when, toward the end of the mediation, the father balked at what he conceded (and the mediator strongly agreed) was an extremely reasonable offer from the florist: to settle the $7,000 claim for $4,000. Only after the florist left the room did the mediator learn that the father's refusal to accept the offer was due to his fear of having to face his angry wife and explain to her that he had agreed to pay that amount of money to a florist who she believed had *"caused us so much embarrassment."*

It obviously would have been better to have obtained this information earlier, by means of pre-mediation screening questions ("*Is there a reason why your spouse won't be attending? Could that be a problem?*") or through similar inquiries during the mediator's opening statement. ("*Is there any reason why this cannot be resolved today? Will you have to consult your wife or your daughter before you can agree to settle this?*") At a minimum, where the parties' mediation statements suggest that the dispute may be of interest to persons not at the bargaining table, the mediator needs to learn about the potential impact of those persons' views on the decision making of the person in the room and on the viability of any agreement that may be reached.

■ §7.5.7 PROBE FOR NEEDS, INTERESTS AND PRIORITIES

As we saw in Chapter 2, when people negotiate, they take positions and demand concrete and tangible things they want. For example: "*Our demand is $2 million in damages, plus attorney's fees*," asserts the lawyer for the recently terminated executive. "*By hook or by crook, the kids are going to live with me*," declares the wife whose husband has just informed her that he is divorcing her to marry a younger woman.

However, more often than not, these demands are surrogates (and often poor or incomplete ones) for the parties' true interests — those less concrete but powerful forces that *really* matter to them: unsatisfied hopes and fears, emotional needs and drives that must be accommodated sufficiently for a party to be "happy enough" to agree to end the dispute.[23]

In comparison to the tangible demands that make up the parties' positions, needs and interests are intangible and personal to every individual. And while needs and interests may vary greatly in their relative importance, they are not negotiable. (Would you try to talk a friend out of needing respect from her spouse? Wanting recognition from her boss? Needing to feel that she is doing something useful with her life?)

Given their power, discovering the parties' needs and interests may hold the key to solving the problem. But they are often difficult to unearth, especially in joint session and early in the process. Why is this so?

First, needs often operate at a subconscious level, especially when they are somehow unacceptable to the individual. In a recent mediation, an elderly widow was embroiled in a dispute with her son and daughter about whether she should continue to live alone or move (as her children wanted) to an assisted-living facility. To the mediator, the old woman seemed very lonely and in need of human stimulation. But because being independent had always been so essential to her self-esteem, she remained consciously unaware of this need until the mediator gently explored it and her apparent unhappiness with her in caucus.

In a similar vein, in a mediation between a store owner and a teenage shoplifter, the victim seemed especially reluctant to accept the young offender's sincere apology and offer to make amends through repayment and community service, despite having been prepared to receive such an offer in pre-mediation "coaching" session. Only when pressed by the mediator on this resistance — especially given his claim to be a religious and forgiving person — did the victim realize that a part of him still harbored a strong need to see the young man punished. After taking a break, the shopkeeper relented, telling the youth, "I hope you take advantage of this second chance. There won't be a third."

---

23. *See generally* CHRISTOPHER W. MOORE, The Mediation Process: Practical Strategies for Resolving Conflict 252-263 (3d ed. 2003).

Second, even when people are aware of their needs and interests, many find it hard to articulate them. For example, a recently fired long-time salesman might be comfortable setting forth his claim for $2 million in lost wages but might not identify "feeling productive," "needing long-term security," "fearing loss of identity" or "being treated with loyalty" as important concerns, without the assistance of a mediator.

Third, powerful strategic factors often make it difficult for the mediator to learn the parties' true interests. This is especially so when the mediator's questions involve sensitive settlement facts — the parties' fears, constraints and vulnerabilities — that could undermine the strength of their publicly stated commitments. For example, the plaintiff in an automobile accident case might be willing to accept far less than the objective value of his claim because he is afraid of trial, is extremely risk-averse, or is out of work and needs money right now to replace his dying furnace. It is often difficult for even the most experienced mediators to unearth such facts, because the parties and their lawyers know that revealing them could undermine their bargaining position. Hence, probing about such interests must generally be done in the privacy of the caucus.

Sometimes learning the parties' true interests will be easier, sometimes harder. In the following extracts, watch first how one of our consumer mediators probed in caucus to see if the defendant contractor was worried about the potential impact of the litigation on his reputation. Then watch how one of our personal injury mediators tried to find out how the plaintiff felt about proceeding to trial. (The plaintiff actually wanted desperately to settle his case and to put the whole incident of his assault behind him.) This second extract takes place at the beginning of the mediator's first caucus with the plaintiff, about thirty-five minutes into the mediation. To what extent did the mediator succeed in learning what he wanted to learn? Could the mediator have probed more effectively or done anything differently to get the information he wanted? What can be learned about potential interests when a party refuses to discuss, or protests strongly about, concerns like reputational harm or risk of loss at trial? **Video Clip 7-G (1–2).**

Why Seek to Discover Interests?   Learning about interests can ease negotiations in two important ways. First, a party's true interests are often less in conflict with those of the opponent than is his stated position. For example, even the most antagonistic divorcing couples generally share an interest in having their children grow up to become happy and productive adults, and most would agree that their kids would be better off developing a good relationship with both parents rather than only one. By continually pointing out shared interests, mediators can reduce the level of tension in many disputes.

Second, in contrast to a demand or position, there are usually several ways in which an interest can be met. We saw this in Chapter 2, with the story of the dog bite case. Positions (*"Get rid of the dog!" "No way!"*) are generally much harder to satisfy than the parties' differing but not necessarily conflicting interests — for example, the dog bite victim's need for physical safety and the dog owner's desire for companionship for his children. A mediation in that case in which these interests were openly discussed could produce negotiations in which an electronic fence, or a chain link fence, or a dog run, or an agreed-upon exercise schedule for the dog were all viable options. Moreover, each party is likely to have certain needs that subjectively are more important than others. Where other issues are on the table, such as compensation for the victim's injuries, and the issues are valued differently by the parties, this sets up the possibility of trades that will give both sides more of what they care about. Each party might be willing to forgo claims based on low-priority interests if they got enough of their higher-priority needs met.

"Narrow settler" and time-constrained mediators often resolve disputes without learning much about the parties' real needs. But agreements built on addressing interests are likely to be more satisfying and thus more durable than simple compromises between two stated positions.

Listening and Probing for Interests.   The process of learning the parties' interests begins during their opening statements, with the mediator's developing tentative working hypotheses about the needs that might explain the parties' public statements and often extreme positions. Sometimes the parties are quite explicit. In the dog bite case, the plaintiff's statement "*I'm scared to cross the street when her dog isn't fenced in*" would be a pretty sure indicator of his interest in physical security. How might a mediator confirm that this is so? By using active listening: "*So it sounds as if your future physical safety is an important concern for you. Am I right?*" If the mediator has misunderstood the plaintiff's statement, he will correct her, no harm done.

Sometimes, however, the mediator must listen more deeply for the underlying message, beyond the words the parties use. Perhaps a topic is repeated several times, signaling its importance. Maybe there is a revealing emotional display or body language suggesting that a topic is particularly significant or upsetting. For example, if the defendant in the dog bite case bristles in response to one of the plaintiff's statements and angrily retorts, "*Well, there's no way we're going to give up our dog!*" the mediator must ask herself: "*Why might she being saying this?*" "*Why in that tone?*" "*What needs might explain this position?*" "*What might most other people in her situation be concerned about?*" With careful listening, the mediator may be able to reframe the position (insistence on keeping the dog) as an interest or need. ("*So is continuing companionship an important goal for you?*" "*No? Well, does having your dog make you feel more secure against intruders?*")

Often, however, the parties do not voluntarily reveal or signal their interests in joint session or even in the early phases of caucusing. When this occurs, the mediator should probe further. Here are some useful questioning devices:

- ■ **"Why" questions.** Open-ended "why" questions are usually very effective in getting at interests: "*Why is it important that you get . . . ?*" "*Why is what Joe has proposed unacceptable?*"

- ■ **Feelings and effects questions.** Asking questions about the impact of the dispute or possible solutions on parties' lives can also yield important information about interests, as in: "*What bothers you most about her conduct?*" "*How is this dispute affecting you?*" "*How might their attempt to enforce this non-competition clause impact your business over the next ten years?*" "*What would you do if you got that amount of money?*"

- ■ **Priority questions.** Asking the parties about their priorities is a way of getting at the relative strength of their different interests, for example: "*What are your goals in this case? What is most important to you? As between this issue and that one, if you had to choose, which one has priority* *and which could you accept less of?"* These kinds of questions force the parties to articulate their preferences and provide criteria with which to evaluate different settlement proposals that may come later.

■ **Asking about or verifying hunches about specific interests.** In §2.4, we provided a list of interests that motivate most human beings. Using their intuition and life experience, mediators identify particular needs or interests they think *might* be motivating the disputants and then ask about them specifically. In Clip 7-G, you saw one of our *Wilson v. DiLorenzo* mediators ask the defendant contractor in caucus whether he was concerned about the possible effect of the plaintiff's lawsuit on his reputation in the plaintiff's community. The question was not directly prompted by anything the defendant had said earlier in the mediation; rather it was the mediator's intuition that, like most contractors, reputational concerns might carry weight with him. Questions based on such hunches are usually "no-lose" propositions for the mediator: She will learn valuable information whether the party agrees, defensively disagrees, or corrects the mediator by revealing other concerns.

■ §7.5.8 PROBE FOR UNCERTAINTY AND DOUBT

As we have noted, parties in conflict generally know a lot about "their" version of the facts and less about their opponent's. They often suffer from egocentric over-confidence and partisan bias about the rightness of their cause and the likely future course of the dispute. Effective mediators expose the participants to the legitimate viewpoints of the other side as well as "third-person" perspectives — ways of seeing the same situation that may differ from *either* side's view. They do so by fleshing out the parties' self-serving statements and conclusions; surfacing weaknesses, contradictions and uncertainties; and where appropriate in the mediation of legal disputes, asking hard questions about how the parties will be able to prove contested aspects of their case at trial.

Many newer and legally trained mediators are naturally drawn in their questioning to try to find out "what happened." To them, conflicting factual accounts are messy and unsettling.[24] They endeavor, as a judge or other fact-finder might, to determine the most plausible version of past events. In the process, they often attempt to reconcile the parties' diverging accounts of the dispute and seek agreement (and sometimes downplay differences) about the facts in order to be able to determine for themselves "who's (more) right." And, while underscoring points of agreement or of clarity can create a climate of cooperation, *disagreement and uncertainty* about the facts may, paradoxically, have greater benefits.

This is because, unlike a judge or arbitrator, the mediator is not trying to resolve the contested legal and factual issues in the case, but rather is seeking to help the parties, if possible, attain an agreement. And shaking the parties' confidence and sowing honest doubt can be among the neutral's most effective

---

24. For some, this discomfort may be a product of the formative first year of law school, in which the facts are often neatly "given" in court opinions, casebook editors' summaries and professorial hypotheticals.

interventions toward this end. It is only after learning that one's opponent's position is stronger than previously thought, or one's own stance weaker, or that some third perspective is equally plausible, that many parties can be persuaded to rethink their positions. If the parties' versions of past events diverge and each is at least somewhat plausible, doesn't each side have some real risk of being disbelieved? Effective neutrals thus actively seek out ambiguity. How?

Probing for Factual Details.   Some of the questioning techniques we have already discussed for expanding on the parties' opening statements are useful for this purpose. One is forcing the parties to unpack conclusions by asking open and narrow questions about what seem to be key topics. In a neighbor-neighbor dispute, suppose that one party complains that the adjoining homeowner *"constantly has loud parties late at night."* The mediator might ask, *"Say more about what you mean by 'constantly'?"* *"How many parties, in, say, the last month?"* *"How do you know they were 'parties'?"* *"What exactly did you hear?"* *"When you say 'late at night,' what times are we talking about exactly?"* Through this kind of questioning process — of both sides — the mediator might learn that there have been three incidents in the last month, that two ended by 10:15 p.m., and that one was a gathering to commemorate the death of the defendant's mother. As one mediation scholar has written, "facts persuade, so develop them."[25]

Another effective approach is to probe for significant chronological details in areas that might affect the parties' rights and responsibilities if the case were to go to trial. In an auto accident case in which the plaintiff's own driving is claimed by the defendant to have contributed to causing the crash, the neutral might ask the plaintiff: *"At what exact times did you consume the three bottles of beer? Did you eat anything else that day? When? How long, exactly, was the interlude between your drinking and driving?"*

Questioning About Evidence.   In the same way, doubt can be sown by questioning the parties closely about the *evidence* they have to support the propositions that they will need to prove if the case goes to trial. In the mediation of the hypothetical auto accident case just discussed, a mediator might ask hard questions about how the plaintiff will prove that the defendant's driving was "negligent." This abstract legal conclusion can only be established through one or more concrete factual propositions — for example, that the defendant was speeding, or talking on his cell phone, or combing his hair at the time the accident occurred, or that his reaction time was impaired by alcohol.

In legal disputes, concrete factual propositions must then be established through actual (and admissible) evidence. If the claim is based on speeding, are there any eyewitnesses who can testify as to the speed that the defendant was driving? If there was an eyewitness, did he have an unobstructed view? Was he paying attention or was he distracted by other activities? Does he wear prescription eyeglasses and, if so, did he have them on?

If there is no *direct* evidence of speeding (an eyewitness, a radar-supported citation for speeding in an admissible police report, etc.), is there any *circumstantial*

---

25. Joseph Stulberg, Taking Charge/Managing Conflict 96 (1987).

evidence of speeding (evidence that the driver was in a rush to get to a meeting, 100-foot skid mark evidence that must be interpreted by an expert, etc.)?

Questioning About Evidentiary Gaps.   Often the *absence* of documents or tangible evidence can be persuasive. In a recent mediation of a landlord-tenant dispute, the tenant asserted, and the landlord denied, that the final month's rent had been paid in cash to the landlord's secretary. Based on this narrative, the mediator asked the tenant whether he had obtained a receipt (as would likely occur in the case of cash payment). Receiving a negative response, the mediator (without saying anything further) was able to create substantial doubt in the tenant's mind as to whether his version would be believed in court, thus promoting a resolution.

You may think that this kind of probing requires expertise in the legal subject matter of the dispute, and sometimes it does. But often it requires little more than ordinary experience with the patterns of daily life. It is a matter of asking yourself, "What else would be true if this were true?"—of reasoning backward from each key factual conclusion that a party is asserting to the potential evidence that *should* exist to support it. If that evidence does not exist, you have created an opening for doubt.

Third-Party Perspectives: Questioning About Alternative Possible Outcomes and Unseen Risks.   In situations in which uncertainty exists with respect to each party's position, another possibility looms: that a third potential outcome—one that will please neither side—may be as or more likely than the ones that the parties have been contemplating. Such possibilities are often best appreciated—and sometimes only seen—from the "fly on the wall" distance that the mediator brings to the conflict. Neutrals who want to help disputants appreciate all of the risks they face actively probe to flesh out such potential risks when they exist.

In a hotly contested child custody mediation, the parents of a two-year old argued bitterly about the site of the father's visits with his daughter. Each parent wanted the contacts to take place at his or her home. When her questioning revealed that each had a live-in lover who was the source of considerable resentment and who might be present at visits, the mediator was able to present a third (and mutually undesired) possible court outcome: that the visits would be ordered to take place in the supervised but austere confines of the court house nursery. The parents quickly agreed to a plan of their own.

Probing for Doubt: Joint Session or Caucus?   Have a look at the following extracts, in which the two mediators in our premises liability case brought out various legal and evidentiary problems in the plaintiff's and defendant's positions through questioning. Sometimes their interventions led to explicit concessions, sometimes not. When should such interventions be carried out in joint session and when privately?[26] What variables guide your answer? **Video Clip 7-H (1–2).**

---

26. For an example of a "no-caucus" mediation model that includes open discussion of the parties' legal risks in joint session, *see* Videotape: Saving the Last Dance: Mediation Through Understanding (Center

Should the Mediator Review Tangible Evidence?   What should the mediator do when the parties ask him to review what they see as probative tangible
evidence (performance evaluations, contracts, receipts, diagrams, photographs,
etc.) they have brought with them? Mediation often takes place without the
parties' having had previous access to each other's proofs. If the mediator anticipates trying to produce movement by creating uncertainty in the mind of an overly
confident party, shouldn't he welcome the opportunity to review such evidence
and to share it with that party?

Our answer is: It depends. If the tangible evidence is not extensive or if there
are a few key documents that are pivotal to the proof, they should be reviewed. For
example, if a landlord has withheld part of a former tenant's security deposit,
claiming that she left the apartment "a mess" and that he had to pay $300 to
get it professionally cleaned, it is certainly worth spending a few minutes reviewing
the tenant's photos of the apartment showing that it was in good order on the day
she left, as well as the landlord's receipt for his cleaning services.

Where the tangible or documentary evidence is extensive, the mediator must
walk a fine line: On the one hand, the mediator wants to give the parties the sense
of "procedural justice," that he has conducted a careful proceeding in which all
parties feel they have been heard. On the other hand, getting bogged down in an
adversarial evidentiary proceeding can be costly in terms of the time it requires and
the atmosphere it reinforces. Transparency may help alleviate this tension:
explaining to the parties that this is a mediation, not a trial; that there is insufficient
time to review and test all possible evidence; and encouraging both sides to present
the evidence they deem most crucial and to summarize the rest.[27]

To the extent you spend joint session time reviewing documents and other
tangible evidence, it is critical that this material be shared with the opposing party.
After all, it doesn't matter if *you* are persuaded by the evidence; it does matter if
they are. Ask, "*Have you seen these photos, Mrs. Hoyle?*" "*Mr. Larsen, may I
share your photographs with Mrs. Hoyle?*"

If a party offers tangible evidence in the opening joint session, should you
review it then? Might later in the process be preferable? What considerations
guide your response? Suppose instead that a party provides you with persuasive
evidence in caucus but says that he or she wants to hold that evidence back in order
to have it as a "secret weapon" in case of a trial? What might you say in such a
situation?

Should the Mediator Hear from Witnesses?   In court-connected mediation,
the parties often bring witnesses with them and ask the mediator to hear the
witnesses' "testimony." Should the mediator agree? As with extensive documents,
in most settings the mediator has no time to take testimony the way a judge in a

---

for Mediation in Law and Harvard Law School Program on Negotiation, 2001). *See also* GARY
FRIEDMAN & JACK HIMMELSTEIN, Challenging Conflict: Mediation Through Understanding (2009) (advocating no-caucus model).

27. Occasionally, one party may wish to present evidence or witnesses and the other side may strenuously object, either because they have no comparable evidence of their own or do not wish to turn the
mediation into a trial-type process. To resolve such a stalemate, the mediator might discuss the potential
benefits (added information that may help make settlement decisions) with the objecting party and the
risks (the mediation ending) with the proponent of the evidence. Ideally, such process issues would have
been resolved before the mediation or in its opening stages. *See* Chapters 4 and 6.

trial might, and may want to lead the process in other, less adversarial directions. In such situations, it should be sufficient to explain his reasons and ask the parties to summarize who their witnesses are and what they would expect them to say.

However, hearing information directly from "the horse's mouth" is usually more persuasive than hearing it characterized secondhand by a party or her lawyer, isn't it? If there is a particularly salient witness who can be brought into the mediation room — the mutually respected next door neighbor who helped the tenant clean her apartment and will testify that it was left in "broom-clean" condition — might not the neighbor's (condensed) live testimony be effective in aiding the process?[28]

Don't Expect a "You're Right; You're Right; I Know You're Right"[29] Moment.   When probing for doubt, do not expect immediate or dramatic shifts in position. Even if your questioning leads the parties to recognize that there are legitimate competing perspectives, competitive bargainers generally will be reluctant to concede this, at least right away. The process of sowing doubt generally tends to produce more subtle signs of softening: an attempt to change the subject, a request for assurance that the other side will be exposed to similar scrutiny, a refusal to discuss certain areas of weakness at all. Moreover, the factual expansion stage we are describing here comes fairly early in the process. If your doubt-sowing probes have been successful, overt shifts in position and new proposals will likely come later on.

The mediator must carry out this form of probing with care. If it is done too tentatively or subtly, it may not achieve its effect. If performed too heavy-handedly or only with a focus on areas of weakness, the parties may feel cross-examined and may thereafter be reluctant to work with the mediator, whose neutrality they may question. The solution is transparency: telling each party exactly what you are doing and why, and assuring them that it will be done evenhandedly and honestly, acknowledging legitimate areas of both strength and weakness on each side.

Finally, as with so many other aspects of the process, there is the potential opportunity cost of going down this road: a premature or prolonged focus on investigating the past and the possible court resolution of a dispute can take valuable time and energy away from other future or interest-oriented approaches to resolving it.

Which Comes First? Probing for Interests or Probing for Doubt?   We have suggested a progression in which the mediator probes for interests before probing for doubt. Why? If parties are willing to be open about their real needs, this can ease the negotiations, reduce the zero-sum nature of the dispute and reduce or even eliminate the need to probe in a more direct or confrontational way. By contrast, probing for doubt can make the parties feel challenged and defensive and can compromise perceptions of the mediator's neutrality. However, depending on the nature of the dispute and the parties' stances, probing for doubt may need

---

28. In some forms of evaluative mediation, where the parties seek the mediator's evaluation of the evidence and possible outcomes, the mediator may wish to invite abbreviated testimony from key lay and expert witnesses so as to be able to provide a more comprehensive and accurate assessment of the matter. We return to the subject of legal evaluation in §9.5.4, *infra*.
29. *When Harry Met Sally* (Castle Rock Entertainment 1989).

to precede any effort to uncover undisclosed needs and interests. Can you think of situations in which this might be the case?

■ §7.5.9 PROBE FOR NEGOTIATION NORMS, STANDARDS AND PAST PRACTICES

Most people think of themselves as adhering to general values, principles or standards as to how they should behave and (as we will discuss further in Chapter 9) want to be seen as acting consistently with those principles. Effective mediators therefore often work from the general to the particular, asking parties to identify such standards and practices before any actual bargaining starts. This is information to which the neutral can return with each participant when the process turns to making and responding to proposals to resolve the problem. This kind of probing sometimes takes place just before or during the bargaining and problem-solving stages of a mediation, because these norms, standards and practices relate to the negotiation proposals that parties make.

Norms and Standards.   For example, in a claim by a rug owner over an expensive, five-year-old Tibetan rug that was allegedly ruined by a rug cleaning service, the mediator, before asking the plaintiff what amount he is seeking in damages, might ask him: "*Do you agree that a new rug loses a certain value as soon as it leaves the showroom?*" "*Would you also agree that it loses additional value each year after that?*" If the plaintiff agrees but later makes an inflated money demand based on the price of the rug in new condition, the mediator can question whether this demand is consistent with his earlier concession. As another example, in an advertising firm's intradepartmental dispute over employees' "face time" at the office as opposed to their working at home, the mediator might ask: "*Can we all agree that maximum creative output by the graphic designers is the company's highest priority?*"

Past Practices.   In some mediations, the kind of dispute being aired is a recurring one for one or both of the participants. Merchants who routinely face customer complaints about goods and services may have established policies for dealing with them. Employers may have standard (even if unofficial) ways of dealing with minor rule infractions. Customary ways of dealing with past disputes can often provide a helpful precedent to guide the resolution of the current one.

Watch how one of our mediators asks the contractor in *Wilson v. DiLorenzo* about his prior practices for resolving customer complaints. What does her probe accomplish? **Video Clip 7-I.**

Probing about past practices during information expansion can be useful in the later resolution-seeking stage of the process. As with questions about general standards, if a party is making proposals that are inconsistent with his own past practices, the mediator can point to these inconsistencies in trying to produce greater movement. ("*Earlier, Frank, I thought you said that your practice is to make your customers happy even if it costs you some money. May I suggest that if you want Bernice to feel that she has been treated well as a customer, now is the time to show it?*")

Questions about past practices sometimes serve another purpose as well: If a party has an established practice that is *itself* an impediment to resolution, the mediator can try to help that party reconsider that precedent or provide a rationale for departing from it. (*"I know that your standard practice has been never to pay for private residential school tuition for special education students unless you are ordered to do so by a judge. But have you taken into account that the plaintiff's attorney's fees are as high as the boy's private school tuition would be in this case and that the Board will be completely on the hook for the fees, and the tuition, if it loses at trial? . . . What about this, then: Suppose that Mr. and Mrs. Asbill would agree to a confidentiality clause stating that they will never disclose to anyone that you agreed in mediation to place their son at Hamilton Academy?"*)

■ §7.5.10 PROBE FOR ALTERNATIVES TO A NEGOTIATED SETTLEMENT AND THE IMPACT OF NON-RESOLUTION

Finally, skillful mediators take time to explore with the parties the economic, social and psychological costs and benefits of settling or not settling the matter in dispute. These conversations usually occur late in the mediation, often after negotiations have begun and sometimes at a point where an impasse may be looming. They almost always take place in caucus, because they concern matters that neither party generally wants to share with the other side.

Because these sorts of inquiries can involve considerations that are distasteful or may seem unjust to the parties (*"Mr. Murphy, even if we agree that your legal position is strong, how much in counsel fees and time will this litigation consume?"*), the mediator must tread lightly. This is not a matter of browbeating the parties into reaching settlement or even subtly influencing the parties to agree that settlement is the best choice. To do her job properly, the mediator needs to have candid, fair-minded discussions with both sides to help them identify and later weigh the pros and cons of settlement as compared to their other options. (Sometimes non-resolution — even with its costs — really is the preferable choice.)

Economic Costs and Benefits.   By economic costs and benefits, we mean the tangible, material consequences of resolution or non-resolution, including:

- ■ **Increased costs.** *"If you are not able to settle this case, will you have to find and hire a lawyer? What do you estimate you will have to spend on legal fees? On expert fees and other trial expenses? How does this consideration affect your thinking?"* Or: *"If you end your mediation without a parenting agreement, will you incur any additional child care expenses? Will these pose any hardship for you? Shall we explore that issue?"*

- ■ **Other financial impacts and "opportunity costs."** *"Who will 'watch the store' while you are sitting in the courtroom? Will you lose any work time while the trial is taking place? Vacation time?"* Or: *"While you are awaiting your student conduct hearing, will you be able to study for finals? Will you have the energy to look for a summer internship?"*

- ■ **"Multiplier" effects.** *"Mr. Manufacturer, this is a standard clause in all of your sales contracts, isn't it? If you litigate this case and lose, might other customers want to challenge the same contract term?" "Mr. Hospital Administrator, have you considered how a newspaper article about the plaintiff's gender discrimination allegations might affect your hospital's ability to hire competent women physicians?"*

Social Costs and Benefits.   We refer here to the effects of settling or not settling on a party's relationships with others, including but not limited to the opposing party. For example: "*Explore with me: If you end up fighting this custody case out in court, how do you see this affecting your kids? Could you harm your relationship with them?*" Or: "*Are you worried at all that if you end up settling your discrimination claim, your co-workers will see you as a sellout? Do you want to talk about that?*"

Psychological Costs and Benefits.   Skilled neutrals also try to help disputants surface and consider the potential personal and emotional impact of continuing a dispute and psychological benefits of achieving closure, and how these compare with any disappointment with the other side's settlement offers. For example: "*Share with me: How does the prospect of going through a trial make you feel? How would it feel not to have to think about this any more? Have you factored that into deciding what you want to do?*" Lawyers often downplay the psychological benefits of ending conflict, but for many disputants the freedom to "move on" can often be an important benefit of settlement.

§7.6 BEYOND CATEGORIES: THE ROLE OF INTUITION AND CURIOSITY

Much information expansion comes about by thorough exploration of the probing categories we have discussed in this chapter. But sometimes important information — maybe even the key information to resolving a difficult dispute — emerges only in response to some intuition, hunch or curiosity that the mediator is willing to pursue.

Have you ever been in the presence of someone or something that, for no apparent reason, made you feel uncomfortable or fearful? While reading a story or watching a film, has something hit you — unconsciously, not as a result of thinking — that made you sense that something important (you're not sure what) was happening that might later figure in the plot? Maybe it was a pause, a glance, a change of rhythm or a just a feeling that something that *should* have happened was missing. We all have such intuitions from time to time. When mediators act on their intuitions, this sometimes helps them unearth critical information.[30] Consider this recent case:

> A week after she moved out of their apartment, a woman sued her ex-boyfriend for $1,600, which she claimed represented half of the cost of the furniture they had bought together a year earlier and which she now needed to furnish her new living quarters. The ex-boyfriend, unemployed and unable to pay her, offered to give her the living room couch, which had cost $1,900 and was in excellent condition, and

---

30. Social science tells us that intuitions — automatic signals as opposed to deliberate step-by-step thoughts or ideas — are triggered by drawing on our reservoir of past experiences and cultural exposures that we carry with us but cannot recall consciously. *See generally* HANS WELLING, *The Intuitive Process: The Case of Psychotherapy*, 15 J. OF PSYCHOTHERAPY INTEGRATION 19 (2005).

arrange for its delivery to her. At her angry rejection of the ostensibly reasonable offer, an impasse seemed imminent.

The mediator called a caucus, starting with the plaintiff. *"I sense that there is something no one wants to say,"* he said. *"Is there something significant about this sofa that no one has mentioned?"* Several teary minutes later, she revealed that she had been told that the defendant and her best friend had commenced an affair on that sofa; as a result, it was too painful to consider owning it. The case settled quickly after that. When the defendant was confronted with the reason why his ex-girlfriend wouldn't accept the sofa, he agreed to borrow the money from his father to repay his debt to her — an option he had previously refused to consider.

It is said that some people are naturally more intuitive than others, and this is probably true. But we think that all mediators can improve upon their natural intuitive tendencies by clearing their minds, by avoiding assumptions and fixed ideas about the problem, by paying attention to details and by being fully "in the present."[31]

Of course, intuitions are merely hypotheses. They need to be explored and confirmed with disputants before being acted upon as though they had validity. Pursuing hunches also requires the mediator to shed inhibitions about being invasive or "prying." So long as the mediator's curiosity is not gratuitous and is explained as part of the process of trying better to understand the parties' conflict, it communicates caring and concern and will be understood that way.[32]

■ §7.7 TO THE MAXIMUM EXTENT POSSIBLE, DEVELOP INFORMATION IN JOINT MEETINGS

As stated in the opening of this chapter, we recommend that, to the maximum extent possible, mediators try to develop information in joint session, rather than in caucus. In advancing this model, we draw a distinction between caucusing during the information-expansion stage and caucusing during negotiations. In negotiation caucuses, which we discuss in Chapter 9, the mediator meets with each party privately, helping them to craft their own negotiation proposals and weigh and evaluate those coming from the other side. If necessary, the mediator also uses the caucus to engage in those persuasion efforts that are best carried out privately.

The separation we draw between "caucusing during information gathering" and "caucusing during negotiations" is, to some degree, an artificial one. All of the categories of information we have discussed in this chapter at least anticipate the negotiation process and seek information that may aid the eventual bargaining. Moreover, information gathering commonly continues during the negotiations. Indeed, some of the categories of information we have discussed here — the parties' needs and interests, the parties' alternatives to a negotiated settlement, the parties' past practices for dealing with similar disputes — often do not arise

---

31. Leonard C. Riskin, *The Contemplative Lawyer: On the Potential Contributions of Mindfulness Mediation to Law Students, Lawyers, and Their Clients*, 7 Harv. Negot. L. Rev. 1 (2002).
32. David E. Reiser, *The First Patient, in* Patient Interviewing: The Human Dimension 3-20 (David E. Reiser & Andrea Klein Schroder eds., 1980).

(or cannot be discussed productively) until the actual bargaining starts. Nevertheless, we think this distinction is useful. First, it underscores the importance of developing information as a separate stage of the process, before trying to solve the problem. Second, it helps highlight the different considerations, costs and benefits in caucusing for different purposes.

The Advantages of Informational Caucusing.   The caucus is arguably the most unique feature of the mediation process. No other "primary" dispute resolution mechanism has it. Especially where the parties have attacked each other or taken extreme competitive stances in the opening joint session, moving immediately into separate meetings seems to offer many advantages. It can provide a respite from the level of hostility. Given the promise of confidentiality, parties are likely to be more open in private than they would be in joint session.

Separate sessions can also provide a safe setting for parties who may be fearful of talking in the presence of the other side or who want the neutral's guidance on whether or how best to convey potentially inflammatory information. This can create intimacy and rapport, which helps the mediator probe for, interpret and evaluate information without having to worry about appearing biased.

The mediator can also use the caucus to "translate" toxic or upsetting statements by the other side. Privately reframing inflammatory information or offering an explanation for it can prevent conflict escalation and promote mutual understanding, in the process opening up the flow of information.

Finally, the mediator may need to address concerns about problematic behavior that may be impeding the process of gathering information. Is one side being overly belligerent? Reluctant to talk? Unable to communicate clearly? Discussions of such topics require privacy.

Given these considerable benefits, it is hardly surprising that many mediators — especially newer ones — seek to move into the "easier" realm of separate sessions as soon as joint sessions begin to feel tense or challenging at all, or whenever they want to broach potentially sensitive topics.

The Disadvantages of Caucusing.   But separating the parties during information gathering has many costs as well. First, it is generally only through face-to-face contact that a party can hear, be persuaded by and develop empathy for the other party's situation. Similarly, face-to-face interaction allows each party to watch the mediator demonstrate empathy for the other side's perspective — a perspective that an overconfident party may otherwise deem unworthy of credence. Keeping everyone together also provides the parties (and the mediator) valuable data that comes from directly observing participants' reactions to what is said.

Where a continuing relationship between the parties is contemplated — in child custody, co-worker and neighbor-neighbor disputes, for example — caucusing minimizes the parties' ability to use the mediation experience as an opportunity to learn to communicate more effectively in future conflicts. When the parties will be dealing with each other going forward, such "educational" effects are one of the most important potential benefits of mediation.[33]

---

33. For this reason, it is not uncommon for family mediators and neighborhood dispute centers to minimize caucuses, if not avoid them entirely.

There are other, less obvious disadvantages to gathering information privately. While avoiding the direct hostility that can characterize joint sessions, caucusing can open the door to heightened *indirect* hostility in the form of self-serving statements and misleading assertions about absent parties.[34] Such distortions and misstatements can have the effect of leading the mediator to form a bias in favor of the party with whom she is meeting.[35]

Caucusing — especially early in the mediation — can also lead to an expectation of private dealings for the remainder of the process. Parties who like the private environment of the caucus may become resistant to a returning to a joint session or to dealing with the other side productively while there. When this occurs, much of the potential of the process may be lost.

Finally, caucusing can pose special challenges for the neutral. When the mediator is meeting with one side, the party not in the room may stew or become suspicious by virtue of being excluded. If parties perseverate and caucuses lengthen, these problems are exacerbated. Caucusing also creates a situation in which only one person — the mediator — knows all of the information that has been revealed. This creates the possibility that the mediator may try to manipulate the process in troubling ways, which we will discuss in Chapter 12.

On balance, then, there is much to be gained by seeking as much information in joint session as possible, for as long as possible, relegating information caucusing to situations of clear need. Such "need" cannot be defined in a neat set of rules. Our guiding principles are these: How hostile or discouraging of openness is the parties' joint presence? Is this factor so strong that it outweighs the potential gains from keeping the parties together? So long as the level of direct hostility is low, no one seems fearful and the parties' communications are not stalled, we think that the costs of caucusing for information outweigh the benefits.

■ §7.8 CONDUCTING THE INFORMATION CAUCUS

Still, the mediator will sometimes view caucusing for information as necessary. Perhaps, despite the best efforts to create a comfortable environment, one or more parties seem reluctant to speak openly. Perhaps the mediator cannot control the aggression in the room. Maybe one of the parties or their lawyers signals or insists that he wants to meet with the mediator alone. Maybe the mediator has learned a lot about the dispute in joint session but believes that there are now topics that can only be explored privately. When the mediator decides to caucus for the purposes of developing information, what are the mechanics and objectives for doing this?

Plan for the Caucus. It is always useful to take at least a few minutes before each caucus to think through one's goals for the caucus and how they will be

---

34. *See* GARY L. WELTON, DEAN G. PRUITT & NEIL B. MCGILLICUDDY, *The Role of Caucusing in Community Mediation*, 32 J. CONFLICT RESOL. 181, 187, 192 (1988) (study showing that disputants often make wild accusations or try to co-opt the mediator in caucus sessions, though caucuses generally include less swearing and fewer angry displays than joint sessions).
35. *Id.* at 187, 196-197 (showing that mediators are more likely to side with a party in a caucus session than in a joint session); *see also* CHRISTOPHER W. MOORE, *The Caucus: Private Meetings That Promote Settlement*, 16 MEDIATION Q. 87, 100 (1987) (warning against the potential danger of mediators abandoning their impartiality in caucus sessions).

achieved. When co-mediating, holding a brief "mediators' caucus" (perhaps after escorting the participants to the waiting area) allows the team to "get on the same page" about what they will seek to accomplish in each private session and how they will go about it. Questions to consider before any round of private meetings include:

■ Whom to meet with first? The party who seems most fearful or uncommunicative? The party whose communication style is belligerent or bombastic? The party who was forced to go second in the opening stage of the mediation? Will this decision be explained to the parties and, if so, how?

■ What are you trying to accomplish in this caucus? To learn more information that has not yet come out? What information? To understand a party's reactions or reticence in joint session? What questions will you ask? What resistance might you encounter?

Prepare the Party Who Will Be Leaving the Room.   Next, the mediator needs to attend to the participants with whom she will not be meeting, including sending or escorting them to where they will wait. Obviously, to preserve the confidentiality of the process, those persons need to be kept out of earshot of the mediation room. Because caucusing can be lengthy, mediators often try to give the departing party a rough estimate of how much time will likely be spent with the other side. What are the pros and cons of doing this?

Some mediators assign "homework" where possible, so that a party's time spent alone is not "dead" time. For example, if a participant seems to be missing certain potentially useful information, maybe he can use this time to track it down. If someone should be at the mediation but isn't, maybe she can be located and brought to the session. What about asking the party to make a list of things not yet discussed or disclosed that she might like to raise confidentially when it is her turn to caucus? Might there be reasons not to do this?

Build Trust and Rapport.   When a mediator begins caucusing with a party, it is always helpful to reiterate the promise of confidentiality that was made at the beginning of the mediation and to give participants an opportunity to speak openly about anything that may be on their minds. Asking questions like: *"How is this process going for you? Is there anything you didn't feel comfortable talking about in joint session that you would like to share?"* helps accomplish this, as does expressing empathy for the parties' perspectives. The mediator's goal in the caucus, especially the first caucus, is to create intimacy and rapport with each party—the sense that *"this is a confidential space in which you can feel free to disclose anything that's on your mind."* This positive connection can be a valuable foundation for later stages of the mediation.[36] As in joint session, this means beginning with party-centered, not mediator-centered, questions.

Work on Communication Problems.   Once the party has been heard, the mediator will want to pursue the goals that caused her to call a caucus in the

---

36. Building trust and intimacy are important tools of persuasion, which we discuss in more detail in Chapter 9.

first place. This might include encouraging disclosure of information that seems to have been suppressed or avoided during joint discussions, interpreting inflammatory information that emerged in joint session so that it can be better received and understood and addressing problem behaviors that made continuing in joint session difficult.[37]

Whatever the mediator's goals, it is important to keep track of time and to be sensitive to the fact that there is another party waiting. When a mediator has a long list of goals, it is usually best to consider whether some of them (e.g., exploring negotiating flexibility while information is still being gathered) can be deferred to a later stage.

Encourage Meaningful Conversations.   An overarching reason for using the caucus format is to encourage meaningful, complex and self-revealing conversations and disclosures that will encourage the participants to look at their situation differently, to reveal and respond to new information and to consider and recognize the need for change.[38] Therefore, the *rhetoric* the mediator uses is important. In general, questions that ask respondents to *"explain," "explore with me," "share with me,"* or *"walk me through your thinking"* are more useful in inducing dialogue, revealing of interests, and analysis than yes-no or other simple questions. *"How would it feel to be done with this dispute?"* is apt to produce more complex thinking than *"Would you like to be done with this dispute?"*[39]

Explore the Wisdom of Sharing More Information.   Disputants often want to avoid disclosing certain facts to the other side, for reasons that may be counterproductive (even if logical on the surface). For example, sometimes parties wish to withhold potentially persuasive information in order to retain an element of surprise at trial, even though that very information, if disclosed, might persuade the other side of the wisdom of settling.

Problematic withholding of information also occurs in situations where the information in question is two-sided. For example, information that a party fears will be inflammatory (an employer's assertion that *"his job performance was abysmal"*) can also, if stated well, be persuasive. A fact that a party feels is embarrassing, demonstrates weakness or creates a risk of exploitation (a doctor's concession that *"my mind may have wandered in performing the surgery because my wife was dying"*) can, if conveyed properly, evoke sympathy. The mediator can use the privacy of the caucus to explore the nature of the information, its potential for helping or hurting the process and — if it is to be transmitted — how, when and by whom this might best be accomplished.

For an example of this process in action, watch how one of the mediators in *Wilson v. DiLorenzo* encourages the defendant contractor, Frank, to disclose information about his family's long-time relationship with his employees, Connie and Sam, to Bernice, the plaintiff homeowner. Reviewing the materials in this chapter, what was the mediator trying to accomplish by encouraging that this

---

37. In extreme cases, you may have to be blunt and inform the party that if the destructive behavior continues, you may have to terminate the mediation.
38. *See* CHARLES D. BRENNAN, Sales Questions That Close the Sale 68-86 (1994).
39. *Id.* at 74.

information be shared? Why might Frank or his lawyer consider the information sensitive? What impact does it seem to have on the negotiations when, much later in the process, Frank decides to reveal it? **Video Clip 7-J.**

Close the Caucus and Determine What Information You May Share with the Other Side.   Before concluding each caucus, the mediator needs to determine what information learned in caucus may and may not be shared with the other side. There are two ways of doing this. One is to ask: "*Is there any information we've talked about in caucus that I can disclose to the other side?*" The alternative is to ask: "*Is there any information we've talked about in caucus that I may not disclose to the other side?*" Is one formulation preferable? Why?

Ordinarily, to maintain balance, the mediator conducts a *round* of information caucuses: If she meets privately with one side, she will also meet with the other. Once the mediator has confirmed what is to be kept confidential, she sends or escorts out the initial caucusing party. The other party is brought in and the process starts all over again. Can you think of situations where a mediator would caucus for information with only one side? Where the number of caucuses held with each side would not be equal?

Decide the Next Format: Continued Caucusing or Joint Session?   In the waning moments of the first round of caucuses, a decision must be made whether or not to return to joint session. If the next phases of the mediation will be conducted by caucus, the mediator will have a good deal of control about how information will be carried back and forth between the parties. But if the process will return to joint session, the mediator may need to spend some of her time in caucus discussing with each party what information will be conveyed and coaching the party on how it can most productively be stated to the other side.

Is joint session versus continued caucusing a decision that should always be made by the mediator? Under what circumstances might it make sense to ask the parties what their preferences are? When should the mediator defer to those preferences? What about negotiating with the parties regarding *conditions* for returning to joint session? What might such a conversation entail?

CHAPTER

8

IDENTIFYING AND FRAMING NEGOTIATING ISSUES, ORGANIZING AN AGENDA

This chapter contains one video clip, totaling approximately three minutes.

■ §8.1 INTRODUCTION

"OK. I think we all have a pretty full sense of each of your perspectives. Obviously, you both have disagreements and concerns that will need to be addressed if we are to resolve this. Is there any reason we shouldn't move in the direction of seeing whether this can be worked out, by identifying what needs to be discussed?"

There comes a time when the mediation must move from understanding the problem to trying to resolve it. How does the mediator know when this point has arrived? Perhaps little new information is coming out through probing, even in caucus. Maybe the parties have begun to repeat themselves or have signaled that they want to begin to negotiate. Maybe time is running short.

In Chapter 6, we recommended that, from the parties' first statements onward, you keep not only a running mental list of possible negotiation issues, but an actual list as well. Taking notes about potential bargaining topics is a way of organizing your own thoughts and later discussions. This list should include not only those subjects that the parties have indicated must be discussed in order to resolve the conflict; it should include those that you think might be productive to add to the negotiations.

In this chapter, we examine in more detail the types of issues that are productive fodder for negotiation, those that are not and how a mediator can frame the mediable issues to aid negotiation and problem-solving. We discuss the mediator's and the parties' respective roles in constructing a negotiation agenda and in organizing the discussions to follow.

This stage of the mediation is often brief. In most negotiations — at least the kinds we are talking about in this book — the issues can be identified, framed and organized into an agenda in a matter of a few minutes or less.[1] Indeed, it is not uncommon for the process of agenda setting to be omitted entirely, especially where time is limited, there appears to be only one topic to discuss or the mediator assumes that "everyone knows what the issues are." We view this as unfortunate. For reasons that follow, we think it desirable to treat the transition from information gathering to problem-solving as a separate and deliberate stage of the mediation process.

■ §8.2 ISSUE IDENTIFICATION AND AGENDA CONSTRUCTION: THE BENEFITS

The creation of an agenda is aimed at providing a structure for the upcoming negotiations and as protection against overlooking important topics. But it can accomplish a great deal more.

Elevating Moods.   Creating an agenda can be a mood elevator, shifting energy from disputing about a past problem to the concrete, here-and-now task of working jointly to resolve it. It can mark a behavioral turning point, from arguing about things that often cannot be resolved by mediation, to negotiating and problem-solving about things that can. Even the most difficult disputes can experience a shift in optimism when the mediator signals this transition.

Bringing Order and Calm.   In situations filled with heated emotions, multiple concerns and disagreements, having an agenda can bring order out of chaos. By distilling messy and seemingly overwhelming factual disputes and feelings down to matters that are concrete and negotiable, the mediator can create a sense of calm.

Expanding Issues.   It can relieve competitive pressure by broadening narrow problems. Drawing up a list of items to be discussed will often prompt participants to raise new issues beyond those already identified. As we have already noted, while a resulting longer agenda can seem to make matters more complicated, it can actually ease the process of resolution by enhancing the possibility of creative and integrative trades.[2]

Ensuring the Presence of Indispensable Parties.   Creating an agenda can identify persons who have not yet been contacted but who may be indispensable to the negotiations. In a suit for money damages alleging unlawful use of force by a police officer, must the local prosecutor sign off if dropping criminal charges is a possible issue to be discussed as part of settling the civil claim? In a wrongful termination of employment case, if job reinstatement is a possible negotiation issue, are company managers with decision authority available by phone?

---

1. Complex, multi-issue disputes—international and environmental disputes, for example—often involve a lengthy process of agenda development, including multiple drafts of potential negotiation issues and their proposed sequence.
2. See §7.5.2, *supra*.

Ensuring That the Matter Is "Ready."   Being asked to commit to an agenda item can bring to the surface concerns about whether or not the issue — or even the whole dispute — is ripe for negotiation. Does a business partner need to see the next quarter's sales figures before considering any proposal to sell his share? Should a divorcing couple get an evaluation from a child psychiatrist before trying to negotiate the details of a custody arrangement? Does a spouse's reluctance to discuss selling the house mean he has not yet come to terms with the reality that a divorce will occur?

Avoiding Misunderstandings.   A pre-negotiation agenda can dispel erroneous assumptions about what is, or is not, in dispute. If participants are forced to be explicit about what they want to see discussed, the chances that a party will add new demands later in the negotiations will be reduced. New demands tacked on late in the bargaining process can produce anger and, sometimes, impasse.

Increasing the Chances of Success.   This stage can have strategic importance. As will be discussed shortly, the choice and labeling of issues placed on the agenda and the sequence in which they are discussed can often affect the success of the upcoming negotiations in significant ways.

■ §8.3 WHAT IS A "MEDIABLE" (NEGOTIABLE) ISSUE?

Mediation is a time-limited process, with participants who seek tangible results. An important part of the mediator's role in setting a negotiation agenda is confining it to issues that are mediable and excluding those that are not. In this chapter we use the terms "mediable issue" and "negotiable issue" interchangeably.[3] A "mediable issue" is simply a contested subject that is capable of being negotiated.

To be negotiable, an issue must have three essential characteristics:

■ **The possibility of more than one outcome.** Obviously, to be subject to negotiation, an issue must have more than one possible solution. A labor management dispute over the size of a cost-of-living wage increase for public sector workers is mediable if the outcome of negotiations could be an increase of, say, 1, 2 or 3 percent per year. If the cost-of-living increase for public sector employees is fixed by statute at 2 percent, there is nothing about this topic to be negotiated. Similarly, a party's "take it or leave it" position, if sincere, cannot be made into a mediation issue.

■ **Tangible and concrete.** To be negotiable, issues must be concrete and tangible enough to be adjusted through a bargaining process of give and take. Lots of topics that are in contention and important to the parties may be too vague or intangible to be negotiated. For example, "job security" is a familiar and often-raised concern in labor contract talks, but until it is restated in concrete terms (e.g., "length of contract" or "grounds for retention, promotion and firing"), it is too abstract a concept to be settled by negotiation.

---

3. Jennifer E. Beer & Eileen Steif, The Mediator's Handbook 115 (3d ed. 1997).

■ **Within the control of the parties to resolve.** To be mediable, an issue must be within the parties' ability to resolve, given their authority and the resources under their control.[4] If a company's health insurance plan is limited by contract to current employees, the issue of extending coverage retroactively to a worker fired last year probably cannot be the subject of productive negotiations. In some situations, court policies or other external constraints may rule an otherwise appropriate negotiation issue out of bounds. For example, family court rules that require divorcing couples to participate in child custody mediation often preclude staff mediators from mediating many of the financial aspects of divorce.

Distinguishing Mediation *Issues* from Information or Discussion *Topics*. As we saw in Chapter 7, many "topics," including historical facts, legal rules, feelings, interests, relationships and values, are important to inquire about and discuss in mediation. But the fact that a specific topic may be a fruitful area for detailed exploration doesn't mean that it is a negotiable issue.[5] Not everything that participants want to discuss or that is productive to explore can be resolved through mediation. Consider the following examples:

■ **Disputed issues of law and fact are not negotiable.** Law-trained mediators often think of "issues" as the disputed legal and factual questions in the appellate decisions they read in law school and in practice. But in mediation, disputes over legal and factual matters or what the most likely court result in a particular case would be are not negotiable. In our premises liability case, Josh Resnick sued his former landlord, Howard Stevens, claiming that an intruder got into his apartment, terrorized him and stole his property because of inadequate security provided by the landlord, including allowing a fire escape in a locked alleyway to hang too close to the ground. In this case, the parties might have a productive exchange of views about whether the intrusion into the plaintiff's apartment was "reasonably foreseeable" given the lack of prior break-ins, or whether it was within the landlord's legal responsibility to "make sure that no one could climb up onto that fire escape." They might argue about various factual and evidentiary issues, such as how the burglar got into the apartment building in the first place and how this fact will be proved. They might argue about who would win if the case went to trial. The parties' views on all such issues might affect their negotiation positions and tactics. But none of these issues could be negotiated. Why not? Because neither the mediator nor the parties can *decide* such questions. (Only a court can.)

■ **The parties' basic values and beliefs are rarely negotiable.** Some of the most difficult conflicts implicate deeply ingrained values or beliefs. For example, in a child custody mediation involving a devout father and a less devout mother, should the children receive religious schooling in their formative years? Must a private university instructor remove the pro-life poster from her office door when her dean demands this in response to the campus

---

4. Joseph B. Stulberg, Taking Charge/Managing Conflict 82 (1987).
5. Negotiable *issues* are often referred to as *topics* as well.

women's organization threat to organize a boycott of her classes? Strongly held views involving questions such as these are extremely difficult to change through persuasion or negotiation. Recognizing these limitations, most mediators steer parties away from trying to resolve value disagreements and redirect them toward issues that can more readily be negotiated.

For example, if divorcing parents are arguing about whether exposure to the mother's lifestyle with her new female partner would be harmful to their young son, an effective mediator might give the parties plenty of time to explore this difficult topic, but then try to move the discussion toward the tangible, interests-based issue of the "time and conditions under which the mother will have custody of the child."[6]

- **The parties' needs and interests are not negotiable.** As we have seen, a party's needs and interests are often at the heart of a conflict and are critically important for the mediator to probe and understand. But they themselves are non-negotiable. A man's fear and concern for personal security in the face of his neighbor's large, unfenced dog might well be a fruitful topic for exploration, but it cannot be negotiated. (What to do about the dog *is* negotiable.) A long-term employee laid off without any warning cannot be expected to "negotiate" her need to be treated with respect, to feel productive or to be concerned about future economic and health care security. (However, mediation could explore such concrete topics as company assistance in securing other employment, varying forms of compensation, including continuing insurance and pension benefits and a process by which her past contributions to the company might be acknowledged.)

- **The parties' habits and character traits are not negotiable.** A person's disputed attitudes, qualities and habits are not realistic topics for negotiation. Thus, a mother's lament that their child's father *"has no interest in being a real dad"* is not mediable. (But the amount of time he spends with the kids and the amount of financial support he provides for them are.) The claim by a group of minority workers that "our supervisor is a racist in hiring" is not negotiable. (But concrete steps that could be taken to increase minority hiring in the department might be.)

Converting Non-Mediable Issues into Mediable Ones. As these examples make clear, effective mediators do not squelch discussion of difficult topics. But at some point in the proceedings, they must work to convert non-mediable issues into mediable ones by (a) focusing on specific conduct that the parties might be persuaded to negotiate about and/or (b) by breaking down abstract propositions into more tangible topics that are amenable to concrete solutions. Such conversion is

---

6. Separating out the more readily negotiable interests-based portions of a values-laden dispute is one of several strategies discussed in LAWRENCE SUSSKIND, *How to Negotiate When Values Are at Stake*, NEGOTIATION (Harvard Program on Negotiation, October 2010), *http://cbuilding.org/publication/article/2010/how-negotiate-when-values-are-stake*.

possible even in disputes raising significant legal issues or deeply held values questions. For example:

> In an actual case a few years ago, male prison inmates objected to the state's plans to deploy female guards for the first time and sued state correctional authorities to enjoin the practice. During the first hour of the court-ordered mediation, inmate representatives regularly repeated their charges of "unconstitutionality" and their assertions of deprivations of rights to "privacy" and "dignity."
>
> Advising the parties that mediation could not resolve such contested and abstract issues, the mediator suggested that the inmates delineate their privacy and dignity concerns in more concrete terms. They complained of the risk of being seen showering, changing for exercise or using the toilet in their cells; being frisked or body-searched by a female; and being surprised when a woman was substituted for a male guard without prior notice. With this information in hand, the mediator proposed the following issues as possible agenda topics: hours of female guard deployment; location of female guard deployment; procedures for frisks and body searches; potential architectural modifications; and a system for notification about guard shifts.[7]

Sometimes this effort may be perceived by the parties as trivializing the real problems that will continue to linger even if such "side issues"[8] are worked out. But at least in some situations, resolving such side issues may take care of the underlying problem in the long run. For example, in a custody dispute, a father's non-mediable attitude of indifference toward his children might change over time if, after successful resolution of issues that can be negotiated—for example, a schedule for overnight stays at his home—he finds that he enjoys spending time with his kids. In a neighbor-neighbor dispute, non-negotiable feelings of animosity and distrust can be softened over time if both sides reliably comply with their negotiated commitments to keep their shared driveway free of trash cans.

Must Non-Negotiable Issues Be Dropped? The Transformative Critique.
Mediators with a transformative orientation argue that limiting mediation to tangible issues that have concrete solutions may cause the process to avoid addressing the more messy, interpersonal and relational matters that often lie at the heart of a dispute. They also attack the control this approach gives the mediator over how the problem will be defined and what will be discussed.[9]

But keep in mind the distinction we have drawn between a *discussion topic* and a *mediable issue*. Just because a topic cannot be resolved as a negotiation issue does not mean that it must be dropped from discussion. To the contrary, the real problem can be explored in depth through an early, open-ended exchange process in which the parties are provided time to discuss whatever is on their minds without

---

7. With this agenda as the guide, resolution on all but one of the issues was reached fairly quickly. Because the question of hours of guard deployment involved potential changes in the union contract covering all prison guards, that topic was deferred as beyond the parties' ability to resolve, at least until the union could be consulted.

8. *See* Beer & Steif, *supra* note 3, at 118.

9. *See* Robert Baruch Bush & Joseph Folger, The Promise of Mediation 66-68 (1994).

mediator structure or interruption; and a party-centered period of information expansion in which the mediator fleshes out the parties' own statements before exploring additional mediator-generated topics. Thus, except in extremely time-limited situations, it is possible to conduct a mediation in which *any* topic the parties want to discuss is fully aired, even though it might not become an issue for negotiation.

Values and Culture: Understandable Even If Not Mediable. Recent psychological research suggests that while there are certain universal moral values — avoiding harm to others, acting fairly, demonstrating loyalty to family and community, respecting authority, avoiding defilement — different cultures tend to weigh and define these values differently.[10] One culture may revere and protect dogs; another may eat them. Sometimes, the bitter conflicts that arise between persons of diverse backgrounds stem from different moral meanings these disputants assign to the same event, idea or action. Once those meanings are discussed and understood, significant progress may be achievable. Consider this case:

A recent employment dispute pitted the management of a Middle Eastern company against a U.S. minority group member seeking greater representation for members of his race in company hiring and advancement. When a company vice president chose one of his nephews over a qualified minority group member for a key promotion, a bitter conflict arose. Charges of nepotism were leveled at the company; it, in turn, thought it would be unfair to promote anyone primarily because of their race. Each side saw the other as acting out of immoral motives.

Probing the cultural underpinnings of the dispute might have revealed that, in the manager's country of origin, it is quite natural — indeed, expected — to hire one's own. The worker, in turn, might have explained his view, shared by most members of his race, of the need to correct historical discrimination. Such an exchange might have served to lower tensions, if not opened the door to actual negotiations. At a minimum, it could have helped each party understand that the other was (as he saw it) acting from laudable, not immoral, motives, driven by universal moral principles: the vice president's loyalty to family and community (not racism) and the worker's desire for fairness (not power).

What's a Mediable Issue?

A Restaurant Inspection. In a recent small-claims case in a major city, a municipal health inspector accused a Korean-American restaurant owner of injuring him by throwing a metal mixing spoon at him during an unannounced inspection. The inspection resulted in the restaurant being shut down for two weeks for various code violations. The angry restaurant owner alleged that it was a neighboring proprietor who had thrown the spoon. Contending that the inspector was hostile to Korean- and other Asian-American restaurant owners in the community, he demanded an end to the system of surprise inspections. He also sought payment for the cost of fixing a cracked neon sign that he alleged had been knocked over by the inspector during a follow-up inspection.

continues on next page >

---

10. STEVEN PINKER, *The Moral Instinct*, N.Y. Times Magazine (Jan. 13, 2008).

The mediable issues are **not**:

- *Who hit the inspector?* This is a disputed fact, not resolvable through mediation.
- *The restaurant owner's injured sense of dignity or the inspector's fear of the owner.* These are interests or feelings.
- *The inspector's alleged racism.* This is an attitude or prejudice.
- *How future inspections will be conducted.* This might have been negotiable, but these parties did not have the authority to change city policy.

Negotiable agenda items **might include**:

- *How the inspector's injury and the owner's sign damage will be addressed.*
- *How the parties will interact and communicate in the future to the extent they will have continued dealings.*
- *Steps that can be taken to improve relations between the inspector and this community.*

■ §8.4 PROPOSING AND FRAMING MEDIATION ISSUES

Who Proposes Mediation Issues?   When the time comes to make the transition from information gathering to negotiation, the mediator could simply invite the parties to identify the issues they wish to negotiate. This approach might be seen as an exercise in party autonomy and could have the advantage of revealing what is most important to the parties.

But simply inviting the parties to propose mediation issues has significant disadvantages as well. Most important, each party is likely to frame the issues it wants to discuss from its own partisan perspective: "*I want to discuss how much they are going to pay us for the disruption to the business they caused.*" "*I want to talk about why our kids should be living in their own home, with me, and not at their grandmother's.*" It may also be an invitation to the parties to act strategically, raising false issues to gain concessions on something they value more.

A better climate is usually achieved by the mediator's summarizing the key mediable issues identified to that point (framed appropriately, as discussed below) and then inviting the parties to make suggestions for additions. By the time of this transition to negotiation and problem-solving, the parties may have worked through difficult emotions to a considerable extent. With increased readiness to move toward resolution, they may be receptive to the mediator's language choices, with the result that their own agenda proposals may then sound like invitations to communicate rather than aggressive demands.

Framing the Issues to Be Negotiated.   The way mediation issues are framed by the mediator can affect how the participants think and negotiate about them.[11] Here are five principles for framing negotiation issues:

- ■ **Frame neutrally.** This is the most fundamental requirement. The mediator must frame each issue in a way that neither incorporates one side's position

---

11. CHRISTOPHER W. MOORE, The Mediation Process 243 (3d ed. 2003), *citing* JEFFREY Z. RUBIN & BERT R. BROWN, The Social Psychology of Bargaining and Negotiation (1975).

nor implies responsibility or blame where there is a dispute about it. Thus, in litigation against a freight company in which there was a dispute over whether frozen meat that had partially thawed during shipping was usable, the mediator would not want to describe the meat as "damaged" or "spoiled" when listing potential negotiation issues. Instead, she might describe the issue to be discussed as "*What shall be done about the partially thawed meat?*" or, more simply, "*Let's talk about the meat.*" In a neighbor-neighbor dispute about a loud stereo being played at night, the issue should be framed as "*Let's talk about the stereo*" rather than "*Let's talk about the loud stereo at night.*"[12]

■ **Frame to promote creativity and problem-solving.** If the participants are to be encouraged to consider multiple options for resolving a disputed issue, the issue should be described in a way that neither suggests nor forecloses possible resolutions, in words that invite but do not contain a solution.[13] For example, in the previous hypothetical neighbor dispute, the issue might be framed as "*How can Mary's desire to listen to her music and Fred's desire to get needed sleep both be accommodated?*" rather than "*Let's talk about the possibility of Mary cutting back on her stereo use at night.*" A proposed agenda topic in a typical personal injury case could be framed: "*How can John's injury be addressed or compensated?*" instead of "*How much will John be paid?*"

■ **Frame in a forward-looking manner.** Instead of using backward-looking words focusing on the problems that led to the mediation, issues can be framed in future-oriented language by focusing on what might be done about them. In a heated eviction dispute about a tenant's withholding all rent for three months because the landlord allegedly ignored his frequent requests for repairs, the issues might be framed as follows: "*One issue, it seems to me, is the status of the lease going forward: whether Mr. Joseph will remain as a tenant. A second issue is what will be done, if anything, concerning the months of rent that were admittedly not paid. A third set of issues has to do with whether any repairs will be made and, if so, a timetable for getting them completed. A fourth possible issue, assuming that Mr. Joseph continues to be a tenant, is coming up with a system for future communication about repair concerns. Do you agree that these are subjects that would be productive to discuss? Are there any issues either of you think we should add?*" Note that the issues are all framed in concrete terms involving future conduct in which the parties will or will not engage — the possible skeleton of a settlement agreement.

■ **Frame to lower competition.** Sometimes, the mediator can define what parties want to talk about in ways that make it sound more like a shared

---

12. The mediator must walk a fine line here. Just as with reframing of emotion-laden statements, care must be taken to ensure that neither party feels that their perspective on any topic has been ignored or minimized through this neutral framing.

13. This expansive approach to naming negotiation issues shares a good deal with successful forms of open-ended questioning aimed at eliciting maximum information during probing.

problem than an invitation to compete in a zero-sum contest. In disputes over arrangements for the care of children, words such as *custody, visitation, primary* and *legal* are loaded with competitive meanings for many couples who are in conflict. ("*If I get 'primary legal custody,' I win, and she loses.*") By contrast, defining the negotiating issues as "developing a joint parenting plan" or "sharing responsibilities for your daughter's care" or "ensuring that both of you have quality time with the kids" may trigger more collaborative approaches. It is common practice for family mediators to use such terms.

▪ **Frame concretely.** Mediation issues defined too vaguely or generally will provide insufficient guidance to stimulate idea generation. Thus, in a dispute between a worker and his boss in which the employee alleges that work is assigned unevenly and feedback on work is always negative and poorly timed and the supervisor responds that the employee is hypersensitive to any criticism of his work, it would likely be unhelpful to identify the issues as "your relationship" or "how you communicate" or even "how supervision will occur in the future." To make progress on the issues, they might more usefully be framed as follows: "*So one issue has to do with work assignments and schedules. Is that correct? And another issue has to do with giving and receiving feedback?*" Note that the second issue is stated as a shared problem, but in behavioral terms that are amenable to negotiation.

▶ ▶ ▶ ▶   **Exercise: Identifying and Framing Issues**

Several members of the board of directors of a cash-strapped nonprofit organization sought to oust its executive director. They complained that he was always out in the field or working remotely and couldn't be found; the nonprofit could no longer afford his salary; he was doing a poor job of raising money; and his relaxed management style left subordinates too free to do their own thing.

In response, the executive asserted: I am in the office when it is necessary; I am more productive telecommuting; I am worth every penny of my salary; I am doing my best to bring in grants and large donors in a difficult economic climate for fundraising; and my approach to management is to hire good people and let them do what they do best.

Identify the mediable issues presented and — in the language you deem most productive — frame them for discussion and negotiation.

§8.5 HOW NEGOTIATION AGENDAS EMERGE

In some types of disputes, the principal issues to be negotiated come pre-packaged. The personal injury mediator knows in advance with virtual certainty that compensation for the injured plaintiff will be the major (perhaps the only) issue to be negotiated. Family mediators know that they must help their divorcing clients resolve all the issues required to obtain a judicially approved marriage dissolution: parenting arrangements, division of real and personal property and other assets, child support, alimony and so forth.

In large-scale commercial disputes, mediators may learn of some of the issues in advance through the parties' pre-mediation written submissions. In other kinds of mediation — involving neighbor-neighbor disputes, low level criminal cases or small claims matters, for example — there may be a good deal of variety in the kinds of issues presented and limited information available to the mediator before talks begin.[14]

But no matter how much a mediator thinks he knows in advance about the potential issues in the case, he must be attentive to additional issues as they arise during the course of discussions. Even cases with "stock" issues often raise additional problems that need to be addressed.

Child custody mediation provides a good example. In order to make progress on all the official issues that must be resolved in a child custody dispute (day, night and weekend time with the kids, holidays and vacations, decision making about schooling and health care, etc.), the mediator must listen carefully for other issues that may need to be addressed: How will the parents talk about each other in front of the kids? How will transitions from one home to another be handled? How will homework be supervised?

Issues such as these often simmer under the surface of a dispute. The parties may be reluctant to disclose, or may even be unaware, of some of the real concerns that are motivating them. They may have a narrow view of mediation that leads them to think that a particular issue would be inappropriate to raise. The intuitive mediator listens carefully for such possible agenda items. Often they come to the surface only after she identifies them as possible problems and asks whether the parties might want to work on them.

With regard to timing, specific agenda topics are frequently discernable from the parties' opening statements. For an example, watch a portion of Bob's opening narrative in the *Fitzgerald* custody mediation. If you were mediating this case and wanted to summarize the negotiable issues that Bob has identified at this point, what are they, and how would you frame them? **Video Clip 8-A.**

In other situations, the issues for negotiation surface more gradually as the mediation unfolds, and sometimes emerge from the most heated interactions or comparatively late in the process, after actual negotiations have begun.[15] Bargaining over one issue (e.g., weekend visits with a child, a claim for unpaid rent) often yields proposals to add other issues to the agenda that might not previously have been thought about or were earlier viewed as unattainable (time with the kids on their birthdays; the method, including non-monetary means, of settling the rent claim.)

Mediators often can play a proactive role in proposing additional issues helpful in achieving agreements or improving their quality. For example, if the amount of money to be paid to settle a claim is hotly contested, proposing the sub-issue of

---

14. As suggested in Chapter 4, it can be useful to hypothesize about potential negotiation issues while preparing to mediate and then confirm or reject these hypotheses as the negotiations go forward.
15. As will be discussed in Chapter 9, one approach to problem-solving — brainstorming possible solutions without negotiating them — can be a powerful way to identify new mediation issues that have not previously been considered.

the timing of payment may open the door to tradeable concessions. Where repairs are a possible solution in a dispute over allegedly shoddy home construction, an often overlooked issue is the kind of warranty that the repairs will carry. By anticipating and addressing problems that might arise in the future, something the parties may overlook, mediators help enhance the durability of agreements. Similarly, when disputing parties anticipate continued dealings with each other, they often fail to consider how they will resolve any potential future problems (Will they agree to negotiate? To mediate? To use some other process?) unless the mediator identifies this as a potential issue to be addressed.

Note, however, that proposing new issues may not affect the parties equally. For example, if the parties have not raised the issue themselves, suggesting that the parties try to negotiate warranty terms covering future repairs may seem to benefit one side at the possible expense of the other. Should a mediator avoid doing this, to avoid any appearance of partiality?[16] If the mediator raises this as a possible new negotiation issue, does this unduly compromise her neutrality or its appearance?

■ §8.6 CONSTRUCTING AN AGENDA: COMPLEXITY VS. MANAGEABILITY

We have already noted the gains that can be derived from expanding the number of negotiable issues. An agenda that contains multiple issues creates possibilities for trading that do not exist when there is only a single item to negotiate. Identifying issues that the parties value differently increases the likelihood that each party's interests will be satisfied.

However, this does not mean that the mediator must list every concern that has been mentioned as a potential negotiating issue. Sometimes, the mediator must also keep the agenda manageable and focus on the issues most critical to resolve. One way to determine the importance of an issue is to consider whether it *must* be decided if resolution is to be achieved or whether it is merely a discretionary subject. If a work stoppage will commence by midnight unless an agreement is reached on wages and benefits, more discretionary issues, such as improving the system for employees' input on workplace safety, may have to be put off until another day.

But sometimes even discretionary issues are of great importance to the parties, and a mediator will sense that little progress will be made on other matters unless they are addressed. One way to determine this is to take note of the frequency or passion with which a topic is raised. Also, if an omitted issue is important enough, a party will generally say so when invited to add to the mediator's list of proposed topics.

---

16. As we have discussed, transformative mediators believe that any mediator intervention that potentially shapes the outcome of a dispute is inappropriate. *See* ROBERT BARUCH BUSH & JOSEPH FOLGER, The Promise of Mediation: Responding to Conflict Through Empowerment and Recognition 104-105 (1994). Some problem-solving mediators share the concern that volunteering their own ideas about possible negotiating issues or settlement terms will undermine their neutrality and impartiality in the parties' eyes. *See* KENNETH M. ROBERTS, *Mediating the Evaluative-Facilitative Debate: Why Both Are Wrong and a Proposal for Settlement*, 39 LOYOLA CHICAGO L. J. 187, 194 (2007).

In evaluating the significance of an issue, it is sufficient that one participant identifies it as important. So long as the issue is negotiable and requires a shared decision, it becomes something all must deal with. In a recent eviction action brought by a landlord against a tenant for nonpayment of rent, the landlord agreed to let the tenant stay on if he paid his overdue rent within two weeks and also (this was an added condition) got rid of his dog, which the landlord claimed was bothering the neighbors with his constant barking. The tenant strongly disagreed that his dog disturbed his neighbors, but because he wanted to remain where he was, he had to deal with the dog as a negotiating issue.

In some situations, one side's insistence that an issue be made part of the agenda can threaten to derail the process before negotiations begin. This can be especially true if the demand is seen as a power play (attempting to force negotiation on an unrelated topic) or tactical (a false demand aimed at getting concessions on other issues). In such circumstances, the mediator's persuasive abilities may be called into play earlier than anticipated to avert a stalemate over what will be negotiated.

Some types of legal disputes — personal injury cases are the paradigmatic example — appear to consist of only one negotiating issue: How much will the defendant pay the plaintiff to settle his claim? Here is where the mediator may want to work to see if, by expanding the information base further, the number of issues can also be expanded. If this is not possible, the mediator will proceed with a search for a negotiated compromise between the parties' stated positions, knowing that this is the best result that can be obtained under the circumstances.

But many other kinds of disputes present a bundle of interrelated issues. This is characteristic of relationships (contractual, family, employment, neighbor-neighbor or labor-management) that generally involve multiple and mutual obligations over a period of time. It is here that the skill of agenda-building is especially important.

Three factors will determine the extent to which a mediator works to expand or contract the number of issues: time limits, the mediator's role orientation and need. In time-constrained situations, the extent to which the problem can be broadened may be limited; the mediation may have to be relegated to one or a few core issues. For example, in the restaurant inspection dispute we discussed earlier, it is unlikely that any mediator would take on the issue of steps to improve community relations if he has four other cases on his docket for that day. Broad problem definitions and multiple issue agendas take time.

In settings not subject to significant time constraints, the mediator's role orientation will play a more central role. The more broadly the neutral defines the problem, the more expansive (and interest-based) the potential agenda is likely to be. Finally, there is the question of need: Most mediators, regardless of philosophy, will seek to expand the issues when faced with a threatened impasse, especially in a single-issue matter.

■ §8.7 ORGANIZING A MULTI-ISSUE AGENDA

Assuming that there are multiple issues to be negotiated, choices have to be made about the order in which they will be considered. If the mediator and the parties had all the time in the world to negotiate, the structuring of the discussions might not matter that much. But most mediations take place under at least some time constraints, and ordering choices sometimes can affect the likelihood of resolution. Here are some options and variables to consider:

Negotiate Issue by Issue, "Easiest" Issue First.   It is common in multi-issue negotiations to discuss issues one at a time. Some commentators take the view that the mediator should generally start with the easiest issues and work gradually toward the harder ones.[17]

There is much to be said for this view. As discussed in Chapter 2, recent evidence suggests that moods can have an important effect on negotiations: Negotiators who are upbeat achieve more and better resolutions than negotiators in bad moods.[18] The theory of starting with easy issues is that if early successes can be achieved, this creates a climate of cooperation and commitment to resolution that may carry over to later, more challenging items. It can also make fighting over differences on later issues seem less attractive, as each side has an investment in the agreements already reached and in not having wasted the time devoted to the earlier topics.[19]

What Is an "Easy" Issue?   What makes an issue potentially easy? Experienced mediators develop an ability to recognize issues as to which there is a high likelihood of obtaining agreement efficiently. Often, the parties' choice of language or nonverbal behavior signals their lack of commitment to a particular position. In addition, an issue is potentially easy when:

- **The parties have shared (or at least non-conflicting) interests regarding the issue.** Where the parties' interests concerning a particular issue are shared, resolution of the issue may be comparatively easy. For example, in the dispute involving the board of directors and the executive director of the struggling nonprofit organization, both parties have something to gain if steps can be identified to beef up the agency's fund-raising and improve the organization's overall financial posture. It might make sense to start the discussions there.

- **The issue lends itself to reciprocal concessions.** An issue may be comparatively easy when concessions of roughly equivalent size are possible, so that each party feels that the exchange is mutual.[20] For example, in *Fitzgerald*, the parties might find "a parenting plan during legal holidays" an easy issue to tackle, because Christmas might be traded for Thanksgiving, Labor Day for Memorial Day, etc. It might make sense to start with this issue, rather than the likely much more contested matter of "primary" or "permanent" custody.

---

17. *See, e.g.*, STULBERG, *supra* note 4, at 87-89.
18. *See* §2.6, *supra. See also* JENNIFER GERARDA BROWN, *The Role of Hope in Negotiation*, 44 UCLA L. REV. 1661 (1997).
19. The principle of starting with easy issues thus builds on what we know about people's general desire to avoid perceived losses. *See* §2.7, *supra.*
20. As we will see in Chapter 9, reciprocity is an important principle of persuasion.

■ **The issue requires a comparatively small concession.** If a concession by one party is required but it is small in relation to the magnitude of the more difficult issue(s) to come, this may make it an easy issue to negotiate. For example, the executive director of the nonprofit might easily agree to spend a few more hours a week in his office if he perceives that this would earn back the trust of board members and help him keep his job.

Note that even small concessions must be perceived as real—that is, representing genuine movement from a prior position—in order to trigger reciprocal concessions. In *Wilson*, the contractor's willingness to let the homeowner keep the kitchen counter top that had been made but not installed or paid for might do little to establish a climate of agreement, since the homeowner knew that the item had been custom made for her and could not be sold by the contractor to any other customer.

■ **Both parties perceive the issue as urgent.** Sometimes an otherwise very difficult issue can be made easier because the parties share a sense of urgency to resolve it. For example, if Bob and Jane Fitzgerald have to enroll their daughter in school by the beginning of September, their August mediation might produce agreement on the child's weekday residence more readily than if the mediation were held in May or June.

■ **Where it is a lower-stakes subpart of a hard issue.** Finally, sometimes difficult issues can be made easier by dividing them into lower stakes, smaller sub-issues. For example, in the *Fitzgerald* custody mediation, the mediator might be able to build momentum toward resolution on the dispute over permanent custody arrangements by proposing that the parties first discuss a temporary four-week plan for how the children will spend the month of August, when pre-school programs are closed. An agreement that is temporary is often easier to negotiate than one that is permanent.

Disadvantages of an Easy-to-Hard Approach. The tendency to work from easier issues to harder ones comes naturally to many mediators. In situations involving conflict, it is human nature to defer difficult subjects at the start. But this easy-to-hard approach to organizing a negotiation is not risk-free. Have you ever been stuck at a meeting in which early agenda items were argued about interminably, leaving more important items to rushed, last-minute consideration? This can readily happen in mediation. In the beginning of the bargaining phase of the process, especially in the absence of trust, even easy early topics may be negotiated competitively, as the parties feel each other out. If too much time is spent haggling over relatively easy matters, more important and difficult ones may get rushed later, creating excessive pressure or even impasse as a result.[21]

Beyond this, momentum (or at least the appearance of momentum) can cut both ways: While it can create an atmosphere of escalating agreement, it can also spawn false hopes. Those given to excessive or unrealistic optimism based on early agreements on easy issues may overreact—in anger or disappointment—when

---

21. *See* William R. Pendergast, *Managing the Negotiation Agenda*, 6 Negotiation J. 135, 138 (April 1990).

the other party later maintains a firm stance on some more difficult or more important deferred issue.

Negotiating Issue by Issue, Most Crucial Issues First.   For these reasons, the opposite strategy — starting out with the core issues — may be a better approach in some situations. If time is limited or the parties are insistent, there may be little choice but to begin with the most central or potentially deal-breaking issues, even if they are the most contentious.

The theory of starting with the most difficult issues is that once they are tackled successfully, less important issues will resolve easily. This approach is most likely to succeed when the parties share a modicum of trust or have a history of successful dealings. They may be able to "cut to the chase" quickly, free of the need to feel each other out.

Negotiating Independent Issues First and Dependent Issues Second.   In some situations, the *connection* between issues will suggest a sequence in which they should be discussed. It is common for the negotiation of one issue to depend on how another has been resolved. If there is an independent issue and a dependent (or contingent) issue to be resolved, it generally makes sense to address the independent issue first. For example:

■ In an employment discrimination case in which lost pay and job reinstatement are requested by the terminated employee, it would seem illogical to devote time and energy to the amount of back wages to be paid until the issue of reinstatement has been negotiated. The plaintiff's damages are contingent on how the issue of reinstatement is resolved: Reinstatement would extinguish any claim for continued lost pay, might soften considerably the worker's feelings about claiming back wages and might, in many cases, be conditioned on a waiver of all damages.

■ In *Wilson v. DiLorenzo*, if the only issues were (a) whether Bernice (the angry homeowner) would permit Frank (the contractor) to complete the kitchen job he started but on which he fell way behind schedule and (b) possible damages to cover the cost of hiring a different contractor to finish the job, it would seem sensible to discuss and try to resolve (a) before taking up (b).

Tackling Dependent Issues First?   Suppose you were mediating a landlord-tenant eviction dispute in which three months' rent was withheld by the tenant because the landlord allegedly ignored repeated complaints about heat problems. In what order would it make sense to address these three issues: (a) whether the tenancy will continue; (b) how much of the rent arrearage the tenant will pay; and (c) how to address future repair problems?

It would seem logical to defer discussion of a process for addressing future repairs until the issues of eviction and rent payment are resolved. After all, the need to create a mutually satisfactory process for addressing future repairs is (technically) contingent on whether the tenant will remain a tenant in the landlord's apartment.

However, success in dealing with an *easier*, though contingent issue — devising a system for handling future repair complaints — might actually help resolve the (theoretically) independent but more difficult issues — whether the landlord will continue to press for eviction and how much the tenant will pay of the past rent. The bottom line: The logic of ordering of issues is hard to generalize. Sometimes the need to create a climate of cooperation outweighs the need to follow a strictly logical sequence of issues.[22]

Negotiating in Packages Rather than Issue by Issue. Regardless of the sequence in which issues are organized, an issue-by-issue approach often encounters resistance. Negotiators are often reluctant to "buy a pig in a poke" on an early issue without knowing what the other party will do on other issues. ("*OK. You want a fifty-cent-an-hour raise each year for all nonsupervisory workers for the next three years. We might or might not be willing to pay that. But we need to hear more about what you have to say about the future of the pension plan, health care benefits and premiums and proposed revisions in seniority rules before we can reach any final agreement on a basic pay scale.*") In effect, the negotiators create packages of issues.

How can progress be made under these conditions? First, on sensing this tentative resistance, the mediator can try to encourage further issue-by-issue negotiation by having the parties agree that no agreement or concession on a single issue will be considered final until all of the issues in the entire matter are resolved.

Alternatively, an issue-by-issue approach can be abandoned entirely in favor of negotiating all issues as a package. Many multi-issue negotiations present issues that could be resolved piecemeal but might more profitably be discussed together. As we have noted, the principal advantage of this approach is value creation: The participants may be able to trade items of less interest to them for ones they value more, with both sides gaining by virtue of the differences in what they value. To continue with our collective bargaining example, if the company's primary objective is to phase out defined benefit pensions for employees and thereby get its long-term financial house in order, and employee representatives place a higher value on securing good current health benefits for all workers than on pension benefits, simultaneous negotiations of both forms of benefits — pensions and health — as a single package would likely prove productive.

When creating a multi-issue mediation agenda, many mediators employ flip charts, computer projections or other visual aids. This can help the parties keep track of all of the issues and help reinforce the ground rule that any agreements are to be considered tentative until all the issues have been resolved to everyone's satisfaction.

Who Creates the Negotiation Agenda? In our discussion of multi-issue negotiations thus far, we have assumed that the mediator controls the structure of the agenda. In high-conflict situations and disputes where the parties are inexperienced bargainers, we think that this approach makes sense. First, if there are strongly held disagreements about the *substantive* issues to be negotiated, it is probably not wise to introduce a *procedural* decision that may simply throw oil

---

22. *See* STULBERG, *supra* note 4, at 92-93.

onto the fire. ("*I want to talk about Megan's speech problems first!*" "*You do, huh? Well, I want to talk about the kids coming back to live with their mother first!*")

Second, if the mediation participants are inexperienced negotiators or poor communicators, their judgment about the most fruitful way to organize the discussions will probably not be as good as the mediator's. Third, if one party is a much more sophisticated negotiator than the other, he or she might try to use the mediator's invitation to propose an agenda as an opportunity to engage in power tactics to take advantage of the other party.[23] For these reasons, the mediator may prefer simply to set out a proposed order of topics and explain the reasons for doing so if asked. In most cases, the parties will defer to the mediator's process expertise.[24]

However, where the conflict dynamics are low, both parties have reasonably good negotiating skills and there is no significant power imbalance, we see no reason why setting the agenda should not be a collaborative process. The mediator can seek real input from the parties on the order in which they would like to discuss issues and how in general they wish to proceed. This is especially so where the mediator isn't sure which topics should be addressed first or whether they should be considered as a package rather than on an issue-by-issue basis. By being transparent — by saying, in effect, "*I'm not sure how best to proceed. Any ideas?*" — he signals to the parties that this is *their* process, and he trusts the parties' knowledge of their own situation.

▶ ▶ ▶ ▶
Review Exercise: Identifying and Framing Issues and Constructing a Multi-Issue Agenda

By this point, you should be reasonably familiar with the facts and central themes that emerged in the *Fitzgerald* custody dispute. (To refresh your recollection, you may wish to review, in addition to Clip 8-A in this chapter, Clip 6-M.) Recall that the mediators handling this matter contracted with the Fitzgeralds for two ninety-minute sessions and that the first session took place in mid-August. A great deal of hurt and anger was expressed in this session, and no progress was made in negotiating a long-term custody agreement. In no particular order, the following main themes emerged:

Bob wants the kids to live with him at his parents' home. He believes that they receive more "structure" there than with Jane. Jane thinks the kids should be living with her. She's their mother, after all, and besides, the kids don't have fun with their grandmother, who isn't particularly warm.

Bob worries about four-year-old Megan's speech development: She doesn't talk much and her enunciation isn't good. Jane is worried too. But Bob tends to blame Megan's delays on Jane's poor housekeeping and lack of structure in the home. Bob

---

23. This can take the form of threatening to walk out if a certain issue is not resolved first, "packing" the early agenda with that party's own concerns to create delay or putting forward false ("red herring") issues to get concessions on real ones. *See* PENDERGAST, *supra* note 21, at 135.

24. Part of this expertise is knowing when an issue is better left *off* the announced agenda. For example, addressing emotional needs by way of apology or other gesture may be best treated as something other than an item open to negotiation. We discuss this in more detail in Chapter 9.

also worries about three-year-old Ryan's toilet-training. Jane thinks (apparently as does the pediatrician) that he will grow out of this.

Jane blames Bob for not helping out with child care and housekeeping responsibilities. Bob sees Jane as listless, possibly depressed and "not into it" as far as parenting is concerned.

Bob is hurt and furious that Jane filed a spousal abuse complaint against him, which resulted in his being thrown out of the house for sixty days. Jane alleges that Bob injured her; Bob denies this, saying that he was only defending himself. Jane says Bob has anger issues. This was the only physical incident between them.

Jane is furious, claiming that Bob "snatched" the kids after the protection-from-abuse order expired. (He took them on a vacation, and then to his parents.) Jane has seen them only seven times since, for an hour a session.

Bob and Jane had each expected that Bob would return home after the temporary order expired. Jane gives signals that she remains open to having Bob come home. Bob seems ambivalent.

Megan needs to start kindergarten in three weeks. The kindergarten in Bob's parents' neighborhood is a half-day program. The kindergarten in Jane's neighborhood is full-day.

Suppose that you were preparing to meet the Fitzgeralds for their second mediation session, aimed at making progress in resolving their custody dispute. What are the mediable issues? How would you frame them? In what sequence would you propose they be addressed? Why?

CHAPTER

9

GENERATING MOVEMENT THROUGH PROBLEM-SOLVING AND PERSUASION

This chapter contains eight video clips, totaling approximately twenty-six minutes.

■ §9.1 INTRODUCTION

Neither a comprehensive agenda nor a sophisticated strategy for discussing negotiation issues can ensure success in producing a mediated resolution. Even if the parties have revealed a great deal of new information, they may cling to positions that must be relaxed or abandoned if resolution is to occur. In the next two chapters, we analyze the mediator's efforts to bring about such movement, through persuasion and problem-solving.

Much of the material in this chapter is based on established persuasion principles from the fields of social psychology, marketing and communications. As you read about specific techniques, ask yourself whether or not, and under what conditions, you would be comfortable with their use. We will return to this topic and explore the ethical limits of proper mediator persuasion in Chapter 12.

■ §9.2 THE PREVALENCE OF PERSUASION IN MEDIATION; PERSUASION AND PROBLEM-SOLVING DEFINED

Many mediation trainees, especially those with a law school background, are at home in a persuasive role. However, over the years some of our students have expressed discomfort with the idea that mediators engage in persuasion at all. To them, the word has a connotation of pressure or excessive influence that the friendlier term "problem-solving" does not.

Some practicing mediators do wield influence — over the outcomes as well as the process of mediation — in quite heavy-handed and, we think, inappropriate ways. Certainly, the idea of persuading the parties to accept a particular proposal

227

just because the *mediator* favors it is antithetical to accepted norms of mediator neutrality.

Nevertheless, as mediation scholar Josh Stulberg has written, "generating movement is the heart of the mediator's work."[1] For most practicing mediators, at least those working with the kinds of disputes that are the main subject of this book, bringing about settlements is the "overriding goal that drives their activities and the primary basis they use to judge themselves."[2] And the process of change that brings about such settlements comes most often through persuasion—in which the mediator plays a key role.

If this strikes you as potentially unseemly, raising visions of sleazy car salesmen pressuring worn-down customers to "close the deal," consider three points:

First, persuasive efforts are used by many we think of as working in the helping professions. The family doctor tries to convince her sedentary and overweight patients to develop a healthier lifestyle. The clergyman guides his parishioners and the therapist counsels her patients to help them confront their personal problems and take productive action to overcome them.

Second, some fairly benign interventions we have already described in this book are exercises in influence and persuasion. For example, mediators commonly engage in persuasion when they urge court-mandated participants to give mediation a good faith try, tout the benefits of mediation in their opening statements to get "buy-in" to the process or model good listening behaviors with the goal of convincing the parties to consider each other's perspectives.

Third, persuasion in mediation is a two-way street. Long before a mediator might try to influence the parties to moderate their demands or consider the other side's point of view, chances are good that each participant will have tried to convince the mediator that he or she is right and the other side is wrong. In many instances, the parties will try to align themselves with the mediator—or negotiate with, deceive and even threaten her—in the hope that she will favor his or her cause. Under such circumstances, persuasion by the mediator can be seen as a way to neutralize the parties' "gaming" of the process.

Persuasion and Problem-Solving Defined.   We use the term *persuasion* in accordance with its common meaning: as an attempt to alter another person's attitudes or actions.[3] It is a mistake, however, to think of persuasion as something one does to someone else. Research demonstrates that most effective persuasion is done *with* others, not *to* them. Competent adults generally cannot be persuaded to do something unless they want to do it. Effective persuasion is therefore an interactive process, in which the persuader must work closely with her subject to evaluate whether the advantages of taking a certain course of action outweigh the disadvantages.[4]

Problem-solving in mediation involves the effort to achieve resolution through more than mere haggling over concessions from stated positions. It too is

---

1. Joseph B. Stulberg, Taking Charge/Managing Conflict 105 (1987).
2. Deborah M. Kolb & Kenneth Kressel, *The Realities of Making Talk Work, in* When Talk Works 470 (1994).
3. Charles J. Stewart & William B. Cash, Jr., Interviewing: Principles and Practices 301 (10th ed. 2003).
4. *Id.* at 302.

interactive. As we use the term, it describes a process that (a) pierces party positions so that each side's interests, priorities and constraints can be understood; (b) develops a variety of potential solutions to the issues confronting the parties; and (c) examines how well those solutions meet, or do not meet, the parties' interests compared to their available alternatives. Problem-solving is thus not *distinct* from persuasion; rather, it is a *mode* of persuasion in which satisfaction of underlying needs, rather than mere compromise, is the goal.

■ §9.3 EFFECTIVE PERSUASION: A CONCEPTUAL OVERVIEW

Before we examine the specific ways in which mediators influence the progress of negotiations, we think it is important to ask a broader question: What generally makes for a persuasive messenger or message in everyday life?[5]

The Messenger: Personal Credibility Matters.   When a political leader you like (or don't) makes an important speech proposing or defending a new policy, how do you react? If you are like most people, your reaction to the message often depends greatly on your evaluation of the *source*. Social psychology tells us that the objective credibility of any persuasive message is important, but the credibility of the source is often more important. Interpersonal persuasion is relational as well as substantive.[6]

When a mediator attempts to establish credibility with the parties early in a negotiation, it is to provide a foundation for persuasive interventions that may come later. As we will see, when it comes time to generate and evaluate proposals, attributes such as likeability and authoritativeness can be key ingredients in the mediator's ability to generate party movement.[7]

The Message: Logic, Data and Evidence Matter.   You have known it since you were a child asking *"why?"*: Mere exhortations and conclusions (*"because daddy says so"*) don't sell. Appeals and arguments are not persuasive unless they are grounded in facts, logic and evidence. In particular, people cannot be persuaded to engage in a new course of action unless they are convinced that the advantages of taking that action outweigh the disadvantages. *"Is this suggested course of action workable? Reasonable? Better than the available alternatives, taking into account my needs, values and beliefs?"*[8]

Suppose that you are about to purchase your first laptop computer. You are prepared to spend up to $750, which is a lot for you. You do not know much about computers. You go to an electronics store and the salesman tries to get you to spend $350 more than you have budgeted to buy the latest fifteen-inch screen model, with a fast processor, lots of memory and a big hard drive, weighing almost

---

5. Many of the ideas in this section are based on the influential book by ROBERT CIALDINI, Influence: The Psychology of Persuasion (1993).

6. GARY WOODWARD & ROBERT DENTON, Persuasion and Influence in American Life 211-213 (4th ed. 2000).

7. CIALDINI, *supra* note 5, at 166-170, 208-229.

8. HERBERT SIMONS, Persuasion in Society 155, 158-159 (2001). Reason is at the center of everything a mediator does, which sounds obvious but can be challenging because of the impact of partisan biases and strong emotions on the negotiation process.

seven pounds. What will it take for you to be convinced to go for the model he wants to sell you?

In order to persuade you, the salesman will need to support his ideas thoroughly, explicitly and by means of evidence.[9] He will need to learn about your specific needs in order to help you select the most appropriate computer for *you*. Will you do a lot of traveling? Are you strong enough to carry a six-pound model, plus any attachments? Will you be editing photos or playing video games? Would a lightweight or tablet computer better suit your needs? The effective salesman tries to create a dialogue with you, working from the general to the specific — from your needs, priorities and criteria for selection to the particular models you might wish to consider.[10]

So it is in mediation. Mediation participants being urged to consider settlement will want to know the specific factors that make their trial or other non-settlement options unattractive and settlement in general preferable. They will also need to be persuaded, based on facts, logic and evidence, why a particular resolution option should be chosen instead of others.

The Role of Feelings in Persuasion.   But persuasion based on reason alone seldom suffices. As we have observed throughout this book, humans are emotional beings. (As a political scientist recently observed, "'feelings' are millions of years older than the kind of conscious thought processes we call 'reason', and they have been guiding behavior far longer."[11]) Thus, attempts to persuade must also appeal to what people are feeling, especially when they are "dug in." Many of the communication tools we have already discussed — helping people to express their feelings productively, listening actively, reframing and disentangling the effect of people's conduct from their intentions, for example — are not only tools to improve the communication flow but persuasive devices as well. The use of such skills evokes empathy and can soothe injured relationships, often making problem-solving and resolution more achievable.

Many successful persuasive appeals play to positive emotions: They attempt to make people feel good through the use of optimism, hope, humor, flattery and appeals to pride. But not all persuasive appeals to emotions are so positive. For example, why do politicians use "attack ads," if not to create fear and anger about their opponents? Why do prosecutors want to show jurors graphic, gory pictures of the victim and crime scene in homicide prosecutions? Because they know that photographs tell a story that words alone cannot convey, appealing to the jury's revulsion (and making conviction more likely). Rightly or wrongly, well-executed appeals to "negative" emotions, such as fear, anxiety and guilt, can be effective too.[12]

---

9. Stewart & Cash, *supra* note 3, at 326.

10. *Id.* at 240 ("The foundation of all persuasion is a thorough understanding of one's audience.").

11. Drew Westin, The Political Brain 53 (2007).

12. Many commentators might take umbrage at a mediator's deliberately appealing to fear and guilt as a mode of persuasion in mediation. Research from other disciplines suggests that a healthy dose of fear can help people reconsider overly confident decisions not in their long term interest. Similarly, induced guilt may help individuals come to terms more fully with the negative effects of their behaviors on others, thereby developing greater objectivity about their situation. That same body of research suggests that, as long as fear and guilt appeals are not exaggerated, both kinds of interventions can help

The Importance of Reciprocity.   Reciprocity is another persuasion norm, and a particularly potent one. The idea that we should repay in kind what another person has given us is pervasive in all human cultures, going back to food and skills sharing at the beginnings of human society.[13] This is why those who don't reciprocate are called "moochers" and "ingrates."[14] Reciprocity works as a tool of human persuasion because most people find it disagreeable to be in a state of indebtedness.[15]

We see examples of the power of reciprocity — positive and negative — in all walks of life. If a schoolmate or work colleague pays for our morning coffee, we may say *"Thanks a lot. I'll get the next one."* The posh resort offers us greatly reduced prices for the weekend getaway if we will just attend their time-share sales presentation, knowing that this "gift" creates a sense of obligation and makes it more likely that we will buy. On the negative side, if your neighbor says he's too busy to help you jump-start your car when your battery dies on a frigid January morning, chances are that when he wants a referral for a good accountant or estate lawyer, you won't break your back trying to find him one.

In negotiation and mediation, reciprocity is a fundamental expectation. If a custody mediator can convince a father to say something nice about the mother, he can then turn to the mother for a reciprocal statement. If a supervisor acknowledges some degree of fault or responsibility in his dealings with an employee, the mediator can point that out, looking for a similar acknowledgment from the subordinate. Perhaps most important, negotiators who fail to make reasonable bargaining concessions in response to their opponent's concessions are considered to have violated the reciprocity norm; when this occurs in mediation, the neutral can use the expectation of reciprocity to urge more meaningful concessions.

The Role of Consistency and Commitment in Persuasion.   In most people's view, consistency is considered a virtue, inconsistency a vice. This is why leaders who "stay the course" are considered strong, while "flip-floppers" are not. According to Cialdini, all human beings have a desire to be perceived by others as acting consistently.[16]

Salespeople understand this. Once they get their customers to take a stand, it is easier to ask them for a commitment to act consistently with that stand. To return to our earlier computer example, if the electronics salesman can get his customer on record as being concerned about long-term reliability and technical assistance issues, he is halfway home to selling him an extended warranty with 24/7 customer support. *"You said you were concerned about these issues,"* he will say. *"I have an inexpensive plan for you that addresses them."* The customer, not wanting to be seen as inconsistent, will be more likely to buy it. (And here, of course, is where the store makes much of its profit.)

---

individuals surface and confront painful thoughts and feelings about which they may have been in denial, and produce more fully considered decisions. For a review of empirical studies of fear and guilt as modes of persuasion and how they might apply in the mediation process, *see* JAMES STARK & DOUGLAS FRENKEL, Changing Minds: The Work of Mediators and Empirical Studies of Persuasion 47-61. *http://papers.ssrn.com/sol3/papers.cfm?abstract_id = 1769167* (Feb. 17, 2011).

13. CIALDINI, *supra* note 5, at 17-18.
14. *Id.* at 19-20.
15. *Id.* at 30, 35.
16. *Id.* at 57-103.

As we will see, effective mediators can exploit the consistency principle as well, from the opening stage (asking questions like "*Are you here today to resolve this problem if possible?*") to later efforts to persuade ("*I wonder: How does that position square with your earlier statements that both parents should have 'quality time' with the kids?*").

Scarcity as a Persuasion Tool.   A friend tells the following story: He and his partner were at a Manhattan art fair, moving about among various booths, unable to decide whether to buy an expensive painting they had admired an hour earlier. An older suburban couple arrived at the booth where the painting hung and casually began to express interest in it. Spying the older couple from across the room, our friend ran back, pulled out his check book and purchased it.

This story is a clear example of the "scarcity principle" in action: Opportunities become more valuable to us when their availability seems limited.[17] Why does the scarcity principle work? Because when people feel that they are losing an opportunity, they fear that they are losing part of their autonomy as human beings.[18]

We see the scarcity principle in action in many human endeavors. The rarer the stamp or classic baseball card, the higher its value. The closer the deadline on the "everything must go; final close-out" sale, the more likely that we will drop everything and go. In negotiations, effective bargainers know that a credible "exploding" offer (i.e., one that will expire soon) can often induce acceptance. This is why, if a car salesman wants to get the best possible price from you on that used Toyota Camry, he will tell you he has another buyer in the wings, and if you want the car, you had better buy it *today* (at his price, of course). Mediators can also harness the power of scarcity by creating deadlines and emphasizing the "now or never" nature of mediation during its later stages.

■ §9.4 SETTING THE TABLE FOR PERSUASION: "CONDITIONING" THE PARTIES

Now let's start to look more closely at how persuasion works in mediation. We begin with another story — from a law professor we know.

When she was a junior in high school, our friend came home one evening and announced to her parents at the dinner table that she wanted to be a high school English teacher. She came from an affluent family and had been given the best of everything. Her parents were unenthusiastic, to say the least. "*High school teachers are underpaid and have very little status in this society,*" her father said. "*I worry that you would be unhappy if all your friends made more money than you did and could afford to do things you couldn't.*" Upset, she ran out of the room. To her, elementary and secondary teaching was a noble profession. For many years after that, she thought about that conversation with indignation.

While in college, our friend flirted with the idea of becoming an English professor but rejected that plan and decided on law school. Then, after a few years in

---

17. *Id.* at 238.
18. *Id.* at 244-246.

law practice, she "drifted" into law school teaching. She hadn't been thinking about a career change, but she heard about a teaching opening at a nearby law school and applied for the position. That was more than twenty years ago, and she has been happy in her work ever since.

How did our friend come to reject high school teaching in favor of the more lucrative, higher-status position of law professor? According to her, there was no "aha!" moment when she realized that, just maybe, she agreed with her parents. Instead, she experienced a gradual change in her thinking, without even being aware of the change.

Noted Harvard educational psychologist Howard Gardner suggests that most "self-persuasion" is like that. It occurs gradually—as a result of small shifts in perceptions and slow, unidentifiable changes in viewpoint—rather than as the result of any single argument or sudden realization.[19]

Bringing about change in mediation is also a gradual process. It is subtle, often encounters resistance and takes time. Effective mediators, even facilitative ones, therefore do not wait until formal bargaining starts to try to induce change. They "condition" the parties for flexibility through a variety of persuasive interventions that start at the opening of the mediation (if not in pre-mediation discussions) and continue throughout the process.[20] How is this accomplished?

Creating a "Seize-the-Day" Atmosphere. First, a mediator who can impress on the parties the feeling that mediation provides a unique and possibly final opportunity to achieve settlement has a leg up in persuading them to reach agreement. This approach harnesses the power of the scarcity principle. Watch how one of our personal injury case mediators uses this *carpe diem* rhetorical theme, beginning at the start of his opening statement and continuing throughout it. **Video Clip 9-A.**

Mediators can also try to cement a shared sense of a special "settlement event"[21] by seeking and obtaining a serious commitment to the process from the parties. Obtaining a *"yes"* response to a question such as *"Would you both like to put this behind you today if possible?"* may help create a pattern of progress over time. If a party later gets stuck and refuses to budge, the mediator can remind her of her earlier stated desire to achieve resolution. This technique thus exploits the consistency principle.

Establishing Deadlines. Mediators also commonly use deadlines to create the sense that time is running out on the (scarce) opportunity to settle. Actual, externally imposed deadlines are the best motivators; this is why so many cases settle with trial dates looming or literally on the courthouse steps. But deadlines imposed by mediators themselves (*"I will end the mediation if substantial progress isn't made by 4 p.m."*) also work to induce settlement. Setting such time limits is not without risks, however. Can you think of any?

---

19. HOWARD GARDNER, Changing Minds 4, 173 (2004).
20. Some of the interventions we analyze in this section have been discussed earlier. Nevertheless, it is useful to review them again, through the distinctive lens of persuasion.
21. DWIGHT GOLANN, Mediating Legal Disputes 41-44, 154-162, 181-184 (1996).

Building Intimacy and Rapport.   A recent survey of thirty highly experienced labor and commercial mediators asked them to identify the "essential strengths and techniques" that most contributed to their ability to settle disputes. More than 75 percent rated their ability to develop rapport with the parties—a relationship of understanding, empathy and trust—as the most important ingredient of their success—much more important than other, often highly touted mediator skills, such as the ability to generate novel solutions to a problem.[22] Attorneys who frequently use mediation seem to agree.[23]

Developing rapport with the parties starts with the mediator's opening statement and continues throughout joint sessions, with many of the listening and communication skills that we have already discussed—active listening, attending to feelings and summarizing, for example. But certain methods of friendly persuasion—techniques used to "move towards persuadees psychologically so that they will be moved to accept the persuader's position or proposal for action"[24]—can most effectively be accomplished in private. *Intimacy* is a powerful factor affecting our willingness to comply with requests.[25] In mediation, a sense of "we-ness"[26] between the neutral and each party can best be established in a caucus.

What are the hallmarks of intimate interactions? Mediators seeking to "connect" with disputants (who are usually strangers) engage in pre- or early mediation small talk in order to trade on shared interests or experiences and demonstrate interest in the disputants and their lives.

Mediators also may invite each participant in caucus to share his or her *personal* reactions to the process as well as to proposals, by asking questions such as *"How is this process working for you so far?" "I have the sense that you weren't entirely comfortable when we were talking together with Mr. Romero. Am I off base?" "Are there things you didn't feel comfortable talking about in joint session that you would like to discuss now?"* These kinds of "just between us" statements convey the message: *"I am here to help you. You can trust and confide in me."*

Conversing, Not Preaching.   Effective persuasion is a "conversation, not a lecture."[27] People differ greatly in their attitudes (about what is good or bad), beliefs (about what is true or likely) and values (about what is important, worthwhile, fair, etc.). Thus, telling individuals what to do is generally not nearly as effective as having discussions with them that are tailored to their unique beliefs and values.

How do mediators discover the disputants' true beliefs and values? By using question forms that invite complex thinking and self-revelation. These include:

---

22. STEPHEN B. GOLDBERG, *The Secrets of Successful Mediators*, 21 NEGOTIATION J. 365 (2005).
23. STEPHEN B. GOLDBERG & MARGARET L. SHAW, *The Secrets of Successful (and Unsuccessful) Mediators Continued: Studies Two and Three*, 23 NEGOTIATION J. 393 (2007). In this follow-up study, mediator friendliness, empathy, likeability and caring were judged the most important ingredients in mediator success by 60 percent of respondents.
24. SIMONS, *supra* note 8, at 74.
25. WOODWARD & DENTON, *supra* note 6, at 221.
26. CIALDINI, *supra* note 5, at 185 ("Compliance professionals are forever trying to establish that we and they are working towards the same goals . . . that 'they, in essence, are our teammates.'").
27. WOODWARD & DENTON, *supra* note 6, at 4. *See also* RODERICK HART, Modern Rhetorical Criticism 9 (1990).

■ **"Explore with me" questions.** In general, questions that ask respondents to "*explain*," "*explore with me*," "*share with me*," or "*walk me through your thinking*" are more useful in inducing dialogue and analysis than simple response "*how do you react to X?*" types of questions. For example: "*If you could create your ideal dream solution here, what would it be?*" Or "*Share your thinking with me: What do you see as the pros and cons of their proposal?*"[28]

■ **Feelings questions.** Questions that ask "*how would it feel to do Y?*" are likely to produce more revealing responses than questions such as "*are you willing to consider doing Y?*"[29] For example: "*How would it feel, after a year and a half of fighting with your homeowners' association over these condo rules, to be done with this dispute?*" or "*You seem conflicted about Patrick's demand that Janie go to religious school next Fall. Could you share with me your feelings about that?*"

Other Ways of "Connecting." Other kinds of "friendly persuasion" that the mediator may attempt, usually in caucus, include the roles of *protector*, *coach*, *ally*, *admirer* and even *advocate*.

Examine the mediators' choice of language in the following excerpts. What exactly are they doing in these video examples to create intimacy and rapport? Do all of these interventions seem sincere? Are they consistent with a neutral and impartial stance? If you were the party at whom these interventions were directed, would you find them persuasive? As a mediator, are there any you would not feel comfortable employing yourself? Could you see yourself trying to connect in these ways with a party you mistrusted or found offensive? **Video Clip 9-B (1–4).**

Conveying Authority. Rapport with the parties, as important as it is, may not suffice as a foundation for persuasion. As we have noted, studies show that mediation and subject-matter expertise are highly valued by users of mediation services.[30] Consumers — both those experienced and inexperienced in disputing — often want their mediators to wield an authoritative voice before they will be willing to be persuaded.[31]

Authority-enhancing statements by mediators can take many forms. Evaluative mediators often talk about their experience litigating similar cases or trumpet their past successes in resolving similar disputes. Sometimes, they confidently predict how a case will be decided if it is not settled through mediation. Facilitative mediators convey authority by emphasizing their mediating experience and the training that equips them for the role and by expressing their general confidence in the parties and the mediation process. Evaluate the following video example. As a newer mediator, would you feel comfortable making these kinds of statements? If not, what can you do to enhance your authority with the parties? **Video Clip 9-C.**

---

28. *See* CHARLES D. BRENNAN, Sales Questions That Close the Sale 68-75 (1994).

29. WOODWARD & DENTON, *supra* note 6, at 68-86; BRENNAN, *supra* note 28, at 99.

30. JOHN LANDE, *How Will Lawyering and Mediation Practices Transform Each Other?* 24 FLA. ST. U. L. REV. 839, 856-879 (1997).

31. *See e.g.*, GOLDBERG & SHAW, *supra* note 23 (47% of attorney users of mediation services value high quality preparation and knowledge of relevant law in their mediators).

Keeping the Mood Positive.   Finally, throughout the mediation, persuasive mediators try to keep the parties hopeful about the process and its chances for success. As we have noted, research suggests that enhancing positive emotions (feeling happy or optimistic) and reducing negative ones (feeling anger or distress) are correlated with improved negotiating conduct and outcomes.[32]

One way to pre-condition the parties to be optimistic is to extol, at the beginning of the process, the positive benefits of mediation, including high settlement rates, high party satisfaction rates and high levels of compliance with mediated agreements. (We saw a good deal of this in connection with mediator opening statements in Chapter 6.) Research supports the validity of such claims about the process even in cases where the parties have been compelled to try mediation.[33]

Employing humor can also pay dividends. Breaking the tension of a mediation by the use of humor can accomplish more than simply increasing the mediator's "likability" quotient. If used appropriately, humor can provide momentary perspective: As serious as the dispute may be to the parties, it is not *deadly* serious; there are other important and pleasurable aspects of life that will go on no matter how it is resolved. Gentle, non-malicious teasing — of a party, a lawyer or at the mediator's own expense — can also be a subtle way of suggesting to the parties that they might consider lightening up on a position or a behavior that could threaten the process. For the parties, sharing a laugh with one's "adversary" can provide a pleasant experience that demonstrates their shared humanity.

Watch how one of the mediators in our premises liability matter uses humor (directed at a lawyer he knew before the mediation) to leaven his otherwise highly directive style. Would you have been comfortable acting the way this mediator did? **Video Clip 9-D.**

■ §9.5 GENERATING MOVEMENT: A "PROGRESSIVE" MODEL OF PROBLEM-SOLVING AND PERSUASION

So much for general conditioning of the parties. In this section, we set out a progressive model of mediator persuasion and discuss more specific approaches aimed at moving the disputants away from problematic perceptions and inflexible commitments.[34]

How is this model a progression? In general, it prefers participant self-persuasion to mediator influence and prescribes a continuum of approaches that move in that direction. Like other models in this book, this one must be applied flexibly to adapt to the circumstances of each case. Nevertheless, we recommend

---

32. CLARK FRESHMAN et al., *Adapting Meditation to Promote Negotiation Success: A Guide to Varieties and Scientific Support*, 7 HARV. NEGOT. L. REV. 67 (2003).

33. CRAIG MCEWAN & RICHARD MAIMAN, *Mediation in Maine: an Empirical Assessment*, 31 ME. L. REV. 237 (1981) (indicating equivalent satisfaction in voluntary and mandatory settings); ROSELLE WISSLER, *Court-Connected Mediation in General Civil Cases: What We Know from Empirical Research*, 17 OHIO ST. J. ON DISP. RESOL. 641, 682-683 (2002) (same).

34. The model of persuasion we present here is informed in part by more than fifty years of empirical studies of persuasion extrapolated from the fields of social psychology, communications, public health and marketing. Little if any of this research comes from the world of mediation, leaving open questions about its validity as applied to the kind of persuasion that this chapter covers.

this progression as the best — if not necessarily the straightest — path to generating real movement.

Our model reflects what research tends to suggest: "soft sells" generally work better (and may be resisted less) than "hard sells."[35] The idea is that lasting change is more likely if people come to their own realization that the decisions they are making are in their interests than if they have to be convinced of this.[36] This model is also consistent with our general belief that party-determined, rather than mediator-directed, decisions are the best prescription for satisfying, durable agreements.[37]

What produces "self-persuasion"? In general, self-persuasion occurs when an alternative point of view penetrates the thinking of the target audience. For most people, it occurs through subtle rather than blunt messages, and through questions that make them think or get "under their skin."

"Ask, Don't Tell."   In reviewing the specific approaches to persuasion that follow, you will notice a pattern: Most of them start with the mediator asking questions that bring the listener into a dialogue and only later move to the mediator's making explicit statements or recommendations. Studies suggest that when audiences are forewarned that a persuasive message is coming, the forewarning tends to make the message less persuasive.[38] People — especially those who are psychologically dug in — often tune out lectures and mount defenses to them, mentally rehearsing their counterarguments while the other person is speaking.[39] They generally react better to questions that permit them to reach their own conclusions in their own time. As one commentator puts it: When trying to persuade, it is generally better to "ask rather than tell."[40]

This progression also tracks and ideally harvests the rewards from the approach to information gathering we outlined in Chapter 7. There, we laid out a sequential process in which the mediator develops information from which first the seeds of empathy, then of satisfaction and finally of doubt, are planted. Here the mediator uses that information in much the same sequence to bring about flexibility in bargaining.

In the pages that follow, we analyze an array of problem-solving and persuasive interventions, ranging from less directive to more directive. Even though our progression starts "soft," none of the forms of persuasion we discuss are free from the mediator's active involvement. And make no mistake: Soft selling will not work in every case. Thus, a mediator concerned about achieving resolutions needs to master more directive modes of influence as well.

---

35. *See* Woodward & Denton, *supra* note 6, at 210-216.
36. *See, e.g.,* Elliot Aronson, *The Power of Self-Persuasion*, 54 Am. Psychol. 875, 882 ("The common theme running through my 40 years of research appears to be the phenomenon of self-persuasion and its enormous power to affect long-term changes in attitudes and behavior.").
37. *See* McEwan & Maiman, *supra* note 33, at 237.
38. William L. Benoit, *Forewarning and Persuasion, in* Mike Allen & Raymond Preiss, Persuasion: Advances Through Meta-Analysis 146 (1996).
39. Simons, *supra* note 8, at 52-53.
40. Stewart & Cash, *supra* note 3, at 327.

■ §9.5.1 PERSUASION BASED ON EMPATHY: ROLE REVERSAL

Role reversal is a method by which each party is asked to step into the shoes of the other party and consider how a situation, issue or position might look from that person's perspective. The goal is to have each person acknowledge — in their own words if possible — that the situation might look differently when viewed from the other side's point of view.

Interventions using role reversal generally ask parties to (a) put aside their own perspective for the moment; (b) try to see the issue the way the other side does (not the way *they* would see it if they were the other side); and (c) articulate that other perspective. Once they have heard themselves say these words, the other side's perspective may become more understandable (even if not totally convincing), and their opposition to it may soften. On a deeper level, role reversals can trigger empathy for the other side and even produce some thawing of strained relationships.

There are many variations on this basic concept, all of which involve the mediator's helping a party see the other perspective even if at first they cannot or will not. As examples, the mediator can help the parties to:

- Consider how their *own* past statements and actions may have been understood (or misunderstood) by the other side, as in: "*If you were your neighbor, how would your conduct look?*" Or "*Put yourself in Mr. Lopez's shoes. What do you think he might have thought when you said [X]? . . . I know you don't agree, but try to say what he could have been thinking.*" If this fails to produces an empathic response: " *. . . Can you understand how he might have thought [Y]?*"

- Consider how the *other party's* past actions might have a different and more innocent explanation, as in "*Looking at it from Ms. Taylor's perspective, why might she have acted the way she did?*" If this doesn't work: "*Is it possible that she acted the way she did because of a concern for her daughter's safety rather than anger at you? . . . Is it possible that communications between the two of you had broken down so much that you misunderstood her intentions?*"

- Better appreciate each other's arguments. A mediator can ask each party, "*If you were the other side, what arguments would you make in support of their position?*" If the party is unable to identify an opponent's arguments: "*If you were the mom, would you argue that your rights as their mother should take precedence over your rights as the kids' grandmother?*"

- Consider how a party's own bargaining proposals might affect or be viewed by the other side — for example: "*If you were the landlord, concerned about avoiding a large, publicized settlement in this case, how would you view your intended demand — that they pay you $30,000, with no promise of confidentiality?*" Consider how the other side's negotiation proposals might look from their perspective, as in "*You say that $7,500 is totally inadequate as an offer to settle this case. I wonder: Is your landlord a wealthy man? . . . And we know that he doesn't have insurance that covers this kind of claim. In light of those factors, do you think that $7,500 is a 'lowball' offer from his perspective?*"

Notice the progression of mediator directiveness in each of these examples. The mediator starts by inviting (through a question) the party to articulate the other side's perspective, without helping by suggesting the "answer." In doing so, she tries to get each party actively engaged in recognizing and articulating the competing view. Only if this fails to produce some understanding of the alternative perspective does the neutral suggest one for the party to consider.

The empirical literature on persuasion supports this approach.[41] Empathy is best developed by *helping*, not *forcing*, parties to recognize the legitimate perspectives of the other side.[42] Role reversal works most effectively when the parties are *invited* to suspend judgment and open their minds to new points of view.

The Challenges of Role Reversal and the Mediator's Role. Getting parties to engage in productive role reversal can be difficult. Some disputants have limited ability to empathize with the perspectives of others or to juggle, even momentarily, two competing perspectives. Some will resist the invitation to reverse roles because they are blinded by their disagreement with the other side's views or are unwilling, for strategic reasons, to concede that any other view may have legitimacy.

Success in this potentially powerful form of persuasion therefore often requires the mediator to prepare the parties for it. For example: "*Ms. Chang, I know how strongly you disagree with what Mr. Snow has said and done. But I'm going to ask you to put your own views on hold for a few minutes. Try to put yourself in his shoes. I know you disagree strenuously with him, but try to imagine and then put into words — his words — how this situation looks to him. If it helps, start with the words 'he thinks' . . . And try not to say 'but' at the end of a sentence. Can you try?*" Some mediators might feel capable of orchestrating such an effort in joint session.[43] However, given the resistance that is to be expected, it may be more productive to do this kind of preparatory work in caucus.

Now watch how one of our child custody mediators, after starting down a more directive persuasion path, shifts gears and tries to get Bob, the father, to consider and articulate Jane's strengths as a mother. Watch Bob struggle as he tries to adopt the mother's perspective even for a few minutes, reverting to his own perspective after each word of praise for her. This excerpt is an excellent example of how self-persuasion works: gradually and, often, despite great resistance. **Video Clip 9-E.**

■ §9.5.2 PERSUASION THROUGH HEALING: APOLOGY

Bernice Wilson, the homeowner in our consumer case, sought money from her contractor to complete the kitchen renovation he never finished. But she was also angry about how she had been treated in the process. Her case is typical: Most claims of past or ongoing wrongdoing involve a combination of tangible (e.g.,

---

41. Role reversal is a form of "counter-attitudinal advocacy" — a role-playing process designed to engage subjects in a process of self-persuasion. Empirical studies amply demonstrate its effectiveness in producing lasting attitude change. *See* STARK & FRENKEL, *supra* note 12, at 10-18, 33-39, summarizing research studies.
42. ROBERT A. BARUCH BUSH & JOSEPH P. FOLGER, The Promise of Mediation: Responding to Conflict Through Empowerment and Recognition 159-161 (1994).
43. GARY J. FRIEDMAN & JACK HIMMELSTEIN, Challenging Conflict: Mediation Through Understanding (2009) (advocating no-caucus mediation model).

pecuniary and proprietary) and intangible (emotional, interpersonal and psychic) harms.

Addressing only the tangible harms will often produce a mediated resolution. But in many cases, the mediator's ability to produce flexibility on tangible issues will depend on addressing intangible injuries as well. Obtaining an apology or some other articulated acknowledgment of a harm done can often be a key ingredient in producing movement. Of course, beyond helping to settle cases, such statements can provide the basis for real healing.[44]

Offering and receiving apologies is another form of party-generated persuasion. To help the parties carry this out, the mediator must first ensure that the injury that needs addressing is identified. Where the parties are open and verbal, the mediator can encourage enough emotional expression to take place so that intangible harms are brought to the surface and the wrongdoer can hear how the victim feels.

Where these psychic harms are not stated explicitly, the mediator must listen actively to see if they lurk beneath the surface, using her intuition (*"There seems to be something he's not saying. In my experience, most victims would feel that their privacy was violated by that conduct. Does he?"*) and, through questions, confirm their existence. She must look for opportunities to help the parties express regret for past mistakes and misunderstandings. She must also draw attention to statements implicitly acknowledging responsibility or regret when they naturally occur in the conversation, repeating or paraphrasing such statements to make sure the other party has heard them. (*"So it seems, Mr. Gomez, that what you're saying is that you didn't expect things to escalate the way they did and that you're sorry for your part in what happened."*)

But none of these efforts or statements by the mediator is a substitute for an effective apology offered *personally* by the offending party to the party who feels wronged. How do mediators, sensing that an apology may be a helpful or necessary element of persuasion, bring one about?

The Challenges of Making Apologies.   First, mediators must appreciate the many reasons why apologizing is difficult for people — even those who do feel sorry about their behavior or its effects. Many people find it hard to acknowledge the guilt or shame they feel as a result of having caused another person injury.[45] Others are inexperienced at giving apologies, a factor that may be influenced by the way apologies are sometimes viewed in American culture. (As John Wayne once said, *"Never apologize, mister. It's a sign of weakness."*[46]) Those who have

---

44. A recent meta-analytic review of 175 studies involving 26,000 participants concludes that apologies are, in general, positively correlated with interpersonal forgiveness. RYAN FEHR, MICHELE GELFAND & MONISHA NAG, *The Road to Forgiveness: A Meta-Analytic Synthesis of Its Situational and Dispositional Correlates*, 136 PSYCH. BULL. 894, 904 (2010). As one article puts it, "[a]pologies are the world's most . . . pervasive conflict resolution technique . . . serving a crucial social lubrication role." CYNTHIA MCPHERSON FRANTZ & COURTNEY BENNIGSON, *Better Late Than Early: The Influence of Timing on Apology Effectiveness*, 41 J. EXP. SOC. PSYCHOL. 201 (2005).

45. *See* CAROL LIEBMAN & NANCY DUBLER, *Bioethics Mediation: A Guide to Shaping Shared Solutions* (2004); DOUGLAS FRENKEL & CAROL LIEBMAN, *Editorial: Words That Heal*, 140 ANNALS OF INTERNAL MED. 482 (2004).

46. Dialogue of Captain Nathan Brittles in *She Wore a Yellow Ribbon* (Argosy Pictures 1949).

been accused of (or sued for) what they feel is a minor offense may feel like victims themselves and thus may be resistant to making amends.

Second, in a legal dispute context, the mediator must be aware of powerful strategic and evidentiary barriers impeding the offering of apologies. Many litigants fear that an apology will be pounced on by their adversary or its lawyer to justify a higher settlement demand.[47] Despite the confidentiality of the mediation process in general, and the explicit protection given to acknowledgments of fault in settlement discussions in many jurisdictions,[48] some litigants are deterred by concern that such a statement could later be admissible at a trial as evidence of fault.[49]

Third, even if a party is open to apologizing, the mediator must understand that certain forms of apology are ineffective, and perhaps counterproductive, as a means of persuasion. Whether as a result of the apologizer's inexperience, embarrassment, resistance or shame, many attempted apologies come out badly. Here are three common examples:

- **The "safe" or partial apology.** *"I'm very sorry this happened to you."* This form of apology is carefully worded, seeking to have it both ways: softening the victim by showing empathy for her situation but taking no responsibility or blame for it. This form of apology is often used to avoid making any admission of fault.

- **The "not responsible" apology.** This takes the partial apology one step further by adding a specific rejection of responsibility to the expression of regret. It is commonly used in personal injury litigation where the defendant strongly contests liability on factual or legal grounds. An excellent example occurred in one of our premises liability mediations, in which defense counsel (after arguing earlier that plaintiff's case was *"a bunch of baloney"*) stated: *"First of all, I'd like Josh to know on behalf of Mr. Stevens and his company that we certainly feel badly about what happened to you. Certainly no one would want that to happen to anyone and we're hopeful that you make a full recovery. At the same time, let's put this in context of what really happened. . . . "* (The attorney went on to argue, among other things, that the plaintiff's losses were caused by his own negligence in leaving his apartment door unlocked.)

- **The apology of justification.** Here the apologizer equivocates, acknowledging responsibility but then explaining or justifying the wrongful conduct.

---

47. One empirical study, involving a hypothesized personal injury case, showed that although receiving an apology from the defendant tended to "soften up" injured plaintiffs, causing them to lower their bottom lines, this had the *opposite* effect on plaintiffs' lawyers, leading them to set higher aspirations for settlement than where no apology was received. JENNIFER ROBBENNOLT, *Attorneys, Apologies, and Settlement Negotiation*, 13 HARV. NEGOT. L. REV. 349 (2008). One limitation of this study is that it involved a full apology that included an express acknowledgement of legal responsibility (*"I am sorry you were hurt. The accident was all my fault. I was going too fast. . . . "*). In our experience, these kinds of "home run" apologies are comparatively rare in legal dispute negotiations. In legal disputing, it is often easier to promote statements of regret around the edges of the conflict — about the parties' interactions and how they have treated each other or about the effects of their conduct — than apologies for conduct that is at the core of the parties' competing legal claims.
48. Fed. R. Evid. 408.
49. *See, e.g.,* JONATHAN R. COHEN, *Advising Clients to Apologize*, 72 S. CAL. L. REV. 1009 (1999); DEBORAH L. LEVI, *Note, The Role of Apology in Mediation*, 72 N.Y.U. L. REV. 1165 (1997).

He says, in effect, "*I'm sorry I did this, but I had good reasons.*" In extreme cases, he tries to blame the victim as part of the justification. A famous example is President Clinton's Monica Lewinsky apology: "*I know that my public comments and my silence about this matter gave a false impression. I misled people, including even my wife. I deeply regret that. I can only tell you that I was motivated by many factors. First, by a desire to protect myself from the embarrassment of my own conduct. I was also concerned about protecting my family. The fact that these questions were being asked in a politically inspired lawsuit, which has since been dismissed, was a consideration too.*" (President Clinton then went on to attack the independent counsel investigation that led to the exposure of his affair.)

What do all of these apologies have in common? They seem to lack any real contrition. They risk leaving the person who is owed an emotional debt feeling shortchanged and angry. And although in some circumstances, a halfhearted apology may be better than none at all, there is recent evidence suggesting that, where fault is clear, "no responsibility" apologies may actually make things worse.[50]

All of this raises the obvious question: What makes for an effective apology — one that will cause the victim to soften in response? Most research suggests that effective apologies are those that (a) appear to be sincere; (b) contain an acknowledgment of the wrongful act and its impact on the victim; (c) accept responsibility; (d) if applicable, promise to refrain from such conduct in the future; and (e) offer compensation for any tangible loss as well.[51] In short, they are *complete* and *unconditional*.

Orchestrating Apologies. How does a mediator orchestrate an apology to maximize its potential for the parties and the process? First, she works to ensure that the needed words will be spoken, and spoken constructively. Having established sufficient intimacy in caucus, the mediator can explore with the disputants whether they have any regrets about their own contributions to the dispute and whether they are willing to share those regrets with the other side. If there is resistance, the mediator might seek to understand and address it. Role reversal, discussed in the previous section, may help a reluctant party appreciate the opponent's need for such words.

In appropriate cases, the mediator can coach an uncomfortable party on how to express an apology in a way that the other party might accept. This can include role-playing as practice and advice about the kind of backsliding or equivocal statements that can make things worse. Note in this regard that effective apologies generally cannot come from agents: The parties themselves, not their representatives, must do the talking.

---

50. *See* Jennifer K. Robbennolt, *Apologies and Legal Settlement: An Empirical Examination*, 102 Mich. L. Rev. 460 (2003).

51. *See, e.g.,* Erin Ann O'Hara & Douglas Yarn, *On Apology and Consilience*, 77 Wash. L. Rev. 1121, 1130-1145 (2002); Steven Scher & John Darley, *How Effective Are the Things People Say to Apologize? Effects of the Realization of the Apology Speech Act*, 26 J. Pscholinguist. Res. 127 (1997).

Next, the mediator must work to maximize the chances that the apology will be well received. In addition to coaching about the content of what is offered, effective mediators understand that an apology that is offered spontaneously and seeks nothing in return is more likely to seem sincere than one that is offered only after it has been requested or that comes across as just another bargaining chip. It is therefore generally not effective to treat potential apologies or other acts of contrition merely as one of a number of issues to be negotiated.[52] And the mediator should avoid another common pitfall: asking the victim if he or she would like to receive an apology (can you think why?), and surely should not do so without some assurance that one will be forthcoming from the other side. Finally, once an apology is made, the mediator must intervene to prevent an angry recipient from rejecting it out of hand and further raising tensions.[53]

If such orchestration seems manipulative and manufactured merely to produce resolution by pleasing (or placating) the victim, consider this: Clinical evidence suggests that the act of apologizing may also allow the *wrongdoer* to reclaim his sense of self-respect or experience the shame needed to deter him from future wrongdoing.[54] Given its healing and restorative (as well as settlement-promoting) potential, the effective management of apologies may be one of the most valuable exercises of process expertise a mediator can offer.

■ §9.5.3 PERSUASION BY APPEALING TO INTERESTS: PROBLEM-SOLVING

As we have emphasized throughout this book, attempting to end conflicts by problem-solving — meeting the parties' real needs — is likely to be less competitive and more likely to produce satisfying, sustainable resolutions than efforts to forge mere compromises on positions. It therefore makes sense to see if solutions can be built on party interests — especially those that are shared or not in conflict — *before* trying to persuade the disputants to make positional concessions on zero-sum issues.[55]

Before problem-solving can occur, however, the disputants must be open with the mediator about their interests. As we have seen, considerable probing by the

---

52. There are exceptions, however. For example, in certain formal and public negotiation contexts involving matters of international diplomacy, the language of "public apologies" might be the subject of direct and intense negotiation. *See* RICHARD B. BILDER, *The Role of Apology in International Law and Diplomacy*, 46 VA. J. INT'L L. 433, 436-441 (2006).

53. Some mediators believe in coaching the prospective recipient of an apology on how to receive it *before* it is actually offered, again through role-playing exercises in caucus. ("*If Mr. Pomeroy were willing to apologize for his role in what happened, do you think you could accept his apology? Would hearing him speak words of apology be helpful? If he said something like [x], what might you say in response?*") However, note that such coaching likely detracts from the spontaneity (and thus the power) of the apology if and when it is offered.

54. *See* BEVERLY ENGEL, The Power of Apology: Healing Steps to Transform Your Relationships 12-14, 132-133 (2002); CHARLOTTE WITVLIET, THOMAS LUDWIG & DAVID BAUER, *Please Forgive Me: Transgressors' Emotions and Physiology During Imagery of Seeking Forgiveness and Victim Responses*, 21 J. PSYCHOL. & CHRISTIANITY 219 (2002). *But see* TYLER OKIMOTO, KYLI HEDRICK & MICHAEL WENZEL, *I Make No Apology: The Psychological Benefits of Refusing to Apologize.* IACM 23rd Annual Conference Paper. Available at SSRN: *http://ssrn.com/abstract=1612866* (July 10, 2010).

55. To relate this section to the previous one, an apology can be viewed as a solution based on satisfying emotional interests. An effective apology can be a powerful interest-based form of persuasion in that it moves the recipient toward being open to dealing with the wrongdoer.

mediator (usually in caucus) is often needed to accomplish even that much. Even if the parties have been forthcoming with the mediator, additional work is often needed to promote real problem-solving with the other side. As we have emphasized, disputants are often reluctant to share their true needs with an opponent out of fear of being exploited. Some are not able to think of interest-based solutions without considerable help from the mediator. Often the parties will not agree to try interest-based bargaining until more conventional distributive bargaining approaches have hit an impasse. If the mediator decides that the conditions are right to try problem-solving, what does this form of persuasion involve?

Getting Needs on the Table: Transparency and Further Probing.   The first step is a return to probing to ensure that interests have been identified. (The process for doing this was discussed in Chapter 7.) Here, however, the mediator can make explicit her goal of problem-solving and articulate the reasons why the parties should buy in: Adversarial bargaining can be difficult and limited; by comparison, the parties may find that interest-based bargaining potentially presents great advantages.

If the mediator is successful at learning more about the parties' interests than has been previously disclosed, she can then seek permission to reveal those interests to the other side. Party hesitation can be addressed by the mediator's promising not to reveal party interests unless she deems it useful or to disguise such interests, without revealing them, as hypothetical mediator proposals. Such "trial balloons" — ideas that appear to have been thought of by the mediator instead of either party — serve a number of useful purposes, which we discuss in Chapter 10.

Encouraging the Parties to Think Creatively.   In addition, parties who are used to thinking only of conventional positional approaches to resolving the matter may need to be encouraged to think more imaginatively, for example:

>   ■ *"Just for a few minutes, forget what you thought was possible or what the other side might be willing to do here or what you think they'll reject. Instead, try to imagine an ideal solution or even several ideas that you'd like, regardless of whether they'd work or you feel silly proposing them."*

>   ■ *"Are there any services or other things that you could use or that you could give — regardless of what you think the other side would think of it — that could be put in the pot here to make this soup we're calling a resolution?"*

When the parties are reluctant to reveal information openly, this is best done in caucus. If conditions warrant, a group brainstorming session might be held in which multiple options can be considered with everyone present.[56]

Thinking Creatively Yourself.   Even if the parties cannot come up with needs-based ideas, the mediator can. After first eliciting proposals from the parties (on

---

56. Interestingly, empirical studies of brainstorming in other contexts have shown that people tend to produce more ideas when working alone than in groups. *See* STARK & FRENKEL, *supra* note 12, at 61-65. Assuming this to be valid, a mediator might be able to "have his cake and eat it too," encouraging disputants to work separately to develop possible creative resolution options, and then convening a group session to compare, expand and refine those ideas. We discuss group brainstorming in Chapter 10.

the theory that they are most familiar with their own needs and must live with the consequences of their decisions), effective mediators often offer their own ideas and refinements. Many newer practitioners aspire to do this but feel stymied.

How does the mediator develop this ability? First, she must be willing to suspend certain social inhibitions and conventions based on standard or legalistic thinking or fear of putting people on the spot. She must use her own imagination and hypothesize solutions that might satisfy the parties' interests — promises, acts, things that the parties can exchange — and then test them out, even if they appear to be a long shot. If such solutions are not apparent, she can indulge her curiosity and do more fact-digging. It is a matter of looking for possible trades that can benefit both parties or at least help one without costing the other, as well as looking for possible ways to bring outside resources to bear on the problem and ease the negotiations.

Case Examples.   The following mediator questions and ideas have generated responses leading to settlements in actual cases — all of which involved difficult disputes:

- ■ *"Ms. Williams, what do you do for a living? . . . Oh, you own a gift shop. Hmm. Do you ever need seasonal help? Could Joey pay off the car damage by helping out before Christmas?"*

- ■ *"Mr. Thomas, I see you're wearing a shirt with a moose logo on it. Does the moose have any special meaning? . . . You have a cottage on a lake in Canada? Is it out of the question to talk about the idea of the Allens using it for a vacation in lieu of the price reduction on the house that they're demanding?"*

- ■ *"I noticed that the child who is out in the waiting room with your husband has a disability. Is she your daughter? . . . If the movers aren't willing to pay you for the items that you claim they lost in delivery, would you be open to their making a donation to the cerebral palsy research foundation instead?"*

This kind of creativity isn't magic, and it can be learned. But it does require imagination, a hunger for finding possible "connections" and sometimes tenaciousness in seeking the next idea when the previous one doesn't fly.

The Limits of Problem-Solving.   Success in shifting the negotiation from positions to needs provides no assurance of smooth sailing thereafter. Interest-based negotiations commonly address only part of the problem; the remaining issues may well be distributive in character.[57] For example, even after a sincere apology or a creative and integrative agreement about the timing and method of payments, the accident victim and the drunk driver must usually still haggle — hopefully less competitively — over the monetary amount to be paid. In a child custody mediation, parents with flexible work schedules might agree to an interest-based approach that helps each parent with child care while the other is working, but still have to divide all non-work and vacation time. In that remaining bargaining,

---

57. *See* §2.2, *supra*, on the tension between problem-solving ("creating value") and competing ("claiming value") that is present in most negotiations.

the parties might return to aggressive tactics, including overly confident assertions about their claims, in order to "win" the distributive aspects of the negotiation. When this occurs, the mediator's only persuasion option may be to attempt to inject more uncertainty into their thinking.

■ §9.5.4 PERSUASION THROUGH DOUBT: PROVIDING FEEDBACK AND EVALUATION

As we discussed in Chapter 2, even the most able and experienced negotiators often come to the mediation table with excessive optimism about their claims. A skilled mediator — the only person in the room with a disinterested perspective — can dampen that overconfidence by exposing the negotiators to honest feedback. Doing so can be viewed as a direct way of conditioning the negotiators to moderate their positions. As stated in Chapter 3, we view properly conducted evaluation as a valuable, often welcomed and sometimes justice-enhancing form of persuasion.

Evaluation Defined.   Most law-trained mediators equate evaluation with assessing the *legal* strengths of the parties' positions. However, even in the narrowest legal matters, mediator evaluation is potentially far broader than that. It can include feedback on the practicality, wisdom, fairness and, in rare cases, morality of a party's proposals or positions. While much evaluation focuses on comparing a party's position to some external standard, mediators also provide evaluative feedback when they point out tensions between a party's actions, statements or positions and their own professed standards or ideals.[58] In this chapter, we focus our discussion primarily on legal evaluation in legal disputes. However, for the most part, the considerations that govern legal evaluations are applicable to all forms of doubt-based persuasion.

Because raising doubt by means of evaluation is a potentially confrontational intervention, we list it last in our "progression."[59] But if a party's overconfidence and refusal to discuss interests is threatening to cripple the mediation, the mediator may have to resort to this approach earlier. However, even within this most mediator-driven type of persuasion lies a "softer to harder" range of choices.

Gradations of Legal Evaluation.   In roughly ascending order of apparent directiveness, legal evaluation includes:[60]

■ **Asking parties to discuss the strengths and weaknesses of their case.** (*"Of all of the claims (defenses) you have, which do you see as the strongest? The weakest? What are the problems, if any, with your claim of fraud? What percentage chance do you see of its being rejected? What is your worst case scenario?"*)

---

58. STARK & FRENKEL, *supra* note 12, at 55-60.
59. This is parallel to the approach to information expansion we presented in Chapter 7, in which probing for doubt comes after probing for empathy and interests.
60. *See generally* JAMES H. STARK, *The Ethics of Mediation Evaluation*, 38 S. TEX. L. REV. 769, 774 (1997); M. SHAW, Evaluation Continuum, Prepared for Meeting of CPR Ethics Commission, May 6-7, 1996 (on file with James Stark).

- **Questioning parties about elements of their case, evidentiary problems, etc.** (*"What evidence do you have to support your claim of inadequate security? Do you have any case law support for your claim for compensatory damages for lost tuition?"*)

- **Asking one party to respond to another party's legal arguments.** (*"Defense counsel argues that the break-in was not reasonably foreseeable because the town has a low crime rate and there had never been a previous break-in at his building. How do you respond to that?"*)

- **Providing legal information without applying it to the facts of the case.** This is often directed at parties who are representing themselves: (*"As the plaintiff in this case, you have to persuade the jury that the defendant's negligence caused you harm by a preponderance of evidence. What this means is. . . ."*)

- **Making a prediction about an *evidentiary* or *procedural* question by applying the law to the facts.** (*"My opinion is that the court will exclude that letter, because it is hearsay." "Anything's possible of course, but I don't think it's likely that the judge will grant your motion for a continuance based on the facts you present."*)

- **Making a prediction about a *substantive* element of the case by applying the law to the facts.** (*"My sense is that the judge will allow the plaintiff to present the jury with the question of whether the duty of reasonable care was breached. It seems to me that, as the defendant, you have significant risk on that issue."*)

- **Making a prediction about possible or probable court outcomes.** (*"If this case gets to a jury, and I think it will, I see the most likely jury award as being in the range of $50,000 to $75,000."*)

- **Proposing or recommending a specific settlement based on analysis of the law and the facts.** (*"It's your decision of course. But if you want my opinion, I think you should accept their $60,000 offer."*)

As you can see, the first three types of evaluation are doubt-raising (and thus self-persuading) *questions* of a kind already discussed in Chapter 7. In the others, the mediator provides increasingly direct and comprehensive feedback to the parties by means of declarative statements.

Note that a mediator evaluation — in legal matters as well as other settings — need not be so technical or specific in its predictions as to require substantive expertise as a foundation. In its most elementary form, the evaluation can simply involve the mediator getting the parties to acknowledge reality: There is risk in uncertainty. Unless a disputant feels that the other side's perspective is *wholly* unworthy of credit or sympathy, even the most headstrong disputant must concede (at least to himself) that the favorable outcome he envisions cannot be ensured.

On the other hand, empirical research on persuasion suggests that the more specific and detailed a statement or appeal is — the more it rests on explicit supporting data and trustworthy sources — the more likely it will be given credence by the recipient.[61] This may suggest the value of industry knowledge as an ingredient of effective evaluation.[62]

The Challenges of Legal Evaluation.   It is hard to do legal evaluation properly and well. First, because it depends on imparting information designed to shake a party's confidence, its "bad news" aspect is often greeted by considerable push back or even anger. Second, if improperly done, evaluation creates the risk that the mediator will be perceived as non-neutral. Third, because of this risk, more directive forms of evaluation tend to be provided in caucus, a setting that presents the potential for questionable mediator conduct. Fourth, even the most experienced subject matter experts must concede that any prediction of court outcomes — especially when lacking the full adversary presentation of a trial — is far from a science.

It is also difficult to provide universal generalizations about how a mediator should provide legal evaluation, because cases and litigants vary so greatly. How intelligent the parties are, whether they are represented by counsel and whether they have had previous encounters with the court system will all affect how explicit an evaluation needs to be in order to be understood. How emotionally entrenched the parties are in their positions, how much they trust the mediator and how invested they are in the mediation process may dictate how direct the mediator should be in her approach. The substantive content of the evaluation itself also matters: An evaluation that strongly favors one side needs to be handled with considerably greater tact than an evaluation that points out substantial risks and problems on both sides of the case.

Providing Effective and Proper Evaluation: Concrete Suggestions.   Nonetheless, here is a list of concrete legal evaluation suggestions based on the literature on persuasion, the writings of other mediation scholars[63] and our own experience:

- ■ **Evaluate only when necessary.** Provide legal evaluation only in a "merits" dispute, when the parties are stuck because they have different predictions of who will prevail or what the specific outcome will be at trial if the case doesn't settle. If the principal barrier to settlement is something else (poor communication, personal hostility, reactive devaluation, etc.), don't evaluate until efforts to address those impediments have been exhausted. Any evaluation still needed at that point may become easier for the parties to accept.

    A related point: the later the evaluation, the better. The longer you wait, the more you will learn about the dispute. The more you know about the dispute, the more informed your evaluation will be. The more informed your evaluation, the more credible it will appear to the disputants, who, when all is said and done, must decide whether it has value to them. And by waiting, the parties may surprise you and reach a

---

61. DANIEL O'KEEFE, *Justification Explicitness and Persuasive Effect: A Meta-Analytic Review of the Effects of Varying Support Articulation in Persuasive Messages*, 35 ARGUMENT. & ADVOC. 61, 68-69 (1998) (Meta-analysis: 23 investigations, 5,358 participants).
62. STARK & FRENKEL, *supra* note 12, at 45-46.
63. *See, e.g.*, MARJORIE CORMAN AARON, *Evaluation in Mediation*, *in* DWIGHT GOLANN, Mediating Legal Disputes: Effective Strategies for Lawyers and Mediators 267-305 (1996).

resolution based on other considerations, before you ever get around to having to make a direct evaluation.

- **If possible, evaluate in caucus.** While it is possible to provide direct feedback in joint session, the caucus setting provides two major advantages. First, the parties will fight your evaluation less if it's given privately rather than in front of a hostile adversary, because there is less potential for loss of face. Second, it is easier to tailor your message, by making it simpler or more complex as needed, or softening it by starting with statements expressing empathy. If you do give feedback in joint session, be sure to ask hard questions of, and point out weaknesses to, *both* sides to maintain the appearance of impartiality.

- **Ask permission.** If you want to give the parties explicit feedback about the strength of their case, it is helpful to ask if they are open to hearing your views. If a party declines, is that the end of the matter? You might feel that you should respect their choice; ultimately it's their case. Besides, you may think, if they don't even want to hear your opinions, what chance is there that they will be persuaded by them? But sometimes a "no" — especially an adamant one — may betray a sensitivity to having a weak case and a desire to avoid exposing it. When this happens, you can choose to accept the decision or try to engage the party in a dialogue about their apparent lack of interest in what may be new and helpful information or at least another perspective to consider.

- **Be transparent and explicitly evenhanded.** How do you react when a doctor simply performs a procedure with no advance explanation? When it comes to more direct forms of evaluation, most disputants will be more open to listening to the mediator's message if she explains what she is about to do and her purpose in doing it. Even more appreciated — especially by those who still wish to "punish" the opponent — may be the knowledge that the other side will receive the same evaluative treatment. Such preparatory explanations can protect against the appearance that the mediator has lost her neutrality. Here is an example of this technique in action, from the *Resnick* mediation: **Video Clip 9-F.**

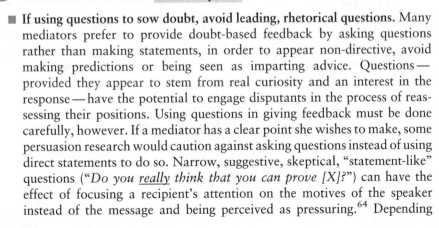

- **If using questions to sow doubt, avoid leading, rhetorical questions.** Many mediators prefer to provide doubt-based feedback by asking questions rather than making statements, in order to appear non-directive, avoid making predictions or being seen as imparting advice. Questions — provided they appear to stem from real curiosity and an interest in the response — have the potential to engage disputants in the process of reassessing their positions. Using questions in giving feedback must be done carefully, however. If a mediator has a clear point she wishes to make, some persuasion research would caution against asking questions instead of using direct statements to do so. Narrow, suggestive, skeptical, "statement-like" questions (*"Do you really think that you can prove [X]?"*) can have the effect of focusing a recipient's attention on the motives of the speaker instead of the message and being perceived as pressuring.[64] Depending

---

64. *See* STARK & FRENKEL, *supra* note 12, at 33-39 (summarizing research).

on the context (e.g., requests for explanations or justifications immediately following a party's strong assertions, posing multiple questions on the same topic) even well-intentioned, ostensibly neutral questions can be perceived this way.

If you were Bob Fitzgerald in the excerpt that follows, how would you react to the mediator's efforts to get you to examine your position? **Video Clip 9-G.**

■ **Use stories, analogies and metaphors.** People tend to understand and accept information more readily when it is conveyed in stories, metaphors and analogies. These devices can be used to make difficult messages simpler and more digestible. They are also a form of self-persuasion: In contrast to a lecture, which may cause the listener to defend against an obvious message, a story, metaphor or analogy conveys the same point more indirectly and subtly, requiring listeners to stop in their tracks and use their mental faculties to ponder the message's meaning and apply it to themselves.[65]

Thus, instead of predicting that "*the judge will probably find against you because the delays were caused by your taking on too many jobs at one time,*" a mediator might say to the contractor in *Wilson*: "*Even the best juggler has trouble keeping too many torches in the air; if one drops, he can get burned.*" Or, in an effort to persuade the same contractor to consider one approach for resolving the *Wilson* dispute, he might draw an analogy to the loyalty-preserving practice that airlines follow when they run into problems selling more tickets than there are seats on given flights. For example: "*Some friends of ours got bumped last month from a flight to Orlando because the airline overbooked it. As I understand it, that's most airlines' regular practice. But not only did the airline put our friends on the next flight out the following morning, they paid for their hotel and gave them a voucher for a free trip anywhere in the continental U.S. in the next year.*"

■ **Provide balanced evaluations.** Research suggests that two-sided refutational statements—arguments that present both sides of an issue while suggesting why one side may be more persuasive than the other—are generally more effective forms of persuasion than one-sided statements.[66] By acknowledging that there is more than one side to any question faced or decision to be made, and by helping an interviewee weigh the pros and cons

---

65. On the use of such figures of speech in mediation, *see* Michael Benjamin & Howard H. Irving, Therapeutic Family Mediation: Helping Families Resolve Conflict 66 (2002).

66. *See* Daniel O'Keefe, *How to Handle Opposing Arguments in Persuasive Messages: A Meta-Analytic Review of the Effects of One-Sided and Two-Sided Messages*, 22 Communication Yearbook 209-249 (1999), listing studies; Mike Allen, *Comparing the Persuasive Effectiveness of One- and Two-Sided Messages, in* Mike Allen & Raymond Preiss, Persuasion: Advances Through Meta-Analysis 96 (1996).

On a related point, recent survey research suggests that attorney consumers of mediation value honesty and integrity in their choice of neutrals and resent those who only emphasize case weaknesses in order to produce movement. (Quoting one respondent, for example: "*I've had mediators come in and say to both sides that their case stinks. No credibility there.*") *See* Goldberg & Shaw, *supra* note 23, at 407, 410.

of those different points of view, with input as to which is more likely to prevail, the persuader appears forthright, helpful and fair.[67]

For example, in the *Resnick* case, there was conflicting evidence about how the burglar got into the building. A balanced, two-sided and non-exaggerated evaluation with the defendant might have sounded something like this: "*You are quite right, Mr. Stevens, that there is no direct evidence of how the burglar got into the building. That could be a real problem for the plaintiff in proving his case. But the circumstantial evidence — the unlocked window on the stairwell and the broken glass indicating forced entry there — is, I fear, a real problem for you. I worry that the judge will let this issue go to the jury and, if the jury hears this evidence, that you face a serious risk of losing on that issue.*"

Here's a related point: If you think the party's case has both strengths and weaknesses, mention the strengths first. Say, "*For what it's worth, I think your claim for emotional distress damages here is quite strong, because your psychologist appears to be a very credible witness. I do have concerns, however, about the viability of your claim for lost tuition expenses.*" Providing good news first softens up your audience for any bad news to follow and furthers the goal of appearing fair and objective. Trying to settle a dispute by "beating up" each party with only negatives is an invitation to resistance.

■ **When delivering bad news, externalize your predictions.** Rather than expressing a pessimistic assessment as your own view of what will happen (which might be read as your view of what *ought* to happen), blame the decision maker and commiserate. For example: "*Unfortunately, I think that the judge will probably not admit this letter into evidence. I think she'll rule that it's inadmissible hearsay.*"

■ **Don't evaluate unless you know what you're talking about.** Although this should go without saying, many neutrals will — out of a desire to produce movement — venture into opinion areas in which they are guessing more than professing. If the main reason to evaluate in mediation is to help parties make more informed decisions, assessments ought to be grounded and accurate. If you are asked a substantive, procedural or evidentiary question to which you don't know the answer or are not sure and the question is crucial to a party's ability to decide on an important concession, try to make arrangements to obtain an answer by adjourning the mediation to do further research or by referring the question to a knowledgeable outside source.

■ **Explain fully and don't pull your punches.** However, if you *are* confident of your predictions and believe that the risks facing one or more parties are so substantial that a direct evaluative statement would be useful, don't

---

67. This generalization must be qualified to take into account the fact that individuals have widely differing capacities to weigh and analyze complex arguments. Persons of average or greater intelligence are in general hard to persuade, but more likely to be persuaded by two-sided arguments. Less intelligent people are in general easier to persuade, but persuasive messages directed at them must be simpler to be understood. SIMONS, *supra* note 8, at 15-16, 37-38. Therefore, you must tailor your arguments to your audience.

undermine the effort by hedging unduly or giving a half-baked answer. Remember that direct language and explicit arguments and conclusions are persuasive.[68] Moreover, persuasion research into the use of fear to change behavior suggests that, instead of overwhelming or shutting down recipients' ability to process a message, an appeal that makes clear the seriousness and likelihood of a threat is far more likely to trigger a search for a solution than one that fails to do so.[69]

It is also important to take the time to explain the rationale for your predictions fully so that the parties can understand and, hopefully, accept them. (Recall: reasons persuade.) In a legal matter, a full explanation of a mediator's prediction would include the rule on which it is based, why the disputed facts would call for applying this rule in this instance and, if the rule itself is questioned or resented, the reason or policy behind the rule. The credibility of the evaluation may be further enhanced by citing authoritative sources.[70] Equally important, a complete explanation of legal norms and their likely application to the situation can appeal to a disputant's sense of the fairness of the outcome that is predicted.

■ **Provide assurance that concessions will be productive.** Even where an evaluative message has reached its target, it may not have persuasive effect unless the recipient thinks that a change in position will be efficacious. In a tough negotiation, parties who think the other side will not be receptive to a change in stance may resist making a next offer. In such situations, an evaluation is not likely to have an effect unless it includes some assurance from the mediator (perhaps gleaned from caucus discussions with the other side) that the contemplated move is likely to produce progress, if not end the conflict.[71]

■ **In rare situations, confront.** Certain rare circumstances warrant bluntness. When a party is taking a stance or making a decision based on offensive views or patently wrong reasoning, the mediator ought to deal with such ideas carefully but directly, in caucus. (*"Mr. Jenkins, you seem to have a conviction that people like Ms. Johnson can be refused the opportunity to rent units in your building, solely on the basis of their race. Where did you get that view from? . . . I see. Well, this is a society where each person is entitled to hold opinions as they wish. But I have to tell you that your views are incompatible with how the law regards housing opportunity and, based on my experience, I can assure you they will not prevail at the hearing. Moreover, if you persist in that stance, and given her reaction, I will have no recourse but to terminate the mediation."*)

---

68. DANIEL O'KEEFE, *Justification Explicitness and Persuasive Effect: A Meta-Analytic Review of the Effects of Varying Support Articulation in Persuasive Messages*, 35 ARGUMENT. & ADVOC. 61 (1998) (23 investigations, 5,358 participants); DANIEL O'KEEFE, *Standpoint Explicitness and Persuasive Effect: A Meta-Analytic Review of the Effects of Varying Conclusion Articulation in Persuasive Messages*, 34 ARGUMENT. & ADVOC. 1 (1997) (32 investigations, 13,754 participants).
69. KIM WITTE & MIKE ALLEN, *A Meta-Analysis of Fear Appeals: Implications for Effective Public Health Campaigns*, 27 HEALTH ED. & BEHAV. 591 (2000).
70. WILLIAM L. BENOIT, *Forewarning and Persuasion, in* ALLEN & PREISS, *supra* note 38, at 149.
71. STARK & FRENKEL, *supra* note 12, at 53-54.

The Range of Evaluation: Video Examples.   As you watch the following efforts to produce movement through evaluation, consider: What do you like and not like about the mediators' different evaluation styles? What are principal differences in their approaches? What factors in each example made it more or less effective? Recalling the approach taken in Clip 9-G, how do you compare efforts to sow doubt through questions as opposed to statements? How, if at all, does the presence of counsel affect the above suggestions for providing effective and proper evaluation? **Video Clip 9-H (1–5).**

CHAPTER 10

CONDUCTING THE BARGAINING, DEALING WITH IMPASSE

This chapter contains nine video clips, totaling approximately fifty-nine-and-a-half minutes.

■ §10.1 INTRODUCTION

In this chapter, we move from general principles and methods of persuasion to the mediator's role in orchestrating the actual bargaining process. After examining the formats that are available for conducting negotiations, we focus on how the neutral can assist the parties' bargaining, recognize potential impasses and seek to overcome them and then forge an agreement even when time is running out.

■ §10.2 CONDUCTING THE ACTUAL BARGAINING: A RANGE OF FORMATS

When it comes time for the parties to engage in actual bargaining, three different processes are available to the mediator:

- **Group brainstorming.** The mediator tries to orchestrate a creative, open-minded, group problem-solving process. In this process, the parties first generate, without evaluation or censorship, multiple possible options for resolving the dispute. They then evaluate the options in hopes of finding a solution by expanding, combining and improving on aspects of them. Significantly, bargaining is deferred until all of the ideas are vetted.

- **Face-to-face negotiation.** The mediator keeps the parties in the same room and moderates a face-to-face negotiation process in which the parties trade offers back and forth one at a time.

- **Caucused negotiation.** The mediator separates the parties and conducts a facilitated negotiation in which he meets with the parties privately, helps them frame offers one at a time and then conveys information and offers back and forth between the two sides in hopes of producing a settlement.

These formats are not mutually exclusive; as we will see, they are combined by practicing mediators in different ways. But they differ in important respects, including the degree of mediator control of what the parties know and the kind of results they are likely to produce.

Some mediators have a preferred procedure they tend to use in most of their cases, based largely on their philosophy about the mediator's proper role. Facilitative mediators who are committed to the goal of interest-based bargaining and nondirected party decision making might prefer to keep the parties together if possible and might try a brainstorming process if the conditions are right. Highly evaluative mediators, focused on achieving settlements, are likely to move to — and stay in — caucuses as soon as it is time to start negotiating.

The mediator's selection of a bargaining format ought to be chosen with deliberation, based on the dispute and party characteristics in each situation. As you read more detailed descriptions of each model and consider their advantages and disadvantages, ask yourself: Do you think you would be equally comfortable managing each format? If not, which format(s) make you uncomfortable? Why?

■ §10.3 GROUP BRAINSTORMING: MULTIPLYING OPTIONS THROUGH COLLABORATION

Most efforts at solving problems through brainstorming, in mediation and elsewhere, follow a two-stage, sequential process: (1) idea generation and (2) evaluation. Based on the work of Alex Osborn,[1] four basic "rules" have become accepted:

- **At first, no criticism.** Generating ideas and critiquing ideas are two separate processes. Criticism of ideas during idea generation is ruled out. ("*Yes, but*" is a no-no.)

- **As many ideas as possible.** The more ideas that can be generated, the better. Doing this quickly seems to promote the flow of ideas and minimize self-censorship and criticism.

- **The wilder the better.** While ideas are being generated, uninhibited and freewheeling discussion is encouraged even if it feels "wild" or "silly." Stimulating the parties to include both ideal and even unattainable outcomes can yield good potential solutions and occasionally gems.

- **Combine and synthesize ideas.** During the idea evaluation stage, combination and improvement of ideas are sought. ("*Yes, and*" is encouraged.) Trading or other bargaining is not allowed.

---

1. *See* ALEX F. OSBORN, Applied Imagination (1957).

More recent empirical work[2] suggests the following specifics for mediators facilitating a group brainstorming process:

Tips for Brainstorming

- Instruct the disputants in the basic rules of brainstorming, verbally or in writing;
- Encourage disputants to work to generate the broadest possible list of ways to resolve the dispute;
- Time permitting, have the parties generate ideas separately, before sharing their ideas as a group.
- Have the parties take turns presenting their proposals;
- Record everyone's ideas as they emerge on a piece of paper, flip chart or by computer projection;
- Encourage everyone to participate equally, by calling on them and reminding them that their participation is important;
- Use humor and optimism to keep everyone's spirit up;
- Interrupt group members when they get off topic and get them back on task;
- Remind group members of the "no criticism" rule if they begin prematurely to evaluate or reject proposals;
- If there is a lull in ideas, restate the problem to be resolved or use silence;
- Encourage evaluation (but not negotiation) of ideas once a complete list of ideas is generated;
- Encourage amendment and synthesis of different ideas, based on the parties' individual and shared needs and interests.

The major advantage of brainstorming over other negotiation models is that it promotes the consideration of multiple options at the same time.[3] Whereas positional bargaining usually causes the disputants to consider only two options (each party's current offer) at any moment — causing the parties to feel as though a concession by them is a gain for the other side — group brainstorming helps the parties generate multiple proposals, consider them simultaneously and then amplify, combine and improve on them.[4] Brainstorming is thus an attempt to resolve a dispute in a way that adds to the parties' joint satisfaction, rather than simply trading concessions or carving up a fixed pie.

---

2. *See, e.g.,* BERNARD NIJSTAD et al., *The Illusion of Group Productivity: A Reduction of Failures Explanation,* 36 EUR. J. SOC. PSYCHOL. 31 (2006); SIGAL G. BARSADE, *The Ripple Effect: Emotional Contagion and Its Influence on Group Behavior,* 47 ADMIN. SCI. Q. 644 (2002); HAMIT COSKUN et al., *Cognitive Stimulation and Problem Presentation in Idea-Generating Groups,* 4 GROUP DYN. THEORY RES. PRACT. 307 (2000); MORRIS GALLAGHER et al., *The Nominal Group Technique: A Research Tool for General Practice?* 10 FAM. PRAC. 76 (1993); NORBERT L. KERR & R. SCOTT TINDALE, *Group Performance and Decision Making,* 55 ANNU. REV. PSYCHOL. 623 (2004); ANNE K. OFFNER et al., *The Effects of Facilitation, Recording and Pauses on Group Brainstorming,* 27 SMALL GROUP RES. 283 (1996); NICOLE L. OXLEY et al., *The Effects of Facilitators on the Performance of Brainstorming Groups,* 11 J. SOC. BEHAV. PERS. 633 (1996).
3. CHRISTOPHER W. MOORE, The Mediation Process 283-284 (3d ed. 2003).
4. *Id.*

A second advantage claimed for the brainstorming process is that it can build a sense of group identity that encourages the participants to set aside their individual interests and analyze a problem collectively. Studies in non-dispute settings suggest that most people enjoy the process and believe it to be effective in building group cohesion and increasing commitment to decisions that are made.[5]

Group brainstorming was employed with considerable success by one of the mediators in *Wilson v. DiLorenzo*. As you watch the pre-brainstorming caucuses and group session, consider the following questions:

To what extent did this mediator follow the facilitation "rules" listed above? What did her presence and involvement add? What did she do that was effective? What might have been done to improve on it? Was there something about this dispute or the disputants that made this case amenable to a group brainstorming approach? What was it about the brainstorming that led to the final outcome? You may recall that Ms. Wilson told this mediator in caucus that she preferred not to have to deal with Mr. diLorenzo or to have him come to her house "ever again." **Video Clip 10-A.**

Variables to Consider.   Group brainstorming will not work in every situation. In what kinds of cases is it likely to be effective? Two variables seem important:

- **Multiple issues? Or only one?** First, do the negotiations that are to commence, at least potentially, have multiple kinds of solutions or options for resolution? Brainstorming — especially the idea of broadening the potential number of options before bargaining starts — seems to require this as a precondition. By contrast, a single issue, zero-sum dispute — for example, a personal injury negotiation solely over money damages — is much less amenable to a brainstorming approach. (Each "idea" generated in sequence would, in effect, simply be a counterproposal to the previous one, quickly transforming the discussions into a competitive bargaining session.)

- **Cognitive, social and negotiating skills of the parties.** Can all of the participants understand the difference between generating ideas and evaluating them? Do the disputants all have reasonable social skills? Are they comfortable asserting positions and working with others? Some people are reluctant to express their ideas in groups, because of social anxiety, sensitivity to group criticism or low self-esteem. Empirical research demonstrates that individuals who are self-confident and reasonably assertive do better in group brainstorming activities than people who are not.[6] For the mediator, then, it is important to look for signs that all parties can hold their own in groups before using brainstorming as a mode of resolving a dispute.

---

5. Corinne Faure, *Beyond Brainstorming: Effects of Different Group Procedures on Selection of Ideas and Satisfaction with the Process*, 38 J. Creative Behav. 13 (2004); Michael Kramer, Chao Lan Kuo & John Dailey, *The Impact of Brainstorming on Subsequent Group Process: Beyond Generating Ideas*, 28 Small Group Research 218 (1997).

6. *See* Thomas J. Bouchard, *Training, Motivation, and Personality as Determinants of the Effectiveness of Brainstorming Groups and Individuals*, 56 J. Appl. Psychol. 324 (1972); L. Mabel Camacho & Paul B. Paulus, *The Role of Social Anxiousness in Group Brainstorming*, 68 J. Pers. Soc. Psychol. 1071 (1995).

Does the Presence of Strong Disagreement or Bad Feelings Matter?   One might assume that brainstorming would not work well when there is strong disagreement or hostility between the parties. But it is not clear how this variable affects the process. On the one hand, at least as far as idea-*generation* is concerned, empirical research in fact suggests that groups in which there is authentic dissent produce more and better ideas than those lacking dissent.[7] On the other hand, some research suggests that, as interpersonal conflicts within a group become more severe, this interferes substantially with cognitive flexibility and creative thinking.[8]

A bigger hurdle may be the competitive orientation of the parties or their counsel. Those deeply committed to distributive bargaining may strongly resist an open, nonjudgmental exploration of many possible settlement ideas, as it is antithetical to asserting a single negotiating position. Asking such participants to "*take a chance and try it*" may be met with swift rejection, at least until a bargaining impasse seems imminent.

■ §10.4 FACE-TO-FACE NEGOTIATIONS

Conducting the bargaining by keeping the parties together for face-to-face (no-caucus) negotiations can be a challenging yet useful format. But because barriers to resolution between the parties often linger when the participants remain together, and because bargaining concessions are often facilitated by privacy, many mediators and parties prefer to conduct negotiations through caucuses. Nonetheless, in the right situations, there may be important reasons to conduct the negotiations with everyone present.

For example, where there is an educational objective in the parties' learning how to communicate and negotiate with each other in anticipation of possible future disagreements, a mediation that keeps them together may be the beginning of a valuable learning experience. For this reason, many family mediators minimize the use of caucuses in child custody mediations. In what other sorts of disputes is this likely to be a factor?

Variables to Consider.   Curiously, little has been written about the conditions that make face-to-face negotiations effective in various mediation settings. In our experience, this process works best when:

- **The dispute is "cool," not "hot."** The parties are not angry with each other, can talk to each other effectively and seem desirous of working together to reach a resolution.

- **There is not a lot of strategic posturing.** Both parties seem willing to talk about their interests candidly or are bargaining competitively but reasonably, not making overly inflated demands of each other.

---

7. CHARLAN NEMETH et al., *Devil's Advocate Versus Authentic Dissent: Stimulating Quantity and Quality*, 31 EUR. J. SOC. PSYCHOL. 707 (2001); CHARLAN NEMETH & BRENDAN NEMETH-BROWN, *Better than Individuals? The Potential Benefits of Dissent and Diversity for Group Creativity*, in Group Creativity: Innovation through Collaboration 63 (PAUL B. PAULUS & BERNARD A. NIJSTAD eds., 2003).
8. CARSTEN K.W. DE DREU & LAURIE R. WEINGART, *Task Versus Relationship Conflict, Team Performance, and Team Member Satisfaction*, 88 J. APPL. PSYCHOL. 741 (2003).

- **There is no need or desire for mediator evaluation.** Both sides are aware of the likely legal outcomes or other non-resolution scenarios, or value personally important norms — such as efficiency, enhancing their relationship or "fairness" over law or other external standards — to guide the resolution of their dispute.

- **There is significant time pressure.** When both parties have their eye on the clock, they may be willing to forgo caucuses and work together to reach a settlement expeditiously.

§10.5 CAUCUSED NEGOTIATION OR "SHUTTLE DIPLOMACY"

The third negotiation format available to mediators is caucused bargaining. In Chapter 7, we discussed how a mediator can use private meetings to develop information that the parties may be reluctant to disclose in joint session. Here, we analyze how keeping the parties separated can be used to promote bargaining and resolution. As we said earlier, the distinction between caucusing for information and caucusing for negotiation often breaks down in practice, because many private sessions will involve both information gathering and negotiation activities. But facilitating the bargaining process remains one of the most important uses of the caucus.

Advantages of Caucused Negotiation.   In general, caucused negotiation has two major advantages over both face-to-face negotiations and group brainstorming. First, for many negotiators, processing the other side's offers and concessions and planning one's own require considerable deliberation and often the mediator's assistance. The privacy of the caucus can facilitate this kind of collaborative planning.

Second, the same cover of privacy allows mediators to use certain kinds of persuasion to influence what proposals are made, how they are presented to the other side and what proposals are accepted — in a way that does not compromise their perceived neutrality.

Variables to Consider.   What kinds of case and participant characteristics suggest the use of caucused negotiations?[9]

- **The single-issue, zero-sum dispute.** If the only issue is how much money the defendant's insurance carrier will pay the overly confident plaintiff for his claim (say, a car accident case in which all of the plaintiff's injuries have healed), generally there are no other solution ideas that could be developed through brainstorming. Face-to-face bargaining is also unlikely to succeed,

---

9. *See generally* JAY FOLBERG et al., Resolving Disputes: Theory, Practice and Law 338-346 (2005); EILEEN M. HOHLT, *Effective Use of Caucus* (1993), *in* Alternative Dispute Resolution: Strategies for Law and Business 335-336 (E. WENDY TRACHTE-HUBER & STEPHEN HUBER eds., 1996); CHRISTOPHER W. MOORE, *The Caucus: Private Meetings That Promote Settlement*, 16 MEDIATION Q. 87 (1987); GARY WELTON et al., *Antecedents and Characteristics of Caucusing in Community Mediation*, 3 INT'L J. CONFLICT MGMT. 303 (1992) (empirical study); GARY L. WELTON et al., *The Role of Caucusing in Community Mediation*, 32 J. CONFLICT RESOL. 181 (1988).

because the parties will likely trade offers sequentially in a competitive "negotiation dance" that may not lead to a convergence of positions without the kind of mediator assistance that is usually best offered in private.

- **When strategic barriers impede open and honest exchange.** Tough, distributive bargaining strategies can jeopardize any face-to-face negotiation, even in disputes that are not zero-sum. In general, parties tend to exhibit more flexibility in their bargaining positions and disclose more information that reveals case weaknesses or their underlying goals and interests in caucus than when facing the "opponent." Privacy similarly eases the mediator's efforts to help the parties assess offers and counteroffers realistically or urge them to take risks in formulating proposals they might be reluctant to make if negotiating face-to-face.

- **When the parties' negotiating behavior is problematic.** Caucused mediation is useful when the negotiators need help in their bargaining. Is one disputant turning off the other by her overly aggressive conduct? Does a participant seem unsure about his ability to negotiate or reluctant even to engage in bargaining? In the privacy of the caucus, a mediator can coach each party on his or her bargaining style and, in some situations, discuss whether the process should even proceed. She can suppress or translate harsh statements and irrational arguments that might otherwise impede negotiations. She can use the caucus to calm negotiators down when they are infuriated by offers they consider insulting. She can help the parties frame offers in ways designed to maximize their chances of acceptance and even propose settlement ideas herself.

- **If the mediator plans to use a directive or evaluative approach.** Caucusing is helpful when mediators want to provide the parties with evaluative feedback. As discussed in Chapter 9, when delivering bad news, evaluative mediators can present a difficult message in an empathic way calculated to make it "go down" more easily. If the other side is not present, the party on the receiving end is less apt to fight the message (because of loss of face) or doubt the mediator's neutrality.

With Whom to Meet First?   In general, the mechanics of negotiation caucuses are similar to those of information-gathering caucuses, discussed in §7.8. But one decision—the decision about which party to meet with first—is governed by different considerations.

Some writers suggest that the first negotiation caucus should be held with the side whose bargaining position seems most inflexible so as to be able to "work on" that party.[10] Some mediators believe that to balance the process, the neutral should begin with the party who, in presenting their opening statement, went second. Others suggest, conversely, that the mediator should begin with the party who initiated the case or the mediation.

---

10. *See* Moore, *supra* note 3, at 92; Walter A. Maggiolo, Techniques of Mediation in Labor Disputes 53 (1971).

But the initiating party (in legal matters, the plaintiff) is often the wrong person with whom to start if generating a change in positions is the goal. He is likely to have made a specific demand (for money, performance of some act, cessation of ongoing behavior or some other change in the status quo) and, unless the defendant has already made a counteroffer, may be unwilling to reduce his demand (and thus "bid against himself"). On the other hand, if the plaintiff's opening demand is so extreme as to threaten an impasse, the first caucus might be with him to attempt to persuade him to reconsider that position. As you can see, this decision can be complex, with potential consequences for the success of the negotiations; it thus requires careful thought.

■ §10.6 USING MIXED NEGOTIATION FORMATS

As we have said, these three bargaining formats are not mutually exclusive; in practice, they are often combined by mediators in various ways. Common examples include:

■ After information expansion efforts in joint session have been exhausted, the mediator may wish to conduct a preliminary caucus with each side to lay the groundwork for and choose the best negotiation format. What are the conflict dynamics? How far apart are the parties actually? Are they willing to reveal more about their interests than they have to this point? Do I need simply to coach one party about her tactics? If, through these caucuses, the mediator learns that face-to-face negotiations or brainstorming might be effective, she can proceed accordingly at that point.

■ Alternatively, the mediator might conduct the negotiations primarily by caucus, but toward the end of the mediation bring the parties back into joint session to bridge any final gaps together. This is very common, at least in cases where the mediator believes that initiating or resuming face-to-face negotiations will not raise tensions or create deal-threatening strategic problems. When used successfully, reconvening the parties toward the end of a mediation can yield a greater sense of ownership in any agreement reached, greater satisfaction with the process as a whole and the feeling of a "high note" ending.

■ A similar mixed format brings the parties back together once a deal in principle has been reached through caucused negotiations, to work out its operational details: When exactly will the payments be made? By check or in cash or by money order? To whom should the check be addressed? Will any confidentiality provisions include family members? If there is to be a press release, who will draft it, and what will it say?

■ §10.7 CONDUCTING THE ACTUAL BARGAINING: THE MEDIATOR'S ROLE

Whatever negotiation format or formats are chosen, effective mediators can play an integral role in orchestrating the actual bargaining. During this phase, the full range of persuasive activity continues as the mediator takes on additional tasks.

As we will see, the approach adopted can vary widely by mediator and dispute. Because much of what the neutral does will be aimed at minimizing the influence of potential barriers to resolution, discussed in Chapter 2, this might be a good time to review that chapter.

Before Trading Offers: Obtaining a General Framework for Agreement?

In some cases, the polarized tone of discussions may prompt concerns about whether the matter is resolvable at all. Multiple negotiable issues may have surfaced, but there appear to be divergent positions on all of them. In such situations, the mediator may wish to put off any bargaining on specifics and instead begin by proposing an agreement on a set of general principles to guide the negotiations.

Where parties have identified interests in common, such guiding principles may be easy to find. For example, parents locked in a bitter feud over future child custody arrangements might be asked to react to the concept that *"each parent should spend quality time with the child."* Where the parties are in a dispute over whether a long-term contract to supply a restaurant with dairy products has been breached, they may still be able to agree that all remaining contractual obligations will be honored going forward.

In other situations, the mediator may be able to surface such shared standards by starting with questions such as: *"Can we agree that whatever resolution we end up reaching, it has to feel fair to both of you?"* More specific commonalities might then be learned, by asking the parties to talk about their vision for the future of their relationship assuming that *"everything is going well."*[11]

While this approach is certainly no guarantee of smooth sailing, it may help soften later disagreements. It applies the consistency principle to ensure that, once the actual bargaining begins, the negotiators behave in accordance with their stated commitments.

During the Bargaining Process: An Overview of Mediator Activities.

The mediator can assist the bargaining in four ways:

- **What is said: the content and timing of proposals.** Effective mediators work with the parties to coach them on the types of offers made, encouraging them to make proposals that are realistic and productive. They also advise on the timing of offers, which can affect their chances of being accepted.

- **What is said: how offers are framed and justified.** In a caucused process, the mediator must decide whether she will communicate settlement proposals on behalf of the parties or have the parties make them directly to each other. In either event, careful attention must be paid to how offers and counter-offers are articulated and justified.

- **What is heard: how offers are received and evaluated.** Effective mediators work with the parties to help them evaluate offers objectively, including exploring the costs of a failure to reach agreement.

---

11. MOORE, *supra* note 3, at 400.

■ **The momentum of the talks: avoiding "no."** Settlement-oriented mediators create a tone of optimism and an expectation of party flexibility, moving the parties determinedly toward resolution.

Let's look more closely at each of these activities. Much of what follows assumes that the negotiation is distributive and conducted mostly through caucuses. As you review the approaches that follow, ask yourself: Which mediator interventions, if any, could also be accomplished in a face-to-face bargaining process? Are there any you could not see yourself doing? Why?

■ §10.8 WHAT OFFERS AND CONCESSIONS WILL BE MADE, AND WHEN?

The conditioning and persuasion approaches discussed in Chapter 9 are designed to encourage the parties to make productive negotiation proposals once they begin bargaining. But for a variety of reasons, including the time it takes for persuasion to take hold, parties often backslide and make ill-considered, adversarial offers that create barriers to resolution. How can a mediator minimize this risk?

Moderating Unproductive Demands or Concessions.   First, as we have noted, it is very common for parties to enter the mediation process with unrealistic expectations about what is possible to achieve in negotiation. Skilled mediators, having learned a great deal in earlier probing about the constraints facing each side and the firmness of their commitments, can coach both parties on their demands and offers and try to moderate them.

Role reversal questions are often useful as a first step, as in "*I wonder: If you were the defendant, how would you respond to an opening demand of two hundred thousand dollars in this case?*" If such questions do not produce the desired result, more direct feedback can be useful, such as: "*I'll convey any number you like, but I'm concerned that if you make that demand, the defendant might just get up and leave.*"

A good illustration of this type of intervention occurred in the *Resnick* mediation, in which a mediator gave defense counsel direct feedback about his proposed first offer. (Prior to this point, the plaintiff was demanding $110,000 and the defense had offered $10,000.) What about this feedback is effective or not effective? If you had been defense counsel, how would you have reacted to it? **Video Clip 10-B.**

The same mediator then gave the plaintiff's attorney even blunter feedback when she proposed to lower her initial demand by only $10,000, to $100,000. If you were the plaintiff's counsel, how might you have reacted? Should this message have been delivered more tactfully? If so, how exactly? **Video Clip 10-C.**

Timing of Offers.   Sometimes a mediator's moderating feedback has to do with the timing of an offer or demand, as well as its substance. For example, in *Resnick*, the defendant's attorney proposed a monetary offer in caucus that the mediator thought was very low. In the same caucus, the lawyer insisted that he would also demand a new term — a confidentiality clause — to settle the case. Watch the mediator's reaction and advice to defense counsel.

 Are the mediator interventions depicted in these three tracks consistent with norms of neutrality and impartiality? Would you feel comfortable employing them? **Video Clip 10-D.**

Urging *Less* Moderation?   If moderating tough positions by hardball bargainers is proper mediator conduct, what about the opposite: urging or helping weak or non-adversarial negotiators to drive a harder bargain? As we noted in Chapter 2, competitive bargainers often feel better about a negotiation — and may be more likely to reach agreement — if that agreement appears to reflect hard-won concessions from the other side.[12] Suppose that the mediator believes that an accommodating party is demanding too little or conceding too much, too quickly. In the interest of obtaining an agreement about which both parties feel good, should he suggest to that party that he consider making larger demands or smaller or more gradual concessions, especially early on in the process? Or is this ethically problematic?

Fleshing Out Offers.   Effective mediators work with the parties to ensure that their proposals are both practical and durable. Asking *"how would that work?"* questions are useful for that purpose. For example, watch how one of our mediators in *Wilson v. DiLorenzo* helps the defendant contractor "unpack" his proposal to offer an extended warranty on his materials. **Video Clip 10-E.**

This is another example of using party-centered, *"say more about that"* questions to flesh out conclusory statements and help the speaker feel heard and be understood.[13]

Providing Time and Space to Consider the Next Move.   Often it is helpful to slow the process down to provide time for the disputants to consider carefully what proposals or counterproposals they want to make next. This can avoid the situation of the angry disputant making a hasty, emotional and counterproductive response to an offer. In other situations, it can serve as a form of "power balancing" by which the mediator gives the less confident negotiator time to think and formulate what he or she wants to say, free from undue pressure by the other side.[14]

---

12. Because they regularly use the tactic themselves, competitive bargainers often assume that their negotiation counterparts are engaging in extreme anchoring, demanding far more than they really want or offering far less than they are willing to give to settle the case. Thus, when an accommodating negotiator's first offer is too close to his own bottom line, his opponent, thinking it to be a mere anchor, may reject the offer and hold out for a lot more. This can create impasse if the misunderstanding about the bargaining zone continues and anger takes over.

13. *See* §7.4.3, *supra.*

14. Mark D. Bennett & Scott Hughes, The Art of Mediation 119 (2d. ed 2005).

Negotiating Challenges: Culturally Driven?

When a mediator senses the need to confront challenges caused by the way the parties are negotiating, it may not suffice merely to address problematic bargaining behaviors. A participant's approach to negotiating may have deeper roots, attributable to culturally ingrained modes of dealing with conflict.

Much has been written on this subject, some of it with a broad brush that paints a rather stereotyped picture of the preferred bargaining styles of entire cultural groups: Some nationalities are deferential and conflict averse; persons from certain cultures gesture physically and negotiate emotionally; women are relational and less competitive and so on. Researchers have attempted to test such assertions, sometimes with results that challenge conventional assumptions. *See, e.g.,* Jeswald W. Salacuse, *Ten Ways that Culture Affects Negotiating Style: Some Survey Results*, 14 Negotiation J. 221 (1998). Obviously, hypotheses in this realm must be tested very carefully: No person should be assumed to be acting in a particular way solely because of their identity or affiliation. Cultures themselves are diverse and negotiating styles can be a product of many factors, including an individual's profession (a subculture itself), personality or the kind of dispute at hand. *See, e.g.,* Jeffrey Z. Rubin & Frank E.A. Sander, *Culture, Negotiation, and the Eye of the Beholder*, 7 Negotiation J. 249 (1991).

But assume that a mediator suspects that culture may be at the root of a party's problematic bargaining approach. Is it appropriate for a neutral to try to address such problems? In the time frame available in a typical mediation, can such problems be dealt with effectively? Would you have the skills to do so? In general, which is easier to address: aggressive conduct that seems to be offending the opponent or passive conduct that seems to be causing a party to "cave in"? Consider this example:

An elderly cabinet maker, a religiously devout recent immigrant, was sued in the local small claims court by a young female customer. To the mediator, the plaintiff's $4,000 claim for poor workmanship seemed spurious, bordering on fraudulent. When the defendant put up no bargaining resistance and appeared to be on the verge of acceding to the plaintiff's demand for full payment of her claim, the mediator called a caucus with him. In the caucus, the man explained that, where he comes from, public conflict is a source of great shame and that bargaining — especially with women — is frowned upon. How would you handle this situation? On what does your answer depend?

§10.9 COMMUNICATING OFFERS: HOW WILL THEY BE FRAMED AND JUSTIFIED, AND BY WHOM?

It is obvious that the way offers are couched can significantly affect how they are received. Effective mediators carefully frame offers — or if the parties will resume face-to-face negotiations, assist them on how to present their own offers — to ensure that information is presented as constructively as possible. For example:

Suppressing Harmful Information.   If the bargaining is done in caucus, mediators can suppress information that may impede negotiations or retard settlement. This includes weeding out harsh statements made by each party about the other side or its case, as well as emotional arguments and irrational proposals that may trigger anger or other psychological barriers.

Suppose in a mediation caucus in a child custody case, the wife tells the mediator, "*You tell my ex-husband that my final offer is that he can see the kids two Saturdays a month and that I view that as generous, considering what a non-father he's been and his incessant drinking and womanizing!*" Must the mediator convey this message verbatim just because the wife has asked her to? The question seems to answer itself: If that were all that the neutral did, her presence would add little, if anything, to the parties' negotiations and, by keeping them apart, might actually set back any progress toward establishing mutual empathy. But how far should the mediator go in toning the message down in order to keep the negotiations moving? Would it be unduly manipulative for the mediator to say to the husband, "*Look, I know that two Saturdays a month is less than you are looking for. But we're really making progress from her earlier proposal, and given the history here, can you understand how she might want you to be reintroduced into your kids' lives in a gradual way?*"

Developing Rationales for Offers and Concessions.   Negotiators sometimes make proposals for settlement that are not justified by reference to any norm, standard or factor in the dispute. Unexplained demands that appear to be plucked out of thin air are typically viewed as arbitrary[15] and can be resented if seen as unreasonable. Such proposals can thus create strategic barriers to settlement. If a negotiator hasn't herself provided a credible rationale to support an intended bargaining proposal, should a mediator help her do so, to "grease the wheels" of the negotiation? ("*You could say that your demand represents what it will cost to repair your car plus the cost of renting a car for a week plus your filing fees.*") While this may aid in the quest for a resolution, is it consistent with the duty of impartiality? We consider this question further in Chapter 12.

Conveying "Good News" First.   If a party is willing to make significant concessions on two out of three of the other side's demands but not the final (most important) demand, it is useful to have the other side hear the good news before the bad. The mediator might then coach the party making only partial concessions to say (or say herself, if conveying offers in caucused negotiation), "*Let me start with what we (they) are willing to do here in the interest of reaching a good faith settlement. We (they) are prepared to offer [A] and [B]. Unfortunately, for the following reasons (supplying the rationale for limiting the offer), we (they) are not able to offer [C].*" Mixed offers are more likely to be received favorably when presented this way.

Making a "Mediator's Proposal."   In order to reduce the likelihood that proposals will be rejected if seen as coming from the opponent, mediators often claim authorship of ideas and suggestions that in reality come from the parties. This approach increases the chance that proposals will be couched productively and that they will be heard with a minimum of cognitive distortion stemming from reactive devaluation or animus toward the other side. To have the desired effect,

---

15. Robert M. Bastress & Joseph D. Harbaugh, Interviewing, Counseling, and Negotiating: Skills for Effective Representation 508-510 (1990).

mediator proposals are usually worded in hypothetical "trial balloon" terms, for example: "*Suppose they were to offer you $150 on your $400 claim?*" Doing this privately has the added benefit of allowing the recipient to reject the proposal and later accept it without loss of face, since it was only tendered (and rejected) hypothetically, and not in the presence of the other party. But this device can raise questions and challenges as well.

▶ ▶ ▶ ▶ **The Mediator as Messenger: Carrier Pigeon or Blind-Bid Auctioneer?**

In a recent, fiercely contested employment discrimination case, the fired employee began the mediation by demanding $150,000 — eight months of back pay ($56,000), seven months of health insurance premiums ($4,000), punitive damages ($80,000) and attorney's fees ($10,000), plus reinstatement to his former position. After several hours of heated argument about the facts and the law, the employer offered $10,000 "nuisance value" to resolve the matter completely. The mediator then caucused with the plaintiff and, after forty-five minutes, was authorized to counter with an offer dropping the claim for reinstatement if the company paid his back pay and attorney's fees claims (a total of $66,000). In your next caucus with the employer, how would you respond as mediator if asked, "*So, where are they?*"

If your instinctive reaction is to convey the counteroffer verbatim to the employer, ask yourself this: What will their most likely reaction be? Even if you are able to sow some doubt or impress on them the potential costs of non-settlement, once they know that the plaintiff is willing to forgo his demand for reinstatement, isn't it likely that they will respond with a very low counteroffer, perhaps "*$15,000 and a confidentiality agreement*"? If time is running short or the employee would be angered by such a response, an impasse might result. How can this scenario be avoided?

Consider the following alternative responses:

(a) "*I made progress with him but we need some from you. Suppose I could get him to back off the reinstatement claim. What would you then be willing to do on the money?*"

(b) "*Let me run by you a possible framework for resolution that has occurred to me: What if you paid him the back wage claim, plus his attorney's fees, and he agrees to go away? If that works for you, I'll try to sell him on it.*"

Both messages are couched as hypotheticals in order to protect information. In example (a), the specific terms offered by the employee are concealed; in (b), the terms are revealed but not their source.

Is such strategic maneuvering deceitful or a form of undue manipulation? If you are not comfortable with this or have concerns about the potential loss of party autonomy, ask yourself: Since the parties are free to refuse this approach and must approve any final resolution, what is the harm if they go along with it? How does this differ from other forms of process management that capitalize on the mediator's knowledge of the parties' strategies, interests and fears? Assuming you are comfortable with this, what would you say when, in response to such a "hypothetical," the employer asks, "*Hmm. Did he offer that?*"

The "Door-In-The-Face" Approach: Inviting Rejection First?   If the mediator becomes the author of ideas for resolution that are transmitted to the parties, must the terms of his hypothetical proposals ("supposals") reflect what he knows the parties will actually accept? Research in the field of persuasion suggests that the ability to reach a target request is enhanced by a person's asking for *more* than he or she wants, having that request rejected and then asking for his or her target.[16] This is more effective than asking for one's target directly. In the above discrimination matter, what would you think of the mediator's asking the employer for their reaction to "*$100,000 with no reinstatement*" on the assumption that, once that figure is rejected, a next offer of "*$66,000 with no reinstatement*" might stand a better chance of being accepted?

■ §10.10   HOW WILL OFFERS BE RECEIVED AND EVALUATED?

Even objectively reasonable, well-justified and well-timed offers are sometimes rejected by litigants, especially when they have been embroiled in a protracted dispute. As we noted in Chapter 5, in a mediation of a few hours' duration, parties often have a hard time emotionally letting go of a conflict that may have been years in the making. In addition, they are often unable to overcome various cognitive barriers that commonly get in the way of accurate perceptions of bargaining offers. Mediators can confront such potentially self-destructive obstacles in a number of ways:

Allowing Venting.   Mediators often have to calm negotiators when they are infuriated by offers they consider insulting. This includes letting them rage against the perceived inadequacy or unjustness of the other side's proposals, then trying to explain those proposals in light of the other side's interests and constraints and giving them time to calm down and formulate counterproposals.

Anticipating and Preempting Negative Reactions.   When the mediator thinks a party is likely to react badly to a proposal, she can try to reduce the chances of a negative response by predicting it. For example: "*You're probably going to be tempted to reject this out of hand, but I think you should give it some thought before doing so. . . .*" Psychologically, this challenge sometimes spurs participants to prove the mediator wrong.[17]

Explaining the Significance of One Party's Offer.   As we have noted, reactive devaluation leads negotiators to discount each other's proposals — even if they are reasonable or would otherwise be acceptable — solely because of their source. Strategic barriers similarly lead to rejection of reasonable offers on the erroneous assumption that the opponent is bluffing. Mediators can overcome such barriers by explaining the significance of each side's concessions to the other side. ("*You know, Mr. Morales shared with me that his wife has just had some experimental medical treatments that their health insurance didn't cover. He wants to be reasonable, but money is very tight for him right now. . . .*") This also sometimes can take the form of leaking the impression, based on caucus discussions with the other side, that "*If you want to make a deal, this may be about as far as you can push him.*"

---

16. *See, e.g.* DANIEL J. O'KEEFE & SCOTT L. HALE, *The Door-in-the-Face Influence Strategy: A Random Effects Meta-Analytic Review,* 21 COMMUNICATION YEARBOOK 1 (1998).
17. HOWARD H. IRVING & MICHAEL BENJAMIN, Therapeutic Family Mediation: Helping Families Resolve Conflict 66 (2002).

Putting Things in Perspective: Focusing on Interests and Exploring the Costs of Not Reaching Agreement.   In helping resistant parties evaluate proposals, effective mediators also try to help them see less than ideal proposals in light of the "big picture," which too often gets lost in the heat of negotiation. How does a particular negotiation proposal relate to each party's broader interests — the profitability of their business, their interest in getting the dispute behind them, their desire to avoid a precedent or bad publicity if possible. It is useful to ask litigants questions such as: "*What will it feel like if we are unable to get this thing resolved today? What would the effect of a failure to resolve this dispute be on your [business][state of mind][litigation expenses] going forward?*"

Watch how one of our mediators framed an offer made by the defendant in the *Resnick* premises liability case, focusing on the dual themes of the desirability of closure and the idea that "money isn't everything." Note also that this mediator leaked his impression, based on confidential discussions with the defendant, about how high defendant might go. Is this appropriate? **Video Clip 10-F.**

Lowering the Perceived Stakes.   In addition to their frequent inability to see the "forest for the trees," parties in mediation often exaggerate what is at stake. For example, a defendant in a civil litigation may balk at the magnitude of the payment demanded to end the lawsuit. But if reminded that nonresolution will also have its costs — in counsel fees, court costs, lost business opportunities and so forth — she may perceive the settlement proposal in a less dramatic light and be more open to considering it.

Similarly, disputants in family and other emotional conflicts often magnify what is at stake. Watch how one of our mediators in the *Fitzgerald* case intervenes in the parents' polarized negotiations over who will have "permanent" custody. **Video Clip 10-G.**

In some situations, the mediator may have to go a step further. Where a complete and final agreement seems unreachable, lowering the *actual* stakes — by proposing that only some of the issues be resolved or that an agreement be temporary in nature — may make at least some concrete progress possible (e.g., "*Would it make sense to try to come up with a parenting plan for the next four weeks, until you come back for your second mediation session?*"). We return to this topic in Chapter 11.

Framing Losses as Gains.   As we discussed in Chapter 2, human beings have a cognitive bias against losing and will take on considerable (even irrational) risk to avoid a perceived loss. Effective mediators can help the parties evaluate potential resolutions more realistically, by pointing out gains to be achieved by settlement. Consider two cases recently mediated:

> • In the first, a child custody dispute, the mother was intent on denying the father any visitation time with their son, because the father had been consistently delinquent in making his child support payments. In her mind, giving up any of "her" time with the son was a loss, especially considering her ex-husband's bad behavior. When the mediators pointed out that earlier in the mediation she

had been complaining about the strain of her 24/7 child care responsibilities, the mother came to see that relinquishing some of her time would actually be a gain for her in terms of reduced stress and greater leisure time. She soon reached an agreement with the father on a visitation plan.

- In the other case, an inexperienced residential landlord was balking at paying his former tenant any money on her claim for the return of her security deposit. He alleged that she had damaged his apartment, that he had been forced to incur costs to evict her and that any money coming out of his pocket on a claim he deemed spurious was a further loss. However, when it was pointed out that by getting rid of this tenant, he had been able to find a much more responsible tenant, who was paying a higher monthly rent, he softened considerably. When the mediators suggested that he could look at this whole incident as a rather inexpensive lesson in how to screen for good tenants and avoid bad ones, he agreed to the former tenant's offer.

Setting Aside "Sunk Costs."   In a similar vein, disputants who are offered attractive proposals to end a dispute often become overly focused on the costs they have already incurred (and will not recover) rather than on the gains achievable by ending the conflict. This often leads them to resist settlement, because it feels like a loss. The mediator must help the parties accept that "sunk" costs are just that: sunk, or gone.

Typical scenario: A defendant who thus far has paid her lawyer $30,000 to defend against a weak defamation claim will never be able to recoup those costs but may be able to end further expense by paying a small amount of compensation to the plaintiff today. Citing the costs already incurred, she refuses.

The challenge is to help such parties focus on the benefits of resolution *going forward* so that they don't throw "good money after bad." As Dwight Golann has suggested, it may be helpful to use the analogy of a poor business or investment decision: At some point, it makes sense to close down the business or to sell the stock at a loss rather than lose even more.[18]

■ §10.11 IN GENERAL: KEEPING THE TALKS MOVING AND AVOIDING "NO"

It is common for mediations to get "stuck" because of the refusal of one or both sides to take a next step. In addition to keeping the parties optimistic and committed to working on the problem, a number of other interventions can be used to keep the talks moving and avoid impasse:

Pointing Out the Expectation of Reciprocity.   If one disputant has made a concession and it's the other side's turn to make a move, it is often effective to point this out. The mediator can appeal expressly to the norm of reciprocity, which

---

18. Dwight Golann, Mediating Legal Disputes: Effective Strategies for Lawyers and Mediators 207 (1996).

everyone understands. For example: *"Mrs. Nguyen has just made a significant concession in offering to accept 50 percent of her claimed damages, even though she and her attorney are confident that she will win at trial. My sense is that she's making a good faith effort to get this case resolved. Like all bargainers, she expects to see you take the next step. If you want to resolve your dispute without litigation, now's the time to show your good faith and make a concession of your own."*

Suggesting Conditional or "Bracketed" Offers.   In a special application of the reciprocity principle, gaps in bargaining positions in situations where no one wants to make the next move can sometimes be narrowed by the parties' agreeing to make a specific concession conditioned on the other side's taking a corresponding (although not necessarily identical) step (e.g., *"Would you go down $2,000 if they came up by $2,000?"*; or union bargaining representative to mediator: *"We'll agree to take 1 percent off our wage demand in year three of the contract, but only if they agree to reinstate vision and disability insurance to the benefits package"*). With the distance separating their positions reduced, the parties may feel more optimistic about the prospects of reaching a settlement and more willing to continue to negotiate. This can be orchestrated by mediators in a series of caucuses or in face-to-face bargaining. Which do you think would be the more hospitable format?

Taking a Break, Changing the Setting.   Sometimes simply calling for a break can ease tensions and help the parties to reevaluate their positions, devise face-saving rationales for a next move or afford them time to consult other advisers or decision makers. Deliberately moving into less formal settings, such as having a meal together, can also help keep things moving. What about deliberately arranging for "impromptu" private conversations with the parties at the copy center or the water cooler as a way to get beyond their current bargaining positions?[19]

Persuading in Steps When Movement is Incremental.   Participants who are engaged in a competitive negotiation "dance" in which they make concessions in a gradual, strategic pattern often need a rationale to justify their next concession. The savvy mediator can aid this process of convergence of offers by providing a new persuasive reason that has not yet been factored into previous concessions. For example, a plaintiff who previously reduced his demand by 25% to reflect the risk of loss at a trial may be persuaded in the next round of the bargaining to lower it further if reminded of his litigation expenses. (In this sense, there may be an element of negotiation between the parties and the mediator at work as well.)

Being Transparent, Harnessing Silence.   When the negotiations get stuck, seeking the parties' help can sometimes be useful. The mediator can simply say, *"It seems as though we're stuck. Anyone have any ideas about how to loosen this logjam?"* and sit back and wait. If the parties really want to resolve matters, the odds are that someone will break the silence.

---

19. *See* JEFFREY KRIVIS, Improvisational Negotiation 316-317 (2006) (recommending arranging for such encounters even in the rest room!).

Pointing Out Inconsistencies.   When the parties have elected mediation but are refusing to consider reasonable compromises, the mediator can point out this seeming contradiction. Appealing to consistency can be an effective motivator. For example: "*By agreeing to enter this process, you've indicated that you want to work this problem out yourselves. I assume you understood that this wouldn't work unless you both put forward proposals that the other side might be open to and that would improve on what had already been rejected before the mediation. Neither of you has budged. So what are we doing here?*"

Similarly, if a party rejects a proposal that meets his previously articulated goals or standards for a resolution, the mediator can challenge the inconsistency. For example: "*Earlier you said that you would be willing to end this, so long as you got your October rent. Mr. Schwartz has now offered to pay that. I'm not sure I understand your reaction.*"

Are you comfortable with the degree of confrontation suggested by these examples? Studies suggest that persistence in pursuit of resolution is considered a valuable mediator trait by attorneys who regularly use mediation.[20] However, tenacity in pursuit of settlement can be taken too far if it crosses the line from effective persuasion into undue manipulation or excessive pressure. When are such lines being approached? We will examine this question in Chapter 12.

■ §10.12 DEALING WITH IMPASSES

No matter how skilled and tenacious the mediator is, he or she will face impasses at the bargaining table. What do we mean by *impasses*, and what should a mediator do when they occur?

Two Definitions of Impasse.   A common dictionary definition of impasse is deadlock,[21] but mediation scholars employ the term in different ways. An *apparent impasse* denotes any situation in which bargaining has broken down or appears likely to,[22] even though in reality further movement is still possible. Perhaps the parties are so far apart that further negotiation appears hopeless, even if there is considerable time left. Perhaps the parties signal that the offers they have made are final, and neither is willing to budge. Perhaps time is starting to run out and the window for additional moves looks too small.

Others use the term impasse to denote situations in which settlement is not possible at all because there is no bargaining zone: The parties are committed to

---

20. *See, e.g.,* Final Report, ABA Section of Dispute Resolution Task Force on Improving Mediation Quality (2008); STEPHEN B. GOLDBERG & MARGARET L. SHAW, *The Secrets of Successful (and Unsuccessful) Mediators Continued: Studies Two and Three,* 23 NEGOTIATION J. 393 (2007) (Patience/persistence listed as most highly-rated process skill by respondents.)

21. *See impasse,* The American Heritage Dictionary of the English Language (4th ed. 2004), *at http://dictionary.reference.com/browse/impasse* (last accessed May 9, 2007).

22. *See, e.g.,* WILLIAM DEVANE LOGUE, *Overcoming Impasse, in* Mediation Practice Book: Critical Tools, Techniques, and Forms 166-170 (HARRY N. MAZADOORIAN ed., 2002); G. RICHARD SHELL, Bargaining for Advantage: Negotiation Strategies for Reasonable People 193-195 (1999); CHRISTOPHER W. MOORE, *Techniques to Break Impasse, in* Divorce Mediation: Theory and Practice 251-275 (JAY FOLBERG & ANNE L. MILNE eds., 1988).

pursuing non-negotiated solutions if their current demands are not met.[23] As one commentator notes (using the term in this more limited sense) "if an impasse can be broken, it really wasn't an impasse."[24]

Of course, like the negotiators they are assisting, mediators deal with imperfect information and often cannot easily distinguish real impasses, in which there is no bargaining zone, from merely apparent ones. Moreover, as we saw in Chapter 2, in situations where rationally there ought to be a bargaining zone, negotiations can break down because of psychological, cognitive and strategic problems. When this happens, "apparent" impasses can become very real indeed.

Analyzing Impasses.   In the sections that follow, we present a two-step analysis a mediator can apply to determine whether (a) it *ought* to make sense to keep going in face of an apparent impasse; and (b) if so, a framework for diagnosing and then addressing remaining barriers to settlement. Almost all of this material is a review of concepts discussed earlier in this book.

■ §10.12.1 STEP ONE: ANALYZE THE CASE OBJECTIVELY TO DETERMINE WHETHER IT "SHOULD" SETTLE

> Imagine that you are mediating a workplace dispute. Two co-workers, Jake and Sam, have been ordered by their boss to utilize the company's mediation program to resolve their constant on-the-job bickering. Their animosity gave rise to a brief fistfight last month. The supervisor has indicated that unless they can work out their problems and avoid any further altercations, both will be fired. After ninety minutes of trying to help them communicate more effectively and resolve the conflict, you have gotten almost nowhere. Jake seems to be approaching the negotiation in good faith, but Sam refuses to acknowledge any responsibility for the problem or to agree to modify his own conduct going forward. How do you decide whether to give up or to persevere? Is this a real impasse or only an apparent one?

Objective Indicators.   The first step for a mediator is to analyze the objective characteristics of the dispute to determine whether it is likely the parties will be able to find a mediated resolution. The main variables in this analysis are (a) whether alternative means exist to resolve the problem if the mediation fails to end the matter; and (b) the extent to which the parties feel free to pursue these other options.[25] If the mediator receives information about the dispute before the mediation begins, this analysis can often be done as part of the mediator's pre-mediation planning, rather than under pressure at the bargaining table.

---

23. *See, e.g.*, JOSEPH STULBERG, Taking Charge/Managing Conflict 151-153 (1987); LEE JAY BERMAN, *Impasse Is a Fallacy* at 1, *http://www.mediationtools.com/articles/impasse.html* (last accessed November 17, 2011).
24. BERMAN, *supra* note 23, at 1. *See also* §2.1, *supra*, on the different meaning of negotiation failures.
25. STULBERG, *supra* note 23, at 152-153.

In some situations, it will be obvious that any impasses are only temporary. For example, when bargaining over a new three-year contract, labor and management representatives might find themselves in a deadlock over wages, benefits and workplace safety rules. The workers might have threatened a work stoppage, and feelings may be running very high. They might even call a strike. But the parties must eventually negotiate a new contract for themselves: No court will do it for them. They have no means to resolve the dispute other than through negotiation.[26] So even if an apparent impasse arises, the mediator knows that he must keep working, assured that sooner or later the parties will find agreement.[27]

At the other end of the spectrum, a disputant's alternatives to a negotiated settlement can sometimes be so attractive that he or she can afford to say (honestly), "*I have nothing to gain from reaching an agreement*" or "*Unless you meet my demands exactly, I'm out of here.*" For example, consider a contractually mandated mediation of a business dispute in which the president of a company threatened with a lawsuit opens the mediation by claiming that the potential gain from postponing resolution and not having to declare a large business loss outweighs any comparable benefit that could be derived from a settlement.[28] Should the neutral continue mediating such a case? Not if, after probing by the mediator, the president's claim appears to be sincere. The company has an alternative available to it that is better than any negotiated settlement that the process can achieve.

Using this analysis in Jake and Sam's hypothetical workplace dispute, does it seem that further mediation will be productive or not?

The answer is: You can't know without asking more questions of Sam (the recalcitrant party) — most likely in caucus. Whether the problems can be resolved through mediation may well turn on Sam's attitudes about his present job and his available alternatives to it. On the one hand, if his attitude is "*I hate this job, and I can get a better one fairly easily,*" the impasse may be real; Sam really may not be willing to take any steps to improve his working relationship with his coworker. On the other hand, if Sam likes his present job well enough or is uncertain about other job prospects, further interventions might help break the logjam; Sam has an unattractive BATNA, and it is in his rational self-interest to try to work things out.[29]

In most mediated disputes involving litigation, the parties' BATNAs are a function of their assessments of the risks and potential benefits of trial, their ability to absorb the costs of litigation, their willingness to accept risk, their need for vindication or closure and other factors we have discussed. Sophisticated competitive negotiators may bluff about such matters. In the face of apparent impasse, the mediator therefore needs to ask probing questions in caucus, monitor the size and rate of concessions, read nonverbal cues and look for signals that further movement is possible.

---

26. This assumes, of course, that the company chooses to keep its doors open.
27. This is an elaboration of an example provided by SHELL, *supra* note 22, at 151.
28. *See* GOLANN, *supra* note 18, at 125.
29. *See* §7.5.10, "Probe for Alternatives to a Negotiated Settlement and the Impact of Non-Resolution." Note also that even if it is rationally in Sam's interests to work things out, additional psychological, cognitive or strategic factors might still prevent resolution.

Other Factors Affecting the Mediator's Decision to Persevere in the Face of Apparent Impasse.   But the decision whether to keep mediating or to give up in the face of apparent impasse is not entirely a matter of objective case assessment. Much depends on the neutral himself and the setting in which he practices.

Mediators fall along a wide spectrum of tenaciousness in pursuing agreements. One scholar has divided the field into "orchestrators" and "deal-makers," with "deal-makers" being the most zealous in their pursuit of settlements.[30] Some mediators view it as their job to use almost any means possible to obtain an agreement, on the assumption that this is what the parties (at least those who chose to mediate) want them to do. For others, the desire to be able to boast of high settlement rates may be a motivating factor. Whatever their motivation, tenacious mediators keep on working through impediments that might be stop signs for more passive neutrals.

The mediation setting and culture matter too. Some mediators have the luxury of scheduling more time or extra sessions if a deadlock arises. By contrast, many mediators working in busy court settings — where litigants are often mandated to try mediation and where caseloads are high — may feel obliged to give mediation the "ole' college try" but at the first hint of impasse, will refer the case back to the court for adjudication. In our Jake-and-Sam workplace mediation, the persistence an in-house mediator demonstrates in the face of apparent impasse might be influenced by company attitudes toward its mediation program, job expectations placed on the mediator, concerns about appearing to pressure employees into agreements and other such factors.

We would say to you: When in doubt about persevering, press on, especially when the parties have selected mediation rather than having been mandated to try it. In our experience, newer mediators are often more pessimistic than they should be about the prospects for settlement, missing cues that further movement is possible. The disputants may grumble, but studies show in general that they prefer to settle their cases rather than leave them unresolved.[31]

■ §10.12.2 STEP TWO: WHEN FACING AN APPARENT IMPASSE, ANALYZE AND ADDRESS THE REMAINING BARRIERS TO SETTLEMENT

If a mediator decides to persevere in the face of an apparent impasse, she may find herself facing a common phenomenon: Disputes that "should" settle do not, at least not easily, due to the lingering presence and power of one or more barriers to resolution. Therefore, the next step is diagnostic, requiring the mediator to ask herself, "*What are the remaining barriers to settlement here? Have I taken all steps possible to address these barriers? Have I done so effectively? Is there any more that I reasonably can do at this stage in the mediation to break the deadlock?*" This must done in real time; as a result, the mediator needs to internalize a diagnostic

---

30. *See generally* Deborah M. Kolb, The Mediators (1983).
31. *See* Roselle Wissler, *Court-Connected Mediation in General Civil Cases: What We Know from Empirical Research*, 17 Ohio St. J. on Disp. Resol. 641, 661, n.77, 700 (2002) (noting, however, that parties do not like feeling pressured by mediators or being subjected to unduly protracted proceedings simply in order to reach settlement).

checklist of potential barriers to settlement and make continued reference to it as the mediation progresses.[32]

Let's review some of the major barriers to settlement that we presented in Chapter 2 and some of the main mediator interventions, discussed in Chapters 6 through 9, that are aimed at addressing them.

A. Strategic Barriers to Settlement

Problem	Signs	Interventions
Informational Barriers	• Someone is lacking important information. • A party is unwilling to share information because he thinks it will "hurt his case" or fears he will be exploited. • The parties are solely focused on "rights and responsibilities."	• Model open communication by open-ended questions and active listening. • Probe, probe, probe for interests. • Use caucuses to pierce positions and encourage greater disclosure. • Explain, where possible, the two-sided nature of withheld information. • Encourage mutual disclosures of harmful information. • Reschedule the mediation to allow disputants to obtain needed information.
Threatening Language	• The negotiators are using personal insults or threats. • The threatened consequences of not settling are escalating.	• Coach the parties on their negotiating behavior. • Point out the risk that threats and insults will produce impasse. • Conduct a caucused mediation so that you can package and convey offers.
Positional Tactics	• Offers are unrealistically high or low. • Few concessions are being made. • Concessions are too small to encourage movement. • Bluffing language is being believed.	• Help the negotiators make reasonable offers based on objective norms and standards. • Encourage larger, bolder moves. • Appeal to principles of reciprocity and scarcity. • Narrow the gap through exchange of conditional or "bracketed" offers.

---

32. It also means that when unresolvable impasses do occur, much useful learning comes from debriefing cases after the fact in order to analyze what else, if anything, might have been done to achieve resolution.

B. Psychological Barriers to Settlement

Problem	Signs	Interventions
Ripeness/ Readiness	• One side seems very indecisive. • A party seems unwilling to consider any options for settlement or goes backwards in making concessions. • The parties are extremely angry or tense.	• Probe for concerns and encourage the expression of feelings. • Use lots of active listening. • Postpone mediation until the parties are "ready."
Emotional Flooding or Contagion	• A party seems unable to think clearly or is unwilling to engage because of great anger. • The heat in the room is rising fast on both sides.	• Call a time-out. • Consider caucused mediation, at least temporarily.
Communication Distortions	• The parties are mishearing each other's messages. • They are having trouble communicating effectively.	• Have the parties repeat back messages to each other. • Intervene to question or correct distortions. • Provide a mediator's interpretation of what was said.
Demonization and Rigid Thinking	• One or both of the parties feels "totally in the right" and their opponent "totally in the wrong." • A party attributes hostile motives to the other. • The parties remain focused on blame and retaliation.	• Reframe angry statements to take the sting out of them. • Encourage "I" statements rather than "you" statements. • Encourage the parties to consider their own contributions to the dispute. • Probe for empathy. • Use role reversal. • Disentangle the effects of a party's conduct from their intent. • Coach the parties on the possibility of making or receiving apologies.

C. Cognitive Barriers to Settlement

Problem	Signs	Interventions
Zero-Sum Bias	• The parties are exaggerating their differences. • Every issue is a source of conflict.	• Probe for interests in caucus. • Point out shared and complementary interests. • Point out shared norms and values. • Probe for additional issues and resources.

Problem	Signs	Interventions
Egocentric/ Partisan Bias	• The parties have excessive confidence in their case. • They are dismissing each other's viewpoints. • Their own offers are "fair" and all opposing offers are "unfair."	• Fully develop the facts in joint session. • Probe for doubt. • Have the parties list case weaknesses as well as strengths. • Have them make the other side's arguments. • Provide an evaluation. • Arrange for an outside evaluation.
Reactive Devaluation	• Offers by the other side are not "real" concessions, are "not good enough" or are rejected reflexively.	• Frame offers to show that they represent real concessions. • Point out how offers satisfy the recipient's expressed interests. • Offer a mediator's "trial balloon" (a "supposal").
Loss Aversion	• The parties are focused on their investment in past costs and expenses. • All financial concessions seem inordinately painful. • The defendant is rejecting a very attractive offer to settle.	• Examine the costs of continuing the dispute. • Point out the risks of litigation. • Point out psychological and social gains from resolution.

D. Cultural Barriers to Settlement

Problem	Signs	Interventions
Lack of Comprehension	• A participant seems confused by the proceedings or by what is being said.	• Call a caucus in order to test assumptions. • Arrange for consultation with support person or language interpreter.
Inappropriate Affect, Hostile Attributions	• A party is inexplicably emotional or withdrawn.	• Caucus to explore cultural assumptions. • Express surprise/concern. • Carefully test for possible cultural explanations.
Culturally Based Disagreements about Rights or "Fairness"	• Parties have diametrically opposite reactions to the same events.	• Call a caucus to explore standards and norms. • Use role reversal. • Suggest consulting an attorney.

Problem	Signs	Interventions
Culturally Influenced Orientations to Conflict and Negotiation	• Disengagement/refusal to negotiate. • Unusually passive or aggressive negotiation tactics.	• Call a caucus to explore negotiation styles and norms. • Coach party on negotiation behaviors.

E. Structural Barriers to Settlement

Problem	Signs	Interventions
Tensions or Disagreements among Party Representatives	• A member of the negotiating team is silent/hostile or backslides.	• Caucus with all representatives to explore intraparty tensions. • Meet separately with "out-group" representative to further explore differences. • Adjourn to allow team to work out differences or to appoint new members.
Missing Constituent/ Stakeholder	• Late, unexplained indecision. • Last-minute reversal of decision made earlier in process.	• Caucus to explore indecision. • Party or mediator contacts missing person(s). • Reschedule to include other stakeholders in the decision or in future proceedings.
Principal-Agent Conflicts	• Agent claims lack of authority to act on behalf of missing principal. • Agent seems to be overriding principal's decisions or giving poor advice.	• Caucus to contact principal or adjourn mediation to ensure principal's attendance. • Caucus separately with the agent. • Caucus separately with the principal.

 Review Exercise: Analyzing Barriers to Settlement in *Fitzgerald*

Now think back to the *Fitzgerald* mediation, portions of which you should have already seen. The Fitzgeralds had demonstrated some commitment to trying to work out their problems cooperatively by agreeing to pay $300 for two ninety-minute mediation sessions rather than accepting free mediation with a court mediator. In her first session, one of our mediators also learned that neither party had a lawyer and that they were far from wealthy. They also needed to act quickly on a parenting plan, because school was starting in six weeks and they needed to know where Megan would be attending kindergarten when the school year began. These factors, plus the general unpleasantness of litigated divorce, all may have suggested that this was a case resolvable through mediation.

In the particular mediation session we are going to focus on, the mediator learned about a heated physical altercation that led to Jane's seeking and obtaining a Protection from Abuse Order and that this was the only incident of alleged abuse, which Bob, for his part, strongly denied. She also heard about an argument that occurred after the Order expired, when Bob, without any advance planning, showed up to take Megan and Ryan on a vacation with him. After the vacation was over, Bob kept the kids to live with him at his parents' house, eight miles away, where they are still residing. Jane has since seen the kids only seven times, for an hour each session.

Five-year-old Megan is delayed in her speech development, and three-year-old Ryan is not yet toilet-trained. The parents disagree about both the seriousness of these delays and their cause. In support of his claim for primary custody, Bob thinks that his mother's home is a cleaner and more "structured" setting than Jane's, and that the kids are doing better in this environment. Jane thinks that Bob's mother is a "clean freak," doesn't play with the kids and that they should be at their own home with their own mother.

In the extract that follows, which took place in the final half hour of the initial ninety-minute session, the mediator attempted to negotiate the specific details of a custody agreement. At the end of the mediation, the parties were far apart, and the discussions had degenerated into heated displays of anger and recrimination.

As you watch the following extract, ask yourself: What barriers prevented these parents from reaching an agreement? If you were the mediator, with this session ending and another ninety-minute session to be scheduled, how might you address these barriers at that next session? **Video Clip 10-H.**

■ §10.13 WHEN TIME IS RUNNING OUT: "END GAME" SETTLEMENT TECHNIQUES

Even where a mediator is able to diagnose and address settlement barriers, situations will arise in which the end game has been reached time-wise: Unless the deadlock is broken quickly, the mediation will end without resolution.

Let's look at a number of last-ditch efforts used by the two mediators in the *Resnick* case and by one of our mediators in *Wilson*. This extended extract provides some illustrations of how mediators can try to overcome tough bargaining and bring about the "final leap" in a positional bargaining process.[33] Watch and consider the comments and questions that follow. **Video Clip 10-I (1–3).**

"Splitting the Difference" and Other "Fair" Settlement Points.   When parties' offers start to converge near the end of a negotiation, a common way to forge a final resolution is to suggest that the parties "split the difference." This move is often used in cases where the parties have a good working relationship, want to work things out efficiently or, as in the *Resnick* case — after a considerable back-and-forth struggle of offers and concessions — are running out of time.[34]

---

33. MOORE, *supra* note 3, at 310-314.
34. SHELL, *supra* note 22, at 190.

Of course, forging a compromise halfway between the parties' last two offers can yield an inequitable result if one side's demands have been artificially high or the other side's artificially low. This device is also better suited to zero-sum bargaining about money or other single issues than to negotiations in which an exploration of interests could (time permitting) lead to more collaborative and optimal solutions.[35] Still, because of its superficial fairness, it is often a useful technique to "get the deal done."

In addition to halfway compromises, there may be other focal points within the bargaining gap that the parties may view as fair; for example, the prevailing wage rate in a comparable industry, the Blue Book® value for a used car in good condition and other objective measures.

Interestingly, recent empirical studies suggest that *round numbers* have some appeal to negotiators as a focal point for settlement. For example, if the mediator proposes a round number within the bargaining range ($10,000 when the plaintiff has asked for actual lost wages of precisely $11,808 and the employer is offering a "nuisance" settlement of $7,500), this may be perceived as a fair settlement point simply because it is seen by both sides as a kind of "rough justice" not directly tied to either party's position, and requiring movement by both sides.[36] Was the first mediator's intervention in Video Clip 10-I consistent with these principles? Was it neutral?

"In Confidence, Give Me Your Best Settlement Offer."   In his book, *Improvisational Negotiation*, mediator Jeffrey Krivis provides a grab bag of impasse-breaking tactics, including this one:

> Obtain in confidence what the parties think is their best settlement offer. . . . Get their permission to float the number to the other party as something coming from you rather than them. This allows you to test the waters before committing and allows you to try a different approach if this fails.[37]

As you saw in Video Clip 10-I, in the second mediation of the *Resnick* case, the mediator used a variation of this technique to try to achieve a settlement. In the last stages of the mediation, with only a few minutes left and the parties still $70,000 apart in their positions, he invited the parties to tell him, in confidence, what their bottom lines were. He then told each of them that if these numbers were less than $20,000 apart, he would have them continue negotiating, but if not, he would terminate the mediation. The parties' next "bids" were, in fact, more than $20,000 apart, and the mediation ended without an agreement.

In general, do you find this to be an effective impasse-avoiding approach? If so, why might it have failed here?

Making a Mediator's Proposal.   If the parties are open to hearing his views, the mediator can make his or her *own* recommendation or proposal to settle the case. This can be combined with a "black box" approach, like that employed in the

---

35. *Id.*
36. Russell B. Korobkin & Chris Guthrie, *Psychology, Economics, and Settlement: A New Look at the Role of the Lawyer*, 76 Tex. L. Rev. 77 (1997) (discussing the role of reference points in a party's decision whether to accept a settlement).
37. Krivis, *supra* note 19, at 317.

clip from *Wilson*, in which each side decides confidentially whether to accept or reject the proposal. In this version, if both parties accept the proposal, a settlement is reached. But if either party rejects the proposal, the mediator announces that no agreement was reached, keeping confidential the fact that one side may have said "yes." This is to protect that party from being disadvantaged in any later negotiations that may occur.

How do you react to this technique? Is it consistent with party self-determination? In the *Wilson* extract, on what did the mediator base his proposed "take figure"? On what should it have been based? If you were a party in a mediation, how would you feel about settling a case this way?

■ §10.14 SOME FINAL THOUGHTS ON IMPASSE

Even in well-conducted mediations, there are many reasons why impasses occur beyond those we have discussed. These include:

Party Indecision. When the time comes to "pull the trigger" on a settlement at the end of a difficult negotiation, parties often become indecisive. In some situations, this may be a last-minute sign of a readiness problem that has escaped detection, or it may be that the parties feel that they have to answer to other persons (justifying their acceptance of a deal) and are reluctant to do so.[38]

Sometimes, in the final moments of legal disputes, the reality of actually "ending it" hits home in a different way. Having to pay money or make some other concession may, at the end, feel unfair to a defendant who still feels in the right. Conversely, accepting a sum of money to settle a protracted conflict may feel empty and unrewarding to a plaintiff. Over time, lawyers become acculturated to the litigation process, in which many forms of human conflict are converted into claims for money damages. But from a litigant's perspective, it is not hard to see why agreeing to receive a sum of money to resolve an emotionally difficult dispute might sometimes feel unsatisfying.

Intraparty Frictions. Frictions and disagreements arising within party ranks also can make it difficult to achieve settlement. If three business partners want to sell their business to an outside concern but cannot agree among themselves on the price or other important terms of the sale, the mediator can try to address these intraparty disagreements in caucus, but resolution may require postponement to allow each party time to obtain outside advice. (Ideally, of course, it would be better to learn about such structural problems before the process begins.)

Planned Impasses. Finally, some negotiators intend to reach impasse no matter what the other party and the mediator do. Planning not to agree to a final settlement *today*, no matter what, is a way that negotiators try to capture a bit more of the bargaining surplus for themselves after the mediation has been concluded but once a bargaining range has been established. On the one hand, this is a risky

---

38. This is why asking questions about other people who must be satisfied with a proposed resolution is an important inquiry earlier in the process. *See* §7.5.6, *supra*.

tactic, because it assumes that the other side's final mediation offer will not be reduced or withdrawn once rejected. On the other hand, by trading on the stress of approaching deadlines or on the extra costs imposed on the other side, negotiators using this tactic can sometimes improve on the ultimate deal they obtain.

In Conclusion: What Is "Success" (and "Failure") in Mediation?   At the end of the process it is very common to find mediators — newer and experienced ones alike — feeling let down, even like failures, when their cases don't settle. A good friend of ours — a former special education mediator — tells of the frustration she experienced whenever a particular "hardball" lawyer was scheduled to appear in one of her one-day cases. Going into a mediation with him, she knew that he would almost never agree to a settlement that day. We asked her, "*Well, did his cases eventually settle, or did they mostly go to a hearing?*" She responded, "*They almost always settled, maybe a week or a month later. But that wasn't much consolation. After devoting five or six hours to each of these cases, I felt for the other side. Besides, I wanted the satisfaction of experiencing the settlement. It was demoralizing not to.*"

We think there is an important moral in this story, which bears on what it means to be "successful" as a neutral. Working as a mediator, trying to forge resolutions to difficult problems, it is only human nature to experience a letdown when you are unable to do so. But remember that even if a dispute does not resolve voluntarily, this may be due to factors — including participants' strongly held principles, strategies and time limitations — that were beyond your control. Also, keep in mind that, as with our friend, your efforts may have improved understanding and narrowed the gap between the parties to the point where a voluntary resolution may yet occur. You may not get to witness the fruits of your labors, but that does not diminish their importance.

CHAPTER

11

CONCLUDING THE MEDIATION

§11.1 INTRODUCTION

At some point, the end comes. (No, not *that* end.) Face-to-face bargaining has produced an agreement, warm laughter, maybe even a hug. A lengthy series of caucuses conducted by the mediator has broken an impasse and has yielded a reluctant compromise between psychologically drained and deflated parties. Or, as a disappointed participant starts to get up to leave, someone — a party or the mediator — declares, *"Sorry; we tried, but we just couldn't get this one done."* Resolution or not, how should the process conclude?

In this chapter, we first talk about the importance of the closing stage of mediation. We then discuss the process of drafting a final settlement agreement. Finally, we consider what the mediator should do if only a partial agreement is possible or if no agreement can be reached at all.

§11.2 THE IMPORTANCE OF CLOSURE

In General. "Closure" serves many valuable purposes when people have invested time, emotion or physical or intellectual effort. We see this in many walks of life: the elaborate closing ceremonies that are held for Olympic athletes, the final plenary session that tries to sum up the central themes of a three-day conference, the celebratory meal held by school or work colleagues when a difficult project has been successfully concluded. Often we experience the importance of closure by its *absence*. How do you feel when a book or a movie ends abruptly or peters out without a conclusion? How about when, at the end of a class or family reunion, people just drift off without a structured opportunity to say goodbye?

In Mediation. Whether or not an agreement is reached in mediation, orchestrating a deliberate ending and leaving adequate time for this final stage are important aspects of the mediator's management of the process. Like a successful opening session, the closing can accomplish a great deal more than drafting an agreement, declaring an impasse or otherwise taking care of the actual business at hand. Research suggests that parties who "own" and feel responsible for coming to their own resolutions are more likely to honor the commitments they make.[1] The way the process ends can also affect the parties' willingness to renegotiate with each other if an agreement is reached but future disputes arise, as well as their ability to continue negotiating if no mediated agreement has been achieved.

Impediments to Closure.   Unfortunately, the end often comes at a point when neither the participants nor the mediator is willing to devote additional time or effort to wrap things up properly. There are at least three reasons for this:

First, where reaching resolution leaves the participants feeling good, they may see no need for any further process and may be happy to dispense with what may be perceived as post-settlement "details." In some cultures, to suggest that the details need to be written down may be viewed by the parties as a sign of distrust.[2]

Second, after completing the hard, emotionally draining work of reaching an accord, participants may be tired and feeling as if the task is finished. If the process was a lengthy one, they may also be in a real rush to leave, anxious to attend to other commitments or save on further transaction costs.

Third, if no resolution was reached, parties who are dejected or angry may be in no mood to remain in the same room with each other, much less discuss the future course of the conflict.

Overcoming These Impediments.   Effective mediators try to work around these hurdles and persuade the parties of the value of at least some sort of closing process. Here are some ways mediators can make the most of the final phase of the mediation process:

- ▪ **Bring the parties back together.** As we discussed in Chapter 10, toward the end of a caucused negotiation, mediators often try to have the final details of an almost-concluded agreement negotiated by the parties face-to-face. This affords them the chance to construct something together — in sharp contrast to the mutual tearing down with which they may have begun the process.

- ▪ **Savor and celebrate success.** If an agreement is reached, mediators can try to create an atmosphere in which the parties savor their success together. This can include congratulatory and complimentary statements by the mediator, stressing the hard work and sacrifices made by all involved and the ways in which the agreements the parties have reached are preferable to their court or other alternatives. This might include efforts to create a good-humored final connection between the parties in which small (or intimate) talk is encouraged, perhaps while documents are being drafted. After protracted mediations, a ceremonial meal or other celebration might even be held.

  The mediator can herself derive great satisfaction from these kinds of ceremonies. Few moments are as professionally rewarding as those that commemorate the thawing of damaged feelings or the restoration of relationships or contain an expression of sincere appreciation to the mediator by disputants-turned-allies.

---

1. *See, e.g.,* CRAIG A. McEWAN & RICHARD MAIMAN, *Mediation in Small Claims Court: Achieving Compliance Through Consent*, 18 LAW & SOC'Y. REV. 11 (1984).
2. *See* CHRISTOPHER W. MOORE, The Mediation Process 353-354 (3d ed. 2003); DWIGHT GOLANN, Mediating Legal Disputes: Effective Strategies for Lawyers and Mediators 336 (1996).

- **Cement the agreement.** In addition to reducing the key elements of the agreement to writing, a mediator can cement a potentially fragile agreement by arranging for the parties to take immediate steps to put it into operation. This can range from suggesting that the first installment in a payment plan be made in cash on the spot, to having the parties call a joint press conference or other public announcement of the resolution (harnessing the commitment and consistency principles).

- **Emphasize the positive.** When agreement has not been reached or when further negotiations are contemplated, the mediator can pave the way for more constructive future dealings between the parties by underscoring — in a final joint session — what *has* been achieved. This includes emphasizing the measurable progress that may have been made toward possible resolution, including partial agreements that were reached on some of the issues, new information that was learned by each of the parties and factual disagreements that may have been clarified. The mediator may also point out less obvious gains, such as the parties' having heard and hopefully appreciated the seriousness of the conflict and the articulation of another perspective on it. Where further talks are envisioned, the mediator can make plans for the next session and, based on the progress already made, express optimism that a resolution can be achieved.

When the parties have reached an oral agreement to settle their dispute, there are normally three important decisions to be made: First, is a written settlement document reflecting the parties' agreements needed? Second, if so, who should draft it? Third, how should it be drafted?

■ §11.3   FORMALIZING AGREEMENTS: IS A WRITING NEEDED?

In some mediation settings, the answer will be clear: If the parties in a court-based mediation want to have their oral agreement ratified as a judgment by the court for purposes of future enforcement, there must be a writing.[3] Many community mediation centers expect their mediators to prepare written agreements for the disputants to sign and provide training to them on how to write agreements in clear and understandable terms.

In other mediation settings — most commonly private ones — the parties will be free to decide whether to have a formal written agreement. Sometimes this can become a point of contention between the mediator and the parties at the conclusion of the mediation. When this occurs, how should the mediator approach the issue?

In rare situations, the parties may have significant strategic, political or public relations reasons to avoid any writing at all. They may want to keep their agreement undocumented in order to be able to maintain to the outside world that they

---

3. On occasion, one party will insist on a court-approved writing while the other objects. (A common objection by debtors stems from wanting to avoid an official court judgment recorded against them.) Unless such differences are resolved, there can be no agreement.

did not settle. However, in most settings where there is a choice, experienced mediators try to adhere to this cardinal rule: No matter how much trust seems to exist, do not let the parties leave without reducing their agreements to *some kind of writing that they have signed.*

Why? Because the absence of a writing is an invitation to future disputes. Even when people are acting in the best of faith, their memories can fade quickly. If some of the negotiations were conducted in caucus or if there were any miscommunications in last-minute, hurried negotiations, there may be genuine uncertainty about the specific commitments each side made. In addition, parties leaving without a formal agreement in hand often have second thoughts about the negotiated outcome or are subject to "Monday morning quarterbacking" by friends, family or constituents with whom they discuss the agreement. When this occurs, recollections of what was agreed to or intended can quickly become distorted by the parties' changed attitudes about the deal itself.[4]

Here's another reason: Post-mediation disagreements about whether an oral settlement agreement was reached or what its terms were can find their way into litigation.[5] Mediators hate to become involved in such disputes, because when they occur, the mediator may be required to testify as to whether an agreement was reached[6] and, in the process, to take the side of one disputant against the other.

■ §11.4 WHO SHOULD DRAFT THE AGREEMENT?

In many situations, the participants will want and expect the mediator to draft any agreement that is reached. Even apart from those expectations, we believe that the mediator should seek to exert control over the drafting process. Effective mediator drafting can demonstrate close attention to detail and enhance the parties' respect for the final resolution. By contrast, allowing the parties to draft the agreement can be an invitation to further bickering, especially when one side seeks to gain an advantage through partisan phrasing of terms or "nibbling" for small added concessions on final details.

However, where lawyers are involved, they commonly offer to "take things from here" by reducing agreed terms to writing, often after the proceedings have concluded. They may have their own preferred language for liability releases and other standard terms or take professional pride in their own drafting ability. They may be motivated by the desire to offer traditional lawyer services to their clients after a process in which, in part, they took a back seat. When attorneys make clear that they want to do the formal agreement drafting, the mediator generally has

---

4. *See, e.g.,* GEORGE A. TALLAND, Disorders of Memory and Learning 18-19 (1969), and FREDERICK C. BARTLETT, Remembering: A Study in Experimental and Social Psychology 38, 191, 213 (1967).

5. *See, e.g., Ryan v. Garcia,* 27 Cal. App. 4th 1006, 33 Cal. Rptr. 2d 158 (Cal. Ct. App. 1994); *Riner v. Newbraugh,* 563 S.E. 2d 802, 211 W. Va. 137 (2002). *See generally* JAMES R. COBEN & PETER N. THOMPSON, *Disputing Irony: A Systematic Look to Litigation about Mediation,* 11 HARV. NEGOT. L. REV. 43 (2006).

6. Establishing whether an oral agreement was reached can require a mediator's testimony about the content of mediation discussions — for example, offers accepted or rejected — that otherwise would be treated as confidential. Courts are split on whether to hear such evidence. *Compare, e.g., Ryan v. Garcia, supra* note 5 with *Few v. Hammock Enters.,* 511 S.E. 2d 665 (N.C. Ct. App. 1999).

little choice but to defer to their wishes.[7] Nevertheless, even here the potential for second thoughts, blurred memories and competitive gaming (if not reneging) during the drafting points to the wisdom of the mediator's recording and having the parties initial at least an *outline* of the agreed terms before they leave the room.[8]

In many of the court, agency and community settings in which volunteers mediate, there is an expectation that there will be a written settlement agreement and that the mediator will draft it. In some of these settings, the basic format of the agreement is outside the participants' control. Courts and agencies with well-developed mediation programs in specialized areas sometimes require the use of preprinted forms containing standard provisions that can be filled in or modified. Where this is not the case, what principles should guide the drafting process?

■ §11.5 DRAFTING SETTLEMENT AGREEMENTS: PRINCIPLES AND OBJECTIVES

The task of drafting a mediation agreement can sometimes be straightforward. Certain agreements need to contain only a simple exchange of promises — for example, "*Mary Hatfield agrees that she will not play her piano later than 9:00 p.m. from Sunday through Thursday. Joseph McCoy agrees that if he believes that Mary has violated this agreement, he will communicate his concerns to her in writing.*"

In other situations, however, the task of agreement drafting can be deceptively complex, especially for inexperienced mediators. If time is limited, the mediator may be tempted to launch right into putting words down on paper or computer. But a settlement agreement is a form of contract, and important choices need to be thought through: How formal or informal should the language be? How detailed or general? To what extent should the agreement try to anticipate things that could go wrong in the future? Answers to these questions would seem to depend on the potential audiences for the agreement and the effect different language choices might have on them.

Audiences. The primary audience for the parties' agreement is, of course, the parties themselves. The language of the agreement they sign has the potential to solidify their commitments, govern their future behavior, help them monitor each other's compliance and avoid further disputes. From this perspective, it would seem that the terms of the settlement agreement should be as specific, detailed and clear as possible.

---

7. Who will do the final document drafting is sometimes determined by contract. Some private mediators include provisions in their retainer agreements specifying whether they will or will not draft the final agreement; in some cases this may be a factor in the parties' selection of the particular neutral. This decision may also reflect legal and ethical concerns. For example, in jurisdictions where drafting final divorce settlements is considered the practice of law, mediators who are not lawyers must limit their drafting of agreement terms to informal summaries or memoranda of understanding and must leave the drafting of final court documents to lawyers retained by the parties. See §12.6, *infra*. Note, however, that the enforceability of such memoranda of understanding, drafted on the premise that a more formal contract will follow, is not a sure thing. *Compare, e.g., Golding v. Floyd*, 261 Va. 190 (2001) *with Snyder-Falkinham v. Stockburger*, 249 Va. 376 (1995).

8. GOLANN, *supra* note 2, at 363-337.

The second principal audience for many agreements is the court, agency or community organization with the authority to enforce the agreement in the event that a party later complains of noncompliance. Focusing on this audience would also seem to point in the direction of producing agreements that are strong: clear, understandable, complete and readily capable of being enforced.

But highly detailed language may be difficult to draft under the pressure of deadlines, with the participants anxious to be done with the mediation and on their way. In addition, the parties often come with potential "shadow" audiences for the agreement: others with whom they may share the document and who may influence what they subsequently think of it. How might this affect drafting choices? Can you think of reasons why, and circumstances when, general settlement terms might be preferable to highly specific ones?

Let's examine these and related drafting issues in action in a setting with which you are familiar. Here is a hypothetical agreement in the version of *Wilson v. DiLorenzo* in which the homeowner agreed to allow the contractor to return and finish the job.

Settlement Agreement
Wilson v. DiLorenzo

1. *Defendant will complete Plaintiff's kitchen renovations in a professional manner. Plaintiff will not unreasonably deny Defendant access to the kitchen for these purposes.*
2. *The renovation will be completed in no more than three days. If it takes longer, Defendant will pay Plaintiff $100 per day for each day the project is delayed.*
3. *Defendant will guarantee the kitchen cabinets for 20 years and labor, countertop, linoleum and lighting for 3 years.*
4. *Plaintiff will receive a $500 reduction in the balance due as compensation for excessive past delays and use of "irregular" cabinets.*
5. *In consideration for the above agreements, Plaintiff will withdraw her claim when the work is finished.*

A Two-Stage Process of Agreement Drafting.   There are typically two stages to the process of drafting settlement agreements. The first involves confirming and expressing in writing those terms that have already been agreed to in the negotiations. This first stage often leads to a second: deciding what to do on realizing that important details may have been overlooked or that the basic agreement might benefit from being strengthened.

The First Stage: Confirm and Put into Words the Agreements That Have Already Been Reached.   Typically, the mediator begins by summarizing what the parties have agreed to and obtains their confirmation or correction. She then proceeds to draft appropriate language that accurately reflects these agreements.

Reducing verbal understandings to the written page presents the mediator with choices. Here are some guiding principles:

■ **Use clear language.** It is obviously important to use language that is not so vague or ambiguous so as to set up the possibility of a new round of fighting (or a reviewing court's having to guess) about the document's meaning. Aiming for clarity also requires avoiding lofty language and unnecessary technical jargon. In the *Wilson* agreement above, does the word *professional* in Paragraph 1 meet these standards? How about *unreasonably*? How, if at all, could each of these sentences be improved? What do you think about the use of the word *consideration* in Paragraph 5?

■ **Be specific.** When the parties read over a draft agreement, they should know with specificity who will do what, in what sequence and when. Important operational details need to be included to provide guidance to the parties and avoid future disagreements. In *Wilson*, this would certainly seem to call for adding a date when the work will begin. What about a starting *time*? Should the "three-day" time limit in Paragraph 2 be refined to specify "work" versus "calendar" days? Does the history of the parties' past dealings suggest answers to these questions?

What about the particulars of the job left to be done and agreed to by the parties: installing the countertop and track lighting, rehanging the cabinets, fixing the linoleum seam and so on? Should these all be delineated in Paragraph 1? If so, how? What about the specifics of the "guarantees" offered in Paragraph 3? If these should be fleshed out in more detail, how would you do it? Is there a point at which increasing the level of contractual detail stops being helpful and instead risks destroying any prevailing atmosphere of trust? How do you know when that line is being approached?

■ **Use language that is mutual, positive, purposeful and personal.** Agreements should be framed in their most positive and balanced light and should include, where possible, reciprocal promises by the parties. When agreements include real commitments by all the parties, not just one, this enhances their apparent fairness and reduces the risk of post-settlement regret.

The mutuality of the agreement can also be enhanced by a preliminary "purpose" provision that sets forth the parties' shared overall objectives in reaching their agreement. While necessarily general and thus not susceptible to being enforced, such provisions can start the drafting on a positive note of joint commitment and may aid later efforts to interpret unclear provisions. What would you think of a preamble to the *Wilson* draft that read: "*The parties, desiring to end their litigation amicably and to have DiLorenzo and Co. complete and Ms. Wilson receive the kitchen renovation originally contracted for, have agreed as follows: . . .*"?

Framing promised acts in positive terms — describing what the parties *will* do rather than what they *will not* do — underscores the contributions each will make to the future relationship and avoids any recitation of troublesome conduct that may have given rise to the conflict in the first place. Agreements should generally be drafted in language that looks forward, not backward, especially in ways that might imply or assign blame for the events that led to the conflict.[9]

Given this guidance, how would you assess the second sentence of Paragraph 1 of the *Wilson* draft? Is this language necessary? Could it be drafted more effectively? How? What about Paragraph 4?

Finally, a personal, nonbureaucratic tone can be set by referring to the parties by name and relationship to the conflict rather than (or perhaps in addition to) their official "role" in the proceedings (plaintiff, defendant, complaining party, etc.). The requirements of a reviewing court or agency might have something to say about this.[10] In *Wilson*, how might the parties be referred to other than as "plaintiff" and "defendant"?

The Second Stage: Strengthen the Existing Agreement or Accept It as "Good Enough"?   If the bargaining has been tough or prolonged or if the agenda failed to identify important issues, the basic agreement reached by the parties may be somewhat skeletal. (This can also occur where the parties' negotiations have been short and amicable.) Important topics — overlooked, omitted or incorrectly assumed to have been included in the deal — may only occur to the participants and the mediator once the drafting process starts. Getting concrete about the agreed general terms often has a tendency to focus the participants' minds on missing details.

However, each time a new and unresolved issue is introduced into the drafting process, it raises the possibility of renewed negotiations that could jeopardize a fragile peace. If the parties don't suggest or inquire about new terms, how is the mediator to decide when to risk "upsetting the apple cart" by introducing additional issues or considerations? At what point should the mediator view her job as done?

The Goal: Practical, Durable Agreements That Will Be Complied With.   To us, the most important consideration in deciding whether to raise any new term is the extent to which it offers the possibility of strengthening the deal by enhancing the likelihood that it will be honored to its conclusion. In every mediation, the mediator's primary goal should be to try to craft a practicable and durable agreement — and to protect against the escalation of the conflict that can come from noncompliance.[11] The extent of contract strengthening needed to achieve these ends depends on the type of agreement that is involved.

---

9. On occasion, a defendant will insist on agreement language that specifically disclaims or, at a minimum, "does not admit" responsibility for the events that spawned the dispute or claim. This reflects the reality that parties often choose mediation in order to avoid such determinations. But in some cases, it can also be a stumbling block to concluding an agreement, especially with a party who feels that he or she is a victim. How can a mediator prevent disagreements over such language from upending a settlement?

10. Court or agency rules or other legal requirements sometimes necessitate using potentially divisive language that has been avoided during the mediation. For example, where child support or school enrollment authorities need official documentation of a parent's rights, it may be necessary to include a term such as *primary custodian* in a parenting agreement. If such a requirement exists, how can the mediator work to ensure that it does not become an insurmountable obstacle to final resolution?

11. MOORE, *supra* note 2, at 348-349.

Types of Agreements.   Agreements differ according to two major variables: (a) how long it will take the parties to fulfill their promises and obligations and (b) how clear (or not) it will be that compliance has occurred. The further into the future the agreement will extend and the more open to interpretation and disagreement the parties' compliance could be, the more important Stage Two strengthening becomes.

- **Completed or executed agreements.** In these agreements, all obligations that are part of the agreement will have been performed and completed at the time the mediation ends. Nothing is left to be done in the future. The simplest agreements involve an act — for example, the payment of an amount of money or giving an apology — in exchange for a signed release from liability and/or the immediate withdrawal of a claim. Such agreements are comparatively rare.

- **Executory agreements.** Most mediation agreements are based on promises whose fulfillment will not occur *at* the mediation session and thus are "executory" or not yet complete; that is, they hinge on a future event. Even a payment by check to resolve a simple monetary dispute is not complete until the check clears. Depending on the nature of these promises, there may be more or less potential for future conflict. At the time that an agreement is signed, terms yet to be satisfied can range from fairly mechanical ones, such as the payment of a specific amount of money on a specific day, to obligations that are far more susceptible to differing interpretations and disagreements, for example, a mechanic's promise to redo automobile engine work to settle a claim by an angry customer.

Building Strong Agreements.   So what makes for a strong agreement? Strong agreements are:

- **Sustainable.** They can withstand changed circumstances arising during the life of the agreement that could interfere with the parties' meeting their obligations. During the second stage of the drafting process, the mediator therefore asks "what if" questions that attempt to anticipate future contingencies that could jeopardize compliance. This can be done by asking the parties *"what could come up that might affect or prevent your performing your commitments under this agreement?"* or by the mediator's trying to foresee these herself. The ability to do this requires placing oneself in the situation and, drawing on one's experience, identifying "future facts"[12] — factors that are internal or external to the parties — that could pose problems. For example: *"Mr. Stankowski, you said earlier that you cannot control your work shifts. What will happen to your proposed child custody schedule if you are assigned to work weekends?"*

  When future contingencies cannot be forecast with precision, the best approach to preserving the agreement is often *procedural*: an agreed

---

12. LOUIS M. BROWN & EDWARD A. DAUER, Planning by Lawyers: Materials on a Nonadversarial Legal Process 485-491 (1978). In anticipating what could frustrate or destroy a mediation agreement in the future, the mediator shares much in common with those who counsel clients in business transactions, helping them anticipate and minimize future disputes.

method of communicating about and resolving future disputes. For example: "*In the event that Mr. or Ms. Stankowski cannot comply with their parenting obligations under this agreement because of future changes in their work schedules, and are unable to resolve any disagreements concerning their parenting plan themselves, they agree to attempt mediation to resolve their differences before initiating court action.*"

■ **Practicable.** In their eagerness to reach an accord, parties sometimes agree to terms that they have not fully considered and may not really be able to perform, even under present circumstances. This is a prescription for non-compliance. In Stage Two of the drafting process, the mediator should therefore ascertain the parties' real capacity to perform their obligations under the agreement. For example: "*Mr. DiLorenzo, is the linoleum that is needed for the work to start on Saturday in stock? If you're not sure, should we make the start date later?*" or "*Ms. Anderson, can you really afford to make these new $170 mortgage payments out of your $400 paycheck each week? Have you considered your other fixed expenses? Shall we talk about them?*" As you can see from these examples, paradoxically sometimes the agreement as a whole can be made stronger — that is, more practicable and durable — by making the parties' substantive commitments weaker.

■ **Complete.** In the parties' desire to reach an agreement, the failure to construct a complete agenda or the hope that certain thorny issues will "disappear" can lead participants, including the mediator, to assume that certain issues have been dropped or conceded as part of the negotiations. Nothing can undermine an agreement more quickly than the late (or even post-signing) discovery that an issue thought to be waived is still, in the mind of one party, unresolved. For example: "*Ms. Wilson, you mean you want your court costs, too? When you said you'd take a $500 price reduction and completion of your kitchen in three days to settle all your claims, didn't that include waiving your claim for repayment of your court filing fee?*"

■ **Acceptable.** Parties who later regret the agreements they sign may be less likely to perform them. (They may also have second thoughts about the mediation process itself.) If the mediator suspects that a party feels that she is about to sign an accord she may later regret, the second stage of drafting should include an inquiry, in caucus, about whether the party has any reservations about concluding the matter that have not yet been raised. In most situations, despite the natural ambivalence that accompanies most compromises, the recalcitrant party will express a desire to complete the agreement. As mediators are often heard to say, the sign of a good settlement is when "everyone is a little unhappy."[13]

But in some cases, there may be warning signals suggesting that the agreement is too fragile to conclude in its current form. Is it a product of a power imbalance? Has a disputant gone along until this moment without thinking how the agreement will look in a day or a month? For example:

---

13. While creative, value-creating, relationship-repairing solutions can truly make the process end on a shared high note, compromise endings — where everyone gives a bit — are much more common.

"Ms. Johnson, in my experience most mothers in your situation would want to have the father at least share the responsibility for transportation. I noticed you were silent in agreeing to his demand that you pick them up and drop them off. Is that really what you want?"

Note also that some mediators, wanting privacy while they write, prefer to ask the parties to leave the mediation room during what may seem like a long and awkward period. But excusing them may come at a price. During the "down time" of drafting, the mood in the room can yield valuable data for the mediator: Are the parties chatting warmly? Is there an icy silence? Any tears? The participants' conduct during the drafting period can provide helpful insight about whether the agreement is truly acceptable to everyone.

■ **Measurable.** When obligations to be performed can be measured by objective standards, there is less risk of a future dispute. However, drafting contractual commitments in measurable, objective terms is often a challenge.

Consider the *Wilson* case. The draft agreement promises that "the defendant will complete the plaintiff's kitchen in a *professional* manner." How might this wording be strengthened to make it more measurable and less subject to future disagreements? One way might be to specify the materials (brand name and/or grade) that will be used in the renovation. What about the quality of the labor and workmanship? A common drafting technique is to incorporate a standard of workmanship that will be complied with—for example, *"All labor will be performed in accordance with the standards of workmanship adopted by the Connecticut Home Building Contractors' Association."* Does this completely resolve the problem?

If not, another common approach, again, is to specify a *procedure* for resolving future disagreements: *"In the event that any dispute arises regarding the quality of Mr. DiLorenzo's workmanship, the parties mutually agree to hire kitchen contractor Phil Formica to appraise the work and resolve the dispute. The parties will equally share the costs of Mr. Formica's appraisal, and all decisions by Mr. Formica shall be final."*[14]

■ **Containing incentives.** In many situations, agreements can be strengthened if they include *positive* incentives to encourage compliance or *negative* consequences for breaching them. We saw an excellent example of a negative incentive in *Wilson*, when the contractor's own lawyer suggested adding a $100 per-day penalty for any delays beyond the agreed period of three days for his client to complete the kitchen.

Now imagine a landlord-tenant case in which a tenant owing his landlord $1,000 in back rent agrees to pay off the debt at the rate of $100 per month over a period of ten months. A landlord wanting the money

---

14. Parties sometimes ask their mediator to serve as a monitor or even binding arbitrator in the event of a future dispute over compliance with the terms of a mediated agreement. (Recall that one of the mediators in the *Wilson* case volunteered to assume that function.) But other mediators resist undertaking such a role. *See* GOLANN, *supra* note 2, at 342. Can you see why?

sooner or concerned about the tenant's financial stability over the long term might agree to offer the tenant a *positive* incentive, to accept only $800, if the money were paid in installments of $200 over a four-month period.

■ **Enforceable and Honored.** Like contracts generally, settlement agreements drafted by mediators and signed by the parties are not self-enforcing. However, in court-connected settings, such agreements are commonly approved by judges as court orders, which can then be enforced like any other decree. For example, in *Wilson*, one mediation ended with a resolution under which the contractor, Mr. DiLorenzo, agreed to pay the homeowner, Ms. Wilson, $1,500, plus court costs, within a specified time. In such a case, it would be common for the mediator to write up the parties' agreement as a proposed court order or judgment to be approved by the presiding judge. Then, if Mr. DiLorenzo failed to pay the judgment within the specified period, the settlement agreement could be enforced, with Ms. Wilson able to garnish Mr. DiLorenzo's bank account or take other collection action permitted by state law. She would not be required to relitigate her original claim.

But suppose that Mr. DiLorenzo wishes to avoid an official judgment on the court records. (This is a very common scenario, especially for those concerned about their credit rating.) In such a case, the parties might mutually agree that Ms. Wilson would withdraw her complaint voluntarily without limiting her right to refile it and seek the entire amount of her original claim later in the event of Mr. DiLorenzo's non-payment.

Note, however, that if Ms. Wilson agreed to these terms and Mr. DiLorenzo failed to pay the agreed-to settlement amount, Ms. Wilson would have to start from scratch, refiling and litigating her claim in order to be able to collect anything. Suppose Ms. Wilson — like many unrepresented parties — is unaware of what she may be giving up by simply agreeing to a $1,500 settlement without a court order behind it. Should the mediator point this out? Is this inconsistent with the duty of impartiality?

If Ms. Wilson understands (or learns) what she is giving up, she might not like the prospect of having to start from the beginning. Or, having originally sued for nearly $15,000, she might feel that, even with a court judgment, she should not be limited to collecting only the settlement amount of $1,500 in the event the contractor failed to pay what he agreed to. To address such concerns, the parties might agree in the event of non-payment to the entry of a court judgment in an amount greater than $1,500. (But here, the contractor might balk.)

Where mediation resolutions involve promises of future conduct other than paying money, unique enforcement concerns may come into play. As we have seen, the second mediation of Ms. Wilson's claim concluded with the contractor's agreeing to complete specified kitchen renovation work within three days and pay a $100 per-day penalty for each day of delay after that. Could this agreement be further strengthened? If so, how? Might such "strengthening" create the risk of standoff? Consider.

■ **Optimal.** The final and potentially most rewarding strengthening move can involve steps to improve on the parties' agreement to try to satisfy more of their needs and interests. For example, in the *Wilson* case, the mediator learned in caucus that the contractor was concerned about potential harm to his reputation in Ms. Wilson's community that could stem from this dispute. Assuming that you thought that tensions had eased sufficiently in the mediation to make this suggestion plausible, what would you think of the mediator's suggesting to the parties that, in addition to their agreed terms, if Ms. Wilson were pleased with the work that he did in completing the job, she would allow the contractor to use photos of her kitchen in his advertising, perhaps in exchange for a further price reduction?

Here's another variation on this theme: In a recent hotly contested employment discrimination case, a fifty-five-year-old worker sought back pay for alleged age discrimination, while his former employer defended the firing on the basis of the employee's poor performance. The claimant confided to the mediator in caucus that, while he needed money right now, he optimally might like to return to the company as a part-time consultant sometime in the future. However, he did not want the employer to know this, because he was afraid that the company might use the information to negotiate for a lower financial settlement and because he believed that they would not really consider him for a future position. No matter how much better an agreement might have emerged if this information were shared, the plaintiff understandably refused to do so.

However, once a settlement agreement was *signed* (in which the defendant agreed to pay the plaintiff $60,000 in damages and the parties knew that they had secured an acceptable resolution), it was then possible to persuade them to let down their guard, disclose their true preferences and consider ways in which the agreed-to deal might be improved for both sides. In the end, the defendant (conceding now that the employee had "*lots of strengths*") agreed to guarantee the plaintiff two years of part-time work as a future consultant in a different company division, in exchange for a slightly reduced cash settlement now—a deal that both parties preferred. A noted negotiation scholar calls this a "post-settlement settlement."[15]

Working to Strengthen Agreements: Risks versus Benefits.   In the abstract, it would seem *always* to be desirable to consider fortifying agreements by adding detailed terms and conditions that make them more durable. (After all, the parties can always reject such suggestions as unnecessary detail, worry or formality.) But such an effort does present certain risks.

First, it can be very time-consuming. As we have said, agreement drafting by the mediator often takes place at the end of long and difficult negotiations, at a time when the parties are anxious to go home or report to work, or (in court-connected cases) a judge is impatiently waiting to review and approve the

---

15. Howard Raiffa, *Post-Settlement Settlements*, 1 Negotiation J. 9-12 (1985).

settlement agreement before leaving for the day. Alternatively, if the mediation was a short one, the parties may not feel that it's worth it to spend a lot of extra time perfecting the agreement's details.

Second, even when the parties indicate their willingness to spend the time to try to improve their agreement and the setting permits it, differences or disagreement over proposals to improve the deal may require further bargaining, including returning to caucuses after having appeared to end on the high note of a joint session. If the mediator tries to introduce too many "what ifs" or strengthening options, this can sometimes kill an already good deal. It is said that "the perfect is the enemy of the good." For these reasons, the mediator may decide to leave well enough alone.

Third, as we have discussed, the potential impact of some strengthening moves may not fall evenly on the parties. Does this mean that the mediator should not suggest them?

The mediator's answer to this question will depend in large measure on how he sees his role. If he views his mission—as we do—as helping to forge durable agreements, he will err on the side of proposing new terms in furtherance of this goal—even if their impact might be seen as disfavoring one side. A transparent explanation of what the mediator is doing, tied to neutral goals the parties are likely to embrace,[16] can help such an effort: "*You can agree, can't you, that a strong agreement—one that's specific, that anticipates potential future problems and that encourages compliance—is better than one that may be easier to agree on now, but is more likely to fail in the future?*" Caucuses can then be used to test or explain potentially delicate new proposals. Parties who have come this far in their negotiations usually want their agreements to succeed. Unless they are not firmly committed to what they have already promised, they will likely see the value—to both parties—of strengthening the deal.

A Post-Agreement Role for the Mediator?   In some situations, parties who have reached an agreement may need future assistance in order to fulfill its conditions or support its compliance. Especially where they have no other advisors, they may turn to the mediator for such help. This can include providing information about or helping to secure outside resources (e.g., anger management counseling for a father whose temper has been a barrier to seeing his children), overseeing future promised acts (e.g. a payment plan over time) or serving as a mediator or arbitrator of future disputes arising under the agreement. Do any of these potential roles raise concerns?

■ §11.6 BETTER THAN NOTHING: PARTIAL AND INTERIM AGREEMENTS

For many reasons—including an impasse on a major issue, an agenda too complex to tackle within a limited time frame or a "readiness" problem—total agreement may be unattainable. In such situations, the mediator may be able to suggest, and

---

16. *See* GOLANN, *supra* note 2, at 341-342.

the parties may be open to accepting a less-than-complete accord that preserves their right to pursue unresolved matters in the future. This can take two forms:

- **Partial agreements.** Some but not all of the issues are finally resolved, with the remaining issues to be negotiated later, submitted to an adjudicator or abandoned. For example, in a dispute over a planned new public art space, agreement might be reached on the total height of the structure, deferring the additional dispute over the environmental impact of increased traffic to an upcoming court hearing. Or, in a divorce mediation, the parents might conclude an agreement on a child custody plan and a process for selling their home, but refer a continuing dispute about division of stocks, bonds and pension assets to an arbitrator with expertise in pension appraisals and financial management.

- **Interim or temporary agreements.** Nothing is resolved finally, but the parties reach an interim agreement on what the status quo will be pending some next step — for example, a court hearing, an extended negotiating deadline or a recommendation from an outside expert. Designed to bring a measure of temporary stability to an uncertain situation, this is not (unless the parties agree otherwise) an audition for a permanent arrangement or a bar to either party's arguing for a different permanent outcome at some point in the future.

  Common examples of this are a union's willingness to work under the current contract while the deadline for any new labor agreement is extended or the agreement of a parent to pay a temporary amount of disputed child support pending a final court hearing. In such situations, even temporary agreements may be hard to come by, if, despite any language negating this, parties fear that a temporary agreement will be seen as a de facto permanent concession.

A Final Note on Mechanics.   In settings in which a court or agency may be called upon later to enforce its terms, the language of an agreement must usually be reviewed and approved by an official of the host institution before it is finalized. In some court settings, the presiding judge will question the parties in court to confirm that they understand the terms of the agreement, have agreed to it voluntarily and know that it can be enforced by a court if it is not complied with.[17] Regardless of the setting, the process is not complete until provisions are made for the parties to receive copies of the signed agreement.

■ §11.7   WHEN NO RESOLUTION IS REACHED

When mediation concludes without a resolution of any kind, the parties' focus will often be on failure — dashed expectations, anger, disappointment, a new round of

---

17. Especially in situations in which the interests of absent third persons may be affected, a reviewing court or agency may conduct an inquiry into the terms of the mediated agreement in order to determine whether to approve it as a binding order. *See, e.g.,* Texas Medical Board's rejection of a mediated agreement purporting to settle allegations of substandard medical practice against a physician, *http:// www.theheart.org/article/1268881.do.*

blaming or a renewed commitment to punish each other in the future. To prevent such an ending from leaving the situation worse off because of the mediation effort, the conclusion of the mediation needs to be managed carefully. What are some ways to accomplish this?

Stressing Accomplishments, Continuing the Effort?   As we said at the beginning of this chapter, even complete "mediation failures" often produce some progress in the conflict, if nothing more than producing a greater appreciation of its seriousness. The astute mediator can attempt to reframe this "failure" into at least a partial success by summarizing what has occurred, and, if appropriate, offering to help further if there is hope of progress through continued mediation. For example:

"Obviously, we weren't able to end things, at least not today. But I want each of you to know that, from where I sit, you both gave it a good faith and full effort and really listened to each other, maybe for the first time. These things are not always easy. Reasonable people can disagree about past events or what should happen in the future, and sometimes it's too much to expect that a conflict that took so long to build up will end in just a couple of hours. For what it's worth, I've seen harder cases, and I think this dispute is resolvable by agreement. But it will take some further reconsidering of each other's perspective, and some further changes in your positions. It's up to you. If you want to give it another shot — and you can tell me confidentially — call me. If you both want to continue, I will be delighted to set up another session. So think about it."

Agreeing to a Different or Streamlined Resolution Process.   Even if there is no further interest in mediation, the parties may be helped to decide on a future method of resolving the dispute that is preferable to the court or other alternative they are facing. If they need a faster binding decision than the public court system or agency will provide, do they want to submit the dispute to a private arbitrator? Might they agree to submit key witnesses to videotaped depositions to cut down on travel costs? If there is a need to see how a key fact or expert witness comes across in testimony, might an abbreviated mini-trial[18] be arranged as a prelude to a possible new round of negotiations? A mediator knowledgeable about the range of ADR processes and the resources available to arrange for them can provide valuable procedural assistance to the parties.

Agreeing to Stipulated Facts.   Sometimes in court-based matters, even if no agreement has been reached on any of the negotiating *issues*, mediators can work with the parties to shorten the time for resolution by developing a list of stipulated or agreed-upon *facts* to take to the judge or hearing officer who will adjudicate the case. For example: *"Mr. Cross and Ms. Blackwell, I'm sorry that we were not able to reach an agreement on Mr. Cross's claim for unpaid rent and Ms. Blackwell's counterclaim for return of her security deposit. You will now have to go into the court, and the magistrate will hear your case. I know you're both concerned about how much time this has taken. It seems to me that you agree on a lot of the*

---

18. *See, e.g.,* James F. Henry, *Mini-Trials: An Alternative to Litigation,* 1 Negotiation J. 13 (1985); Golann, *supra* note 2, at 348.

underlying facts but disagree about what should happen in this case. Would it be useful to list the facts that both agree on? . . . Good. Okay, now Ms. Blackwell, you concede that you didn't pay your final month's (August's) rent and that you caused the wall gashes that Mr. Cross paid $650 to repair. But you disagree that it should have cost that much. Is that correct? . . . And Mr. Cross, you acknowledge that you were holding two months of security deposit received from Ms. Blackwell and that you deducted the August rent and the $650 from that amount. You also acknowledge that Ms. Blackwell returned her keys and gave you a forwarding address on August 31 but that you only mailed the check for the balance on the 46th day after Ms. Blackwell returned her keys, despite the state law requiring landlords to return deposit balances within thirty days. Is that correct? . . . "

Informing About Next Steps.   Where the mediation is ending without an agreement of any sort, the mediator's task is complete when she informs the parties what will happen next. If the dispute is already in litigation, the future course of events may be clear: A court date or a conference with the judge lies ahead, efforts at information discovery will commence or resume, an outside agency will begin an investigation of the dispute, one side will move to have the case dismissed and so forth. In other situations, the future of the dispute may be less clear, and nothing further will take place unless a party takes the next voluntary step — for example, by initiating a court claim, going to the newspapers or calling a work stoppage.

Where the next steps are known, the mediator ought to clarify them, especially when the parties are unrepresented and the mediator will play no further role. For example: *"As you know, you have a court date next Tuesday at 9:30. There is nothing to prevent you from continuing to talk between now and then and even settling this matter."* When unrepresented parties will proceed to a court or agency, it may also be prudent to emphasize that the court may know nothing about their dispute or settlement efforts and that they will have to start over again in explaining their perspectives to the judge or hearing officer. For example: *"Remember, if you go to court, you will have to start at the beginning. I do not inform the judge about anything that was said here, because it was all confidential."* And, although it may not be the most upbeat note on which to conclude, in cases where things end in tension, the mediator's final contribution to the process may simply be to ensure that the parties can leave the mediation site separately and safely.

CHAPTER

12

THE ETHICS OF MEDIATING

This chapter contains four video clips, totaling approximately seven minutes.

■ §12.1 INTRODUCTION: IS MEDIATION A REGULATED PROFESSION?

Up to now, we have concerned ourselves primarily with questions of mediation skill and technique. But technique alone provides us with no anchor to ground decisions about how to act when confronted with difficult ethical challenges. This chapter will analyze such in-role or micro ethics questions, many of which have no clear or agreed-upon answers.

Unlike the traditional professions, such as law, medicine and accountancy, mediation is a comparatively new field of professional endeavor. No state in the country licenses mediators. No state subjects all of its practicing mediators to a binding ethical code with a formal disciplinary body to enforce rules and impose sanctions for rules violations. In theory, the potential of malpractice liability exists as a mechanism to police instances of mediator misconduct, but in practice, it is very rare.[1]

By the same token, the regulation of mediation is increasing. At least twenty-seven states have court-connected mediation programs that include statutory or judicially adopted standards of ethical conduct for court-appointed neutrals.[2] (The vast majority of these ethics codes have been adopted within the past ten years, with significant variations in language from state to state.) Most states with court- and agency-connected mediation programs also have statutes or court rules that regulate the qualifications of mediators eligible to receive appointments.[3]

---

1. MICHAEL MOFFITT, *Suing Mediators*, 83 B.U. L. REV. 147, 153-154 (2003).
2. SUSAN NAUSS EXON, *How Can a Mediator Be Both Impartial and Fair?: Why Ethical Standards of Conduct Create Chaos for Mediators*, 2006 J. DISP. RESOL. 387, 395, 423-429. A handful of states now have formal disciplinary boards to enforce state ethical codes for court mediators. *See, e.g.,* FLORIDA RULES OF PROFESSIONAL CONDUCT FOR CERTIFIED AND COURT APPOINTED MEDIATORS R. 10.700-.880 (2011).
3. SARAH R. COLE, CRAIG A. MCEWEN & NANCY H. ROGERS, Mediation: Law, Policy & Practice §§11-4-11-8 (2001).

Some mediator organizations and private ADR providers have adopted their own standards of conduct[4] for mediators who are members of their associations or who serve as neutrals on their panels. Groups focused on specialized areas such as child custody mediation and the mediation of claims arising under the Americans with Disabilities Act sometimes have their own specialized set of standards.[5] Thus, anyone wanting to "hang out a shingle" as a mediator needs to consult the existing standards in his or her state and practice area.

This regulatory picture is further complicated by questions about the extent to which practicing mediators are bound by ethics rules imposed by their own professions of origin. For example, until 2005, it was unclear whether and how the American Bar Association Model Rules of Professional Conduct governing lawyers applied to lawyers when they served in neutral roles. No provision of the Model Rules expressly referred to mediation. One commentator noted that the Rules as a whole were a poor guide for lawyer mediators, because they were drafted with client representation, not mediation or other ADR activities, in mind.[6]

In 2005, the ABA amended the Model Rules to add two new rules pertaining expressly to mediators. Rule 2.4, "Lawyer Serving as Third-Party Neutral," recognizes the role of the mediator and requires lawyer mediators when speaking to mediation parties to distinguish their role clearly from that of representative counsel. Rule 1.12, "Former Judge, Arbitrator, Mediator or Other Third-Party Neutral," provides guidance to mediators for resolving certain kinds of potential conflicts of interest stemming from having previously served in a neutral capacity.[7] Other questions about how the Model Rules apply to lawyers engaged in mediation remain unresolved.

The closest thing to a "universal" or "general" set of standards for mediators are the Model Standards of Conduct for Mediators (Model Standards), first promulgated in 1994 and revised in August 2005. A joint effort of the American Bar Association's Section of Dispute Resolution, the American Arbitration Association and the Association for Conflict Resolution (a leading organization in the field), the Model Standards are "designed to serve as fundamental ethical guidelines for persons mediating in all practice contexts. They serve three primary goals: to guide the conduct of mediators; to inform the mediating parties and to promote public confidence in mediation as a process for resolving disputes."[8]

We reproduce here some of the major provisions of these Standards.[9] Read them now to get an overall sense of mediation regulation before you tackle the Problems discussed later in this chapter.

---

4. Susan Exon's 2006 survey lists thirteen states as having professional organizations that have adopted standards for general civil mediation. EXON, *supra* note 2, at 395. According to her survey, as of December 2006, thirty-six states had mediation standards of conduct imposed either by the courts for court-connected mediation, by private mediation organizations for their members or both.
5. *See* ABA-ACR-AFCC Model Standards of Practice for Family and Divorce Mediation (2001) at Appendix C, *infra*; ADA Mediation Guidelines (Feb. 16, 2000), which can be found at *http:// www.mediate.com.*
6. MARGARET L. SHAW, *Ethical Obligations and Responsibilities of the Mediator and Mediation Provider Organizations; Mediator Immunity.* (Unpublished materials on file with authors.)
7. Amendments to Rules 1.12 and 2.4 of the Model Rules are contained in Appendix E, *infra*. These provisions are also discussed in §12.2, *infra*.
8. Preamble, The Model Standards of Conduct for Mediators (2005).
9. The Standards in their entirety are set out in Appendix B, *infra*.

The Model Standards of Conduct for Mediators (August 2005)
Note on Construction

These Standards are to be read and construed in their entirety. There is no priority significance attached to the sequence in which the Standards appear.

The use of the term "shall" in a Standard indicates that the mediator must follow the practice described. The use of the term "should" indicates that the practice described in the standard is highly desirable, but not required, and is to be departed from only for very strong reasons and requires careful use of judgment and discretion. . . .

Various aspects of a mediation, including some matters covered by these Standards, may also be affected by applicable law, court rules, regulations, other applicable professional rules, mediation rules to which the parties have agreed and other agreements of the parties. These sources may create conflicts with, and may take precedence over, these Standards. . . .

These Standards, unless and until adopted by a court or other regulatory authority, do not have the force of law. Nonetheless, the fact that these Standards have been adopted by the respective sponsoring entities, should alert mediators to the fact that the Standards might be viewed as establishing a standard of care for mediators.

Standard I. Self-Determination

A. A mediator shall conduct a mediation based on the principle of party self-determination. Self-determination is the act of coming to a voluntary, uncoerced decision in which each party makes free and informed choices as to process and outcome. Parties may exercise self-determination at any stage of a mediation, including mediator selection, process design, participation in or withdrawal from the process, and outcomes. . . .

   2. A mediator cannot personally ensure that each party has made free and informed choices to reach particular decisions, but, where appropriate, a mediator should make the parties aware of the importance of consulting other professionals to help them make informed choices.

B. A mediator shall not undermine party self-determination by any party for reasons such as higher settlement rates, egos, increased fees, or outside pressures from court personnel, program administrators, provider organizations, the media or others.

Standard II. Impartiality

A. A mediator shall decline a mediation if the mediator cannot conduct it in an impartial manner. Impartiality means freedom from favoritism, bias or prejudice.

B. A mediator shall conduct a mediation in an impartial manner and avoid conduct that gives the appearance of partiality.

   1. A mediator should not act with partiality or prejudice based on any participant's personal characteristics, background, values and beliefs, or performance at a mediation, or any other reason.

   2. A mediator should neither give nor accept a gift, favor, loan or other item of value that raises a question as to the mediator's actual or perceived impartiality. . . .

C. If at any time a mediator is unable to conduct a mediation in an impartial manner, the mediator shall withdraw.

Standard III. Conflicts of Interest

A. A mediator shall avoid a conflict of interest or the appearance of a conflict of interest during and after a mediation. A conflict of interest can arise from involvement by a mediator with the subject matter of the dispute or from any relationship between a mediator and any mediation participant, whether past or present, personal or professional, that reasonably raises a question of a mediator's impartiality.

B. A mediator shall make a reasonable inquiry to determine whether there are any facts that a reasonable individual would consider likely to create a potential or actual conflict of interest for a mediator. . . .

C. A mediator shall disclose, as soon as possible, all actual and potential conflicts of interest that are reasonably known to the mediator and could reasonably be seen as raising a question about the mediator's impartiality. After disclosure, if all parties agree, the mediator may proceed with the mediation. . . .

D. If a mediator's conflict of interest might reasonably be viewed as undermining the integrity of the mediation, a mediator shall withdraw from or decline to proceed with the mediation regardless of the expressed desire or agreement of the parties to the contrary.

E. Subsequent to a mediation, a mediator shall not establish another relationship with any of the participants in any matter that would raise questions about the integrity of the mediation. When a mediator develops personal or professional relationships with parties, other individuals or organizations following a mediation in which they were involved, the mediator should consider factors such as time elapsed following the mediation, the nature of the relationships established, and services offered when determining whether the relationships might create a perceived or actual conflict of interest.

Standard IV. Competence

A. A mediator shall mediate only when the mediator has the necessary competence to satisfy the reasonable expectations of the parties.

1. Any person may be selected as a mediator, provided that the parties are satisfied with the mediator's competence and qualifications. Training, experience in mediation, skills, cultural understanding and other qualities are often necessary for mediator competence. . . .

3. A mediator should have available for the parties information relevant to the mediator's training, education, experience and approach to conducting a mediation. . . .

Standard V. Confidentiality

A. A mediator shall maintain the confidentiality of all information obtained by the mediator in mediation, unless otherwise agreed to by the parties or required by applicable law.

1. If the parties to a mediation agree that the mediator may disclose information obtained during the mediation, the mediator may do so.

2. A mediator should not communicate to any non-participant information about how the parties acted in the mediation. A mediator may report, if required, whether parties appeared at a scheduled mediation and whether or not the parties reached a resolution. . . .

B. A mediator who meets with any persons in private session during a mediation shall not convey directly or indirectly to any other person, any information that was obtained during that private session without the consent of the disclosing person.

C. A mediator shall promote understanding among the parties of the extent to which the parties will maintain confidentiality of information they obtain in a mediation. . . .

Standard VI. Quality of the Process

A. A mediator shall conduct a mediation in accordance with these Standards and in a manner that promotes diligence, timeliness, safety, presence of the appropriate participants, party participation, procedural fairness, party competency and mutual respect among all participants. . . .

4. A mediator should promote honesty and candor between and among all participants, and a mediator shall not knowingly misrepresent any material fact or circumstance in the course of a mediation.

5. The role of a mediator differs substantially from other professional roles. Mixing the role of a mediator and the role of another profession is problematic and thus, a mediator should distinguish between the roles. A mediator may provide information that the mediator is qualified by training or experience to provide, only if the mediator can do so consistent with these Standards. . . .

9. If a mediation is being used to further criminal conduct, a mediator should take appropriate steps including, if necessary, postponing, withdrawing from or terminating the mediation. . . .

B. If a mediator is made aware of domestic abuse or violence among the parties, the mediator shall take appropriate steps, including, if necessary, postponing, withdrawing from or terminating the mediation.

C. If a mediator believes that participant conduct, including that of the mediator, jeopardizes conducting a mediation consistent with these Standards, a mediator shall take appropriate steps including, if necessary, postponing, withdrawing from or terminating the mediation.

NOTES AND QUESTIONS

1. Writing in 1994, mediation scholar Robert Baruch Bush observed that, despite the proliferation of mediator ethics codes around the country, all codes suffered from two major problems: First, they were typically framed at a level of generality that failed to provide concrete guidance to mediators. Second, they sometimes were internally inconsistent; where values were in conflict, mediators were often told to choose both values.[10]

---

10. ROBERT A. BARUCH BUSH, *The Dilemmas of Mediation Practice: A Study of Ethical Dilemmas and Policy Implications*, 1994 J. DISP. RESOL. 1, 43-44 (1994).

2. Have the drafters of the 2005 Model Standards succeeded in resolving these problems? Consider this critique:

> [F]or a document that purports to provide ethical guidelines for practitioners, the Model Standards ignore the very prospect of any ethical tensions in the practice of mediation. Instead, they merely set out a series of absolute, hortative prescriptions, such as the following: "Mediators shall conduct a mediation based on the principle of party self-determination." "A mediator shall conduct a mediation in an impartial manner and avoid conduct that gives the appearance of partiality." "A mediator shall conduct a mediation in a manner that promotes diligence, timeliness, safety, presence of the appropriate participants, party participation, procedural fairness, party competency and mutual respect among all participants. . . ."
>
> But . . . [c]omplex cases and the reality of human interaction produce instances in which two or more competing values are pitted against one another . . . The first failing of the Model Standards is that their structure suggests that such tensions do not arise. . . . Instead, the standards tell us, in absolute terms, that we who mediate are simply to uphold every one of these standards at an absolute level. . . .
>
> Perhaps the Model Standards could maintain their current structure if the sponsoring organizations were willing to articulate an overarching ethical norm — a single value that would trump others. But that's not what the Model Standards include — probably because there is nothing close to a consensus among mediation practitioners about which values should be seen as highest. Is impartiality more important than party self-determination? More important than informed consent? More important than "procedural fairness"? Lawyers may be able to say that they are foremost officers of the court. Doctors may be able to say that they first ought to do no harm. Mediators, at the moment at least, have yet to articulate such an overarching ethic.[11]

3. How do you read the Model Standards? Are they written at an appropriate level of specificity? Do they envision a particular approach to the mediator's role? Do they seem helpful as guidance? You will be in a better position to assess these questions after working through the Problems (most of which are based on actual cases) in this chapter.

However one reads the Standards, they state explicitly that "until adopted by a court or other regulatory agency, they do not have the force of law." This means that, at present, almost all mediators have considerable discretion to bring their own personal values to bear on the task of mediating. In our view, this factor, coupled with the inability of any ethics code to "answer" many tough dilemmas, make mediation ethics a rich and important topic to explore.

---

11. Michael L. Moffitt, *The Wrong Model, Again: Why the Devil Is Not in the Details of the New Model Standards of Conduct for Mediators*, Disp. Resol. Mag. 31 (Spring 2006).

■ §12.2 SHOULD I MEDIATE THIS CASE? ISSUES OF COMPETENCE, CONFLICTS OF INTEREST AND DISCLOSURE

> ### Problem One: What Must the Mediator Disclose?
>
> You are a mediation clinic student nervously arriving at court for your first assignment in the court's small-claims mediation program. You have completed thirty hours of pre-mediation training, including conducting one videotaped mediation simulation. Prior to enrolling in the clinic, you also took a negotiation course in which you completed seven out-of-class negotiation simulations. A court staff mediator is available in her office to answer questions or work through problems that may arise during student mediations.
>
> The caseload is light this week, and there is only one case available for you to mediate. The parties have been sent to mediation by the presiding magistrate, who urged them to try mediation to see whether the case can be settled. How will you introduce yourself to the parties? Will you voluntarily disclose that you are a student? Why or why not? What precisely will you say if one the parties asks, *"So how many cases have you mediated?"*
>
> Are the Model Standards helpful here? Should court-based mediators, working with parties who have no choice as to selection of the neutral, have a heightened duty to inform parties of their experience and background?

Conflicts of Interest and Disclosure. Standard III of the Model Standards makes clear that mediators have an affirmative obligation to disclose promptly any potential or actual conflicts of interest, to seek the consent of the parties to continue mediating in the face of a possible conflict and to withdraw notwithstanding party consent if the mediator's conflict of interest "might reasonably be viewed as undermining the integrity of the mediation." It also counsels mediators not to establish post-mediation relationships with the parties that might raise questions about the integrity of the proceedings.[12]

For an example of a conflict of interest disclosure in *Wilson v. DiLorenzo*, click on **Video Clip 12-A.**

Was this disclosure necessary, in your opinion? Was it desirable? Was it adequately detailed, given the circumstances?

---

12. In 2005, the ABA revised the MODEL RULES OF PROF'L CONDUCT to address two types of post-mediation entanglements by lawyers who serve as mediators: subsequent legal representation of mediation participants; and negotiating for future employment with a party or a party's lawyer while serving as a mediator. ABA Model Rule 1.12 states: ". . . a lawyer shall not represent anyone in connection with a matter in which the lawyer participated personally and substantially as a . . . mediator or other third party neutral, unless all parties to the proceeding give informed consent, confirmed in writing." It further provides: "A lawyer shall not negotiate for employment with any person who is involved as a party or as lawyer for a party in a matter in which the lawyer is appearing personally and substantially as a . . . mediator or third party neutral." Sections of the ABA MODEL RULES OF PROF'L CONDUCT expressly referring to mediators are set out in Appendix E, *infra*.

Now consider this recent case:

Problem Two: What if I Know One of the Parties?

You are assigned to mediate a campus dispute arising from a fight between two undergraduate students at a campus bowling alley. Under the campus disciplinary code, if the students are unable to resolve their differences through mediation, the matter will be referred for further disciplinary proceedings by the university.

One of the participants in the fight is a good friend and fraternity mate of your brother, who is three years younger than you are. You are somewhat close to your brother. You have met your brother's friend casually once or twice, most recently about six months ago. (He struck you as immature.) No other mediators are presently available to mediate this dispute; if other mediators have to be found, it will mean a delay of two or three weeks.

Would you be willing to mediate this dispute, if both parties agreed, after disclosure? Why or why not? If you decided you were comfortable mediating, what *specifically* would you say to the parties to secure their informed consent to your serving as the mediator? If you were unwilling to mediate solo, would your answer change if you could co-mediate with a partner who had no prior connection to any of the parties?

Are there conflicts of interest that mediation parties should not be able to consent to or waive? Can you think of examples? What factors are important in determining this?

---

§12.3 DO I HAVE ANY RESPONSIBILITY FOR THE "FAIRNESS" OF THE PARTIES' AGREEMENT?

Impartiality and Neutrality versus Fairness: The Problem of Unequal Bargaining Power.   Imagine that you are mediating a small-claims case in which a retired government lawyer sues his neighbor, a community college dropout, for $500 to replace a nine-year-old bicycle the plaintiff claims the defendant irreparably damaged when she ran over it while backing up her car. The defendant, whose insurance deductible is $1,000, is prepared to pay the entire $500 out of her own funds, wrongly assuming that she is responsible for the full replacement cost of the bike rather than its depreciated value (which is virtually nothing). If you were the mediator, what would you do?

The ideal of a wholly impartial mediator who does nothing more than facilitate the parties' discussions and help them make self-determined decisions rests on an assumption that the parties have roughly equal bargaining power.[13] But much

---

13. Empirical studies suggest that negotiations between persons with relatively symmetrical power produce higher settlement rates, more effective bargaining patterns and higher satisfaction than negotiations involving persons with asymmetrical power. ROBERT S. ADLER & ELLIOT M. SILVERSTEIN, *When David Meets Goliath: Dealing with Power Differentials in Negotiations*, 5 HARV. NEGOT. L. REV. 1, 16-19 (2000) (collecting studies).

mediation, including much mandatory mediation, occurs between parties with unequal power. ADR critic Jerold Auerbach has attacked mediation on the ground that "compromise is an equitable solution only between equals; between unequals, it inevitably reproduces inequality."[14]

What are the differing sources of power in negotiation? What, if anything, can and should a mediator do to balance power? What does it mean for an agreement to be "fair"? What, if anything, should a mediator do if a negotiation between parties with unequal power threatens to produce an unfair agreement? Can a mediator be concerned with fairness while also remaining impartial and neutral? No more important — or contested — ethical questions confront the practicing mediator.[15]

The Meaning and Sources of "Power" in Negotiation.   When people think about power, they often think about its objective trappings: wealth, position, influential friends and so forth. There is no doubt that such endowments can bestow considerable negotiating advantage. As Roger Fisher has observed, "by and large, negotiators who have more wealth, more friends and connections, good jobs, and more time will fare better in negotiations than those who are penniless, friendless, unemployed, and in a hurry."[16]

But objective power or status in the world does not necessarily translate into leverage at the bargaining table. Negotiating power can result from the legitimacy of one's arguments, a good alternative to negotiation or creative ideas for resolution.[17] It can derive from a sense of righteous indignation, a determination not to give in or the ability to appeal to moral principle. It can result from personal traits such as self-confidence, quick-wittedness or good communication skills. It can result from having the status quo or a body of legal rules on one's side. Real power does not provide any bargaining leverage unless its holder is aware of it. Conversely, conveying the *perception* that one has power can provide a negotiator bargaining leverage even if it not real.[18] Thus, assessing who has actual power at the bargaining table is a complex task.[19]

Even more important, power relationships are fluid and dynamic, not static, in most negotiations. Because power derives from many sources, it often shifts (sometimes from moment to moment) depending on the stage of the negotiations

---

14. Jerold Auerbach, Justice Without Law 136 (1983). Of course, unequal power also produces injustices in litigated cases. *See generally* Herbert M. Kritzer & Susan Silbey, In Litigation: Do the "Haves" Still Come Out Ahead? (2003) (studies tending to show, across a wide spectrum of litigation, that "repeat players," which tend to be relatively wealthy institutions with long-term lawyers, fare better in litigation than "one-shotters," who tend to be individuals with fewer resources and no lawyers or "one-shot" lawyers). But some ADR critics worry that the impact of resource and power disparities may be greater in informal dispute resolution procedures, because they lack the openness and formality associated with courts. *See, e.g.,* Richard Abel, *Informalism: A Tactical Equivalent to Law,* 19 Clearinghouse Rev. 375 (1985).
15. As suggested in §3.8, *supra,* we suspect that the way individual mediators approach these difficult issues may be correlated with whether they will adopt a facilitative or evaluative view of their role.
16. Roger Fisher, *Negotiating Power: Getting and Using Influence,* 27 Am. Behav. Sci. 149, 151 (1983).
17. *Id.*
18. G. Richard Shell, *Bargaining for Advantage* 107-108 (1999).
19. On sources of power in negotiation, *see, e.g.,* Fisher, *supra* note 16; Adler & Silverstein, *supra* note 13; Bernard Mayer, *The Dynamics of Power in Mediation and Negotiation,* 16 Mediation Q. 75 (1987); Mark D. Bennett & Scott Hughes, The Art of Mediation 117-118 (2d ed. 2005).

and the topic under discussion. A recently jilted wife may be at a significant power disadvantage during the early stages of a multi-session divorce mediation if she is in a state of shock and denial about her husband's decision to divorce her and is bargaining about complex financial questions about which her husband knows more than she does. Later on, if her denial turns to rage after she learns that her husband has a new woman "friend," the balance of power may be all on her side: The husband's apparent advantage in knowledge may be more than offset by the guilt or shame he feels. As two prominent scholars have written (closely analyzing power relationships in lawyer-client interviews): "power is not a 'thing' to be possessed; it is continuously enacted and re-enacted, constituted and reconstituted. The enactments and constitution are subtle and shifting; they can be observed only through close attention to the micro-dynamics of individual . . . encounters."[20]

Nevertheless, there will be occasions at the bargaining table when the power disparity will be significant, obvious and completely one-sided. What should the mediator do when these occasions arise? One commentator asks, "Is the mediator a 'disinterested referee' or an 'empowerment' specialist?"[21] If there is a conflict between the mediator's duty to act impartially and his duty to promote "party participation" and "procedural fairness," which duty takes precedence?

"Procedural" Power Balancing.   As we have noted, almost everything a mediator does — from deciding who gets to speak first, to controlling the length of time each person speaks, to steering the conversation in certain directions and not others — can affect the substance, and potentially the outcome, of the discussions.

Consider this recent case two of our students mediated:

Problem Three: "Procedural" Power Balancing?[22]

The would-be tenant was a first-generation immigrant from Brazil who spoke broken and somewhat limited English, was small in stature and totally unfamiliar with United States courts. He filed a small-claims court action against a large local realty company for its failure to return $2,250 he had put down on an apartment he had rented. He appeared at the mediation by himself. The defendant was represented by the property manager, who was large and burly, by an assistant property manager and by the company lawyer, who was loud and aggressive.

The parties agreed that the monthly rent for the unit was $750 and that the plaintiff's payment of $2,250 covered the first and last month of the yearlong lease, plus an additional $750 security deposit. They disagreed about what had transpired between them: The plaintiff claimed that the defendant had pulled a "bait and switch" on his scheduled move-in day, offering him a much less attractive apartment than the one he agreed to rent. The defendant admitted that the company had switched apartments but blamed this on the plaintiff's announcing his intention not

---

20. Austin Sarat & William Felstiner, *Symposium: Enactments of Power: Negotiating Reality and Responsibility in Lawyer-Client Interactions*, 77 Cornell L. Rev. 1447, 1453 (1992).

21. Jacqueline M. Nolan-Haley, *Court Mediation and the Search for Justice Through Law*, 74 Wash. U. L.Q. 47, 93 (1994).

22. For useful suggestions on various procedural methods to balance power, *see* Bennett & Hughes, *supra* note 19, at 118-120.

to move in three days before the lease term was set to begin, and then showing up on his original move-in date, having changed his mind again. They also claimed that the new apartment they later offered was "identical." Finally, they defended on the ground that the plaintiff had signed an agreement that stated in bold letters: **"Failure to rent will result in forfeiture of the entire deposit"** and that by refusing the substitute apartment, he was entitled to nothing. (The plaintiff claimed that he did not understand this and that it was unfair in any event.)

Mediator questioning revealed that the defendants had been able re-rent the original apartment within forty-eight hours of the plaintiff's changing his mind, and that, while they claimed spending an extra $200 in advertising fees, they had no receipts in support of that claim. Defense counsel offered plaintiff $500 to settle the case, and then began to exert pressure on him, including threatening him in the hallway during a mediator caucus, calling him *"dishonest,"* and stating that if he insisted on going to court, *"we will see that you get nothing."*

If I were the mediator in this case, my comfort level at taking the following *procedural* steps at this point to balance power would be ("VC" means very comfortable, "SC" means somewhat comfortable, "SU" means somewhat uncomfortable and "VU" means very uncomfortable):

  a. if not obtrusive, arrange to sit next to the plaintiff, if I wasn't already doing so. (VC) (SC) (SU) (VU)
  b. to reduce "ganging up," insist that the assistant property manager leave the room and wait outside. (VC) (SC) (SU) (VU)
  c. rule all threatening statements by the defendants out of bounds. (VC) (SC) (SU) (VU)
  d. call time-outs more often, to give the plaintiff extra time to think through his situation and decide what he wants to do. (VC) (SC) (SU) (VU)
  e. mediate only in caucus to protect the plaintiff from the more powerful defendants. (VC) (SC) (SU) (VU)

Informational Power Balancing.   If you would be at least somewhat comfortable with all (or even most) of these steps, what about acting to ensure that a weaker party has the *information* he needs to make an informed decision and achieve a reasonably fair outcome? The problem is especially acute when one party is represented by counsel and the other is not. Commentators disagree sharply about the propriety of such interventions.

Arguing in favor of at least some forms of "informational" power balancing, Jacqueline Nolan-Haley writes:

> Parties choose the legal system to resolve disputes primarily because they want what courts have to offer, namely, a resolution of their disputes based on principles of law. When parties are required to resolve disputes differently, through the mediation process, their bargaining should be informed by knowledge of law. . . . [H]ow legal rights are acknowledged or ignored determines in large measure whether parties achieve "equivalency" justice in court mediation. . . . The few rules and statutes that specifically refer to unrepresented parties require that mediators encourage them to consult with independent legal counsel. However . . . the "independent counsel" rule is an illusory concept for the

majority of Americans who cannot afford lawyers. Thus, there is no real system in place to protect unrepresented parties in court mediation. Will those whose cases are shunted from the courtroom to the mediation room receive a fair shake? I believe they will if their bargaining is informed by law. If not, court mediation is an impoverished alternative to judicial adjudication that demeans both the courts and the mediation process.[23]

Arguing strongly against any efforts by the mediator to protect the rights of the parties, Robert A. Baruch Bush observes:

[I]f we adopt the protection-of-rights conception, mediators cannot effectively serve this role without undermining their usefulness altogether. . . . [M]ediators who try to protect substantive rights and guarantee that agreements are fair must adopt substantive positions that inevitably compromise their impartiality, either in actuality or in the parties' eyes. . . . The mediator has to create an effective environment for bargaining, develop information, and persuade parties to explore different options, search for areas of agreement and exchange, and finally accept something different from their initial demands; and the ability to do all this depends on maintaining the trust and confidence of both parties in the mediator's complete impartiality. Thus, making protection of rights the mediator's primary and direct role prevents the mediator from serving many other crucial functions. . . .[24]

Do you find one perspective more persuasive than the other? Why? Consider the following variation on the previous case:

Problem Four: "Informational" Power Balancing?

You take a mediator's caucus and decide to consult the court clerk about the enforceability of the deposit forfeiture clause that the plaintiff signed. The clerk (a lawyer with ten years of experience as chief housing court clerk) informs you that most judges view such clauses as against public policy and not enforceable. Moreover, he says that state law is clear that all unused deposits are the property of and to be held in trust for tenants, and that landlord deductions from security deposit accounts — as well as all other charges and "penalties" — may only be made for "provable, actual damages" suffered by the landlord. Of course, the tenant in this case does not know any of this.

If I were the mediator in this case, here's how I would feel about taking the following *informational* steps to balance power:

a. telling the defendant's representatives in caucus about the likely non-enforce-ability of the forfeiture clause and encouraging them to make an offer more reflective of the likely trial outcome. (VC) (SC) (SU) (VU)

---

23. Nolan-Haley, *supra* note 21 at 51, 100.
24. Robert A. Baruch Bush, *Ethical Standards in Mediation*, 41 Fla. L. Rev. 253, 259 (1989). Does preserving impartiality and its appearance "trump" the goal of informed party decision making? Specifically interpreting the Model Standards, Reporter Joseph Stulberg argues, similarly to Professor Bush, that under their structure, "If a party or counsel ask me for my assessment of the law governing a contested matter, I can respect that exercise of party self-determination (Standard I(A)) and, if qualified, provide that information (Standard VI(A)(5)), but I can do so only if I can remain impartial (Standard II(B)), so Standard II takes priority." *See* Joseph Stulberg, *The Model Standards: A Reply to Professor Moffitt*, Disp. Resol. Mag. 34 (Spring 2006).

b. asking the plaintiff in caucus whether he has consulted a lawyer or would like to do so. (VC) (SC) (SU) (VU)

c. suggesting to the plaintiff in caucus that he might want to talk to the clerk about the forfeiture clause during the next defendant caucus (without telling him why). (VC) (SC) (SU) (VU)

d. telling the plaintiff in caucus that you have consulted with the clerk, and the clause is almost certainly not enforceable. (VC) (SC) (SU) (VU)

e. telling both parties in joint session that you have consulted with the clerk, and the clause is almost certainly not enforceable. (VC) (SC) (SU) (VU)

Balancing Bargaining Ability.   A third variation on the problem of power imbalance arises when the mediator becomes aware of significant disparities in the parties' native bargaining ability or knowledge about negotiation. This can be especially pronounced when people are required to enter a court mediation process that they do not fully understand. What kind of negotiation "coaching," if any, is appropriate to assist a weaker party?

Problem Five: Power Balancing by Negotiation Coaching?

In the previous case, assume that you decided that you were not comfortable telling the tenant about the non-enforceability of the forfeiture clause. But you are concerned enough about the power imbalance that you are considering terminating the mediation and sending the parties to court. In your first caucus with the tenant, you plan to explore whether he wishes to continue with the process. But before you can do that, he blurts out that he will accept the $500 being offered by the defendants as full and final settlement of his $2,250 claim.

If I were the mediator in this case, here's how I would feel about making the following statements:

a. "You know that you needn't accept the realty company's offer and that, although it could lead them to end the negotiations, you have the right to make a counteroffer, don't you?" (VC) (SC) (SU) (VU)

b. (Assuming the tenant is open to making a counteroffer): "You know, if they respond to any counteroffer you make, it's likely to be an offer that's higher than $500 but lower than what you have asked for. So it probably makes sense to ask for more than what you are actually willing to accept, so that you have some negotiation room. Shall we talk about that?" (VC) (SC) (SU) (VU)

c. "Also, whatever counteroffer you make is more likely to be taken seriously if it's explained by a convincing rationale. What are some reasons or justifications you could come up with to support a new demand number higher than $500?" (VC) (SC) (SU) (VU)

d. "Can't come up with any? Well, here are three possible examples: You could offer to accept $750 on the assumption that, win or lose, it will likely cost the defendant that much in additional attorney's fees if they take the case to trial. Or you could ask for $1,500, saying it's fair to let the realty company keep your

continues on next page >

> first month's rent. Or you could take the position that you will only pay for
> actual damages that the company can prove it suffered when you decided not
> to rent the apartment." (VC) (SC) (SU) (VU)

"Process" Fairness versus "Outcome" Fairness.   Compare your answers to
Problems Three, Four and Five. Were they similar or different? Mediators
sometimes distinguish between power balancing to ensure the fairness or integrity
of the *process*, as opposed to the fairness of the *outcome*. Is the distinction a valid
one? For example, is balancing information more offensive to ideals of impartiality
and neutrality than balancing the process? Why or why not? Is negotiation coaching in Problem Five a form of insuring process fairness, outcome fairness or both?

Assuming that you felt some obligation to protect *unrepresented* parties from
an unfair settlement, would you feel the same compulsion in a legal matter where
one party's lawyer is outmatched by the opponent's? For example, suppose in
Problem Four that the tenant had an attorney who didn't know about the non-
enforceability of the security deposit forfeiture clause. As the mediator would you
act any differently than if the tenant were unrepresented? Why or why not? If you
would act differently, what *precisely* would you do in each scenario?

What Is a "Fair" Agreement Anyway?   In each of the above problems, any
urge to act as more than an impartial referee may arise out of concern about the
potential for an unfair agreement. In a legal dispute, is a mediation outcome that
varies significantly from the likely court result necessarily "unfair"? Because of
their training, many lawyer mediators naturally think so.

However, it is important to point out that parties in mediation often reject
legal, industry or other "objective" norms as the most important guide to the right
outcome, because these values conflict with their personal notions of fairness
(*"The law may say that I'm entitled to double my security deposit because of
the landlord's technical violations of the statute, but, honestly, all I really want
back is the amount I gave him."*) or because other benefits of a mediated resolution
(privacy, certainty, putting the dispute to rest quickly, etc.) outweigh the potential
gains from asserting legal rights. The question for the mediator in legal disputes is
how much assistance is appropriate in helping the parties make *informed* decisions
about whether to vindicate their legal rights or to forego them?

Neutrality versus Fairness: The Problem of Affected Third Parties.   Yet
another fairness problem arises when equally matched negotiators want to craft an
agreement that, while not unlawful, may be harmful to the rights of third parties.
For example, the culture among many family mediators is that "outcome neutrality" takes a backseat to the "best interests of the child" when parents want to make
an arrangement that may be detrimental to their children. Family mediation codes
are sometimes to similar effect.[25] Thus, because some child development experts

---

25. For example, the 2001 ABA Model Standards of Practice for Family and Divorce Mediation, while
stating that mediation "is based on the principle of self-determination," also assert that "[a] family
mediator shall assist participants in determining how to promote the best interests of children."

view it as developmentally harmful for infants and young toddlers to be shuttled back and forth each night between separated, high-conflict parents,[26] some family mediators might urge parents not to agree to such terms or even terminate the mediation rather than help to effectuate them.

In what other situations, if any, is it appropriate for a mediator to depart from the norm of outcome neutrality by taking into account the interests of persons or groups not at the table? For example, should a mediator sign off on a confidential settlement of a lawyer-client fee dispute if the discussions reveal that the lawyer's drug dependency has likely harmed and might be continuing to harm other unsuspecting clients? Writing in the early 1980s about environmental mediation, MIT professor Lawrence Susskind argued that "environmental mediators ought to accept responsibility for ensuring that . . . the interests of parties not directly involved in negotiations, but with a stake in the outcome, are adequately represented and protected."[27] Writing in sharp response, Joseph Stulberg replied that "most mediators believe that a commitment to impartiality and neutrality is the defining principle of their role. . . . [The] demand for a non-neutral intervenor is conceptually and pragmatically incompatible with the goals and purposes of mediation."[28] With whom do you agree? In an environmental dispute, what variables might affect your answer?

Is "Outcome Neutrality" Actually Achievable, or Is It Just an Ideal?
Several research studies suggest that even when the parties are considering resolutions that could not reasonably be characterized as immoral, unconscionable or harmful to third parties, mediators often favor certain outcomes over others and steer the parties, consciously or unconsciously, toward outcomes that the mediators find acceptable.[29] Some commentators suggest that neutrality is more a myth than a reality in mediation.[30] Would it be better and more honest for mediators to abandon the pretense of neutrality altogether and, instead of subtle manipulation, simply state at the outset, "*Look, obviously I can't impose a result here, but once we get to the point of considering options on how to resolve this matter, if I have an opinion, I'll share it with you candidly, if you like. Would that be OK with both of you?*"

Substantive Fairness and the Model Standards.
The Model Standards say nothing about the problem of unfair agreements. By contrast, some mediation

---

26. *See, e.g.,* Judith Wallerstein, Julia Lewis & Sandra Blakeslee, The Unexpected Legacy of Divorce: A 25 Year Landmark Study 216-217 (2000).

27. Lawrence Susskind, *Environmental Mediation and the Accountability Problem,* 6 Vt. L. Rev. 1, 18 (1981).

28. Joseph B. Stulberg, *The Theory and Practice of Mediation: A Reply to Professor Susskind,* 6 Vt. L. Rev. 85, 86 (1981).

29. *See* David Greatbatch & Robert Dingwall, *Selective Facilitation: Some Preliminary Observations on a Strategy Used by Divorce Mediators,* 23 Law & Soc'y. Rev. 613 (1989) (micro-analysis of divorce mediation in which mediators steer parties toward a division of two properties under which the wife would keep the marital home); Joseph P. Folger & S. Bernard, *Divorce Mediation: When Mediators Challenge the Divorcing Parties,* 10 Mediation Q. 5 (1985). On the difficulty in general of achieving neutrality in divorce mediation, *see* Alison Taylor, *Concepts of Neutrality in Family Mediation: Contexts, Ethics, Influence, and Transformative Process,* 14 Mediation Q. 215 (1997).

30. *See* Sara Cobb & Janet Rifkin, *Deconstructing Neutrality in Mediation,* 16 Law & Soc. Inquiry 35, 37 (1991) (arguing that mediator neutrality is a "folk concept" lacking any empirical support).

ethics codes around the country authorize the mediator to indicate nonconcurrence with or to refuse to draft an agreement that the mediator believes is unconscionable or inherently unfair.[31] Which approach is preferable, in your view?

▪ §12.4 MEDIATION AND THE PROBLEM OF CRIMINAL AND OTHER UNLAWFUL CONDUCT

Perhaps you are not troubled by possible unfairness created by various kinds of imbalances at the bargaining table, or maybe you believe that duties of impartiality and neutrality tie the mediator's hands in trying to correct any imbalances or unfairness that may be encountered. What about situations in which a neutral is being asked to help the parties craft an unlawful agreement? Or situations in which a mediated agreement may enable one or both of the parties, without your assistance, to continue to act unlawfully in the future? Consider these cases:

Problem Six: Problematic Agreements

In the following (real case) scenarios, indicate your comfort level with continuing to serve as a mediator and helping the parties settle their dispute on the terms they propose. What considerations guide your answer? Would it matter if, under court or agency rules, you were expected to sign the agreement as mediator? If you would not be comfortable helping the parties consummate their deal, what *specifically* would you do?

a. The parties in an employment discrimination claim filed with the EEOC agree to characterize the bulk of the payments to be made to the plaintiff as (non-taxable) "compensation for physical injury" instead of (taxable) lost wages so as to reduce the plaintiff's income tax burden in the coming fiscal year. Both are represented by able counsel. The plaintiff has claimed he suffered "health problems" on account of being fired but has presented no evidence in the mediation of any medical treatment received or of damages other than the pay he lost. In exchange for this characterization, the plaintiff has agreed to accept $10,000 less than his earlier communicated "final" settlement demand. You are a mediator in private practice who is appointed to handle approximately ten mediations a year at the local EEOC office on a reduced fee basis. (VC) (SC) (SU) (VU)

b. You are a staff mediator in a local small claims court where mediations take place an hour before the scheduled court hearing. The plaintiff, an elderly widow we will call Mrs. Rosen, sues for return of $1,000, allegedly loaned to a younger man, Mr. Schwartz. There is no written loan agreement. In mediation, when confronted with Mrs. Rosen's righteous anger, he quickly admits that he borrowed the money and now offers to repay the debt in full, half in cash immediately, the balance over two months.

---

31. *See* EXON, *supra* note 2, at 403-405, collecting statutes.

In caucus with the plaintiff to discuss the defendant's proposed payment plan, Mrs. Rosen now tells you that Mr. Schwartz is a scam artist who preys on vulnerable widows by taking them out to dinners, romancing them and then "borrowing" money with no intention of paying it back. She has learned that he did this with four other women in her neighborhood (who have not themselves sued) and is continuing to do it with others. She then takes out a cell phone and calls one of these alleged victims, who, on the phone with you, confirms that the same thing happened to her (conduct, that if proven, constitutes larceny). Despite all of this, Mrs. Rosen tells you that she wants to accept the offer and settle her case quietly. If this happens, the parties will sign an agreement and there will be no court hearing. (VC) (SC) (SU) (VU)

c. You are a mediation trainee co-mediating a landlord-tenant dispute in your local housing court. The landlord has brought an eviction action against two unmarried co-tenants for non-payment of the last two months' rent, totaling $1,800. Under state law, tenants are subject to eviction upon proof that they have failed to pay their rent on a timely basis. The male tenant, the single father of an eleven-year-old son, admits that he did not pay rent during this two-month period because he was injured on the job and was unable to work. The female tenant is unemployed and has never contributed to the monthly rent. All parties are unrepresented. If the case is not settled, it will go to trial this afternoon.

The male tenant offers to pay the entire $1,800 rent arrearage today if the eviction case is withdrawn. The landlord agrees to accept this offer, but only if the tenants agree (a) that the girlfriend will vacate the apartment within thirty days and (b) that the apartment will not be occupied in the future by anyone other than the tenant and his son. The landlord states that she only recently learned that the girlfriend is an African American and that she does not approve of interracial cohabitation. Rental discrimination on the basis of race is unlawful under both state and federal fair housing laws, but it is not a crime. In caucus, the male tenant indicates that while he is repulsed by the landlord's attitudes, he wants to accept the deal because he doesn't want an eviction on his record and needs to *"keep my son in his local school."* The girlfriend says, *"Look, he needs the apartment and he pays the bills, so whatever he says, I'll do."* (VC) (SC) (SU) (VU)

Standard VI(A) of the Model Standards provides: "If a mediation is being used to further criminal conduct, a mediator should take appropriate steps including, if necessary, postponing, withdrawing from or terminating the mediation." Note first the use of the word "should" rather than "shall" in this Standard. This formulation presumably means that the mediator may exercise discretion in deciding how to proceed in the face of different kinds of proposed criminality, including doing nothing. Is this desirable? Note also that this language only addresses *criminal* agreements, not otherwise *unlawful* ones. Do you agree with the way the drafters of the Standards have drawn these lines?

Withdrawal of the Mediator or Termination of the Mediation as Responses to Serious Party Imbalance or Criminality.   Standard II of the

Model Standards directs mediators to withdraw from or terminate a mediation if the mediator's ability to act impartially is compromised, as would likely occur in some cases of serious party imbalance, and as just noted, Standard VI affords mediators the discretion to withdraw from or terminate the mediation to avoid participating in a settlement that "furthers criminal conduct."

In the case of criminal agreements, what ends are served by withdrawal if the parties can negotiate the same unlawful terms themselves after the mediator departs? In cases of serious power imbalance or other unfairness, what good does termination of the mediation accomplish if, as research suggests, the stronger party is likely to come out ahead anyway if the matter then proceeds to court?[32] Is mediator withdrawal designed to serve justice? To relieve the mediator from having to make tough ethical judgments? To protect the good name of mediation? On a process level, if you intended to withdraw from a mediation based on an imbalance of legal information or bargaining ability, how exactly would you explain or announce this to the parties?

Before the 2005 amendments to the Model Standards were promulgated, mediation scholar Jon Hyman proposed that the drafters include a specific provision expressly urging mediators to discuss questions of fairness, justice and morality with the parties.[33] This suggestion did not find its way into the Standards. Should it have been included? In Problem Six (c) above, what might such a "justice" conversation sound like?

Note finally that the confidentiality protections in Standard V(A) of the Model Standards contain no exception for disclosure of unfair or unlawful agreements or problematic conduct by participants, unless such revelations are "otherwise . . . required by applicable law." Thus, the Standards' drafters appear to have taken the view that, unless state or federal law expressly requires otherwise, preserving the confidentiality of the process trumps any duty or discretion on the part of the mediator to blow the whistle on unfair, unlawful or criminal agreements, or offensive or coercive party behavior, no matter how egregious. Do you agree with this balancing of competing values? For example, suppose the mediator in Problem Six (c) withdraws from the mediation rather than assist the parties in concluding a racially discriminatory settlement agreement. Should the mediator be afforded *discretion* to inform the state's human rights commission about the landlord's practices? Why or why not? Would it matter if the mediator knew that the landlord owned many rental properties around the city? What if the mediator were later subpoenaed as part of a civil rights investigation of that landlord's rental practices? Should she be allowed or compelled to testify as to what she learned in mediation? We take up the topic of mediation confidentiality in the section that follows.

---

32. KRITZER & SILBEY, *supra* note 14.
33. *See* JON HYMAN, *The World of Conflict Resolution: A Mosaic of Possibilities*, 5 CARDOZO J. CONFLICT RESOL. 205-206 (2004). These ideas are further elaborated in HYMAN, *Swimming in the Deep End: Dealing with Justice in Mediation*, 6 CARDOZO J. CONFLICT RESOL. 19 (2004).

■ §12.5 ETHICAL AND POLICY ISSUES REGARDING CONFIDENTIALITY

Of all the ethical and policy issues pertaining to mediation, none is as difficult to describe concisely as confidentiality. That confidentiality is essential to mediation is considered axiomatic by most practitioners and commentators.[34] However, no consensus exists regarding its implementation or limits. There are many variations in approach from state to state, and judicial protection of mediation confidentiality has been uneven at best.

The Costs and Benefits of Mediation Confidentiality. An often-cited article[35] makes the following primary arguments for protecting confidentiality in mediation:

> *Effective mediation requires candor.* . . . Mediators must be able to draw out baseline positions and interests which would be impossible if the parties were constantly looking over their shoulders. Mediation often reveals deep-seated feelings on sensitive issues. Compromise negotiations often require the admission of facts which disputants would never otherwise concede. Confidentiality ensures that parties will voluntarily enter the process and further enables them to participate effectively and successfully.
>
> *Fairness to the disputants requires confidentiality.* The safeguards present in legal proceedings, qualified counsel and specific rules of evidence and procedure, for example, are absent in mediation. In mediation, unlike the traditional justice system, parties often make communications without the expectation that they will later be bound by them. . . . Mediation thus could be used as a discovery device against legally naive persons if the mediation communications were not inadmissible in subsequent judicial actions. . . .
>
> *The mediator must remain neutral in fact and in perception.* The potential of the mediator to be an adversary in a subsequent legal proceeding would curtail the disputants' freedom to confide during the mediation. Court testimony by a mediator, no matter how carefully presented, will inevitably be characterized so as to favor one side or the other. This would destroy a mediator's efficacy as an impartial broker.
>
> *Privacy is an incentive for many to choose mediation.* Whether it be protection of trade secrets or simply a disinclination to "air one's dirty laundry" in the neighborhood, the option presented by the mediator to settle disputes quietly and informally is often a primary motivator for parties choosing this process.

---

34. *See, e.g.,* Lawrence R. Freedman & Michael L. Prigoff, *Confidentiality in Mediation: The Need for Protection,* 2 Ohio St. J. on Disp. Resol. 37 (1986); Ellen E. Deason, Reply: *The Quest for Uniformity in Mediation Confidentiality: Foolish Consistency or Crucial Predictability,* 85 Marq. L. Rev. 79, 80-85 (2001); Alan Kirtley, *The Mediation Privilege's Transition from Theory to Implementation: Designing a Mediation Privilege Standard to Protect Mediation Participants, the Process and the Public Interest,* 1995 J. Disp. Resol. 1 (1995); Michael Prigoff, *Toward Candor or Chaos: The Case of Confidentiality in Mediation,* 12 Seton Hall Legis. J. 1 (1988). *But see* Eric D. Green, *A Heretical View of the Mediation Privilege,* 2 Ohio St. J. on Disp. Resol. 1, 32 (1986). ("Although most mediators assert that confidentiality is essential to the process, there is no data of which I am aware that supports this claim, and I am dubious that such data could be collected.")
35. Freedman & Prigoff, *supra* note 34, at 37-39.

As persuasive as these arguments may be, recognizing a principle that broadly prohibits the mediation participants from testifying about what occurred during the mediation process comes at a high price to courts and to the public:

- It may deprive the courts of critical evidence. For example, a disputant in a mediation who alleges that he agreed to the settlement terms only after being coerced to do so by a mediator would have little recourse if confidentiality were strictly enforced. Obtaining relevant information about what occurred during the mediation is often necessary if the court is going to be able to "do justice."[36]

- It may prevent other potential litigants and the general public from learning important information. In a products liability context, for example, should a mediator be free to refuse to testify about what a crib manufacturer said during the successful mediation of a previous lawsuit about an allegedly defective crib design when cribs of the same design were subsequently kept on the market and one later allegedly killed an infant? Commentator David Luban has noted that such information can be important not only because it "might save lives" but also because it "informs public deliberation about an issue of substantial political significance."[37]

Sources of Confidentiality in Mediation.   Confidentiality in mediation can emanate from a variety of sources. Federal and state rules of evidence provide protection against disclosure in court of certain party communications made as part of a settlement effort. In private mediation and in some court and agency settings, confidentiality agreements signed by the parties can expand the scope of protection of the process by contract.[38] Almost all states now have confidentiality statutes that apply to at least some forms of mediation, although what degree of protection is afforded, to what kinds of communications, in what forms of mediation, subject to what exceptions, varies greatly from state to state. In an attempt to create some uniformity of approach, the National Conference of Commissioners on Uniform State Laws disseminated the Uniform Mediation Act[39] in 2003, recommending that it be enacted in all the states. As of 2011, ten states plus the District of Columbia had approved some version of the Act.[40]

Rules of Evidence.   The Federal Rules of Evidence have been adopted in all the federal courts. They also provide the model, with minor exceptions, for the rules of

---

36. In the frequently cited case of *Olam v. Congress Mortgage Co.*, 68 F. Supp. 2d 1110 (N.D. Cal. 1999), the court compelled a mediator to testify in a case in which the plaintiff alleged that she signed a "memorandum of understanding" during a court-sponsored voluntary mediation under duress and sought to avoid its enforcement. In compelling the mediator to testify, the court argued that the mediator is positioned in this case to offer what could be crucial, certainly very probative, evidence about the central factual issues in this matter. There is a strong possibility that his testimony will greatly improve the court's ability to determine reliably what the pertinent historical facts actually were. Establishing reliably what the facts were is critical to doing justice. . . .

37. David Luban, *Settlements and the Erosion of the Public Realm*, 83 Geo. L.J. 2619, 2653 (1995).

38. Where mediation is internal to an organization such as a university, hospital or other large employer, the scope of confidentiality may be determined by the unique and overriding needs of the host institution.

39. *See* Appendix D, *infra* for excerpts from the Act.

40. *See*   *http://www.nccusl.org/LegislativeFactSheet.aspx?title = Mediation%20Act*   (last   visited August 23, 2011).

evidence adopted in forty-two states. Under the Rules, both "offers to compromise" and "evidence of conduct or statements made in compromise discussions" are not admissible to prove "liability for or invalidity of [a] claim or its amount."[41] This provision is designed to exclude evidence of settlement offers ("*We offer to settle this case for $30,000*") that may be weak (if not misleading) proof of legal responsibility at a trial and to encourage frankness in discussing the underlying facts of the dispute ("*We admit that our crib could have been designed differently*"), so as to promote the voluntary resolution of disputes.

Suppose you were mediating our premises liability case, *Resnick v. Stevens Realty*. In joint session, defense counsel stated, "*Ok. So what if our maintenance man says that the fire escape stairs were only about a foot and a half above ground? You still have to prove how the intruder could have gotten into the alley, which we keep securely locked. In light of that, we won't pay a penny more than $50,000. And that's our final offer.*" If the case did not settle, but instead proceeded to trial, would Josh Resnick be permitted (or could you as the mediator be compelled) to testify as to any of the above statements as evidence of Stevens' liability? In jurisdictions adopting Rule 408, the presumptive answer would be no.

Rule 408 thus provides a great deal of protection against subsequent disclosure of settlement discussions in court proceedings. But many would argue that even more protection is needed. Why?

First, the rule only protects against the giving of testimony regarding settlement offers and settlement statements in *trials*.[42] It does not prevent the information from being used or pursued further in pre-trial discovery (and thus potentially brought — albeit less directly — into a trial). If the above statements in mediation led to later deposition questioning of the defendant ("*In our mediation last month, Mr. Stevens, I believe your attorney conceded that, according to the building's maintenance man, the fire escape stairs were only a foot and a half above ground. Is that correct? . . . What's the name, address and telephone number of the maintenance man he referred to? . . . Was it you who spoke to the maintenance man about this subject? . . . Tell me everything you remember about that conversation. . . . Have you had any other conversations about the fire escape stairs with anyone other than your attorney?*"), all such questions would be unobjectionable. The legal standard for permissible discovery is whether the questions asked are "reasonably calculated to lead to the discovery of admissible evidence,"[43] not whether they themselves would be admissible at a trial.

Second, Rule 408 does not preclude disclosure of settlement information for any purpose other than proof of "liability for, invalidity of, or amount of a [disputed] claim." For example, if, after their handshake agreement, either party in *Resnick* later claimed that no settlement had been reached, statements made

---

41. *See* Fed. R. Evid. 408 (Dec. 1, 2006). Rule 410 provides comparable protection in criminal plea negotiations. In states not adopting the Federal Rules of Evidence, some protect only offers to settle, not factual statements and admissions made during settlement discussions. *See, e.g.,* Conn. Code Evid. §4-8 (2000).

42. Because Rule 408 is a rule of evidence, applying only to court testimony, it does not apply to statements made to the press or public. Thus, if Josh Resnick wanted to tell his family, friends, former neighbors or the local newspaper about Mr. Stevens' monetary offer or his mediation statements, he could do so freely, consistent with this rule.

43. Fed. R. Civ. Pro. 26(b)(1).

during mediation that might support or refute such a claim would not be inadmissible under Rule 408.[44]

Confidentiality Agreements.   For these reasons, private mediators and ADR provider organizations often try to create an additional privacy protection for the mediation process by crafting confidentiality provisions for the parties to sign as part of their initial agreement to mediate. Such provisions can be useful, because they enable the parties to tailor the scope of secrecy to their needs in a specific dispute.[45] But these clauses are subject to limitations, the most important of which is that no private contract can create an enforceable privilege not to testify if a judge decides that the testimony of a party or mediator is required at trial. The general rule is that the courts have the right to every person's evidence and that only legislatures or courts themselves can create enforceable privileges to refuse to testify. In addition, even if confidentiality agreements are enforceable against the parties who signed them, they may not be enforceable against non-signatories.

Mediation Confidentiality and Privilege Statutes.   Mediators, attorneys and policy makers seeking additional protection for mediation confidentiality have therefore sought to persuade state legislatures to provide it. Today, virtually every state has enacted some form of mediation confidentiality or privilege legislation. The details and scope of protection afforded by state mediation confidentiality or privilege statutes vary so greatly that it is difficult to generalize about them. Among the most significant variables are the following:

- **What types of mediations are covered by statute?** Some state statutes extend confidentiality to all forms of mediation, public and private. More commonly, however, only mediations sponsored by state courts and agencies are covered. Some states afford confidentiality only to mediations conducted by mediators with specific credentials, such as lawyers or persons who have completed court-approved mediation training programs.

- **What stages of mediation are covered by statute?** Some statutes provide confidentiality only to statements made or conduct at the bargaining table. Other statutes afford protection to conversations during pre-mediation screening and intake procedures and/or post-mediation conversations regarding reconvening the mediation or enforcing an agreement.

- **What information is protected by statute?** Sometimes mediation confidentiality statutes are structured like testimonial privileges and protect only oral communications between the parties themselves or between the parties and the mediator. Other statutes are broader, providing protection for documents and other submissions to the mediator in preparation for mediation, mediator notes and impressions, the identities of the parties in mediation and, occasionally, communications made by non-parties attending the mediation.

---

44. *See* Fed. R. Evid. 408(b); *see, e.g., Uforma/Shelby Bus. Forms, Inc. v. NLRB*, 111 F.3d 1284 (6th Cir. 1997) (Rule 408 is inapplicable when the claim is based on a wrong committed during the course of settlement discussions).
45. Note, *Protecting Confidentiality in Mediation*, 98 Harv. L. Rev. 441, 450 (1984).

■ **Who holds the privilege?** Only holders of a privilege or their designated agents have standing to invoke the privilege or to waive it. Some mediation statutes grant the privilege only to the disputants to prevent their statements and the statements of the mediator from being used in future proceedings. Other statutes afford the mediator an independent privilege to prevent the parties from revealing the mediator's statements, even if the parties are willing to waive their own privilege. A surprising number of statutes are silent on this important question.

■ **What exceptions to confidentiality are recognized by statute?** Almost all mediation confidentiality statutes are subject to exceptions — often significant and wide-ranging ones. These range from specific exceptions for parties seeking to enforce a mediation agreement or set it aside on grounds of perjury, fraud or duress; to exceptions in order to prove child or domestic abuse or threats of violence during the mediation process; to broad or elastic exceptions for certain case categories — for example, all criminal cases or all cases in which the "interests of justice" outweigh the need for confidentiality.[46]

The net effect of all this legislation is a far-from-uniform approach to mediation confidentiality. Given the leeway some courts have to balance other interests against claims of mediation confidentiality, the protection provided to the process is far from ironclad.[47]

Confidentiality in Action. Given this complex and less-than-clear picture, what, if anything, should a mediator tell the parties at the start of the process about the *limits* of confidentiality?

Problem Seven: Describing Mediation Confidentiality

You are a mediator in a community mediation program in a state in which a recently enacted (and yet-to-be court-interpreted) statute, applicable to all mediations that are not court-ordered, provides in part that

All oral or written communications received or obtained during the course of a mediation shall be confidential. No mediator shall be

continues on next page >

---

46. *See generally* COLE, MCEWAN & ROGERS, *supra* note 3, at §9.12, for an excellent survey of this subject, which provides much of the basis for the above discussion.

47. A recent study suggests that the courts may be less reliable protectors of confidentiality than might be supposed. In 2006, James Coben and Peter Thompson studied 1,223 federal and state court cases dealing with mediation between 1999 and 2003. Overall, the authors uncovered 152 court opinions during this time period in which courts considered a confidentiality claim. Of these claims, confidentiality was upheld in whole or in part in just 50 percent of the cases. Although some, perhaps most, of the decisions rejecting confidentiality are no doubt correct, the authors note critically that "few of these decisions involve a reasoned weighing of the pros and cons of compromising the mediation process." Instead they provide a relatively cursory justification for the result reached. *See generally* JAMES R. COBEN & PETER N. THOMPSON, *Disputing Irony: A Systematic Look at Litigation About Mediation*, 11 HARV. NEGOT. L. REV. 43 (2006).

compelled to disclose any such communications unless the disclosure is necessary to enforce a written agreement that came out of the mediation, the disclosure is required by statute or regulation or the disclosure is required because the court finds that the interest of justice outweighs the need for confidentiality.

You are assigned to mediate a dispute that included a physical altercation between two seniors at an urban high school and was referred to mediation by local police. You have no more than ninety minutes in which to conduct the mediation. In your opening statement, what, if anything, would you say about mediation confidentiality? (Rank your answers from 1 to 4, with 1 being the best answer:)

a. Say nothing at all about confidentiality unless asked, because I wouldn't want to mislead the participants about the uncertain scope of protection.

b. Promise confidentiality (e.g., *"Everything you say here is confidential"*; *"What's said in this room stays in this room"*), without more; getting bogged down in complicated exceptions might confuse the participants and deter candid discussions.

c. Promise confidentiality, making a general reference to limits (e.g., *"There are some exceptions, but they don't come up very often"*) and leaving it to the participants to ask about those exceptions if they want to.

d. Try to provide a full description of the rule, its exceptions and the uncertainty of court enforcement.

What factors affected your choice?

As suggested earlier, subsequent in-court testimony as to what was said at a mediation may not be the only concern for unwary participants. Consider this case:

Problem Eight: Confidentiality and Discovery

You are mediating a claim for damages and a restraining order arising out of an incident in which the ex-lover of a female police officer allegedly hit her with her billy club, threatened her with more harm, stormed out of their apartment and then left threatening messages on her telephone answering machine. At the court-mandated mediation (which is taking place two hours before the potential trial in the case), the plaintiff appears with her lawyer and the defendant is unrepresented. After the mediator's opening, in which the parties were promised that *"what's said in this room stays in this room,"* the plaintiff's attorney presents a summary of his client's claims and the history of the dispute. The mediator then turns to the defendant for his opening statement. As the defendant starts an emotional and lengthy defense, talking unguardedly about his feelings and conduct, the plaintiff's lawyer begins to take notes furiously on his legal pad. What, if anything, will you say or do at this point?

"External" versus "Internal" Confidentiality. The preceding discussion of confidentiality has focused on "external" confidentiality: the principle of keeping those *outside* the mediation process — judges, other litigants or their lawyers, the press and so forth — from learning about what took place in mediation. But as we have seen, mediators also commonly promise an additional level of privacy through the caucus process, during which they promise each party not to share information *with the other party* unless he or she consents. This type of protection, which has been labeled "internal" confidentiality,[48] raises difficult questions as well.

"Leaking." One question has to do with subtle messages from the mediator that do not exactly reveal confidential caucus communications but nonetheless may signal important strategic information to the other side. Have a look at one of our mediators in the *Resnick* case conveying the defendant's last offer to the plaintiff and "interpreting" for the plaintiff and his lawyer what further bargaining room might exist. **Video Clip 12-B.**

Did this mediator's conduct violate his earlier promise to the parties to keep confidential "what you discuss with the mediator"? Does it matter that he did not at any time reveal what the parties actually *said*, but only his impressions of what they would and would not *do*? Does the fact that sophisticated parties sometimes expect their mediator to "move the discussions" in this way affect your response? If this mediator's actions made you uncomfortable, consider the comments of Judge Richard Posner on mediation as an aid to settlement:[49]

> Since the mediator can meet with the parties separately and his discussions with them are confidential, they are likely to be more candid with him than they would be with each other, enabling him to form a more accurate impression of the actual strengths and weaknesses of their respective positions than they can and to communicate this impression to them in a credible fashion. He can thus help them to converge to a common estimate of the likely outcome of the case if it is litigated to judgment. *To do this, however, the mediator must be not only a conduit of information between the opposing sides but also an impediment to transparent communication between them. When a mediator formulates a proposal to one party, that party will infer that the proposal reflects information conveyed to the mediator by the other party. But so long as the information is fuzzied up by the mediator, that other party will be giving up less in the way of strategically valuable information (should mediation fail and the case go to trial) than if he had to communicate with his opponent face to face.* (Emphasis supplied.)

Internal Confidentiality: Any Limits? Promising a party that "*I won't reveal anything you tell me privately in caucus unless you give me express permission to*

---

48. MICHAEL MOFFITT, *Ten Ways to Get Sued: A Guide for Mediators*, 8 HARV. NEGOT. L. REV. 81, 108 (2003) (distinguishing external and internal confidentiality).
49. RICHARD POSNER, Economic Analysis of Law 576 (6th ed. 2003).

do so" can sometimes put the mediator in a difficult if not untenable bind. Consider this scenario:

Problem Nine: Confidentiality that Assists Fraud

You are mediating a small claims case between a plumbing contractor and a homeowner concerning the contractor's $3,000 claim for unpaid services plus interest at 12 percent. The original contract called for payment in full upon completion of the job and made no provision for the payment of interest. In caucus with the homeowner, he admits the debt and proposes to pay it in fifteen monthly payments of $200, plus interest at the rate of 6 percent on the outstanding principal balance. He then states: *"Confidentially, it doesn't much matter what the payment plan is, because I am planning to consult a lawyer in the next couple of weeks in order to declare bankruptcy. I'll make payments until my bankruptcy petition is filed, but after that, this guy will be lucky to get ten cents on the dollar. Of course, I don't want you to tell him that!"*

This troubles you sufficiently that you place a quick call to a bankruptcy lawyer you know to check out your hunches. Based on that call, you advise the homeowner that he needs to be aware that the refinancing of a debt under false pretenses may prevent the discharge of the debt under federal bankruptcy laws and that when the plumbing contractor discovers his bankruptcy petition, he might decide to sue him for fraud. In response, the homeowner says, *"Thanks for the tip, but let me worry about that. Just convey my proposal to pay the debt on these terms. If you aren't comfortable, I'll propose it to him myself."*

If you were the mediator, what *specifically* would you do?

---

§12.6 PURSUING SETTLEMENT: WHAT ARE THE ETHICAL LIMITS?

Standard I(B) of the Model Standards states that "A mediator shall not undermine party self-determination by any party for reasons such as higher settlement rates, egos, increased fees, or outside pressures from court personnel, program administrators, provider organizations, the media or others." In our experience, this is a great deal easier said than done.

First, mediators in high-volume courts and agencies are often under substantial pressure, whether stated or otherwise, to "move the docket." Second, from a psychological standpoint, just as winning is more enjoyable than losing, mediators tend to see cases they are able to resolve as "notches in their belt." Third, because they want to succeed in resolving their dispute, consumers of private mediation services often select mediators based on their settlement rates. But this shared definition of a "successful" mediation raises an important question: How far may the mediator go, and what tactics may he or she use, in the pursuit of a negotiated resolution?

Voluntary Decisions: How Much Pressure Is Too Much?   As we saw in Chapters 9 and 10, mediators employ a wide variety of persuasive tactics in seeking settlement. Sometimes they use the waning moments of mediation to take advantage of the scarcity principle to obtain final resolution. Sometimes they use more overt tactics, including various exhortations to "keep moving" that can significantly raise the pressure on disputants. Some pull procedural levers — round-the-clock sessions, for example — to close a deal. When does the use of pressure in mediation cross the line into coercion?

The question is a difficult one to answer. Just because an agreement is reached under circumstances in which a party seems to feel pressured does not necessarily mean that the mediator has acted inappropriately. Pressure can result from the parties' having scheduled insufficient time for the mediation, taking into account the complexities of the case. A pressured decision toward the end of a mediation session can be the product of the parties' failing to negotiate in earnest early on. Or it can be a function of the difficulty a party has in finally letting go of conflict or in making decisions about distasteful compromises.

Review the following segments of the closing portion of the mediation of *Resnick v. Stevens Realty*. The entire mediation lasted approximately two hours and fifteen minutes. The first ninety minutes or more were spent on factual exchanges and legal and evidentiary assessments of the case. When actual bargaining began, the plaintiff led off with a demand of $110,000, and the defendant countered with an offer of $30,000. In the final stages of the mediation, the mediator engaged in shuttle diplomacy, by going back and forth rapidly between the parties and trying to find a convergence point at which they might be willing to settle.

As you watch selected portions of this caucus with the plaintiff and his lawyer, ask yourself: Did any of the mediator's interventions cross the line from appropriate persuasion into inappropriate pressure or coercion? Be specific. If none of the mediator's specific interventions crossed that line, did his approach as a whole? Why or why not? **Video Clip 12-C.**

Note that we did not show you the private consultations that took place between the client and his lawyer, because as mediators, you would not have seen them. Is a mediator entitled to apply more pressure when dealing with represented parties on the assumption that their counsel will "protect" them?[50] Suppose that the plaintiff in this case had taken a similarly aggressive position, but was not represented. What, if anything, should the mediator have done differently?

Informed Decisions: What Is Adequate Disclosure? Mediator persuasion sometimes takes the form of manipulating the information available to the disputants through both active statements and passive non-disclosures. Let's begin with the problem of strategic silence, which could lead the parties to make decisions without important relevant information. Consider this actual case:

Problem Ten: Mediator Non-Disclosure of Information

The parties to a complex construction dispute agreed to try court-appointed mediation two days before its scheduled trial date. An hour before the mediation was scheduled to begin, the presiding judge informed the mediator that an unexpected

continues on next page >

---

50. We focus on what an attorney can do to protect a client at the bargaining table in §13.7, *infra*.

emergency would cause at least a two-month delay in the trial. The parties did not know this. The mediator thought to himself, *"If I tell the lawyers the trial is off, the pressure to settle now will be substantially dissipated."* In response to a lawyer's reference in the opening joint session to *"our trial the day after tomorrow,"* the mediator said nothing. I am:

  a. very comfortable with what the mediator did;
  b. somewhat comfortable with what the mediator did;
  c. somewhat uncomfortable with what the mediator did;
  d. very uncomfortable with what the mediator did.

How useful are the Model Standards in helping a mediator decide what to do in such a case? On the one hand, if one takes seriously the duty to conduct a mediation "based on the principle of party self-determination"[51] and "procedural fairness,"[52] it seems hard to justify the mediator's silence. Weren't the parties and their lawyers entitled to know about the court delay in order to make an informed, self-determined choice whether to go forward with the mediation that day or to postpone it? For all the mediator knew, a postponement to allow the parties to engage in further trial preparation might have made future negotiations between them that much more productive.

On the other hand, if one takes a close look at the mediator's general disclosure obligations in the Model Standards, they fall far short of stating any general duty to provide the parties with useful or salient information. Standard VI(A)(4) states: "A mediator should promote honesty and candor between and among all participants, and *a mediator shall not knowingly misrepresent any material fact or circumstance in the course of a mediation*." (Emphasis supplied.) This language, which tracks both the formal rules governing negotiations by lawyers[53] and the law of fraud,[54] draws a distinction between affirmative misrepresentations of "material facts" (prohibited) and "passive" non-disclosures — that is, remaining silent in the face of another's ignorance of important information (generally not prohibited, at least between bargaining equals). Some negotiation scholars have criticized this minimalist, "only positive fraud is barred" approach to negotiation ethics.[55]

---

51. Standard I, §12.1, *supra*.
52. Standard VI(A), *id.*
53. *See* Rule 4.1(a), ABA Model Rules of Prof'l Conduct (2002), portions of which are set out in Appendix E, *infra*. The rule states: "In the course of representing a client a lawyer shall not knowingly make a false statement of material fact or law to a third person."
54. A very useful summary of the ethics of negotiation and the law of fraud is contained in G. Richard Shell, *Bargaining for Advantage* 196-227 (2d ed. 2006).
55. *See, e.g.*, Gerald Wetlaufer, *The Ethics of Lying in Negotiation*, 72 Iowa L. Rev. 1219 (1990). Some contend that lawyers who appear at mediations in a representative capacity should owe a higher duty of truth-telling than is expected of lawyers in unassisted negotiations. Arguments in favor of such a "candor in mediating" requirement include protecting the integrity of mediation, encouraging its greater use and insulating the mediator from having to deal with untruthful information. By and large, such efforts have failed to catch on. The American Bar Association's Standing Committee on Ethics and Professional Responsibility recently concluded that lawyers do not owe a higher duty of candor to the mediator in caucused mediation than they owe to opposing counsel in conventional, face-to-face negotiations. Formal Opinion 06-439 (April 11, 2007). But doesn't caucused mediation pose a greater risk of distortion than ordinary negotiation if the mediator "massages" and then selectively leaks (already untruthful) information to a party that can neither hear nor directly assess its source? If so, does this warrant a different standard of truth-telling?

Whatever one's reactions to these standards when applied to lawyer negotiators, how appropriate are they when applied to mediators? The rules governing lawyer negotiators are premised on notions of zealous representation of the client and adversary relationships between the lawyers. How applicable are these premises to the mediator? Is the mediator, even when acting in a persuasive mode, *negotiating against* the parties? How much silence is acceptable in the name of getting an agreement? In Problem Ten, what if the lawyers learned the next day of the mediator's concealment? If such non-disclosures were commonplace, what impact would this have on the public's perception of mediation?

Informed Decisions: "Tailored" Evaluations. What about a case in which the mediator *does* provide information to the parties but "tailors" her evaluations or other messages to give them more impact? We talked about these kinds of persuasive interventions generally in Chapters 9 and 10. At what point does this kind of message "packaging" cross the line into impermissible deception or misrepresentation? Consider this case:

Problem Eleven: Tailoring Legal Evaluations

A complaint alleging breach of employment contract and wrongful ("without cause") termination and seeking back pay and emotional distress damages was filed by a fired teacher against his former employer, a private paralegal school owned by a lawyer. It was the subject of a pre-litigation mediation required by the terms of the teacher's contract. The complainant, a young attorney who had never practiced law, was very intelligent and appeared on his own; the school was represented by its lawyer-owner. After four hours of factual exchange, evidentiary presentations and extreme positional bargaining, the defendant offered $15,000 to settle the case, but the complainant was still demanding $30,000.

The mediator thought to himself, *"The economic damages for lost pay in this case are fixed at about $20,000. If this case went to trial, it's unlikely that a jury would award damages for emotional distress. The only real question in this case is whether the defendant acted unlawfully when it fired him from his job. On that issue, I'd say the plaintiff has a 75 percent chance of prevailing."*

In caucus with the defendant, the mediator said, *"From where I sit, you have a very weak case on liability and a very significant chance of losing."* In caucus with the plaintiff, the mediator said, *"From where I sit, you have real risks in your case on liability and a significant chance of losing."* I am:

   a. very comfortable with what the mediator did;
   b. somewhat comfortable with what the mediator did;
   c. somewhat uncomfortable with what the mediator did;
   d. very uncomfortable with what the mediator did.

At first glance, the mediator's inconsistent statements seem deceptive. But are they really? What if the mediator honestly thinks that accepting this offer is in the plaintiff's best interest, especially given the difficulty of representing himself at a trial or finding a contingent fee lawyer in such a case. Should that matter?

This case example illustrates the difficulty of drawing clear lines about what is acceptable and unacceptable mediator "persuasion" and of effectively regulating it. The harnessing of uncertainty is one of the central ways that professionals — and mediators are no exception — gain power for themselves.[56] In the hands of a skillful mediator and in the hurly-burly (and unrecorded privacy) of mediation, questions of deception and truth-telling can be subtle and all-but-impossible to police.

We have endorsed the appropriate, careful use of evaluation because we believe that parties' decisions should be well informed where possible and because many disputants welcome it. But if mediators deliberately exaggerate the risks of non-settlement or the benefits of settlement in their evaluations — even for laudable purposes — this is a cause for concern, especially in the case of unrepresented parties on whose trust and confidence the mediator may be trading.

Informed Decisions: "Stunted" Legal Evaluations.   A related ethical issue for evaluative mediators involves their tendency to provide "stunted" evaluations. In our experience, mediators are often comfortable providing legal information or predictions that emphasize each party's potential litigation *risks*, because these kinds of evaluations generally narrow the bargaining range between the parties. But they often fail to include legal information or advice that acknowledges each party's *strengths*, because doing so might pull the parties farther apart.[57]

Watch as one of the mediators in *Wilson v. DiLorenzo* gives the defendant and his attorney a very direct and negative evaluation about his failure to comply with contractual deadlines and the litigation risks (including the risk of punitive damages) that this might entail for him. Note that the mediator states that he has said none of this to the (unrepresented) plaintiff in order not to "build her case." If one believes that informed decision making is an important ingredient of self-determination, can this approach toward Ms. Wilson be justified? **Video Clip 12-D.**

Self-Determined Decisions: Battling Lawyer Interference.   Sometimes the parties may be fully informed about the pros and cons of the options available to them, but are impeded in making autonomous decisions by their own lawyers or other advisors, who may or may not be acting for "client-centered" reasons. What, if anything, should the mediator do when this occurs? Consider this case:

Problem Twelve: Circumventing the Lawyer

You are mediating an automobile accident case in which a meek and mild-mannered plaintiff, who suffered a serious back injury in the accident, is being represented by a very pugnacious lawyer. Liability on the part of the defendant is all but conceded, but damages are disputed. The plaintiff's attorney has made it clear from the beginning of the mediation that he expects to do almost all of the talking and

---

56. Sissela Bok, Lying: Moral Choice in Public and Private Life 19-20 (1999).
57. *See generally* James H. Stark, *The Ethics of Mediation Evaluation: Some Troublesome Questions and Tentative Proposals, From an Evaluative Lawyer Mediator*, 38 S. Tex. L. Rev. 769 (1997).

negotiating for his client and will consult with the client only if he sees reason to do so. The attorney has also taken very aggressive negotiating positions throughout the mediation, with the result that, after more than two-and-a-half hours, the parties are still $100,000 apart, with the defense offering $250,000 to resolve the case, and the plaintiff's lawyer demanding $350,000. Throughout the mediation, the plaintiff has given strong nonverbal signals that he wants to avoid a trial.

In caucus, the insurance company attorney representing the defendant now makes what she says is *"one last-ditch effort to settle this case: We will offer $300,000, but if the plaintiff doesn't accept it now, the offer will be withdrawn and we will go to trial."* When you then caucus with the plaintiff and his counsel and convey the offer, the plaintiff opens his mouth as if to accept it, but counsel places his hand on the plaintiff's sleeve and says, *"Tell her this is our answer: We're going to trial!"*

If I were the mediator in this case, I would say (rank your answers from 1 to 5, with 1 being the best answer):

  a. "It looked as if you were about to say something, Mr. Peterson, but your attorney interrupted you. What were you about to say?"

  b. "I have a sense that you'd like to accept this, Mr. Peterson, but you are concerned about disappointing your lawyer. Am I wrong?"

  c. "With your permission, counsel, and before terminating the mediation, I would like to talk privately for a few minutes with your client. Could you briefly step outside?"

  d. "With your permission, Mr. Peterson, and before terminating the mediation, I'd like to talk for a minute with your lawyer. Could you briefly step outside?"

  e. Nothing. The client has selected his attorney and established a relationship with him. It is not my role to intrude in the attorney-client relationship.

Information versus Advice.   Standard VI of the Model Standards provides in part that:

> mixing the role of a mediator and the role of another profession is problematic and thus a mediator should distinguish between the roles. A mediator may provide information that the mediator is qualified by training or experience to provide, only if the mediator can do so consistent with these Standards.

The Standards, in common with a number of other codes and the views of some commentators,[58] condone the mediator's providing the parties with *information*, but not *advice*. What does this mean?

The dichotomy between *information* and *advice* is not very helpful to the practicing mediator.[59] While the distinction may be blurry for many neutrals, it is particularly murky for lawyer mediators. Almost *any* information a mediator provides to a party in a legal matter, even of the most general or objective kind ("As

---

58. *See, e.g.*, ABA-ACR-AFCC Model Standards of Practice for Family and Divorce Mediation, Standard VI(B), *infra* at Appendix C (". . . a mediator may provide the participants with information that the mediator is qualified by training or experience to provide. The mediator shall not provide . . . legal advice.")
59. STARK, *supra* note 57, at 784-786.

in most noncriminal cases, you, as the plaintiff, will have the burden of persuasion at a hearing" or "*You know, of course, that it will take nine months or so to get a trial date*" or "*The letter from your neighbor is technically hearsay because its author won't be present to be cross-examined about it.*"), is usually not plucked out of the air. Rather, it is calculated to *advise* the party about the risks and disadvantages of litigation should the case go to trial. Some argue that it is only when legal principles are applied to the facts of a particular case that (permissible) information becomes (impermissible) advice.[60] But many mediation parties, especially those who are unrepresented, need to have general legal principles applied to the facts of the case in order to understand what the mediator is talking about. ("*So does that mean my neighbor's letter won't be accepted by the judge?*" "*Unfortunately, probably not.*") If mediation is working correctly when it promotes informed party decision making, should the ethics of the mediator's intervention turn on the relative *explicitness* of the mediator's information?

Is Mediation the "Practice of Law"?   The distinction between providing information and advice in some mediation ethics codes becomes more understandable when one considers the fact that (a) many practicing mediators are not lawyers; (b) unauthorized practice of law rules that prohibit the practice of law by non-lawyers exist in almost all states but vary greatly around the country and (c) advice-giving constitutes the "unauthorized practice of law" in some states, but not others. This state of affairs has created considerable uncertainty about the kinds of behaviors in which non-lawyer mediators may appropriately engage.

Courts around the country have developed five different tests to determine what the practice of law is:[61]

- The "*Commonly Understood*" Test. This broad (and circular) test asks whether the activity in question is commonly understood to be part of the practice of law in the community. Factors would include whether lawyers in the community, rather than non-lawyers, routinely provide the particular service.

- The "*Client Reliance*" Test. This test asks whether the parties who receive a particular service subjectively believe that they are receiving "legal" services. Evidence of such reliance may be established by examining advertisements or written materials received by the person pertaining to the services in question.

- The "*Affecting Legal Rights*" Test. This test subsumes within "the practice of law" all activities that may affect a person's legal rights — an extremely broad test. Mediations involving litigation matters by definition involve parties' legal rights.

---

60. *See, e.g.*, CARRIE MENKEL-MEADOW, *Is Mediation the Practice of Law?* 14 ALTERNATIVES TO HIGH COST LITIG. 57, 61 (1996).
61. This section is adapted from the Connecticut Council for Divorce Mediation (CCDM) Mediation Standards (2001), for which James Stark served as Reporter. They can be found at *http://www.ctmediators.org/standards.htm#mediation*. *See also* DAVID HOFFMAN & NATASHA AFFOLDER, *Mediation and UPL: Do Mediators Have a Well-Founded Fear of Prosecution?* DISP. RESOL. MAG. 162-165 (Winter 2000); Virginia Guidelines on Mediation and the Unauthorized Practice of Law (Dept. of Dispute Resolution Services of the Supreme Ct. of Virginia, 1999) at pp.2-4.

- The *"Attorney-Client Relationship"* Test. This much narrower test asks whether the relationship between the person providing services and the person receiving them is tantamount to an attorney-client relationship. Applying this test in the context of mediation, one might ask whether the party to the mediation reasonably views him- or herself as a "client" and the mediator as his or her "lawyer."

- The *"Applying Law to Facts"* Test. This test asks whether the service involves relating the law to specific facts, as some contend occurs when a mediator evaluates the strengths and weaknesses of the parties' legal claims by applying legal principles to the particular fact situation.

The "applying law to facts" test is widely adopted, though by no means universal.[62] In states that adhere to it, mediators who are not licensed attorneys in that state (or admitted to practice under a local student practice rule) make legal predictions about the potential resolution of legal issues at their peril. However, almost all mediation ethics codes, including the Model Standards, are written for both lawyer and non-lawyer mediators. Does it make sense to subject lawyer mediators to the same restrictions on the giving of legal advice as non-lawyer mediators? Why or why not?

■ §12.7   ON DEVELOPING JUDGMENT: SOME CONCLUDING THOUGHTS

Although it may not appear so from reading this chapter, some ethical questions confronting mediators do have ready answers. For example, if you have a potential stake in the outcome of a case, you should disclose it. If a party shows clear signs that he or she is unable to understand the mediation process, you should promptly terminate it. If your idea of mediating is to "beat up the parties" to settle on terms *you* find acceptable even if the parties don't, you should probably find yourself a new vocation.

Given the early state of its development as a distinct profession, however, it is fair to say that there are a great many unanswered questions about the ethics of mediating. Lawyers, therapists and other "helping" professionals who face tough ethics dilemmas can usually consult a substantial body of regulatory guidance and/or more experienced practitioners for answers. And because they ordinarily work with the same client over a period of months or years, they usually have the luxury of time to seek such guidance. Mediators, by contrast, often have to make split-second decisions. As a beginning mediator, facing a difficult ethical question in the hurly-burly of a mediation, what can you do?

There are no panaceas. When co-mediating or mediating under supervision, you can take a mediator's caucus to discuss carefully what to do next. On the rare occasions when you can postpone or reschedule a mediation, you can try to find

---

62. For example, the District of Columbia Court of Appeals appears to have adopted the narrower "attorney-client relationship" test in concluding that mediation is not the practice of law because "ADR services are not given in circumstances where there is a client relationship of trust and reliance; and it is common practice for providers of ADR services explicitly to advise participants that they are not providing the services of legal counsel." D.C. Ct. App. R. 49, comment (1995).

respected mediators or ADR organizations to consult. However, even if you are able to get help, the lack of professional consensus on some very fundamental ethical questions affords you great discretion to act based on your own personal judgment and sense of your professional role. Put differently, you will still be faced with tough choices, implicating competing visions about the most important goals and characteristics of "good" mediation.

Ultimately, as in all your professional work, your own experiences will be your best teacher. Take the time to review them carefully, if possible with a trusted colleague or mentor. Over time, developing habits of careful reflection on one's work enables professionals to develop confidence in their capacity to make good decisions when confronted with difficult challenges.

CHAPTER 13

REPRESENTING CLIENTS IN MEDIATION

This chapter contains eight video clips, totaling approximately twenty-five minutes.

■ §13.1 INTRODUCTION

Having spent most of this book examining mediation from the perspective of the mediator, we now shift our focus to the lawyers who guide their clients through the process.

Those of you who are studying mediation because you see yourselves as party representatives in the process may welcome what seems to be a shift in gears. You have learned about the mediator's goals and the means by which she seeks to accomplish them at each stage in the process. Now you are in a position to use that knowledge to explore how lawyers can help their clients use mediation effectively to resolve their disputes. Conversely, if you see yourself working as a neutral, appreciating what the parties' lawyers are doing in a mediation can only enhance your effectiveness. This chapter can therefore also be viewed as completing our analysis of the mediator's skills.

These are the main questions we will explore in this chapter:

- As a representative attorney, how should you advise your clients about whether to enter mediation? What factors would you have them consider in making this choice?

- If a decision is made to mediate, how should you prepare the client — an individual or an organization — for the process?

- What makes for effective client representation at the mediation table? How can a lawyer best use the mediation process to achieve the client's objectives?

- Overall, is mediation representation just another form of "advocacy"?[1] How, if at all, does it differ from lawyering in other settings?

---

1. JOHN W. COOLEY, Mediation Advocacy (2d ed. 2002).

In order to analyze these questions concretely, we will make liberal use of video clips, particularly from our premises liability case, *Resnick v. Stevens Realty*. Although most of the discussion in this chapter assumes that all parties in a dispute are represented by lawyers who are present at the mediation, we will also consider how the presence of an unrepresented opposing party might affect the lawyer's role in the process. Throughout this chapter, we will make frequent reference to the following problem (based on an actual case):

▶ ▶ ▶ ▶   **A Campus Death: The *Yanni* Case**

Nineteen-year-old Robert Yanni, a freshman at a local university, was despondent after breaking up with his high school girlfriend shortly before his first semester exams. (She had e-mailed him that she had met another guy at the college she was attending.) Late one evening he went to see his resident advisor, a physics graduate student in charge of his dorm floor. After listening to Robert's tearful concerns about "hating his life" and "not being able to deal with things," the RA suggested that Robert contact the Campus Counseling Center, a branch of the university-operated student health service, where psychologists and clinical social workers provide free counseling services to students experiencing personal difficulties. When Robert asked for help in contacting the service, the RA placed the call and left a message with the night receptionist requesting that Robert be called back.

Robert never received the return call. He was last seen in the shower room at 9:30 a.m. the next morning. His body was found at 11 a.m. that day in a dumpster loading area behind the dormitory. He had apparently jumped to his death from his ninth-floor dormitory room window. A note left behind stated that he couldn't "take the pressure any more." His cell phone recorded a voice mail message from the counseling center at 11:23 a.m.

Robert's parents filed a wrongful death suit against the University (and the Dean for Student Life and the Director of Student Health) some six months later. They alleged that Robert's death had been foreseeable, preventable and the result of, among other things, inadequate RA training in detecting and dealing with suicidal students and the counseling center's failure to respond adequately in following up on the phone message. The University filed a summary judgment motion seeking to have the case dismissed; that motion was denied by the trial judge.

Discovery in the case has recently been completed. It revealed that Robert Yanni had a history of treatment for depression during his senior year of high school and that he had been prescribed medication for that condition. (His parents claimed that they did not know about the prescription.) It further showed that, while all RAs receive suicide awareness training before they take on the role of RA, the RA in question was studying for a big final exam in a course he was in danger of failing on the evening he was consulted. It also indicated that Robert had missed several recent after-dinner dorm hall meetings and that although his roommate had reported that Robert was "sleeping a lot," and "seems sad and withdrawn," the RA had not checked up on him.

The counseling center's time logs showed that the office receptionist had called in sick the morning in question; the return call came from a temporary fill-in obtained at 10 a.m. from another department. It also revealed that two other university students, one an undergraduate and one a graduate student, had taken their lives during the last three years. During the past ten years, the school has enjoyed a big jump in the national rankings, with greatly heightened competition among applicants for admission and for top grades once admitted.

You are outside counsel for the University and all other named defendants.[2] The University is self-insured and can pay any judgment against any or all defendants up to $100 million. Trial (preceded by a pre-trial conference with the judge) is scheduled to take place in the next six months. Your review of this matter and the applicable law has led you to conclude that the University has a substantial likelihood, perhaps 80 percent, of winning at trial. The Yanni family is represented by a very aggressive, publicity-seeking plaintiff's lawyer. He has demanded $12 million to resolve the matter. There have been no settlement talks.

A nationwide survey of all college and university suicide lawsuits filed and resolved formally over the last five years (a total of fifty cases nationwide) reveals that the defendant university was exonerated, either by summary judgment or defense verdict, in thirty-five (70%) of the cases. In the remaining fifteen cases, plaintiffs received favorable verdicts, with damage awards that ranged from a high of $13.2 million to a low of $545,000, with a median verdict of $2.15 million. Data on out-of-court settlements were not available and are not included in this survey, but your research assistant, who talked to several university counsel around the country, is under the impression that both court filings and pre-filing settlements in these kinds of cases are on the rise.

The University is being pressured by other schools in its league to fight this case in order to avoid any further precedent for colleges being found responsible for student suicides and other harms over which it feels it has no real control (and for which the students' families are often responsible in this era of high-pressure child rearing). The University has already invested almost $120,000 in lawyers' fees and other expenses in this case. Because this is a complex matter that will require significant expert testimony, you estimate that the additional costs of defense if the case goes to trial could run as high as $500,000.

■ §13.2 DECIDING WHETHER TO ENTER MEDIATION: THE ROLES OF LAWYER AND CLIENT

Clients often consult lawyers at the early stage of their involvement in a dispute, without any sense that choices exist in terms of dispute resolution processes that might be used.[3] This means that lawyers play a crucial gatekeeper role in deciding whether and how to discuss alternative options. What is the proper role of the

---

2. Representation of multiple defendants is ethically permissible if, as here, the clients share a common understanding of the facts and the same legal theory, have consented to the common defense and the (vicariously liable) University has agreed not to pursue its right of indemnification in the event of a settlement or a plaintiff's verdict in the case.
3. Parties who are ordered to try mediation do not, of course, have such choices. Similarly, parties who have entered into contractual relationships containing pre-dispute mediation or arbitration clauses have, in effect, already made the decision to use a particular process before, or in lieu of, litigation.

lawyer and the client in the decision to pursue one or another dispute resolution option? Must the lawyer initiate a discussion of non-trial options such as mediation? Even if the lawyer thinks such options are inadvisable or doomed to fail?

The ABA Model Rules of Professional Conduct (MRPC) provide a useful starting point in analyzing these questions, distinguishing between the *objectives* of the representation (presumably to be decided by the client) and the *means* by which those ends should be pursued (presumably to be decided by the lawyer, in consultation with the client).[4] Under the MRPC, the decisions whether to settle a matter or not, and on what terms, are expressly reserved to the client. (After all, it *is* the client's case.) By contrast, decisions such as what witnesses to call at trial or what arguments to stress on appeal would presumably be the lawyer's. (Is this not the expertise that the client is buying?) How helpful do you find the Rules' ends-means distinction in deciding how much voice the client should have in choosing, or forgoing, mediation?

Some lawyers consider the decision about whether to enter mediation as a tactical matter concerning the means by which to try to achieve client-determined objectives. Under this view, the lawyer's procedural expertise would warrant her having wide latitude over such process choices.

But is this the kind of decision that the lawyer can or should make on her own? Even when making purely tactical decisions, the rules contemplate consulting the client, especially if they might affect the cost of the representation or have adverse effects on others.[5] More to the point: Is a decision about whether to pursue mediation merely one of means? Isn't the *way* in which a matter is resolved sometimes an important aspect of the client's overall goals? For example, the decision to obtain a divorce is clearly an objective to be decided by the client. But for a client seeking to minimize family pain, might not dissolving the marriage *by avoiding adversarial process* be an objective in itself?[6] Viewed this way, clients—not lawyers—ought to control such choices and should be advised about the choices in enough detail so they can make them in an informed way.[7]

In a few states, any doubt over this ends-means debate has been resolved by language in rules of professional conduct that urge, if not require, lawyers to present dispute resolution process choices to the client for consideration.[8] A lawyer practicing in such a state might therefore be subjected to professional discipline for failing to advise a client about mediation, even if she were convinced that it would be a complete waste of the client's time and resources. Is such a rule desirable?

Having elected to take a mediation course, you might be surprised at the need to regulate lawyers or promote ADR processes in this way. If so, consider a number of factors that may cause at least some lawyers to be hostile or resistant to mediation:

---

4. *See* Rule 1.2 of the Delaware MODEL RULES OF PROF'L CONDUCT in Appendix E, *infra*. Delaware's rules are in all substantive respects identical to the ABA Model rules.
5. Those rules note that lawyers usually defer to clients when such factors are present. *See, e.g.*, Delaware MODEL RULES OF PROF'L CONDUCT R. 1.2(a), 2.1 and 1.4 and Comments, in Appendix E, *infra*.
6. DAVID LUBAN, *Paternalism and the Legal Profession*, 1981 WIS. L. REV. 454, 459 n.9.
7. *See* Model Rule 1.4 Appendix E, *infra*.
8. *See, e.g.*, COLO. RULES OF PROF'L. CONDUCT R. 2.1; HAW. RULES OF PROF'L CONDUCT R. 2.1; VA. RULES OF PROF'L. CONDUCT R. 1.2 cmt. 1.

The Lawyer's "Standard Philosophical Map." In an often-cited 1982 article,[9] Leonard Riskin observed that most lawyers are trained to think in terms of zealous representation of the client and the traditional litigation paradigm, with its wins and losses, and focus on rights and duties instead of persons and zero-sum (usually money judgment) outcomes. Professor Riskin argued further that lawyers often tend to view non-material values (honor, respect, dignity, etc.) as irrelevant by themselves and reduce these values to mere amounts of money. Lawyers socialized to think this way put people and events into "categories that are legally meaningful" and discount the overall effects of litigated outcomes on relationships. "Many lawyers," Professor Riskin concluded, "therefore tend not to recognize mediation as a viable means of reaching a solution; and worse, they see the kinds of unique solutions that mediation can produce as threatening to the best interest of their clients."[10] What influences or factors might account for a lawyer's having such a view of legal conflict? To what extent is this still the prevailing paradigm in the legal profession today?

Lawyer-Client Conflicts of Interest. Conflicting personal or professional interests may also interfere with a lawyer's objectivity about process choices. Some observers point to the lawyer's billing arrangement with the client as such an influence.[11] In this line of reasoning, lawyers who charge by the hour are disinclined to promote a process that might end a dispute quickly. Those representing clients on a contingent fee basis may have differing incentives that lead them to steer their clients away from non-monetary solutions. (*"There is no one-third contingency fee in an apology."*)

Do you share this view of lawyers' ethics? Is a defense lawyer who prolongs a matter in order to "milk" its discovery or other hourly billing potential necessarily operating in his own best financial interests? Is it impossible for a plaintiff's lawyer to protect herself financially against her client's willingness to accept less-than-full monetary value in exchange for satisfying non-monetary interests?

Other Professional Inhibitors. A lawyer's resistance to mediation may also be explained by noneconomic concerns. Some lawyers feel inhibited by the presence of the parties at a mediation; they prefer conventional lawyer-lawyer negotiations. They enjoy the freedom to say less-than-flattering things about their own client to appeal to the opponent or paint their absent client as the "bad cop" to justify their own hard-line advocacy or, generally, to negotiate without being observed by their clients. They may also prefer it if the *other side*'s client is not there. As one lawyer put it in a study of Maine divorce mediation: "It's easy to be Tarzan over the telephone, it really is. . . . You can call my client a slut or a crook over the telephone, but it's real different to have the guts to do that when they're sitting across from you. . . . Not only do the norms of mediation diminish the most aggressive conduct by attorneys, but seeing the other side makes posturing more difficult. . . ."[12]

---

9. Leonard L. Riskin, *Mediation and Lawyers,* 43 Ohio St. L.J. 29 (1982).
10. *Id.* at 45.
11. *See, e.g.,* Charles B. Wiggins & L. Randolph Lowry, Negotiation and Settlement Advocacy 224 (1997).
12. Craig A. McEwan et al., *Bring in the Lawyers: Challenging the Dominant Approaches to Ensuring Fairness in Divorce Mediation,* 79 Minn. L. Rev. 1317, 1368 (1995).

Washington lawyer Deanne Siemer observes that lawyers may feel a substantial loss of control when they are required to mediate their client's disputes:

> In the normal litigation context, the court rules confer a certain power on lawyers to set schedules, propound demands, and force action on the part of the opponent. The [mediation] process appears to interfere with or suspend that control. . . .
>
> In litigation, the danger of the unexpected during oral presentations is rather limited. Court appearances are very stylized "discussions." One side speaks; then the other side speaks; then the judge decides. [Mediation] discussions can be quite free-flowing. They may wander into subjects having to do with what is really bothering one of the parties, perhaps covering ground not at issue in the lawsuit at all. The mediator or neutral evaluator can guide the discussion in directions that are unpredictable. . . . Lawyers who specialize in litigation . . . seek to avoid the unexpected. . . . [13]

Another factor, according to Siemer, may be the desire to avoid exposing the client to a process that invites his or her active participation:

> Both lawyers and clients perceive this as a danger. The client has hired a lawyer to speak for him or her. That protection may be stripped away when the mediator calls upon the client to state his or her own views. The lawyer, knowing the client's weaknesses, may be apprehensive that, no matter how much coaching is done, the client will expose those weaknesses during the . . . process to the advantage of the other side if [mediation] fails.
>
> Some clients are fairly unappealing as people. These attributes can be seen by the other side to some extent in the formal context of a deposition, but they may be more apparent during a free-format [mediation]. . . . This gives the opposing lawyer an additional opportunity to size up the jury appeal of the case and could cause the settlement price to go up. Lawyers believe that unattractive clients will affect the leanings of the mediator or neutral evaluator as to an appropriate outcome for a settlement, giving additional support to the other side. [14]

"The Devil Made Me (Not) Do It."   Finally, some lawyers claim that their *clients'* expectations make it difficult for them to propose mediation, even when they think a case may warrant it. The following summarizes a 1989 survey of lawyers' perceptions of what clients want and how the lawyers react to these client expectations:

> Our participants told us . . . [that b]y the time [clients] come to a lawyer they have already tried informal routes for resolving their troubles. They dislike coming to lawyers, and so they do it only after deciding that litigation — which is what we are known to do — is what they need to have done. Even though most people don't know how unsatisfying litigation can be, it is that expectation about what they need that brings them into the law office. And . . . clients often (always?) have an emotional need for catharsis, for vindication, for a day in court. Some clients even seem to want punishment for their adversary; and at the very least a clear-cut victory is often more satisfying than a "resolution."
>
> The lawyers respond accordingly: Particularly for the new client, the lawyer believes that he or she has to be the meanest S.O.B. in the valley, or the client won't

---

13. Deanne C. Siemer, *Perspectives of Advocates and Clients on Court-Sponsored ADR*, *in* Emerging ADR Issues in State and Federal Courts 169 (1991).
14. *Id.* at 170.

remain a client: "For you I'll kill. I do it all the time." To suggest ADR to a client may therefore be to appear incompetent or inadequate, or (even worse) to be saying to a client, who expects the full treatment, "Your case just isn't important enough."[15]

Are these lawyers' responses a case of circular reasoning based on a flawed premise? If lawyers fail to have explicit conversations with their clients about what they want, isn't there a danger that they will proceed based on what they assume about (or project on to) those clients? Might those assumptions be a product of the lawyer's urge to legitimize her own needs or "standard map"?[16]

How accurate do you think these lawyers' comments from the 1980s remain in this era of increased mediation use and client (especially those that have in-house corporate counsel) sophistication? If you think today's legal consumers are more savvy, what might be the consequences of *failing* to discuss the option of mediation with a client who is knowledgeable about such matters?

All of these comments suggest a scenario in which the lawyer is seeking to protect himself or his client from a settlement-oriented process he doesn't control. As students of the mediation process, you may find this troubling. But what about the reverse situation: lawyers who push or manipulate reluctant clients *into* mediation in order to enlist the mediator's support in overcoming the client's unreasonableness? Is this more justified? Why or why not?

Given this range of lawyer attitudes, we think that *how* a lawyer discusses ADR options with her client is more important than whether there is, or should be, a professional obligation to do so. "*Ms. Smith, let me tell you about mediation and why it's a bad idea in your case*" might fulfill a state-imposed advising duty, but unless it reflects an objective analysis of the pros and cons of using mediation in that matter, could poorly serve the client's interests.

Problem One: Counseling About Choice of Process

You are outside counsel for the University in the *Yanni* matter. Your designated contacts are Eric Binder, a young lawyer in the University's Office of General Counsel, and Adrian Winter, the University's Vice-President for Risk Management. Both are relatively new to their offices and to litigation of this sort.

You have a meeting scheduled this week with Mr. Binder and Ms. Winter. Because the University's motion for summary judgment in the *Yanni* matter was recently denied, you expect to be asked about next steps in the case. If you are asked about the possibility of mediation, what do you see as the considerations for and against? Prepare a checklist of points you would like to discuss with these client representatives.

---

15. EDWARD A. DAUER, *Impediments to ADR*, 18 COLO. LAW. 839 (1989).
16. Other lawyer-client dynamics may add to the difficulties in discussing settlement and mediation as a means to accomplish it. If, at the outset of a relationship, lawyers project great optimism about a victorious outcome in hopes of being retained by a prospective client, the client's inflated expectations may make both attorney and client more reluctant to discuss settlement and mediation at a later point in the representation. *See* BENNETT G. PICKER, *Navigating Relationships: The Invisible Barriers to Resolution, http://www.mediate.com/articles/pickerrelationships.cfm?nl = 209.*

■ §13.3 INITIATING MEDIATION

Problem Two: Proposing Mediation

Suppose that after a few minutes of discussion, Ms. Winter expresses considerable interest in mediation but asks *"If we propose it, won't it seem as if we're desperate to avoid a trial?"* How will you respond? If it is ultimately decided that you will initiate the topic with plaintiff's counsel, will you phone, write, or email? What *precisely* will you say?

The idea of proposing mediation to an opponent—especially to one who seems intent on gaining maximum advantage—is often unpalatable to lawyers who fear looking weak.[17] But is proposing mediation necessarily a sign of lack of confidence in one's case?

This question is more complex than may appear at first glance. Obviously, on the one hand, signaling a willingness to enter mediation implies some willingness to negotiate. On the other hand, in a "vanishing trial"[18] culture in which fewer than 5 percent of civil cases ever enter the courtroom and where managerial courts routinely pressure litigants to settle their differences, couldn't a proposal to mediate (if communicated well) be seen as both a statement of reality and even of strength and confidence? Is suggesting mediation any more "wimpy" than initiating conventional unassisted negotiations? Indeed, might it be less so?

Tactically, there may be ways of initiating mediation without appearing to do so. What do you think about the idea of contacting a judge, law clerk or provider of dispute resolution services and asking them to try to bring an opponent to the table? Would your response depend on whether the opponent knew (or could surmise) that you had initiated the idea? Would you feel comfortable doing this in a way that disguised your role in having the other side contacted?

When to Mediate.   At the conclusion of the successful mediation of a prolonged and costly lawsuit, clients are often heard to ask *"Why didn't we do this sooner?"* In other words, lawyers must not only grapple with whether and how to enter mediation, but also when. Some situations present little choice: Timing may be dictated by the terms of a pre-dispute contract clause between the parties or by a court's mandatory mediation rules. Other situations—a family business unraveling because of inter-generational squabbling, not-yet-public allegations of sexual harassment by the respected CEO of a major cultural institution—may seem (at least from one side's perspective) to call for mediating as soon as possible, before a lawsuit is filed and the dispute becomes public. For matters already in litigation, mediation tends to take place at moments of heightened (and shared) loss or risk aversion: just before a ruling on a motion that could end

---

17. According to a 2007 survey of corporate and organizational disputing, outside corporate counsel consider mediation their top ADR choice, but when they don't choose it, fear of "conveying weakness" is the most likely reason why. *See* 25 ALTERNATIVES TO HIGH COST LITIG. 98 (June 2007).
18. MARK GALANTER, *The Vanishing Trial: An Examination of Trials and Related Matters in Federal and State Courts*, 3 J. EMPIRICAL LEGAL STUD. 459 (2004).

the case, prior to discovery that will be costly in relation to the size of the case or on the eve of trial.

The timing — and often the delaying — of mediation can also be a function of deliberate strategy. Instead of considering mediation (or resolution generally) at the outset of a matter, some lawyers prefer to conduct a full-court litigation press early in the case to be able to convey a strong bargaining stance later, when the inevitable settlement talks do take place. (This can also play to the client's desire to inflict a degree of punishment on the opponent before being willing to let go of the conflict.) Such delays can also often be explained by the perceived need to complete sufficient investigation and discovery in order to be able to evaluate the trial prospects accurately prior to mediating. But as we've already seen, lawyers' heightened (and arguably irrational) needs to gain certainty and to avoid losses can lead them to conduct excessive discovery.[19]

When does a lawyer have enough information to make an adequate assessment of the case for settlement purposes? One commentator cites what he calls the "80-20" rule as guidance: The initial basic rounds of discovery cost only 20 percent of a potential discovery budget but typically yield 80 percent of the available relevant information. This, he asserts, should be sufficient to inform most settlement decisions.[20]

Would you feel comfortable going to trial based on that imperfect level of knowledge? If not, would you nevertheless feel comfortable settling (and advising your client to settle) the same claim on that basis? If your answers are different, what explains this? Are there ways (short of spending the other 80 percent of the discovery budget) to settle the claim, assured that no "smoking guns" are being concealed by your opponent?

This reason for putting off early mediation has been questioned by mediator Tom Arnold. He points out how the mediation process can itself be used to address concerns about missing information:

> Get and give critical discovery, but don't spend exorbitant time or sums in discovery and trial prep before seeking mediation. Mediation can identify what's truly necessary discovery and avoid unnecessary discovery.
>
> One of my own war stories: With a mediation under way and both parties relying on their perception of the views of a certain neutral vice president who had no interest in the case, I leaned over, picked up the phone, called the vice president, introduced myself as the mediator, and asked whether he could give us a deposition the following morning. "No," said he, "I've got a board meeting at 10:00." "How about 7:30 a.m., with a one-hour limit?" I asked. "It really is pretty important that this decision not be delayed." The parties took the deposition and settled the case before the 10:00 board meeting.[21]

---

19. *See* §2.7 *supra.*

20. Jeffrey M. Senger, Federal Dispute Resolution: Using Alternative Dispute Resolution with the United States Government 76-77 (2004).

21. Tom Arnold, *Twenty Common Errors in Mediation Advocacy*, 13 Alternatives to High Cost Litig. 69 (1995).

Problem Three: Choosing the Right Mediator

Assume that the parties in the *Yanni* case have agreed to enter mediation and that they prefer to choose a neutral rather than have one appointed by the court or by a private provider of such services. Several options have surfaced:

1. A lawyer-mediator who frequently represents plaintiffs and who has been proposed by counsel for the Yannis.
2. A retired judge who has presided over trials and settlements of hundreds of tort cases.
3. A lawyer-psychologist who practices mediation in family and employment disputes.

As counsel for the University, do any of these seem to be appealing choices? Who would be your first, second and third choice? Why? If you could specify the qualifications of an ideal mediator for the *Yanni* matter, what would they be? Why?

Selecting a Mediator.   Choosing an appropriate neutral to mediate the client's case is obviously a critical decision. Once a specific individual or a list of potential neutrals is identified, most writers on the subject view the lawyer as responsible for screening them via reference checking and, if possible, telephonic or even in-person interviews.[22] Topics of these (usually ex parte) discussions might include the candidates' preferred orientation/style, expectations concerning pre-mediation submissions, the duration and structure (joint vs. caucus) of sessions and their methods of dealing with threatened impasses. What role, if any, should the client have in the actual vetting process? What role should the client have in the final selection of a mediator? What considerations guide your answer?

Some writers urge the mediation representative to go further and use such interviews as an opportunity to begin to persuade or "spin" the neutral about their case and their opponent while developing rapport.[23] Do you see any problems in doing this?

■ §13.4 PREPARING FOR THE PROCEEDINGS

Deciding Who Should Attend.   In Chapter 4 we discussed the mediator's considerations for who must and should be present at a mediation in order to enhance the likelihood of a successful resolution. Each side's lawyer must make similar decisions, albeit from a partisan perspective and based partly on his or her overall strategy for the mediation, as discussed later in this chapter.

---

22. *See, e.g.,* BENNETT G. PICKER, *The Ten Most Common Mistakes Made by Mediation Advocates,* The Legal Intelligencer (Apr. 19, 2007).
23. *See, e.g.,* JERRY SPOLTER, *A Mediator's Tip: Talk to Me!* THE RECORDER 4 (Mar. 8, 2000).

Lawyers representing individual clients have few choices. The person whose complaint or grievance has triggered the dispute — and who thus is the one whose interests are at stake and who can end it — must be present. Mediations in which a resolution will turn on the continuation or resumption of a relationship require the presence of all who are needed to make the deal sustainable. But in some situations, additional participants may be desirable. What about a support person for the indecisive client who may need help in "pulling the trigger" on settlement at the end?

Organizational clients pose different considerations. The larger the entity, the greater the number of choices. Clearly, the party must be represented by someone with authority to resolve the dispute (or in some situations, the ability to speak with assurance about being able to get an agreement ratified). Beyond this, organizational parties can be represented or personified by many "types," depending on their role in the underlying dispute or in making the decision about whether to settle, and on the strategy for what is to be said at the mediation. Where the stakes are not seen as huge, it may be difficult to secure the presence of the busy person — the department head, the CEO, the board chair — in whom actual authority to settle may rest. What problems might be presented by such an individual's absence?

Regardless of the kind of client involved, where the stakes warrant it and agreement on a procedure can be reached, what about bringing in a key expert or other likely witness for an abbreviated preview of key testimony?

Problem Four: Who Should Attend?

Recall that in addition to representing the University in the *Yanni* matter, you represent the Dean for Student Life and the Director of Student Health as well. Of the following possible University participants, who should and who should not attend the mediation? Is there anyone *not* on this list who should attend? What considerations guide your answer? How large or small a defense contingent do you want at the table?

1. The President of the University. An extremely busy, charismatic, hard-headed former business school dean, the President has indicated that he would like to stay out of the case if at all possible and could only give a half day (at most) to the process.

2. The Provost of the University. A world-class classics scholar, the Provost (the University's second-in-command and chief campus administrator) is warm and empathic. She feels that what happened in the *Yanni* matter could have been avoided.

3. Ms. Winter. As head of the University's risk management effort, she has taken the lead in the early stages of this case and would ordinarily be the settlement decision maker for the institution. She is also the administrator who (together with the general counsel) coordinates the school's dealings with its peers over issues of mutual concern, such as exposure to suits like the *Yanni* case.

4. The Dean for Student Life. He is angry and upset that he has been sued and is strongly of the view that all RA training programs that he organized,

continues on next page >

> including the suicide training program, are "state of the art." (You have a very
> impressive expert witness who will support this.)
> 5. The Director of Student Health. Has feelings similar to those of the Dean for
>   Student Life but is more irascible and potentially uncontrollable. So far as she
>   is concerned, the phone call the RA placed gave no hint of any emergency
>   and, as a result, the response time of the return call was reasonable.
> 6. The RA. The RA has graduated and moved across country but presented
>   quite well at his deposition last year. Good combination of empathy
>   and insistence that Robert, while upset about his girlfriend, showed no
>   signs of severe depression, much less suicidal ideation. Told you after the
>   deposition that he "couldn't stand" plaintiff's counsel. Would rather not be
>   involved.

Deciding What to Submit and What to Bring.   By its very nature as a settlement device, a mediation is not a trial. Yet mediations in litigation-based disputes with counsel for all parties often take on certain attributes of trials. Whether
due to the lawyers' training in courtroom advocacy or the parties' expectation that
the mediator will adopt an evaluative style, legal argumentation tends to be the
dominant form of discourse, at least until information is expanded and non-
monetary interests are revealed. As a result, when there is time to prepare, the
stakes are high enough and the mediator is identified in advance, it is not uncommon for the lawyers to prepare partisan pre-mediation submissions to the neutral
and to plan for exhibits, documents and even witnesses that might be produced
during the proceedings.

Pre-Mediation Submissions.   Pre-mediation statements, or "briefing papers"[24]
as they are sometimes called, serve to educate the mediator about the dispute in
order to shorten his learning curve. For most lawyers, this conjures up the idea of
summarizing the case factually and legally. In this respect, the mediation brief
might resemble a shortened version of what might be filed in the trial. (Indeed,
some lawyers simply submit excerpts from court papers already filed in the
matter.)

Here is an excerpt from the defendant's pre-mediation submission in *Resnick
v. Stevens Realty*. (It is based on the submission filed in the actual case on which
Resnick was based.) By way of background: The insurance claims adjuster had
reluctantly given defense counsel total settlement authority of $75,000, but was
hoping to pay less, have the settlement be confidential (out of concern about
encouraging more litigation of this type) and conclude the matter this month
(so he could get credit for closing it in the current accounting period). On the
question of liability stemming from the intruder's entry into the plaintiff's apartment building, his (and counsel's) big concern was how a low-hanging fire escape
ladder would look to a jury. Moreover, Howard Stevens was very worried about

---

24. HAROLD I. ABRAMSON, Mediation Representation: Advocating as a Problem-Solver in any Country
or Culture 271 (2d ed. 2010).

heightened local publicity about a trial over an assault and security concerns in one of his buildings even if he won.

What do you think of the submission below? What were its author's objectives?

Defendant's Confidential Memorandum to the Mediator

This memorandum is for the mediator only, and is not to be disclosed to any other party in this matter.

The defendant views this case as yet another attempt by an overly ambitious plaintiffs' bar to stretch the law beyond its proper bounds and to make defendants, in this case landlords, the insurers against every bad event that happens to their tenants. Nevertheless, the defense is willing in good faith to seek an amicable resolution. . . .

Liability.   The plaintiff's liability case is extraordinarily weak. Under New Jersey law, landlords can be liable for harm caused to their tenants or customers when the harm is foreseeable, when the landlord knew or should have known of the risk and where the landlord fails to provide reasonable security. *See Trentacost v. Brussel*, 82 N.J. 214 (1980); *Butler v. Acme Markets*, 89 N.J. 270 (1982); *Clohesy v. Food Circus Supermarkets*, 149 N.J. 496 (1997). But the harm must be foreseeable; that is, based on the defendant's awareness or knowledge (actual or constructive) of the risk of injury. *See J.S. v. R.T.H.*, 155 N.J. 330, 338 (1998).

In this case, Stevens Realty had no reason to think that the building was unsafe. There was no such special risk and no such notice here. There had been no previous burglaries in the building. The building was not located in a high crime area. Bloomfield is a safe town, with a low crime rate. There is no evidence that anyone complained to Stevens Realty about unsafe or risky conditions in the building.

Moreover, we can only speculate how the burglar entered the building. The plaintiff has no more than attenuated inference to explain that. The roommate, who is not available, may have left the two exterior front doors open, because he did not have his key. There is nothing to indicate that the burglar somehow got access to the fire escape and entered through a fire escape window. Only one fire escape window was broken or open, and the glass from that window had fallen *out* onto the fire escape, rather than into the building, suggesting that the burglar may have broken it as part of his escape, but not as part of his entry.

More importantly, the building was well secured, with two locked exterior doors in the front, one locked exterior door in the rear and a locked door to the side courtyard. All the locks were functioning. The hallways' windows to the fire escape had sash locks. The record suggests that, rather than having any security defect, the front door to the building may have been left unlocked or propped open by plaintiff's roommate.

The plaintiff's case is further weakened by the plaintiff's contributory negligence. (Citations omitted.) The plaintiff permitted his roommate to leave the apartment door open, allowing the burglar simply to walk in. Under New Jersey law, if the plaintiff's contributory negligence is greater than the defendant's negligence, recovery is precluded. (N.J.S.A. 2A:15-5.1) (2004). In this case, the defendant has committed no negligent act, and the plaintiff's negligence in leaving his front door open was the height of foolishness.

In short, defendant has a strong case for judgment NOV, or for reversal on appeal, in the unlikely event that the plaintiff obtains a jury verdict.

Damages.   Being the victim of a burglary is always traumatic, and defendant sympathizes with the surprise and upset the plaintiff must have felt. But the damages sought here are way out of proportion to the injuries actually suffered. The plaintiff only lost $350 and an iPod. Thankfully, he was not physically hurt beyond some bruised wrists.

The plaintiff's claimed psychological injuries are highly speculative. The purported post-traumatic stress disorder (PTSD) did not begin until the plaintiff, a man in his mid-20s, had voluntarily given up his education and moved back to Long Island to live with his parents. Nor is it at all clear that the burglary caused the plaintiff to drop out of school. He had been an indifferent student at college and had not shown much ambition or direction in the years between college and enrolling at Rutgers. His purported depression could just as well have been brought on by the stress of having to be in school again or bad feelings from not being able to change the direction of his life. . . .

Negotiations.   Despite the foregoing, the defendant is interested in resolving this matter in an expeditious manner. It would be a nuisance to have to continue with it; $10,000 seems to be a reasonable sum for settlement.

———————————

Most evaluative mediators, expecting to assess the matter legally, would surely welcome this kind of information. But, from defense counsel's perspective, what other information, if any, might it have been useful to include?

Think back to the mediator's objectives for the early and middle stages of the process. If the mediator is to help resolve the conflict, she must be able to diagnose its real causes. If she is to engage in persuasion by other than mere legal evaluation, learning the parties' interests, potential flexibility and the history of previous attempts to resolve the dispute could be invaluable. If solution is to be achieved, the barriers that need overcoming must be identified.

Now ask yourself: As defense counsel in *Resnick*, would you feel comfortable revealing this kind of information in advance to the mediator? Would you (confidentially) disclose all of your concerns and settlement flexibility in your pre-mediation statement? On what might this depend?

When it comes to such disclosures, do you see the mediator as your client's ally? As an opponent? As something else? If the mediator, despite being neutral, is seen as a proactive agent of settlement at (almost) any cost, does the lawyer put his client at risk if he appears open and reasonable (as opposed to resolutely dug in) on first impression? (Recall the discussion in Chapter 12 of "leaked" confidences.) Or could that be an advantage?

Suppose in the *Yanni* case that University representatives — despite wanting to settle the case — were, in your judgment, taking an unreasonably inflexible position. Might this affect how much information you would be willing to share in writing with the mediator in advance, taking into account that you would also be sending the University's representatives a copy of your submission? Why or why not? Would you be comfortable calling the mediator and telling him this information behind your client's back?

Witnesses and Documentary Evidence.   A high-stakes, lawyered mediation sometimes includes the option of presenting witnesses, documents, exhibits and even video deposition excerpts for the mediator and opposing party to see. If the merits are hotly contested, winning the "battle of the evaluation" or persuading a stubborn and overconfident opponent may turn on preparing a mediation preview of the expected litigation proof. Consider this advice:

> Like trial, mediation has a *primacy* effect. The evidence and people whom the mediator actually observes tend to be more vivid, and thus have more impact on decision making, than data that the neutral merely hears about. Documents and the personalities of the people in the room are thus likely to have much more impact on a mediator than outside evidence. There is also a *melding* effect. When the mediator cannot personally observe a witness, she must place the person in a category ("nurse," "retired accountant," etc.), then make an assumption about how a fact-finder would react to a typical member of that group. . . . As a result, if you want a mediator to give full weight to a witness or piece of evidence, you must place it directly in front of him. . . .[25]

In addition, the mediation representative's planning ought to anticipate all of the issues — monetary or otherwise — that must be addressed for the matter to be resolved. Drafting a proposed settlement agreement or term sheet before the process starts can ensure that no important items are overlooked.[26] Is there standard language — a release from liability, a confidentiality clause, a dispute resolution clause — that the client would want to include in any agreement that is reached? If so, the representative seeking an efficient resolution ought to come equipped with that.

Much of this preparation advice to lawyers seems to assume that the neutral will adopt a law-driven, evaluative approach in mediating such disputes. Would you do the same kind of preparation when expecting to work with a facilitative or transformative neutral? Are there disadvantages to such litigation-style preparation? Might your investment in such planning efforts make it harder to get beyond adversarial positioning and narrow problem definition? It has been suggested that transactional lawyers, who are experienced in constructing business deals that build on the interests of their clients, make the best mediation representatives.[27] Does an emphasis on trial-type mediation presentations suggest that litigators can best represent clients in high-stakes disputes?

▪ §13.5 PREPARING THE CLIENT FOR MEDIATION

For litigators, preparing their clients to participate in an active way as witnesses in trials and hearings is considered a "fundamental duty of representation and a basic element of effective advocacy."[28] The same goes — perhaps even more strongly — for lawyers whose clients will take part in mediation. But this calls for an understanding of the various potential roles that a client may play during the

---

25. Dwight Golann, *How to Borrow a Mediator's Powers*, 30 Litigation 41, 46 (Spring 2004).
26. *See* Picker, *supra* note 22.
27. Jay Folberg, Dwight Golann, Lisa Kloppenberg & Thomas Stipanowich, Resolving Disputes: Theory, Practice, Law 317 (2005).
28. John S. Applegate, *Witness Preparation*, 68 Tex. L. Rev. 277, 279 (1989).

process. What are these? It may be helpful to recall Frank DiLorenzo in the *Wilson* matter and Josh Resnick, the plaintiff in the premises liability case.

- **Client.** Together with his lawyer, the represented party (or organizational party representative) is a member of a more or less coordinated team effort to achieve the client's objectives. This usually translates into an agreed allocation of responsibilities at the mediation table and a game plan for handling the unexpected.

- **Witness.** The client may be needed to "make the case" and, in doing so, play an important part in the persuasion effort, especially if there has been little previous information exchange. The opponent (and the neutral) may be using the mediation in part to size up the client and the mediation "testimony" he offers. This is especially so where key facts are disputed, damages are in doubt or subjective or restoration of a relationship is a possible outcome.

- **Negotiator.** Even with counsel present, the absence of formal rules and prescribed roles can turn the client into an active player in the bargaining, who can lead the dispute toward (or away from) resolution.

- **Final Decision Maker.** This is the fundamental role, inherent in the definition of mediation (and clienthood). Whatever other tasks he assumes during the proceedings, the client or its representative must decide whether to settle, and on what terms.

This combination of roles makes preparation for mediation different from, and arguably more complicated than, other processes in which the client may have previously taken part. Even clients who have been to mediation before may have experienced a different style of mediation than the one being planned for. Effective preparation of the client must therefore start with the basics: What will happen and what will the client be expected to do?

Problem Five: The Client's Role at the Mediation

Assume that it has been decided (regardless of your views in the previous Problem) that the President of the University and the Dean for Student Life should attend the *Yanni* mediation. You e-mail the President to propose it. After the President consults with general counsel, his administrative assistant calls you and confirms his willingness to attend. You then call the Dean. He seems anxious to be present, adding *"I'm looking forward to seeing these parents. First they pressure their kids to be perfect to meet some sick need of their own, then they sue us when the kids crack!"*

It is now two weeks later and you are to meet with the President and the Dean to discuss the roles that they (and you) will play at the mediation. What will you tell each of them? What specific tasks do you want them to take on? What, if anything, should they *not* do? For what will you take primary responsibility? Why?

The Client's Role: How Active? To What End? In What Tone?   In thinking about these questions, it may be useful to start with the conventional wisdom on how mediation differs from unassisted negotiation. By this point in your studies, these ideas will be familiar to you:

> When attorneys attempt to settle their clients' disputes without using mediation, the clients remain very much in the background. While the attorney is ethically required to obtain the client's approval for any settlement, the attorney typically negotiates the deal on her own, merely consulting the client occasionally. The client is not present for the negotiation and therefore is unable to hear firsthand what the other side's position is; experience the other side's anger; assess the arguments of the opposing attorney; explain the potential importance of non-monetary relief; voice his own feelings; or give or receive an apology.
>
> By contrast, in a mediation the client potentially can do each of these things and more, thereby enabling a settlement that would not otherwise have been possible. Mediation can permit the client to communicate directly with the opposing party and its attorney, and eliminate the erroneous transmissions that inevitably occur when one person acts as the agent for another.
>
> Usually mediation can serve this beneficial purpose only where clients are permitted to play an active role in the mediation. If a client attending the mediation does not express his or her own views in his or her own voice, neither the client nor the opposing party will secure many of the mediation's potential benefits. Where the attorneys "take over" the mediation and silence their own clients, they remove one of the mediation's primary potential benefits, recasting the mediation primarily as a negotiation among attorneys.[29]

These comments capture mainstream thinking on the desirable role for the mediation client, at least among mediation teachers and theorists. Do you agree with them? Do they assume certain kinds of disputes or disputants? Are there cases and situations in which the client's role and participation should be deemphasized and the lawyer's heightened? If so, what might these be? Note that mediations can be unpredictable and proceed in unexpected directions even with a mediator who is a known quantity. Assuming that a lawyer has planned to give her client a significant voice in the mediation, what situations arising at the table might warrant altering this planned division of responsibilities?

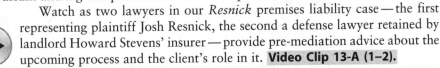 Watch as two lawyers in our *Resnick* premises liability case — the first representing plaintiff Josh Resnick, the second a defense lawyer retained by landlord Howard Stevens' insurer — provide pre-mediation advice about the upcoming process and the client's role in it. **Video Clip 13-A (1–2).**

Both lawyers departed from the conventional wisdom and prescribed rather limited client participation. (This is common in personal injury mediations.) Taking each lawyer separately, what factors might have accounted for their wanting to employ such a strategy? Was the strategy of each lawyer sound? Why or why not?

Managing the Client's Tone. You may also have noticed in this segment that defense counsel cautioned his client against displaying anger at the table. Was this good advice? Are there situations in which the display of a client's anger might be helpful?

---

29. Jean R. Sternlight, *What's a Lawyer to Do in Mediation?* 18 Alternatives to High Cost Litig. 1 (2000).

Many clients approach mediation with the same goal as they approach litigation: to win as much as they can. But of course a "win" in mediation is different from one in court. A favorable settlement is the presumptive goal here but, by definition, it can only occur with the assent of the other side. The other party is in the room and may be strongly affected not only by *what* you and your client say, but *how* it is said. The fact that one's client has elected to enter mediation may also create certain expectations concerning the kind of conduct that will be exhibited at the table.

Does it necessarily follow that mediation calls for a different (more civil? more gentle?) *style* of conversation, negotiation or advocacy than what is typically used in trials or unassisted negotiations?

Managing Client Expectations, Anticipating Client Reactions.   Here is a closely related point: Effective preparation often requires representative lawyers to *anticipate* their client's potential emotional reactions and cognitive distortions at the table, even when they are not displayed during pre-mediation counseling. Where the lawyer envisions strong client reactions — to the other side, the mediator or to specific topics or proposals that may come up — she may have to work with the client beforehand to protect him from behavior and decisions that he might later regret.

 Watch as two lawyers in our premises liability case prepared the plaintiff for the upcoming mediation. What were each lawyer's concerns? What do you think of each lawyer's counseling? **Video Clip 13-B (1–2).**

Problem Six: Establishing Settlement Authority

As defense counsel in the *Yanni* case, you will need to consult with appropriate University officials in order to obtain instructions regarding authority to resolve the matter at mediation. What will you discuss with them in establishing mediation settlement parameters? Will you press for a specific bottom line in advance of the mediation? Why or why not?

Obtaining Bargaining Authority.   A basic premise of entering mediation voluntarily is the idea that, under the right conditions, each side prefers a negotiated resolution to the litigation or other alternative. Preparing the client to mediate ought therefore to include at least some discussion of what those conditions are — that is, possible resolution parameters. This is necessary in order to get a sense of the client's overall goals (which may have shifted over the course of the representation) and to choose the negotiating approach most likely to accomplish them in the mediation.

Clients are often unrealistic about or unaware of what can reasonably be accomplished through mediation. Effective pre-mediation counseling should therefore include the lawyer's prediction of the costs, benefits and outcome of the court or other alternative, and invite the client's questions and reactions. It can also involve discussion of interest-based solutions that the client has not yet identified or may not have thought possible.

Where an organizational client includes factions that disagree on how the dispute should be resolved or where responsibility will lie for implementing or funding it, the representative may have to play a (mediative) counseling role in getting these "ducks in a row" so that the client and the lawyer can speak with one voice at the table. (Such decisions may also help determine who will actually attend the mediation.) Where possible solutions to the problem might require the approval of different constituents within an organization—for example, where resolution of a damages claim for a shipment of defective merchandise might also include an agreement to renegotiate the parties' existing supply contract—obtaining authority may require multiple consultations and sign-offs.

At the end of the discussion of possible resolution parameters, the lawyer can try to pin the client down to a specific bottom line or instead plan to enter the mediation with a more general and flexible sense of the range of acceptable outcomes, to be revisited in the light of what transpires during the proceedings. As a lawyer going into a mediation with a client, what do you think are the pros and cons of each approach? Which would you prefer? If you were the mediator in the *Yanni* matter, which kind of authority would you want the two lawyers to have obtained in advance? Why? Are there particular situations in which it may be crucial for a lawyer to get precise (rather than general) authority from her client before the mediation begins? What are they?

Watch as one of the plaintiff's lawyers in *Resnick* counsels her client regarding settlement authority. **Video Clip 13-C.**

Should this lawyer have tried to pin the client down more precisely? Or was her approach preferable? What do you think was motivating her counseling?

▶▶▶▶   **Preparing the Client for Mandatory Mediation: What Constitutes "Good Faith" Participation?**

You represent Patricia McDermott in a child custody dispute. Bitter litigation resulted in a divorce decree issued by the court eleven months ago under which Mrs. McDermott was awarded primary physical custody of the couple's two teen-aged daughters, ages thirteen and fifteen. Her ex-husband, Sandy, who lives three miles away, was granted overnight visitation rights with the two girls one night a week, usually on Fridays. He is now petitioning the court to modify the decree to allow him full weekend visits on alternating weekends. The presiding judge has assigned the case to mandatory mediation.

Your client's immediate response to the judge's mediation order is *"Over my dead body! As it is, Sandy takes the kids overnight barely half the Fridays he was awarded. If the judge orders this change, I'll have no choice but to comply. But I'll be damned if I will negotiate this voluntarily!"* You are fairly confident that Mr. McDermott's petition will be denied if the case goes to trial. As Patricia McDermott's attorney, how will you counsel her about attending and conducting herself at the mandated mediation? What exactly will you say to her?

As noted earlier, mediation is increasingly being required of disputants before they are permitted to invoke the power of a court or administrative agency to seek a compelled resolution. Mandatory mediation schemes, which have generally been upheld when challenged, commonly include the obligation to participate in "good faith." This obligation can pose considerable challenges for lawyers whose clients are

continues on next page >

opposed to participating. How does the lawyer prepare and protect such a client? What level of participation constitutes "good faith"?

Courts that have ruled on the subject have generally not required very much beyond the parties' attendance at the mediation, compliance with pre-mediation submission rules and, with organizational clients, ensuring the presence of someone with settlement authority. *See* John Lande, *Using Dispute System Design Methods to Promote Good Faith Participation in Court-Connected Mediation Programs*, 50 UCLA L. Rev. 69, 84-85 (2002). As with other areas of counseling, the lawyer thus has a wide range of choices in providing guidance. Would you be comfortable telling your resistant client that *"it's OK to show up and just say 'no'"*? Would it matter if there were research showing that, at least in the divorce context, disputants forced to mediate exhibit the same level of participation during the process and the same high level of satisfaction as those who mediate voluntarily? *See* Jessica Pearson & Nancy Theonnes, *Divorce Mediation: An Overview of Research Results*, 19 Colum. J.L. & Soc. Probs. 451 (1985). How, if at all, would your advice to Mrs. McDermott differ from what you would say to a similarly (and appropriately) confident businessman resistant to participating in a mandated mediation in a commercial matter in which he had been sued?

▪ §13.6 DEVELOPING AN OVERALL NEGOTIATION STRATEGY

Before the actual mediation begins, the lawyer representative and the client must formulate an overall strategy for the negotiation. This can be a difficult task, especially in situations where little is known about the mediator and the other side. Recall from Chapter 2 the two major strategic approaches available to negotiators:

- ▪ *Distributive* or *competitive* negotiation, characterized by tough "information bargaining" — seeking information to expose the opponent's weaknesses, interests or flexibility while hiding and manipulating information that might expose one's own — and negotiating about positions, including making high demands and making grudging concessions, in order to get the greatest share of the presumed "fixed pie" that is to be divided.

- ▪ *Problem-solving* or *integrative* negotiation, characterized by more open sharing of information and sometimes creative brainstorming, with the goal of discovering shared and differing interests that might facilitate value-creating trades and increase the size of the "pie" for everyone.

Recall also our discussion in Chapter 2 about how both strategic barriers (principally stemming from the fear of exploitation by a competitive opponent) and cognitive distortions (especially the assumption that "if it's good for them, it must be bad for me") often make it difficult for negotiators to engage in problem-solving negotiation, even when the problem being negotiated has real integrative potential. The result: inefficient or failed adversarial negotiations in which negotiators fail to discover each other's true interests or achieve optimal (or any) solutions to their clients' problems.

Note finally that strategy and style, while sometimes related, are analytically distinct and should not be confused with each other: One can employ a tough distributive strategy on a problem while maintaining a cordial, friendly interpersonal style; and one can have a pugnacious, aggressive demeanor while pursuing problem-solving ends.

However, our focus here is not on negotiations in general;[30] rather, it is on bargaining during mediation. The key questions in preparing for this setting are: Is this arena different? If so, how? Is there a general strategy or approach that should be followed in all mediation situations?

Some writers urge lawyers to take a problem-solving approach whenever they represent clients in mediation:

> You should be a persistent problem-solver. It is relatively easy to engage in simple problem-solving moves such as responding to a demand with the question "why?" in order to bring to the surface the other party's interests. But it is much more difficult to stick to this approach throughout the mediation process, especially when faced with an adversarial, positional opponent. Trust the problem-solving approach. When the other side engages in adversarial tactics or tricks — a frequent occurrence in practice — you should react with problem-solving responses, responses that might even convert the other side into a problem-solver. . . .
>
> For the skeptics [who think that problem-solving does not work for most legal cases because cases are primarily about money], I offer four responses.
>
> First, . . . [w]hether a dispute is largely about money varies from case to case. . . . Second, you have little chance of discovering whether your client's dispute is about more than money if you approach the dispute as if it is only about money. Such a preconceived view, backed by a narrowly focused, adversarial strategy, will likely blind you to other parties' needs and inventive solutions. . . . Third, if the dispute or any remaining issues at the end of the day turn out to be predominately about money, then at least you will have followed a representation approach that may have created a hospitable environment for dealing with the moneyed issues. A hospitable environment can even be beneficial when there is no expectation of a continuing relationship between the disputing parties. Fourth and most important, the problem-solving approach provides a framework for resolving moneyed issues. . . . If [the usual problem-solving initiatives] fail, you might then turn to a traditional positional dance . . . that has been refined to serve a problem-solving process by focusing on objective standards and justifications while avoiding tricks.[31]

What do you think of this as an across-the-board prescription? Is it realistic? Does every negotiated dispute have significant problem-solving potential?[32] What if your client insists that she is not interested in cooperative problem-solving,

---

30. Those who want to learn about effective negotiating skills generally might consult any number of excellent texts on the subject. Among them are Donald G. Gifford, Legal Negotiation: Theory and Practice (2d ed. 2007); Gary Goodpaster, A Guide to Negotiation and Mediation (1997); Roger Fisher & William L. Ury, Getting to Yes (2d ed. 1991); Melissa L. Nelkin, Understanding Negotiation (2d ed. 2003); Howard Raiffa, The Art and Science of Negotiation (2005); G. Richard Shell, Bargaining for Advantage: Negotiation Strategies for Reasonable People (2d ed. 2006); Robert H. Mnookin, Scott Peppet & Andrew Tulumello, Beyond Winning: Negotiating to Create Value in Deals and Disputes (2000).

31. Abramson, *supra*, note 24, at 6-7.

32. Most legal disputes do, at least in theory and as a partial solution. For example, in the *Resnick* mediation, did Mr. Stevens, the landlord, own any desirable rental properties in the Long Island

wanting instead to obtain the most advantageous distributive outcome possible? Even when representing a flexible client in a case with problem-solving potential, is it risky to begin with and persist in using a problem-solving strategy when dealing with a stranger (or a possible "trickster")?

If a one-size-fits-all negotiation strategy for all mediations strikes you as a bit utopian, the question remains whether strategic planning for mediation is any different from strategic planning for conventional, unassisted negotiation. We think so, at least in this respect: *Effective mediation representatives plan in advance ways to enlist the neutral's help in resolving their clients' disputes.*

Planning to Use the Mediator.   Recall the basic definition of the mediation process — *assisted* negotiation. If negotiations were likely to succeed without assistance, mediation wouldn't be needed in the first place. In planning a mediation strategy, then, the guiding questions — regardless of whether your client is seeking maximum personal gain, optimal mutual benefit or something in between — are: What difference could the presence of a mediator make? How can I enlist the neutral to assist me in accomplishing my client's goals? How might the presence (and hoped-for help) of the mediator affect my own behavior and that of my client?

Before the process starts, this means:

- Attempting to identify existing barriers to resolution and communicating them to the mediator. In doing this, the representative should be open to the possibility that her own judgment or conduct or that of her client is itself posing a problem, at least as viewed by the other side. (A perceptive mediator will, of course, add her own diagnosis later, including barriers to which you or your client may be contributing without realizing it.)

- Thinking in advance about information you are willing to share with the mediator, even if you are not willing to share it (at least not yet) with the other side, and how and when you will do so.

- Thinking in advance about ways to use the mediator as a conduit of information: as a carrier of signals or messages to the other side or as a source of indirect information about the other side's flexibility.

Problem Seven: A Plan for the *Yanni* Mediation

Assume that you have the University's reluctant authority to settle the *Yanni* case at mediation for up to $2.5 million on a confidential basis. You also have broad authority to propose other possible integrative solutions, including those that might address the possible psychological needs of the Yannis so long as they don't raise the total settlement cost to the University — for example, a privately funded scholarship or suicide prevention program in their son's name. You have not responded to Plaintiff's $12 million demand. From their depositions, the Yannis

---

community to which Josh Resnick had subsequently moved? A problem-solving lawyer or mediator might inquire about this. *See, e.g.,* Carrie Menkel-Meadow, *Toward Another View of Legal Negotiation*, 31 UCLA L. Rev. 754 (1984).

seem to be different people at different moments: aggrieved, guilt-ridden parents who seem non-litigious; passive clients easily led by their lawyer and his self-righteous, angry accusations.

Based on what you know, what are the major considerations that come to mind in planning an overall negotiating strategy to be used in representing the University at the *Yanni* mediation? Specifically:

a. What are the likely principal barriers to resolving this matter? How can mediation overcome them?

b. How open will you be at the outset, both to the mediator and to the other side, about your client's interests, potentially harmful information or your settlement authority?

c. What might your opening offer be, and what factors would influence that decision?

d. Will you make your first offer in person or through the mediator in caucus? On what factors does your answer depend?

■ §13.7 AT THE TABLE: REPRESENTING THE CLIENT'S INTERESTS[33]

Problem Eight: Party Opening in *Yanni*

Outline the content of the opening statement that will be given for the University at the *Yanni* mediation. Who will deliver it? What kind of tone should be struck?

The Parties' Opening Statements: The Lawyer as Sword? Successful advocacy at the beginning of mediation requires appreciating the impact that the lawyer's and client's initial statements can have on the audiences present. Consider these views regarding the appropriate tone for lawyers and their clients to strike in the opening stages of mediation and who the primary audience is:

> . . . [T]here is a need for the opening presentations to clearly and effectively communicate the "other side of the story" to the opposition. Many clients to a dispute might be quite pleased with a lawyer that relieves built up feelings and relates their positions in ominous, scolding, or even threatening terms. An overly

---

33. Lawyers who represent clients in mediated disputes do not always appear at the bargaining table. In certain kinds of cases, state laws or judicial rules may preclude representative counsel from attending mediations with their clients. *See, e.g.*, South Dakota Codified Laws §25-4-59; Montana Code Ann. §40-4-302(3). Divorcing parties, seeking to save costs, often mediate without lawyers present and instead hire lawyers to play the role of nonattending consultant on future negotiation moves the client might make. In other cases, divorcing parties consult with their own lawyers at the end of the process as "review counsel" to review the proposed agreement and advise whether to sign it, suggest revisions, etc. What is the appropriate role of such a "review" attorney? To compare the *substance* of the agreement to the likely alternative court outcome, factoring in costs, time and possible ill will engendered by not signing? To ensure that the *process* that produced the agreement was a fair one? Can a reviewing lawyer properly advise the client about any of this without having investigated the facts herself or having observed firsthand the other party and the actual mediation process?

aggressive tone or demeanor to an opening presentation in a mediation, however, can serve to "turn off" the opposition and the critical task of expanding their understanding of the dispute is not achieved. . . .

Accordingly, the best overall theme and tone of opening presentation in mediation would probably be a matter-of-fact-description of the case to be presented at trial—firmly and unequivocally stated. It should clearly set forth the principal contentions underlying the position asserted, and the facts, principal documents, and expert opinions that support those contentions. There should be minimal argument—let the facts do the arguing. . . .[34]

. . . The "judge" or "jury" you should be trying to persuade in mediation is not so much the mediator as the adversary. If you want to make the other party sympathetic to your cause, most often at least it is best not to hurt him. For the same reason, plenary sessions should demonstrate your client's humanity, respect, warmth, apologies, and sympathy. Stay away from inflammatory issues, which are better addressed by the mediator in private caucuses with the other side.[35]

Both of these commentators see the opposing party as the principal audience in the opening session. Are there situations in which you would view the mediator as the main opening-session audience? If so, what are they?

Assuming that trying to persuade the neutral is one of your objectives, what approach is most effective? Consider this advice:

Your strongest ally, if you can make him or her an ally, is the mediator. It is the mediator's neutral voice that is most powerful in carrying your argument to the other side. This is true even if the mediator asks a lawyer to put on the chalkboard the strongest points of the case, then unveils the board to the other side.

The mediator knows you . . . are trying to manipulate, or con, him or her. Manipulation is as much a given as the coffee machine. But often—perhaps usually—the mediator is aware of the con. Good advocates know when to stop the con, show some trust, and make a straighter, and more reasonable, argument. Honesty can buy an advantage.[36]

Regardless of who the primary audience is, all three commentators counsel the lawyer to make temperate presentations at the beginning stages of a mediation. Are reasonableness and honesty always the best policies at the outset? Are there situations where using early hardball tactics might be wiser? Can you imagine a scenario where "hanging tough" might actually help in making the mediator an aide in achieving resolution?

Watch as one of the lawyers representing plaintiff Josh Resnick makes an opening statement together with his client. **Video Clip 13-D.**

What message do you think the lawyer was trying to send? Was it successful? Why or why not? Assume that there is a good defense argument that Josh was contributorily negligent in allowing his apartment door to remain unlocked at the

---

34. Lawrence M. Watson, Jr., Effective Advocacy in Mediation: A Planning Guide for a Civil Trial Mediation, *http://www.summitsolutions.us/resources/Watson_Effective_Adv.pdf.*
35. Arnold, *supra* note 21, at 69.
36. Robert M. Smith, *Advocacy in Mediation: A Dozen Suggestions*, 26 San Francisco Atty. 14 (June-July 2000).

time of the assault. If you were representing Josh, would you have mentioned this in your opening? Why or why not? If so, in what words?

Now watch opening remarks on the question of damages by a defense lawyer in the *Resnick* case. (It comes after a discussion of liability issues and a statement by plaintiff's counsel in which she likened her client's condition to the post-traumatic stress flashbacks suffered by combat veterans of the Vietnam War.) **Video Clip 13-E.**

What were this lawyer's likely objectives in this statement? Were they accomplished? If you had been defending Stevens Realty, would you have delivered these messages differently? If so, in what words?

In contrast to these two lawyer-dominated openings, clients sometimes take the lead in making opening statements, even in cases involving lawyers. For example, you may recall the *Wilson* case, in which, after plaintiff Bernice Wilson presented her opening, defense counsel sat back as his client, Frank DiLorenzo, related the entire defense opening with almost no attorney interjections and then summed up: "*I think that tells DiLorenzo's side of the story. I am comfortable with having Frank do that, and we are ready to proceed.*" Were there any reasons to treat Howard Stevens's role in the *Resnick* opening differently from Frank DiLorenzo's role in *Wilson*? What are the variables that make one or another approach advisable?

Protecting the Client: The Lawyer as Shield?   If presenting a client's case in a manner that takes maximum advantage of the process is part of the representative's role, lawyers in mediation must often play a defender role as well. Starting with the opening session, this obviously involves the effort to rebut contested assertions and neutralize any overreaching by the other side. Those who represent clients who are vulnerable or disadvantaged in terms of their bargaining ability know this role well. But the role of protector can also take the form of making sure that the mediator does not place the client at a disadvantage. This can occur when mediators apply excessive pressure or try to bypass the lawyers and draw the parties directly into the discussion under circumstances in which the lawyer would prefer to control matters.

Watch these four video excerpts from the *Wilson* and *Resnick* mediations. Was each lawyer's intervention advisable? Effective? If not, why not? What, if anything, would you have done differently as the lawyer in these situations? In the excerpts involving Josh Resnick, could pre-mediation client preparation have obviated the need for these interventions on his behalf? **Video Clip 13-F (1–4).**

■ §13.7.1 ENLISTING THE MEDIATOR'S HELP IN THE BARGAINING PROCESS[37]

Mediation representatives whose clients seek to gain maximum advantage have little choice but to bargain competitively (although not offensively). Those whose

---

37. The content of this section draws on the authors' experiences and, in considerable part, on DWIGHT GOLANN, *How to Borrow a Mediator's Powers*, 30 LITIGATION 41 (Spring 2004). This practitioner-oriented article is recommended in its entirety.

clients have more flexible or problem-solving goals are also usually inclined to begin the negotiations competitively to avoid exposing their clients to an opponent's possible exploitation. But while this may be a rational initial strategy, it can erect barriers to resolution and create a risk of impasse. Can mediators be helpful in mitigating some of these strategic and psychological barriers to settlement? If so, how can lawyers enlist that help?

Relying on the Mediator as a Calming Influence?   Contrary to much of the conventional thinking about mediation representation, some view mediation as a safe place to bargain aggressively — safer even than in conventional negotiations — because the parties are generally too invested in the process to leave quickly, and the mediator can be expected to hold things together in case they begin to fall apart. As Dwight Golann puts it:

> [A] mediator can "scrape the other side off the ceiling" when they erupt at their opponent's unreasonableness. Lawyers sometimes take advantage of this dynamic to play tough cop, knowing that a good mediator will instinctively take on the good cop role and cushion the impact of a tough bargaining strategy to keep the process alive.[38]

Can a representative be sanguine that all neutrals have such good instincts? Some less savvy mediators might respond differently — for example, by failing to see through the tactics and aligning themselves against the more aggressive party or even by terminating the mediation prematurely. What about the opposing party's likely reaction? Some opposing lawyers might not be counted on to act as a calming influence or respond well to the "good cop" interventions of the neutral. Finally, what are the pros and cons of a "bad cop" approach if the other side is unrepresented?

Using the Mediator to Send Signals of Flexibility.   Generally in a tough distributive negotiation, neither side wants to be the first to take the risk of acknowledging case weaknesses or signaling a willingness to be flexible — information that might be useful in breaking the cycle of competition. Can the mediator help with this?

Negotiators who are flexible or who seek a problem-solving outcome may be able to resolve the tension between competing and cooperating by pursuing an aggressive stance publicly while signaling cooperation in private — that is, by confiding in the neutral that their tough stance will be softened upon some assurance of mutual cooperation. Given the likelihood that the neutral will be inclined to leak this to the opponent, such a strategy might also include trying to shape exactly what the mediator will say to the other side.

Watch as a defense lawyer in *Resnick*, after refusing for an hour to budge from the offer she had made prior to the mediation, does this. Were defense counsel's "marching orders" to the mediator sufficiently clear and concrete? **Video Clip 13-G.**

Using the Mediator to Disclose Interests and Float Ideas.   A similar approach can often be used in situations where revealing undisclosed interests

---

38. *Id.* at 43.

might be seen as undercutting a strong position taken, typically on a zero-sum issue like a plaintiff's damages claim. One example would be a fired worker seeking lots of money in back pay for alleged discrimination but who is reluctant to reveal her real interest in being rehired by the defendant employer. Confiding these interests to the mediator and asking the mediator to float them to the employer as hypothetical (mediator) ideas could allow the negotiator to engage in problem-solving efforts without compromising his "official" stance.

Seeking Information and Guidance from the Mediator Before Bidding. Distributive negotiators hate to make concessions in an informational vacuum. On the one hand, they want to avoid overpaying (or accepting too little) by misreading the other side's intentions or needs. On the other hand, they may be concerned about alienating the opponent and jeopardizing the chances of resolution by over-looking psychological needs or maintaining too aggressive a position for too long. Those with problem-solving goals have similar informational needs. All basically come down to wanting to learn more than they know about the opponent before they make their next move. Typically, negotiators want to know:

- whether a particular demand or offer is likely to help or harm the negotiations;

- how best to couch a particular proposal;

- whether now is the right time to make a move;

- what the other side might accept or be interested in;

- whether it is time for the clients or the lawyers to talk to each other alone; and

- whether/when it is safe to disclose flexibility or undisclosed interests.

If the mediator has spent time in caucus with the other side or has received a revealing pre-mediation submission from them, she may be in a good position to provide, at least indirectly, the information that is sought.[39] Most lawyers want the mediator to do just that if it will assist the negotiations. As one commentator observes:

> In practice, most lawyers designate very few facts as confidential and appear to expect a mediator to reveal at least some of what is said in private caucuses. You might, for instance, tell a mediator, "At this point, $500,000 is as low as we'll go. You can tell them 500." The neutral might well interpret that to mean he could tell the other side that you were reducing your demand to $500,000, and also that he saw you as probably willing to go further if you received an appropriate response. A mediator, in other words, usually feels able not merely to report what a party is saying but also to give an *interpretation* of its intentions.[40] (Emphasis added.)

Sometimes lawyers seek such assistance directly, asking the mediator for specific guidance on the next offer they should make, rather than for general information about the other side. Watch such an interchange between one of

---

39. We discussed the ethics of this kind of indirect leaking of confidential information in Chapter 12.
40. GOLANN, *supra* note 37, at 45.

the defense lawyers in *Resnick* and the mediator. At the point you are observing, the plaintiff was demanding $90,000 to settle the claim, and the last defense offer was $30,000. **Video Clip 13-H.**

On what might a mediator have based his guidance to defense counsel? The other side's last demand? His sense of a next step that would keep the momentum of the negotiations going? His view of a "fair" final result and the next offer that would be most likely to produce it? If you were the mediator, would you have answered the lawyer's questions as this one did? Would you have answered them at all?

Note three things about seeking a mediator's bargaining guidance: First, to the extent that you act on a mediator's advice, you are substituting his judgment for your own observations concerning the other side's mood, resolve or on what would be an appropriate next move. Second, you are trusting the mediator not to be manipulative or biased. Third, as Professor Golann has noted, if you use the mediator in this way, there is every likelihood that the mediator will "take this as permission to provide the opponent with the same kind of information about you." Therefore, he advises, you should "[d]iscuss with the mediator what he will say to your opponent about you, and identify any information you do not want communicated."[41]

Using the Mediator to Overcome Cognitive Barriers.   As we have seen, neither side to the dispute is likely to view it objectively. To the contrary, their assessments of the facts, the law, their chances of prevailing and the reasonableness of their proposals are likely to be impaired by biases that make them overconfident, if not unrealistic. We have also seen how negotiators face the risk that what they have to say and offer will be heard in a distorted way by the other side. Solely by virtue of their status as "opponents," their otherwise fair, accurate or even generous ideas and offers will be reactively devalued. Finally, the parties' ability to process information and make decisions in a rational way may be compromised by other forces — for example, loss aversion, which can lead to rejection of offers that "should" be accepted. As representative counsel, how can you use the neutral to minimize the potential impact of these cognitive distortions on the bargaining process?

First, of course, you must be aware that these distortions may be at work. (As readers of this book, you should be by now.) Second, having identified potential cognitive barriers, you can turn to the only person in the room who can trade on dispassion, distance and trust — the mediator — and can ask him to communicate things to the other side that are likely to be discounted if you said them yourself. This can take the form of asking him to convey your proposals as his own ideas or to vouch for offers you want to make. Third, you can solicit the mediator's efforts — through evaluation or other forms of persuasion — to help the other side see the dispute or assess a specific proposal more realistically. Most neutrals welcome such requests and appreciate being provided with the ammunition with which to carry out these tasks.

There are other variations on the theme of using the mediator to overcome barriers to settlement. How might you enlist the mediator's help if the

---

41. *Id.*

overconfident or loss-averse party is *your own client*? What if you sense that the other party is being realistic about her chances of prevailing or is potentially interested in an attractive offer you have made but that *her lawyer*'s judgment and advice on these topics is getting in the way of progress?

Seeking Help to Avoid Deadlock.   Parties who maintain a tough competitive stance throughout the negotiations — by not budging much from their initial positions — may find themselves nearing the end of the mediation quite far apart yet still holding on to considerable negotiating authority. Even though both sides may want to reach an agreement today and neither has walked out, no one is willing to make the final leap needed to avoid impasse. Assuming there is an actual overlap in the parties' authority, terminating the mediation without a deal would represent a bargaining failure.

Mindful of this, with the clock winding down, mediators or client representatives may begin to use the scarcity of time to accelerate concessions. As the threat of an impasse looms, the representative looking to settle but not wanting to make another public concession might ask the mediator to try to break the apparent deadlock by employing one of two confidential gap-closing devices we saw mediators initiate in Chapter 10. (To review, see Video Clip 10-H.)

In the first, a lawyer might ask the mediator to provide both parties a "take number" — the mediator's proposal for resolving the case based on all the information he has learned in public and private sessions (and possibly his own evaluation of the matter). In *Wilson*, we saw one of the mediators do this of his own accord.

As a second impasse-breaking strategy, the representative lawyer might ask the neutral to obtain, in confidence, both sides' bottom lines (or, at least, a considerable concession) in hopes of producing significant progress, if not a deal. (We saw a mediator-initiated example of this in *Resnick*.) The mediator can then announce that a settlement is attainable (i.e., there is a bargaining zone given the parties' overlapping bottom lines) or, if there is no current overlap, whether, in his view, there has been sufficient narrowing of the gap in positions to warrant continuing the mediation.

If one of these devices will be employed, the client (presumably after being advised by his lawyer) then has to decide what to do: whether to accept the recommended settlement or, in the second scenario, how to proceed — overlap or not. Can you think of reasons why a lawyer (with the client's assent) would turn down a mediator's "take number" even though it is, in fact, acceptable to the client? Are there reasons why, despite the fact that the device is confidential and the client wants to settle the matter at mediation, a lawyer might lie about his client's bottom line and reveal less than his total authority?

■ §13.7.2 SUGGESTING CHANGES TO THE GAME

Negotiating impediments cannot always be overcome by eliciting these kinds of interventions from the neutral. Despite the fact that mediators are said to be "in charge of the process," situations may arise in which the conventional mediation model or a mediator's process decisions are not meeting the challenges of the dispute. This creates an opening for the representative lawyer to suggest modifications to the existing format—even unconventional ones—that might work better for the client or enhance the chances of resolution. For example:

- Are plenary sessions not working? Perhaps the mediation should be conducted entirely by caucus (or vice versa).

- Is the lawyers' stormy and distrustful relationship hurting the process? Maybe the lawyers will agree to leave the room and make themselves available to the client-negotiators only for private consultations. Conversely, if the parties are the problem, maybe the lawyers should talk alone for a while.

- Does the mediator's expertise fall short in some way? Maybe he can be asked to bring in a consultant or co-mediator with complementary expertise.

- Is the believability of a key witness the sticking point? Perhaps a mini-trial can be held to assess the witness' condensed testimony, with the parties' decision makers present.

For many representative lawyers, the notion of "creating your own sundae" in these ways is foreign: They are used to a rule-bound litigation system in which virtually every step—from pleading, motion and discovery through trial and appeal—is prescribed by rule. Despite all of the action in litigation, trial lawyers are rather passive players, at least when it comes to control of the actual procedures. Mediation, by contrast, is free from such rigid constraints. With very few exceptions, the process can be tailored to each situation, limited only by the participants' collective imagination.

■ §13.8 CLOSING THE CIRCLE: PROCESS PLURALISM REVISITED

As the above discussion and video excerpts from *Resnick* suggest, effective mediation representation requires the lawyer to take an active part in shaping the process. Such active representation in a hard-fought dispute might include seeking to confer with the neutral at key moments and asking him to do things—carry messages, make proposals, answer questions, massage or interpret information in desired ways, give hints, evaluate—at points in the mediation when the neutral might not have thought of doing so himself.

Is there a cost to using the process and the mediator in these ways? It would seem so. Such advocacy generally requires dealing with the mediator privately. In a heavily caucused approach, the parties rarely see and speak to each other. Important communications are delegated to the neutral, and the parties must rely on his recommendations and feedback in order to make the next bargaining move. Much of the available information is also filtered through the mediator, to be conveyed, reframed, translated or distorted. Lawyers who use the mediator in these ways appear to be ceding almost total control over the process—and even the shaping of the outcome—to the neutral. On the surface, this seems at odds with much of what mediation claims to add to the world of dispute resolution.

Yet, when given the opportunity, sophisticated lawyers deliberately choose mediators who are effective at doing such things, because they are aware of the barriers to resolution that are present in their clients' disputes and want to enlist the neutral's help in overcoming them. (Those same savvy advisors will also recognize situations where a more open, party-driven process is called for and will seek a mediator who is adept at conducting that kind of proceeding.) For them and the neutrals they enlist, the goal of furthering the disputants' objectives outweighs strict adherence to any particular process model.

And so we complete the circle, returning to the main theme of this book: Sound judgment and decision making in the mediation arena — by providers and consumers alike — require an appreciation for the diverse ways in which the process can effectively be conducted and an ability to apply that knowledge to the unique circumstances of each dispute. We hope that this text and its interwoven video case studies have provided you with an understanding of these choices and of the unique contribution that mediation can make in improving communications, restoring relationships and resolving difficult conflicts.

VIDEO CLIP TRANSCRIPTS
FOR ANALYSIS*

Chapter-by-Chapter Menu

Where it appears: M = Mediator; P = Plaintiff; PL = Plaintiff's Lawyer; D = Defendant; DL = Defendant's Lawyer; A = Attorney.

CHAPTER 6 CLIPS

Clip 6-A: Mediator Opening: Child Custody Case

(Sam Rossito, in Fitzgerald v. Fitzgerald)

Sam:	Mr. and Mrs. Fitzgerald, I am Sam Rossito. It's nice to meet both of you. Please call me Sam. How would you like me to address you?
Bob:	Bob is ok.
Jane:	Jane is fine.
Sam:	Ok. They just give me a little bit of information before we begin and I know you have a daughter and a son but they didn't tell me what the names of your children are, but it would be nice for me to know ...
Jane:	Megan and Ryan.
Sam:	Megan. Ok. So before we began, I think it's real important to talk a little bit about what this process is to make sure that this is something that you want to participate in and that you fully understand what the process is about. Ok, so let me just, I know

---

* This appendix contains transcripts of all DVD tracks appearing in the Chapter-by Chapter menu, beginning with Chapter 6. Chapter 3 contains "play all" video clips (3-A and 3-B) whose transcripts are too lengthy to be reproduced here. Any deviations between the transcript and the actual DVD are unintentional.

that you have signed agreements to mediate, but I just want to talk about it a little bit more. And also to give you an opportunity to ask questions of me or any questions of the process.

Jane: Ok.

Sam: So, for the most part what mediation is, it's really an informal process to see perhaps whether or not you can resolve this dispute before someone like the judge would resolve this for you. And when I say informal, like there is no one here taking down, a stenographer or anything or anything like that. So, it is just an informal conversation to try to understand this problem a little bit better and maybe we can come up with some ideas that maybe you can work this out in a way that really does work for the two of you.

Now, let me tell you what I am not. I think that's a good way to understand my position. First of all, I am not a judge. This isn't about you tying to convince me or telling me, you know, what's important for you and why you think you are right, because I am not the decision maker. I'm really here as a facilitator to help the two of you to discuss this, to maybe understand probably a little bit more, help you carve out an agreement. So, I am not the decision maker here. And by the same token, what I am also not is, I not an advocate for either of you. I am not here to protect one person against the other person, or if I think that one person may, in my opinion, be giving up something they shouldn't be giving up, I'll take their side. That is not what this is about. It is really about the two of you trying to come up with something, if you want to, that might resolve this. So essentially what I am considered would be a facilitator to facilitate the discussion.

Now, if you reach an agreement about the matters that are presented here, then that would be written down and you would sign that and that would be how this matter is resolved and then we could just present this the judge and that would become what is called your custody order. And if you don't reach an agreement, that is ok, what will happen is it will go to the next phase, which means it will go before the judge and the judge will make that decision. Many people find that by working this out together without having a judge do it, gives you a little bit more control over it. You don't know what the judge is going to decide. The judge might decide something that neither of you want. So this gives you an opportunity to work it out. The other thing you might want to keep in mind that if you do work this out — I mean your children are young, they are three and five, you have a lot of years ahead of you to deal with each other, so perhaps if you can work out the matters that are in front of us today without intervention of a court then perhaps it will kind of set the tone of the future when other matters come up and hopefully you will be able to work them out too without getting courts and lawyers involved . . .

Sam:	Ok, great. Now would you like to establish any rules in a sense of how you want to talk to each other? Let me give you an example. I sort of gave an example before. Some couples like to say 'well you know what, I think it's a good rule that one person speaks at a time' and I could sort of enforce that or at least remind you if you start to talk at the same time. You don't have to have this rule, it's just a possibility.
Bob:	If we don't do it that way I don't think that anything is going to get done here.
Sam:	So we will have that rule and if I see it, then I will sort of remind you if I see things happening. And again, it's very natural to just want to say something just as you feel it. But, sometimes it's not the best way of understanding what is happening with the other person. Let me give you an example of some other rules people use. You may or may not want to use them because it may not be your style. Some people don't like to use curse words. Some people want to keep the volume down. And it may just depend upon your style, what works for you. You know, maybe things that have worked for you in the past that you may want to introduce as way of setting rules for how you want to talk about things.

Clip 6-B: Ice Breaking and Mediator Self-Introduction

1. (Craig Lord, in Wilson v. DiLorenzo)

Mediator:	Based on the papers I see here, I can sort of guess that you are Bernice Wilson, is that right?
Ms. Wilson:	Yes, I am.
Mediator:	Which one is Mr. DiLorenzo?
Mr. DiLorenzo:	I am.
Mediator:	And you are Mr. Bowen?
Mr. Bowen:	Yes.
Mediator:	Good morning.
Bowen:	Good morning.
Mediator:	Well the most important question is, did you have a nice weekend?
Wilson:	Um, not really.
Mediator:	Not really?
Wilson:	No.
Mediator:	Well, we can take some steps today make your week better than your weekend then hopefully.

Mediator:	How about you, Mr. DiLorenzo?
DiLorenzo:	I'm good, thanks.
Mediator:	Ok, Mr. Bowen, you had a good weekend?
Bowen:	Yes, of course.
Mediator:	Good, ok. You know, it was a little difficult for me to get here today. The rain just tied up the traffic. I can't believe how that traffic just gets tied up in center city. Did you have any problems in getting here?
DiLorenzo:	No, you know, we left plenty of time. I had my coffee, good to go. Good to go. Thanks for asking.
Mediator:	How about you, Ms. Wilson?
Ms. Wilson:	I had all the same traffic I think you did.
Mediator:	Ok, alright. Well, again, we'll make it better by coming here today.

2. **(Judith Meyer, in Wilson v. DiLorenzo)**

Mediator:	You are all here. Well, first let me tell you, um, I've met Mr. Bowen before. He and I, I work as a full time neutral, so that you know that. I am here because Small Claims Court has referred this case to mediation and apparently if we don't, we've got ninety minutes to work on this more or less, but when the Court is ready, he'll basically tell us that he is ready and if the case isn't settled, he'll be eager to have you in front of him, but I've met Barry because I work as full time neutral on other cases in arbitration that we did involved in a partnership dispute and Barry and I in fact, sometimes see each other at Bar conferences because we are both very interested and into alternative dispute resolution theory and practice, so I need to tell you that. Are you ok with that? Can we use first names? Is that comfortable?
DiLorenzo:	That's fine.
Wilson:	That's fine.
Mediator:	And you can call me Judy. . . .

Clip 6-C: Describing the Process

1. (Cheryl Cutrona, in Wilson v. DiLorenzo)

Mediator:	Good afternoon everybody. My name is Cheryl Cutrona and I am going to be your volunteer mediator today. Um, I understand that you have chosen to mediate your dispute prior to your scheduled court date, is that correct?
Wilson:	Wonderful, wonderful.

Ms. Wilson:	Correct.
Mediator:	Ok, and you have about, somewhere between and hour and hour and a half before you have to go into the courtroom, if you don't settle here right?
Mr. Bowen:	Right.
Ms. Wilson:	Correct.
Mediator:	Ok, well then let's get started. Have any of you ever been in mediation before?
Bernice:	No, I haven't.
DiLorenzo:	No.
Mr. Bowen:	Yes.
Mediator:	Yes? Well, good. So you know a little bit about it. Let me tell the other folks just how it works. Ok? Um, mediation is a voluntary dispute resolution process during which the parties try to find a mutually agreeable outcome to whatever the situation happens to be that brought them here today. If you reach an agreement, I will help you put it into writing and a copy of the agreement will be given to the judge so that he can incorporate it into his court order, so it will have the same effect as a court order.
	As a mediator I consider everything that is said in here today to be private and confidential. What that means is I won't repeat anything that I hear outside of this dispute resolution program. It also means that I will not be willing to testify in court in regard to this case.
	The mediation process that I prefer to use involves giving each of you uninterrupted time to present your perspective on the situation. After that we will discuss the situation, clarify the issues. Um, I have provided some paper and pens for each of you so that if you think of something that you want to say while someone else is speaking you can just take some notes to remind you what you want to say when it is your turn to speak.
	There may come a time during the process where I will want to speak to each of you privately; that is called a caucus. Um, the caucus has a sort of an extra layer of confidentiality. Anything that is said to me during that time will not be repeated to other side unless you give me specific permission to do that. Other than asking you respect each other's uninterrupted time at the beginning of the sessions, I don't really have any ground rules for the mediation session, but I would like to ask you if there is anything that would make you feel more comfortable today . . .

2. **(Chuck Forer, in Resnick v. Stevens Realty)**

   M: Now, I have read the papers that your lawyers both provided
                           to me and they both did a very, very good job about telling
                           me about the case and telling me about their side of the case.
                           But in the next couple hours, I really want to hear not only
                           from your lawyers, but also from you because you brought
                           the case and you're defending the case and my guess is that
                           you have something you want to say and get off your chest
                           and I bet you you have something you want to say and get off
                           your chest. So in the course of this afternoon, I'm really
                           looking both to your lawyers and to you to tell me what this
                           case is about and why you believe your side is right and why
                           the other side is wrong.

Clip 6-D: Touting the Advantages of Mediation

1. **(Craig Lord, in Wilson v. DiLorenzo)**

   Mediator: I think that you both made a wise choice by agreeing to
                           participate in this mediation program. You may or may not
                           know, we've had a great success rate here. We've had a
                           success rate well over 75%, and I think that's because people
                           come in here and they realize that going to court is really
                           rolling the dice and if you come in here and you can talk
                           things through in a calm, relaxed fashion, you have a lot
                           better chance of getting a result that you can live with. If you
                           go to court, what usually happens is somebody walks out of
                           there very unhappy. Here we hope to get you to a point
                           where you walk out of here and you are just a little bit
                           unhappy, not really unhappy. So that is our objective and of
                           course, I am doing this — I am volunteering for this because I
                           really believe this is a much more effective way of resolving
                           disputes than going to court and that's why I'm volunteering
                           my time, and I don't get paid for this or any other
                           compensation.

2. **(Sam Rossito, in Fitzgerald v. Fitzgerald)**

   M: ... And if you don't reach an agreement, that is ok, what
                           will happen is it will go to the next phase, which means it will
                           go before the Judge and the Judge will make that decision.
                           Many people find that by working this out together without
                           having a Judge do it, gives you a little bit more control over
                           it. You don't know what the Judge is going to decide. The
                           Judge might decide something that neither of you want. So
                           this gives you an opportunity to work it out. The other thing
                           you might want to keep in mind that if you do work this

out — I mean your children are young, they are three and five, you have a lot of years ahead of you to deal with each other, so perhaps if you can work out the matters that are in front of us today without intervention of a court then perhaps it will kind of set the tone of the future when other matter come up and hopefully you will be able to work them out too without getting courts and lawyers involved.

3. **(Harris Bock, in Resnick v. Stevens Realty)**

M: The most, I think, valuable thing that mediation brings, in my view and in my experience, has nothing to do with money. One of the most valuable things that a mediation brings is resolution. We're all most concerned in our lives with things that we don't know what the future's going to be, are anxious about, don't know how it's going to turn out, and that's what a lawsuit is all about for people. You really don't know how it's going to turn out. You really don't know what the result's going to be and it produces a great deal of anxiety because of that. You think about it when you get up sometimes, think about it when you go to sleep sometimes. It's just something that's there and nagging at you and doesn't go away. Well, today we have a special window of opportunity. We have this time to try and get together and try and be realistic, to try and take that and put that aside. *(To Plaintiff)* Resolving the case is not going to make you better, you know, and make everything perfect all of a sudden, but resolving the case will say, "Well, I've completed that aspect of the matter. I've accomplished that. Now it's time to close the book on the matter and move on with my life."

Clip 6-E: Describing the Mediator's Role

1. **(Cheryl Cutrona, in Wilson)**

M: My role as a mediator is to just facilitate the discussion, clarify the issues, and help you find a resolution. If you do reach an agreement, like I said, I will help you put it in writing. I am not a judge, I don't make a ruling or predict the outcome of your case if you go to trial. Um, and while I am an attorney, I am not here to offer legal advice or representation. I don't take sides or evaluate your positions or anything like that.

2. **(Judith Meyer, in Wilson)**

M: I am not here as a fact finder, a law giver, a judge. If we do not consensually, if you do not consensually come to a resolution, then this case will go its normal course to trial and possibly appeal, but my job and your job really, your job with my help, is to try to come to a consensual resolution here, one that you have control over, one that you have input into, one that works for you, one that makes sense and one that doesn't lead to some else's idea of whatever justice is.

3.   (Sam Rossito, in Fitzgerald)

M: First of all, I am not a judge. This isn't about you tying to convince me or telling me, you know, what's important for you and why you think you are right, because I am not the decision maker. I am really here as a facilitator to help the two of you to discuss this to maybe understand probably a little bit more and maybe help you carve out an agreement. So, I am not the decision maker here. And by the same token, what I am also not is, I not an advocate for either of you, I am not here to protect one person against the other person, or if I think that one person may, in my opinion, be giving up something they shouldn't be giving up, I'll take their side. That is not what this is about. It is really about the two of you trying to come up with something, if you want to, that might resolve this.

4.   (Harris Bock, in Resnick)

M: First of all, my name's Harris Bock and I've been practicing law for thirty-two years or so and I was very involved in litigation, probably for the first fifteen years. But, for the last fifteen years or so, I've given my entire time to try and resolve cases in a more reasonable way. . . . And from that experience, from my daily work I have a fair amount of expertise with regard to issues that are involved in cases, and valuations that take place with regard to cases. My job is to assist you, the parties, in terms of sharing some of that expertise with you, trying to help you to understand what goes into a valuation of a case, why lawyers and other people who value cases, do so in a way. That is primarily my job because the attorneys on both sides, not that they don't know about this because they do know about it and that's what they do on an ongoing basis, but they see things as your attorney. They see things on your behalf. I see things on behalf of everybody. I'm the only one here that is looking at the matter somewhat objectively. Third party who has some knowledge of the case and going to be assisted with some additional knowledge of the case, and I look at it objectively and I have those clear glasses without Plaintiff side on it and without Defense side on it, to help and assist you with regard to resolving the case.

Clip 6-F: Establishing Ground Rules

1. **(Mary Hanna, in Fitzgerald)**

   M: One of my ground rules, if you don't mind my referring to it in that way, is to ask each of you to speak and allow the other the opportunity to complete their thought or complete statement without interruptions. So that is why I have provided note pads and pencils for you so that if you have a concern or you perceive a particular situation differently than the other then you make a little notation and we can come back to that rather than just having an outburst. That sometimes happens. These are very emotional issues, I understand that. But it is very helpful for me to be able to hear one of you at a time. . . .

   Finally, I prefer that you describe your relationship and your concerns about the children in terms of your own experience, your own feelings. Sometimes we refer to these as "I" messages: that "I feel" a particular way, "I am upset" that such-and-such has happened, rather than blaming one another. I think frequently, we tend to cast the responsibility away from ourselves. And if you try to think of your concerns for the children in terms of your own reaction that would be particularly helpful to me.

2. **(Sam Rossito, in Fitzgerald)**

   M: Ok, great. Now would you like to establish any rules in a sense of how you want to talk to each other? Let me give you an example. I sort of gave an example before. Some couples like to say 'well you know what, I think it's a good rule that one person speaks at a time' and I could sort of enforce that or at least remind you that if you start to talk at the same time.

   Jane: That's a good rule.

   M: You don't have to have this rule, it's just a possibility.

   Bob: If we don't do it that way I don't think that anything is going to get done here.

   M: OK. So we will have that rule and I will remind you of it if I see things happening. And again, it's very natural to just want to say something just as you feel it. But, sometimes it's not the best way of understanding what is happening with the other person. Let me give you an example of some other rules that people use. You may or may not want to choose from them because it may not be your style. Some people don't like to use curse words. Some people want to keep the volume down. And it may depend upon just your style, what works for you. You know, maybe things that have worked for you in the past that you may want to introduce as way of setting rules for how you want to talk about things.

Clip 6-G: Describing Confidentiality

1.   (Don Weinstein & Jean Biesecker, in Fitzgerald)

Jean: One of the really, I kind of think neat things about the mediation process is that it creates an opportunity, kind of a safe haven for moms and dads to come together and have a conversation without any of your conversation being recorded. Notice that this is a little bit different, probably than a court room, even if you've never been in a court room yourself, maybe on TV you've seen that. Um, so that we don't have stenographers here, you know taking down your conversation. We don't have anyone here with a tape recorder taking down our conversation. And as a result of that, it creates a real private opportunity to talk with each other about whatever the concerns are that bring you here today around your children. And because of that, we know that you really have your children's best interest in mind here. And so you've, you're looking to this process to help you create some type of schedule, I'm assuming, for you to see your children. Um, and so talking again about kind of the privacy of this process, means that it's confidential. And because it's confidential, Don and I don't make any reports to the court about what your conversation is here. The only thing the court's going to know after our time together is whether or not you reached an agreement. . . .

There are some exceptions, though, to the confidentiality and I think those were reviewed in the mediation agreement. I just want to make sure you're clear about what those are. Primarily, the confidentiality provisions have to do with safety issues, and protection issues, both for your person as well as property. So that if Don and I hear conversation or if we believe there's a viable threat made by one person to the other, then we have an obligation to report that. The same way, if we believe that we, that there's conversation we hear and any child may be at risk, we have an obligation to report that. And that also extends to damage to any personal property, or your home where you're living or your car, whatever. Other confidentiality provisions have to do with Don and my notes. They cannot be used, ah, in court. You can't request us to come to court and testify about conversations that occurred here today. And you can't request us to bring any of our notes. To the extent that we may, you may have brought paperwork here to the mediation today and you had that before you came in, that you could certainly use at any subsequent hearing. And again, that's to kind of protect this process, so that you're going to have the freedom to perhaps talk and have a conversation with each other that you may, prior to today, not have had an opportunity to do. OK?

2. **(Chuck Forer, in Resnick)**

M: At some point we may break up into what we lawyers or mediators call caucuses, and in those caucuses I'm going to be meeting individually and privately with one side or the other. So I might meet with you and your lawyer, or I might meet with you and your lawyer. Both when we're all together and in the caucuses themselves, everything that we say and everything that we do is private and confidential. Let me, let me make sure you understand what that means. First, if we meet in a caucus where I'm just meeting with you, I will ask these folks to leave the room, so it will just be the three of us and we're going to talk and we're going to let our hair down. In the course of that caucus, I may ask you questions. You may ask me questions. I may say things. You may say things, but I want you to understand and I want to assure you that anything that takes place in a private caucus stays within the three of us. If you say something to me, it will only stay with me and I will not repeat it to the other side, until and unless you let me do that.

In fact, typically what I do is I will in a sense rehearse with you what I'm going to say and how I'm going to say it. Why is that important? That's important because in my experience I find that if people can really be truthful and if they can really be honest and if they can really be frank, we can make a lot of progress. And I believe that people can be frank and truthful, not only with their attorneys but with me, if they have that hundred percent assurance that what they say to me will not go to the other side.

But we're also going to be confidential when all five us are meeting, and what that means is that anything that we say and anything that we do today can't be communicated outside this room. Yes, there's some exceptions. If one of you tries to beat up the other person or if we enter into an agreement and one side decides that he or she isn't going to follow that agreement, but by and large, everything that we say and everything that we do today is confidential. What that means is, if you offer a billion dollars to settle this case and you turn it down because you want two billion dollars, you can't later on outside this room and to someone else, say to someone or say to the judge or say to the jury or say to anybody, "He offered me a billion dollars. That shows that he thinks he had a pretty weak case." And nor can you say that if he demands fifty-seven cents to settle this case, nor can you use that fact at any later point to say, "He must have a pretty lousy case, if all he wants is fifty-seven cents."

Clip 6-H: Inviting the Parties to Speak: Forms of Questions

1.   (Cheryl Cutrona, in Wilson)

Mediator:	Alright, well um, Bernice since you are the initiating party what I would like to do is have you have your uninterrupted time first, and like I said if you have any, you know what I didn't give you paper did I?
Barry:	Well, Frank can share mine.
Frank:	We're ok, we're ok.
Mediator:	Ok, ok.
Frank:	Thanks.
Bernice:	Alright, ok. I found DiLorenzo and Sons in the Yellow Pages. Um, I was looking through, wanted to get my kitchen remodeled, found them in the Yellow Pages. They had a big ad, "licensed, bonded, and insured." I thought that was a great thing, called them. A gentleman by the name of Sam contacted me, set up an appointment to come out and give me a consultation. Came out to my home, gave me a consultation, drew a drawing of my kitchen of what the renovated kitchen would look like. The renovations would include new cabinets, using my existing appliances — my stove, refrigerator, the sink and faucet — then I would get a new floor, a linoleum floor, as well as four foot track lighting across the ceiling with three cans in it, he called them. They are like round lights. Um, I agreed with that. At that time I chose the type of cabinets I wanted. He left me — and I chose them from samples that he had — he left me additional samples for the linoleum floor and for the counter top that would be installed, because I wasn't sure exactly which colors I wanted at that time. He said the contract would be sent out to me. He quoted me a price at that time of $7,995.00, I agreed with that price.

Um, on August 22nd I received the contract. At that time I had to pay a $500.00 deposit, which I did, and um, at that time I also called the office and let the secretary know what my choices were for the counter top and what my choices were for the linoleum, so that I wouldn't be holding anything up. I was told that initially, during the initial consultation, that work would take about two weeks. When I received the contract, it said that it would take four weeks. Ok, it's a little discrepancy there, but I was fine with that. And I was told by Sam that work would begin within a week. A week went by, and I didn't hear anything. I let ten days go by, and didn't hear anything so I called to find out what was going on. I was told that the cabinets weren't in yet, so that they couldn't start. They didn't begin work on home until October 1st. . . . |

2. (Craig Lord, in Wilson)

Mediator:	We all agree that the kitchen is not done, is that in dispute?
Mr. Bowen:	That's not in dispute.
Mediator:	OK.
Mr. Bowen:	It would be done if she would just let us in the house; I mean, we're only minutes away.
Mediator:	OK. There's no—we are just trying to see what's in agreement. Ok, the kitchen is not finished. Now, is there a dispute, Mr. Bowen, about whether the contractor agreed to complete the work in four weeks?
Mr. Bowen:	Well, if possible, we try our very best and I'm sure Mr. DiLorenzo will tell you that there were circumstances here that prevented that from happening. It certainly wasn't our intention to inconvenience Ms. Wilson and, uh, we did try and would try to get it done very quickly now.
Mediator:	When did the work begin?
Ms. Wilson:	Work began October 1st. Now, I understand, I was told that they couldn't begin work until the counter tops, till the cabinets were delivered, excuse me.
Mediator:	I just want to stop you for a minute.
Ms. Wilson:	Yes.
Mediator:	Counsel, is there any dispute as to when the work started?
Mr. Bowen:	No, there is no dispute about that.
Mediator:	All right. Now, Ms. Wilson, I want to go over a couple of things with you.
Ms. Wilson:	Yes.
Mediator:	Why don't you just tell me in your own words what the basis of your complaint is here.
Ms. Wilson:	Um, I hired DiLorenzo and Sons to remodel my kitchen. Um, I wanted to have my kitchen remodeled so that I could entertain in my home more often. August 22nd, actually I should go back and say that after I called them, a gentleman came out and gave me a consultation, I selected cabinets, um, he measured my kitchen and drew a sketch of what the remodeled kitchen would look like. I liked what he had done, I liked the estimate and the figure that he came up with. I agreed to go with them, he left me samples for the linoleum floor and for the laminate counter top. Um, because I couldn't choose at that time, I wasn't exactly sure what colors I wanted, and then he said they would get back to me with the contract. They got back to me with the contract. At

that time, August 22nd, I signed the contract and paid the $500.00 deposit. Um, and I was told the work would start within one week of me signing the contract, by Sam. And, um, that at that time I also called the office and let the receptionist know what laminate I wanted, what counter top I wanted and what flooring I wanted so that I wouldn't hold up any process. Signed it, got all that information in. Um, work was supposed to start in a week. Work didn't start. Ten days later no work started.

3. **(Don Weinstein & Jean Biesecker, in Fitzgerald)**

Don: As I've mentioned before, the process really begins with getting some snapshot of where things are, why you're here. You're here for child custody. Not for any other issues.

Jane: Yeah.

Bob: Right.

Don: Um, how do you see that issue? Very briefly, what is it you're hoping will be accomplished as part of the discussion today? And then what we'll do is go on to elaborate further, and then discuss options, and then bring closure by developing some memorandum.

Bob: Well, I would hope we could just come to an agreement about custody and visitation.

Jane: I'm hoping that the children can finally come home and then work out with as much access as schedules permit. You know, I'm most upset that they've been taken from their home where they live.

Clip 6-I: Represented Parties: Who Should Speak?

(Chuck Forer, in Resnick)

M: I have read the papers that your lawyers both provided to me and they both did a very, very good job about telling me about the case and telling me about their side of the case. But in the next couple hours, I really want to hear not only from your lawyers, but also from you because you brought the case and you're defending the case and my guess is that you have something you want to say and get off your chest and I bet you you have something you want to say and get off your chest. So in the course of this afternoon, I'm really looking both to your lawyers and to you to tell me what this case is about and why you believe your side is right and why the other side is wrong. . . .

M: But before we can go around the room, is there anything about these ground rules or anything about what I've just said that troubles you, that you have a question about or that you feel that in some way you can't follow?

PL: Yes.

M: Okay. What's your problem?

PL: I'm very uncomfortable with the idea that this is supposed to be an exchange where the clients themselves are talking to each other about the case. I don't feel that it is appropriate and I don't feel that it's helpful to put Josh into a position where he's talking, not simply about how he's doing and what his plans are, but actually revisiting right now before the group assembled here the night of this assault on him and have him talk about it and have that be productive in any way.

I understand that what we're here to do is to talk about money because ultimately what drives cases on both sides is money and I'm more than happy to engage in good faith in the process of talking about our strong points and our weak points, their strong points and their weak points. But I don't see this as a forum in which it's appropriate to ask Josh now to talk about why he's brought this case, as though he — as though he's privy to all the information, all the depositions.

M: That's fine. You know, I understand exactly what you're saying, and let me — let me respond in a couple respects. First, as I said at the outset, everything that we're doing today is voluntary. I can't force you and I can't force your client to do anything and if you feel uncomfortable at any time, or if you don't want to do something that I suggest, just respectfully say no and I'm not going to force you to do it. . . . I just want you to understand that I don't want you to do anything that makes you feel uncomfortable. If you feel comfortable, by all means, you know, let us hear what you have to say and if you feel comfortable doing that only in confidential session with the three of us, because remember you may well have that opportunity, by all means do that. But in no sense do I want to force you or ask you to do something that is going to make you feel uncomfortable. Do you feel comfortable with that?

PL: Um, with what you just —

M: Yeah, and with how we're going to proceed. Yeah, I mean you had a concern and I think I responded to your concern. Do you feel comfortable with that?

PL: I feel comfortable with the position that I made clear to you.

Clip 6-J: Listening for Diagnosis

(Don Weinstein & Jean Biesecker, in Fitzgerald)

Bob:	How am I supposed to trust you to give them back when I bring them over?
Jane:	Because you're treating me the way you know you reacted! And that's not fair!
Bob:	I didn't react any way.
Jane:	Yes, you did. You took them.
Bob:	You put an order on me. I had every right. That order was gone, there wasn't even anything legal! I ...
Jane:	But you could have asked me! You could have! I could have packed their clothing.
Bob:	Wait a minute, hold on here ... I could have moved in after June 30th again ...
Jane:	You could have!
Bob:	Right ...
Jane:	And you didn't want to!
Bob:	Oh no? Oh, that's not true.
Jane:	And you even ...
Bob:	Oh, no, no, no, no ...
Jane:	I just thought you were going to come back and you didn't!
Bob:	What do you mean, you thought I was going to come back?!
Jane:	Because the order was over!
Bob:	You didn't want me back, you made that very clear—
Don (M):	(*trying unsuccessfully to interrupt*). OK ... OK.
Jane:	How do you know? You didn't even ask ...

Clip 6-K: Exchange

(Cheryl Cutrona, in Wilson)

Mediator:	Ok, is there anything you would like to add?
Barry:	No, I think that tells the DiLorenzo side of the story. I am comfortable with having Frank do that and we are ready to proceed.

Mediator:	All right. Is there anything you would like to say in response?
Bernice:	Um, I agree that there was a total lack of communication, but one thing and I understand that we are in mediation to work this through and I am trying to table my anger. I'm trying so hard but I went through this, he did not go through this. I dealt with other people, not him. You know what I mean? Even though it is still the same company, you are the owner of the company, still, I didn't deal with you and you weren't involved from the onset of this until now. . . . Because what I don't understand is yes, I understand a fire is beyond your control, it is completely beyond your control, but all of your business didn't stop, so if this is the place where you always get the counter tops from, this is the place where all of your stuff comes from, then you should have been there to be able to receive my phone calls because you had no work.
Frank:	No, that is not true.
Bernice:	You know what I mean.
Frank:	No! Bernice I said to you that I do a lot of business.
Bernice:	Right, you have a lot of jobs.
Frank:	It's not always, it's not all just kitchens and this and that, but I had other things going on. Those counter tops and things were ready. Let's communicate now, let's fix it. Let's fix it.
Mediator:	Well tell us, you said that you know, "I went through this, he didn't." Say some more about that.
Bernice:	Well I went through . . .
Mediator:	Went through what?
Bernice:	I went through making fifty million phone calls, cause see, the thing that really kills me is that had my check bounced, had the money not been there, you better believe I would have received a phone call. Had my answering machine not worked and the check bounced, they would have been sending me a letter in the mail. It would have been a certified letter in the mail. It could have been a sheriff at my door, could have been anything. So those things to me, my answering machine did not—for, on Connie's behalf one day, the tape wasn't working. One day. Same day I fixed that tape, but like you said, you weren't there, you didn't have the conversations with me, like I said, you weren't there.

Clip 6-L: Active Listening

1. (Sam Rossito, in Fitzgerald)

Jane: Um, we made an agreement before we got married. It was something that we both agreed that we wanted children and that I would stay home to raise them. I have a small part-time business that I do out of the home. And that was a choice that both of us made. Um, I am available. Now when Bob says that he wants custody it's really his mother having custody. That's not something that I am comfortable with. The children need to live in their home, ok, where they were born. That's where all their things are. That's where all their friends are and I already have the time available to take care of my children. We don't agree on how that care is. He says they have a much more structured environment. It's one more of fear rather than joy and play. Um, his mother does not deal well with kids. Yes. His mother does not deal well with children. Um, she's — when he says the house is immaculate, the woman has a fetish when it comes to cleaning. You can't even leave a crumb anywhere. They do not feel comfortable to play. They never used to like going there. They love their grandpa. I mean your dad is an amazing guy, but your mom is a problem. And don't look so shocked. You know that. . . .

Jane: But on the weekend . . .

Bob: Can I talk just for a moment?

Jane: No, not right now. You are going to get your chance. That's why you are writing notes. So, I mean, I'm not comfortable with them living in South Philly as a primary place for those reasons. I know that Bob has issues with my parenting which he has made abundantly clear. I think what it comes down to are different styles. I come — both of my parents worked so, the way that my sister and I were raised was much more — my mother always said and maintained that dust and dishes were always going to be there but the opportunity for you to interact and have fun with your children when they are little is fleeting. So I didn't dust today? I'll dust tomorrow. So I put a puzzle together with the kids today. That's more important than dusting. That's more important to me. If you want a "Leave It to Beaver", I can't do that and I never maintained to do that and I will not do that because I am not your mother. And the way that our children are raised they are much more happy and they are wonderful children. And Megan is going to be fine. The pediatrician says there is no problem and that if she continues to have speech problems by second grade and I told you all this. It's gone in one ear and out the other. If second grade, she continues to have a speech problem, then we will look at a speech pathologist. But right now he believes that children develop at their own pace. And with Ryan in diapers, you know, it's not that I have not been concerned about these things too. I have talked to the pediatrician, the person who is trained to know how these things work and he said don't be worried, boys train later than girls and he'll be fine. He'll show an interest. Don't push it. That's the worst thing you can do. And, um, that he's— nobody goes to college in diapers with a bottle. You know, no one goes to first grade with diapers and a bottle. He will be fine. To let him advance at his own pace.

Sam: So let me just kind of get a sense of what you are saying. What it sounds like what is important for you, Jane, it sounds like it is important for Bob to know that you sort of made a decision as far as having a different style of being with the children in terms of housekeeping. And that you could spend more time cleaning and all that but you feel that that will take away from your time to be with the children, the joyful moments and things like that.

Jane: Yes.

Sam: So you feel that you have a different parenting style than his mother . . .

Jane: Yes.

Sam: You feel that if they were with his mother, it may be clean, but it they wouldn't feel. . . .

Jane: Relaxed.

Sam: Relaxed and playfulness and perhaps, love.

2. **(Cheryl Cutrona, in Wilson)**

Bernice: The next time I heard from them, from October 8th, the next time I heard from a work person, a workman or anyone from DiLorenzo and Sons, except for the 19th when the secretary called to say the counter top would be ready in a couple days, was on October 31st when they wanted to come in the next day and finish the job. And I told them no. Thank you but no thank you. And it was Connie that I spoke with, I believe that's her name, the secretary and we had a very heated discussion. And I explained to her all of my concerns and I felt as though I was speaking on deaf ears because she wasn't the person in charge. And I hadn't heard from Sam again. So I didn't know what had happened to him, it was like he fell of the face of the earth and now I'm here. And the next day I filed a small claims.

Mediator:	Ok, so it sounds like what I hear you saying is that you've been frustrated because you anticipated that this was only going to take a couple months and it's been — or a couple of weeks, and it's now been a couple months and you're still without a completed kitchen.
Bernice:	Correct.

Clip 6-M: 'I' Statements

(Don Weinstein & Jean Biesecker, in Fitzgerald)

Jane:	Wait a minute. Wait a minute. Every time I try to talk about it ... You want a "Leave It to Beaver" 50's house. I can't do that. We have two kids that are close in age. I have different priorities than you do ...
Bob:	Yeah — you sure do!
Jane:	Yeah, well let's face it. Your biggest problem isn't with the kids. Your biggest problem is because you can't eat off the kitchen floor. That's what your problem is. And every time I say ...
Bob:	That's an issue too.
Jane:	If you've got an issue, why don't we get some help in because I can't do it all ...
Bob:	That is something we can talk about too.
Jane:	"My mother never needed any help, so why do you need help and I can't afford it!" Bob, you never, you never pitch in to clean anything. I know, I never realized that I married you to become your house maid.
Bob:	Somehow ...
Jean (M):	Jane, can I ask a question here? When you're talking with Bob right now, what I'm hearing a lot of conversation about is what he's not doing. Can you talk about what it is that you need from him? In a like, an "I" kind of statement instead of looking at him and saying, "You aren't doing all of these things." Can you think of a way to talk with him about what you need?
Jane:	(Crying.) Now I'm crying and I don't like to do that. I know that you think I'm a rotten mother. I know that. And it kills me. And I need you to stop comparing me to your mother. I'm not your mother! I mean, I need you to not assume that I'm lazy. I need you to say that I'm worth something and that's all I get from you is what I don't do and what you think I don't do, and how rotten I am. You have no idea and I ask

for help and it's like, you know, if my mom can do it, why can't you? All her kids weren't as close in age and I'm not superwoman and I have different priorities. Just because my priorities are different, it doesn't mean that they're wrong.

Bob: I never thought you were a bad person or a horrible mother and I never wanted to . . .

Jane: That's what you said . . .

Clip 6-N: Dealing with Strong Emotions

1. (Mary Hanna, in Fitzgerald)

Jane: I'm sorry. I have to say something here. I have a real problem with his mother mainly. Cause, it's not your dad, it's his mother being the primary care giver.

Bob: You've always had a problem with my mother.

Jane: I know, I know but it's not just that. It's not just that.

Bob: Oh no. I think it is . . .

Jane: I don't—I have real issues with her. First of all her age, she's not a young woman. They are two little kids.

Bob: She's still very healthy and spry.

Jane: Well . . .

Bob: She still manages to clean the house.

Jane: And that's about all she does. Um, and that's a real problem. She does not play. She has no patience for the kids, um . . .

Bob: Oh, that's not true.

Jane: Yes, it's very true. I've watched it. I really don't want her being the primary care giver. I don't like some of the things she is saying to the kids that get back to me. I don't like it.

Bob: Well . . .

Jane: And I don't want her to be—I resent it because these are two happy, easy kids and I don't like what I am seeing them become.

Bob: I don't like what I see them become either.

Jane: Well then maybe you should get a little more involved!

Mary: Ok, Jane. . . .

Bob: I am as absolutely involved as I can be.

Jane: Oh, really? Really?

Bob: Yeah. I work all day. I don't know what you do all day. Because I have home and I find the place a mess, I find the kids crying. . . .

Jane: Well, you know. . . .

Bob: I find the TV blaring. . . .

Jane: Yeah, you're speaking of one incident.

Bob: The kids are underdeveloped.

Jane: You're making all this up.

Bob: I wonder what you have been doing with them for the past five years.

Jane: Oh, you don't want to go there, you don't want to go there.

Bob: I've tried to and you never talk to me about it.

Mary: Time out, time out. I think what I has said at the beginning was that in order for me to be helpful, I needed to have one of you talk at a time. I appreciate the fact that you are engaging directly with each other. But I think this may be a little premature for our purposes and what I would ask is that we go back to trying to keep the thoughts and reactions to each other's comments either on paper or at least, to give me the opportunity to hear . . .

Jane: I did ask if I could interrupt and say something. I did ask.

Mary: Well it is also apparent that to me that at this time that there are real concerns that you have, apparently about Bob's mother.

Jane: Yes.

Mary: . . . as a care giver and I'm not clear that I have a full understanding other than just the fact that you are concerned. I don't know based on you comments right now, whether that means that she is not attentive to the children or whether they are physically at any risk in her care or just what the nature of that concern is. Um, I also heard Bob express some frustration and concern about some issues and I would like to hear a little bit more about them. I also have to caution you: I'm not a therapist, so I am not here to solve problems and to listen to um, extended discussion about longstanding arguments. To the extent that there are concerns that have to do with the care of the children and how you are going to work out those issues, I would hope to be helpful in trying to get you to be able to hear what the other has to say and to understand those concerns. To allow you to go on and get back into what may be preexisting arguments that may not specifically be based with the children, um I not really in a position to address that.

2. (Sam Rossito, in Fitzgerald)

Sam: So we were talking about an incident where, from what I understood you said, Jane, is that there was an agreement to bring the children back and that for some reason it didn't happen.

Bob: Oh, the first time? Is that what you are talking about?

Jane: I'm talking about July 2nd when we had agreed on two hours and it turned into 2 months.

Sam: Ok, would it be helpful for you to know why that happened?

Jane: Yeah, it would be because he never did tell me, he just said I have a week, I have two weeks, whatever it was, vacation.

Bob: I had just found out that I had gotten a couple of. . . . You know that I could have a week's vacation, which I didn't originally have. It was because one of the other manager had gotten . . . had canceled his vacation, so I my boss told me that I could have some time off around the 4th of July. So I thought, great. So, you know, when I came to pick up the kids, I uh . . . The restraining order was gone. I mean I could have moved back in technically, if I wanted to.

Jane: Yes, you could have.

Bob: Right. So there wasn't any big deal anymore. There was no legal clamps or anything going on. And so, I just went ahead and I wanted to pick up my kids and take them away for few days on vacation. There was no reason that I shouldn't do that. And uh, so, I did that and uh, of course, as I feared, her immediate reaction was violent and strident and basically, she got into a physical match with my sister and I. And, it was another ugly scene that she created in front of the kids that, yes, I'm sorry, that didn't need to be that way. All I wanted to do was do what I had a perfect right to do. Hey. I got some time off. I wanted to take the kids for a few days around the 4th of July and she made a big production out of it. A big scene and it was ugly. They were in the car. Yes, so what?

Jane: They didn't have any clothes. Like we can afford for you to outfit them for three days. Megan didn't have her "whitey," Ryan didn't have his blanket. You hadn't made any plans. You could have called me and said "Hey, I've got these days off. What do you think?" And you know what? With the way things were going, I would have said yes.

Bob: Oh. Not the way that . . .

Jane: Had I denied you once when you called after . . .

Bob: When you throw me out for sixty days it makes me feel a little like "she's going to say no to this, I think she's going to say no to this". . . .

Jane: Would you look at since the first time you took them out. Had I ever said, "no you can not take them?"

Bob: You had said. . . .

Jane: No! Answer the question.

Bob: Yes. You had made the rules about when I was going to see them.

Jane: No, I never I did. It was whatever you called. Whenever you called—whenever you called and had time.

Bob: I wasn't the point that . . .

Jane: Yes, it was . . .

Bob: No it wasn't . . .

Jane: The very first time it was but after that it was fine. . . .

Bob: Let's not make it about . . .

Sam: Time out, time out . . .

Jane: Oh, that's such bullshit!

Sam: Ok, alright Jane. There's real strong feelings about this and I can understand why this would happen what happened right here. But, as another part of you knows, nothing is going to get resolved by doing what just happened. So, let's try to look at this and see well what is this raising. What I heard—and again, this is looking to how can we take this and move forward. Is this—I heard that one of the problems Jane, is that this was sort of—this idea of taking the children was sort of sprung on you without a previous agreement about planning it. Because if you had planned it, you know, I guess you are thinking that the children would have the clothing, you would have known the time—but it's kind of chaos right now, it sound like. Right?

Jane: Yes.

Sam: There's nothing that is established so you know, Bob, you might say "well, I have a right to see my children for a week." Which there is nothing wrong with that. Maybe you do, but if there is no plan, I think there could certainly cause the things that happened.

Bob: I can understand that.

Sam: So, do you want to um, talk about—try to establish so sort of plan going forward? Some sort of schedule?

Bob:	I think we need one.
Jane:	Yes.

3. (Don Weinstein & Jean Biesecker, in Fitzgerald)

Don:	What's the arrangement now?
Jane:	There is no arrangement.
Don:	No arrangement. Where are they living now?
Bob:	They're living with me at my parents', where I stay, at my parents' place.
Don:	And do you see them?
Jane:	I've seen them for seven hours since the second of July.
Jean:	That was after the Order?
Jane:	The Order ended on the 30th and the children left on the second, with Bob. And what's happened is, that Bob will bring, because I don't have a car and Bob and the children are at his folks place in South Philly — and I'm in Germantown — Um, Bob will bring Megan and Ryan and uh, to the house, for like a meal or something, for exactly an hour. And that's only happened seven times since the second of July. And he sits outside the whole time in the car.
Bob:	That's partly ... I mean that's been partly your decision about how often you wanted to see the kids. I didn't, you know, you're acting like I am, have kept you from seeing them except for the seven hours and that's not so.
Jane:	Yeah, well. It is so.
Bob:	No, it's not.
Don:	How was that decided? ...
Bob:	I've given you other opportunities ...
Jane:	It wasn't decided!
Don:	How did that arrangement take shape? From what you describe, you seem — what, one hour?
Jane:	One hour. For seven different occasions. And, um, basically it's based around Bob's schedule and what's convenient for Bob. Because I don't drive. It's not that I don't drive, I don't have a car.
Bob:	Right, so I bring the kids to her.
Jane:	But the fact that you sit outside in front the whole time, you don't give me more than an hour with them and you're there the whole time. We never get to relax, we never get to have ... it's very uncomfortable and it's not ...

Bob:	I'm doing what I can. I have to bring the kids to you and I have to bring them back. So, you know, I'm doing what I can.
Jane:	Like sitting out on the curb, and they know you're there. That's not good. That doesn't give me any time.
Don:	Let me just understand again. They're with you and your parents.
Bob:	Right.
Don:	You bring them one hour a week to see Jane.
Bob:	Right.
Don:	And ... then ... it's that arrangement 'till the next week. She's seen them one hour ...
Bob:	That's the way it's worked out. Between her schedule and mine.
Jane:	I don't have a schedule!
Bob:	Well, you know, I don't see you calling them and you're saying, "I want to see the kids."
Jane:	Yeah, I talk to the children every day, but I'm supposed to have you bring them while you're working?
Bob:	No.
Jane:	I can't do that.
Bob:	I can't either. I'm sorry. I'm only one person. I can only be in one place at a time.
Jane:	I know you're only one person but, you know the whole point is, is that, you uprooted them. You took them away from their home.
Bob:	Excuse me. You separated them from their father. You uprooted the whole household.
Jane:	Uh, no. No.
Bob:	Yes, you did. And nobody asked you to come up with some order about abuse just because you and I had a, a disagreement.
Jane:	It wasn't a disagreement. The fact that ...
Bob:	Yes, it was.
Jane:	... it was pretty intense.
Bob:	Well, you might have, that might have been a rage problem, but it wasn't because ...
Jane:	Oh no. No. No.

Bob:	You, you told the judge I was choking you. That's ridiculous.
Jane:	You were!
Bob:	I wasn't choking you.
Jane:	I don't think you ... Was it my body, or was it your body? It was my body!
Bob:	It was my body getting hit by your fists. That's why ...
Jane:	Because I was trying to get you to let go of me!
Bob:	Let go of you.
Jane:	Because you had your arm across my throat!!
Bob:	I couldn't let go of you! You were pummeling me.
Jane:	I begged you to let go of me because I couldn't breathe.
Bob:	Oh, I see ...
Don:	OK, let's get back ...
Jean:	Can I just ask a question? Is this pretty much how you're able to have a conversation since you've left the house?
Bob:	Sounds pretty bad, doesn't it? ...
Bob:	I'm saying, I think you've done your best and you had your shot and now it's time to give me a shot.
Jane:	Hey, but your shot is your mother. . . .
Bob:	Just in the afternoons.
Jane:	No. That's—No! No! No!
Bob:	Just in the afternoons ...
Jane:	No! No!
Bob:	I don't see what the problem is.
Jane:	That's the problem. Your mother.
Bob:	I know. I knew you were going to have this—you had the same reaction whenever I wanted to come and see the kids initially.
Jane:	No I did not.
Bob:	No, no, no, everything is no, no, no ...
Jane:	One day I said no, one day ...
Bob:	Oh here we go. . . .
Jane:	I was concerned that you weren't going to bring them back, and you know what, I was right.
Bob:	No you weren't.

Jane: I was right.

Bob: No you weren't. I brought them back.

Jane: Yeah, but then the next time — the last time you didn't bring them back.

Bob: The last time ...

Jane: You agreed and you didn't keep up your end of the bargain.

Bob: I kept up my end of the bargain. ...

Jane: You did not!

Bob: Every single time ...

Jane: No! Except the last time.

Bob: I would have to live by your laws ...

Jane: No! It wasn't always my laws ...

Bob: Your rules for a couple of weeks. At first, at first it was two in a half weeks before I even saw my kids.

Jane: You didn't even bother calling! They mean so much to you.

Jean: Can I, can I just ask a question? Is this, is this conversation working?

Jane: No!

Jean: Yeah, yeah.

Bob: No it's not.

Jean: What do you think, what do you think needs to change? What do you think need to happen?

Jane: Well I have no power at all because he's got the kids. I have no power at all.

Bob: Now you know what it feels like.

Jane: But you were still able to see them whenever you had time.

Bob: You can see the kids all the time.

Jane: No. Yeah, yeah, how am I supposed to get down there?

Bob: I will get them to you.

Jane: Well that's so generous and that's so helpful.

Bob: I'm doing what I can.

Jane: You are the one that has mobility. Why can't they be in their home and you come home every night for dinner?

Bob: They are in their home.

Jane: No they are not. They are in your mother's home!

Bob:	They are in my home.
Jane:	No they are not.
Jean:	Do you know what I am hearing conversation about? I am hearing conversation that talks about power, control and I have also heard betrayal.

Clip 6-TM-1: Opening the Process: Mindfulness

(Sam Rossito, in Fitzgerald)

Sam:	Bob, Jane, now that we have talked about this process and that you both want to begin, um, what we may want to do, I find this helpful for some couples, because you know, we kind of come here from our, wherever we came from and we are kind of active, we are kind of nervous. I find it useful to take a moment of silence before we begin … So just kind of sit up straight in your chairs and have your eyes closed. Have your feet flat on the floor and have your palms resting on your thighs. So being silent isn't just an absence of sound but also to have silent thoughts. So just let go of all of the thoughts that you have right now, the expectation of what you think might happen, thoughts from the past. Just for this moment just be present in this room. (Silence) Notice your breathing. Just feel the air coming through your nostrils. (Silence) Just take all that active energy up in the head and just sort of bring it down to the base of the spine. Move your awareness down into the belly and the base of the spine area. (Silence) And now bring your awareness up to your heart. Just feel what is there in your heart for a few moments. (Silence) Now bring your awareness up to the point that is between your eyebrows. Now just be still here for a few moments. (Silence) Now just slowly open your eyes. … Ok. So who would like to begin?

Clip 6-TM-2: Listening and Note Taking Exercise

(Fitzgerald v. Fitzgerald)

Jane:	On July 2nd, Bob and his sister Rose came to pick Megan and Ryan for what was supposed to be a regular visit like we had been doing, um, and after he got the children in the car and all strapped down, um, he says that he is going to Rose's for the 4th of July and that, uh, that he is going to keep them for the week, and I have nothing to say about that. And, I said that I wasn't comfortable with that, we haven't talked about it, the kids weren't packed, nothing was prepared. And, um, I was going to, you know, I had thought about going up to

Lancaster to my parents for the 4th of July and um, I said if you weren't going to come back in two hours that I wasn't comfortable with you leaving with the children at all. Like we had agreed, the two hours that we had agreed to. And he just went off and I went over to the car. Rose was starting to get into the car and I asked her to please move so I could get the children out and she called me certain names that she always tends to use and then she went to pull the door shut and slammed it on my leg. Um, at that, Bob threw me away from the car. I stumbled and I fell. And then he jumped in the car and drove off at which point the kids were both screaming and crying.

Um, I called the police. They said that there was nothing that I could do because they asked me if I had a custody order and I said, you know, I don't think I do. I said I have this protection order but it expired on the 30th. And they said there is nothing that you can do, you have to go and file a petition for custody, which I never thought we were ever going to get to that point. Um, I just thought that we were going to have the two months apart and then we would have some time to reevaluate where we wanted to begin our relationship and then Bob would move back and everything would be fine. I—I tried to call the house. I was not permitted to speak with the children. When I finally got Bob he just kept saying that he had a right to see his kids and I couldn't dictate to him what his, you know, what his access to the children was going to be. I said I'm not dictating anything. You call when you want to see them, I never say no, you come over and see them. Um, and he said now he wasn't going to bring them back at all until I agreed to his visitation demand and he never articulated what those were because he was screaming and yelling on the phone and being egged on in the background by his mother and sister. I could hear them, Bob.

And, um, so I didn't see my kids for a long time. On the 8th of July—I wasn't even allowed to talk to them either— on the 8th of July I went and filed a petition for custody and I believe Bob did so at some point that week as well and, um when we met with the Judge on the 29th, he offered mediation as a possibility and we both amazingly agreed to try it and that's why we are here. Point of fact, um, since July 2nd I have only seen my kids for seven hours and each time that Bob would bring them to the house he would sit outside in the car, in front of the house the whole time. Whenever Bob had the children, we would agree on a time limit . . .

Jane: . . . So Bob had to leave the house on the 24th of April but the actual, I guess the official thing that in front of a judge, that was on May 1st, and he called, I think it was on the 8th, which is just about a week later. He called and said he wanted to see the kids. He hadn't tried to call prior to that and I admitted at that point that I was not real comfortable, you know I didn't know if I could trust him or not. He called back again two days later and he kind of demanded, but I was still uncomfortable but the kids really missed him and I realized it wasn't fair for me to ... to deny them access and so I said that he could come the next day. Which he did. And we had set up a time.

Sam M: ... How do you see the situation? Why are you here? What would ... What's the situation from your point. ...

Bob: It's hard. I mean she's presenting everything, of course, with her own slant on it that's making me sound like, you know, the bad guy, and her like the victim. But uh, let me just start with what totally shocked me. Let's go back to the very beginning um, when I was thrown out of the house. I've had issues with Jane's housekeeping and the way she's been taking care of the kids. I have a five year old who barely talks and when she does you can't even hardly understand her. And she's about to enter school. I have a three year old who is still very dependent on diapers, who's not been properly toilet trained. She's with the kids all day, she's not giving them the kind of structure that they need and I come into this, you know, with some issues about that. So, I come home and is so often the case, things are pretty much in chaos. I mean, if Jane's been home all day, the house is a mess, the breakfast dishes are still in the sink, Toys everywhere. Food strewn around on the floor. The kids are sitting there crying, the TV is blaring, and Jane is in the kitchen talking on the phone. With a friend of hers. Not any crisis, nothing important. She was just chatting. And, uh, so I come in. I try to calm the kids down and stop them from crying. I turn the TV down, I come into the kitchen, I hang out patiently. I wait for, like five minutes hoping that she will realize that it's time to wrap it up, and you know, maybe acknowledge my existence, and uh, let's talk about dinner and things like that. But she's sitting there, in this mess of a kitchen, chatting on the phone and uh, finally, I just try to interrupt her and say, "can we talk?" And she just throws up her hands, you know, like don't, don't disturb me, you know, like, what I'm doing is more important. Well, you know, after the homecoming I'd already received, I was, that made me a little bit angry, yes. So I took the phone away from her and I hung it up. There was nothing violent about it. I just took the phone away from her and I hung it up. And I asked her what was going on? What she'd been doing all day and why the kids were crying and why the house was a mess ... And I felt these are issues that need to be addressed.

And she had an immediate violent reaction, which she often does. And she starts yelling at me. And uh, she either yells at me or she ignores me. So, she just gave some sarcastic remark. She's always sarcastic. Very sarcastic remark about, you know, that she'd just been watching Oprah and lounging around, and you know, sipping her mint juleps and eating bonbons all day. And then she just turns around and walks out of the room. And this is typical. This is what she does. She'll make a sarcastic comment with a little bomb, and then turn around and walk out of the room and avoid the whole thing. So, you know, it had reached a point where I really felt like this needed to be addressed.

So, I, I actually took her by the shoulders and turned her around and said, please talk to me. And, uh, she just glared at me. She just basically wouldn't acknowledge, wouldn't speak, wouldn't do any of it. And uh, then next thing I knew, she was, she was actually trying to get away from me, and she was starting, she was swinging at my face. And uh, trying to punch me. And so I had to, I had to restrain her a little bit, I had to hold her against the wall. She was screaming. The kids were starting to wonder what was going on. A very unpleasant situation for the kids to be in. Because, we'd never had to get physical before. And it was very upsetting to me. And so, I was just trying to keep her from punching me in the face, and just restraining her a little bit and finally when she calmed down and stopped screaming and waving her fists, I let go of her immediately. And what did she do? She just turned right around and bolted out of the house. And disappeared! Just disappeared. Never said where she was going. Didn't come back the entire night. And, you know, the kids were wondering where mom was. And I was wondering where mom was. I had no idea. And uh, she had us all very worried. Frankly, I didn't know if, I didn't know what had happened to her. So, you know, I was trying to address some important issues that had mostly to do with the kids, and partly to do with our relationship. And she just, again, refuses to talk. She disappeared. She got us all very worried.

And then what happened, she shows up the next day . . . Meanwhile, I had no idea where she was, so I had to stay home from work the next day, to watch the kids. And so I'm there. Waiting. For some word, some phone call, something. She shows up on the front porch that afternoon with the police, throwing me out of the house. With something about abuse! Some kind of an abuse thing. And I'm like, I can't believe that, I just couldn't believe that she even, would even say that about me, let alone go and get some kind of a legal document about it. I was absolutely . . . blown away. Um, but I didn't put up any argument, I just packed my bags and went to my folks.

Bob: Well, I would like them, I would like custody of the children and I would like to um, I would like to be able to see them on a daily basis and have them um, have them be in my living situation now as their regular home as a home base. I think the environment there is much better for the kids. They're getting more attention. The kind of attention that they need. I've noticed a real improvement in the kids just since I've had them. In terms of making verbal advancement and her social advancement. And I have seen Ryan actually acknowledging that you know it's time to go to the bathroom — things like that. I have been seeing more progress just in the time that I have had them along with my folks then in all the years that Jane's been raising them, so I want to see them — I will try to get back to the point here. I'm sorry. I want them to be with me. I think that they are getting the attention that they need with me. So I would like for them to be with me on a daily basis. And um, I want to be able to spend good quality time with them um, after work and on weekends. I'm home, you know every evening and I'm home on the weekend and I want to be able to play with them and help them with their homework and you know, do everything that needs to be done. . . .

Jane: Now when Bob says that he wants custody it's really his mother having custody. That's not something that I am comfortable with um the children need to live in their home. Ok? Where they were born. That's where all their things are. That's where all their friends are and I already have the time available to take care of my children. We don't agree on how that care is. He says they have a much more structured environment. It's one more of fear rather than joy and play. Um, his mother does not deal well with kids. Yes. His mother does not deal well with children, um, she's — when he says the house is immaculate, the woman has a fetish when it comes to cleaning. You can't even leave a crumb anywhere. They do not feel comfortable to play. They never used to like going there. . . .

Clip 6-TM-3:   Active Listening Exercises

1. **(Craig Lord, in Wilson)**

Mediator: Now let me ask you a couple of other things about your complaint. When you say you have been defrauded by the contractor, what do you mean by that?

Ms. Wilson: There was information that I wasn't told. I wasn't told anything about this fire. I wasn't told anything about any of this information. They just weren't returning my phone calls and I felt as though they had taken my money and they had done half of the job and also as I was saying earlier, from the 25th to the 31st, I had a friend of mine come over. I was telling everyone at work about this. I was telling people everywhere because I didn't know what to do and they were giving me advice. A friend of mine, her son is very handy, he does some carpentry stuff on the side, he came over and looked at it. Now, before he had come over, I had noticed that one of the cabinets, uh, was moving away from the wall, um separating. And that there was a $2\frac{1}{2}$ inch space where the stove was supposed to go that seemed a little bit too narrow. I called again, left a message. No one returned my call, because I was concerned — is the cabinet going to fall off of the wall? Well, the friend's son comes over and looks at it and says, "this wall should have been put in, a new wall should have been put in. These walls are old, this is not going to hold, this is eventually going to fall off of the wall." Then he shows me on the back of the cabinets where it said that these are second rate or irregular. Now, I didn't know that I was paying for second rate materials.

2. **(Cheryl Cutrona, in Wilson)**

Frank: Another thing I'm going to say to you is, you know, Connie, maybe doesn't do the best work. And she does miss some things. So I will assume responsibility for that. Sam maybe doesn't, he tries to close things and he wants to do good for the company because he knows how rough it's been since my dad and uncle are no longer with the business. So he tries to close things too, but they are loyal to my family, I'm loyal to them and I trust them with certain things. I have been finding that as the years have gone by they are maybe not doing as well as they used to in the past but, I'm never going to let them go. They're in the company until they die, and that is just the way it is. I will take responsibility on that.

3. **(Don Weinstein & Jean Biesecker, in Fitzgerald)**

Jane: And the fact that we disagree how to do that is the crux of the problem.

Jean: Disagree on how to do what?

Jane: How to raise children. We have very, we unfortunately discovered that we have very different views.

Bob: We do.

Jean: OK.

Don: What are some of the areas of disagreement?

Bob: Well, here's the thing. We have a five year old daughter, almost six. She's getting ready to start kindergarten and she barely talks. And when she does, she's hard to understand. And, ah, it's clear to me that she is behind in her development. And I would like her to see a specialist. And, you know, we have a three year old who's very dependent on diapers still. I think that he should be further along with his toilet training. And you know, like Jane says, this is what she does. This is supposed to be what she's supposed to be helping to develop, all day long when she's with the kids. And I don't see it happening. I see kids that are behind. And it concerns me. . . .

Jane: Well, first of all, I'm concerned about Megan too, but that's why I took her to the pediatrician. I mean I bring it up every time we have our visits and the opinion of a medical doctor doesn't matter to Bob. It's not good enough. . . .

4.   **(Chuck Forer, in Resnick)**

M: Let me ask you another question when it comes to settlement. Who is paying any settlement here? Mr. Stevens, are you? Do you have insurance?

DL: Universal's paying.

M: Okay.

DL: Universal Insurance Company is paying.

M: Okay.

DL: Would be paying, I should say.

M: Okay.

D: But I'm—I'm kicking in five thousand.

M: Okay, so you have a five thousand dollar kick in?

D: Yup.

M: Okay. Are you prepared to kick that money in?

D: Well, I guess I have to.

M: Yeah, okay. Okay.

D: If I have to, but I'll tell you all along, I mean at some point you just have to take a stand on some of these things. I mean, I've been—from what I'm told, you know, the insurance company will handle it from now on, but I don't really want to get the reputation, either, as somebody who runs a shoddy operation, and has unsecured buildings and I wouldn't want that to be publicized. You know, I don't know whether I would want to take — the way I feel now, I would rather take the chance in some ways of going to court and winning and going to court and losing, but it's not up to me. It's up to the insurance.

Clip 6-TM-4:   Productive Reframing Exercises

1.   (Don Weinstein & Jean Biesecker, in Fitzgerald)

Bob:	. . . I understand that.
Jean:	Can I ask a question here? Um, one of the things that I thought I heard talked about early on, at least from Jane's perspective, was that there was an agreement when you had the children that it probably would be best for one parent, to the extent that would be possible, to be in the home with the children.
Jane:	Yes.
Jean:	Do you, do you share that view?
Bob:	I certainly did share that view. And until I saw my kids weren't developing normally. And I thought well ok. And I saw Jane's increasing, sort of lack of energy with the kids and it just doesn't seem like she is really into it. And I just think . . .
Jane:	Bob you are making that decision . . .
Bob:	I think I would be a better parent.
Jane:	Bob, Bob, Bob . . .

2.   (Don Weinstein & Jean Biesecker, in Fitzgerald)

Jean:	Ok. Let's talk about what's important for you as parents. What do you want to see happen here?
Bob:	I think that, as I've stated that, I feel that Jane has done her best. I think she has given a shot as being their all day care taker and I think as a result they are behind where they should be in their development. And I not saying that it's because she's a bad person. I think she loves the kids. But I just think that she is maybe not the greatest parent or maybe just not real into it. I see her being kind of low energy around the kids and kind of whatever. She doesn't seem to have the enthusiasm for it that she had at the beginning. And that's my concern. I think she might be a little burnt out. Sorry, I think you are getting a little burnt out and you are just like kind of letting them go.

Jane:	Maybe if you jumped in a little bit and helped.
Bob:	I've tried to help.
Jane:	No you're not, no you're not.

Clip 6-TM-5: Screening for Domestic Violence

(Don Weinstein & Jean Biesecker, in Fitzgerald)

Jean:	Ok, I know that before you came into the room the court clerk had an opportunity to give you the agreement to mediate and I believe that you signed that. So we are going to take a few minutes during our time today to take a look at that again. But what we are going to ask first to do is have an opportunity to meet with both of you individually, which is really a routine procedure for all moms and dads who participate in this court mediation program. And the purpose of having that time together is to, for Don and I to assess whether or not we believe that your family is the one that is really appropriate for the court mediation program. Um, and that's important because you are both going to need to be spending some time together this afternoon having a conversation and we want to take a look at where you are right now in your family and what concerns that you bring, and that the mediation process is the right place for you. Ok. So having said that, knowing that we need to meet with each one of you individually, who would like to go first? How would you like to work?
Bob:	I don't care. Would you like to go first?
Don:	The process will take about five minutes with each.
Jane:	That's fine. Ok.
Bob:	Should I leave?
Jean:	If you would, please. Thanks; we will come and get you. I believe that there's a few chairs in the hallway. Thanks, Bob. (Bob leaves the room.)
Jean:	Hi, Jane.
Jane:	Hi.
Jean:	As I said, this is really a routine procedure that we do with all families through the court. And one of the things that we know is that domestic violence and child abuse is part of many families and what we want to take a look at and ask some question, which we will ask both of you and of Bob, it will be the same questions, um is to take a look at the possibility that there may be any kind of violence between

you and Bob that might make it difficult for you to sit in the room together because we are going to be spending a fair amount of time together this afternoon. Um, so I am going to be asking you some questions to kind of take a look at, um whether or not there may be some issues or concerns you have about participating actively and having a voice in our time together this afternoon. Does that sound ok?

Jane: Yes that is fine.

Jean: Ok, um, when you and Bob may have a disagreement, are you able to talk with each other without getting into arguments?

Jane: Not recently, no. We have been having trouble in our marriage for easily, about maybe three years. Since uh — it was getting bad once we had Megan and then when we had Ryan it just really started to deteriorate even more. Um, we do tend to argue. I usually try to walk away and I prefer not to argue in front of the kids. I mean there is nothing wrong with children seeing parents having a disagreement, but if it is going to get into screaming and angry accusations and things like that back and forth, then I don't believe that is something kids need to necessarily be exposed to.

Don: No.

Jane: So more often than not I will walk away if I feel that the temperature is getting high. I'm not always successful with that but I try.

Jean: Ok, when you have these arguments, are they frightening for you? Do have any fears?

Jane: The last time we did, yes it was frightening, and it got physical, which it had never done before. Um, and that is what precipitated actually the whole reason that we are here to begin with. Um, I had a protection from abuse order for Bob and that was supposed to be rescinded on the 30th of June. Not rescinded, I guess that's not the right word.

Don: Expired.

Jane: Expired. Thank you.

Don: So it was issued May 1st.

Jane: Yeah, May 1st. And, um, that was expired and I thought you know that two months was going to give us time to kind of cool down and really decide where we wanted to go with our lives. And ...

Don: So it wasn't terminated, it ended after sixty days.

Jane: Yeah. And as I said that was the only time that we had ever gotten physical. We've argued, but he never, ever approached me like that before and it scared me. It did scare me. Now, do I feel that he would hurt me again? I don't know, I don't think so, but I don't know.

Don: Have there been any incidents after that expired?

Jane: Just one. On the 2nd of July, Bob came to pick up the kids for what was supposed to be like a regular visit and it wasn't anything formal, it's something that as the time went along, we just kind of, you know, he'd call and say he wanted to see the kids X amount of time and I would be like, ok, fine, and he would take the kids and they would go have fun and everything. And, um, he came on the 2nd, and after he had Ryan and Megan in the car, um, he said that he was going to keep them for a week. We had not discussed it, the kids weren't packed, they had nothing, you know, with them. And, you know, I had been kind of bantering about going up my folks in Lancaster for the 4th of July because they are not too far from Dutch Wonderland and the kids like that place. And I said no. If you are not going to bring them back after you know, the two hours that we had agreed upon then I don't want you to take them. I tried to get the children out of the car. His sister closed the door on my leg and then Bob, he pulled me away from the car and threw me, um, back against the house. Um, I don't know. He's got a volatile nature in a sense. He loses his temper quickly. Um, vocally, but those are the only two times he's ever been physical and you know . . .

Jean: Do you have any concerns that in voicing your opinion and expressing your opinion during mediation today that when you leave here there may be any repercussions or there may be . . .

Jane: Physical repercussions?

Jean: Yes.

Jane: I don't think so. I don't think there would be a physical threat. I think both of those incidents — well, the first incident, I still really have trouble understanding why it escalated to the degree that it did. But the second incident, I think, I don't know whether he was just trying to get me out of the way and he was, emotions were high, you know. I don't think he meant to do that. And like I said, we've been together nine years. You know, we've been married for seven, um, and this is, these are the only times anything like this has happened.

Don: So you feel comfortable enough in moving forward with this process?

Jane: I think so yes. I hope so.

Jean:	It would be important that if at any time during our mediation today and our time together that you did feel uncomfortable, um, that you certainly have the right to say that this process isn't working for me or that you need to leave the room or that you need to end it.
Jane:	Ok.
Jean:	You have that control. This is your time. This is your process. . . .
Don:	Hi Bob.
Jean:	Hi Bob.
Bob:	Hi.
Don:	Bob, we are aware that anyone referred from the courts, um, needs to feel that they are able to move forward with the process of mediation. We are aware that there had been a protection order that had been made first. So with that in mind and we realize that is has expired. We want to make sure that everyone is feeling comfortable with moving forward with discussion here. Um, do you feel comfortable in these confined quarters in this meeting to be able to discuss some of the issues that you feel may be coming up?
Bob:	Yeah. I'm comfortable with talking about the issues and I am hoping we can come to a reasonable decision.
Don:	Right and that's the purpose of mediation.
Bob:	Yeah.
Don:	Is there any sense of discomfort or is there any sense of safety of welfare or whatever or any issues that we should be aware of if the two of you were meeting.
Bob:	Well, I think with the two of you between us and the table, I think it would help because it seems like we've been, you know, tempers have been a little hot lately. Um, I don't know how much of our story you know, but, um, I guess what sort of started all this was an argument that we had that really got, that ended up getting physical, which I think surprising to both of us because it's not something that we normally did and . . .
Don:	You've been married nine years?
Bob:	Seven.
Don:	Seven years. And that happened recently.
Bob:	Well yeah. That happened April 23rd actually. I can remember it well. The day before Jane had me thrown out of the house which was a deep shock to me. I mean she just suddenly became very militant and I was very surprised by that.

Don:	Was that the incident?
Bob:	No. The incident was the day before. I had come home and things were very much in disarray. Which is getting more and more common. Um, you know, the house was a mess, the kids were unattended. They were crying actually when I walked in. There were toys and food and things all over the place. The TV was blaring. The kitchen was a mess and she was sitting in the kitchen talking on the telephone. And I came in and all of this was, I guess it's been building for a while. I came in and I was a little dismayed to see this again. And so, I tried to quiet the kids down and turn the TV down and went into the kitchen and just patiently waited for about five minutes hoping that she would sort of wrap it up and we could talk about what we were going to do about dinner and thing like that. And she really just didn't acknowledge me at all and I tried to sort of interrupt at one point to see if I could get her to wrap it up and she just put up a hand, like, don't disturb me. Like she resented me. And so, finally I just got fed up and I just took the phone away and hung it up. And said look, we have to talk about some things. And her way more and more has been to avoid and not discuss issues. We've got some things we need to talk about and once again she was sort of defiant and sarcastic. She made a sarcastic remark.
Don:	It was that incident that led to the protection order?
Bob:	Yeah.
Don:	It lasted for only sixty days. It's expired so that hopefully you both feel that you can move forward with the mediation process.
Bob:	I think we can.
Don:	You feel safe enough here?
Bob:	Yeah. Like I said, I was shocked at that whole, that whole order. I couldn't believe that she — I mean we both got a little hot, tempers got a little high and it got a little bit physical, but I mean, nobody was injured or anything and fortunately, neither one of us was injured because I mean, she was being much more violent toward me than I was toward her. I was just trying to restrain her and I get hit with the order.
Don:	It's important for mediation, for both of you to feel comfortable in order for mediation to move forward. So if you both feel comfortable, then we really can begin with the process. We know that you signed the Agreement to Mediate, but we wanted to make sure you both felt comfortable enough to move forward.
Jane:	If you could just wait outside for a few minutes and let Don and I talk together, and then we'll come and get both of you. Are you comfortable waiting in the hallway?

CHAPTER 7 CLIPS

Clip 7-A: Information Gathering: Past Versus Future?

(Mary Hanna, in Fitzgerald)

Mary: Time out, time out. I think what I had said at the beginning was that in order for me to be helpful, I needed to have one of you talk at a time. What I appreciate is the fact that you are engaging directly with each other. But I think this is a little premature for our purposes and what I would ask is that we go back to trying to keep the thoughts and reactions to each other's comments either on paper or at least, to give me the opportunity to hear ...

Jane: I did ask if I could interrupt and say something. I did ask.

Mary: Well it is also apparent to me at this time that there are real concerns that you have, apparently about Bob's mother ...

Jane: Yes.

Mary: ... as a care giver and I'm not clear that I have a full understanding other than the fact that you are concerned. I don't know based on you comments right now, whether that means that she is not attentive to the children or whether they are physically at any risk in her care or just what the nature of that concern is. Um, I also heard Bob express some frustration and concern about some issues and I would like to hear a little bit more about them. I also have to caution you, I'm not a therapist, so I am not here to solve problems and to listen to um, extended discussion about longstanding arguments. To the extent that there are concerns that have to do with the care of the children and how you are going to work out those issues, I would hope to be helpful in trying to get you to be able to hear what the other has to say and to understand those concerns. To allow you to go on and get back into what may be preexisting arguments that may not specifically be based with the children, I'm not really in a position to address that.

Clip 7-B: Questioning: Chronological

(Craig Lord, in Wilson)

Mediator: Ok, so what happened after that?

Ms. Wilson: No one came on the 2nd of October. Um, I called all day long. I had my neighbor keep an eye on the house to see if anyone had arrived. I had to get to work. Can't be late to work. Jobs are hard to come by, didn't want to lose mine. Um, and, my neighbor called me at work. I'm not allowed to receive calls phone calls at work, but she called me to tell me no one had showed up. I called DiLorenzo and Sons almost—I tried to call them every hour on the hour, kept getting the answering machine. 3:30 in the afternoon, I finally spoke to the receptionist and she informed me that, oops, they didn't make it today. There was something else that tied them up. She gave me no formal explanation and told me they would be there the next day. October 3rd, they came in and that was their second day of work. And October 3rd, they put up a couple of the cabinets and they put down part of the linoleum floor. They did not complete the linoleum floor. They left the area where the stove and the doorway are open.

Mediator:	All right, let's stop there for a second. Now, Mr. DiLorenzo do you, I mean, have anything to add to the version of the events for October1st?
DiLorenzo:	I would, I would ...
Mediator:	Wait, wait, wait, let me finish the question for October 1st.
DiLorenzo:	I would actually like to be able to say my side of the story the same way that she is.
Mediator:	You will have that opportunity.
DiLorenzo:	OK.
Mediator:	You will have that opportunity. But everyone gets a chance in order. But I am taking you back to October 1st and I would like to know, you know, she has described what happened on October 1st, would you like to add anything to that?
DiLorenzo:	No, I will wait until it is my turn.
Mediator:	I would like you to add now because the problem is by the time I get to the end I will forget all the details, so I would just like to know what happened, how did the work start?
DiLorenzo:	We do more than one job a day. The only way that we can affordably offer this kind of work is to do several jobs at the same time, all right. It's just the nature of the business. It's a small niche that we have found. We are able to give things to people that they can't normally afford. A normal kitchen, even with the work that we are doing would cost three to four times what we are able to get it done at.

Clip 7-C: Questioning: Topical

Topical Questioning: Broad

1.   **(Harris Bock, in Resnick)**

PL:	In this matter, the burglar was able to gain access to what was supposed to be a secure building, through a fire escape

that led to an unsecured hallway window, and was allowed really to gain access to the premises. What happened that night was, as Josh was asleep in his bed, the intruder woke him with a large knife to his neck, threatening him with bodily harm. He then proceeded to tie him up, proceeded to put clothes stuffed in his mouth, as he rummaged through the apartment, and over the course of fifteen minutes, as Josh lay there, not knowing whether he would live or die, the intruder then, before leaving, basically said that if he told anyone about what happened, he threatened to kill him. Certainly this was a situation full of terror, and following these events, Josh experienced post-traumatic—

M: Let's—let's just stop there for a second. Let me tell you about in terms of a lawsuit. A lawsuit has basically two chapters to every lawsuit. Two chapters to the Book of the Lawsuit. Number one is liability or responsibility. In order to recover in a lawsuit, you as the plaintiff have to show that the other party's responsible in some way. Just because you got injured on Mr. Stevens' property or because you're a tenant there, he's not a guarantor of your safety. He has to take what the law calls reasonable care with regard to that aspect of the matter on your behalf, and that's what you have to show with regard to the liability aspect. That's what portion of the case we're talking about right now and we're going to address that in the first way. The we'll get onto what we call damages. Damages is assuming there is liability and responsibility, what was the harm suffered by that with regard to that? So why don't you focus in—

PL: If I can—

M: On—

PL: I can do it any order. The point of the recitation really here is to lay out what happened. The event and we can get now really to the point that Josh, who then suffered a post-traumatic stress disorder, is here because this was a preventable event.

M: Then why don't you lay that out for us—

PL: I'll be glad to do that.

M: And tell us what you think, in your view, Mr. Stevens, did that factually or legally imposes liability upon him?

PL: This is a premises liability case. . . .

Topical Questioning: Narrow

2. **(Mary Hanna, in Fitzgerald)**

Mary: So you mentioned that your mother was the primary care taker.

Bob:	During the day, yeah.
Mary:	Does she primarily keep them at home? Is there a yard? Is there a playground nearby?
Bob:	Yeah. There is a yard and a playground nearby, all of that. And she really enjoys being with the kids and she gives them a nice structured environment which I think is helpful, which I think is exactly what they've needed more of.
Mary:	Now when you say it's a "structured environment," what exactly does that mean?
Bob:	Well that they have a schedule, they have a routine. She's trying to help them to um, I've actually seen an improvement between what I have been doing with the kids and what she's been doing with the kids. I've seen an improvement in their development.
Mary:	What's the structure that you are referring to?
Bob:	Well they have a, they get up a certain time. They eat their meals at a certain time and you know, they have some free time. They have structured play time and that kind of thing. So she's doing a nice job of structuring their day and trying to encourage Ryan to tell her when it is time for him to go to the bathroom, so that he doesn't have to be completely dependent on diapers. So he can begin to develop his toilet training a little bit better. And she's been, as I have been, trying to engage Megan in more you know, conversation. Just trying to draw her out more and get her to be more verbal. Because those are areas that I think they need more concentration on.
Mary:	Your concern as I am hearing it right now is that there be a structured set of activities for the children during the course of the day?
Bob:	Yeah.
Mary:	That is a fair statement?
Bob:	Yes.
Mary:	Can you hold that thought for a minute?
Bob:	Sure.
Mary:	Let me check with Jane. What kind of activities, what was their routine during the course of the day when they were with you?
Jane:	In the morning they would wake up when they wake up, they weren't awoken. They woke up when they woke up. They would have their breakfast.
Mary:	Approximately what time?

Jane:	They would usually be up sometime around seven thirty, eight o'clock they would wake up. Because they would go to bed around seven thirty and eight in the evening. They would sleep about twelve hours. They're good at that. Um, they get up, they have breakfast. We will either put a puzzle together, maybe Ryan is old enough for Candy Land, we'd play Candy Land. If it is a nice day then we would go out for a walk. If play group was scheduled, usually play group would start around ten-ish and go 'til just about after lunch. The kids would all have lunch together. Then come home, we'd have nap. Then when we would get up from naps—usually they would go down for nap around one, they would get up around three and then in the afternoon they would just play and you know, maybe play a puzzle, maybe play a game, maybe we would go outside again, you know, whatever, whatever was comfortable. We would do a lot of reading, contrary to what Bob is indicating. And you know, Megan is a quiet kid, it's not that she is not encouraged to speak, she's definitely encouraged to speak, but that's not where she is right now.

Clip 7-D: Probing for Empathy

(Cheryl Cutrona, in Wilson)

Mediator:	Is there anything you would like to add?
Barry:	No, I think that tells DiLorenzo's side of the story. I am comfortable with having Frank do that and we are ready to proceed.
Mediator:	Alright. Is there anything you would like to say in response?
Bernice:	Um, I agree that there was a total lack of communication, but one thing . . . and I understand that we're in mediation to work this through and I am trying to table my anger. I'm trying so hard but I went through this, he did not go through this. I dealt with other people, not him. You know what I mean? Even though it is still the same company, you are the owner of the company, still, I didn't deal with you and you weren't involved from the onset of this until now. . . .
	Because what I don't understand is yes, I understand a fire is beyond your control, it is completely beyond your control, but all of your business didn't stop, so if this is the place where you always get the counter tops from, this is the place where all of your stuff comes from, then you should have been there to be able to receive my phone call because you had no work.
Frank:	No, that is not true.

Bernice:	You know what I mean.
Frank:	No! Bernice I said to you that I do a lot of things at work.
Bernice:	Right, you have a lot of jobs.
Frank:	It's not always, it's not all just kitchens and this and that, but I had other things going on. Those counter tops and things were ready. Lets communicate now, let's fix it. Let's fix it.
Mediator:	Well tell us, you said that you know, "I went through this, he didn't." Say some more about that. Went through what?
Bernice:	I went through making fifty million phone calls, cause see, the thing that really kills me is that had my check bounced, had the money not been there, you better believe I would have received a phone call. Had my answering machine not worked and the check bounced, they would have been sending me a letter in the mail. It would have been a certified letter in the mail. It could have been a sheriff at my door, could have been anything. So those things to me, my answering machine did not — for, on Connie's behalf one day, the tape wasn't working. One day. Same day I fixed that tape, but like you said, you weren't there, you didn't have the conversations with me, like I said, you weren't there. Um ...
Frank:	I'm here now.
Bernice:	Exactly, you are, you are here now, but you know, it kills me that it's so — I definitely understand why I am here, but I am just still so upset. ...
Mediator:	I guess I hear you say you still doesn't understand why all of your phone calls were not answered.
Bernice:	Yes!
Mediator:	Maybe you can explain that.
Frank:	I, I can't. I wish I could give you a decent answer, and I said there were three screw ups. Two beyond my control. I can't be in all places at the same time. Perhaps I was a little over-extended, but it's the nature of my business. Sometimes you're juggling balls and one's going to fall.

Clip 7-E: Probing for Future Dealings

(Cheryl Cutrona, in Wilson)

Mediator:	What could they do to make you trust them at this point?
Bernice:	Really nothing. There is nothing that they could do to make me trust them. I would love to sever ties with them altogether. To just end the relationship and have it be over and done with. To say, ok, um, my ultimate would be for them to um, give me additional monies to hire a new

	contractor. I know what I am suing for is really high, but that is not really what I want. I mean ...
Mediator:	Is there anything that you said during this caucus that you don't want me to repeat to the other side or you're probably to be bringing this up anyway?
Bernice:	Yeah, I'd like them not to know the lowest amount that I wanted to go. I would really want them not to know that. And I would prefer not to deal with them, to have them come back in my house ever again. That's what I would prefer.
Mediator:	Are you totally ruling that out or is that —
Bernice:	That's my preference, that's my preference.
Mediator:	So you are willing to negotiate it?
Bernice:	I am willing to negotiate. If I can't get what I want, then I am willing to negotiate because my ultimate goal is to have my kitchen done.

Clip 7-F: Probing for Readiness

(Don Weinstein & Jean Biesecker, in Fitzgerald)

Bob:	This whole thing didn't have to become a federal issue. If I wasn't thrown out of the house and told I was an abuser. If we can just have an adult conversation about this a long time ago, and we could have agreed to it, we could have done this. And it could have been over.
Jean:	Bob, you keep, you've come back to that several times during our session today. I'm wondering, for you, what will be helpful in getting past that? What will it take to feel, I don't know ... what needs to happen for you to be able to move beyond the point in time and the feelings that have been left with you when you were asked to leave the house. You've come back to it several times and I hear it's a really ...
Bob:	It's what started this whole thing.
Jean:	Right. And what do you think is going to end it? What will it take to put an end to that?
Bob:	(Sighing). Well, I think we need to, I think we need to come to some agreements. Albeit, maybe compromises, but we have to come to some agreements — albeit compromises — about the kind of environment to raise our kids in and I think, I mean obviously I think the most ideal thing in the world is if we could live together again. If we could all be a family together in the same place. I, I don't know. I don't know.
Don:	But under different conditions.

Bob:	Well, yeah!
Jean:	What does that sound like to you?
Jane:	That's what I thought we were going to do.
Jean:	So that's something you would like to see happen as well?
Jane:	That's right. That's what I thought we were going to do.
Bob:	Well, we never really discussed it. It was just, you know, I was out and that was it.
Don:	Have the both of you ever gone for help?
Jane:	I wanted to and he didn't.
Jean:	I'm hearing him say that that's something he would be interested in doing.
Jane:	And I think that we owe that to our children.
Don:	How about to each other?
Bob:	Yeah!
Don:	Well, there's a lot of hurt so right now you can't make that decision. But it is something to think about.

Clip 7-G: Probing for Interests

1. (Cheryl Cutrona, in Wilson)

Mediator:	Ok Frank and Barry I just want to remind you what I said in my opening statement. This part of the mediation had an extra layer of confidentiality. You can feel free to talk frankly because I won't repeat anything that I hear.
Frank:	Ok.
Mediator:	I just wanted to ask you a question: Sounds like she said that she was telling her friends, her people at church all about her situation. Are you concerned at all about your reputation?
Frank:	Yeah I'm worried about my reputation. If people, if somebody is going to go around, because the community that Bernice lives in is a community where I have found my niche. I mean, these people, the people can't afford, they're low and middle income families that can't afford to get all the finer things in a kitchen, but I can give them a kitchen that will have that look, and be 1/8 of the price.

2. (Chuck Forer, in Resnick)

M:	And I want to just reiterate what I said. If you feel more comfortable now talking to me, by all means interrupt me,

M: interrupt your attorney and let it go, but of course I wanted to spend this time talking with you in private, in confidence about the case. . . .
            Let me ask this, and again this is in confidence. Do you really want to go to trial on this case?

PL: Absolutely.

M: Does your client want to go to trial? I don't mean to win the case, but you said at the outset that you didn't want your client, you know, having to go through and relive this incident, and I can fully understand and I can fully sympathize with that. He certainly doesn't want to relive that incident with five of us, but does he want to relive that incident with seventeen of us when there's a judge and a jury? I don't mean to say that, you know, maybe, you know, you will do really well at trial and win the case. My question really is, is this something that you want to go through again in front of twelve strange people or thirteen strange people or more because of course there's other people in a courtroom as well.

P: Well, I mean, I think —

PL: Would you mind if I interrupt you?

P: No.

PL: Would it be okay if I respond to that?

M: Yeah.

PL: Josh and I have talked about this and it's not something that Josh is dying to do. Josh is not someone who is feeling right now a burning desire to have his story told, and to have the story be out there and to demonize Mr. Stevens. But Josh also understands the importance of the process. He understands the importance of the civil litigation process, and he is in a position where if this can be settled for an amount that's going to be reasonable, for an amount that's going to make sense for him, for an amount that does something about, coming somewhere in the ballpark of helping not so much to replace the year that he's lost, but to address it, then he's willing to do that. But he's also more than willing and would be more than prepared to go through trial. Is it his first choice? Of course not.

M: Okay.

PL: Of course not. But is he willing to do it? Absolutely.

M: Okay.

PL: Now, did I speak out of turn?

P: No, that makes — that's exactly what — yeah.

Clip 7-H: Probing for Doubt

1. **(Harris Bock, in Resnick)**

M: So how do you know how the burglar gained entrance?

PL: Well, there is available evidence with regard to really what people saw and really this is the only way that he could have come in. There was evidence of repairs to the window on the landing or the hallway window area after this event, where the burglar likely came in. And there was another person in another apartment on the third floor, who shortly before this event heard someone who was likely the intruder jiggle her door and before they went up to the fourth floor. But by everything we know, all the evidence leads to the conclusion that the access to this secure building, otherwise, was through this fire escape that was low to the ground, in an area where there was no real lighting on the side. So it was dark at night, and the likely entry point was on the second floor. There is a hallway window with a landing that was totally unsecured.

          Now, there were gates or window gates and locks on all the other windows from the fire escape, but this window had no locks, no pins or other device to keep it secure from entry.

M: But I think — I guess what comes to mind right away to me is if he — if he got into the building, how did he get into Josh's apartment?

PL: As some of the information we provided shows, because this was a secure building, the tenants inside believed it to be safe. They believed, based on reliance on the landlord's representation at the time of rental and otherwise, that no one really could come in and intrude, and Josh's roommate, who wanted to go out briefly, ran out, was going to be back shortly and said that he was going to leave his front door open.

M: So Josh knew that the door was open?

PL: He was aware of that fact, but in reliance really on —

M: You felt comfortable, Josh, with that?

P: Uh-hmm.

M: Yeah? . . .

PL: We believe that what is compelling in this case in terms of liability is that during the six year period that Stevens was involved with owning this property, not only did they make the building less safe, they did nothing really to inspect or make improvements to insure what they were marketing —

M: Were there any burglaries before this one?

PL: Not on this — in this building.

M: So we have six years of basically —

PL: Basically nothing being done.

M: Okay, but six years where they didn't have any problems, either . . .

2.   (Chuck Forer, in Resnick)

PL: And this is really the important thing, right? For them to sit there for a week of trial and say, "Ah, we have no idea how it happened. We have no idea where the guy came in, where the guy went out." You know, in the face of, you know, one big, fat broken window that leads to the fire escape, that just by the way is really the only part of the exterior of the building that's this unprotected, I mean, you know, what are the chances? Coincidence? I think not.

M: Is there any any other physical evidence? In other words, we have this broken window. I understand — you know, I understand where you're coming from about that. Is there any other evidence that you can point one way or the other to that talks about how this crime took place? There's no fingerprints? There's no —

PL: There's no fingerprints. There's no evidence elsewhere of any kind of forced entry. There was some talk about perhaps some tar that may have come from the roof that was on one part of the sash, I believe, again of the broken window. That evidence, you know, I'm going to be straight with you here because we're trying to get something done. I'm not exactly sure that that necessarily comes in. It's both second or third hand and not well substantiated.

Clip 7-I: Probing for Standards, Norms or Past Practices

(Cheryl Cutrona, in Wilson)

Mediator: Well let me ask you a question then, and this is just between us. I'm sure, you know, you have been in business for how long?

Frank: Well it's a family, my dad and uncle came over in 1935 and they founded the business not — shortly after that, so for a while.

Mediator: So when consumers have complaints, how do you usually settle them, what do you do?

Frank:	Well, I mean, I try to make them happy. I tell my people to make the customer happy. Do what, if it is going to cost me a hundred dollars you know, if they don't like the handle on a cabinet, if they don't like that, you give them new ones, you throw it in. It's not as if I make a million dollars on every thing. I'm not a rich man, I'm not getting rich on this. I don't have a vacation home down in Carolina or anything like that, you know. I make enough to get by, you know, and live a decent life.

Clip 7-J: Caucusing: Encouraging Disclosure

(Cheryl Cutrona, in Wilson)

(In caucus)

Frank:	Another thing I going to say to you is you know Connie, maybe doesn't do the best work. And she does her best at some things. So I will assume responsibility for that. Sam maybe doesn't, he tries to close things and he wants to do good for the company because he knows how rough since my dad and uncle are no longer with the business. So he tries to close things too, but they are loyal to my family, I'm loyal to them and I trust them with certain things and I have been finding that as the years go by they are maybe not doing as well as they did in the past but, I'm never going to let them go. They're in the company until they die and that is just the way it is. I will take responsibility on that ...
Mediator:	Ok. Is there anything else you think I should know before I go out and meet with ...
Frank:	I was candid to you about Connie and Sam and how that they are older and that they might have dropped the ball and that I was busy on another job. She doesn't need to know any of that but I mean, I told you things that, I, you know.
Barry:	(Pointing at Bernice's chair) I just hope that she's as candid with you as we have been.
Mediator:	Oh, I'm just wondering if that might actually help you to tell her that. About Sam and Connie and your loyalty. I mean, your loyalty to them speaks well for you.
Frank:	Am I going to tell her that she scared the hell out of Connie?
Mediator:	Well, I don't know if you want to do that, but I think the fact that you are so loyal to them, that they have been long term employees speaks well for you. I don't understand your hesitancy in terms of telling her that.
Frank:	I'm trying to protect them.

Barry:	Let's leave it at that for now.
Mediator:	All right.

(In later joint session)

Frank:	Connie and Sam worked for my dad. You see how old Sam is?
Bernice:	Yes.
Frank:	Connie is older than him and I have a loyalty to them and they mess up sometimes. I'm never going to fire them, I have to keep them on, I want to keep them on. I love them like they are my uncle and my aunt, so no matter what they do they are there.
Bernice:	I understand that and I respect that because they are family.
Frank:	And I will be responsible, well they are not literally family . . .
Bernice:	But still.
Frank:	But they are family to me.
Bernice:	Yes.
Frank:	And I think that they messed up here and I have been more often than not having to pick up some pieces after them, so I take full responsibility as the owner of the establishment for what happened, but I love them and I don't, and they are part of the issue.
Bernice:	OK.
Frank:	So, my cell phone number. . . .

Clip 7-TM-1:   T-Funneling Exercise

(Craig Lord, in Wilson)

Mediator:	Now let me ask you a couple of other things about your complaint. When you say you have been defrauded by the contractor, what do you mean by that?
Ms. Wilson:	There was information that I wasn't told. I wasn't told anything about this fire. I wasn't told anything about any of this information. They just weren't returning my phone calls and I felt as though they had taken my money and they had done half of the job and also as I was saying earlier, from the 25th to the 31st, I had a friend of mine come over. I was telling everyone at work about this. I was telling people everywhere because I didn't know what to do and they were giving me advice. A friend of mine, her son is very handy, he does some carpentry stuff on the side, he came over and

looked at it. Now, before he had come over, I had noticed that one of the cabinets, uh, was moving away from the wall, um separating. And that there was a $2\frac{1}{2}$ inch space where the stove was supposed to go that seemed a little bit too narrow. I called again, left a message. No one returned my call, because I was concerned — is the cabinet going to fall off of the wall? Well, the friend's son comes over and looks at it and says, "this wall should have been put in, a new wall should have been put in. These walls are old, this is not going to hold, this is eventually going to fall off of the wall." Then he shows me on the back of the cabinets where it said that these are second rate or irregular. Now, I didn't know that I was paying for second rate materials. And, yes . . .

Mediator:	It actually had a label on it?
Ms. Wilson:	It was labeled on the back corner.
Mediator:	It said second rate?
Ms. Wilson:	It said second rate.
Mediator:	Boy, that's a bad advertising program.
Ms. Wilson:	Exactly.
Mediator:	Second rate?
Ms. Wilson:	Yes. It said irregular, second rate.
Mediator:	Well, maybe irregular.
Ms. Wilson:	I did not know that I was going to get irregular. I didn't know that I was getting less than quality merchandise. And even though I did select those cabinets, I like those cabinets, but I just didn't know, I wasn't informed and that's how I feel I was defrauded. Because I wasn't made aware of a lot of things that were going on.
Mediator:	Anything else apart from irregular cabinets?
Ms. Wilson:	The fact that the linoleum, he told me that there was going to be a big humongous seam, because they were going to have to put a patch piece of linoleum down on the floor.
Mediator:	Who told you that?
Ms. Wilson:	The gentleman, the son who came in, my friend's son who came in. He says — and also not only did he say it, but from the estimates that I've received, um, when they came in, the contractors came in and looked, they said they agreed with him, and told me: one, the walls would have to be — new sheet rock would have to be put in. That two, the linoleum would leave a seam, so that they would have to cut the linoleum differently and put down so that there would be no seam.

Clip 7-TM-2:   Probing for Readiness Exercise

(Mary Hanna, in Fitzgerald)

Mary: What would you propose as being a more, I believe your term was equitable? A more equitable arrangement for the children to have contact with you and be involved with you.

Jane: Well, obviously, in the best of all worlds, I want them living back home because, first of all, I've been their primary caretaker since, well, before birth, since pregnancy. And um, they're my children and they don't need to be raised by a grandmother if I'm alive. Um, and I have, whether Bob agrees with how I'm parenting or not, that's my goal. That's what I do. That's what I live for. And to have been denied access to them like this for such a long time . . . Um, I mean I'm just rambling around the house. You know, I'm not at work. I don't have a place to go. They're echoing all over the house. And um, and um. What? I mean in the best of all worlds, I thought Bob was moving home. In July, that's what I thought was going to happen. I never expected this. Um, and I don't think it's fair to deprive the children of either parent. Um . . .

Bob: I agree.

Jane: And uh, the way he may be upset with the fact that he had to leave the house, but you know, any time, except for the first time, anytime that he wanted to see the children, I said yes. I never said . . .

Bob: But . . .

Jane: The very first time that you called, I hesitated because I wasn't sure I could trust you.

Bob: I've already been through this . . .

Jane: No, but I mean . . .

Bob: . . . every step of the way.

Jane: But the point I'm trying to make is that you never gave me that same consideration.

Mary: Jane, the question that I posed was, what would you like to see that would be a more acceptable arrangement than what you have at the present time? Given the fact that you, at the moment, are separated.

Jane: I mean, I would like them to live at home. And as far as I'm concerned, Bob can come have dinner every night with the kids. Help put them to bed like we always did. And then he can . . . go home. To South Philly. If that's what he wants to do. And on the weekends, if he wants to take them all

	weekend, that's fine. If he wants to, since I have them all during the week, I don't want to deprive him of the time that he has. If he wants them on the weekends, that's fine. But, it should come down to, the kids shouldn't be put in the middle. They shouldn't be confused ...
Mary:	Thank you. Bob, uh, you have, in effect, created the particular schedule that they have at the present time, in terms of how often they go to the house, and how often they see their mother. Um, is this, is this an ideal arrangement, from your perspective? For the children to ...
Bob:	No, this is not an ideal arrangement. I think that from the time that I was asked to leave the house it was not an ideal arrangement. Um, and part of the reason, I haven't limited her to only seeing the kids seven hours in the last six weeks. Or whatever it's been. That's been partly her doing as well. Partly her schedule.
Jane:	I don't. ...
Bob:	And it's partly mine. Partly her preference of what's good for her and what's not good for her. And I know that, even when she had the kids and I was visiting, um, you know, she was very happy to have the time away from the kids. The time off, the time to herself to do some other things. And that's fine. I don't begrudge her that. I think maybe she needs more time away. 'Cause I'm feeling like ... I've been getting the impression that maybe she's not that enthused about parenting as she once was ... a little burnt out. ...
Mary:	Well, let me ask you ... let me ask you. Jane has just said that she would like the children to be in the marital residence, in the family home, ah, on a full time basis and if I understood her correctly, she was saying you were welcome to come to either have dinner with them or to have dinner and to help put them to bed, if that's feasible.
Bob:	What she's saying is ... now. I mean, she just never said that before.
Mary:	But she's said it now.
Bob:	Well, it's the first I've heard of that.
Jane:	Because the only thing that you ...
Bob:	... move back in
Jane:	The only thing ...
Bob:	You threw me out of the house. And you just sort of assumed that I was going to know when I was supposed to move back in.
Jane:	I thought we were going to have some conversations.

Bob:	Oh, conversations that you never wanted to have before!
Jane:	. . . and you didn't want to do it!
Bob:	All of a sudden you want to have conversations!
Jane:	No! Counseling! I've been after you for that forever!
Bob:	I've been after you to have a conversation with me, like an adult person. And you haven't been able to do it.
Jane:	. . . too condescending.
Bob:	Con . . . Oh!
Mary:	All right. There . . .
Bob:	Now that I have the kids, it seems like she's bringing out all this stuff about wanting me to come home . . .
Jane:	Oh! Well, yes . . .
Bob:	It's amazing . . .

CHAPTER 8 CLIPS

Clip 8-A: Party Openings: Negotiating Issues Revealed

(Sam Rossito, in Fitzgerald)

Sam:	How do you see the situation? Why are you here? What would . . . What's the situation from your point of view?
Bob:	All right, I mean she's presenting everything, of course, with her own slant on it that's making me sound like, you know, the bad guy, and her like the victim. But uh, let me just start with what totally shocked me. Let's go back to the very beginning um, when I was thrown out of the house. I've had issues with Jane's housekeeping and the way she's been taking care of the kids. I have a five year old who barely talks and when she does you can't even hardly understand her. And she's about to enter school. I have a three year old who is still very dependent on diapers, who's not been properly toilet trained. She's with the kids all day, she's not giving them the kind of structure that they need and I come into this, you know, with some issues about that. So, I come home and as is so often the case, things are pretty much in chaos. I mean, Jane's been home all day, the house is a mess, the breakfast dishes are still in the sink, toys everywhere, food strewn around on the floor. The kids are sitting there crying, the TV is blaring, and Jane is in the kitchen talking on the phone. With a friend of hers. Not any crisis, nothing important. She was just chatting. And, uh, so I come in. I try to calm the kids down and stop them from crying. I turn

the TV down, I come into the kitchen, I hang out patiently. I wait for, like 5 minutes hoping that she will realize that it's time to wrap it up, and you know, maybe acknowledge my existence, and uh, let's talk about dinner and things like that. But she's sitting there, in this mess of a kitchen, chatting on the phone and uh, finally, I just try to interrupt her and say, "can we talk?" And she just throws up her hands, you know, like "don't, don't disturb me, you know, like, what I'm doing is more important." Well, you know, after the homecoming I'd already received, I was, that made me a little bit angry, yes.

So I took the phone away from her and I hung it up. There was nothing violent about it. I just took the phone away from her and I hung it up. And I asked her what was going on, what she'd been doing all day and why the kids were crying and why the house was a mess . . . And I felt these are issues that need to be addressed. And she had an immediate violent reaction, which she often does. And she starts yelling at me. And uh, she either yells at me or she ignores me. So, she just gave some sarcastic remark. She's always sarcastic. . . .

CHAPTER 9 CLIPS

Clip 9-A: Conditioning for Persuasion: "Seize the Day"

(Harris Bock, in Resnick)

M: Okay. Glad everybody could get here today and we're here for a very special day . . .
(To Plaintiff:) For someone such as yourself that was injured in a case and has something, I have to say that first off, I think I speak for everybody, that we, you know, really feel bad about that situation. No one feels good about it. No one thinks it's anything but a very serious situation and we're hopeful that you can get it behind you as much as possible. But we're here today to recognize the realities of the situation and although there's certainly a lot of emotion for you involved, as in continuing emotion, we have to approach the thing in a way as to distill the matter and try and leave the emotion outside a little bit and recognize that we're here to try and get the case resolved. . . .

The most I think valuable thing that mediation brings, in my view and in my experience, has nothing to do with money. One of the most valuable things that a mediation brings is resolution. We're all most concerned in our lives with things that we don't know what the future's going to be, are anxious about, don't know how it's going to turn out, and that's what a lawsuit is all about for people. You really don't know how it's going to turn out. You really don't know what the result's going to be and it produces a great deal of anxiety because of that. You think about when you get up sometimes, think about it when you go to sleep sometimes. It's just something that's there and nagging at you and it doesn't go away. Well, today we have a special window of opportunity. We have this time to try and get together and try and be realistic, to try and take that and put that aside. Resolving the case is not going to make you better, you know, and make everything perfect all of a sudden, but resolving the case will say "Well, I've completed that aspect of the matter. I've accomplished that. Now it's time to close the book on the matter and move on with my life."

Clip 9-B: Conditioning for Persuasion: "Connecting"

1.   (Craig Lord, in Wilson)
(Caucus with Defendent)

Mediator:	Listen, I think I made some progress with the Plaintiff, just so you know.
DiLorenzo:	Right.
Mediator:	My brother has run a contracting company for the past 25 years, so I am not unknowledgeable when it comes to these situations.
DiLorenzo:	OK . . .
Mediator:	And I told her that, you know, actually, Mr. DiLorenzo made efforts to keep her functioning with the refrigerator out in the shed and the stove in the living room and there are plenty of contractors that wouldn't even do that. So I think I got her off that issue. We talked about that right away. Because I understand that, I mean you can't redo a kitchen and keep everything in place, I mean it just doesn't work.
DiLorenzo:	Thank you.

2.   (Harris Bock, in Resnick)

M:	It's a terrible event. Everyone—no one—no one—no one disputes that, but the question of course with regard to every event, no matter how bad it is, what's the ongoing impact?
PL:	I understand that.
M:	What's the interference with, you know, ongoing lifestyle and plans and things of that nature?
PL:	But I think the point that I would like to make is that a jury will have to consider as part of the economic—as part of the

	damages here what was recurrent nightmares, the recurrent reliving of this event on an ongoing basis for six months, to the point where he was unable to function, as Dr. Geller will explain. And I agree with you that Josh took the steps necessary to improve his situation and that is to his credit.
M:	Absolutely.
PL:	And another six months of treatment, where he continued to work on the recurrent nightmares, the anxiety. He had to move home. He dropped out of school. He couldn't have contact with people and that is a significant loss for a young man who's on the brink of what is a bright future with all of his goals. And I think that a jury—
M:	I still hope your future's bright. . . .

3. (Harris Bock, in Resnick)

M:	I know it's tough going through with this and whatever, and I'm hopeful that, you know, we can move forward with regard to this case and get it resolved. I know you take pride in the building that you have.
D:	I do.
M:	I know you feel strongly about that, but you know, you really have to understand that we can't be resolving cases on a personal basis. We're here to resolve the case on what makes sense under the circumstances, what's good for all the people involved and, you know, being involved in litigation is not a fun thing for a person to do. Not a fun thing for somebody to want and, you know, all that work that you've done with regard to having a reputation for a safe building and a building that people like and a landlord that cares about his people, you know, one little article in the newspaper can do a lot of harm.
D:	That's exactly right.
M:	I mean a lot of harm.
D:	That's right. . . .

4. (Harris Bock, in Resnick)

M:	Now, I represented when I was practicing, I was just like Judy. I was representing people that were injured. In my view, with regard to people that are injured, is that they always come out on the short end of the stick. The other side doesn't get the long end of the stick, but the person that's injured gets the short end of the stick, and that's the kind of the cards that you got. You didn't choose them or whatever,

PL: but you were there that day and you got the short end of the stick. And those are the cards you have to deal with, having got that short end of the stick, but having understood that, we want to come out as reasonably as we can on your situation.

PL: I'm going to talk to Josh, and you can assume ...

M: I'm on your side. I'm with you guys, you know. (*Moves to seat next to Plaintiff and Counsel.*) I'm with you guys. I'm here, you know. I'm not on the other side.

PL: I'm asking—

M: But I want to try and get the job done. That's what we're here to do.

Clip 9-C: Conditioning for Persuasion: Conveying Authority

(Harris Bock, in Resnick)

M: First of all, my name's Harris Bock and I've been practicing law for thirty-two years or so. I was very involved in litigation, probably for the first fifteen years, but for the last fifteen years or so, I've given my entire time to try and resolve cases in a more reasonable way. . . .

M: And from that experience, from my daily work, I have a fair amount of expertise with regard to issues that are involved in cases, and valuations that take place with regard to cases. My job is to assist you, the parties, in terms of sharing some of that expertise with you, trying to help you to understand what goes into a valuation of a case, why lawyers and other people who value cases, do so in such a way. That is primarily my job because the attorneys on both sides, not that they don't know about this because they do know about and that's what they do on an ongoing basis, but they see things as your attorney. They see things on your behalf. I see things on behalf of everybody. I'm the only one here that is looking at the matter somewhat objectively. Third party who has some knowledge of the case and going to be assisted with some additional knowledge of the case, and I look at it objectively and I have those clear glasses without Plaintiff sides on it and without Defense side on it, to help and assist you with regard to resolving the case. . . .

M: You've heard your very able counsel tell you what they have to say, but they say it in a little different way. You know, they kind of sugarcoat it a little bit to you in terms of what's on the other side. You're not going to get any sugarcoating from me. I'm not here to win your popularity contest today, or whatever.

Clip 9-D: Conditioning for Persuasion: Using Humor

(Harris Bock, in Resnick)

DL:	(Referring to Plaintiff's Counsel:) She has the burden of proof. She has to prove—
M:	You know what burden of proof is? Has that been explained to you a little bit?
D:	Yes.
M:	Okay. All right, that's just the person going forward with regard to the case has to prove more likely than not what they say is true. Different from a criminal case. Different from a criminal case. Criminal case, you know beyond a reasonable doubt. We're not talking about that here. Just like they say when a case goes to court, law is a simple balance scale. All he has to tip the edge in his favor, that's preponderance of the evidence, and that's what we talk about burden of proof. Not beyond a reasonable doubt. Get that out of your mind in a civil case.
DL:	But if the balance scales stay the same, in equipoise, the verdict has to be for the Defendant.
M:	What was that?
DL:	Equipoise.
M:	Equipoise, is that a disease? [laughs]
DL:	I learned that in law school.

Clip 9-E: Role Reversal

(Sam Rossito, in Fitzgerald)

Sam:	Let me ask it this way. In what ways is Jane a good mother? When you see her interacting with the children, what would you say positive about Jane as a mother? I've heard Jane say the children love to play with you, they have a ball. And I heard her say some really nice things about how the children, how they interact with you and they just have a ball with you.
Bob:	Right ...
Sam:	What are things that you could say about Jane that, that are positive?
Bob:	Well, I know Jane loves the kids. There's no question in my mind about that. There's no question in my mind. And, and, you know, in many ways she means well, but I just don't

think that she's giving them ... Well. Let me stay on the point. Um, I think that if there's a, if one of the children is having a problem or something, or if they need nurturing or cuddling or whatever, she's very good with that. I mean she's very affectionate with them in that way. And, I think that's great. Um, and, you know, I'm sure the kids enjoy the fact that she's fairly permissive with them, you know, to a certain extent. But I just, I'm sorry I have to throw in the other side of the coin here. I just feel like, you know, that she has to be a little bit less permissive with them and give them a little more structure. And pay a little more of quality attention to them. But I think that she gives ... I think that she gives like nurturing attention but I don't think she gives enough structure to them.

Clip 9-F: Legal Evaluation: Preparatory Explanation

(Chuck Forer, in Resnick)

M: I want to say a couple things before we start. My job as a mediator I think, is at some points to be a so-called devil's advocate. So what that means is generally when I'm with one side or the other, to ask them tough questions. Now, just because I ask a tough question, doesn't mean I know or don't know the answer to that question and it doesn't mean that I think you have a terrible case or a great case. For every tough question I ask of one side in the mediation, I ask another tough question to the other side.

But I believe that it's helpful in a mediation to really evaluate your case and to really understand the good points and bad points about your case, because only in that way can you make the best decision possible when it comes to whether you want to go ahead and try the case or whether you want to go ahead and settle the case. Okay? So I just want to give that little introduction.

Clip 9-G: Persuasion: Questions vs. Statements

(Sam Rossito, in Fitzgerald)

Sam: So Bob, as I said before, anything that you say here today, uh, in this period, is confidential. Unless you, after we're done, you say yeah, it's OK to disclose this.

Bob: OK.

Sam: Um, I guess, Bob, what I wanted to talk about is uh, that your proposal is that essentially the children be with ... be away from their mother and with other people, um, pretty much

	five days a week. So, mom, she is ... home for large chunks of time and her children are with someone who is not a parent.

Bob: Right. But I mean they love their grandmother too. I mean, hey ...

Sam: Do you, um ... Where do you, I mean where do you think the children would be most comfortable? Do you think they would. ... How would that play out? With the children not being with their mother during those large chunks of time when mother is home, she's available?

Bob: I know she's available. She's available now and they're living with her now. Um, and I'm seeing these problems already in their development. And I just don't think that, you know, the more I've had a chance to think about all of this, since we've, we've sort of been separated, that I really think that I'm going to do a better job parenting them. ...

Sam: Have you thought about how, let's say if you, if, if you didn't reach an agreement today, uh in terms, let's say that you wanted to uh, go forth with your position that the children should be with your mother during the day when mom is home ... Have you thought about how this might play out before a judge? Maybe talk to a lawyer about standards that a judge would use, or what the rules and laws are about, you know, any preferences with parents opposed to grandparents. Have you talked to anyone about this?

Bob: Well, no, I haven't talked to anybody in the legal profession about it, but um, my concern is that I don't want the kids to be in one place during the day, half a day, and then be in another place the other half a day. You know, during the evening and over night. I want them to have that consistency, so that they know where their home is in other words. And I think it would be confusing, uh, for them to be split that much where they're there every day. And again, it's going to be under Jane's influence which I think is ... lax. It might perpetuate the problems that are al. ... that are ... I mean, that wouldn't be any different than my just living at home and, you know ... She's got the kids all day just like she had. I feel she had her chance at that. And she's not doing a very good job. And you know, if that played out before a judge, and, and, I wouldn't want to get into all the legal ramifications of that. And bringing in child experts and things, and fighting in court. I'd hate to see that have to happen. But, I think that what I'm seeing is that she is being a little negligent as a mother. ...

Sam: Do you think that, however you can portray how Jane has negatively affected the children is so strong that a judge would say that they should not live with their mother during the week? Do you think you can make that strong a case? . . .

Bob: Well, it's not that, it's not that she's cruel to them or anything, you know. And I don't, frankly, I don't know who would prevail in a case like that but . . . I think that, from my point of view anyway, I feel like I have a very good case. . . .

Bob: I feel like maybe she's getting a little burned out. I really question if she's really into it. I mean, as far as being a parent.

Sam: Hmm.

Bob: I really question how much she's into it. I know she wanted to have a family at the outset. . . .

Clip 9-H: Legal Evaluation: Varied Approaches

1.   (Chuck Forer, in Resnick)

DL: I mean, you don't need an expert to explain to you that glass on the outside means someone was going out. Whereas, glass on the inside means someone was going in.

M: Okay. Now, let's go back to my question which is if the judge lets the jury make an inference as to the meaning of this glass and that the jury could find out that someone came in from the outside, what do you think as a lawyer are the chances that the judge would admit the evidence of these bars that Mr. Gonzales put on after the incident? My real question is do you think that comes in? Does that evidence come in?

DL: He may or may not. I mean, I feel that it's a toss-up. Some judges may well let that in. I'm just being perfectly frank with you. Some judges may well let that in and some judges may feel that it's, you know, there's a test to be done. There's a balancing test to be done and some judges may feel that it doesn't, you know, it doesn't cut it and they would keep it out. So to be honest, I think there's a possibility certainly that that evidence could come in.

M: And if that evidence does come in, what's your sense as to whether that's good or bad for your case?

DL: I think —

M: The jury hears, after the incident that Mr. Gonzales, who's worked for you for four years, put these security bars. Do you think that helps your case or hurts your case?

D: I'd like to see this guy prove that that was the window that somebody came in, after climbing over a ten foot wall and getting into the alleyway and climbing up the fire escape and coming directly into the — into the hallway there through that window.

DL: Well, he won't be able to prove that.

M: Well, I mean, I think don't we all agree that at the end of the day, would you say it's a fair statement that whatever evidence, whatever physical evidence there is — we have the broken window. We have the undisputed fact that there was a broken window. At some point. I understand you don't know when it occurred, but the undisputed fact of a broken window and we have the undisputed fact of this criminal incident.

DL: Uh-hmm.

M: And isn't it fair that at the end of the day, each side is going to argue to the jury whatever inferences they want the jury to make, and at the end of the day, the jury will conclude that whatever story makes more logical common sense, is what occurred? As opposed to — as opposed to either side coming up with direct evidence as to what occurred. A witness who said, "This is what I saw."

DL: Of course.

M: Neither side has that.

2. (Craig Lord, in Wilson)

Mediator: All right, Ms. Wilson, I have a couple of questions that I wanted to discuss with you separately. Do you have any, um, witnesses to testify today or is it just you?

Ms. Wilson: Um, it is just me, but I do have a statement.

Mediator: From whom?

Mrs. Wilson: I have a statement from Miss Archer, who has dealt with DiLorenzo and Sons before and had problems with them.

Mediator: In another case?

Ms. Wilson: In another case. And I also have someone that I could call. Ms. Jenkins, I could call her. She works around the corner from this building, and I could call her in and she has had dealings with DiLorenzo and Sons in the past and was very unhappy. But, at this point it is just myself and my letter.

Mediator: Ok, well let me just say this. I, you know, the judge will have to make his own rulings, but I doubt he is going to let that in. Um, it's what we. . . .

Ms. Wilson: You don't think he will allow my letter?

Mediator:	I don't think he will. No. It is what we call hearsay. You know the basic idea of the court is when somebody testifies, the other side has to be able to ask them questions, so when you bring in a letter, you can't question the letter.
Ms. Wilson:	Even if it is notarized, and all of that? It doesn't matter?
Mediator:	No, not usually, not normally. You can ask the judge, but I suspect he won't let that in.

3. (Harris Bock, in Resnick)

M:	In addition, I think that the thing with your roommate, you know. Have you ever really talked to your roommate about that? Now, we're confidential here.
P:	I mean, not. We sort of lost touch with each other since I moved out. I moved out very shortly after—after the incident. So—
M:	I know that, you know, living in a place that you feel comfortable with regard to that and you maybe had that comfort feeling when you left the door open, but can you see how someone sitting on the jury might think that, "Hey, if he would have locked the door, this would have never happened"?
P:	Yeah, I meant I dealt with that quite a bit.
M:	And how have you dealt with it?
P:	Well, I spoke with Mr.—I mean Dr. Geller about—about the incident and sort of I've had a lot of trouble with responsibility about the incident, and I sort of put a lot of the blame on myself for leaving the door open and it's something I've spent a lot of time dealing with.
M:	And if you yourself put some blame on yourself, do you see how a jury could do that as well?
P:	Yes.
M:	And it's a real factor we have here.
P:	Yeah, yeah.
M:	And—
PL:	Has—I don't mean to interrupt.
M:	No, no.
PL:	I mean clearly there is a legal issue of contrib, but it wasn't Josh but his roommate who left the door open.
M:	But he left it open, but he allowed it to remain open. He could have got up off the sofa and locked the door.

4. **(Craig Lord, in Resnick)**

Mediator: Well, look. The fact of the matter is you are still a little bit ahead, and I think that she has a very good case here that you breached the contract in terms of performance. So, I think a court is likely to award her money here, how far they are going to go, are they going to get into the failure to have the registration issue, I can't predict that. It's a possibility. But, you know, when you have this ... under Connecticut law, as I am sure your counsel will tell you, that you know, one of the terms of the contract like this must have is it must have a starting date and a completion date, and if you violate that, you know, you can even kick over into the Unfair Trade Practices Law, that is failure to comply with the contract provisions is a per se violation of that law and you can get damages and punitive damages. Not sure the court is going to award that, but I think the court is going to say this woman was inconvenienced, upset, aggravated because the contractor didn't perform within the time that he was supposed to perform. Had you performed within the time you were supposed to perform, then I think some of these things that she is complaining about wouldn't amount to much, you would have an explanation.

Mr. Bowen: You know, it would be years before she got a nickel, because if this case doesn't go our way this afternoon we going to take an appeal. We have the right to a *de novo* appeal, we'll have a jury trial, she'll need to get a lawyer. I mean, if she is prepared to be reasonable, we are prepared to be reasonable. But if she is not going to be reasonable, we will just litigate this.

Mediator: Well, I mean, listen, your client is always entitled to spend his money on legal fees if he wants, that's his privilege ... um
 ...

Mr. Bowen: So far I haven't heard anything about what it is that you think will get this case settled.

5. **(Harris Bock, in Resnick)**

M: Give us an idea of the damages with regard to—

PL: Give you an idea of the damages, as we see them. There are always certain economic losses in these cases. That's in this case the smallest part of this case. We've listed out—

M: I think I saw them in your papers, you had—

PL: What the damages are. If you just calculate lost tuition, reduced income, and the medical expenses, the security deposit, it comes to the neighborhood of sixteen thousand dollars.

M:	What is his reduced income? I didn't see anything about that.
PL:	Well, he's going back. He was making twenty-seven thousand five hundred dollars. He's now gotten a job for less.
M:	At the time of the events, he wasn't working at all.
PL:	Well, he left a job to do this Master's Degree program to make forty thousand a year.
M:	But he wasn't working at the time of the occurrence, right?
PL:	That's correct.
M:	Just so I understand the facts.
PL:	So he has now lost the opportunity of making even more money—
M:	But he said he—
PL:	By graduating from graduate school.
M:	He may not have even liked the program. He was only there a couple months. So we don't know — we don't have any track record to as to what he would be earning.
PL:	Except that—except that his grades were good. He was motivated and this was the event that triggered his leaving. But if we factor in, I guess the point with economic damages, I think a jury will be able to see a low of sixteen thousand of losses, and if you factor in that for six months he really was at a standstill, wasn't going to school, wasn't working, that's another almost fourteen thousand. That could bring economic damages with a sympathetic jury to thirty thousand, and given that although Josh is doing well, we don't know what the future holds. He remains at risk. There may be future economic losses that a jury will have to consider.
M:	I don't know if you have the basis for any future economic loss. I don't see any reports or any real medical basis for that, as I understand it.

CHAPTER 10 CLIPS

Clip 10-A: Group Brainstorming

(Cheryl Cutrona, in Wilson)

Mediator:	Um, well it looks like we've got several issues that we need to discuss here. I know that we have cabinets, the linoleum, time frames, start dates, end dates, who is going to do the job. Um, what I would like to do is just sort of clear your mind of what you wanted when you walked in the door this morning, ok? Coming to mediation is a time to negotiate, be open minded, think about um, all of the options. So what I would like to do is, I

would like to just brainstorm with you. And brainstorming is just a way to generate options. Quickly, without judging, I want you to come up with ideas. They don't all have to be what you would want to do, what you don't want to do, just anything that comes to your mind of how you could settle this so that you can all leave here feeling that you have accomplished something and that you are satisfied with the outcome. So what we will do is see if we can get at least ten things without making any judgments until we get ten things on the paper, alright? Does that sound like a good way to go from here?

Bernice:	Yeah.
Frank:	It's ambitious.
Mediator:	Alright, well let's see what we can come up with. Sometimes it works, sometimes it doesn't, but I have faith in you guys. Um, let's start with you Bernice, what's one thing that would be good in terms of trying to settle this?
Bernice:	Um, one thing that would be good . . .
Mediator:	It doesn't have to be the whole thing, but one piece of it. What would you like . . .
Bernice:	Ok, starting back at zero, my kitchen's back to the way that it was and I get my money back. They get their stuff back and I get my money back.
Mediator:	Ok. So put everything back the way that it was and get your money back?
Bernice:	Yes.
Mediator:	Refund, and the total amount was 39. . . .
Bernice:	97.
Mediator:	Ok. One thing that would. . . .
Frank:	For me to personally do the work and give guarantees.
Mediator:	Ok. So Frank would do work and make guarantees, guarantees on . . .
Frank:	On work and material.
Mediator:	Work and material. Ok.
Bernice:	Um, that they would give me a refund, a partial refund of what I've paid for my time and inconvenience. To finish the job with another contractor.
Mediator:	Ok.
Frank:	We finish the job and give her a partial refund.
Mediator:	Ok. Um . . .

Bernice:	I don't know um, something else, ten things and we are already at number five. I feel like I'm in school and I can't think. Um, um,
Mediator:	Maybe Frank can come up with something else.
Barry:	I can come up with one.
Mediator:	Ok, fine.
Barry:	We get three more competing, completing contractors.
Mediator:	So three more estimates?
Barry:	Three more estimates to do the job that was actually bid in this case. Not some other job that somebody could dream up.
Mediator:	Ok.
Bernice:	They get those three estimates and pay for it.
Mediator:	(*Laughing.*) Ok, we will see how that works. Three estimates and pay for it.
Barry:	Pay for what?
Bernice:	For them to complete the job.
Mediator:	Well these don't have to be realistic, we are brainstorming here. (*All laugh.*)
Barry:	Yeah, you are going to have to be realistic.
Mediator:	Alright, well anyone else?
Frank:	Walk away from the deal as is.
Mediator:	Walk away how?
Frank:	I walk away with the money that I have, she walks away with the all the materials and the work as is.
Mediator:	Ok.
Bernice:	I walk away with the materials, a refund.
Mediator:	Materials and …
Bernice:	A partial refund.
Mediator:	Ok. Two more to go.
Frank:	Sure, I, I finish the job and get double the quote, since we're going there.
Mediator:	One more. Do you have anything?
Frank:	I let my, I let my crew finish it and I, I let my crew finish it and we keep an open door policy with Bernice that if there is any issues, she can come directly to me. I will give her my cell phone number and I will give her a discount on future work

	she may want done, say a bathroom.
Mediator:	Ok, well, thank you. Ten things. Is there anything on here that we absolutely, should I read it back or you all remember what they are?
Frank:	I remember the ones that I think are outrageous. I have one and Bernice has one.
Mediator:	Alright, well is there anyone that is too outrageous to consider?
Frank:	I think one of Bernice's. . . .
Barry:	Number six.
Frank:	Right.
Mediator:	Three estimates and you guys pay for it.
Frank:	Right.
Mediator:	Alright so should we cross that one off?
Bernice:	Yeah.
Mediator:	Alright, we will cross that one off.
Bernice:	That one gave me a nice little chuckle inside.
Mediator:	Made you feel good.
Bernice:	Yeah it really did.
Mediator:	All right, anything else that we don't want to do?
Frank:	I don't think that Bernice wants to have me finish the work for $16,000.00
Bernice:	Double the quote. No, no way.
Mediator:	Well let's look at some of the more realistic ones. Um, put everything back and refund the $3997.00. How do you guys feel about that one? What would that look like?
Frank:	You want to reinstall all of the cabinets?
Bernice:	See that's the thing because I would have to have someone finish the work anyway. So I wouldn't want them to reinstall the cabinets. I would love my refrigerator and my stove and my water turned back on. That would be very nice. But re-installing the cabinets, no. Having things, everything removed that they put in, but they couldn't remove the, I am sure that they could remove the linoleum floor, but who would want to, um that could be done. You know the cabinets that they put in thus far because the counter top isn't in there. The rest of the cabinets aren't in.
Mediator:	I think I am losing track. Put everything back would mean what then? Just the stove, the refrigerator and ...

Bernice:	Turn the water back on.
Frank:	You can turn the water back on but there is no sink because there is no counter top. The old counter top is gone.
Bernice:	Oh.
Frank:	There is no way to have a sink unless you put in another one in.
Bernice:	But if they put in my old counter top, just rested my old counter top up there back up there. It has to be some kind of way. That they could ...
Barry:	Not without the old base cabinets back in. There would be nothing to put the counter top on top of.
Bernice:	Sure.
Mediator:	So then this one isn't realistic.
Bernice:	Yeah, it's not realistic. Let's take that one off.
Mediator:	Frank would do the work and make guarantees on the work and material. Why don't you say some more about the guarantees so that Bernice understands a little bit more about what you are saying with guarantees.
Frank:	I would give a twenty year guarantee on the cabinets and a three year guarantee on the work, if anything comes up. I would be back to do it. I would put that in writing.
Mediator:	What about the linoleum?
Frank:	The linoleum floor, I think we mentioned this, I will do everything possible to make you happy in the installation of the linoleum. I think that there is going to be an issue and I said this to Cheryl, that you've been looking at this and this, so even when I make it this and this it is still going to look like this and this to you in your mind. If you want, I will switch it this way, but it's going to mean that you are going to have not one long seam, but two. Um, now ...
Mediator:	So you haven't seen the linoleum yet, so ...
Frank:	She picked a pattern that is easily when they are together it blends beautifully.
Mediator:	So what you are saying is that if it's laid wrong in your estimate, you would re-lay it to make it look right so that the seam that you are concerned about would not be a problem. Is that what I am hearing you say?
Frank:	I will do my best to, I will personally go there and we will look together at every option there is for laying the floor so that as little will be seen as possible.

Mediator:	And could you do that this afternoon?
Frank:	I'm prepared to get changed, I wouldn't need to get changed into my work clothes, I'm prepared to go like this and start.
Mediator:	If that were the option selected would that be something that you would be willing to do is have him come out and take a look today and see how he could ...
Bernice:	If that were the option selected, yeah. I would be willing to have him come out and look at it today if that were the option but we are just going through all of them.
Mediator:	Alright, so this one we are not ruling out this one?
Bernice:	I'm not ruling out that one.
Mediator:	Ok, all right. Well let's go to the next one. Partial refund for time and inconvenience. Bernice finishes the work with other contractors.
Frank:	We didn't mention in that the materials. What happens with them?
Bernice:	I think there's another one that mentions the partial refund and materials.
Mediator:	So we could combine these two then.
Bernice:	Yes. ...
Frank:	So we keep everything there and we give her money back?
Mediator:	Partial refund and somebody else finishes the job.
Barry:	Somebody else finishes the job?
Mediator:	Yes.
Barry:	Ok.
Frank:	Well it would depend on, I mean. ...
Mediator:	It would depend on how much the partial is?
Frank:	I mean everything I am doing as you suggested. I'm coming in here and I'm open.
Mediator:	Uh huh, ok.
Frank:	Ok, so that of course, would depend on the amount we are talking about.
Mediator:	All right, so this is still a possibility.
Frank:	With me.
Mediator:	Frank finishes job and gives Bernice partial refund.
Bernice:	And for that one would you finish the job with the same guarantees and ... ?

Frank:	Absolutely.
Bernice:	I have a question about that that I didn't ask before.
Mediator:	Go ahead.
Bernice:	The guarantee, a twenty year guarantee. How do you give a twenty year guarantee?
Frank:	I will replace the cabinet if something goes wrong with the cabinet that is a result of the defect and not the result of misuse or an accident or someone purposely damages it, if it is a result of how it's hung and that we find that the defect, say it's split in the back and that it's hanging, I will replace the cabinet, free of charge. . . .
Bernice:	So that if, God forbid, something happens to DiLorenzo & Sons, the company itself, the warranty would still be good?
Barry:	It's only good if DiLorenzo & Sons stays open.
Mediator:	Well how long have you been in existence?
Frank:	Well this is the second generation.
Mediator:	Since, since. . . .
Frank:	For like 30 years. More.
Bernice:	And you are not planning on going out of business?
Frank:	I'm not planning on going out of business or dying any time soon.
Bernice:	Ok, just checking, cause you never know. It could be a year, you know, the warranty could be good for a year.
Mediator:	Alright, so twenty years or as long as you are in existence if that is shorter than that.
Frank:	Yup.
Mediator:	Plus three years on the work. Say some more about what that means on the work. . . .
Frank:	Well, I mean if I in soldering, doing the plumbing, soldering something, it comes loose and she develops a leak, I'll fix it. . . .
Bernice:	Ok, so what kind of partial refund?
Mediator:	On the partial refund for time and inconvenience or the partial refund for if Frank finishes the job and gives partial refund.
Bernice:	Yes.
Frank:	I'll tell you what, I was looking at, from what I heard from the reports that Sam wrote up and from what he told me, it looks to me as though you are probably going to need a new stove or a

new refrigerator in a couple of years, $500.00 would buy that. So when you cross that path if you are smart about it, you got your $500.00 in the bank, you don't have to put it on your credit card, there's your new stove or your new refrigerator.

Mediator:	So that would read Frank finishes the job and gives Bernice $500.00 back?
Frank:	She is going to have, she is going to need new appliances soon.
Mediator:	And she keeps the materials?
Barry:	Well if he finishes the job. . . .
Mediator:	Oh that's when he finishes the job.
Frank:	Yeah, we were still talking about that I thought.
Mediator:	Ok.
Bernice:	And that's $500.00 less. That would be instead of $3997.00, that would be $3497.00 balance?
Frank:	Correct.
Mediator:	$3497.00 would be covering . . .
Bernice:	Them finishing the job.
Mediator:	Ok.
Frank:	That's right. . . .
Frank:	And I said to Cheryl when you were out of the room, I want to see you look at me and say, "I'm happy with the work you did." I want to see that from you and that is where I am willing to go.
Bernice:	Well number seven is just walk away as is. I just can't walk away as is and . . .
Mediator:	So we will take that one off.
Frank:	And I won't get that look from her if I walk away.
Mediator:	All right. So that won't make either of you happy, that's not a win/win. . . .
Mediator:	So what do you want to look at first? Frank would do the work? I think the two major differences is Frank doing the work or Frank not doing the work.
Bernice:	Right.
Frank:	I'll do the work if you want me. If you want me Bernice. . . .
Bernice:	Ok, actually what I would like to look at first is um, is what kind of partial refund I would I get if I kept the materials and had someone else do the job. . . .

Clip 10-B: Giving Feedback on Size of Offers

(Harris Bock, in Resnick)

DL: The provable economic losses are sixteen grand. Judy Greenwood's going to get a legal fee out of the jury, although it's not technically supposed to be part of our calculation, they're probably going to figure that out.

M: That increases the damages because they figure . . .

DL: I know it does. I'm going to point that out. I'm going to point that out. So if you threw another eight thousand bucks on it as a third, another third. That would get you to twenty-four thousand total. I would be willing to round that up some more because there is some more stuff in this case, there's some risk. So I'd go up to thirty thousand dollars and I think that would—I think they ought to take that money and run with it. That's not a hundred and ten thousand, but that's thirty thousand dollars in actual cash.

M: Not my responsibility to value the case or whatever. When I sit as the arbitrator, I make decisions and I value the case. As a mediator, we kind of assist, move it along a little bit and stuff like that, you know. From that viewpoint, I think it's light and I don't think you're going to settle case. That's a little bit less than I wanted to take back for starters, but you know, I'm here to do your bidding and I'll certainly discuss that with them.

Clip 10-C: Encouraging Meaningful Concessions

(Harris Bock, in Resnick)

PL: Okay, we'll come off a hundred and ten. We'll come back at a hundred.

M: I think that's unrealistic. Let's make some progress with regard to the matter. You know, that's really unrealistic. That's going to retard negotiation, rather than jump start. Let's get into the, you know, category that makes some sense. Really.

PL: They're at thirty.

M: Do you want to talk for a minute? Why don't you talk for a minute and I'll come right back. . . .

M: I don't want you to feel pressure, but I know you feel pressure. But we've got to move along here, and it's a fluid situation, as I said. Let's go. Where are we going right now?

PL: In an effort to try to get this resolved, and I understand that they're not going to go to six figures, which I think I've told

	you is — six figures plus is the real value. I mean we would be willing to compromise, and we will come back at ninety thousand dollars.
M:	That's still too high. I think it's still too high.
PL:	Well, I think that it is important to recognize what he's gone through and I think there is risk here.
M:	Again —
PL:	For them, as well. . . .
M:	I don't want to be arguing with you because I have empathy for you and I want, you know, I want to do right by you. On the other hand, we want to, you know, we want to — doing right is getting the thing resolved at a reasonable thing. I'm happy to go back at ninety, but I think seventy-five would probably make a lot more sense to try and get this job done today. Up to you as to what you want to do. You know, really, I'm bound by yours. You just take my suggestions a little bit and do with them what they are. You know, I'm the one who does this all the time and I have a little experience.
PL:	We may not be able to get this resolved today, although we would like to.

Clip 10-D: Giving Feedback on the Timing of Offers

(Chuck Forer, in Resnick)

M:	This is your apartment building. In a sense, this is all about you. What's your take in all this?
D:	I got — I certainly do want to make sure that if we do settle here, that as little as possible gets floating out into the world and especially into my other buildings.
DL:	But you mean, you're referring to the confidentiality clause?
D:	Yeah.
DL:	Right, we certainly would have a confidentiality clause. You know, as I said, I'm not — you know, even if this case were tried, you know, to a verdict in front of a jury, I don't know how big a deal that would be. But if we are going to settle, then certainly a confidentiality clause would be part of that agreement. And I don't see that as being an obstacle in this case. I mean, I don't see, you know, that this, that the Plaintiff has some axe to grind and that he needs to make it public. I don't think that's part of his concern.
M:	At this point, if it's okay with you, I'm not going to raise the confidentiality with the other side.

DL:	Okay.
M:	At this point.
D:	All right.
M:	And the reason I say that, and again, it's my judgment and if you disagree you tell me and I'll do your bidding, to be perfectly honest with you. I just think they're going to be upset enough with ten thousand.

Clip 10-E: Fleshing Out Specifics of Proposals

(Cheryl Cutrona, in Wilson)

Mediator:	Frank would do the work and make guarantees on the work and material. Why don't you say some more about the guarantees so that Bernice understands a little bit more about what you are saying with guarantees?
Frank:	I would give a twenty year guarantee on the cabinets and a three year guarantee on the work, if anything comes up. I would be back to do it. I would put that in writing.
Mediator:	What about the linoleum?
Frank:	The linoleum floor, I think we mentioned this, I will do everything possible to make you happy in the installation of the linoleum. I think that there is going to be an issue and I said this to Cheryl, that you've been looking at this and this, so even when I make it this and this it is still going to look like this and this to you in your mind if you want, I will switch this way, but it's going to mean that you are going to have not one long seam, but two. Um, now . . .
Mediator:	So you haven't seen the linoleum yet, so . . .
Frank:	She picked a pattern that is easily when they are together it blends beautifully.
Mediator:	So what you are saying is that if it's laid wrong in your estimate, you would re-lay it to make it look right so that the seam that you are concerned about would not be a problem. Is that what I am hearing you say?
Frank:	I will do my best to, I will personally go there and we will look together at every option there is for laying the floor so that as little will be seen as possible. . . .
Bernice:	Ok, so even if God forbid, something happened to DiLorenzo and Sons, the company itself, that warranty would still be good?
Barry:	It's only good if DiLorenzo and Sons stays open.

Mediator:	Well how long have you been in existence?
Frank:	Well this is the second generation.
Mediator:	Since, since. . . .
Frank:	For like 30 years. More.
Bernice:	And you are not planning on going out of business?
Frank:	I'm not planning on going out of business or dying any time soon.
Bernice:	Ok, just checking cause you never know. It could be a year, you know, the warranty could be good for a year.
Mediator:	Alright, so twenty years or as long as you are in existence if that is shorter than that.
Frank:	Yup.

Clip 10-F: Assessing Offers: Underscoring Interests

(Harris Bock, in Resnick)

M:	So we've got to move on. They've now put fifty thousand on the case, and I think that they're in the low range of reasonableness with regard to it. I still there's, you know, a little more there, but not a whole lot, and we're going to get down to a figure that, you know, this is our last shot, kind of take it or leave it basis and things of that nature. So we want the bottom type situation as to where you're going to go in the case right now, and see if you can deal with it.
PL:	Do you think you can get them to go to seventy-five thousand?
M:	No.
PL:	Because if you can, I will talk to Josh about recommending it.
M:	I don't think that's going to happen. I don't think that's going to happen. . . .
PL:	I have a question for you. Could you recommend to them that they go to seventy-five?
M:	My recommendation really is not in the midst of the mediation, in terms of recommendation. You know, I assist, I push. I really don't —
PL:	Do you think if you could discuss that with them, and I haven't — I don't have authority for this, but Josh and I could talk and maybe lay out to them that if they could go to that number . . .

M: I talked about that number, and I don't think it's going to get—I don't think we're going to get there. We're going to have to get somewhere between fifty and seventy-five to get this case settled, if you want to get it settled. Fifty is not acceptable to you. Seventy-five is not acceptable to them . . .

M: And I do have children and whatever, and as I tell my children all the time, but you know, anything that you can—anything that you can buy with money can't be that important, and money is going to be the ultimate thing here and money is important, but you know, Josh going on and finding his way and not having to deal with this case, which may drag on for a couple years for an appeal, or something like that. You know, hopefully—hopefully the difference that we're talking about moneywise is going to be inconsequential in terms of his life and, you know, his life has been interrupted already by this incident, by this trauma. I don't want to have another trauma going along.

Clip 10-G: Lowering the Perceived Stakes

(Mary Hanna, in Fitzgerald)

Bob: They need to know, they need to be in the best place for them. And I'm not sure that living there with you is the best place for them to be permanently.

Jane: But you're not the one to make that decision.

Mary: Let me ask . . .

Bob: I'm just telling you what my feeling is.

Mary: Bob, Bob, you just mentioned . . .

Bob: I think they should be with me.

Mary: If I could interrupt. You just mentioned "permanently." And I must say that in parenting arrangements, particularly when we have very young children, you have a long road ahead, a lot of years as parents of minor children. And there are many things that can occur in the lives of the children over their growth and development. Megan is just approaching elementary school age. So there's a lot of opportunity for the two of you as parents to spend time with them and to have an input with them. And I think when I hear the word "permanent," in the context of parenting and working with children, it almost seems foreign. Because if there's anything about children, it's a lack of permanence. Children are growing and developing and so things change just in their own environment, in their own experiences.

Clip 10-H: Analyzing Barriers to Settlement

(Mary Hanna, in Fitzgerald)

Mary: What would you propose as being a more, I believe your term was equitable? A more equitable arrangement for the children to have contact with you and be involved with you?

Jane: Well, obviously, in the best of all worlds, I want them living back home because, first of all, I've been their primary caretaker since, well, before birth, since pregnancy. And um, they're my children and they don't need to be raised by a grandmother if I'm alive. Um, and I have, whether Bob agrees with how I'm parenting or not, that's my goal. That's what I do. That's what I live for. And to have been denied access to them like this for such a long time ... Um, I mean I'm just rambling around the house. You know, I'm not at work. I don't have a place to go. They're echoing all over the house. And um, and um. What? I mean in the best of all worlds, I thought Bob was moving home. In July, that's what I thought was going to happen. I never expected this. Um, and I don't think it's fair to deprive children of either parent. Um ...

Bob: I agree.

Jane: And uh, the way he may be upset with the fact that he had to leave the house, but you know, any time, except for the first time, anytime that he wanted to see the children, I said yes. I never said ...

Bob: But ...

Jane: The very first time that you called, I hesitated because I wasn't sure I could trust you.

Bob: I've already been through this ...

Jane: No, but I mean ...

Bob: ... every step of the way.

Jane: But the point I'm trying to make is that you never gave me that same consideration.

Mary: Jane, the question that I posed was, what would you like to see that would be a more acceptable arrangement than what you have at the present time. Given the fact that you, at the moment, are separated.

Jane: I mean, I would like them to live at home. And as far as I'm concerned, Bob can come have dinner every night with the kids. Help put them to bed like we always did. And then he can ... go home. To South Philly. If that's what he wants to do. And on the weekends, if he wants to take them all weekend, that's fine. If he wants to, since I have them all during the week, I don't want to deprive him of the time that he has. If he wants them on the weekends, that's fine. But, it should come down to, the kids shouldn't be put in the middle. They shouldn't be confused. . . .

Mary: Thank you. Bob, uh, you have, in effect, created the particular schedule that they have at the present time, in terms of how often they go to the house, and how often they see their mother. Um, is this, is this an ideal arrangement, from your perspective? For the children to . . .

Bob: None of this is an ideal arrangement. I think that from the time that I was asked to leave the house it was not an ideal arrangement. Um, and part of the reason, I haven't limited her to only seeing the kids seven hours in the last six weeks. Or whatever it's been. That's been partly her doing as well. Partly her schedule.

Jane: I don't . . .

Bob: And it's partly mine. Partly her preference of what's good for her and what's not good for her. And I know that, even when she had the kids and I was visiting, um, you know, she was very happy to have the time away from the kids. The time off, the time to herself to do some other things. And that's fine. I don't begrudge her that. I think maybe she needs more time away. Cause I'm feeling like . . . I've been getting the impression that maybe she's not that enthused about parenting as she once was. She seems a little burnt out . . .

Mary: Well, let me ask you . . . let me ask you. Jane has just said that she would like the children to be in the marital residence, in the family home on a full time basis and if I understood her correctly, she was saying you were welcome to come to either have dinner with them or to have dinner and to help put them to bed, if that's at all feasible.

Bob: Well, she's saying this now. I mean, she just never said that before.

Mary: But she's said it now.

Jane: You were supposed to move back in. . . .

Bob: Well, it's the first I've heard of that.

Jane: Because the only thing that you . . .

Bob: . . . move back in

Jane: The only thing . . .

Bob: You threw me out of the house. And you just sort of assumed that I was going to know when I was supposed to move back in.

Jane: I thought we were going to have some conversations.

Bob:	Oh, conversations that you never wanted to have before!
Jane:	. . . and you didn't want to do it!
Bob:	Oh, you want to have conversations!
Jane:	No! Counseling! I've been after you for that forever!
Bob:	I've been after you to have a conversation with me, like an adult person. And you haven't been able to do it.
Jane:	You're . . . too condescending.
Bob:	Con . . . Oh!
Mary:	Alright. There . . .
Bob:	Now that I have the kids, it seems like she's bringing out all this stuff about wanting me to come home . . .
Jane:	Oh! Well, yes . . .
Bob:	It's amazing.
Mary:	Let me interrupt for a minute. Do we need to um, do we need to take a break? Would it be at all beneficial to have a few minutes to calm down or to talk together without me being present. Are there some things that would be useful for you to say to each other? Um . . .
Bob:	I don't know that we could accomplish. I've been trying to do that for years and it hasn't been working, so . . .
Mary:	As I said before, I'm not here in the role of a therapist. It looked as though there was a glimmer of an opening, an opportunity there for a moment and maybe there is, but counseling is something that you can always consider . . .
Bob:	Can't go back to the way it was. The next thing you know is the cops are going to come and throw me out again.
Mary:	I don't know if you've seen these before. This is something called the Universal Calendar.
Jane:	Universal . . . ?
Mary:	Well, it's a Universal Calendar because it's not based on a particular month or a particular year, it allows you to fill in dates and times. Or, specifically, what I was going to suggest is that you might each want to take a look at this and mark down . . . Maybe Jane, you could put either a J for your initial or M for mom. And either B for Bob or F for father. Um, times, days when you think it would be to the children's advantage, as well as something that would fit with your individual schedules. We might take a minute or two now to have you look at this and think about what your schedule might be. I think an offer was made, your response, if I

understood correctly was that that was an enticement back to the family home. Ah, it might be that it would be within your discretion as to how much or how often, if this is even something that you want to consider? Ah, what it would look like if you were going to spend some time there. Or, if you have a counter proposal that would be useful to put out? ...

Bob: I do have a counter proposal. I, I, see, first of all we have to agree on what home is. And, and Jane is still sticking with where she lives right now as home. And that doesn't necessarily mean home to me. I've been thrown out of that, and as long as she ...

Jane: The kids haven't ...

Bob: Well, sometimes ... they've been separated from their father because of it. And when you had control of the situation, things were very different than the way you're making them out to be right now. All of the sudden, when I have the kids, "Oh yeah, come on over as much as you want." But we have to agree on some things or you know, it's, we're just on shifting sands again and I'd be walking into, blindly into a situation I don't know how it's going to go from one day to the next.

Mary: I see you ...

Bob: And also, again, without getting too much into old issues, I mean I still have issues with her as a parent. So, I want to be the primary care taker. I want to have the kids with me.

Jane: But you're not there!

Bob: I am there every evening and on the weekends and my mother is there ...

Jane: Which is what I'm offering!

Bob: ... in the afternoons.

Mary: OK, Bob, may I ask something? That you think perhaps in terms of the children's definition of where home is and at least, from what I recall here, Jane has indicated that the children still identify the marital residence as their home and perhaps where you are with your parents is grandma and grandpa's home. Now I don't know, you haven't specifically said that, but I would imagine since they were ah, I think there was conversation here that they keep asking ...

Jane: They keep asking me when they're coming home.

Mary: ... with your folks' place. So ...

Bob: They refer to it as home too so, you know, that's the thing. I want to take the confusion out of their equation.

Mary:	Well, I don't know that we can sit here and make a decision about what is or is not confusing to the children. I think that perhaps some consistency is one thing. But that's my value. And I think that the two of you have to, ah, come to some terms as to the frequency, the length of time that the children are going to spend with each of you. I noticed that Jane said before that these were her children. And I would correct you Jane. I would correct Bob if he said the same thing. They're your children. Together. And, I have no hesitation in saying that my values say, ah, as parents of these two children, the children need both of you. . . .
Mary:	Excuse me Bob. If you're saying that you feel that the children are, um, developing in a more positive way in the care of your mother, where you are, um, and you, what would you then want to provide as opportunities for the children to spend with their mother?
Bob:	Well, you know, I have to bring them to her. Because I know public transportation is tough for her to get down. She doesn't have a car. So I have to bring the kids to her. And so it does have to be a mutual schedule thing. And is a mutual schedule thing the way it is right now. And ideally, of course I want her to see them more often than what they are now. It's just, it's not enough.
Mary:	And what would be enough from your perspective?
Bob:	I was thinking something along the lines of an evening a week and a whole weekend day.
Jane:	Oh, gee honey, thanks!
Mary:	A whole weekend day? Would there be any reason that the children could not stay over night with her?
Bob:	I'd rather not. Because I don't think they should go from bed to bed. I think they should know that, you know, this is their bed, this is their home and then when they go there, it's a place that they're visiting.
Jane:	Do you realize that you created this whole situation of them not knowing where their home is?
Bob:	Don't go there with me! Creating . . . anything . . . You created the entire thing by throwing me out of the house in the first place and dividing this family!
Jane:	No. No, no, no. The point is, that you, I may have disrupted your life but I didn't disrupt theirs.
Bob:	No, no, no. You disrupted all of our lives.
Jane:	No, because I . . .
Bob:	By taking the father out of the home, you disrupted their lives.

Jane:	The oh-so-involved-father! The oh-so-involved-father.
Bob:	Yes! More involved than you, obviously.
Jane:	No, I don't think so.
Bob:	What I see, what ...
Jane:	The amount of interest that you're showing right now is more than you've done in five years.
Bob:	Oh really?
Jane:	Yes!
Bob:	Yeah.
Jane:	Yes.
Bob:	Interesting.
Mary:	Can we turn that into a positive ...
Bob:	I haven't seen you show any interest in the kids in five years!
Jane:	Oh really?
Mary:	Jane?
Bob:	Yeah, you just kind of let them go on their own.
Jane:	You changed all their diapers. That's amazing.
Bob:	Yeah, you're good at the mechanical stuff.
Mary:	... we, could we channel this interest, whether it's new interest or ongoing interest, into something that is meaningful for the children?
Bob:	That's what I'm trying to do here. I want the kids to be ...
Mary:	Then I come back to a specific question. You have proposed ah, that the mother see the children for one night during the week. Is that correct?
Bob:	Yes.
Mary:	And is that for an overnight?
Bob:	Well ... no. I'd rather not. ...
Mary:	Your proposal would be? Would look like what? And can you perhaps just use the calendar ...
Bob:	I don't know, just say. I don't know, it doesn't matter to me. Whatever night is good for her ...
Mary:	Well, you're making, I'm asking you the proposal. What you would feel would be acceptable from your point of view? And perhaps while he's doing that, if you wanted to make a notation of what it was that you had suggested. So that we

	have a specific proposal from each one of you. We can kind of work from that, from that perspective.

Bob: OK, ah, say it's the middle of the week maybe, or, so Jane Wednesday evening and Jane all day Saturday. Something like that. That's better than she gave me at the outset.

Mary: And how often would that occur?

Bob: Every week!

Mary: Every week?

Bob: Yeah! . . .

Mary: Ah, you mentioned you would be the one providing the transportation.

Bob: Right.

Mary: So what time would you be picking up the children after work and what time would you get to Germantown? . . .

Mary: And on a weekend, what would you be thinking of?

Bob: As soon as the kids want to go over there, you know, in the morning. As early as they want to go over there.

Jane: So if they wake up at 6:30 and they're excited to see mom, then you would be ready to um, jump in the car . . .

Bob: I would do it. If that's what they wanted, yup.

Mary: So, 7 a.m., they could be at Germantown. . . .

Bob: Sure, yup!

Mary: And then you would leave them for the day?

Bob: Leave them for the day.

Mary: And you would come back . . . on Sunday?

Bob: Well, no, not overnight. After dinner I would pick them up and then come back home. Again, I don't want that confusion. I want them to know where their bed is.

Mary: OK. So you're thinking in terms of a Saturday. I'm saying 7:00 a.m. just for the sake of conversation, until maybe 7:00 p.m. Is that what I heard you say? Or did I misperceive . . .

Bob: Sure. That's fine.

Mary: OK.

Bob: It's far more than I ever got.

Mary: Um, Jane, you have much more detailed schedule. But it was an every day schedule. That the children will be with you?

Jane: And they'll see their father every day.

Mary:	And the father would come ... And that would be, am I correct that what you're anticipating would be his choice to come?
Jane:	He could come every night. It would be up to him.
Mary:	OK. And all day you're suggesting?
Jane:	If he would want either Saturday or Sunday, he could have all day, even an overnight if he wanted.
Mary:	Well, you know, it appears to me as though we're really going to have to give this some further thought. And I, I think we're running out of time for today, which suggests to me that we will come back. Are you willing to proceed to a second session? ...
Bob:	Sure. (Jane nods.)
Mary:	Good. I thank you very much. I think the fact that you have at least agreed to come back is a very positive one and I look forward to meeting with you again. Take care.

Clip 10-I: "End Game" Settlement Techniques

1.   (Harris Bock, in Resnick)

M:	All right, I got them down. They'll take seventy-five. That's, you know, kind of where we thought a little bit. I know you wanted to be lower, but if you pay the seventy-five, they'll take that today.
DL:	No, sir. I told you we'd pay sixty and it's the limit.
M:	You said — you said, your value — you thought the value was for sixty, was what it was worth, and I can appreciate that, and you know, I'm not disagreeing with that, but we're talking about getting the case settled. We've got them down a figure that is in that range of reasonableness.
DL:	I tell you what I'll do. I'll make a call and I'll see if I can — if they say they will take splitting the difference.
M:	No, they said they'd take seventy-five and the mediator is of the opinion that seventy-five is a reasonable figure. You make the call. You tell them they picked me for the mediator. You know, take some guidance. Tell them that seventy-five, the mediator says seventy-five is a reasonable figure.
DL:	Harris, halfway between seventy-five and fifty is sixty-two five. I will make a call and I'll say to the — I've got to get some more authority, but I'll recommend sixty-two five and I think that's a fair number and they should take it.

M:	Let's—I'll go back. Let's go back with a little bit more than half. Make them think that they're getting one. Doesn't mean that much to the carrier. Let's go with sixty-five.
DL:	Okay, let me try.
M:	Let's go with that, and you pay for the mediation. . . .
DL:	But, before I do that, I got to know that they will take that sixty-five.

2. **(Chuck Forer, in Resnick)**

M:	Let me ask you this, because we are very late and we're about to close down. . . .
M:	Are you prepared to tell me—recognizing that it's not going to leave this room, are you prepared to tell me what your bottom line number is, recognizing I'll ask them and in my judgment, if I feel you're kind of close, I'll keep you here.
DL:	I think that's worthwhile. I mean, you're telling me that I would tell you my bottom line number and that you wouldn't communicate it to them?
M:	I'm not going to communicate it to them. . . .
DL:	How will you make a determination that they're too far apart? How will you do that?
M:	You know what, I could tell both of you—I could simply make—I could simply tell both of you that I believe your numbers are not that far from one another, in my judgment. If they're within twenty or twenty-five thousand dollars, I'll do that, without saying exactly how far apart they are.
DL:	Within twenty or twenty-five?
M:	That's what I propose. How's that? That you give me your number. They'll give me—and let's say twenty, and if they're within twenty thousand, we'll keep on talking. If not, we won't talk. How's that?
DL:	Okay, if they're within twenty thousand.

3. **(Craig Lord, in Wilson)**

Mediator:	All right, so, what I think here I should do is, I am going to—I am going to give you both a number and it's going to be a number that I think, considering everything and where the parties are and I'm not telling where you are and I'm not telling you where he is except, you know—he doesn't mind me conveying the fact that he is willing to throw in some of these physical things. I will give you a number, I will give you

some time to think about it, and then I only want to know yes or no from you.

Ms. Wilson: Ok.

Mediator: If, you know, you say yes and he says yes — then the case is settled.

Ms. Wilson: Ok.

Mediator: If you say no or he says no, then the case if over and I will take that from you individually so that you won't be giving up anything in terms of future bargaining. If you tell me that you'll take X dollars, and he doesn't say he will pay it, then I won't tell him what you said. You follow me?

Ms. Wilson: Ok, yes.

Mediator: So by you telling me that you are not giving anything up.

Ms. Wilson: Ok.

Mediator: Because he won't know unless he settles the case. Same thing works opposite.

Ms. Wilson: Ok.

Mediator: If you say you won't take it but he says he'll pay it, you will never know whether he agreed to pay it.

Ms. Wilson: Right.

Mediator: And, that way he is not giving up anything either. So, um, what I would like you to do is this: I would like you to step out for one minute, and, well actually I think I am going to give you the number now.

Ms. Wilson: Ok.

Mediator: What I am going to recommend — you don't have to, you will have some time to think about it — but I am going to recommend that you accept his offer to take the base cabinets, the linoleum and the counter top which he apparently already has and has paid for, and $1500.00. And by my calculations, that will give you enough to hire a new contractor, have him do the sheet rock work, which is extra, and probably have a little bit left over for your aggravation. And it's not a perfect solution, but litigation is not a place where people get perfect remedies. . . .

(Caucus with Defendant)

Mediator: Ok, and by the same token if she accepts my recommenda-tion and you don't, you know, you won't know that she accepted it. So, a lot of people get to this stage and they're afraid, "well geez, I'm bidding against myself. I am putting my cards on the table." Well, you are only putting them on the table privately to me. Ok?

DiLorenzo:	Ok, I like that.
Mediator:	Now I have worked hard on her. I worked on her with some of the things on the irregular cabinets, I worked with her on the linoleum, I've told her the kitchen is going to look better whoever completes it. I've talked all that. But, here is my recommendation. I don't want you to react until you get a chance to talk to your counsel. Ok? My recommendation is that you do deliver the items you talked about. The remaining linoleum to match up with what's left, the countertop that's been ordered, and the remaining base cabinets that you already have. And instead of paying her $1500.00, I'm sorry $1000.00, I want you to pay her—I want you pay her $1,575.00.
Mr. Bowen:	Where does that number come from?
Mediator:	That is sort of my recommendation. My recommendation. And it's not with the idea that she is going to have a windfall on this, at all. Now, what I would like for you to do is, you know, I'm sure your counsel will tell you more than I do what the vagaries of litigation are and if it goes against you what the problems can be, the expenses and everything. This is to end of it right here and now. Settlement check. Ten days, is that reasonable? Counsel, if we agree?
Mr. Bowen:	Mr. DiLorenzo, ten days, if we agree?
DiLorenzo:	Yes. . . .

(Caucus with Plaintiff)

Mediator:	Ms. Wilson, I—just understand that court is ready to get started, so I am running out of time. You've seen, I have tried to listen to everybody and work with you and come up with something that pulls you out of a difficult situation and courts don't have the ability to wave the magic wand, and you know, make everything all like it never happened, but we try to do something here that you can live with. So can you live with my recommendation?
Ms. Wilson:	I can live with your recommendation.
Mediator:	Ok, alright. What I want you to do is—now remember, I don't know what his position is. He won't know that you said that unless he goes along with it, ok. So just step out and ask him to come in and we are almost over.
Ms. Wilson:	Ok. One thing I do want to know—
Mediator:	What's that?
Ms. Wilson:	Is that there will be some type of document drawn up stating that the cabinets and the countertop and all of that will be . . .

Mediator:	That will be part of the settlement process and if you want I will throw in my time to take a look at that too.
Ms. Wilson:	Ok, that will be fantastic. . . .

(Caucus with Defendant)

Mediator:	Counsel, where are we?
Mr. Bowen:	We have given this some thought, um . . .
Mediator:	By the way, we only have, um, you know, we are down to the . . .
Mr. Bowen:	It's more than we want to spend, really. Um, it's probably, three, four hundred dollars more than we want to spend. If we do this, it really puts us in a hole, um, but we have decided for the sake for the sake of bringing an end to the litigation, we would be agreeable to a payment of $1575.00. But there is a condition on that: we must insist on confidentiality. He does work in this community and we can't have Ms. Wilson telling everyone that she got a settlement for her kitchen.
Mediator:	All right, let me ask you this. Your offer includes delivering the materials that we talked about: the linoleum, the cabinets and the counter top, is that right?
DiLorenzo:	Uh huh.
Mr. Bowen:	That's right, yes it does.
Mediator:	Ok, and you would want her to agree that she would keep confidential the amount of the settlement as well as the fact of the settlement?
Mr. Bowen:	Yes. We don't want to be hearing about this from other people in the community.
Mediator:	If there's disputes about the confidentiality agreement, can I arbitrate those disputes?
Mr. Bowen:	That would be fine.
Mediator:	Ok, alright. Ask her to come in for just a minute, please?

(Caucus with Plaintiff)

Mediator:	I just have one thing that I neglected to mention to you. It's my fault for not doing this. In connection with settlements in commercial cases like this, the parties customarily agree to a confidentiality agreement. That would require you to agree that you won't discuss the fact that the case settled or discuss the amount of the settlement. Now, like I say, this is something that people agree to. Are you pretty good at keeping your lips sealed when you have to?

Ms. Wilson:	Most definitely. Yes, I am.
Mediator:	Can you live with something like that?
Ms. Wilson:	Yes.
Mediator:	By the way, if there are any disputes over it, they have agreed that I can arbitrate it. Will you be agreeable to that too?
Ms. Wilson:	Oh, yes.
Mediator:	That means, you know, if there is some dispute over the papers, I will take a look at it, make my suggestions, and ask the parties to go along with it. Ok?

(Parties reconvene together)

Mediator:	All right, I am pleased to announce that we have a settlement in the case. I think that everybody has operated in good faith. Um, I appreciate your taking the time. It always makes me feel good when I volunteer my time and that the parties like you work to get a case settled.
Ms. Wilson:	Thank you very much.
Mediator:	Now the terms of the settlement, just so that you can have them down, it will be a — Mr. DiLorenzo will within 10 days deliver the remaining cabinets, the linoleum to finish out the floor and the counter top. There will be a payment of $1575.00 and there will be a confidentiality agreement where you agree not to discuss the fact that there was a settlement or the amount with anybody and both of you have agreed, that is plaintiff and defendant, that if there is any disputes about the confidentiality agreement that I will arbitrate, that I will say what is fair, and that will be the end of it. Ok. Agreed, counsel?
Mr. Bowen:	Yes, that's fine.

CHAPTER 12 CLIPS

Clip 12-A: Conflict of Interest Disclosure

(Judith Meyer, in Wilson)

Mediator:	You are all here, well, first let me tell you, um, I've met Mr. Bowen before. He and I, I work as a full time neutral, so that you know that. I am here because the Small Claims Court has referred this case to mediation and apparently if we don't, we've got ninety minutes to work on this more or less, but when the Court is ready, they'll basically tell us that he is ready and if the case isn't settled, he'll be eager to have you in front of him. But I've met Barry because I work as a full time

neutral on other cases: an arbitration that we did involved a partnership dispute. And Barry and I, in fact, sometimes see each other at Bar conferences because we are both very interested and into alternative dispute resolution theory and practice, so I need to tell you that. Are you ok with that?

Clip 12-B: Confidentiality: "Leaking" Information in Pursuit of Settlement

(Harris Bock, in Resnick)

DL:	Okay, now I'm going to ask you something you may not want to answer.
M:	Uh-hmm.
DL:	What do you think the right number is?
M:	Well, if it's the right number for them or whatever, I can only guess as to, you know, what will settle the case or something like that. I think that the value of the case is somewhere between sixty and seventy-five, and if you got it for sixty, you'd be getting a good deal. If you got it for seventy-five, you'd be getting a reasonable deal.
DL:	Yeah, I was going to say I thought the value of this case was sixty. That's what I was going to say, but I can't put sixty on the table because they're going to come back and say sixty, then—
M:	Well, I can't give you the authority and I can't tell you what to offer specifically because, you know, I don't know how much authority you have and I have an ethical issue with regard to knowing what you got or whatever. But I don't think that anybody would be terribly disappointed if you put fifty on the table right now and tried to see where they would be.
DL:	All right. I think that's what we should do. . . .

(Caucus with Plaintiff):

M:	OK. So we've got to move on. They've now put fifty thousand on the case, and I think that they're in the low range of reasonableness with regard to it. I still there's, you know, a little more there, but not a whole lot, and we're going to get down to a figure that, you know, this is our last shot, kind of take it or leave it basis and things of that nature. So we want the bottom type situation as to where you're going to go in the case right now, and see if you can do it.
PL:	Do you think you can get them to go to seventy-five thousand?

M:	No.
PL:	Because if you can, I would talk to Josh about recommending it.
M:	I don't think that's going to happen.

Clip 12-C: Mediator Pressure to Settle

(Harris Bock, in Resnick)

PL:	Okay, we'll come off at a hundred and ten. We'll come back at a hundred.
M:	I think that's unrealistic. Let's make some progress with regard to the matter. You know, that's really unrealistic. That's going to retard negotiation, rather than jump start. Let's get into the, you know, category that makes some sense. Really.
PL:	They're at thirty.
M:	Do you want to talk for a minute? Why don't you talk for a minute and I'll come right back. . . .
M:	I don't want you to feel pressure, but I know you feel pressure. But we've got to move along here, and it's a fluid situation, as I said. Let's go. Where are we going with now?
PL:	In an effort to try to get this resolved, and I understand that they're not going to go to six figures, which I think I've told you is — six figures plus is the real value. I mean we would be willing to compromise, and we will come back at ninety thousand dollars.
M:	That's still too high. I think it's still too high.
PL:	Well, I think that it is important to recognize what he's gone through and I think there is risk here.
M:	Again —
PL:	For them, as well.
M:	I don't want to be arguing with you because I have empathy for you and I want, you know, I want to do right by you. On the other hand, we want to, you know, we want to — doing right is getting the thing resolved at a reasonable thing. I'm happy to go back at ninety, but I think seventy-five would probably make a lot more sense to try and get this job done today. Up to you as to what you want to do. You know, really, I'm bound by yours. You just take my suggestions a little bit and do with them what they are. You know, I'm the one who does this all the time and I have a little experience.

PL: We may not be able to get this resolved today, although we would like to. . . .

PL: I think you've even said that is low, okay? Particularly given the real value before the jury. There was a case a hundred and thirty-seven thousand. There's a hundred, a hundred and ten. We're discounting what is a case you've told us will go to a jury —

M: Judy, Judy, we've been through that. We've been through that already, let's — you know, come on. We've got to move on. We've got a couple minutes left. . . .

PL: Okay. I'm going to talk to Josh and you can assume from —

M: I'm on your side.

PL: Okay.

M: I'm with you guys, you know. I'm with you guys. You know, I'm here. I'm not on the other side.

PL: I'm asking —

M: But I want to try and get the job done. Which is what we're here to do.

Clip 12-D: "Stunted" Legal Evaluation

(Craig Lord, in Wilson)

Mediator: Now, there is a couple of things that I really want to focus on here. Because I think that the essence of the problem that you have here is the contract that was signed. I don't know who filled this out. I assume that one of your men fills them out in the field, but what it says is: "The work to be performed by us will, if possible, begin on or before August 29th." And then it says: "The work to be performed by us will be substantially completed, if possible, on or before the following approximate estimated date: September 27th." So, I mean I recognize that it says, "if possible." I recognize that it says, in both of these, start date and a completion date. But, you know, and I didn't want to get into this in front of her cause I am not trying to build her case while she is here.

DiLorenzo: OK.

Mediator: But, I've gotta just trying to be independent about this, I've got a real issue with that because, you know, we are in agreement that the work started August 1st, which is, you know, substantially later than —

DiLorenzo: October 1st.

Mediator: I'm sorry, October 1st, which is, you know, well over a month later than what was stated it would start.

Mr. Bowen:	She never asked for her money back. She never said "You haven't started on time. I don't want you to do the work. I've lost trust in you. I have no confidence." She let us start.
Mediator:	But that—that is not an excuse for a breach. As a matter of fact, I believe, maybe you Counsel have an opinion on this, the Connecticut Consumer Protection Act, I'm sorry, Unfair Trade Practices Act makes failure to comply with the contract provision a *per se* violation. And, you know, if the court would find that the provision for completion—for commencement or completion of the work had been violated, they could award not only actual damages, but attorney's fees, which she doesn't have an attorney, or punitive damages. . . .

CHAPTER 13 CLIPS

Clip 13-A: Preparing the Client for the Process and His Role

1. (Dave Kwass, with Josh Resnick)

A:	Now, in approaching the mediation process, as I said, you're not—this is not going to be like the deposition. You remember the deposition, where the defense lawyers—
P:	Mm-hm.
A:	—you know, tried to beat you over the head with this, that and the other thing. This is not going to be like that.
P:	Mm-hm.
A:	The mediator may ask you some, sort of softball questions about how you're doing, how you're feeling, what your plans are. I don't—I'd be very, very surprised if a mediator wanted to ask you the questions today about specifically what happened or why the front door was left open, or this kind of stuff. I'd be very, very surprised.
P:	Mm-hm.
A:	And frankly, I probably would want to try to move the conversation elsewhere.
P:	Right.
A:	Because today's not the day for rehashing that.
P:	Gotcha.

2. (Terry Lefco, with Howard Stevens)

DL:	All right. Now, if during this mediation—well, here's how it works. We go in there. The mediator will be there. You and I

will be there. Josh Resnick and his lawyer will be there. The mediator will probably make some sort of an opening statement explaining who he or she is and, you know, the way they intend to work. Then he'll probably invite both sides to make some sort of an opening presentation and then he'll probably start to work with both sides separately. You don't have to say anything initially. I'm going to make the opening presentation. When we get into private session, he may talk to you directly.

D: About what kind of thing?

DL: Well, I don't know. We'll have to wait and see, but I'll—I mean I, I'll be there with you, so I can guide that discussion.

D: Okay.

DL: As far as you talking directly to Josh, if the opportunity comes up to express your feelings that you're sad and, you know, that you and Carol were unhappy that this happened to him.

D: Try and smooth his feelings out.

DL: Yeah, you could do that, but other than that I wouldn't want you saying anything directly —

D: To him.

DL: To him or to his lawyer. Don't get into a fight with his lawyer. Okay?

D: Okay.

DL: Okay?

D: Yeah.

DL: And if you need to talk to me privately at any point, just say, "I need to talk to my counsel privately." Get up and we walk out.

D: And why would I—why would I?

DL: I don't know. You know, something may come up. You may want to say something, but you may want to say to me beforehand, "Should I say this?"

D: Uh-hmm.

DL: And if that comes up, which it might, then we'll just go outside and discuss it.

Clip 13-B: Preparing the Client: Managing Expectations, Anticipating Reactions

1. **(Dave Kwass, with Josh Resnick)**

P: I'm really eager to get this over with. I would like to be able to settle today. That would be ideal for me. Just because I want to move on with my life. So I just want you to know that's where I sort of stand with this.

A: Right, but of course—and I hear you, and I absolutely respect that, and that makes a lot of good sense to me. And I also know, not from being on the client-side Josh, but from being on the lawyer-side, I know what it's like for clients to go through trial. And litigation stinks. And trials some times even more. Trials are inevitably emotional roller-coaster rides, when the case is going good you feel great, when the case is going bad you feel awful, and ultimately it often has nothing to do with how the jury perceives it anyway. It's quite remarkable, but I understand what you're saying. We also want to make sure that we're able to put some money in your pocket and it's an amount that's going to—you know nothing is going to fairly compensate you for what you've lost, there isn't an amount of money that I could hand you and say, "Here. Sorry you lost a year."

P: Yeah.

A: You know. And the other part of this is we're not going to get an apology from them, and in fact what we'll probably get, if there's a settlement agreement, is this legal document that says that their liability is expressly denied and they're making this settlement only for economic reasons, not because they think they did anything wrong.

P: Yeah.

A: And then they're also likely to insist on confidentiality, not that you'd want to go tell anyone, "Hey, I got this many thousand dollars from this landlord that I sued" but they are very, very likely to insist on confidentiality. And you know, to the extent that you have an interest in making sure that Stevens Realty behaves better in the future, I'm hoping that this is going to be something that they'll remember—

P: Mm-hm.

A: —but I need to tell you honestly, defendants don't always internalize the message. They don't always get it. Being sued carries with it, I think, so much of, you know, an ego-injury, that all they've been thinking about is defending themselves, they're not thinking about, how can we make this better? How can we avoid the next Josh Resnick assault situation? And that's a shame. But, let's see how well we can do, let's see how far we can push them, and if it's a number that feels right to you, then we'll see what we can do a deal today.

2. **(Judy Greenwood, with Josh Resnick)**

   A: Our goal here is to get you fair and reasonable value for your case, and there is a range really, in every case, where you

P:	would consider it reasonable. If we go to this mediation, and it can happen, it happens in many mediations, where you go and you go through a process, and a resolution is not reached. I want you to understand that there will be a pre-trial conference down the road, the case will then get listed for trial, so this is not really the end of the road.

A: OK. And if the other side doesn't come to a number that we, together, feel is fair and reasonable, we say "No."

Clip 13-C: Obtaining Settlement Authority

(Judy Greenwood, with Josh Resnick)

A: Let me talk to you a little bit about numbers, OK? I think I told you that there's no one number that is written in stone in a case this. If we go to court, it's unclear what a jury will do, in terms of the case. I feel good about the case. I think that it's more likely than not that we'll prevail, but then the question becomes, beyond the economics, what value can we get a jury to put on this case?

P: Uh-huh.

A: And I think that you make a good appearance, you are a sympathetic plaintiff so to speak.

P: Mm-hm.

A: I think jurors will like you. And I think Dr. Geller will be a good witness and an advocate for us.

P: Mm-hm.

A: So I think we can do well in court. . . .

A: There was a similar case, not in New Jersey but in another location, where the jury awarded I think it was $137,000 to a plaintiff.

P: Mm-hm.

A: There have been other cases where they've awarded less and depending on the facts, you know, somewhere they've gone higher, but that seemed to be a close situation. And that was a good result.

P: Mm-hm.

A: My guess from reading that case is that the jury there, which was favorable for the plaintiff, awarded some economic losses plus maybe $100,000 for pain and suffering not "pain and suffering" so to speak but for the terror of the event, the

Post-Traumatic Stress Disorder and somehow came up with a figure like that. . . .

A: And, you know, certainly going into this mediation, I would like to know from you that if there are numbers reached of a hundred and — or a hundred and ten thousand — that if I came to you, you would give me authority to settle this case.

P: Absolutely, yeah, I mean . . .

A: OK.

P: I would even, you know, probably go a little lower than that, just to get it over with today, you know, so . . .

A: Now that is probably good value. The other side, in my view, will never reach those numbers. . . .

A: I mean, and, I understand that fifteen thousand to twenty thousand, as you say, is just the economics, but on top of that you've lost a year of your life.

P: Yeah.

A: And you continue to have problems, and we don't know really what the future holds for you.

P: Mm-hm.

A: And I do think that is a significant injury, that a jury, you know, will compensate. Let me ask you this without pinning you down too much before this mediation. If the mediator got the other side to a range that was close to a six-figure number.

P: Mm-hm.

A: OK. Seventy-five to a hundred thousand dollars —

P: Mm-hm.

A: — somewhere in there, is that something that you would be willing to consider, let me put it that way, to settle this case early? And I'm not asking you for any authority on that now.

P: Yeah. Um, yeah, I think so. . . .

A: So, when we go into this mediation, they will come back with low numbers.

P: Yeah, yeah.

A: OK, are you going to be able to say "No" to them?

P: If they're — yeah, if it doesn't — if I don't think it's fair. Yeah, absolutely.

A: OK. What I don't want to happen at this mediation is where you feel pressured . . .

P:	. . . to take something that I don't feel comfortable with.
A:	Right.
P:	OK.
A:	Or that is less than fair value for the case.
P:	OK.
A:	OK? . . .
A:	I think your approach, or the approach that we're going to take here, is a reasonable one. My job is to try to maximize your recovery here. I do agree that below seventy thousand is really getting off the mark.
P:	OK.
A:	I do agree that a six-figure — hundred, hundred and ten thousand — is a good result.
P:	OK.
A:	I'd like to see closer to the higher range, I always do . . .
P:	Mm-hm.
A:	. . . in the case, but I understand where you're coming from, and we'll factor that into the approach we take. . . .

Clip 13-D: Lawyer Opening: Plaintiff

(Dave Kwass, in Resnick)

M:	Okay? Why don't we start?
PL:	Okay. Well, I'll tell you what, let me start by asking you a couple of questions and see if we can begin that way and if that is going to work.
M:	That's makes sense.
PL:	Why don't you tell Mr. Stevens and the group here what you're up to right now and how you're doing.
P:	Um. Yeah, sure. Right now I'm living on Long Island. I'm working at a university in the library. Um, I say I'm on the road to recovery. I've been through counseling for the last six months and I'm just — just reached the end of that counseling. I'm — I don't know where I am — you know, before this I was headed into a Master's program. I was about three months into the Master's program, but now I'm not so sure what direction I'm headed, but I'm just sort of getting my footing again and trying to find — find a direction.

PL: From our perspective, this is a case about plans and this is a case about planning. There was not good planning for security at the apartment building where Josh was living. There was not good planning in terms of looking at a living situation, a communal living situation and thinking carefully about the risks to the people who were living in that apartment building. This is a case about taking the time to perform some kind of a risk analysis, a hazard analysis, a security—to develop a security plan and then to follow through with making sure that it's implemented, with making sure that the residents who live in the apartment building understand it and can live with it, and to make sure that it continues to be in full force, in full effect for the protection of the people who live there.

This is a case about plans, about the interruption of Josh Resnick's plans. His plans to complete a Master's Degree. His plans to work as a professional. His plans to continue to develop academically and socially and that's why we're here today, because of the absence of planning on security matters by Stevens Realty has led to an interruption of the plans of Josh Resnick.

Clip 13-E: Lawyer Opening: Defendant

(Terry Lefco, in Resnick)

DL: First of all, I'd like Josh to know on behalf of Mr. Stevens and his company that we certainly feel badly about what happened to you. Certainly no one would want that to happen to anyone and we're hopeful that you make a full recovery. At the same time, let's put this in context of what really happened. What really happened is we have a burglary in which I think three hundred and fifty dollars of cash and an iPod were stolen. Those are the financial, the monetary damages of, direct damages of this burglary. . . .

DL: Yeah, and the underlying facts—the underlying activity took about fifteen minutes. He was threatened. A knife was put at his throat. His wrists were bound with his belt. The burglar then left. He was released and that's the end of the story. Now, I'm at a loss to figure out the plaintiff's economic damages calculation. Miss Greenwood said sixteen thousand dollars for something. She talked about lost income. As you pointed out, he didn't have any lost income. He wasn't working. . . .

DL: The question is was he going to continue with this thing and plaintiff's theory is, but for this accident today, I suppose I'd be an architect or a city planner or something. But that

DL: doesn't square with the facts. He was an indifferent student. He was not doing particularly well. He wasn't particularly motivated in the subject matter. So to say "Well, he would have gone forward," is a pretty big leap. . . .

DL: I think that post-traumatic stress disorder is certainly a real problem and people have it, but to analogize this plaintiff's situation to a Vietnam veteran returning from the war and having flashbacks of the Tet Offensive or something is frankly going to be offensive. If there's anybody on that jury who was around then, they will compare what this plaintiff went through with what those people went through and will say "Give me a break."

DL: . . . and I think the jury will say, "Josh, we feel bad for you, but you left the door open. You knew that your roommate was going out without his keys. You must have known he was going to leave the front door open, too. If you didn't think of that, we're really sorry, but it's not your landlord's fault," and that's why all of these damages are not going to go anywhere, or they're going to be so substantially diminished by the jury in some sort of compromise, that the plaintiff's not going to ring the bell on this case.

Clip 13-F: Protecting the Client

1. ([Lee Rosengard ("Barry Bowen"), in Wilson])

Mediator: Now, Mr. DiLorenzo, do you want to pick up from October 7th or 8th when I think we have agreed that most of the cabinet tops were in and some linoleum was in and some linoleum work remained to be done and the counter top was on order. Tell us what happened, say, from there up then . . .

Mr. Bowen: I'm going to interrupt at this point. Ms. Wilson was given an opportunity to tell her story in an orderly fashion and I think it is only fair that Mr. DiLorenzo be given that same opportunity, so I am going to ask you to indulge him. Let him start from the beginning.

Mediator: What would you have me do differently?

Mr. Bowen: I would like him to tell his story. In — in one telling.

Mediator: Tell your story from the start to up to October . . .

DiLorenzo: Thank you, because I feel like I was getting cross-examined and I am not having an opportunity to speak. So thank you both. We — I'm the second generation in this business. I'm proud of the business. It was founded by my father and my uncle. We can't do the kinds of work in Hartford that we would like to now, there's not a whole lot of new building on. So we found a way to help the community and provide something to the community so that we could better their own properties and feel better about the place they live in Hartford.

2. **(Judy Greenwood, in Resnick)**

M: I don't want to be arguing with you because I have empathy for you and I want, you know, I want to do right by you. On the other hand, we want to, you know, we want to — doing right is getting the thing resolved at a reasonable thing. I'm happy to go back at ninety, but I think seventy-five would probably make a lot more sense to try and get this job done today. Up to you as to what you want to do. You know, really, I'm bound by yours. You just take my suggestions a little bit and do with them what they are. You know, I'm the one who does this all the time and —

PL: We may not be able —

M: I have a little experience.

PL: We may not be able to get this resolved today, although we would like to. . . .

M: You know, you're still over what I think is the upper end value of the case for settlement purposes. For settlement purposes.

P: Do you think we could go to like eighty just —

PL: Uh, uh — him — why don't we talk privately?

M: Okay. All right.

PL: Can we talk privately for a minute?

M: Okay, but we've got to move along.

P: Okay. . . .

PL: My view is that I think we should come down to ninety.

P: Okay.

PL: All right, and then put the ball back in their court.

P: Okay, to see where they go.

PL: To see where they go.

P: Okay.

PL: Okay?

P: That makes sense.

PL: All right. Again, are you feeling pressured?

P:	A little, but I mean —
PL:	I can sense that, all right?
P:	Yeah. Okay.
PL:	And that's what I don't want to happen here.

3. (Dave Kwass, in Resnick)

M:	And I want to just reiterate what I said. If you feel more comfortable now talking to me, by all means interrupt me, interrupt your attorney and let it go, but of course I wanted to spend this time talking with you in private, in confidence about the case. . . .
M:	Let me ask this, and again this is in confidence. Do you really want to go to trial on this case?
PL:	Absolutely.
M:	Does your client to go to trial? I don't mean to win the case, but you said at the outset that you didn't want your client, you know, having to go through and relive this incident, and I can fully understand and I can fully sympathize with that. He certainly doesn't want to relive that incident with five of us, but does he want to relive that incident with seventeen of us when there's a judge and a jury? I don't mean to say that, you know, maybe, you know, do you really well at trial and win the case. My question really is, is this something that you want to go through again in front of twelve strange people or thirteen strange people or more because of course there's other people in a courtroom as well.
P:	Well, I mean, I think —
PL:	Would you mind if I interrupt you?
P:	No.
PL:	Would it be okay if I respond to that?
M:	Yeah.
PL:	Josh and I have talked about this and it's not something that Josh is dying to do. Josh is not someone who is feeling right now a burning desire to have his story told, and to have the story be out there and to demonize Mr. Stevens. But Josh also understands the importance of the process. He understands the importance of the civil litigation process, and he is in a position where if this can be settled for an amount that's going to be reasonable, for an amount that's going to make sense for him, for an amount that does something about, coming somewhere in the ballpark of helping not so much to

replace the year that he's lost, but to address it, then he's willing to do that. But he's also more than willing and would be more than prepared to go through trial. Is it his first choice? Of course not.

M: Okay.

PL: Of course not. But is he willing to do it? Absolutely.

M: Okay.

PL: Now, did I speak out of turn?

P: No, that makes — that's exactly what — yeah.

4. (Judy Greenwood, in Resnick)

M: Okay, here's where we are. At a final situation with regard to that. You know, they were willing to pay the sixty-two five. I said, okay, we talked and sixty-two five is not going to do it. At my behest, terrible behest, I said "Let them feel they're coming out, sixty-five." Go make the call and we'll be able to get it if you take the sixty-five. No more negotiation. That's it. Here it is right now in front of you. Again, I think it's in the reasonable range, and we're doing better than I thought we would do in this situation today, but it's up to you where you want to go. So it's not anything, sixty-seven, it's not sixty-eight. Sixty-five, that's where we are. . . .

PL: Okay. Josh, it's lower than I wanted to get for you.

P: Uh-huh.

PL: And then the question is, I'd be happier if we were in the seventy to a hundred thousand, and I'm always happier on the high end.

P: Yeah.

PL: There is an element of pressure that every client feels in this situation.

P: Uh-hmm.

PL: Okay?

P: Yeah.

PL: And I want to talk to you without you feeling like you have to do anything. . . .

PL: Okay. How do you feel about the sixty-five thousand? It is lower . . .

P: Yeah, yeah.

PL: . . . than what we talked about . . .

P:	Yeah.
PL:	. . . initially, but it's close.
P:	Yeah.
PL:	So tell me what you think and I'm comfortable any way you want to go.
P:	Yeah. Well, I mean, I think that there's five thousand difference between what we said and what they're offering and to get it done and over with, I mean, I just—I don't want to have to deal with it for the next two years.
PL:	Okay.
P:	And I would like to take that.
PL:	Okay, and you're comfortable with that?
P:	Yeah, I am.
PL:	You don't feel pressured.
P:	No.

Clip 13-G: Using the Mediator: Sending a Signal

(Lauren Levin-Geary, in Resnick)

M:	Put another way, is it fair to say that you really have more than ten thousand dollars that you're willing to put on this case but because of where the Plaintiff started out, you're not prepared to put that number on the table right now?
DL:	Right. You know, you've put me in a little bit of an awkward position I feel. You know, they've come—they've put a number out there that I feel, you know, is in outer space for this case.
M:	I understand.
DL:	You know, it is. I mean, I have to be frank with you. I mean I probably would be willing to offer more money, if I thought that they were being reasonable, but given that this is where they are, I don't see—I don't see going anywhere from here.
M:	Okay, well, let me ask. Let me put it this way. There's different ways to communicate a ten thousand dollar offer to them.
DL:	Uh-hmm.
M:	One way is to say "The Defense thinks your case stinks. They think that you guys are here, you know, it's 1-800-LAWYER and you just want to hit the jackpot. They'll give you ten

	thousand dollars. Take it or leave it because, you know, they'll probably spend more than ten thousand to defend this case, but they're sick of you and they have to make some kind of an offer." That's one way.
DL:	Uh-hmm.
M:	Another way I can present is to say "I've spoken to the Defendants — the Defendant, and the Defendant really wants to try to settle this case. The Defendant is troubled by what they believe to be a very high demand. They really want to talk very serious turkey. At this point they're willing to offer ten thousand dollars, but I the Mediator, think that there's more money there. How much more I don't know, but I think there's more money there and if you the Plaintiff really want to try to settle this case for below a hundred and ten, I think you should make another demand."
DL:	Well, let me say this: I wouldn't say to the Plaintiff, "Defense really wants to settle this case," because I don't feel that way. At least not — at least not for what they're looking at. Do we want to settle the case? Yes. We want to settle the case for a number closer to my number than a number closer to the Plaintiff's number. . . .

Would I like to move the case? Yes. |
M:	Okay.
DL:	So I think that — and also, I like the way you phrased it when you said that, you the Mediator suspected that there was more money back there, because I think that, you know, that kind of puts the idea out there without like definitively saying that there is more money out there.
M:	Okay.
DL:	And that they need to make a counter, and that it has to be, you know, it has to be reflective of this case, and I don't feel like the money that they're asking for is reflective of this case.

Clip 13-H: Using the Mediator: Seeking Bargaining Guidance

(Terry Lefco, in Resnick)

DL:	Well, look, here's — I mean you got to put a — can I rely on you, that if we put more money on the table, that it's going to — that you would — not a promise, but your honest belief that it's going to provoke a substantial reduction by them?
M:	I can't represent what it's going to do. Am I going —
DL:	Not a hundred percent. Do you think that it might —

M: Am I going to hope that it assists in the process of negotiation? Yes, I'm hopeful that it will.

DL: Then you'll try. You'll try to help us to do that.

M: I'm trying on both sides. . . .

DL: . . . Okay, now I'm going to ask you something you may not want to answer.

M: Uh-hmm.

DL: What do you think the right number is?

M: Well, if it's the right number for them or whatever, I can only guess as to, you know, what will settle the case or something like that. I think that the value of the case is somewhere between sixty and seventy-five, and if you get in for sixty, you'd be getting a good deal. If you got it for seventy-five, you'd be getting a reasonable deal. . . .

DL: Yeah, I was going to say I thought the value of this case was sixty. That's what I was going to say, but I can't put sixty on the table because they're going to come back and say sixty, then . . .

M: Well, I can't give you the authority and I can't tell you what to offer specifically because, you know, I don't know how much authority you have and I have an ethical issue, you know, knowing what you got or whatever. But I don't think that everybody would be terribly disappointed if we put fifty on the table right now and tried to see where they would be.

DL: All right. I think that's what we should do.

Clip 13-TM: "End Game" Settlement Strategies

(Resnick v. Stevens Realty: Chuck Forer Version)

(Caucus with Defendant)

DL: So you want to know my bottom line number. Thirty-five.

M: Thirty-five. So you understand, if they're within twenty of that, I'll keep you here. If they're not, we go home.

DL: Good enough. Fair enough.

M: Okay.

DL: Should we leave?

M: Yes. . . .

(Caucus with Plaintiff)

M: So if you want to try, you have nothing to lose because if you're more than twenty thousand dollars apart, I say, "You know, that's it," and you haven't lost anything because I don't tell them. I'm a black box. They don't get that number in any event.

PL: Are you willing to give that a shot?

P: Sure, yeah.

PL: Why don't you give me a second with Josh.

M: Okay. I'll be right back. [pause] . . .

(Dave Kwass counsels Josh Resnick)

PL: Well, it seems to me that right now the ball game is not to necessarily give him our bottom, bottom, because I think we don't necessarily know what our bottom bottom is.

P: Yeah.

PL: But we want to be, if that's what you're feeling, then it seems to me the important thing is that we try to be — we try to put ourselves into a range that will be within twenty of them. . . .

P: Uh-hmm.

PL: So with that said, you know, my inclination would be to come back at seventy-five and let that play out. It seems to me I'd like to —

P: Okay.

PL: I really would like to see this get above sixty.

P: Okay.

PL: Preferably to the sixty-five kind of a range.

P: Uh-hmm.

PL: It may be that we end up just outside of the twenty on that, but there still might be some things they could do. Or if, you know, we want to assure ourselves that we're going to get to that twenty position, it may be that we come down to seventy, or we can split the difference and —

P: Yeah, I really would like if we came down to seventy. If you think that they're at fifty, then maybe we can keep, you know —

PL: Keep the talks going?

P: Yeah, I would like to do that.

PL: Well, if that's what you want to do.

P: I would.

PL: I think that's in the range. . . .

APPENDIX

B

MODEL STANDARDS OF CONDUCT FOR MEDIATORS (SEPTEMBER 2005)*

Preamble

Mediation is used to resolve a broad range of conflicts within a variety of settings. These Standards are designed to serve as fundamental ethical guidelines for persons mediating in all practice contexts. They serve three primary goals: to guide the conduct of mediators; to inform the mediating parties; and to promote public confidence in mediation as a process for resolving disputes.

Mediation is a process in which an impartial third party facilitates communication and negotiation and promotes voluntary decision making by the parties to the dispute.

Mediation serves various purposes, including providing the opportunity for parties to define and clarify issues, understand different perspectives, identify interests, explore and assess possible solutions, and reach mutually satisfactory agreements, when desired.

Note on Construction

These Standards are to be read and construed in their entirety. There is no priority significance attached to the sequence in which the Standards appear.

The use of the term "shall" in a Standard indicates that the mediator must follow the practice described. The use of the term "should" indicates that the practice described in the Standard is highly desirable, but not required, and is to be departed from only for very strong reasons and requires careful use of judgment and discretion.

---

*These model standards were drafted by representatives of the American Arbitration Association, American Bar Association Section of Dispute Resolution and the Association for Conflict Resolution (ACR) and have been approved by all three organizations. The Reporter's notes — which are not part of the approved Standards — can be found at www.moritzlaw.osu.edu/programs/adr/msoc/.

The use of the term "mediator" is understood to be inclusive so that it applies to co-mediator models.

These Standards do not include specific temporal parameters when referencing a mediation, and therefore, do not define the exact beginning or ending of a mediation.

Various aspects of a mediation, including some matters covered by these Standards, may also be affected by applicable law, court rules, regulations, other applicable professional rules, mediation rules to which the parties have agreed, and other agreements of the parties. These sources may create conflicts with, and may take precedence over, these Standards. However, a mediator should make every effort to comply with the spirit and intent of these Standards in resolving such conflicts. This effort should include honoring all remaining Standards not in conflict with these other sources.

These Standards, unless and until adopted by a court or other regulatory authority, do not have the force of law. Nonetheless, the fact that these Standards have been adopted by the respective sponsoring entities should alert mediators to the fact that the Standards might be viewed as establishing a standard of care for mediators.

STANDARD I. SELF-DETERMINATION

A. A mediator shall conduct a mediation based on the principle of party self-determination. Self-determination is the act of coming to a voluntary, uncoerced decision in which each party makes free and informed choices as to process and outcome. Parties may exercise self-determination at any stage of a mediation, including mediator selection, process design, participation in or withdrawal from the process, and outcomes.

> 1. Although party self-determination for process design is a fundamental principle of mediation practice, a mediator may need to balance such party self-determination with a mediator's duty to conduct a quality process in accordance with these Standards.
>
> 2. A mediator cannot personally ensure that each party has made free and informed choices to reach particular decisions, but, where appropriate, a mediator should make the parties aware of the importance of consulting other professionals to help them make informed choices.

B. A mediator shall not undermine party self-determination by any party for reasons such as higher settlement rates, egos, increased fees, or outside pressures from court personnel, program administrators, provider organizations, the media, or others.

STANDARD II. IMPARTIALITY

A. A mediator shall decline a mediation if the mediator cannot conduct it in an impartial manner. Impartiality means freedom from favoritism, bias, or prejudice.

B. A mediator shall conduct a mediation in an impartial manner and avoid conduct that gives the appearance of partiality.

> 1. A mediator should not act with partiality or prejudice based on any participant's personal characteristics, background, values and beliefs, or performance at a mediation, or any other reason.

2. A mediator should neither give nor accept a gift, favor, loan, or other item of value that raises a question as to the mediator's actual or perceived impartiality.

3. A mediator may accept or give de minimis gifts or incidental items or services that are provided to facilitate a mediation or respect cultural norms so long as such practices do not raise questions as to a mediator's actual or perceived impartiality.

C. If at any time a mediator is unable to conduct a mediation in an impartial manner, the mediator shall withdraw.

STANDARD III. CONFLICTS OF INTEREST

A. A mediator shall avoid a conflict of interest or the appearance of a conflict of interest during and after a mediation. A conflict of interest can arise from involvement by a mediator with the subject matter of the dispute or from any relationship between a mediator and any mediation participant, whether past or present, personal or professional, that reasonably raises a question of a mediator's impartiality.

B. A mediator shall make a reasonable inquiry to determine whether there are any facts that a reasonable individual would consider likely to create a potential or actual conflict of interest for a mediator. A mediator's actions necessary to accomplish a reasonable inquiry into potential conflicts of interest may vary based on practice context.

C. A mediator shall disclose, as soon as practicable, all actual and potential conflicts of interest that are reasonably known to the mediator and could reasonably be seen as raising a question about the mediator's impartiality. After disclosure, if all parties agree, the mediator may proceed with the mediation.

D. If a mediator learns any fact after accepting a mediation that raises a question with respect to that mediator's service creating a potential or actual conflict of interest, the mediator shall disclose it as quickly as practicable. After disclosure, if all parties agree, the mediator may proceed with the mediation.

E. If a mediator's conflict of interest might reasonably be viewed as undermining the integrity of the mediation, a mediator shall withdraw from or decline to proceed with the mediation regardless of the expressed desire or agreement of the parties to the contrary.

F. Subsequent to a mediation, a mediator shall not establish another relationship with any of the participants in any matter that would raise questions about the integrity of the mediation. When a mediator develops personal or professional relationships with parties, other individuals, or organizations following a mediation in which they were involved, the mediator should consider factors such as time elapsed following the mediation, the nature of the relationships established, and services offered when determining whether the relationships might create a perceived or actual conflict of interest.

STANDARD IV. COMPETENCE

A. A mediator shall mediate only when the mediator has the necessary competence to satisfy the reasonable expectations of the parties.

1. Any person may be selected as a mediator, provided that the parties are satisfied with the mediator's competence and qualifications. Training, experience in mediation, skills, cultural understandings, and other qualities are often necessary for mediator competence. A person who offers to serve as a mediator creates the expectation that the person is competent to mediate effectively.

2. A mediator should attend educational programs and related activities to maintain and enhance the mediator's knowledge and skills related to mediation.

3. A mediator should have available for the parties information relevant to the mediator's training, education, experience, and approach to conducting a mediation.

B. If a mediator, during the course of a mediation, determines that the mediator cannot conduct the mediation competently, the mediator shall discuss that determination with the parties as soon as is practicable and take appropriate steps to address the situation, including, but not limited to, withdrawing or requesting appropriate assistance.

C. If a mediator's ability to conduct a mediation is impaired by drugs, alcohol, medication, or otherwise, the mediator shall not conduct the mediation.

Standard V. Confidentiality

A. A mediator shall maintain the confidentiality of all information obtained by the mediator in mediation, unless otherwise agreed to by the parties or required by applicable law.

1. If the parties to a mediation agree that the mediator may disclose information obtained during the mediation, the mediator may do so.

2. A mediator should not communicate to any non-participant information about how the parties acted in the mediation. A mediator may report, if required, whether parties appeared at a scheduled mediation and whether or not the parties reached a resolution.

3. If a mediator participates in teaching, research, or evaluation of mediation, the mediator should protect the anonymity of the parties and abide by their reasonable expectations regarding confidentiality.

B. A mediator who meets with any persons in private session during a mediation shall not convey directly or indirectly to any other person, any information that was obtained during that private session without the consent of the disclosing person.

C. A mediator shall promote understanding among the parties of the extent to which the parties will maintain confidentiality of information they obtain in a mediation.

D. Depending on the circumstance of a mediation, the parties may have varying expectations regarding confidentiality that a mediator should address. The parties may make their own rules with respect to confidentiality, or the accepted practice of an individual mediator or institution may dictate a particular set of expectations.

STANDARD VI. QUALITY OF THE PROCESS

A. A mediator shall conduct a mediation in accordance with these Standards and in a manner that promotes diligence, timeliness, safety, presence of the appropriate participants, party participation, procedural fairness, party competency, and mutual respect among all participants.

1. A mediator should agree to mediate only when the mediator is prepared to commit the attention essential to an effective mediation.

2. A mediator should only accept cases when the mediator can satisfy the reasonable expectation of the parties concerning the timing of a mediation.

3. The presence or absence of persons at a mediation depends on the agreement of the parties and the mediator. The parties and mediator may agree that others may be excluded from particular sessions or from all sessions.

4. A mediator should promote honesty and candor between and among all participants, and a mediator shall not knowingly misrepresent any material fact or circumstance in the course of a mediation.

5. The role of a mediator differs substantially from other professional roles. Mixing the role of a mediator and the role of another profession is problematic and thus, a mediator should distinguish between the roles. A mediator may provide information that the mediator is qualified by training or experience to provide, only if the mediator can do so consistent with these Standards.

6. A mediator shall not conduct a dispute resolution procedure other than mediation but label it mediation in an effort to gain the protection of rules, statutes, or other governing authorities pertaining to mediation.

7. A mediator may recommend, when appropriate, that parties consider resolving their dispute through arbitration, counseling, neutral evaluation, or other processes.

8. A mediator shall not undertake an additional dispute resolution role in the same matter without the consent of the parties. Before providing such service, a mediator shall inform the parties of the implications of the change in process and obtain their consent to the change. A mediator who undertakes such role assumes different duties and responsibilities that may be governed by other standards.

9. If a mediation is being used to further criminal conduct, a mediator should take appropriate steps including, if necessary, postponing, withdrawing from, or terminating the mediation.

10. If a party appears to have difficulty comprehending the process, issues, or settlement options, or difficulty participating in a mediation, the mediator should explore the circumstances and potential accommodations, modifications, or adjustments that would make possible the party's capacity to comprehend, participate, and exercise self-determination.

B. If a mediator is made aware of domestic abuse or violence among the parties, the mediator shall take appropriate steps including, if necessary, postponing, withdrawing from, or terminating the mediation.

C. If a mediator believes that participant conduct, including that of the mediator, jeopardizes conducting a mediation consistent with these Standards, a mediator shall take appropriate steps including, if necessary, postponing, withdrawing from, or terminating the mediation.

STANDARD VII. ADVERTISING AND SOLICITATION

A. A mediator shall be truthful and not misleading when advertising, soliciting, or otherwise communicating the mediator's qualifications, experience, services, and fees.

    1. A mediator should not include any promises as to outcome in communications, including business cards, stationery, or computer-based communications.

    2. A mediator should only claim to meet the mediator qualifications of a governmental entity or private organization if that entity or organization has a recognized procedure for qualifying mediators and it grants such status to the mediator.

B. A mediator shall not solicit in a manner that gives an appearance of partiality for or against a party or otherwise undermines the integrity of the process.

C. A mediator shall not communicate to others, in promotional materials or through other forms of communication, the names of persons served without their permission.

STANDARD VIII. FEES AND OTHER CHARGES

A. A mediator shall provide each party or each party's representative true and complete information about mediation fees, expenses, and any other actual or potential charges that may be incurred in connection with a mediation.

    1. If a mediator charges fees, the mediator should develop them in light of all relevant factors, including the type and complexity of the matter, the qualifications of the mediator, the time required, and the rates customary for such mediation services.

    2. A mediator's fee arrangement should be in writing unless the parties request otherwise.

B. A mediator shall not charge fees in a manner that impairs a mediator's impartiality.

    1. A mediator should not enter into a fee agreement which is contingent upon the result of the mediation or the amount of the settlement.

    2. While a mediator may accept unequal fee payments from the parties, a mediator should not use fee arrangements that adversely impact the mediator's ability to conduct a mediation in an impartial manner.

STANDARD IX. ADVANCEMENT OF MEDIATION PRACTICE

A. A mediator should act in a manner that advances the practice of mediation. A mediator promotes this Standard by engaging in some or all of the following:

    1. Fostering diversity within the field of mediation.

2. Striving to make mediation accessible to those who elect to use it, including providing services at a reduced rate or on a pro bono basis as appropriate.

3. Participating in research when given the opportunity, including obtaining participant feedback when appropriate.

4. Participating in outreach and education efforts to assist the public in developing an improved understanding of, and appreciation for, mediation.

5. Assisting newer mediators through training, mentoring, and networking.

B. A mediator should demonstrate respect for differing points of view within the field, seek to learn from other mediators, and work together with other mediators to improve the profession and better serve people in conflict.

MODEL STANDARDS OF PRACTICE FOR FAMILY AND DIVORCE MEDIATION (2001)*

Overview and Definitions

Family and divorce mediation ("family mediation" or "mediation") is a process in which a mediator, an impartial third party, facilitates the resolution of family disputes by promoting the participants' voluntary agreement. The family mediator assists communication, encourages understanding and focuses the participants on their individual and common interests. The family mediator works with the participants to explore options, make decisions and reach their own agreements.

Family mediation is not a substitute for the need for family members to obtain independent legal advice or counseling or therapy. Nor is it appropriate for all families. However, experience has established that family mediation is a valuable option for many families because it can:

- increase the self-determination of participants and their ability to communicate;

- promote the best interests of children; and

- reduce the economic and emotional costs associated with the resolution of family disputes.

Effective mediation requires that the family mediator be qualified by training, experience and temperament; that the mediator be impartial; that the participants reach their decisions voluntarily; that their decisions be based on sufficient factual data; that the mediator be aware of the impact of culture and diversity; and that the best interests of children be taken into account. Further, the mediator should also be prepared to identify families whose history includes domestic abuse or child abuse.

---

* These model standards—but not the comments to them—were approved by the ABA House of Delegates in February 2001 and have also been adopted by the Association for Conflict Resolution (ACR) and the Association of Family and Conciliation Courts (AFCC).

These Model Standards of Practice for Family and Divorce Mediation ("Model Standards") aim to perform three major functions:

1. to serve as a guide for the conduct of family mediators;
2. to inform the mediating participants of what they can expect; and
3. to promote public confidence in mediation as a process for resolving family disputes.

The Model Standards are aspirational in character. They describe good practices for family mediators. They are not intended to create legal rules or standards of liability. The Model Standards include different levels of guidance:

- Use of the term "may" in a Standard is the lowest strength of guidance and indicates a practice that the family mediator should consider adopting but which can be deviated from in the exercise of good professional judgment.

- Most of the Standards employ the term "should" which indicates that the practice described in the Standard is highly desirable and should be departed from only with very strong reason.

- The rarer use of the term "shall" in a Standard is a higher level of guidance to the family mediator, indicating that the mediator should not have discretion to depart from the practice described.

STANDARD I

A family mediator shall recognize that mediation is based on the principle of self-determination by the participants.

A. Self-determination is the fundamental principle of family mediation. The mediation process relies upon the ability of participants to make their own voluntary and informed decisions.

B. The primary role of a family mediator is to assist the participants to gain a better understanding of their own needs and interests and the needs and interests of others and to facilitate agreement among the participants.

C. A family mediator should inform the participants that they may seek information and advice from a variety of sources during the mediation process.

D. A family mediator shall inform the participants that they may withdraw from family mediation at any time and are not required to reach an agreement in mediation.

E. The family mediator's commitment shall be to the participants and the process. Pressure from outside of the mediation process shall never influence the mediator to coerce participants to settle.

STANDARD II

A family mediator shall be qualified by education and training to undertake the mediation.

A. To perform the family mediator's role, a mediator should:
   1. have knowledge of family law;

2. have knowledge of and training in the impact of family conflict on parents, children and other participants, including knowledge of child development, domestic abuse and child abuse and neglect;

3. have education and training specific to the process of mediation;

4. be able to recognize the impact of culture and diversity.

B. Family mediators should provide information to the participants about the mediator's relevant training, education and expertise.

STANDARD III

A family mediator shall facilitate the participants' understanding of what mediation is and assess their capacity to mediate before the participants reach an agreement to mediate.

A. Before family mediation begins, a mediator should provide the participants with an overview of the process and its purposes, including:

1. informing the participants that reaching an agreement in family mediation is consensual in nature, that a mediator is an impartial facilitator, and that a mediator may not impose or force any settlement on the parties;

2. distinguishing family mediation from other processes designed to address family issues and disputes;

3. informing the participants that any agreements reached will be reviewed by the court when court approval is required;

4. informing the participants that they may obtain independent advice from attorneys, counsel, advocates, accountants, therapists or other professionals during the mediation process;

5. advising the participants, in appropriate cases, that they can seek the advice of religious figures, elders or other significant persons in their community whose opinions they value;

6. discussing, if applicable, the issue of separate sessions with the participants, a description of the circumstances in which the mediator may meet alone with any of the participants, or with any third party and the conditions of confidentiality concerning these separate sessions;

7. informing the participants that the presence or absence of other persons at a mediation, including attorneys, counselors or advocates, depends on the agreement of the participants and the mediator, unless a statute or regulation otherwise requires or the mediator believes that the presence of another person is required or may be beneficial because of a history or threat of violence or other serious coercive activity by a participant;

8. describing the obligations of the mediator to maintain the confidentiality of the mediation process and its results as well as any exceptions to confidentiality;

9. advising the participants of the circumstances under which the mediator may suspend or terminate the mediation process and that a participant has a right to suspend or terminate mediation at any time.

B. The participants should sign a written agreement to mediate their dispute and the terms and conditions thereof within a reasonable time after first consulting the family mediator.

C. The family mediator should be alert to the capacity and willingness of the participants to mediate before proceeding with the mediation and throughout the process. A mediator should not agree to conduct the mediation if the mediator reasonably believes one or more of the participants is unable or unwilling to participate;

D. Family mediators should not accept a dispute for mediation if they cannot satisfy the expectations of the participants concerning the timing of the process.

Standard IV

A family mediator shall conduct the mediation process in an impartial manner. A family mediator shall disclose all actual and potential grounds of bias and conflicts of interest reasonably known to the mediator. The participants shall be free to retain the mediator by an informed, written waiver of the conflict of interest. However, if a bias or conflict of interest clearly impairs a mediator's impartiality, the mediator shall withdraw regardless of the express agreement of the participants.

A. Impartiality means freedom from favoritism or bias in word, action or appearance, and includes a commitment to assist all participants as opposed to any one individual.

B. Conflict of interest means any relationship between the mediator, any participant or the subject matter of the dispute, that compromises or appears to compromise the mediator's impartiality.

C. A family mediator should not accept a dispute for mediation if the family mediator cannot be impartial.

D. A family mediator should identify and disclose potential grounds of bias or conflict of interest upon which a mediator's impartiality might reasonably be questioned. Such disclosure should be made prior to the start of a mediation and in time to allow the participants to select an alternate mediator.

E. A family mediator should resolve all doubts in favor of disclosure. All disclosures should be made as soon as practical after the mediator becomes aware of the bias or potential conflict of interest. The duty to disclose is a continuing duty.

F. A family mediator should guard against bias or partiality based on the participants' personal characteristics, background or performance at the mediation.

G. A family mediator should avoid conflicts of interest in recommending the services of other professionals.

H. A family mediator shall not use information about participants obtained in a mediation for personal gain or advantage.

I. A family mediator should withdraw pursuant to Standard IX if the mediator believes the mediator's impartiality has been compromised or a conflict of interest has been identified and has not been waived by the participants.

Standard V

A family mediator shall fully disclose and explain the basis of any compensation, fees and charges to the participants.

A. The participants should be provided with sufficient information about fees at the outset of mediation to determine if they wish to retain the services of the mediator.

B. The participants' written agreement to mediate their dispute should include a description of their fee arrangement with the mediator.

C. A mediator should not enter into a fee agreement that is contingent upon the results of the mediation or the amount of the settlement.

D. A mediator should not accept a fee for referral of a matter to another mediator or to any other person.

E. Upon termination of mediation a mediator should return any unearned fee to the participants.

Standard VI

A family mediator shall structure the mediation process so that the participants make decisions based on sufficient information and knowledge.

A. The mediator should facilitate full and accurate disclosure and the acquisition and development of information during mediation so that the participants can make informed decisions. This may be accomplished by encouraging participants to consult appropriate experts.

B. Consistent with standards of impartiality and preserving participant self-determination, a mediator may provide the participants with information that the mediator is qualified by training or experience to provide. The mediator shall not provide therapy or legal advice.

C. The mediator should recommend that the participants obtain independent legal representation before concluding an agreement.

D. If the participants so desire, the mediator should allow attorneys, counsel or advocates for the participants to be present at the mediation sessions.

E. With the agreement of the participants, the mediator may document the participants' resolution of their dispute. The mediator should inform the participants that any agreement should be reviewed by an independent attorney before it is signed.

Standard VII

A family mediator shall maintain the confidentiality of all information acquired in the mediation process, unless the mediator is permitted or required to reveal the information by law or agreement of the participants.

A. The mediator should discuss the participants' expectations of confidentiality with them prior to undertaking the mediation. The written agreement to mediate should include provisions concerning confidentiality.

B. Prior to undertaking the mediation, the mediator should inform the participants of the limitations of confidentiality such as statutory, judicially or ethically mandated reporting.

C. As permitted by law, the mediator shall disclose a participant's threat of suicide or violence against any person to the threatened person and the appropriate authorities if the mediator believes such threat is likely to be acted upon.

D. If the mediator holds private sessions with a participant, the obligations of confidentiality concerning those sessions should be discussed and agreed upon prior to the sessions.

E. If subpoenaed or otherwise noticed to testify or to produce documents, the mediator should inform the participants immediately. The mediator should not testify or provide documents in response to a subpoena without an order of the court if the mediator reasonably believes doing so would violate an obligation of confidentiality to the participants.

STANDARD VIII

A family mediator shall assist participants in determining how to promote the best interests of children.

A. The mediator should encourage the participants to explore the range of options available for separation or post-divorce parenting arrangements and their respective costs and benefits. Referral to a specialist in child development may be appropriate for these purposes. The topics for discussion may include, among others:

1. information about community resources and programs that can help the participants and their children cope with the consequences of family reorganization and family violence;

2. problems that continuing conflict creates for children's development and what steps might be taken to ameliorate the effects of conflict on the children;

3. development of a parenting plan that covers the children's physical residence and decision-making responsibilities for the children, with appropriate levels of detail as agreed to by the participants;

4. the possible need to revise parenting plans as the developmental needs of the children evolve over time; and

5. encouragement to the participants to develop appropriate dispute resolution mechanisms to facilitate future revisions of the parenting plan.

B. The mediator should be sensitive to the impact of culture and religion on parenting philosophy and other decisions.

C. The mediator shall inform any court-appointed representative for the children of the mediation. If a representative for the children participates, the mediator should, at the outset, discuss the effect of that participation on the mediation process and the confidentiality of the mediation with the participants. Whether the representative of the children participates or not, the mediator shall provide the representative with the resulting agreements insofar as they relate to the children.

D. Except in extraordinary circumstances, the children should not participate in the mediation process without the consent of both parents and the children's court-appointed representative.

E. Prior to including the children in the mediation process, the mediator should consult with the parents and the children's court-appointed representative about whether the children should participate in the mediation process and the form of that participation.

F. The mediator should inform all concerned about the available options for the children's participation (which may include personal participation, an interview with a mental health professional, the mediator interviewing the child and reporting to the parents, or a videotaped statement by the child) and discuss the costs and benefits of each with the participants.

Standard IX

A family mediator shall recognize a family situation involving child abuse or neglect and take appropriate steps to shape the mediation process accordingly.

A. As used in these Standards, child abuse or neglect is defined by applicable state law.

B. A mediator shall not undertake a mediation in which the family situation has been assessed to involve child abuse or neglect without appropriate and adequate training.

C. If the mediator has reasonable grounds to believe that a child of the participants is abused or neglected within the meaning of the jurisdiction's child abuse and neglect laws, the mediator shall comply with applicable child protection laws.

    1. The mediator should encourage the participants to explore approriate services for the family.

    2. The mediator should consider the appropriateness of suspending or terminating the mediation process in light of the allegations.

Standard X

A family mediator shall recognize a family situation involving domestic abuse and take appropriate steps to shape the mediation process accordingly.

A. As used in these Standards, domestic abuse includes domestic violence as defined by applicable state law and issues of control and intimidation.

B. A mediator shall not undertake a mediation in which the family situation has been assessed to involve domestic abuse without appropriate and adequate training.

C. Some cases are not suitable for mediation because of safety, control or intimidation issues. A mediator should make a reasonable effort to screen for the existence of domestic abuse prior to entering into an agreement to mediate. The mediator should continue to assess for domestic abuse throughout the mediation process.

D. If domestic abuse appears to be present the mediator shall consider taking measures to insure the safety of participants and the mediator including, among others:

    1. establishing appropriate security arrangements;

    2. holding separate sessions with the participants even without the agreement of all participants;

3. allowing a friend, representative, advocate, counsel or attorney to attend the mediation sessions;

4. encouraging the participants to be represented by an attorney, counsel or an advocate throughout the mediation process;

5. referring the participants to appropriate community resources;

6. suspending or terminating the mediation sessions, with appropriate steps to protect the safety of the participants.

E. The mediator should facilitate the participants' formulation of parenting plans that protect the physical safety and psychological well-being of themselves and their children.

STANDARD XI

A family mediator shall suspend or terminate the mediation process when the mediator reasonably believes that a participant is unable to effectively participate or for other compelling reason.

A. Circumstances under which a mediator should consider suspending or terminating the mediation, may include, among others:

1. the safety of a participant or well-being of a child is threatened;

2. a participant has or is threatening to abduct a child;

3. a participant is unable to participate due to the influence of drugs, alcohol, or physical or mental condition;

4. the participants are about to enter into an agreement that the mediator reasonably believes to be unconscionable;

5. a participant is using the mediation to further illegal conduct;

6. a participant is using the mediation process to gain an unfair advantage;

7. if the mediator believes the mediator's impartiality has been compromised in accordance with Standard IV.

B. If the mediator does suspend or terminate the mediation, the mediator should take all reasonable steps to minimize prejudice or inconvenience to the participants which may result.

STANDARD XII

A family mediator shall be truthful in the advertisement and solicitation for mediation.

A. Mediators should refrain from promises and guarantees of results. A mediator should not advertise statistical settlement data or settlement rates.

B. Mediators should accurately represent their qualifications. In an advertisement or other communication, a mediator may make reference to meeting state, national or private organizational qualifications only if the entity referred to has a procedure for qualifying mediators and the mediator has been duly granted the requisite status.

Standard XIII

A family mediator shall acquire and maintain professional competence in mediation.

A. Mediators should continuously improve their professional skills and abilities by, among other activities, participating in relevant continuing education programs and should regularly engage in self-assessment.

B. Mediators should participate in programs of peer consultation and should help train and mentor the work of less experienced mediators.

C. Mediators should continuously strive to understand the impact of culture and diversity on the mediator's practice.

UNIFORM MEDIATION ACT (EXCERPTS)*

SECTION 2. DEFINITIONS

In this [Act] . . .

(2) "Mediation communication" means a statement, whether oral or in a record or verbal or nonverbal, that occurs during a mediation or is made for purposes of considering, conducting, participating in, initiating, continuing, or reconvening a mediation or retaining a mediator. . . .

(7) "Proceeding" means

    (a) a judicial, administrative, arbitral, or other adjudicative process, including related pre-hearing and post-hearing motions, conferences, and discovery, or

    (b) a legislative hearing or similar process. . . .

SECTION 4. PRIVILEGE AGAINST DISCLOSURE; ADMISSIBILITY; DISCOVERY

    (a) Except as otherwise provided in Section 6, a mediation communication is privileged as provided in subsection (b) and is not subject to discovery or admissible in evidence in a proceeding unless waived or precluded as provided by Section 5.

    (b) In a proceeding, the following privileges apply:

        (1) A mediation party may refuse to disclose, and may prevent any other person from disclosing, a mediation communication.

        (2) A mediator may refuse to disclose a mediation communication, and may prevent any other person from disclosing a mediation communication of the mediator.

---

*Approved and recommended for enactment in all the states by the National Conference of Commissioners on Uniform State Laws in August 2001. Most Comments have been omitted. The complete document can be viewed at www.law.upenn.edu/bll/ulc/mediat/UMA2001.htm.

(3) A nonparty participant may refuse to disclose, and may prevent any other person from disclosing, a mediation communication of the nonparty participant.

(c) Evidence or information that is otherwise admissible or subject to discovery does not become inadmissible or protected from discovery solely by reason of its disclosure or use in mediation.

SECTION 5. WAIVER AND PRECLUSION OF PRIVILEGE

(a) A privilege under Section 4 may be waived in a record or orally during a proceeding if it is expressly waived by all parties to the mediation and:

(1) in the case of the privilege of a mediator, it is expressly waived by the mediator; and

(2) in the case of the privilege of a nonparty participant, it is expressly waived by the nonparty participant.

(b) A person that discloses or makes a representation about a mediation communication which prejudices another person in a proceeding is precluded from asserting a privilege under Section 4, but only to the extent necessary for the person prejudiced to respond to the representation or disclosure.

(c) A person that intentionally uses mediation to plan, attempt to commit or commit a crime, or to conceal an ongoing crime or ongoing criminal activity is precluded from asserting privilege under Section 4.

SECTION 6. EXCEPTIONS TO PRIVILEGE

(a) There is no privilege under Section 4 for a mediation communication that is:

(1) in an agreement evidenced by a record signed by all parties to the agreement;

(2) available to public under [insert statutory reference to open records act] or made during a session of a mediation which is open, or is required by law to be open, to the public;

(3) a threat or statement of a plan to inflict bodily injury or commit a crime of violence;

(4) intentionally used to plan a crime, attempt to commit a crime, or conceal an ongoing crime or ongoing criminal activity;

(5) sought or offered to prove or disprove a claim or complaint of professional misconduct or malpractice filed against a mediator;

(6) except as otherwise provided in subsection (c), sought or offered to prove or against a mediation party, nonparty participant, or representative or a party based on conduct occurring during a mediation; or

(7) sought or offered to prove or disprove abuse, neglect, abandonment, or exploitation in a proceeding in which a child or adult protective services agency is a party unless the

[Alternative A: [State to insert, for example, child or adult protection] case is referred by a court to mediation and a public agency participates.]

[Alternative B: public agency participates in the [State to insert, for example, child or adult protection] mediation.]

(b) There is no privilege under Section 4 if a court, administrative agency, or arbitrator finds, after a hearing in camera, that the party seeking discovery or the proponent of the evidence has shown that the evidence is not otherwise available, that there is a need for the evidence that substantially outweighs the interest in protecting confidentiality, and that the mediation communication is sought or offered in:

(1) a court proceeding involving a felony [or misdemeanor]; or

(2) except as otherwise provided in subsection (c), a proceeding to prove a claim to rescind or reform or a defense to avoid liability on a contract arising out of the mediation.

(c) A mediator may not be compelled to provide evidence of a mediation communication referred to in subsection (a)(6) or (b)(2).

(d) If a mediation communication is not privileged under subsection (a) or (b), only the portion of the communication necessary for the application of the exception from nondisclosure may be admitted. Admission of evidence under subsection (a) or (b) does not render the evidence, or any other mediation communication, discoverable or admissible for any other purpose.

SECTION 7. PROHIBITED MEDIATOR REPORTS

(a) Except as required in subsection (b), a mediator may not make a report, assessment, evaluation, recommendation, finding, or other communication regarding a mediation to a court, administrative agency, or other authority that may make a ruling on the dispute that is the subject of the mediation.

(b) A mediator may disclose:

(1) whether the mediation occurred or has terminated, whether a settlement was reached, and attendance;

(2) a mediation communication as permitted under Section 6; or

(3) a mediation communication evidencing abuse, neglect, abandonment, or exploitation of an individual to a public agency responsible for protecting individuals against such mistreatment.

(c) A communication made in violation of subsection (a) may not be considered by a court, administrative agency, or arbitrator.

SECTION 8. CONFIDENTIALITY

Unless subject to the [insert statutory references to open meetings act and open records act], mediation communications are confidential to the extent agreed by the parties or provided by other law or rule of this State.

Comments:

The evidentiary privilege granted in Sections 4-6 assures party expectations regarding the confidentiality of mediation communications against disclosures in subsequent legal proceedings. However, it is also possible for mediation communications to be disclosed outside of proceedings, for example to family members, friends, business associates, and the general public. Section 8 focuses on such disclosures.

SELECTED EXCERPTS, DELAWARE LAWYERS' RULES OF PROFESSIONAL CONDUCT (AS AMENDED THROUGH MAY 2010)*

RULE 1.2 SCOPE OF REPRESENTATION AND ALLOCATION OF AUTHORITY BETWEEN CLIENT AND LAWYER

(a) Subject to paragraphs (c) and (d), a lawyer shall abide by a client's decisions concerning the objectives of representation and, as required by Rule 1.4, shall consult with the clients as to the means by which they are to be pursued. A lawyer may take such action on behalf of the client as is impliedly authorized to carry out the representation. A lawyer shall abide by a client's decision whether to settle a matter. In a criminal case, the lawyer shall abide by the client's decision, after consultation with the lawyer, as to a plea to be entered, whether to waive jury trial and whether the client will testify. . . .

Comment

Allocation of Authority between Client and Lawyer

[1] Paragraph (a) confers upon the client the ultimate authority to determine the purposes to be served by legal representation, within the limits imposed by law and the lawyer's professional obligations. The decisions specified in paragraph (a), such as whether to settle a civil matter, must also be made by the client. See Rule 1.4(a)(1) for the lawyer's duty to communicate with the client about such decisions. With respect to the means by which the client's objectives are to be pursued,

---

* These provisions are in all significant respects identical to the corresponding A.B.A. Model Rules of Professional Conduct as amended through August 2007.

the lawyer shall consult with the client as required by Rule 1.4(a)(2) and may take such action as is impliedly authorized to carry out the representation.

[2] On occasion, however, a lawyer and a client may disagree about the means to be used to accomplish the client's objectives. Clients normally defer to the special knowledge and skill of their lawyer with respect to the means to be used to accomplish their objectives, particularly with respect to technical, legal and tactical matters. Conversely, lawyers usually defer to the client regarding such questions as the expense to be incurred and concern for third persons who might be adversely affected. Because of the varied nature of the matters about which a lawyer and client might disagree and because the actions in question may implicate the interests of a tribunal or other persons, the Rule does not prescribe how such disagreements are to be resolved. Other law, however, may be applicable and should be consulted by the lawyer. The lawyer should also consult with the client and seek a mutually acceptable resolution of the disagreement. If such efforts are unavailing and the lawyer has a fundamental disagreement with the client, the lawyer may withdraw from the representation. See Rule 1.16(b)(4). Conversely, the client may resolve the disagreement by discharging the lawyer. See Rule 1.16(a)(3).

[3] At the outset of a representation, the client may authorize the lawyer to take specific action on the client's behalf without further consultation. Absent a material change in circumstances and subject to Rule 1.4, a lawyer may rely on such an advance authorization. The client may, however, revoke such authority at any time. . . .

RULE 1.4 COMMUNICATION

(a) A lawyer shall:

(1) promptly inform the client of any decision or circumstance with respect to which the client's informed consent, as defined in Rule 1.0 (e), is required by these Rules;

(2) reasonably consult with the client about the means by which the client's objectives are to be accomplished;

(3) keep the client reasonably informed about the status of the matter;

(4) promptly comply with reasonable requests for information; and

(5) consult with the client about any relevant limitation on the lawyer's conduct when the lawyer knows that the client expects assistance not permitted by the Rules of Professional Conduct or other law.

(b) A lawyer shall explain a matter to the extent reasonably necessary to permit the client to make informed decisions regarding the representation.

Comment

[1] Reasonable communication between the lawyer and the client is necessary for the client effectively to participate in the representation.

Communicating with Client

[2] If these Rules require that a particular decision about the representation be made by the client, paragraph (a)(1) requires that the lawyer promptly consult with and secure the client's consent prior to taking action unless prior discussions with the client have resolved what action the client wants the lawyer to take. For example, a lawyer who receives from opposing counsel an offer of settlement in a civil controversy or a proffered plea bargain in a criminal case must promptly inform the client of its substance unless the client has previously indicated that the proposal will be acceptable or unacceptable or has authorized the lawyer to accept or to reject the offer. See Rule 1.2(a).

[3] Paragraph (a)(2) requires the lawyer to reasonably consult with the client about the means to be used to accomplish the client's objectives. In some situations — depending on both the importance of the action under consideration and the feasibility of consulting with the client — this duty will require consultation prior to taking action. In other circumstances, such as during a trial when an immediate decision must be made, the exigency of the situation may require the lawyer to act without prior consultation. In such cases the lawyer must nonetheless act reasonably to inform the client of actions the lawyer has taken on the client's behalf. Additionally, paragraph (a)(3) requires that the lawyer keep the client reasonably informed about the status of the matter, such as significant developments affecting the timing or the substance of the representation.

[4] A lawyer's regular communication with clients will minimize the occasions on which a client will need to request information concerning the representation. When a client makes a reasonable request for information, however, paragraph (a)(4) requires prompt compliance with the request, or if a prompt response is not feasible, that the lawyer, or a member of the lawyer's staff, acknowledge receipt of the request and advise the client when a response may be expected. Client telephone calls should be promptly returned or acknowledged.

Explaining Matters

[5] The client should have sufficient information to participate intelligently in decisions concerning the objectives of the representation and the means by which they are to be pursued, to the extent the client is willing and able to do so. Adequacy of communication depends in part on the kind of advice or assistance that is involved. For example, when there is time to explain a proposal made in a negotiation, the lawyer should review all important provisions with the client before proceeding to an agreement. In litigation a lawyer should explain the general strategy and prospects of success and ordinarily should consult the client on tactics that are likely to result in significant expense or to injure or coerce others. On the other hand, a lawyer ordinarily will not be expected to describe trial or negotiation strategy in detail. The guiding principle is that the lawyer should fulfill reasonable client expectations for information consistent with the duty to act in the client's best interests, and the client's overall requirements as to the character of representation. In certain circumstances, such as when a lawyer asks a client to consent to a representation affected by a conflict of interest, the client must give informed consent, as defined in Rule 1.0(e).

[6] Ordinarily, the information to be provided is that appropriate for a client who is a comprehending and responsible adult. However, fully informing the client according to this standard may be impracticable, for example, where the client is a child or suffers from diminished capacity. See Rule 1.14. When the client is an organization or group, it is often impossible or inappropriate to inform every one of its members about its legal affairs; ordinarily, the lawyer should address communications to the appropriate officials of the organization. See Rule 1.13. Where many routine matters are involved, a system of limited or occasional reporting may be arranged with the client.

Withholding Information

[7] In some circumstances, a lawyer may be justified in delaying transmission of information when the client would be likely to react imprudently to an immediate communication. Thus, a lawyer might withhold a psychiatric diagnosis of a client when the examining psychiatrist indicates that disclosure would harm the client. A lawyer may not withhold information to serve the lawyer's own interest or convenience or the interests or convenience of another person. Rules or court orders governing litigation may provide that information supplied to a lawyer may not be disclosed to the client. Rule 3.4 (c) directs compliance with such rules or orders.

RULE 1.12 FORMER JUDGE, ARBITRATOR, MEDIATOR OR OTHER THIRD-PARTY NEUTRAL

(a) Except as stated in paragraph (d), a lawyer shall not represent anyone in connection with a matter in which the lawyer participated personally and substantially as a judge or other adjudicative officer or law clerk to such a person or as an arbitrator, mediator or other third-party neutral, unless all parties to the proceeding give informed consent, confirmed in writing.

(b) A lawyer shall not negotiate for employment with any person who is involved as a party or as lawyer for a party in a matter in which the lawyer is participating personally and substantially as a judge or other adjudicative officer or as an arbitrator, mediator or other third-party neutral. A lawyer serving as a law clerk to a judge or other adjudicative officer may negotiate for employment with a party or lawyer involved in a matter in which the clerk is participating personally and substantially, but only after the lawyer has notified the judge or other adjudicative officer.

(c) If a lawyer is disqualified by paragraph (a), no lawyer in a firm with which that lawyer is associated may knowingly undertake or continue representation in the matter unless:

(1) the disqualified lawyer is timely screened from any participation in the matter and is apportioned no part of the fee therefrom; and

(2) written notice is promptly given to the parties and any appropriate tribunal to enable them to ascertain compliance with the provisions of this rule.

(d) An arbitrator selected as a partisan of a party in a multimember arbitration panel is not prohibited from subsequently representing that party.

Comment

[1] This Rule generally parallels rule 1.11. The term "personally and substantially" signifies that a judge who was a member of a multi-member court, and thereafter left judicial office to practice law, is not prohibited from representing a client in a matter pending in the court, but in which the former judge did not participate. So also the fact that a former judge exercised administrative responsibility in a court does not prevent the former judge from acting as a lawyer in a matter where the judge had previously exercised remote or incidental administrative responsibility that did not affect the merits. Compare the Comment to Rule 1.11. The term "adjudicative officer" includes such officials as judges pro tempore, referees, special masters, hearing officers and other parajudicial officers, and also lawyers who serve as part-time judges. Compliance Canons A(2), B(2), and C of the Model Code of Judicial Conduct provide that a part-time judge, judge pro tempore or retired judge recalled to active service, shall not "act as a lawyer in a proceeding which the judge has served as a judge or in any other proceeding related thereto." Although phrased differently from this Rule, those Rules correspond in meaning.

[2] Like former judges, lawyers who have served as arbitrators, mediators or other third-party neutrals may be asked to represent a client in a matter in which the lawyer participated personally and substantially. This Rule forbids such representation unless all of the parties to the proceedings give their informed consent, confirmed in writing. See Rule 1.0(e) and (b). Other law or codes of ethics governing third-party neutrals may impose more stringent standards of personal or imputed disqualification. See Rule 2.4.

[3] Although lawyers who serve as third-party neutrals do not have information concerning the parties that is protected under Rule 1.6, they typically owe the parties an obligation of confidentiality under law or codes of ethics governing third-party neutrals. Thus, paragraph (c) provides that conflicts of the personally disqualified lawyer will be imputed to other lawyers in a law firm unless the conditions of this paragraph are met.

[4] Requirements for screening procedures are stated in Rule 1.0(k). Paragraph (c)(1) does not prohibit the screened lawyer from receiving a salary or partnership share established by prior independent agreement, but that lawyer may not receive compensation directly related to the matter in which the lawyer is disqualified.

[5] Notice, including a description of the screened lawyer's prior representation and of the screening procedures employed, generally should be given as soon as practicable after the need for screening becomes apparent.

COUNSELOR

RULE 2.1 ADVISOR

In representing a client, a lawyer shall exercise independent professional judgment and render candid advice. In rendering advice, a lawyer may refer not only to law but to other considerations such as moral, economic, social and political factors, that may be relevant to the client's situation.

Comment

Scope of Advice

[1] A client is entitled to straightforward advice expressing the lawyer's honest assessment. Legal advice often involves unpleasant facts and alternatives that a client may be disinclined to confront. In presenting advice, a lawyer endeavors to sustain the client's morale and may put advice in as acceptable a form as honesty permits. However, a lawyer should not be deterred from giving candid advice by the prospect that the advice will be unpalatable to the client.

[2] Advice couched in narrow legal terms may be of little value to a client, especially where practical considerations, such as cost or effects on other people, are predominant. Purely technical legal advice, therefore, can sometimes be inadequate. It is proper for a lawyer to refer to relevant moral and ethical considerations in giving advice. Although a lawyer is not a moral advisor as such, moral and ethical considerations impinge upon most legal questions and may decisively influence how the law will be applied.

[3] A client may expressly or impliedly ask the lawyer for purely technical advice. When such a request is made by a client experienced in legal matters, the lawyer may accept it at face value. When such a request is made by a client inexperienced in legal matters, however, the lawyer's responsibility as advisor may include indicating that more may be involved than strictly legal considerations.

[4] Matters that go beyond strictly legal questions may also be in the domain of another profession. Family matters can involve problems within the professional competence of psychiatry, clinical psychology or social work; business matters can involve problems within the competence of the accounting profession or of financial specialists. Where consultation with a professional in another field is itself something a competent lawyer would recommend, the lawyer should make such a recommendation. At the same time, a lawyer's advice at its best often consists of recommending a course of action in the face of conflicting recommendations of experts.

Offering Advice

[5] In general, a lawyer is not expected to give advice until asked by the client. However, when a lawyer knows that a client proposes a course of action that is likely to result in substantial adverse legal consequences to the client, the lawyer's duty to the client under Rule 1.4 may require that the lawyer offer advice if the client's course of action is related to the representation. Similarly, when a matter is likely to involve litigation, it may be necessary under Rule 1.4 to inform the client of forms of dispute resolution that might constitute reasonable alternatives to litigation. A lawyer ordinarily has no duty to initiate investigation of a client's affairs or to give advice that the client has indicated is unwanted, but a lawyer may initiate advice to a client when doing so appears to be in the client's interest.

RULE 2.4 LAWYER SERVING AS THIRD-PARTY NEUTRAL

(a) A lawyer serves as a third-part neutral when the lawyer assists two or more persons who are not clients of the lawyer to reach a resolution of a dispute or other matter that has arisen between them. Service as a third-party neutral may include service as an arbitrator, a mediator or in such other capacity as will enable the lawyer to assist the parties to resolve the matter.

(b) A lawyer serving as a third-party neutral shall inform unrepresented parties that the lawyer is not representing them. When the lawyer knows or reasonably should know that a party does not understand the lawyer's role in the matter, the lawyer shall explain the difference between the lawyer's role as a third-party neutral and a lawyer's role as one who represents a client.

Comment

[1] Alternative dispute resolution has become a substantial part of the civil justice system. Aside from representing clients in dispute-resolution processes, lawyers often serve as third-party neutrals. A third-party neutral is a person, such as a mediator, arbitrator, conciliator or evaluator, who assists the parties, represented or unrepresented, in the resolution of a dispute or in the arrangement of a transaction. Whether a third-party neutral serves primarily as a facilitator, evaluator or decision maker depends on the particular process that is either selected by parties or mandated by a court.

[2] The role of a third-party neutral is not unique to lawyers, although, in some court-connected contexts, only lawyers are allowed to serve in this role or handle certain types of cases. In performing this role, the lawyer may be subject to court rules or other law that apply either to third-party neutrals generally or to lawyers serving as third-party neutrals. Lawyer-neutrals may also be subject to various codes of ethics, such as the Code of Ethics for Arbitration in Commercial Disputes prepared by a joint committee of the American Bar Association and the American Arbitration Association or the Model Standards of Conduct for Mediators jointly prepared by the American Bar Association, the American Arbitration Association and the Society of Professionals in Dispute Resolution.

[3] Unlike nonlawyers who serve as third-party neutrals, lawyers serving in this role may experience unique problems as a result of differences between the role of a third-party neutral and a lawyer's service as a client representative. The potential for confusion is significant when the parties are unrepresented in the process. Thus, paragraph (b) requires a lawyer-neutral to inform unrepresented parties that the lawyer is not representing them. For some parties, particularly parties who frequently use dispute-resolution processes, this information will be sufficient. For others, particularly those who are using the process for the first time, more information will be required. Where appropriate, the lawyer should inform unrepresented parties of the important differences between the lawyer's role as third-party neutral and a lawyer's role as a client representative, including the inapplicability of the attorney-client evidentiary privilege. The extent of disclosure required under this paragraph will depend on the particular parties

involved and the subject matter of the proceeding, as well as the particular features of the dispute-resolution process selected.

[4] A lawyer who serves as a third-party neutral subsequently may be asked to serve as a lawyer representing a client in the same matter. The conflicts of interest that arise for both the individual lawyer and the lawyer's law firm are addressed Rule 1.12.

[5] Lawyers who represent clients in alternative dispute-resolution processes are governed by the Rules of Professional Conduct. When the dispute-resolution process takes place before a tribunal, as in binding arbitration (see Rule 1.0 (m)), the lawyer's duty of candor is governed by rule 3.3. Otherwise, the lawyer's duty of candor toward both the third-party neutral and other parties is governed by Rule 4.1.

TRANSACTIONS WITH PERSONS OTHER THAN CLIENTS

RULE 4.1 TRUTHFULNESS IN STATEMENTS TO OTHERS

In the course of representing a client a lawyer shall not knowingly:
   (a) make a false statement of material fact or law to a third person; or
   (b) fail to disclose a material fact when disclosure is necessary to avoid assisting a criminal or fraudulent act by a client, unless disclosure is prohibited by Rule 1.6.

Comment

Misrepresentation

[1] A lawyer is required to be truthful when dealing with others on a client's behalf, but generally has no affirmative duty to inform an opposing party of relevant facts. A misrepresentation can occur if the lawyer incorporates or affirms a statement of another person that the lawyer knows is false. Misrepresentations can also occur by partially true but misleading statements or omissions that are the equivalent of affirmative false statements. For dishonest conduct that does not amount to a false statement or for misrepresentations by a lawyer other than in the course of representing a client, see Rule 8.4.

Statements of Fact

[2] This Rule refers to statements of fact. Whether a particular statement should be regarded as one of fact can depend on the circumstances. Under generally accepted conventions in negotiation, certain types of statements ordinarily are not taken as statements of material fact. Estimates of price or value placed on the subject of a transaction and a party's intentions as to an acceptable settlement of a claim are ordinarily in this category, and so is the existence of an undisclosed principal except where nondisclosure of the principal would constitute fraud.

Lawyers should be mindful of their obligations under applicable law to avoid criminal and tortious misrepresentation.

Crime or Fraud by Client

[3] Under Rule 1.2(d), a lawyer is prohibited from counseling or assisting a client in conduct that the lawyer knows is criminal or fraudulent. Paragraph (b) states a specific application of the principle set forth in Rule 1.2 (d) and addresses the situation where a client's crime or fraud takes the form of a lie or misrepresentation. Ordinarily, a lawyer can avoid assisting a client's crime or fraud by withdrawing from the representation. Sometimes it may be necessary for the lawyer to give notice of the fact of withdrawal and to disaffirm an opinion, document, affirmation or the like. In extreme cases, substantive law may require a lawyer to disclose information relating to the representation to avoid being deemed to have assisted the client's crime or fraud. If the lawyer can avoid assisting a client's crime or fraud only by disclosing this information, then under paragraph (b) the lawyer is required to do so, unless the disclosure is prohibited by Rule 1.6.

APPENDIX

F

TOLMAN SCREENING MODEL (MODIFIED)*

1. Mediation often occurs with both (spouses)(partners)(parents)(interested adults) in the same room together. Do you have any concerns about mediating in the same room together with your (spouse)(partner)(child's other parent)(the other adult involved)?

The rationale for this question is that it may tap reluctance to participate in mediation because of physical abuse without directly asking for it. Thus, it may be effective as a broad screening question, even if abuse victims are reluctant to directly disclose abuse. One the other hand, reasons other than abuse may result in concerns about mediation, and these would have to be sorted out in further screening.

2. Are you fearful of your (spouse)(partner)(child's other parent)(other adult involved) for any reason?

This question taps the subjective perspective of the respondent. It does not assume fear is a result of physical abuse, nor is it limited to fear of physical harm. It may identify fears of various types (taking children away, fear of humiliation, fear of the other parent harming himself, etc.)

3. Has your (spouse)(partner)(child's other parent)(other adult involved) ever threatened to hurt you in any way?

This question is similar to question #2 in that it asks about threats in a broad manner, not limited to physical abuse. It adds information about the other parent's behavior (or the behavior of any other adult involved), rather than focusing on the subjective perspective of the respondent.

---

*Copyright 1989 by Richard M. Tolman, Ph.D. Reprinted with permission. We have modified the original Tolman Screening Model to make it usable across a wide range of domestic matters, including child custody disputes involving unmarried adults.

4. Has your (spouse)(partner)(child's other parent)(other adult involved) ever hit you or used any other type of physical force towards you?

This question directly asks about physical abuse, though it does not use the term abuse. Many individuals who experience physical abuse may not label it with that term. This question is more neutral in its terminology and may elicit more positive responses. On the other hand, further screening may clarify the physical force used as non-abusive. For example, a person's use of physical force may be legitimately self-defensive.

5. Have you ever called the police, requested a protection from abuse order, or sought help for yourself as a result of abuse by your (spouse)(partner)(child's other parent) (other adult involved)?

An affirmative answer to this question would demonstrate that abuse is a significant problem. However, serious abuse might have occurred even if it is answered negatively.

6. Are you currently afraid that your (spouse)(partner)(child's other parent)(other adult involved) will physically harm you?

This repeats #2, except that it more pointedly asks about physical abuse. An affirmative answer to #2 and a negative answer to #6 would point the screening towards a clarification of the nature of the respondent's fears. It also may clarify that while the respondent experienced abuse in the past, (s)he is not currently fearful. This also would indicate a direction for further screening.

7. Mediation is a process in which (spouses)(partners)(parents)(the adults involved) work together with a neutral third person to negotiate details of their (divorce)(separation)(parenting arrangements). Do you believe you would be able to communicate with your (spouse)(partner)(child's other parent)(other adult involved) on an equal basis in mediation sessions?

This question indicates the respondent's subjective perspective about ability to mediate. A negative response would lead to further screening about the reasons for the inequality. If previous questions about abuse were answered negatively, but this question is answered positively, it may indicate that the reason for inequality is not physical abuse, but some other factors, including psychological maltreatment. This could then be clarified further. On the other hand, if abuse questions are answered positively, but this question is answered negatively, it might reflect the respondent's belief that the abuse has not hampered her ability to use mediation effectively.

(If the mediation will affect children, also ask the following questions.)

8. Has your child's other parent (or any other adult involved) ever threatened to deny you access to your children?

9. Do you have any concerns about the children's emotional or physical safety with you or the other parent (or any other adult involved)?

10. Has the department of children or family services ever been involved with your family?

Chapter-by-Chapter Video Clip List

■ **CHAPTER 3**

Clip 3-A: *Wilson v. DiLorenzo Full Length* (Craig Lord)
Clip 3-B: *Wilson v. Dilorenzo Full Length* (Cheryl Cutrona)

■ **CHAPTER 6**

Clip 6-A: *Mediator Opening: Child Custody Case* (Sam Rossito)
Clip 6-B (1-2):   *Ice Breaking and Mediator Self-Introduction* (Craig Lord, Judith Meyer)
Clip 6-C (1-2):   *Describing the Process* (Cheryl Cutrona)
Clip 6-D (1-3):   *Touting the Advantages of Mediation* (Craig Lord, Sam Rossito, Harris Bock)
Clip 6-E (1-4):   *Describing the Mediator's Role* (Cheryl Cutrona, Judith Meyer, Sam Rossito, Harris Bock)
Clip 6-F (1-2):   *Establishing Ground Rules* (Mary Hanna, Sam Rossito)
Clip 6-G (1-2):   *Describing Confidentiality* (Don Weinstein & Jean Biesecker, Chuck Forer)
Clip 6-H (1-3):   *Inviting the Parties to Speak: Forms of Questions* (Cheryl Cutrona, Craig Lord)
Clip 6-I: *Represented Parties: Who Should Speak?* (Chuck Forer)
Clip 6-J: *Listening for Diagnosis* (Don Weinstein, Jean Biesecker)
Clip 6-K: *Exchange* (Cheryl Cutrona)
Clip 6-L (1-2):   *Active Listening* (Sam Rossito, Cheryl Cutrona),
Clip 6-M: *"I" Statements* (Don Weinstein & Jean Biesecker)
Clip 6-N (1-3):   *Dealing with Strong Emotions* (Mary Hanna, Sam Rossito, Don Weinstein & Jean Biesecker)
Clip 6-TM-1:   *Opening the Process: Mindfulness* (Sam Rossito)
Clip 6-TM-2:   *Listening and Note Taking Exercise* (Sam Rossito)
Clip 6-TM-3:   *Active Listening Exercises* (Craig Lord, Cheryl Cutrona, Don Weinstein & Jean Biesecker, Chuck Forer)
Clip 6-TM-4:   *Productive Reframing Exercises* (Don Weinstein & Jean Biesecker)
Clip 6-TM-5:   *Screening for Domestic Violence* (Don Weinstein & Jean Biesecker)

■ CHAPTER 7

■ CHAPTER 8

■ CHAPTER 9

■ CHAPTER 10

■ CHAPTER 12

■ CHAPTER 13

INDEX